THE ENCYCLOPEDIA

of the

REPUBLICAN PARTY

★ ★ ★ ★ ★ ★ ★ ★ ★ ★

Volume Two

Edited by

GEORGE THOMAS KURIAN

JEFFREY D. SCHULTZ
Associate Editor

Sharpe Reference

An imprint of M.E. Sharpe, INC.

CONTENTS

Volume 2

Garfield–Arthur Poster, 1880. *Source:* Smithsonian Institution.

CONVENTIONS

— 1856 —

The decline of the Whig Party and the centrality of the slavery issue brought to life a new party. In February 1856 in Pittsburgh, Pennsylvania, the embryonic Republican Party held its first meeting, to which each state was permitted to send one representative. It was determined at that meeting to call a convention later in the year in Philadelphia, at which time each state would be given six delegates and three additional ones for each congressional district.

The issue of slavery was clearly central to the gathering in June as no delegates from the southern states were in attendance. The territory of Kansas was given full participation in recognition of its slavery struggles.

In contrast to the Democratic Conventions, a simple majority was enough to win the nomination as the party's standard-bearer.

While the major figures, Salmon P. Chase of Ohio and William H. Seward of New York, had withdrawn from contention before the convention began, Senator John C. Frémont of California and Supreme Court

Meeting that Led to the Formation of the Republican Party, Lafayette Hall, Pittsburgh, February 22, 1856. *Source:* Library of Congress.

Justice John McLean of Ohio remained in the race. Frémont had little trouble in securing the nomination as the party's first presidential candidate.

In an informal ballot, former Senator William L. Dayton of New Jersey led former Representative Abraham Lincoln of Illinois in the vice presidential race. When the official roll call was taken, Dayton's nomination was made unanimous.

The Republican platform was a decidedly pro-North, antislavery document. It called for the admission of Kansas as a free state and the prohibition of slavery in the territories. The party also called upon Congress to fund internal improvements and encourage the development of a transcontinental railroad. In addition, the party supported the idea of buying or taking Cuba from Spain.

— 1860 —

When the Republicans convened in Chicago in May 1860 in the new 10,000-seat hall known as the Wigwam, they were already aware of the splintered Democratic Convention in Charleston, South Carolina. Delegates from the northern states, territories and several southern states (Maryland, Delaware, Virginia, Kentucky, Missouri, and Texas) were in attendance.

Several debates over the credentials of southern delegations and over the majority rule were raised. Specifically, the question arose as to the number of delegates to which southern states were entitled as they were not very strongly Republican. The convention voted to recommit the credentials report so as to downplay the role of southern states. Without all possible delegates in attendance, a debate arose over what constituted the majority. The convention, after much discussion, adopted the rule that a majority would be of those delegates present and not of the total number possible.

The front-runner, William H. Seward of New York, narrowly led over Abraham Lincoln of Illinois after the second roll call. Lincoln had gained national recognition through his famous debates with Senator Stephen A. Douglas in the 1858 Senate race. On the third ballot, Lincoln captured the lead and the nomination.

Senator Hannibal Hamlin of Maine was declared the unanimous nominee for the vice presidency after the second round of balloting. He defeated Cassius M. Clay of Kentucky when the New England states began a bandwagon movement for his nomination.

Nearly one-half of the platform of 1860 addressed the issue of slavery. While the Republicans opposed the extension of slavery into the territories, they believed that states' rights protected slavery where it already existed. In addition, the platform adopted measures similar to those of its first platform in 1856 supporting internal improvements and a transcontinental railroad.

— 1864 —

When the Republicans met in Baltimore in June 1864, many were dissatisfied with President Abraham Lincoln's prosecution of the Civil War. Nonetheless, there was little doubt that Lincoln would be the party's nominee.

Non-Republicans who supported the president were encouraged to attend the convention, which billed itself as the Union Party. Delegations from all the Northern states, the territories, the District of Columbia and several Southern states (Arkansas, Florida, Louisiana, South Carolina, Tennessee, and Virginia) were in attendance. Credentials fights brewed over the Southern delegations' participation. In the end, Arkansas, Louisiana and Tennessee were given full privileges, including voting. Florida and Virginia were seated although not permitted to vote. South Carolina was not seated.

Lincoln easily captured the nomination on the first roll call, receiving all the votes except Missouri's 22, which it cast for General Ulysses S. Grant. After the roll, Missouri switched its votes, making the nomination unanimous.

The vice presidential nomination went to Democrat Andrew Johnson, former senator and military governor of Tennessee. Johnson beat a field that included the incumbent vice president, Hannibal Hamlin of Maine, and former Senator Daniel S. Dickinson of New York.

The party platform was adopted without debate. Central to the platform was the party's pledge to prosecute the war vigorously. In addition, the party endorsed the abolition of slavery through a constitutional amendment.

— 1868 —

Several blacks representing southern states were in attendance at the first post–Civil War Republican Convention in Chicago in May 1868.

General Ulysses S. Grant, who had been considered by the Democrats as a possible nominee a year earlier, was the only candidate placed in nomination. He received all 650 votes cast.

The National Union Republican Convention at Crosby's Opera House, Chicago, May 21, 1868. Grant Is the Republican Candidate for President. *Source:* Library of Congress.

Eleven names were placed in nomination for the second spot on the ticket. The two leading candidates were Senator Benjamin F. Wade of Ohio and Speaker of the House Schuyler Colfax of Indiana. On the fifth ballot, Colfax achieved the necessary majority vote.

The Republican platform adopted many of the radical measures supported by congressional Republicans. It criticized President Andrew Johnson, arguing that he deserved to be impeached. In what can be viewed as a hypocritical plank, the platform endorsed the right of blacks to vote in the South while leaving black suffrage to the states' discretion in other regions. Finally, in what would be a recurring plank, the Republicans endorsed a policy of hard money.

— 1872 —

When the Republicans met in Philadelphia in June 1872, they did so without the liberal, reform wing of the party, which had left to form its own Liberal Republican Party, whose nominee for president was Horace Greeley. Without this element, the renomination of President Ulysses S. Grant was unanimous.

Senator Henry Wilson of Massachusetts defeated incumbent Vice President Schuyler Colfax in a very close, though single-roll-call ballot.

Much of the platform praised the accomplishments of the Republicans in Reconstruction. The platform did contain some more liberal planks that sought to ensure the rights of women and the extension of black suffrage in all states, not just the defeated South.

— 1876 —

The Republican Convention held in Cincinnati, Ohio, in June 1876 saw the rejoining of the short-lived Liberal Republicans in large measure. The convention was highlighted by a speech by freedman Frederick Douglass, who criticized the Republicans for freeing the slaves without giving them the means for equality.

Two contending delegations arrived from the state of Alabama. One was committed to House Speaker James G. Blaine of Maine; the other, to Senator Oliver P. Morton of Indiana. The convention, following the recommendation of the majority report, seated the pro-Blaine delegation.

The party was nearly equally divided into its three wings. The radical Republicans were led by Senator

The Republican National Convention, Cincinnati, Ohio, June 14–16, 1876. The Chairman Is Announcing the Nomination of Governor Hayes for President. *Source:* Library of Congress.

Roscoe Conkling of New York and supported Morton. The half-breeds were led by Blaine. The third group, the reformers, were led by former Treasury Secretary Benjamin H. Bristow of Kentucky.

Blaine led after the initial ballot. During the second round, three delegates from Pennsylvania objected to the unit rule, which bound them to vote as a block. The chair released the delegates from the rule, a decision that was upheld in a voice vote. The immediate effect of the abolition of the unit rule was a boost for Blaine. As balloting continued, Blaine's delegate count grew. However, dark-horse candidate Governor Rutherford B. Hayes of Ohio also showed increased strength. On the seventh ballot, anti-Blaine delegates rallied behind Hayes and gave him enough votes for victory.

Despite five candidates' being placed in nomination for vice president, it was clear during the first ballot that Representative William A. Wheeler of New York would easily win. The roll call was suspended, and he was declared the nominee by acclamation.

The party's most controversial plank involved its call for a congressional investigation of Oriental immigration. In addition, the platform continued its support for hard money, the use of the tariff for both revenue and industrial protection, the abolition of polygamy, and the extension of civil rights. A new plank calling for a con-stitutional amendment forbidding the use of public land for nonpublic schools was added.

— 1880 —

For the first time, the Republican Convention that assembled in Chicago in June 1880 was limited to Republicans only. The party was divided into two camps: those led by Senator Roscoe Conkling of New York who sought to renominate former President Ulysses S. Grant and those who opposed Grant's renomination.

The convention featured more than 50 credentials disputes, seven of which went to the floor for resolution. The most important one was the case from Illinois in which the Grant forces tried to bar anti-Grant delegates from being seated. By a very narrow margin, the anti-Grant delegates were seated.

The rules committee recommended that the unit rule not be used. The Grant forces wanted the unit rule as the former president had majorities in several large, key states. However, after an attempt by the Grant forces to proceed without considering the rules committee recommendation was defeated, the report was adopted by acclamation.

Despite these procedural defeats, after the first ballot

Grant was in the lead with 304 votes, followed closely by Senator James G. Blaine of Maine with 284 votes. After 28 roll-call ballots, there had been little change.

When balloting continued the next day, on the 34th ballot Representative James A. Garfield of Ohio received 16 votes from Wisconsin. Garfield objected, stating that he was not a candidate, but his protest was ruled out of order by the chair. The Ohio representative continued to gain votes on the next roll call, with his total rising to 50. On the 36th ballot, Garfield received 399 votes, enough to win the nomination.

The easy winner of the vice presidential nomination was Chester A. Arthur of New York, the choice of the Grant forces.

The party platform continued its support of a tariff for revenue and protection. It argued that the Constitution was more than a mere contract as the Democrats had argued in their platform. In an amendment taken from the floor, the platform called for the "thorough, radical and complete" reform of the civil service.

— 1884 —

As the Republicans gathered in Chicago in June 1884, calls to the convention included instructions on how and when delegates should be selected. The national committee believed that this would avoid the credentials fights that occurred at the 1880 convention.

Once again, Senator James G. Blaine of Maine was a leading candidate. However, there continued to be strong opposition to him, particularly from the incumbent president, Chester A. Arthur. The strength of these two sides was immediately put to a test over the selection of a temporary chair. The anti-Blaine forces succeeded in having John R. Lynch of Mississippi elected. Lynch was the first black ever to serve as temporary chair of a national convention.

However, on the first ballot, Blaine took a commanding lead, with $334\frac{1}{2}$ votes to Arthur's 278. Most of Arthur's supporters were from the South, where the administration had extensive patronage power. After three more ballots, in which Blaine slowly gained strength, the Maine senator secured the nomination.

Senator John A. Logan of Illinois, the only candidate, easily won the vice presidential nomination.

The party platform adopted by the Republicans had changed little from the previous one in 1880. It supported a tariff for revenue and protection of American industry. The platform called for reform of the civil service and restrictions on Chinese immigration. And bor-

The Republican National Convention, Chicago, June 2, 1880, at the Exposition Building. *Source:* Library of Congress.

The Republican National Convention, Chicago, June 3–6, 1884. Scenes from Opening Night.
Source: Library of Congress.

rowing from the 1880 Greenback Party, it encouraged the regulation of railroads and an eight-hour workday.

— 1888 —

When the Republicans assembled in Chicago in June 1888, the party's 1884 standard-bearer, Senator James G. Blaine of Maine, had already removed his name from contention. This withdrawal left the nomination wide open.

On the first ballot, 14 candidates received votes, the leaders being Senator John Sherman of Ohio, Circuit Judge Walter Q. Gresham of Indiana, and former Governor Russell A. Alger of Michigan. The convention recessed until the next morning after the third ballot.

The next day, the fourth roll call saw former Senator Benjamin Harrison of Indiana leap into second place. There was little change on the fifth ballot. A motion to adjourn until Monday was approved.

On Monday, the voting showed little change on the sixth roll call. However, on the seventh roll call, delegates who had been voting for Blaine shifted their votes to Harrison, giving the Hoosier the lead for the first time. On the eighth ballot, a bandwagon move-

ment had begun for Harrison, and he easily captured the nomination.

Former Representative Levi P. Morton of New York was the easy victor for the vice presidential nomination over two rivals.

The central issue of the platform was the tariff. The Republicans continued to favor its use for both revenue and protectionist purposes. It also supported the coinage of both gold and silver. In addition, the party opposed the practice of polygamy in the territories.

— 1892 —

While President Benjamin Harrison was unpopular with many in the party, as the delegates convened in Minneapolis, Minnesota, in June 1892, there was little doubt that he would be renominated. Two preballoting events showed the strength of the Harrison forces. In selecting a permanent chair of the convention, Harrison supporters had former Representative William McKinley elected without opposition. Second, in a credentials dispute over six Alabama delegates, the pro-Harrison forces prevented the seating of the delegates.

While there were no other official candidates, two alternatives to Harrison received votes. McKinley and former Republican standard-bearer James G. Blaine of Maine each received support. However, the nomination easily went to Harrison on the first roll call.

For the first time, the party selected a candidate for the national ticket without a roll call. By acclamation Whitelaw Reid, former editor of the *New York Tribune* and ambassador to France, received the vice presidential nomination when incumbent Vice President Levi P. Morton did not actively seek renomination.

The platform distinguished the party from its rivals in two major areas. First, the Republicans continued their long-standing support for a revenue and protectionist tariff. Second, the party sympathized with the prohibition movement.

— 1896 —

The currency issue was the dominant one to shape the conventions of both parties. As the Republicans gathered in St. Louis, Missouri, in June 1896, the gold forces were clearly in control of the events.

For more than a year, Marcus "Mark" Hanna of Ohio, Governor William McKinley's campaign manager, had been courting delegates throughout the country. His adept backroom political dealings had gathered enough support for the Ohio governor that the party's nomination was never in doubt. While four other candidates were placed in nomination, McKinley easily won the nomination on the first roll call.

A McKinley supporter, former state legislator Garret A. Hobart of New Jersey, easily won the party's nomination for vice president.

In sharp distinction to the Democratic platform, the Republican platform called for the coinage of only gold until an international agreement could be made on bimetallism. An attempt to adopt a 16-to-1 ratio as the Democrats had was soundly defeated. The defeat of the minority silver forces, led by Senator Henry M. Teller of Colorado, resulted in a walkout by 24 delegates from western states. The remainder of the platform was adopted on a voice vote.

— 1900 —

In order to heal the political wounds of the delegate walkout in 1896, Senator Edward O. Wolcott of Colorado was selected as the temporary chair of the Republican Convention that met in Philadelphia in June 1900.

Republican National Convention, Minneapolis, June 1892. *Source:* Library of Congress.

Republican National Convention, Chicago, 1904. Former Governor Black of New York Names Roosevelt for President. *Source:* Library of Congress.

With no opposition, President William McKinley received all 926 votes to be the party's standard-bearer. However, with the death of Vice President Garret A. Hobart in 1899, there was no clear candidate for the second spot. McKinley asked his campaign manager, Mark Hanna, to remain on the sidelines in the selection process. Much to Hanna's dismay, the delegates chose the reformer Governor Theodore Roosevelt of New York. The powerful New York machine, led by Senator Thomas C. Platt, captured all but one vote for Roosevelt, the hero of the Spanish-American War.

The platform adopted by the convention praised the accomplishments of the McKinley administration. It supported expansionism and the creation of the Department of Commerce. The party continued to favor the gold standard and protective duties.

— 1904 —

With the death of Senator Mark Hanna of Ohio in February, the nomination of President Theodore Roosevelt faced no opposition going into the June 1904 Chicago convention.

As expected, Roosevelt was unanimously nominated as the party's standard-bearer. Senator Charles W.

Fairbanks of Indiana, the leadership's preference, received the vice presidential nomination by acclamation, though there was support for other candidates.

The platform of 1904 offered little that was different from previous Republican documents. It extolled the virtues of the party's expansionist foreign policy and its commitment to the gold standard. The platform was adopted without dissent.

In a successful attempt to rally the delegates behind Roosevelt, a message from the secretary of state to the American consul in Morocco was read aloud by the chair of the convention. The message asserted: "We want either Perdicaris alive or Raisuli dead." The note referred to Ion Perdicaris, an American citizen who had been captured by the Moroccan Chieftain Raisuli. The cheap ploy rallied the party faithful behind their presidential nominee.

— 1908 —

As the delegates convened in Chicago in June 1908, there was once again little doubt as to who would be the party's standard-bearer. President Theodore Roosevelt, while declining to seek renomination, had personally selected Secretary of War William Howard Taft of Ohio.

The preconvention work featured 230 of the 980 delegate seats' being contested. In the end, all disputes were resolved without the need to have a floor vote. In addition, vote allocation was an issue. An amendment to the rules to base vote allocation on population rather than the electoral vote was defeated by a coalition of southern delegates and Taft supporters.

On the first ballot, Taft was the runaway winner over the six other candidates placed in nomination. Representative James S. Sherman of New York, a conservative, easily captured the vice presidential nomination.

The detailed minority plan of the Wisconsin delegation, led by Senator Robert M. La Follette, was divided into separate sections for consideration. However, the more conservative delegation handily defeated the more liberal proposals of the Wisconsin progressive. In the end, the majority report, which praised the party's achievements in making the United States the wealthiest nation on earth, was adopted by a voice vote.

— 1912 —

The June 1912 Republican Convention in Chicago was a showcase for the feud that had developed between former President Theodore Roosevelt and his hand-picked successor, President William Howard Taft. While Roosevelt had dominated the primaries, Taft controlled the national committee. This split in power produced one of the most interesting conventions ever.

Credentials disputes involved 254 of the 1,078 delegates. More than 90% of these disputes (involving 235 delegates) were settled in favor of Taft. In another test of strength, the conservative Taft forces succeeded in having their candidate, Senator Elihu Root of New York, selected as temporary chair. The Roosevelt forces decided to challenge 72 of the delegates' credentials on the floor. Of the four cases that eventually required a roll call, all the decisions favored Taft.

Roosevelt, sensing defeat, encouraged his supporters to remain at the convention but to refrain from participating. Pro-Roosevelt supporters in the galleries rubbed sandpaper together and blew horns, mimicking the sound of steamrollers.

President Taft's name was placed in nomination by former Lieutenant Governor Warren G. Harding of Ohio. The only other name placed in nomination was that of Senator Robert M. La Follette of Wisconsin, the other recognized leader of the progressive wing of the party. Even with most of Roosevelt's delegates abstaining, Taft easily won the nomination on the first ballot.

Despite his failing health, Vice President James S. Sherman was renominated. As a precaution, the con-

vention passed a resolution empowering the national committee to fill the second spot, if necessary.

The party platform praised the Republican administrations from William McKinley to Taft, though it did not offer any strikingly new planks. A more progressive minority report introduced by the Wisconsin delegation was tabled by a voice vote.

— 1916 —

The Republican Convention held in Chicago in June 1916 featured extensive behind-the-scenes negotiations to heal the split between the more conservative wing and the progressive wing, which had bolted and formed its own party in 1912. The Republican National Committee was willing to make changes in order to attract the progressives.

In a preconvention move, the committee restructured vote allocation to take into account Republican voting strength. The net result of this was the South's loss of more than one-third of its 1912 votes. However, there were limits to the committee's willingness to compromise. Under no circumstances could the party leadership accept the nomination of Theodore Roosevelt as president.

In order to smooth over differences, a five-member Republican committee met with leaders of the progressive wing. When the committee reported back that the progressives were adamant about their desire to nominate Roosevelt, the convention chair, Senator Warren G. Harding of Ohio, instructed them to continue with the talks.

In the meantime, the presidential nominating had begun, with the leader being Supreme Court Justice Charles Evans Hughes, the former governor of New York. While Hughes did not actively seek the nomination, many considered him to be the ideal candidate as he had a progressive background and had not been part of the ill-fated 1912 convention. After the first ballot, Hughes took the lead, though he was well short of the simple majority necessary. When the second ballot produced little change, the convention called for a recess.

In a surprise move, Roosevelt suggested the name of conservative Senator Henry Cabot Lodge of Massachusetts. The progressives immediately broke off negotiations and by acclamation nominated Roosevelt and John P. Parker of Louisiana. Roosevelt, however, declined the nomination on the grounds that Hughes's positions on several major issues were acceptable.

As the Republicans reconvened the next day, Hughes was overwhelmingly nominated on the third ballot, with the nomination being declared unani-

Republican National Convention, Chicago, 1920. *Source:* National Archives.

mous. Former Roosevelt Vice President Charles W. Fairbanks of Indiana easily captured the party's nomination for vice president.

Once again a progressive Wisconsin delegation proposed a minority platform that denounced dollar diplomacy and supported woman suffrage and a constitutional amendment to establish initiatives, referenda and recalls. On a voice vote, the measure was defeated. In its place, the party adopted the majority report, which criticized the Wilson administration. The party promised neutrality in the growing European hostilities while calling for a strong national defense.

— 1920 —

With the passage of the 19th Amendment almost assured, female delegates were present for the first time in large numbers as the Republicans met for their fifth consecutive convention in Chicago in June 1920.

When the presidential balloting began, there was no clear front-runner. Eleven different names were placed in nomination, including the eventual winner, Senator Warren G. Harding of Ohio, who was sixth after two ballots. The initial leaders were Major General Leon-

ard Wood of New Hampshire, Senator Hiram Johnson of California, and Governor Frank Lowden of Illinois. The first two split the party's progressive votes between them.

After four ballots, no candidate was anywhere near the simple majority needed to secure the nomination. The permanent chair, Henry Cabot Lodge of Massachusetts, entertained another motion to adjourn. In a closely divided voice vote, the chair ruled that the motion had passed.

During the recess, party leaders met throughout the night in the hotel suite of National Committee Chairman Will Hays, hoping to resolve the growing deadlock. Harding emerged with the help of Lodge as the compromise candidate who was acceptable to both the conservative and progressive wings of the party.

As balloting resumed the next day, Harding's vote total continued to grow. On the ninth ballot, a large number of Lowden supporters shifted their votes to Harding. Although not enough to give the Ohioan the nomination, the switch created a movement that secured the nomination for Harding on the tenth roll call.

A delegate from Oregon, standing on his chair, nominated Governor Calvin Coolidge of Massachusetts as the party's vice presidential candidate. The governor had gained national fame for his handling of the 1919 Boston police strike. A pro-Coolidge celebration ensued, and the Massachusetts governor was easily nominated.

For the third consecutive convention, the Wisconsin delegation offered its minority report as the party platform. Once again, the report was defeated by a voice vote. The platform that was adopted harshly criticized the Wilson administration's handling of both the war and its peace settlement. The party praised the Republican Senate for blocking U.S. entry into the League of Nations; however, it did not rule out U.S. support for League decisions. In order to balance the budget, the Republicans favored the consolidation of several federal departments. They continued their support for a protectionist tariff. This majority report was adopted by a voice vote.

— 1924 —

The Republican Convention of June 1924 in Cleveland, Ohio, had two firsts: the convention was broadcast over the radio, and women were elected to the national committee as part of a rules change calling for one woman and one man from each state.

President Calvin Coolidge was easily chosen as the party's nominee, capturing all but 35 votes. The balloting for the vice presidential nomination was a different story. Former Illinois Governor Frank O. Lowden took the lead on the first ballot. However, he announced that he was not interested in the post. On the second ballot, nonetheless, he received a majority of the votes. A brief recess was called to see if Lowden would reconsider. He steadfastly refused. On the third roll call, former Budget Bureau Director Charles G. Dawes garnered enough votes for the nomination.

As was becoming customary, the Wisconsin delegation submitted a minority platform, which was rejected without a roll-call vote. The Wisconsin platform was a reflection of the delegation's more progressive bent. It encouraged government ownership of railroads and water power and a progressive income tax.

The platform that was adopted praised the Republican administration for being fiscally conservative and promised a tax cut. The party acknowledged and condemned the corruption of the Harding administration but defended those whom it believed to be innocent people. In foreign policy, the platform encouraged participation in the World Court while shunning the League of Nations.

— 1928 —

As Republicans gathered in June 1928 for their convention in Kansas City, Missouri, President Calvin Coolidge lived up to his billing as "Silent Cal" when he announced his intention not to seek renomination. "I do not choose to run for president in 1928." With that, Commerce Secretary Herbert Hoover of California quickly filled the void that the president had left.

The strength of the Hoover forces was put to an earlier test when 18 pro-Hoover delegates from Texas were challenged. By a strong majority, the motion to remove them was defeated. Even though six names were placed in nomination, Hoover won with an overwhelming majority. Hoover's chief rival, former Illinois Governor Frank O. Lowden, who had been the party's first choice for vice president in 1824, withdrew from the race before the first roll call because he could not support the party's stance on agriculture.

Senator Charles Curtis of Kansas was easily nominated for the second spot on the ticket.

Despite the death of Wisconsin's progressive leader Robert M. La Follette, the delegation once again submitted a minority report for consideration. The report, presented by Senator Robert M. La Follette Jr., was never even voted upon.

Two proposals from the floor were heard. The first proposal favored the repeal of Prohibition. It was tabled by a voice vote. The second was a resolution for the adoption of principles similar to the McNary–Haugen bill, which had been twice vetoed by Coolidge. On a roll-call vote, the resolution was soundly defeated.

The majority platform was adopted by a voice vote as it had originally been written. The document promised continued prosperity and concluded with a strong statement in support of self-reliance and local government.

— 1932 —

With the economic depression worsening, the Republicans gathered in Chicago in June 1932 with little hope of electoral victory and no alternative to President Herbert Hoover. Hoover was easily renominated as the party's standard-bearer. Vice President Charles Curtis faced competition from Major General James G. Harbord of New York, though in the end his renomination was made unanimous.

The party platform of nearly 9,000 words was the longest in the Republicans' history to date. It was not a stellar document. Its plank on Prohibition was ambiguously worded, calling for enforcement of Prohibition while advocating a national referendum on it. The Republicans argued that the depression could best be countered by continued governmental fiscal frugality. They explained that the depression was the result of worldwide economic affairs and that the Hoover administration was responding with great leadership. The last plank called on congressional Republicans to support the party's program in their actions, warning of the perils of internal dissent.

— 1936 —

As Republicans gathered in Cleveland, Ohio, in June 1936, there was little doubt who would be the party's standard-bearer in the election. Governor Alfred M. Landon of Kansas was the overwhelming choice for the nomination as he was the only Republican governor reelected in 1934. Landon, a moderate Republican, was teamed with Colonel Frank Knox of Illinois, publisher of the *Chicago Daily News*.

The party's platform began with the alarming words "America is in peril." It then proceeded to describe the threat the Roosevelt administration posed to constitutional government, local self-rule, and the power of the Supreme Court. The party's solutions were not that different from the ones it had articulated in its 1932 platform, though it did support in concept social security, unemployment insurance and control of agricultural production.

— 1940 —

The Republican Convention held in Philadelphia in June 1940 had no clear candidates for the top spot on the ticket. When balloting began, ten names were placed into nomination. After the first roll call, Manhattan District Attorney Thomas E. Dewey led Senator Robert A. Taft of Ohio. The party's eventual nominee, Wendell L. Willkie of Indiana, was a distant third.

Willkie, a political novice, had never run for office before his bid for the White House. A lifelong Democrat, Willkie switched parties in 1938 in opposition to President Franklin Delano Roosevelt's policy of public power projects. Most considered his chances of capturing the nomination to be slim since he had missed most of the primaries.

Republican National Convention, Philadelphia, 1940. Hoover Addresses the Convention. *Source:* National Archives.

However, as the balloting continued, Dewey lost ground to Taft and Willkie. On the fourth ballot, Willkie surpassed both Dewey and Taft. On the fifth ballot, the race was between Taft and Willkie, and when Michigan shifted its votes to Willkie, a bandwagon began. A motion to make his nomination unanimous was adopted.

Senate Minority Leader Charles L. McNary of Oregon was Willkie's preferred running mate. The Oregon senator had supported several pieces of New Deal legislation. He easily won the nomination on the first ballot.

The platform was adopted without debate. In most respects it mirrored the one adopted by the Democrats at their convention. However, the platform did criticize the Roosevelt administration for being unprepared for war, if necessary.

— 1944 —

The Republicans met in Chicago in June 1944 with the United States at war. The nomination for president was easily won by Governor Thomas E. Dewey of New York, who received all the votes except one that was cast by a Wisconsin delegate for General Douglas MacArthur. The unanimous choice of the convention for the number-two spot was Governor John W. Bricker of Ohio. Bricker had been a candidate for the presidency but withdrew from the race before the first roll call.

For the first time at a Republican convention, the nominee appeared before the delegates to accept the nomination personally. Much of Dewey's acceptance speech was an attack on the Roosevelt administration.

The party's platform was accepted without debate. With the war in Europe continuing, the Republicans called for the United States to be a responsible participant in any postwar international organization. In addition, the party endorsed the creation of a Jewish state in Palestine.

The domestic agenda called for passage of the Equal Rights Amendment, a two-term limit on the presidency, and the establishment of a Fair Employment Practice Commission and also denounced the centralizing effect of the New Deal.

— 1948 —

The Republican Convention was held in Philadelphia in June 1948. The front-runner was the party's 1944 standard-bearer, Thomas E. Dewey. However, in contrast to 1944, Dewey faced competition for the nomination from Senator Robert A. Taft of Ohio and former Minnesota Governor Harold E. Stassen.

After the first ballot, Dewey held a substantial lead over his rivals. The second ballot increased his lead, but his vote total was still short of the majority necessary to garner the nomination. Being confident of his renomination, Dewey's organization allowed for a recess so that the anti-Dewey forces could organize themselves. However, his opponents were unable to form a coalition around any one alternative. Both Taft and Stassen withdrew from consideration before the third ballot. On that ballot, Dewey won the nomination unanimously.

Governor Earl Warren of California was the personal choice of Dewey for the vice presidential nomination. Warren accepted the nomination by acclamation on the condition that the responsibilities of the post would be increased under Dewey.

The Republican platform of 1948 did not spend a great deal of verbiage criticizing the Truman administration. Instead, it praised the 80th Congress and outlined the party's agenda for the country. The planks supported the Taft–Hartley Act, the Marshall Plan, membership in the United Nations, and recognition of Israel. In addition, the platform continued its pledge to end segregation in the military and pass legislation to outlaw lynching.

— 1952 —

The July 1952 Republican Convention, held in Chicago, placed the conservative and moderate/liberal wings of the party in direct conflict.

The conservative forces favored Senator Robert A. Taft of Ohio, while the moderate and liberal wings preferred General Dwight D. Eisenhower of Texas, who had resigned his commission as supreme commander of the North Atlantic Treaty Organization (NATO) earlier in the year in order to pursue the nomination.

Prior to the presidential balloting, there were two tests of the factions' relative strength. The first was over the voting rights of challenged delegates. The Taft forces favored the 1948 rule that allowed challenged delegates to vote in all cases except their own. Eisenhower's supporters offered what was termed the fair-play amendment, which stipulated that only those delegates who received two-thirds support from the credentials committee could vote. After a counteroffer by the Taft forces, the fair-play amendment was adopted by a voice vote.

The second test of strength came in regard to challenged delegates from Georgia, Louisiana, and Texas. After a heated debate on the Georgia delegates, a roll-call vote supported the Eisenhower minority report.

Republican National Convention, Chicago, July 1952. Eisenhower's Acceptance. *Source:* National Archives.

The other two challenges also went Eisenhower's way on voice votes.

After the initial roll call, five men had received votes. Eisenhower was in the lead and needed only nine more votes to secure the nomination, although Taft was a close second. However, before the second roll could be called, Minnesota switched 19 of its votes to Eisenhower, starting a bandwagon that resulted in Eisenhower's unanimous nomination for president.

Thirty-nine-year-old California Senator Richard M. Nixon was chosen by Eisenhower as his running mate. Nixon was nominated by acclamation.

The party platform was adopted on a voice vote. The 6,000-word document attacked the Roosevelt and Truman administrations. In addition, the planks called for American military preparedness and declared that there were no communists to be found in the Republican Party. On the domestic front, the platform endorsed a reduction in federal power, a civil rights agenda, and states' rights.

— 1956 —

As the Republicans gathered in San Francisco in August 1956, the issue of who would be the party's

nominee for president had been settled with President Dwight D. Eisenhower's strong recovery from his heart attack. When the delegates voted, he received all 1,323 votes.

A preconvention move by former Governor Harold E. Stassen of Minnesota, Eisenhower's disarmament adviser, to replace Vice President Richard M. Nixon with Governor Christian A. Herter of Massachusetts did not receive support from the party leaders. On the first round of the vice presidential balloting, Nixon was unanimously renominated.

Several southern delegates withdrew from the convention in opposition to the party's civil rights plank, which recounted the advances made in desegregation under Eisenhower's leadership. The plank also endorsed the Supreme Court rulings and committed the party to enforcement of civil rights laws. In other domestic areas, the platform lauded the balanced budget and reductions in taxes. The party favored revisions to the Taft–Hartley Act and the elimination of agricultural surpluses.

In the area of foreign affairs, the Eisenhower administration was praised for its efforts to stem the spread of communism by ending the Korean War. The party was staunchly pro-Israel, in contrast to the Democrats. The planks also spoke of the military preparedness of the United States as a counter to the Democratic charges that budget cutting limited U.S. readiness.

— 1960 —

Vice President Richard M. Nixon was clearly going to win the Republican nomination for president as the delegates gathered in Chicago in July 1960 for their convention.

Nixon's two chief rivals, Senator Barry Goldwater of Arizona and Governor Nelson A. Rockefeller of New York, had both withdrawn from the race. Despite his withdrawal, Goldwater's name was still placed in nomination. On the first roll call, Nixon received all the votes except ten from the Louisiana delegation that went to Goldwater. However, on a voice vote, the nomination was made unanimous.

Rockefeller was Nixon's first choice as a running mate. However, being unable to convince him to take the post, Nixon chose United Nations Ambassador and former Senator Henry Cabot Lodge Jr. of Massachusetts.

The 1960 Republican platform was, in large part, the result of a secret meeting between Nixon and Rockefeller in which the two worked out many of the major issues. The "compact of Fifth Avenue," as it has been called because the meeting was held in Rockefeller's New York City apartment, dealt equally with national defense and domestic issues.

The agreement upset party conservatives, especially Goldwater, who called the agreement "the Munich of the Republican Party." Two specific planks were the most controversial. The original civil rights plank was strengthened with language that supported civil rights demonstrations and job equality for blacks. Nixon threatened the committee with a floor fight if the upgraded language was not adopted. The committee, in the end, adopted the stronger Nixon–Rockefeller language. In the defense plank, the compact sought and received language supporting the necessity of a rapid upgrade of the military. The entire platform—which included planks supporting a balanced budget, flexible farm supports, passage of the Equal Rights Amendment, and support for local autonomy—was approved by a voice vote without any minority reports.

— 1964 —

The cracks between the conservative and moderate/liberal wings of the Republican Party that had begun to show at the 1960 Republican Convention were dramatically apparent at the July 1964 San Francisco gathering.

Senator Barry Goldwater of Arizona, leader of the conservative movement in the party, held a substantial lead going into the convention. His chief opponent for the nomination was Governor William W. Scranton of Pennsylvania, the leader of the moderates. Two days before the balloting, a Scranton staff member sent a letter allegedly from Scranton to Goldwater attacking the senator's ideology as dangerous. The letter challenged Goldwater to a debate. While Scranton had not penned the letter, he decided to support the call for a debate. Goldwater, however, refused.

While seven others were nominated, Goldwater easily garnered enough votes to win the nomination over Scranton, who came in a distant second.

Goldwater selected Representative William E. Miller of New York as his running mate, in part because "he drives [Lyndon] Johnson nuts." Miller won all but three delegate votes, becoming the first Roman Catholic nominated on the Republican ticket.

In his acceptance speech, Goldwater stuck to his conservative themes. "I would remind you that extremism in the defense of liberty is no vice. And . . . moderation in the pursuit of justice is no virtue." He hoped that the call to liberty and justice would propel the party toward a more defined and conservative path.

The 1964 platform was challenged by moderate forces in the platform committee, where more than 70 different amendments were submitted. However, when the platform came to the floor of the convention, moderates challenged only three issues.

The first issue considered was extremism. A minority report condemning specific groups like the John Birch Society, the Ku Klux Klan and the Communist Party was submitted by Senator Hugh Scott of Pennsylvania and defended in the debate by Governor Nelson A. Rockefeller of New York. Rockefeller's speech was not well received by the conservative majority, who booed him throughout his presentation. This substitute plank as well as another one that did not specify groups, submitted by Governor George E. Romney of Michigan, was handily defeated on a standing vote.

A more extensive substitute civil rights plank offered by Scott was defeated, as was another by Romney. The original plank that supported the Civil Rights Act of 1964 but qualified its extent was retained.

Scott's final attempt to modify the conservative platform was in the area of nuclear weapons. The substitute amendment wanted a clear statement that the president had the sole authority to authorize the use of nuclear weapons. Goldwater favored the original plank, which gave greater authority to North Atlantic Treaty Organization commanders. On a standing vote the Scott substitute was defeated.

The final platform was divided into four parts. The first two were critical of the Democrats in the areas of foreign and domestic affairs. The last two sections offered the Republican alternatives in both domestic and foreign policy. The platform, which was approved on a voice vote, contained planks that included a call for the immediate removal of the Berlin Wall, a reduction in federal spending, a pledge to end deficit spending, and support for a constitutional amendment allowing school prayer.

— 1968 —

Unlike the Democratic Convention in Chicago, which saw violent protests, the Republican Convention in Miami Beach, Florida, in August 1968 was calm.

The race for the nomination was among three candidates, former Vice President Richard M. Nixon of California, Governor Nelson A. Rockefeller of New York, and Governor Ronald Reagan of California. The liberal Rockefeller and the conservative Reagan were

unable to reach any compromise that could keep Nixon from being nominated. On the first roll call, Nixon garnered 25 more votes than were necessary to capture the Republican nomination.

Nixon surprised many by selecting Governor Spiro T. Agnew of Maryland as his running mate. Agnew had initially supported Rockefeller in the race but announced his support for Nixon at the beginning of the convention. The only other candidate for the post was Governor George Romney of Michigan. Agnew easily outdistanced Romney for the nomination.

The 1968 party platform was adopted without debate. Its planks struck a middle ground, avoiding the starkly conservative tones of the 1964 document. Much of the document dealt with Vietnam and the Johnson administration's handling of it. The original hard-line language was replaced with a call for the de-Americanization of the efforts in Vietnam. The platform also addressed the issue of crime, which the party believed the Johnson administration had ignored. On two important issues affecting youth, the party called for the lowering of the voting age to 18 and a reduction in the time during which young men would be eligible for the draft.

Republican National Convention, Miami Beach, Florida, 1968. *Source:* Wide World.

— 1972 —

Although the August 1972 convention had originally been scheduled for San Diego, California, the lack of facilities and the corporate giant ITT's pledge of $400,000 to the campaigns brought the Republicans back to the same Miami Beach, Florida, convention center where the 1968 convention had been held.

The renomination of President Richard M. Nixon and Vice President Spiro T. Agnew was assured. In fact, in the presidential nominating, Nixon received all but one vote, which was cast by a New Mexico delegate for antiwar candidate Representative Paul N. McCloskey Jr. of California. Agnew received all but two abstentions and one vote for veteran newscaster David Brinkley.

The only event that occasioned debate was a new delegate-allocation rule. The Republican National Committee approved a new vote-allocation system submitted by Senator John G. Tower of Texas and Reprentative Jack F. Kemp of New York to give bonus delegates to states that voted for the Republican presidential candidate. A substitute plan offered by Representative William A. Steiger of Wisconsin that favored bonus delegates for gubernatorial and congressional voting strength was defeated. The original rule, which favored small southern and western states, was adopted.

Two amendments to the platform were offered from the floor. The first, calling for a prohibition on deficit spending, was defeated. The second proposal, supporting self-determination for American Indians, was approved by a voice vote.

The 1972 platform was also approved by a voice vote of the delegates. The platform, drafted largely by the White House, criticized not only the Democratic nominee, Senator George McGovern of South Dakota, but the administrations of John F. Kennedy and Lyndon B. Johnson. Generally, its language was conservative, while the actual proposals were moderate. In its domestic agenda, the Republicans opposed busing students for the purpose of desegregation, gun control, and the legalization of marijuana. Additionally, it supported tax reform, the Equal Rights Amendment, and national health insurance. On the foreign policy side, the Vietnam War was the central issue, with the Republicans pledging not to forsake the South Vietnamese and demanding the return of all prisoners of war and those missing in action.

— 1976 —

The delegates who convened in Kansas City, Missouri, in August 1976 were relatively evenly split between moderate and conservative forces. The moderates supported President Gerald R. Ford of Michigan, while the conservatives backed former Governor Ronald Reagan of California. Both candidates arrived at the convention early in order to pursue delegates.

The Reagan forces failed by 111 votes to pass a rule that would have required the announcement of running mates by the presidential contenders prior to the nominating ballots. Under the unsuccessful provision, any candidate failing to announce a running mate would have his delegates freed from their commitment. The vote was dramatic, as the Reagan-backed proposal led early on but lost ground when New York, Ohio, and Pennsylvania voted generally against the measure. At the tail end of the roll call, the opponents' lead diminished, but the proposal finally went down to defeat when Florida and Mississippi—both of which had passed on the initial call—voted against the measure.

In the actual presidential balloting, Ford defeated Reagan by a mere 17 votes. However, on a voice vote, the nomination was made unanimous.

Republican National Convention, Kansas City, Missouri, 1976. President Ford and Running Mate, Senator Robert Dole of Kansas, Face Supporters at the Closing Session. *Source:* White House.

When Reagan showed no interest in the number-two spot, Ford turned to Senator Robert Dole of Kansas to replace the unpopular Vice President Nelson A. Rockefeller. On the roll-call vote, Dole easily beat out a field of 30 other candidates, including the distant second-place vote getter, Senator Jesse A. Helms of North Carolina.

In his acceptance speech, Ford defended his record since assuming the presidency in 1974. Furthermore, he issued a challenge to the Democratic candidate, Governor James E. "Jimmy" Carter of Georgia, to debate openly the differences between the two men's visions of America.

The 1976 platform was a moderately conservative document that both praised Ford's administration and attacked the Democratic Congress. Two minority planks produced some controversy. The first was a proposal to eliminate all references to abortion. The platform supported a constitutional amendment guaranteeing the right to life. After a 12-minute debate, the minority proposal was defeated and the constitutional amendment language remained.

In the area of foreign policy, a second minority report was proposed, which criticized Ford and Secretary of State Henry A. Kissinger for their activities. The Ford campaign, deciding not to engage in a protracted debate on foreign policy, allowed the measure to pass on a voice vote without mounting any opposition.

The remainder of the platform was also adopted on a voice vote. It continued to support limited government and took credit for the favorable direction of the economy.

— 1980 —

As the Republicans gathered at Joe Louis Arena in Detroit in July 1980 for their convention, the eventual nominee, former Governor Ronald Reagan of California, was clearly going to be the party's standard-bearer.

The only drama of the event was the question of who would occupy the number-two spot on the ticket. For much of the convention, it looked as if former President Gerald R. Ford would take the post, creating what many termed "the dream ticket." Ford, in several interviews, indicated that he would accept the position only if its duties were substantially enhanced. He did not want to be a figurehead. Reports indicated that Ford wanted a role closer to that of a chief of staff, with broad leadership, especially in domestic affairs.

In addition to the new role for the vice presidency, there was the question of the 12th Amendment's pro-

hibition against a state's electoral college voters' casting their votes for a president and vice president from the same state. Ford had moved to California after his loss of the White House in 1976. Reagan's staff had researched the issue thoroughly and offered two solutions. The first solution was that the amendment did not bar non-California electors from voting for both of the California residents. The second solution had Ford moving back to Michigan or to his home in Colorado.

Reagan was on the phone pushing the former president to make up his mind when the roll-call vote on his nomination for president was made. In the end, the Reagan–Ford ticket fell apart.

With Ford's withdrawal, Reagan turned to his chief competitor for the nomination, George Bush of Texas, whose credentials included two terms in the House of Representatives, ambassador to the United Nations, head of the United States liaison office in Beijing, and director of the Central Intelligence Agency. Bush offered geographical balance, with his strength in the Midwest and Northeast, as well as giving the Republican ticket extensive Washington experience, though some were not happy with the choice of the moderate Bush over more conservative alternatives. In the balloting for the nomination, Bush easily received enough votes. Conservative Senator Jesse Helms of North Carolina, however, did receive very modest support.

The 1980 Republican platform was generally a compromise document crafted to cloud the differences between the conservative and moderate wings of the party. Additionally, several planks were changed or omitted to reflect the views of the party's standard-bearer. The most notable of these changes and omissions were the silence on the Equal Rights Amendment, which had been supported by the party since 1940, and the plank against the reinstatement of the draft at this time.

However, the majority of the document was agreeable to almost all Republicans. The platform was highly critical of the Carter administration. It took a hard-line stance on defense issues and on abortion, with the party favoring a constitutional amendment to protect the unborn and the appointment of only antiabortion federal judges. The party also attempted to reach out to traditionally Democratic voters like organized labor, blacks, and the poor by making stronger commitments to workers, civil rights enforcement and urban renewal.

Though attempts were made to change the platform's Equal Rights Amendment stance and the staunchly prolife plank, these efforts failed. In the end, the entire platform was adopted by a voice vote.

— 1984 —

The Republican Convention of August 1984 in Dallas was a festive occasion as the party's nominees, President Ronald Reagan and Vice President George Bush, were the beneficiaries of an improving economy and renewed United States leadership in foreign affairs.

Many of the convention's speakers, including former President Gerald R. Ford, focused on the service of Walter F. Mondale, the Democratic Party's nominee, as vice president under Jimmy Carter. From the Republican perspective, voters could choose to return to the malaise of the Carter administration or accept the shining future the Republicans had crafted.

In addition to the constant linking of Mondale with the failed Carter years, the Republicans used special events and speakers to counter the placement of Representative Geraldine A. Ferraro of New York on the Democratic ticket. In a well-received appearance, Democrat-turned-Republican Ambassador to the United Nations Jeane J. Kirkpatrick gave an impressive foreign policy address. In addition, the keynote address was delivered by U.S. Treasurer Katherine D. Ortega.

For the first time in the party's history, the nominees were selected on a joint roll-call vote.

The 1984 platform's nearly 30,000 words were largely shaped by the White House. The party's domestic agenda was broad. The document continued its call for tax cuts and reforms leading to a flat tax, with some exemptions such as home mortgage interest. The commitment was in sharp contrast to Mondale's pledge to raise taxes to balance the budget. The platform also criticized the Federal Reserve Board for what it saw as a too restrictive monetary policy. Despite attempts to include an Equal Rights Amendment plank, it was omitted because of Reagan's opposition to it. The party supported the abolition of both the Department of Energy and the Department of Education. It sought to appoint only judges who opposed abortion on demand. Additionally, the platform included support for students' right to engage in voluntary school prayer.

On the foreign policy side, the platform criticized the Carter–Mondale administration's record. It called attention to the real threat that the Soviet Union posed to world peace. The planks also included support for the Reagan administration's policy in Central America, especially in El Salvador.

— 1988 —

President Ronald Reagan addressed the gathered delegates at the Superdome on the opening day of the August 1988 GOP Convention held in New Orleans. Reagan praised the party's nominee, Vice President George Bush, for the important roles he had played in the administration. In response to the "Where was George?" speech of the Democratic nominee, Governor Michael S. Dukakis of Massachusetts, Reagan repeatedly replied that "George was there."

The convention featured a keynote address by Governor Thomas H. Kean of New Jersey as well as speeches by evangelist Pat Robertson, United Nations Ambassador Jeane J. Kirkpatrick, and former President Gerald R. Ford.

The most dramatic issue of the convention was whom Bush would select as his vice presidential running mate. Bush had planned on keeping his choice secret until the last day of the convention. However, at the Belle Chasse Naval Air Station, after saying good-bye to President Reagan, Bush announced his choice of Senator J. Danforth Quayle of Indiana. The selection of the young senator was unexpected, creating a stir to find out more about him.

Three specific issues caused much consternation over his selection. The first involved a 1980 incident in Florida in which Quayle and two colleagues were seen with lobbyist Paula Parkinson, who later posed for *Playboy* and claimed to have had sex with members of Congress. Quayle denied any sexual involvement with Parkinson. However, he handled the press's inquiries in a less than convincing manner.

The second controversy surrounded Quayle's personal wealth. As an heir to the Pulliam publishing fortune, his net worth had been estimated by some at $200 million. Quayle chose to downplay his wealth as an issue.

Finally, there were questions about his service in the Indiana National Guard during the Vietnam War. There were allegations that his family used its influence to get him assigned to the National Guard in order to avoid the draft. Quayle denied the charge, stating that the decision to join the guard had more to do with his plans to attend law school, get married, and start a family.

In the meantime, Vice President Bush received the renomination of his party after his name had been placed in contention by Senator Phil Gramm of Texas and seconded by actress Helen Hayes, Penn State football coach Joe Paterno, and Columba Bush, the vice president's Mexican American daughter-in-law.

James A. Baker III, Bush's national campaign chairman, was busy with damage control from the early announcement of Quayle as Bush's choice for the number-two spot. There was much speculation that the campaign was going to drop Quayle from the ticket. Baker, however, was sent on a series of interviews to dispel the rumors.

After a number of congressional colleagues spoke highly of the young senator, Quayle was nominated by acclamation in order to avoid opposition. In his acceptance speech, Quayle answered many of his critics concerning his military service. Attacking the liberal legacy of the Democratic Party, Quayle was able to rally the delegates behind him.

Bush's acceptance speech, in which he also attacked the liberal agenda of the Democrats and included the ill-fated "Read my lips. No new taxes" promise, ended with the Pledge of Allegiance, a shot at the Democratic nominee's veto of a bill requiring Massachusetts public school students to recite the pledge.

The 1988 platform, adopted without debate, included planks to freeze government spending, reform welfare, establish a youth training wage, and defend the right to own a gun. In addition to its extensive domestic agenda, the platform addressed issues of security and foreign relations on every continent as well as the Strategic Defense Initiative.

— 1992 —

The August 1992 Houston convention opened with a strong speech by former President Ronald Reagan. In his opening remarks, Reagan reminded delegates and the nation of the accomplishments of 12 years of Republican leadership. The foreign policy accomplishments of the Gulf War and the end of communism were contrasted with the failures of the last Democratic president, Jimmy Carter.

Despite opposition to the right-to-life plank, the entire platform was adopted on a voice vote without debate. Much of the domestic agenda reflected the theme of family values, including calls for tax credits for school choice and for young children. Additionally, the domestic planks dealt with AIDS research; welfare reform; stiffer penalties for criminals, especially drug offenders; and continued business deregulation. The foreign policy planks praised the accomplishments of the Reagan and Bush administrations and called for continued strong Republican leadership.

While a preconvention move to dump Quayle from the ticket had failed, many leading Republicans—including Housing and Urban Development Secretary Jack F. Kemp of New York, Governor William F. Weld of Massachusetts, and political commentator Patrick J. Buchanan of Virginia—took the opportunity to lay the foundations for future political aspirations. Buchanan, who had challenged President George Bush in the primaries, gave a rousing speech in which he dedicated his activities to the reelection of the Bush–Quayle ticket.

The Astrodome crowd heard from many speakers, including Marilyn Quayle—who gave a speech that attacked the activities of Democratic nominee Bill Clinton—Barbara Bush, evangelist Pat Robertson, Governors Tommy G. Thompson of Wisconsin and John Engler of Michigan, and GOP fund-raiser and AIDS victim Mary Fisher.

Labor Secretary Lynn Martin placed Bush's name into nomination. The president was renominated with all but 44 of the votes, as 18 votes went to Buchanan, three went to other candidates, and New Hampshire delegates did not cast the state's 23 votes.

The acceptance speeches of the party's nominees did not live up to the advance billing. Quayle attacked his critics and contrasted his Vietnam activities to those of Clinton. Bush tried to defend his broken "no new taxes" pledge by blaming the Democrat-controlled Congress. Sticking to his strong suit, Bush emphasized his foreign policy successes, especially the Gulf War.

PLATFORMS

— 1856 —

This Convention of Delegates, assembled in pursuance of a call addressed to the people of the United States, without regard to past political differences or divisions, who are opposed to the repeal of the Missouri Compromise; to the policy of the present Administration; to the extension of Slavery into Free Territory; in favor of the admission of Kansas as a Free State; of restoring the action of the Federal Government to the principles of Washington and Jefferson; and for the purpose of presenting candidates for the offices of President and Vice-President, do

Resolved: That the maintenance of the principles promulgated in the Declaration of Independence, and embodied in the Federal Constitution are essential to the preservation of our Republican institutions, and that the Federal Constitution, the rights of the States, and the union of the States, must and shall be preserved.

Resolved: That, with our Republican fathers, we hold it to be a self-evident truth, that all men are endowed with the inalienable right to life, liberty, and the pursuit of happiness, and that the primary object and ulterior design of our Federal Government were to secure these rights to all persons under its exclusive jurisdiction; that, as our Republican fathers, when they had abolished Slavery in all our National Territory, ordained that no person shall be deprived of life, liberty, or property, without due process of law, it becomes our duty to maintain this provision of the Constitution against all attempts to violate it for the purpose of establishing Slavery in the Territories of the United States by positive legislation, prohibiting its existence or extension therein. That we deny the authority of Congress, of a Territorial Legislation, of any individual, or association of individuals, to give legal existence to Slavery in any Territory of the United States, while the present Constitution shall be maintained.

Resolved: That the Constitution confers upon Congress sovereign powers over the Territories of the United States for their government; and that in the exercise of this power, it is both the right and the imperative duty of Congress to prohibit in the Territories those twin relics of barbarism—Polygamy, and Slavery.

Resolved: That while the Constitution of the United States was ordained and established by the people, in order to "form a more perfect union, establish justice, insure domestic tranquility, provide for the common defense, promote the general welfare, and secure the blessings of liberty," and contain ample provision for the protection of the life, liberty, and property of every citizen, the dearest Constitutional rights of the people of Kansas have been fraudulently and violently taken from them.

Their Territory has been invaded by an armed force;

Spurious and pretended legislative, judicial, and executive officers have been set over them, by whose usurped authority, sustained by the military power of the government, tyrannical and unconstitutional laws have been enacted and enforced;

The right of the people to keep and bear arms has been infringed.

Test oaths of an extraordinary and entangling nature have been imposed as a condition of exercising the right of suffrage and holding office.

The right of an accused person to a speedy and public trial by an impartial jury has been denied;

The right of the people to be secure in their persons, houses, papers, and effects, against unreasonable searches and seizures, has been violated;

They have been deprived of life, liberty, and property without due process of law;

That the freedom of speech and of the press has been abridged;

The right to choose their representatives has been made of no effect;

Murders, robberies, and arsons have been instigated and encouraged, and the offenders have been allowed to go unpunished;

That all these things have been done with the knowledge, sanction, and procurement of the present National Administration; and that for this high crime against the Constitution, the Union, and humanity, we arraign that Administration, the President, his advisers, agents, supporters, apologists, and accessories, either *before* or *after* the fact, before the country and before the world; and that it is our fixed purpose to bring the actual perpetrators of these atrocious outrages and their accomplices to a sure and condign punishment thereafter.

Resolved: That Kansas should be immediately admitted as a state of this Union, with her present Free Constitution, as at once the most effectual way of securing to her citizens the enjoyment of the rights and privileges to which they are entitled, and of ending the civil strife now raging in her territory.

Resolved: That the highwayman's plea, that "might makes right," embodied in the Ostend Circular, was in every respect unworthy of American diplomacy, and would bring shame and dishonor upon any Government or people that gave it their sanction.

Resolved: That a railroad to the Pacific Ocean by the most central and practicable route is imperatively demanded by the interests of the whole country, and that the Federal Government ought to render immediate and efficient aid in its construction, and as an auxiliary thereto, to the immediate construction of an emigrant road on the line of the railroad.

Resolved: That appropriations by Congress for the improvement of rivers and harbors, of a national character, required for the accommodation and security of our existing commerce, are authorized by the Constitution, and justified by the obligation of the Government to protect the lives and property of its citizens.

Resolved: That we invite the affiliation and cooperation of the men of all parties, however differing from us in other respects, in support of the principles herein declared; and believing that the spirit of our institutions as well as the Constitution of our country, guarantees liberty of conscience and equality of rights among citizens, we oppose all legislation impairing their security.

— 1860 —

Resolved, That we, the delegated representatives of the Republican electors of the United States, in Convention assembled, in discharge of the duty we owe to our constituents and our country, unite in the following declarations:

1. That the history of the nation during the last four years, has fully established the propriety and necessity of the organization and perpetuation of the Republican party, and that the causes which called it into existence are permanent in their nature, and now, more than ever before, demand its peaceful and constitutional triumph.

2. That the maintenance of the principles promulgated in the Declaration of Independence and embodied in the Federal Constitution, "That all men are created equal; that they are endowed by their Creator with certain inalienable rights; that among these are life, liberty and the pursuit of happiness; that to secure these rights, governments are instituted among men, deriving their just powers from the consent of the governed," is essential to the preservation of our Republican institutions; and that the Federal Constitution, the Rights of the States, and the Union of the States must and shall be preserved.

3. That to the Union of the States this nation owes its unprecedented increase in population, its surprising development of material resources, its rapid augmentation of wealth, its happiness at home and its honor abroad; and we hold in abhorrence all schemes for disunion, come from whatever source they may. And we congratulate the country that no Republican member of Congress has uttered or countenanced the threats of disunion so often made by Democratic members, without rebuke and with applause from their political associates; and we denounce those threats of disunion, in case of a popular overthrow of their ascendancy as denying the vital principles of a free government, and as an avowal of contemplated treason, which it is the imperative duty of an indignant people sternly to rebuke and forever silence.

4. That the maintenance inviolate of the rights of the states, and especially the right of each state to order and control its own domestic institutions according to its own judgment exclusively, is essential to that balance of powers on which the perfection and endurance of our political fabric depends; and we denounce the lawless invasion by armed force of the soil of any state or territory, no matter under what pretext, as among the gravest of crimes.

5. That the present Democratic Administration has far exceeded our worst apprehensions, in its measureless subserviency to the exactions of a sectional interest, as especially evinced in its desperate exertions to force the infamous Lecompton Constitution upon the protesting people of Kansas; in construing the personal relations between master and servant to involve an unqualified property in persons; in its attempted enforcement everywhere, on land and sea, through the

intervention of Congress and of the Federal Courts of the extreme pretensions of a purely local interest; and in its general and unvarying abuse of the power intrusted to it by a confiding people.

6. That the people justly view with alarm the reckless extravagance which pervades every department of the Federal Government; that a return to rigid economy and accountability is indispensable to arrest the systematic plunder of the public treasury by favored partisans; while the recent startling developments of frauds and corruptions at the Federal metropolis, show that an entire change of administration is imperatively demanded.

7. That the new dogma that the Constitution, of its own force, carries slavery into any or all of the territories of the United States, is a dangerous political heresy, at variance with the explicit provisions of that instrument itself, with contemporaneous exposition, and with legislative and judicial precedent; is revolutionary in its tendency, and subversive of the peace and harmony of the country.

8. That the normal condition of all the territory of the United States is that of freedom: That, as our Republican fathers, when they had abolished slavery in all our national territory, ordained that "no persons should be deprived of life, liberty or property without due process of law," it becomes our duty, by legislation, whenever such legislation is necessary, to maintain this provision of the Constitution against all attempts to violate it; and we deny the authority of Congress, of a territorial legislature, or of any individuals, to give legal existence to slavery in any territory of the United States.

9. That we brand the recent reopening of the African slave trade, under the cover of our national flag, aided by perversions of judicial power, as a crime against humanity and a burning shame to our country and age; and we call upon Congress to take prompt and efficient measures for the total and final suppression of that execrable traffic.

10. That in the recent vetoes, by their Federal Governors, of the acts of the legislatures of Kansas and Nebraska, prohibiting slavery in those territories, we find a practical illustration of the boasted Democratic principle of Non-Intervention and Popular Sovereignty, embodied in the Kansas–Nebraska Bill, and a demonstration of the deception and fraud involved therein.

11. That Kansas should, of right, be immediately admitted as a state under the Constitution recently formed and adopted by her people, and accepted by the House of Representatives.

12. That, while providing revenue for the support of the general government by duties upon imports, sound policy requires such an adjustment of these imports as to encourage the development of the industrial interests of the whole country; and we commend that policy of national exchanges, which secures to the workingmen liberal wages, to agriculture remunerative prices, to mechanics and manufacturers an adequate reward for their skill, labor, and enterprise, and to the nation commercial prosperity and independence.

13. That we protest against any sale or alienation to others of the public lands held by actual settlers, and against any view of the free-homestead policy which regards the settlers as paupers or suppliants for public bounty; and we demand the passage by Congress of the complete and satisfactory homestead measure which has already passed the House.

14. That the Republican party is opposed to any change in our naturalization laws or any state legislation by which the rights of citizens hitherto accorded to immigrants from foreign lands shall be abridged or impaired; and in favor of giving a full and efficient protection of the rights of all classes of citizens, whether native or naturalized, both at home and abroad.

15. That appropriations by Congress for river and harbor improvements of a national character, required for the accommodation and security of an existing commerce, are authorized by the Constitution, and justified by the obligation of Government to protect the lives and property of its citizens.

16. That a railroad to the Pacific Ocean is imperatively demanded by the interests of the whole country; that the Federal Government ought to render immediate and efficient aid in its construction; and that, as preliminary thereto, a daily overland mail should be promptly established.

17. Finally, having thus set forth our distinctive principles and view, we invite the co-operation of all citizens, however differing on other questions, who substantially agree with us in their affirmance and support.

— 1864 —

1. *Resolved*, That it is the highest duty of every American citizen to maintain against all their enemies the integrity of the Union and the paramount authority of the Constitution and laws of the United States; and that, laying aside all differences of political opinion, we pledge ourselves, as Union men, animated by a common sentiment and aiming at a common object, to do everything in our power to aid the Government

in quelling by force of arms the Rebellion now raging against its authority, and in bringing to the punishment due to their crimes the Rebels and traitors arrayed against it.

2. *Resolved*, That we approve the determination of the Government of the United States not to compromise with Rebels, or to offer them any terms of peace, except such as may be based upon an unconditional surrender of their hostility and a return to their just allegiance to the Constitution and laws of the United States, and that we call upon the Government to maintain this position and to prosecute the war with the utmost possible vigor to the complete suppression of the Rebellion, in full reliance upon the self-sacrificing patriotism, the heroic valor and the undying devotion of the American people to the country and its free institutions.

3. *Resolved*, That as slavery was the cause, and now constitutes the strength of this Rebellion, and as it must be, always and everywhere, hostile to the principles of Republican Government, justice and the National safety demand its utter and complete extirpation from the soil of the Republic; and that, while we uphold and maintain the acts and proclamations by which the Government, in its own defense, has aimed a deathblow at this gigantic evil, we are in favor, furthermore, of such an amendment to the Constitution, to be made by the people in conformity with its provisions, as shall terminate and forever prohibit the existence of slavery within the limits of the jurisdiction of the United States.

4. *Resolved*, That the thanks of the American people are due to the soldiers and sailors of the Army and Navy, who have periled their lives in defense of the country and in vindication of the honor of its flag; that the nation owes to them some permanent recognition of their patriotism and their valor, and ample and permanent provision for those of their survivors who have received disabling and honorable wounds in the service of the country; and that the memories of those who have fallen in its defense shall be held in grateful and everlasting remembrance.

5. *Resolved*, That we approve and applaud the practical wisdom, the unselfish patriotism and the unswerving fidelity to the Constitution and the principles of American liberty, with which ABRAHAM LINCOLN has discharged, under circumstances of unparalleled difficulty, the great duties and responsibilities of the Presidential office; that we approve and indorse, as demanded by the emergency and essential to the preservation of the nation and as within the provisions of the Constitution, the measures and acts which he has adopted to defend the nation against its open and secret foes; that we approve, especially, the Proclamation of Emancipation, and the employment as Union soldiers of men heretofore held in slavery; and that we have full confidence in his determination to carry these and all other Constitutional measures essential to the salvation of the country into full and complete effect.

6. *Resolved*, That we deem it essential to the general welfare that harmony should prevail in the National Councils, and we regard as worthy of public confidence and official trust those only who cordially indorse the principles proclaimed in these resolutions, and which should characterize the administration of the Government.

7. *Resolved*, That the Government owes to all men employed in its armies, without regard to distinction of color, the full protection of the laws of war—and that any violation of these laws, or of the usages of civilized nations in time of war, by the Rebels now in arms, should be made the subject of prompt and full redress.

8. *Resolved*, That foreign immigration, which in the past has added so much to the wealth, development of resources and increase of power to the nation, the asylum of the oppressed of all nations, should be fostered and encouraged by a liberal and just policy.

9. *Resolved*, That we are in favor of the speedy construction of the railroad to the Pacific coast.

10. *Resolved*, That the National faith, pledged for the redemption of the public debt, must be kept inviolate, and that for this purpose we recommend economy and rigid responsibility in the public expenditures, and a vigorous and just system of taxation; and that it is the duty of every loyal state to sustain the credit and promote the use of the National currency.

11. *Resolved*, That we approve the position taken by the Government that the people of the United States can never regard with indifference the attempt of any European Power to overthrow by force or to supplant by fraud the institutions of any Republican Government on the Western Continent and that they will view with extreme jealousy, as menacing to the peace and independence of their own country, the efforts of any such power to obtain new footholds for Monarchical Government, sustained by foreign military force, in near proximity to the United States.

— 1868 —

The National Union Republican Party of the United States, assembled in National Convention, in the city of Chicago, on the 20th day of May, 1868, make the following declaration of principles:

First—We congratulate the country on the assured success of the reconstruction policy of Congress, as evinced by the adoption, in the majority of the States lately in rebellion, of constitutions securing equal civil and political rights to all, and regard it as the duty of the Government to sustain those constitutions, and to prevent the people of such States from being remitted to a state of anarchy or military rule.

Second—The guaranty by Congress of equal suffrage to all loyal men of the South was demanded by every consideration of public safety, of gratitude, and of justice, and must be maintained; while the question of suffrage in all the loyal States properly belongs to the people of those States.

Third—We denounce all forms of repudiation as a national crime; and national honor requires the payment of the public indebtedness in the utmost good faith to all creditors at home and abroad, not only according to the letter, but the spirit of the laws under which it was contracted.

Fourth—It is due to the labor of the nation, that taxation should be equalized and reduced as rapidly as the national faith will permit.

Fifth—The National Debt, contracted as it has been for the preservation of the Union for all time to come, should be extended over a fair period of redemption, and it is the duty of Congress to reduce the rate of interest thereon whenever it can be done honestly.

Sixth—That the best policy to diminish our burden of debt, is to so improve our credit that capitalists will seek to loan us money at lower rates of interest than we now pay and must continue to pay so long as repudiation, partial or total, open or covert, is threatened or suspected.

Seventh—The Government of the United States should be administered with the strictest economy; and the corruptions which have been so shamefully nursed and fostered by Andrew Johnson call loudly for radical reform.

Eighth—We profoundly deplore the untimely and tragic death of Abraham Lincoln, and regret the accession of Andrew Johnson to the Presidency, who has acted treacherously to the people who elected him and the cause he was pledged to support; has usurped high legislative and judicial functions; has refused to execute the laws; has used his high office to induce other officers to ignore and violate the laws; has employed his executive powers to render insecure the property, the peace, the liberty, and life of the citizen; has abused the pardoning power; has denounced the National Legislature as unconstitutional; has persistently and corruptly resisted, by every means in his power, every proper attempt at the reconstruction of the States lately in rebellion; has perverted the public patronage into an engine of wholesale corruption; and has been justly impeached for high crimes and misdemeanors, and properly pronounced guilty thereof by the vote of thirty-five senators.

Ninth—The doctrine of Great Britain and other European powers, that because a man is once a subject, he is always so, must be resisted, at every hazard, by the United States, as a relic of the feudal times, not authorized by the law of nations, and at war with our national honor and independence. Naturalized citizens are entitled to be protected in all their rights of citizenship, as though they were native-born; and no citizen of the United States, native or naturalized, must be liable to arrest and imprisonment by any foreign power, for acts done or words spoken in this country; and, if so arrested and imprisoned, it is the duty of the Government to interfere in his behalf.

Tenth—Of all who were faithful in the trials of the late war, there were none entitled to more especial honor than the brave soldiers and seamen who endured the hardships of campaign and cruise, and imperilled their lives in the service of the country. The bounties and pensions provided by law for these brave defenders of the nation, are obligations never to be forgotten. The widows and orphans of the gallant dead are the wards of the people—a sacred legacy bequeathed to the nation's protecting care.

Eleventh—Foreign immigration, which in the past, has added so much to the wealth, development of resources, and increase of power to this nation—the asylum of the oppressed of all nations—should be fostered and encouraged by a liberal and just policy.

Twelfth—This Convention declares its sympathy with all the oppressed people which are struggling for their rights.

Thirteenth—We highly commend the spirit of magnanimity and forgiveness with which men who have served in the rebellion, but now frankly and honestly co-operate with us in restoring the peace of the country, and reconstructing the Southern State Governments upon the basis of impartial justice and equal rights, are received back into the communion of the loyal people; and we favor the removal of the disqualifications and restrictions imposed upon the late rebels, in the same measure as the spirit of disloyalty will die out, and as may be consistent with the safety of the loyal people.

Fourteenth—We recognize the great principles laid down in the immortal Declaration of Independence as the true foundation of Democratic Government; and we hail with gladness every effort toward making these principles a living reality on every inch of American soil.

— 1872 —

The Republican party of the United States, assembled in National Convention in the city of Philadelphia, on the 5th and 6th days of June, 1872, again declares its faith, appeals to its history, and announces its position upon the questions before the country.

First. During eleven years of supremacy it has accepted with grand courage the solemn duties of the time. It suppressed a gigantic rebellion, emancipated four millions of slaves, decreed the equal citizenship of all, and established universal suffrage. Exhibiting unparalleled magnanimity, it criminally punished no man for political offenses, and warmly welcomed all who proved loyalty by obeying the laws and dealing justly with their neighbors. It has steadily decreased with firm hand the resultant disorders of a great war, and initiated a wise and humane policy toward the Indians. The Pacific railroad and similar vast enterprises have been generously aided and successfully conducted, the public lands freely given to actual settlers, immigration protected and encouraged, and a full acknowledgement of the naturalized citizens' rights secured from European Powers. A uniform national currency has been provided, repudiation frowned down, the national credit sustained under the most extraordinary burdens, and new bonds negotiated at lower rates. The revenues have been carefully collected and honestly applied. Despite large annual reductions of the rates of taxation, the public debt has been reduced during General Grant's Presidency at the rate of a hundred millions a year, great financial crises have been avoided, and peace and plenty prevail throughout the land. Menacing foreign difficulties have been peacefully and honorably composed, and the honor and power of the nation kept in high respect throughout the world. This glorious record of the past is the party's best pledge for the future. We believe the people will not intrust the Government to any party or combination of men composed chiefly of those who have resisted every step of this beneficent progress.

Second. The recent amendments to the national Constitution should be cordially sustained because they are right, not merely tolerated because they are law, and should be carried out according to their spirit by appropriate legislation, the enforcement of which can safely be entrusted only to the party that secured those amendments.

Third. Complete liberty and exact equality in the enjoyment of all civil, political, and public rights should be established and effectually maintained throughout the Union, by efficient and appropriate State and Federal legislation. Neither the law nor its administration should admit any discrimination in respect of citizens by reason of race, creed, color, or previous condition of servitude.

Fourth. The National Government should seek to maintain honorable peace with all nations, protecting its citizens everywhere, and sympathizing with all people who strive for greater liberty.

Fifth. Any system of the civil service under which the subordinate positions of the Government are considered rewards for mere party zeal is fatally demoralizing, and we therefore favor a reform of the system by laws which shall abolish the evils of patronage, and make honesty, efficiency, and fidelity the essential qualifications for public positions, without practically creating a life-tenure of office.

Sixth. We are opposed to further grants of the public lands to corporations and monopolies, and demand that the national domain be set apart for free homes for the people.

Seventh. The annual revenue, after paying current expenditures, pensions, and the interest on the public debt, should furnish a moderate balance for the reduction of the principal and that revenue, except so much as may be derived from a tax upon tobacco and liquors, should be raised by duties upon importations, the details of which should be so adjusted as to aid in securing remunerative wages to labor, and to promote the industries, prosperity, and growth of the whole country.

Eighth. We hold in undying honor the soldiers and sailors whose valor saved the Union. Their pensions are a sacred debt of the nation, and the widows and orphans of those who died for their country are entitled to the care of a generous and grateful people. We favor such additional legislation as will extend the bounty of the Government to all our soldiers and sailors who were honorably discharged, and who, in the line of duty, became disabled, without regard to the length of service or the cause of such discharge.

Ninth. The doctrine of Great Britain and other European Powers concerning allegiance—"Once a subject always a subject"—having at last, through the efforts of the Republican party, been abandoned, and the American idea of the individual's right to transfer allegiance having been accepted by European nations, it is the duty of our Government to guard with jealous care the rights of adopted citizens against the assumption of unauthorized claims by their former governments; and we urge continued careful encouragement and protection of voluntary immigration.

Tenth. The franking privilege ought to be abolished, and the way prepared for a speedy reduction in the rates of postage.

Eleventh. Among the questions which press for attention is that which concerns the relations of capital and labor, and the Republican party recognizes the duty of so shaping legislation as to secure full protection and the amplest field for capital, and for labor—the creator of capital—the largest opportunities and a just share of the mutual profits of these two great servants of civilization.

Twelfth. We hold that Congress and the President have only fulfilled an imperative duty in their measures for the suppression of violent and treasonable organizations in certain lately rebellious regions, and for the protection of the ballot-box, and therefore they are entitled to the thanks of the nation.

Thirteenth. We denounce repudiation of the public debt, in any form or disguise, as a national crime. We witness with pride the reduction of the principal of the debt, and of the rates of interest upon the balance, and confidently expect that our excellent national currency will be perfected by a speedy resumption of specie payment.

Fourteenth. The Republican party is mindful of its obligations to the loyal women of America for their noble devotion to the cause of freedom. Their admission to wider fields of usefulness is viewed with satisfaction, and the honest demand of any class of citizens for additional rights should be treated with respectful consideration.

Fifteenth. We heartily approve the action of Congress in extending amnesty to those lately in rebellion, and rejoice in the growth of peace and fraternal feeling throughout the land.

Sixteenth. The Republican party proposes to respect the rights reserved by the people to themselves as carefully as the powers delegated by them to the State and to the Federal Government. It disapproves of the resort to unconstitutional laws for the purpose of removing evils, by interference with rights not surrendered by the people to either the State or National Government.

Seventeenth. It is the duty of the general Government to adopt such measures as may tend to encourage and restore American commerce and ship-building.

Eighteenth. We believe that the modest patriotism, the earnest purpose, the sound judgment, the practical wisdom, the incorruptible integrity, and the illustrious services of Ulysses S. Grant have commended him to the heart of the American people, and with him at our head we start to-day upon a new march to victory.

Nineteenth. Henry Wilson, nominated for the Vice-Presidency, known to the whole land from the early days of the great struggle for liberty as an indefatigable laborer in all campaigns, an incorruptible legislator and representative man of American institutions, is worthy to associate with our great leader and share the honors which we pledge our best efforts to bestow upon them.

— 1876 —

When, in the economy of Providence, this land was to be purged of human slavery, and when the strength of government of the people by the people and for the people was to be demonstrated, the Republican party came into power. Its deeds have passed into history, and we look back to them with pride. Incited by their memories, and with high aims for the good of our country and mankind, and looking to the future with unfaltering courage, hope, and purpose, we, the representatives of the party, in national convention assembled, make the following declaration of principles:

1. The United States of America is a nation, not a league. By the combined workings of the national and state governments, under their respective constitutions, the rights of every citizen are secured at home and abroad, and the common welfare promoted.

2. The Republican party has preserved these governments to the hundredth anniversary of the nation's birth, and they are now embodiments of the great truth spoken at its cradle, that all men are created equal; that they are endowed by their Creator with certain inalienable rights, among which are life, liberty, and the pursuit of happiness; that for the attainment of these ends governments have been instituted among men, deriving their just powers from the consent of the governed. Until these truths are cheerfully obeyed, and if need be, vigorously enforced, the work of the Republican party is unfinished.

3. The permanent pacification of the Southern section of the Union and the complete protection of all its citizens in the free enjoyment of all their rights, are duties to which the Republican party is sacredly pledged. The power to provide for the enforcement of the principles embodied in the recent constitutional amendments is vested by those amendments in the Congress of the United States; and we declare it to be the solemn obligation of the legislative and executive departments of the government to put into immediate and vigorous exercise all their constitutional powers for removing any just causes of discontent on the part of any class, and securing to every American citizen complete liberty and exact equality in the exercise of all civil, political, and public rights. To this end we imperatively demand a congress and a chief executive whose courage and fidelity to these duties shall not falter until these results are placed beyond dispute or recall.

4. In the first act of congress, signed by President Grant, the national government assumed to remove any doubt of its purpose to discharge all just obligations to the public creditors, and solemnly pledged its faith "to make provisions at the earliest practicable period, for the redemption of the United States notes in coin." Commercial prosperity, public morals, and the national credit demand that this promise be fulfilled by a continuous and steady progress to specie payment.

5. Under the constitution, the President and heads of departments are to make nominations for office, the senate is to advise and consent to appointments, and the house of representatives is to accuse and prosecute faithless officers. The best interest of the public service demands that these distinctions be respected; that senators and representatives who may be judges and accusers should not dictate appointments to office. The invariable rule for appointments should have reference to the honesty, fidelity, and capacity of the appointees, giving to the party in power those places where harmony and vigor of administration require its policy to be represented, but permitting all others to be filled by persons selected with sole reference to the efficiency of the public service and the right of citizens to share in the honor of rendering faithful service to their country.

6. We rejoice in the quickened conscience of the people concerning political affairs. We will hold all public officers to a rigid responsibility, and engage that the prosecution and punishment of all who betray official trusts shall be speedy, thorough, and unsparing.

7. The public school system of the several states is the bulwark of the American republic; and, with a view to its security and permanence, we recommend an amendment to the constitution of the United States, forbidding the application of any public funds or property for the benefit of any school or institution under sectarian control.

8. The revenue necessary for current expenditures and the obligations of the public debt must be largely derived from duties upon importations, which, so far as possible, should be so adjusted as to promote the interests of American labor and advance the prosperity of the whole country.

9. We reaffirm our opposition to further grants of the public lands to corporations and monopolies, and demand that the national domain be devoted to free homes for the people.

10. It is the imperative duty of the government so to modify existing treaties with European governments, that the same protection shall be afforded to the adopted American citizen that is given to native-born, and all necessary laws be passed to protect emigrants, in the absence of power in the states for that purpose.

11. It is the immediate duty of congress fully to investigate the effects of the immigration and importation of Mongolians on the moral and material interests of the country.

12. The Republican party recognizes with approval the substantial advances recently made toward the establishment of equal rights for women, by the many important amendments effected by Republican legislatures in the laws which concern the personal and property relations of wives, mothers, and widows, and by the appointment and election of women to the superintendence of education, charities, and other public trusts. The honest demands of this class of citizens for additional rights, privileges, and immunities should be treated with respectful consideration.

13. The constitution confers upon congress sovereign power over the territories of the United States for their government. And in the exercise of this power it is the right and duty of congress to prohibit and extirpate in the territories that relic of barbarism, polygamy; and we demand such legislation as will secure this end and the supremacy of American institutions in all the territories.

14. The pledges which our nation has given to our soldiers and sailors must be fulfilled. The grateful people will always hold those who imperilled their lives for the country's preservation in the kindest remembrance.

15. We sincerely deprecate all sectional feeling and tendencies. We therefore note with deep solicitude that the Democratic party counts, as its chief hope of success, upon the electoral vote of a united South, secured through the efforts of those who were recently arrayed against the nation; and we invoke the earnest attention of the country to the grave truth, that a success thus achieved would reopen sectoral strife and imperil national honor and human rights.

16. We charge the Democratic party with being the same in character and spirit as when it sympathized with treason; with making its control of the house of representatives the triumph and opportunity of the nation's recent foes; with reasserting and applauding in the national capitol the sentiments of unrepentant rebellion; with sending Union soldiers to the rear, and promoting Confederate soldiers to the front; with deliberately proposing to repudiate the plighted faith of the government; with being equally false and imbecile upon the over-shadowing financial question; with thwarting the ends of justice, by its partisan mismanagements and obstruction of investigation; with proving itself, through the period of its ascendancy in the

lower house of congress, utterly incompetent to administer the government;—and we warn the country against trusting a party thus alike unworthy, recreant, and incapable.

17. The national administration merits commendation for its honorable work in the management of domestic and foreign affairs, and President Grant deserves the continued hearty gratitude of the American people, for his patriotism and his eminent services in war and in peace.

18. We present as our candidates for President and Vice-President of the United States two distinguished statesmen, of eminent ability and character, and conspicuously fitted for those high offices, and we confidently appeal to the American people to intrust the administration of their public affairs to Rutherford B. Hayes and William A. Wheeler.

— 1880 —

The Republican party, in National Convention assembled, at the end of twenty years since the Federal Government was first committed to its charge, submits to the people of the United States this brief report of its administration:

It suppressed a rebellion which had armed nearly a million of men to subvert the national authority. It reconstructed the Union of the States, with freedom instead of slavery as its corner-stone. It transformed 4,000,000 human begins from the likeness of things to the rank of citizens. It relieved Congress from the infamous work of hunting fugitive slaves, and charged it to see that slavery does not exist. It has raised the value of our paper currency from 38 per cent to the par of gold. It has restored upon a solid basis payment in coin of all national obligations, and has given us a currency absolutely good and equal in every part of our extended country. It has lifted the credit of the Nation from the point where six per cent bonds sold at eighty-six to that where four per cent bonds are eagerly sought at a premium.

Under its administration, railways have increased from 31,000 miles in 1860, to more than 82,000 miles in 1879.

Our foreign trade increased from $700,000,000 to $1,115,000,000 in the same time, and our exports, which were $20,000,000 less than our imports in 1860, were $265,000,000 more than our imports in 1879.

Without resorting to loans, it has, since the war closed, defrayed the ordinary expenses of Government besides the accruing interest of all public debt, and has disbursed annually more than $30,000,000 for soldiers' and sailors' pensions. It has paid $880,000,000 of the public debt, and, by refunding the balance at lower rates, has reduced the annual interest-charge from nearly $150,000,000 to less than $89,000,000. All the industries of the country have revived; labor is in demand; wages have increased, and throughout the entire country there is evidence of a coming prosperity greater than we have ever enjoyed.

Upon this record the Republican party asks for the continued confidence and support of the people, and this Convention submits for their approval the following statement of the principles and purposes which will continue to guide and inspire its efforts.

1. We affirm that the work of the Republican party for the last twenty-one years has been such as to commend it to the favor of the Nation; that the fruits of the costly victories which we have achieved through immense difficulties should be preserved; that the peace regained should be cherished; that the Union should be perpetuated, and that the liberty secured to this generation should be transmitted undiminished to other generations; that the order established and the credit acquired should never be impaired; that the pensions promised should be paid; that the debt so much reduced should be extinguished by the full payment of every dollar thereof; that the reviving industries should be further promoted, and that the commerce already increasing should be steadily encouraged.

2. The Constitution of the United States is a supreme law, and not a mere contract. Out of confederated States it made a sovereign nation. Some powers are denied to the Nation, while others are denied to the States; but the boundary between the powers delegated and those reserved is to be determined by the National and not by the State tribunal.

3. The work of popular education is one left to the care of the several States, but it is the duty of the National Government to aid that work to the extent of its constitutional power. The intelligence of the Nation is but the aggregate of the intelligence in the several States, and the destiny of the Nation must be guided, not by the genius of any one State, but by the aggregate genius of all.

4. The Constitution wisely forbids Congress to make any law respecting the establishment of religion, but it is idle to hope that the Nation can be protected against the influence of secret sectarianism while each State is exposed to its domination. We, therefore, recommend that the Constitution be so amended as to lay the same prohibition upon the Legislature of each State, and to forbid the appropriation of public funds to the support of sectarian schools.

5. We affirm the belief, avowed in 1876, that the duties levied for the purpose of revenue should so discriminate as to favor American labor; that no further grants of the public domain should be made to any railway or other corporation; that slavery having perished in the States, its twin barbarity, polygamy, must die in the Territories; that everywhere the protection accorded to a citizen of American birth must be secured to citizens by American adoption; that we deem it the duty of Congress to develop and improve our seacoast and harbors, but insist that further subsidies to private persons or corporations must cease; that the obligations of the Republic to the men who preserved its integrity in the day of battle are undiminished by the lapse of fifteen years since their final victory. To do them honor is, and shall forever be, the grateful privilege and sacred duty of the American people.

6. Since the authority to regulate immigration and intercourse between the United States and foreign nations rests with the Congress of the United States and the treaty-making power, the Republican party, regarding the unrestricted immigration of the Chinese as a matter of grave concernment under the exercise of both these powers, would limit and restrict that immigration by the enactment of such just, humane and reasonable laws and treaties as will produce that result.

7. That the purity and patriotism which characterized the earlier career of Rutherford B. Hayes in peace and war, and which guided the thoughts of our immediate predecessors to him for a presidential candidate, have continued to inspire him in his career as Chief Executive; and that history will accord to his administration the honors which are due to an efficient, just and courteous discharge of the public business, and will honor his vetoes interposed between the people and attempted partisan laws.

8. We charge upon the Democratic party the habitual sacrifice of patriotism and justice to a supreme and insatiable lust for office and patronage; that to obtain possession of the National Government, and control of the place, they have obstructed all efforts to promote the purity and to conserve the freedom of the suffrage, and have devised fraudulent ballots and invented fraudulent certification of returns; have labored to unseat lawfully elected members of Congress, to secure at all hazards the vote of a majority of the States in the House of Representatives; have endeavored to occupy by force and fraud the places of trust given to others by the people of Maine, rescued by the courage and action of Maine's patriotic sons; have, by methods vicious in principle and tyrannical in practice, attached partisan legislation to appropriation bills,

upon whose passage the very movement of the Government depended; have crushed the rights of the individual; have advocated the principles and sought the favor of the Rebellion against the Nation, and have endeavored to obliterate the sacred memories of the war, and to overcome its inestimably valuable results of nationality, personal freedom and individual equality.

The equal, steady and complete enforcement of the law, and the protection of all our citizens in the enjoyment of all privileges and immunities guaranteed by the Constitution, are the first duties of the Nation. The dangers of a solid South can only be averted by a faithful performance of every promise which the Nation has made to the citizen. The execution of the laws, and the punishment of all those who violate them, are the only safe methods by which an enduring peace can be secured and genuine prosperity established through the South. Whatever promises the Nation makes the Nation must perform. A Nation cannot safely relegate this duty to the States. The solid South must be divided by the peaceful agencies of the ballot, and all honest opinions must there find free expression. To this end honest voters must be protected against terrorism, violence or fraud. And we affirm it to be the duty and the purpose of the Republican party to use all legitimate means to restore all the States of this Union to the most perfect harmony that may be possible, and we submit to the practical, sensible people of these United States to say whether it would not be dangerous to the dearest interests of our country at this time to surrender the administration of the National Government to a party which seeks to overthrow the existing policy, under which we are so prosperous, and thus bring distrust and confusion where there is now order, confidence and hope.

9. The Republican party, adhering to the principle affirmed by its last National Convention, of respect for the constitutional rules governing appointments to office, adopts the declaration of President Hayes that the reform of the civil service should be thorough, radical and complete. To this end it demands the co-operation of the Legislative with the Executive Departments of the Government, and that Congress shall so legislate that fitness, ascertained by proper practical tests, shall admit to the public service.

— 1884 —

The Republicans of the United States in National Convention assembled renew their allegiance to the principles upon which they have triumphed in six successive Presidential elections; and congratulate the American people on the attainment of so many results in legislation and administration, by which the Republican party has, after saving the Union, done so much to render its institutions just, equal and beneficent, the safeguard of liberty and the embodiment of the best thought and highest purpose of our citizens.

The Republican party has gained its strength by quick and faithful response to the demands of the people for the freedom and equality of all men; for a united nation, assuring the rights of all citizens; for the elevation of labor; for an honest currency; for purity in legislation, and for integrity and accountability in all departments of the government, and it accepts anew the duty of leading in the work of progress and reform.

We lament the death of President Garfield, whose sound statesmanship, long conspicuous in Congress, gave promise of a strong and successful administration; a promise fully realized during the short period of his office as President of the United States. His distinguished services in war and peace have endeared him to the hearts of the American people.

In the administration of President Arthur, we recognize a wise, conservative and patriotic policy, under which the country has been blessed with remarkable prosperity; and we believe his eminent services are entitled to and will receive the hearty approval of every citizen.

It is the first duty of a good government to protect the rights and promote the interests of its own people.

The largest diversity of industry is most productive of general prosperity, and of the comfort and independence of the people.

We, therefore, demand that the imposition of duties on foreign imports shall be made, not "for revenue only," but that in raising the requisite revenues for the government, such duties shall be so levied as to afford security to our diversified industries and protection to the rights and wages of the laborer; to the end that active and intelligent labor, as well as capital, may have its just reward, and the laboring man his full share in the national prosperity.

Against the so-called economic system of the Democratic party, which would degrade our labor to the foreign standard, we enter our earnest protest.

The Democratic party has failed completely to relieve the people of the burden of unnecessary taxation by a wise reduction of the surplus.

The Republican party pledges itself to correct the inequalities of the tariff, and to reduce the surplus, not by the vicious and indiscriminate process of horizontal reduction, but by such methods as will relieve the tax-payer without injuring the laborer or the great productive interests of the country.

We recognize the importance of sheep husbandry in the United States, the serious depression which it is now experiencing, and the danger threatening its future prosperity; and we, therefore, respect the demands of the representatives of this important agricultural interest for a readjustment of duties upon foreign wool, in order that such industry shall have full and adequate protection.

We have always recommended the best money known to the civilized world; and we urge that efforts should be made to unite all commercial nations in the establishment of an international standard which shall fix for all the relative value of gold and silver coinage.

The regulation of commerce with foreign nations and between the States, is one of the most important prerogatives of the general government; and the Republican party distinctly announces its purpose to support such legislation as will fully and efficiently carry out the constitutional power of Congress over inter-State commerce.

The principle of public regulation of railway corporations is a wise and salutary one for the protection of all classes of the people; and we favor legislation that shall prevent unjust discrimination and excessive charges for transportation, and that shall secure to the people, and the railways alike, the fair and equal protection of the laws.

We favor the establishment of a national bureau of labor; the enforcement of the eight hour law, a wise and judicious system of general education by adequate appropriation from the national revenues, wherever the same is needed. We believe that everywhere the protection to a citizen of American birth must be secured to citizens by American adoption; and we favor the settlement of national differences by international arbitration.

The Republican party, having its birth in a hatred of slave labor and a desire that all men may be truly free and equal, is unalterably opposed to placing our workingmen in competition with any form of servile labor, whether at home or abroad. In this spirit, we denounce the importation of contract labor, whether from Europe or Asia, as an offense against the spirit of American institutions; and we pledge ourselves to sustain the present law restricting Chinese immigration, and to provide such further legislation as is necessary to carry out its purposes.

Reform of the civil service, auspiciously begun under Republican administration, should be completed by the further extension of the reform system already established by law, to all the grades of the service to which it is applicable. The spirit and purpose of the reform should be observed in all executive appointments; and all laws at variance with the objects of existing reform legislation should be repealed, to the end that the dangers to free institutions, which lurk in the power of official patronage, may be wisely and effectively avoided.

The public lands are a heritage of the people of the United States, and should be reserved as far as possible for small holdings by actual settlers. We are opposed to the acquisition of large tracts of these lands by corporations or individuals, especially where such holdings are in the hands of non-residents or aliens. And we will endeavor to obtain such legislation as will tend to correct this evil. We demand of Congress the speedy forfeiture of all land grants which have lapsed by reason of non-compliance with acts of incorporation, in all cases where there has been no attempt in good faith to perform the conditions of such grants.

The grateful thanks of the American people are due to the Union soldiers and sailors of the late war; and the Republican party stands pledged to suitable pensions for all who were disabled, and for the widows and orphans of those who died in the war. The Republican party also pledges itself to the repeal of the limitations contained in the arrears act of 1879. So that all invalid soldiers shall share alike, and their pensions begin with the date of disability or discharge, and not with the date of application.

The Republican party favors a policy which shall keep us from entangling alliances with foreign nations, and which gives us the right to expect that foreign nations shall refrain from meddling in American affairs; a policy which seeks peace and trade with all powers, but especially with those of the Western Hemisphere.

We demand the restoration of our navy to its old-time strength and efficiency, that it may in any sea protect the rights of American citizens and the interests of American commerce; and we call upon Congress to remove the burdens under which American shipping has been depressed, so that it may again be true that we have a commerce which leaves no sea unexplored, and a navy which takes no law from superior force.

Resolved, That appointments by the President to offices in the Territories should be made from the *bona-fide* citizens and residents of the Territories wherein they are to serve.

Resolved, That it is the duty of Congress to enact such laws as shall promptly and effectually suppress the system of polygamy within our Territories; and divorce the political from the ecclesiastical power of the so-called Mormon church; and that the laws so enacted should be rigidly enforced by the civil authorities, if possible, and by the military, if need be.

The people of the United States, in their organized capacity, constitute a Nation and not a mere confederacy of States; the National Government is supreme within the sphere of its national duties; but the States have reserved rights which should be faithfully maintained. Each should be guarded with jealous care, so that the harmony of our system of government may be preserved and the Union kept inviolate.

The perpetuity of our institutions rests upon the maintenance of a free ballot, an honest count, and correct returns. We denounce the fraud and violence practiced by the Democracy in Southern States, by which the will of a voter is defeated, as dangerous to the preservation of free institutions and we solemnly arraign the Democratic party as being the guilty recipient of fruits of such fraud and violence.

We extend to the Republicans of the South, regardless of their former party affiliations, our cordial sympathy; and we pledge to them our most earnest efforts to promote the passage of such legislation as will secure to every citizen, of whatever race and color, the full and complete recognition, possession and exercise of all civil and political rights.

— 1888 —

The Republicans of the United States assembled by their delegates in National Convention, pause on the threshold of their proceedings to honor the memory of their first great leader—the immortal champion of liberty and the rights of the people—Abraham Lincoln; and to cover also with wreaths of imperishable remembrance and gratitude the heroic names of our later leaders who have been more recently called away from our councils—Grant, Garfield, Arthur, Logan, Conkling. May their memories be faithfully cherished!

We also recall with our greetings, and with prayer for his recovery, the name of one of our living heroes, whose memory will be treasured in the history of both Republicans and of the Republic—the name of that noble soldier and favorite child of victory, Philip H. Sheridan. In the spirit of those great leaders and of our own devotion to human liberty, and with that hostility to all forms of despotism and oppression which is the fundamental idea of the Republican party, we send fraternal congratulations to our fellow Americans of Brazil upon their great act of emancipation, which completed the abolition of slavery throughout the two American continents. We earnestly hope that we may soon congratulate our fellow-citizens of Irish birth upon the peaceful recovery of home rule for Ireland.

We reaffirm our unswerving devotion to the National Constitution and the indissoluble Union of the States; to the autonomy reserved to the States under the Constitution; to the personal rights and liberties of citizens in all the States and Territories of the Union, and especially to the supreme and sovereign right of every lawful citizen, rich or poor, native or foreign born, white or black, to cast one free ballot in public elections, and to have that ballot duly counted. We hold the free and honest popular ballot and the just and equal representation of all the people to be the foundation of our Republican government and demand effective legislation to secure the integrity and purity of elections, which are the fountains of all public authority. We charge that the present Administration and the Democratic majority in Congress owe their existence to the suppression of the ballot by a criminal nullification of the Constitution and laws of the United States.

We are uncompromisingly in favor of the American system of protection; we protest against its destruction as proposed by the President and his party. They serve the interests of Europe; we will support the interests of America. We accept the issue, and confidently appeal to the people for their judgment. The protective system must be maintained. Its abandonment has always been followed by general disaster to all interests, except those of the usurer and the sheriff. We denounce the Mills bill as destructive to the general business, the labor and the farming interests of the country, and we heartily indorse the consistent and patriotic action of the Republican Representatives in Congress in opposing its passage.

We condemn the proposition of the Democratic party to place wool on the free list, and we insist that the duties thereon shall be adjusted and maintained so as to furnish full and adequate protection to that industry throughout the United States.

The Republican party would effect all needed reduction of the National revenue by repealing the taxes upon tobacco, which are an annoyance and burden to agriculture, and the tax upon spirits used in the arts, and for mechanical purposes, and by such revision of the tariff laws as will tend to check imports of such articles as are produced by our people, the production of which gives employment to our labor, and releases from import duties those articles of foreign production (except luxuries), the like of which cannot be produced at home. If there shall remain a larger

revenue than is requisite for the wants of the government we favor the entire repeal of internal taxes rather than the surrender of any part of our protective system at the joint behests of the whiskey trusts and the agents of foreign manufacturers.

We declare our hostility to the introduction into this country of foreign contract labor and of Chinese labor, alien to our civilization and constitution; and we demand the rigid enforcement of the existing laws against it, and favor such immediate legislation as will exclude such labor from our shores.

We declare our opposition to all combinations of capital organized in trusts or otherwise to control arbitrarily the condition of trade among our citizens; and we recommend to Congress and the State Legislatures in their respective jurisdictions such legislation as will prevent the execution of all schemes to oppress the people by undue charges on their supplies, or by unjust rates for the transportation of their products to market. We approve the legislation by Congress to prevent alike unjust burdens and unfair discriminations between the States.

We reaffirm the policy of appropriating the public lands of the United States to be homesteads for American citizens and settlers—not aliens—which the Republican party established in 1862 against the persistent opposition of the Democrats in Congress, and which has brought our great Western domain into such magnificent development. The restoration of unearned railroad land grants to the public domain for the use of actual settlers, which was begun under the Administration of President Arthur, should be continued. We deny that the Democratic party has ever restored one acre to the people, but declare that by the joint action of the Republicans and Democrats in Congress about 60,000,000 acres of unearned lands originally granted for the construction of railroads have been restored to the public domain, in pursuance of the conditions inserted by the Republican party in the original grants. We charge the Democratic Administration with failure to execute the laws securing to settlers the title to their homesteads, and with using appropriations made for that purpose to harass innocent settlers with spies and prosecutions under the false pretense of exposing frauds and vindicating the law.

The government Congress of the Territories is based upon necessity only to the end that they may become States in the Union; therefore, whenever the conditions of population, material resources, public intelligence and morality are such as to insure a stable local government therein, the people of such Territories should be permitted as a right inherent in them to form for themselves constitutions and State government, and be admitted into the Union. Pending the preparation for Statehood, all officers thereof should be selected from the *bona-fide* residents and citizens of the Territory wherein they are to serve. South Dakota should of right be immediately admitted as a State in the Union under the constitution framed and adopted by her people, and we heartily indorse the action of the Republican Senate in twice passing bills for her admission. The refusal of the Democratic House of Representatives, for partisan purposes, to favorably consider these bills is a willful violation of the sacred American principle of local self-government, and merits the condemnation of all just men. The pending bills in the Senate to enable the people of Washington, North Dakota and Montana Territories to form constitutions and establish State governments, should be passed without unnecessary delay. The Republican party pledges itself to do all in its power to facilitate the admission of the Territories of New Mexico, Wyoming, Idaho and Arizona to the enjoyment of self-government as States, such of them as are now qualified, as soon as possible, and the others as soon as they may become so.

The political power of the Mormon Church in the Territories as exercised in the past is a menace to free institutions too dangerous to be longer suffered. Therefore we pledge the Republican party to appropriate legislation asserting the sovereignty of the Nation in all Territories where the same is questioned, and in furtherance of that end to place upon the statute books legislation stringent enough to divorce the political from the ecclesiastical power, and thus stamp out the attendant wickedness of polygamy.

The Republican party is in favor of the use of both gold and silver as money, and condemns the policy of the Democratic Administration in its efforts to demonetize silver.

We demand the reduction of letter postage to one cent per ounce.

In a Republic like ours, where the citizen is the sovereign, and the official the servant, where no power is exercised except by the will of the people, it is important that the sovereign—the people—should possess intelligence. The free school is the promoter of that intelligence which is to preserve us a free Nation; therefore, the State or Nation, or both combined, should support free institutions of learning sufficient to afford every child growing up in the land the opportunity of a good common school education.

We earnestly recommend that prompt action be taken by Congress in the enactment of such legislation as will best secure the rehabilitation of our American merchant marine, and we protest against the passage by Congress of a free ship bill as calculated to work injustice to labor by lessening the wages of those engaged in preparing materials as well as those directly employed in our shipyards. We demand appropriations for the early rebuilding of our navy; for the construction of coast fortifications and modern ordinance and other approved modern means of defense for the protection of our defenseless harbors and cities; for the payment of just pensions to our soldiers; for necessary works of National importance in the improvement of harbors and the channels of internal, coastwise, and foreign commerce; for the encouragement of the shipping interests of the Atlantic, Gulf and Pacific States, as well as for the payment of the maturing public debt. This policy will give employment to our labor, activity to our various industries, increase the security of our country, promote trade, open new and direct markets for our produce, and cheapen the cost of transportation. We affirm this to be far better for our country than the Democratic policy of loaning the government's money, without interest, to "pet banks."

The conduct of foreign affairs by the present Administration has been distinguished by its inefficiency and its cowardice. Having withdrawn from the Senate all pending treaties effected by Republican Administrations for the removal of foreign burdens and restrictions upon our commerce, and for its extension into better markets, it has neither effected nor proposed any others in their stead. Professing adherence to the Monroe doctrine it has seen with idle complacency the extension of foreign influence in Central America and of foreign trade everywhere among our neighbors. It has refused to charter, sanction or encourage any American organization for construction of the Nicaragua Canal, a work of vital importance to the maintenance of the Monroe doctrine and of our National influence in Central and South America, and necessary for the development of trade with our Pacific territory, with South America, and with the islands and further coasts of the Pacific Ocean.

We arraign the present Democratic Administration for its weak and unpatriotic treatment of the fisheries question, and its pusillanimous surrender of the essential privileges to which our fishing vessels are entitled in Canadian ports under the treaty of 1818, the reciprocal maritime legislation of 1830, and the comity of nations, and which Canadian fishing vessels receive in the ports of the United States. We condemn the policy of the present Administration and the Democratic majority in Congress toward our fisheries as unfriendly and conspicuously unpatriotic, and as tending to destroy a valuable National industry, and an indispensable resource of defense against a foreign enemy. "The name American applies alike to all citizens of the Republic and imposes upon all alike the same obligation of obedience to the laws. At the same time that citizenship is and must be the panoply and safeguard of him who wears it, and protect him, whether high or low, rich or poor, in all his civil rights. It should and must afford him protection at home and follow and protect him abroad in whatever land he may be on a lawful errand."

The men who abandoned the Republican party in 1884 and continue to adhere to the Democratic party have deserted not only the cause of honest government, of sound finance, of freedom and purity of the ballot, but especially have deserted the cause of reform in the civil service. We will not fail to keep our pledges because they have broken theirs, or because their candidate has broken his. We therefore repeat our declaration of 1884, to wit: "The reform of the civil service, auspiciously begun under the Republican Administration, should be completed by the further extension of the reform system already established by law, to all the grades of the service to which it is applicable. The spirit and purpose of the reform should be observed in all executive appointments, and all laws at variance with the object of existing reform legislation should be repealed, to the end that the dangers to free institutions which lurk in the power of official patronage may be wisely and effectively avoided."

The gratitude of the Nation to the defenders of the Union cannot be measured by laws. The legislation of Congress should conform to the pledges made by a loyal people and be so enlarged and extended as to provide against the possibility that any man who honorably wore the Federal uniform shall become the inmate of an almshouse, or dependent upon private charity. In the presence of an overflowing treasury it would be a public scandal to do less for those whose valorous service preserved the government. We denounce the hostile spirit shown by President Cleveland in his numerous vetoes of measures for pension relief, and the action of the Democratic House of Representatives in refusing even a consideration of general pension legislation.

In support of the principles herewith enunciated we invite the co-operation of patriotic men of all parties, and especially of all workingmen, whose prosperity is seriously threatened by the free-trade policy of the present Administration.

Resolution Relating to Prohibition
Offered by Mr. Boutelle, of Maine:

The first concern of all good government is the virtue and sobriety of the people and the purity of their homes. The Republican party cordially sympathizes with all wise and well-directed efforts for the promotion of temperance and morality.

— 1892 —

The representatives of the Republicans of the United States, assembled in general convention on the shores of the Mississippi River, the everlasting bond of an indestructible Republic, whose most glorious chapter of history is the record of the Republican party, congratulate their countrymen on the majestic march of the nation under the banners inscribed with the principles of our platform of 1888, vindicated by victory at the polls and prosperity in our fields, workshops and mines, and make the following declaration of principles:

We reaffirm the American doctrine of protection. We call attention to its growth abroad. We maintain that the prosperous condition of our country is largely due to the wise revenue legislation of the Republican congress.

We believe that all articles which cannot be produced in the United States, except luxuries, should be admitted free of duty, and that on all imports coming into competition with the products of American labor, there should be levied duties equal to the difference between wages abroad and at home. We assert that the prices of manufactured articles of general consumption have been reduced under the operations of the tariff act of 1890.

We denounce the efforts of the Democratic majority of the House of Representatives to destroy our tariff laws by piecemeal, as manifested by their attacks upon wool, lead and lead ores, the chief products of a number of States, and we ask the people for their judgment thereon.

We point to the success of the Republican policy of reciprocity, under which our export trade has vastly increased and new and enlarged markets have been opened for the products of our farms and workshops. We remind the people of the bitter opposition of the Democratic party to this practical business measure, and claim that, executed by a Republican administration, our present laws will eventually give us control of the trade of the world.

The American people, from tradition and interest, favor bimetallism, and the Republican party demands the use of both gold and silver as standard money, with such restrictions and under such provisions, to be determined by legislation, as will secure the maintenance of the parity of values of the two metals so that the purchasing and debtpaying power of the dollar, whether of silver, gold, or paper, shall be at all times equal. The interests of the producers of the country, its farmers and its workingmen, demand that every dollar, paper or coin, issued by the government, shall be as good as any other.

We commend the wise and patriotic steps already taken by our government to secure an international conference, to adopt such measures as will insure a parity of value between gold and silver for use as money throughout the world.

We demand that every citizen of the United States shall be allowed to cast one free and unrestricted ballot in all public elections, and that such ballot shall be counted and returned as cast; that such laws shall be enacted and enforced as will secure to every citizen, be rich or poor, native or foreign-born, white or black, this sovereign right, guaranteed by the Constitution. The free and honest popular ballot, the just and equal representation of all the people, as well as their just and equal protection under the laws, are the foundation of our Republican institutions, and the party will never relax its efforts until the integrity of the ballot and the purity of elections shall be fully guaranteed and protected in every State.

SOUTHERN OUTRAGES

We denounce the continued inhuman outrages perpetrated upon American citizens for political reasons in certain Southern States of the Union.

FOREIGN RELATIONS

We favor the extension of our foreign commerce, the restoration of our mercantile marine by home-built ships, and the creation of a navy for the protection of our National interests and the honor of our flag; the maintenance of the most friendly relations with all foreign powers; entangling alliances with none; and the protection of the rights of our fishermen.

We reaffirm our approval of the Monroe doctrine and believe in the achievement of the manifest destiny of the Republic in its broadest sense.

We favor the enactment of more stringent laws and regulations for the restriction of criminal, pauper and contract immigration.

MISCELLANEOUS

We favor efficient legislation by Congress to protect the life and limbs of employees of transportation companies engaged in carrying on interstate commerce, and recommend legislation by the respective States that will protect employees engaged in State commerce, in mining and manufacturing.

The Republican party has always been the champion of the oppressed and recognizes the dignity of manhood, irrespective of faith, color, or nationality; it sympathizes with the cause of home rule in Ireland, and protests against the persecution of the Jews in Russia.

The ultimate reliance of free popular government is the intelligence of the people, and the maintenance of freedom among men. We therefore declare anew our devotion to liberty of thought and conscience, of speech and press, and approve all agencies and instrumentalities which contribute to the education of the children of the land, but while insisting upon the fullest measure of religious liberty, we are opposed to any union of Church and State.

We reaffirm our opposition, declared in the Republican platform of 1888, to all combinations of capital organized in trusts or otherwise, to control arbitrarily the condition of trade among our citizens.

We heartily indorse the action already taken upon this subject, and ask for such further legislation as may be required to remedy any defects in existing laws, and to render their enforcement more complete and effective.

We approve the policy of extending to towns, villages and rural communities the advantages of the free delivery service, now enjoyed by the larger cities of the country, and reaffirm the declaration contained in the Republican platform of 1888, pledging the reduction of letter postage to 1 cent at the earliest possible moment consistent with the maintenance of the Post Office Department and the highest class of postal service.

We commend the spirit and evidence of reform in the civil service, and the wise and consistent enforcement by the Republican party of the laws regulating the same.

NICARAGUA CANAL

The construction of the Nicaragua Canal is of the highest importance to the American people, both as a measure of National defense and to build up and maintain American commerce, and it should be controlled by the United States Government.

TERRITORIES

We favor the admission of the remaining Territories at the earliest practicable date, having due regard to the interests of the people of the Territories and of the United States. All the Federal officers appointed for the Territories should be selected from bona-fide residents thereof, and the right of self-government should be accorded as far as practicable.

ARID LANDS

We favor the cession, subject to the homestead laws, of the arid public lands, to the States and Territories in which they lie, under such Congressional restrictions as to disposition, reclamation and occupancy by settlers as will secure the maximum benefits to the people.

THE COLUMBIAN EXPOSITION

The World's Columbian Exposition is a great national undertaking, and Congress should promptly enact such reasonable legislation in aid thereof as will insure a discharge of the expenses and obligations incident thereto, and the attainment of results commensurate with the dignity and progress of the Nation.

INTEMPERANCE

We sympathize with all wise and legitimate efforts to lessen and prevent the evils of intemperance and promote morality.

PENSIONS

Ever mindful of the services and sacrifices of the men who saved the life of the Nation, we pledge anew to the veteran soldiers of the Republic a watchful care and recognition of their just claims upon a grateful people.

HARRISON'S ADMINISTRATION

We commend the able, patriotic and thoroughly American administration of President Harrison. Under it the country has enjoyed remarkable prosperity and the dignity and honor of the Nation, at home and abroad, have been faithfully maintained, and we offer the record of pledges kept as a guarantee of faithful performance in the future.

— 1896 —

The Republicans of the United States, assembled by their representatives in National Convention, appealing for the popular and historical justification of their claims to the matchless achievements of thirty years of Republican rule, earnestly and confidently address themselves to the awakened intelligence, experience and conscience of their countrymen in the following declaration of facts and principles:

For the first time since the civil war the American people have witnessed the calamitous consequence of full and unrestricted Democratic control of the government. It has been a record of unparalleled incapacity, dishonor and disaster. In administrative management it has ruthlessly sacrificed indispensable revenue, entailed an unceasing deficit, eked out ordinary current expenses with borrowed money, piled up the public debt by $262,000,000 in time of peace, forced an adverse balance of trade, kept a perpetual menace banging over the redemption fund, pawned American credit to alien syndicates and reversed all the measures and results of successful Republican rule. In the broad effect of its policy it has precipitated panic, blighted industry and trade with prolonged depression, closed factories, reduced work and wages, halted enterprise and crippled American production, while stimulating foreign production for the American market. Every consideration of public safety and individual interest demands that the government shall be wrested from the hands of those who have shown themselves incapable of conducting it without disaster at home and dishonor abroad and shall be restored to the party which for thirty years administered it with unequaled success and prosperity. And in this connection, we heartily endorse the wisdom, patriotism and success of the administration of Benjamin Harrison. We renew and emphasize our allegiance to the policy of protection, as the bulwark of American industrial independence, and the foundation of American development and prosperity. This true American policy taxes foreign products and encourages home industry. It puts the burden of revenue on foreign goods; it secures the American market for the American producer. It upholds the American standard of wages for the American workingman; it puts the factory by the side of the farm and makes the American farmer less dependent on foreign demand and price; it diffuses general thrift, and founds the strength of all on the strength of each. In its reasonable application it is just, fair and impartial, equally opposed to foreign control and domestic monopoly to sectional discrimination and individual favoritism.

We denounce the present tariff as sectional, injurious to the public credit and destructive to business enterprise. We demand such an equitable tariff on foreign imports which come into competition with the American products as will not only furnish adequate revenue for the necessary expenses of the government, but will protect American labor from degradation and the wage level of other lands. We are not pledged to any particular schedules. The question of rates is a practical question, to be governed by the conditions of time and of production. The ruling and uncompromising principle is the protection and development of American labor and industries. The country demands a right settlement, and then it wants rest.

We believe the repeal of the reciprocity arrangements negotiated by the last Republican Administration was a National calamity, and demand their renewal and extension on such terms as will equalize our trade with other nations, remove the restrictions which now obstruct the sale of American products in the ports of other countries, and secure enlarged markets for the products of our farms, forests, and factories.

Protection and Reciprocity are twin measures of American policy and go hand in hand. Democratic rule has recklessly struck down both, and both must be re-established. Protection for what we produce; free admission for the necessaries of life which we do not produce; reciprocal agreement of mutual interests, which gain open markets for us in return for our open markets for others. Protection builds up domestic industry and trade and secures our own market for ourselves; reciprocity builds up foreign trade and finds an outlet for our surplus. We condemn the present administration for not keeping pace [faith] with the sugar producers of this country. The Republican party favors such protection as will lead to the production on American soil of all the sugar which the American people use, and for which they pay other countries more than one hundred million dollars annually. To all our products; to those of the mine and the fields, as well as to those of the shop and the factory, to hemp and wool, the product of the great industry sheep husbandry; as well as to the foundry, as to the mills, we promise the most ample protection. We favor the early American policy of discriminating duties for the upbuilding of our merchant marine. To the protection of our shipping in the foreign-carrying trade, so that American ships, the product of American labor, employed in American shipyards, sailing under the stars and stripes, and manned, officered and owned by Americans, may regain the carrying of our foreign commerce.

The Republican party is unreservedly for sound money. It caused the enactment of a law providing for the redemption [resumption] of specie payments in 1879. Since then every dollar has been as good as gold. We are unalterably opposed to every measure calculated to debase our currency or impair the credit of our country. We are therefore opposed to the free coinage of silver, except by international agreement with the leading commercial nations of the earth, which agreement we pledge ourselves to promote, and until such agreement can be obtained the existing gold standard must be maintained. All of our silver and paper currency must be maintained at parity with gold, and we favor all measures designated to maintain inviolable the obligations of the United States, of all our money, whether coin or paper, at the present standard, the standard of most enlightened nations of the earth.

The veterans of the Union Armies deserve and should receive fair treatment and generous recognition. Whenever practicable they should be given the preference in the matter of employment. And they are entitled to the enactment of such laws as are best calculated to secure the fulfillment of the pledges made to them in the dark days of the country's peril.

We denounce the practice in the pension bureau so recklessly and unjustly carried on by the present Administration of reducing pensions and arbitrarily dropping names from the rolls, as deserving the severest condemnation of the American people.

Our foreign policy should be at all times firm, vigorous and dignified, and all our interests in the western hemisphere should be carefully watched and guarded.

The Hawaiian Islands should be controlled by the United States, and no foreign power should be permitted to interfere with them. The Nicaragua Canal should be built, owned and operated by the United States. And, by the purchase of the Danish Islands we should secure a much needed Naval station in the West Indies.

The massacres in Armenia have aroused the deep sympathy and just indignation of the American people, and we believe that the United States should exercise all the influence it can properly exert to bring these atrocities to an end. In Turkey, American residents have been exposed to gravest [grievous] dangers and American property destroyed. There, and everywhere, American citizens and American property must be absolutely protected at all hazards and at any cost.

We reassert the Monroe Doctrine in its full extent, and we reaffirm the rights of the United States to give the Doctrine effect by responding to the appeal of any American State for friendly intervention in case of European encroachment.

We have not interfered and shall not interfere, with the existing possession of any European power in this hemisphere, and the ultimate union of all the English speaking parts of the continent by the free consent of its inhabitants; from the hour of achieving their own independence the people of the United States have regarded with sympathy the struggles of other American peoples to free themselves from European domination. We watch with deep and abiding interest the heroic battles of the Cuban patriots against cruelty and oppression, and best hopes go out for the full success of their determined contest for liberty. The government of Spain, having lost control of Cuba, and being unable to protect the property or lives of resident American citizens, or to comply with its Treaty obligations, we believe that the government of the United States should actively use its influence and good offices to restore peace and give independence to the Island.

The peace and security of the Republic and the maintenance of its rightful influence among the nations of the earth demand a naval power commensurate with its position and responsibilities. We, therefore, favor the continued enlargement of the navy, and a complete system of harbor and sea-coast defenses.

For the protection of the equality of our American citizenship and of the wages of our workingmen, against the fatal competition of low priced labor, we demand that the immigration laws be thoroughly enforced, and so extended as to exclude from entrance to the United States those who can neither read nor write.

The civil service law was placed on the statute book by the Republican party which has always sustained it, and we renew our repeated declarations that it shall be thoroughly and heartily, and honestly enforced, and extended wherever practicable.

We demand that every citizen of the United States shall be allowed to cast one free and unrestricted ballot, and that such ballot shall be counted and returned as cast.

We proclaim our unqualified condemnation of the uncivilized and preposterous [barbarous] practice well known as lynching, and the killing of human beings suspected or charged with crime without process of law.

We favor the creation of a National Board of Arbitration to settle and adjust differences which may arise between employers and employed engaged in inter-State commerce.

We believe in an immediate return to the free homestead policy of the Republican party, and urge the passage by Congress of a satisfactory free homestead measure which has already passed the House, and is now pending in the Senate.

We favor the admission of the remaining Territories at the earliest practicable date having due regard to the interests of the people of the Territories and of the United States. And the Federal officers appointed for the Territories should be selected from the bona-fide residents thereof, and the right of self-government should be accorded them as far as practicable.

We believe that the citizens of Alaska should have representation in the Congress of the United States, to the end that needful legislation may be intelligently enacted.

We sympathize fully with all legitimate efforts to lessen and prevent the evils of intemperance and promote morality. The Republican party is mindful of the rights and interests of women, and believes that they should be accorded equal opportunities, equal pay for equal work, and protection to the home. We favor the admission of women to wider spheres of usefulness and welcome their co-operation in rescuing the country from Democratic and Populist mismanagement and misrule.

Such are the principles and policies of the Republican party. By these principles we will apply it to those policies and put them into execution. We rely on the faithful and considerate judgment of the American people, confident alike of the history of our great party and in the justice of our cause, and we present our platform and our candidates in the full assurance that their selection will bring victory to the Republican party, and prosperity to the people of the United States.

— 1900 —

The Republicans of the United States, through their chosen representatives, met in National Convention, looking back upon an unsurpassed record of achievement and looking forward into a great field of duty and opportunity, and appealing to the judgment of their countrymen, make these declarations:

The expectation in which the American people, turning from the Democratic party, intrusted power four years ago to a Republican Chief Magistrate and a Republican Congress, has been met and satisfied. When the people then assembled at the polls, after a term of Democratic legislation and administration, business was dead, industry paralyzed and the

National credit disastrously impaired. The country's capital was bidden away and its labor distressed and unemployed. The Democrats had no other plan with which to improve the ruinous conditions which they had themselves produced than to coin silver at the ratio of sixteen to one. The Republican party, denouncing this plan as sure to produce conditions even worse than those from which relief was sought, promised to restore prosperity by means of two legislative measures—a protective tariff and a law making gold the standard of value. The people by great majorities issued to the Republican party a commission to enact these laws. This commission has been executed, and the Republican promise is redeemed. Prosperity more general and more abundant than we have ever known has followed these enactments. There is no longer controversy as to the value of any Government obligations. Every American dollar is a gold dollar or its assured equivalent, and American credit stands higher than that of any other nation. Capital is fully employed and labor everywhere is profitably occupied. No single fact can more strikingly tell the story of what Republican Government means to the country than this. That while during the whole period, of one hundred and seven years from 1790 to 1897 there was an excess of exports over imports of only $383,028,497, there has been in the short three years of the present Republican Administration an excess of exports over imports in the enormous sum of $1,483,537,094.

And while the American people, sustained by this Republican legislation, have been achieving these splendid triumphs in their business and commerce, they have conducted and in victory concluded a war for liberty and human rights. No thought of National aggrandizement tarnished the high purpose with which American standards were unfurled. It was a war unsought and patiently resisted, but when it came the American Government was ready. Its fleets were cleared for action. Its armies were in the field, and the quick and signal triumph of its forces on land and sea bore equal tribute to the courage of American soldiers and sailors, and to the skill and foresight of Republican statesmanship. To ten millions of the human race there was given "a new birth of freedom," and to the American people a new and noble responsibility.

We indorse the Administration of William McKinley. Its acts have been established in wisdom and in patriotism, and at home and abroad it has distinctly elevated and extended the influence of the American nation. Walking untried paths and facing unforeseen responsibilities, President McKinley has been in every situation the true American patriot and the upright statesman, clear in vision, strong in judgment, firm in action, always inspiring and deserving the confidence of his countrymen.

In asking the American people to indorse this Republican record and to renew their commission to the Republican party, we remind them of the fact that the menace to their prosperity has always resided in Democratic principles, and no less in the general incapacity of the Democratic party to conduct public affairs. The prime essential of business prosperity is public confidence in the good sense of the Government and in its ability to deal intelligently with each new problem of administration and legislation. That confidence the Democratic party has never earned. It is hopelessly inadequate, and the country's prosperity, when Democratic success at the polls is announced, halts and ceases in mere anticipation of Democratic blunders and failures.

We renew our allegiance to the principle of the gold standard and declare our confidence in the wisdom of the legislation of the Fifty-sixth Congress, by which the parity of all our money and the stability of our currency upon a gold basis has been secured. We recognize that interest rates are a potent factor in production and business activity, and for the purpose of further equalizing and of further lowering the rates of interest, we favor such monetary legislation as will enable the varying needs of the season and of all sections to be promptly met in order that trade may be evenly sustained, labor steadily employed and commerce enlarged. The volume of money in circulation was never so great per capita as it is to-day. We declare our steadfast opposition to the free and unlimited coinage of silver. No measure to that end could be considered which was without the support of the leading commercial countries of the world. However firmly Republican legislation may seem to have secured the country against the peril of base and discredited currency, the election of a Democratic President could not fail to impair the country's credit and to bring once more into question the intention of the American people to maintain upon the gold standard the parity of their money circulation. The Democratic party must be convinced that the American people will never tolerate the Chicago platform.

We recognize the necessity and propriety of the honest co-operation of capital to meet new business conditions and especially to extend our rapidly increasing foreign trade, but we condemn all conspiracies and combinations intended to restrict business, to create monopolies, to limit production, or to control prices; and favor such legislation as will effectively restrain and prevent all such abuses, protect and promote competition and secure the rights of producers, laborers, and all who are engaged in industry and commerce.

We renew our faith in the policy of protection to American labor. In that policy our industries have been established, diversified and maintained. By protecting the home market competition has been stimulated and production cheapened. Opportunity to the inventive genius of our people has been secured and wages in every department of labor maintained at high rates, higher now than ever before, and always distinguishing our working people in their better conditions of life from those of any competing country. Enjoying the blessings of the American common school, secure in the right of self-government and protected in the occupancy of their own markets, their constantly increasing knowledge and skill have enabled them to finally enter the markets of the world. We favor the associated policy of reciprocity so directed as to open our markets on favorable terms for what we do not ourselves produce in return for free foreign markets.

In the further interest of American workmen we favor a more effective restriction of the immigration of cheap labor from foreign lands, the extension of opportunities of education for working children, the raising of the age limit for child labor, the protection of free labor as against contract convict labor, and an effective system of labor insurance.

Our present dependence upon foreign shipping for nine-tenths of our foreign carrying is a great loss to the industry of this country. It is also a serious danger to our trade, for its sudden withdrawal in the event of European war would seriously cripple our expanding foreign commerce. The National defense and naval efficiency of this country, moreover, supply a compelling reason for legislation which will enable us to recover our former place among the trade-carrying fleets of the world.

The Nation owes a debt of profound gratitude to the soldiers and sailors who have fought its battles, and it is the Government's duty to provide for the survivors and for the widows and orphans of those who have fallen in the country's wars. The pension laws, founded in this just sentiment, should be liberally administered, and preference should be given wherever practicable with respect to employment in the public service, to soldiers and sailors and to their widows and orphans.

We commend the policy of the Republican party in maintaining the efficiency of the civil service. The Administration has acted wisely in its efforts to secure for public service in Cuba, Puerto Rico, Hawaii, and the Philippine Islands, only those whose fitness has been determined by training and experience. We believe that employment in the public service in these territories should be confined as far as practicable to their inhabitants.

It was the plain purpose of the fifteenth amendment to the Constitution, to prevent discrimination on account of race or color in regulating the elective franchise. Devices of State governments, whether by statutory or constitutional enactment, to avoid the purpose of this amendment are revolutionary, and should be condemned.

Public movements looking to a permanent improvement of the roads and highways of the country meet with our cordial approval, and we recommend this subject to the earnest consideration of the people and of the Legislatures of the several states.

We favor the extension of the Rural Free Delivery service wherever its extension may be justified.

In further pursuance of the constant policy of the Republican party to provide free homes on the public domain, we recommend adequate national legislation to reclaim the arid lands of the United States, reserving control of the distribution of water for irrigation to the respective States and Territories.

We favor home rule for, and the early admission to statehood of the Territories of New Mexico, Arizona, and Oklahoma.

The Dingley Act, amended to provide sufficient revenue for the conduct of the war, has so well performed its work that it has been possible to reduce the war debt in the sum of $40,000,000. So ample are the Government's revenues and so great is the public confidence in the integrity of its obligations that its newly-funded two per cent bonds sell at a premium. The country is now justified in expecting, and it will be the policy of the Republican party to bring about, a reduction of the war taxes.

We favor the construction, ownership, control and protection of an Isthmian Canal by the Government of the United States. New markets are necessary for the increasing surplus of our farm products. Every effort should be made to open and obtain new markets, especially in the Orient, and the Administration is warmly to be commended for its successful efforts to commit all trading and colonizing nations to the policy of the open door in China.

In the interest of our expanding commerce we recommend that Congress create a Department of Commerce and Industries, in the charge of a Secretary with a seat in the Cabinet. The United States Consular system should be reorganized under the supervision of this new Department upon such a basis of appointment and tenure as will render it still more serviceable to the Nation's increasing trade.

The American Government must protect the person and property of every citizen wherever they are wrongfully violated or placed in peril.

We congratulate the women of America upon their splendid record of public service in the volunteer aid association and as nurses in camp and hospital during the recent campaigns of our armies in the East and West Indies, and we appreciate their faithful co-operation in all works of education and industry.

President McKinley has conducted the foreign affairs of the United States with distinguished credit to the American people. In releasing us from the vexatious conditions of a European alliance for the government of Samoa, his course is especially to be commended. By securing to our undivided control the most important island of the Samoan group and the best harbor in the Southern Pacific, every American interest has been safeguarded.

We approve the annexation of the Hawaiian Islands to the United States.

We commend the part taken by our Government in the Peace Conference at The Hague. We assert our steadfast adherence to the policy announced in the Monroe Doctrine. The provisions of The Hague Convention were wisely regarded when President McKinley tendered his friendly offices in the interest of peace between Great Britain and the South African Republic. While the American Government must continue the policy prescribed by Washington, affirmed by every succeeding President and imposed upon us by The Hague treaty, of nonintervention in European controversies, the American people earnestly hope that a way may soon be found, honorable alike to both contending parties, to terminate the strife between them.

In accepting by the Treaty of Paris the just responsibility of our victories in the Spanish war, the President and the Senate won the undoubted approval of the American people. No other course was possible than to destroy Spain's sovereignty throughout the West Indies and in the Philippine Islands. That course created our responsibility before the world, and with the unorganized population whom our intervention had freed from Spain, to provide for the maintenance of law and order, and for the establishment of good government and for the performance of international obligations. Our authority could not be less than our responsibility; and wherever sovereign rights were extended it became the high duty of the Government to maintain its authority, to put down armed insurrection and to confer the blessings of liberty and civilization upon all the rescued peoples.

The largest measure of self-government consistent with their welfare and our duties shall be secured to them by law.

To Cuba independence and self-government were assured in the same voice by which war was declared, and to the latter this pledge shall be performed.

The Republican party, upon its history, and upon this declaration of its principles and policies confidently invokes the considerate and approving judgment of the American people.

— 1904 —

Fifty years ago the Republican party came into existence dedicated among other purposes to the great task of arresting the extension of human slavery. In 1860 it elected its first President. During twenty-four years of the forty-four which have elapsed since the election of Lincoln the Republican party has held complete control of the government. For eighteen more of the forty-four years it has held partial control through the possession of one or two branches of the government, while the Democratic party during the same period has had complete control for only two years. This long tenure of power by the Republican party is not due to chance. It is a demonstration that the Republican party has commanded the confidence of the American people for nearly two generations to a degree never equalled in our history, and has displayed a high capacity for rule and Government which has been made even more conspicuous by the incapacity and infirmity of purpose shown by its opponents.

The Republican party entered upon its present period of complete supremacy in 1897. We have every right to congratulate ourselves upon the work since then accomplished, for it has added lustre even to the traditions of the party which carried the government through the storms of civil war.

We then found the country after four years of Democratic rule in evil plight, oppressed with misfortune, and doubtful of the future. Public credit had been lowered, the revenues were declining, the debt was growing, the administration's attitude toward Spain was feeble and mortifying, the standard of values was threatened and uncertain, labor was unemployed, business was sunk in the depression which had succeeded the panic of 1893, hope was faint and confidence was gone.

We met these unhappy conditions vigorously, effectively, and at once. We replaced a Democratic tariff law based on free trade principles and garnished with sectional protection by a consistent protective tariff, and industry, freed from oppression and stimulated by the encouragement of wise laws, has expanded to a degree never before known, has conquered new markets, and has created a volume of exports which has surpassed imagination. Under the Dingley tariff labor has been fully employed, wages have risen, and all industries have revived and prospered.

We firmly established the gold standard which was then menaced with destruction. Confidence returned to business, and with confidence an unexampled prosperity.

For deficient revenues, supplemented by improvident issues of bonds, we gave the country an income which produced a large surplus and which enabled us only four years after the Spanish War had closed to remove over one hundred millions of annual war taxes, reduce the public debt, and lower the interest charges of the Government.

The public credit which had been so lowered that in time of peace a Democratic administration made large loans at extravagant rates of interest in order to pay current expenditures, rose under Republican administration to its highest point and enabled us to borrow at 2 per cent even in time of war.

We refuse to palter longer with the miseries of Cuba. We fought a quick and victorious war with Spain. We set Cuba free, governed the island for three years, and then gave it to the Cuban people with order restored, with ample revenues, with education and public health established, free from debt, and connected with the United States by wise provisions for our mutual interests.

We have organized the government of Puerto Rico,* and its people now enjoy peace, freedom, order, and prosperity.

In the Philippines we have suppressed insurrection, established order, and given to life and property a security never known there before. We have organized civil government, made it effective and strong in administration, and have conferred upon the people of those islands the largest civil liberty they have ever enjoyed.

By our possession of the Philippines we were enabled to take prompt and effective action in the relief of the legations at Peking and a decisive part in preventing the partition and preserving the integrity of China.

The possession of a route for an Isthmian canal, so long the dream of American statesmanship, is now an accomplished fact. The great work of connecting the Pacific and Atlantic by a canal is at last begun, and it is due to the Republican party.

*Please note that to avoid confusion, the editors have changed the original spelling of Puerto Rico (Porto Rico) to its current form.

We have passed laws which will bring the arid lands of the United States within the area of cultivation.

We have reorganized the army and put it in the highest state of efficiency.

We have passed laws for the improvement and support of the militia.

We have pushed forward the building of the navy, the defense and protection of our honor and our interests.

Our administration of the great departments of the Government has been honest and efficient, and wherever wrongdoing has been discovered, the Republican administration has not hesitated to probe the evil and bring offenders to justice without regard to party or political ties.

Laws enacted by the Republican party which the Democratic party failed to enforce and which were intended for the protection of the public against the united discrimination or the illegal encroachment of vast aggregations of capital, have been fearlessly enforced by a Republican President, and new laws insuring reasonable publicity as to the operations of great corporations, and providing additional remedies for the prevention of discrimination in freight rates, have been passed by a Republican Congress.

In this record of achievement during the past eight years may be read the pledges which the Republican party has fulfilled. We promise to continue these policies, and we declare our constant adherence to the following principles:

Protection, which guards and develops our industries, is a cardinal policy of the Republican party. The measure of protection should always at least equal the difference in the cost of production at home and abroad. We insist upon the maintenance of the principle of protection, and therefore rates of duty should be readjusted only when conditions have so changed that the public interest demands their alteration, but this work cannot safely be committed to any other hands than those of the Republican party. To intrust it to the Democratic party is to invite disaster. Whether, as in 1892, the Democratic party declares the protective tariff unconstitutional, or whether it demands tariff reform or tariff revision, its real object is always the destruction of the protective system. However specious the name, the purpose is ever the same. A Democratic tariff has always been followed by business adversity: a Republican tariff by business prosperity. To a Republican Congress and a Republican President this great question can be safely intrusted. When the only free trade country among the great nations agitates a return to protection, the chief protective country should not falter in maintaining it.

We have extended widely our foreign markets, and we believe in the adoption of all practicable methods for their further extension, including commercial reciprocity wherever reciprocal arrangements can be effected consistent with the principles of protection and without injury to American agriculture, American labor, or any American industry.

We believe it to be the duty of the Republican party to uphold the gold standard and the integrity and value of our national currency. The maintenance of the gold standard, established by the Republican party, cannot safely be committed to the Democratic party which resisted its adoption and has never given any proof since that time of belief in it or fidelity to it.

While every other industry has prospered under the fostering aid of Republican legislation, American shipping engaged in foreign trade in competition with the low cost of construction, low wages and heavy subsidies of foreign governments, has not for many years received from the Government of the United States adequate encouragement of any kind. We therefore favor legislation which will encourage and build up the American merchant marine, and we cordially approve the legislation of the last Congress which created the Merchant Marine Commission to investigate and report upon this subject.

A navy powerful enough to defend the United States against any attack, to uphold the Monroe Doctrine, and watch over our commerce, is essential to the safety and the welfare of the American people. To maintain such a navy is the fixed policy of the Republican party.

We cordially approve the attitude of President Roosevelt and Congress in regard to the exclusion of Chinese labor, and promise a continuance of the Republican policy in that direction.

The Civil Service Law was placed on the statute books by the Republican party, which has always sustained it, and we renew our former declarations that it shall be thoroughly and honestly enforced.

We are always mindful of the country's debt to the soldiers and sailors of the United States, and we believe in making ample provision for them, and in the liberal administration of the pension laws.

We favor the peaceful settlement of international differences by arbitration.

We commend the vigorous efforts made by the Administration to protect American citizens in foreign lands, and pledge ourselves to insist upon the just and equal protection of all of our citizens abroad. It is the unquestioned duty of the Government to procure for all our citizens, without distinction, the rights of travel and sojourn in friendly countries, and we

declare ourselves in favor of all proper efforts tending to that end.

Our great interests and our growing commerce in the Orient render the condition of China of high importance to the United States. We cordially commend the policy pursued in that direction by the administrations of President McKinley and President Roosevelt.

We favor such Congressional action as shall determine whether by special discrimination the elective franchise in any State has been unconstitutionally limited, and, if such is the case, we demand that representation in Congress and in the electoral college shall be proportionately reduced as directed by the Constitution of the United States.

Combinations of capital and of labor are the results of the economic movement of the age, but neither must be permitted to infringe upon the rights and interests of the people. Such combinations, when lawfully formed for lawful purposes, are alike entitled to the protection of the laws, but both are subject to the laws and neither can be permitted to break them.

The great statesman and patriotic American, William McKinley, who was re-elected by the Republican party to the Presidency four years ago, was assassinated just at the threshold of his second term. The entire nation mourned his untimely death and did that justice to his great qualities of mind and character which history will confirm and repeat.

The American people were fortunate in his successor, to whom they turned with a trust and confidence which have been fully justified. President Roosevelt brought to the great responsibilities thus sadly forced upon him a clear hand, a brave heart, and earnest patriotism, and high ideals of public duty and public service. True to the principles of the Republican party and to the policies which that party had declared, he has also shown himself ready for every emergency and has met new and vital questions with ability and with success.

The confidence of the people in his justice, inspired by his public career, enabled him to render personally an inestimable service to the country by bringing about a settlement of the coal strike, which threatened such disastrous results at the opening of Winter in 1902.

Our foreign policy under his administration has not only been able, vigorous, and dignified, but in the highest degree successful.

The complicated questions which arose in Venezuela were settled in such a way by President Roosevelt that the Monroe Doctrine was signally vindicated, and the cause of peace and arbitration greatly advanced.

His prompt and vigorous action in Panama, which we commend in the highest terms, not only secured to us the canal route, but avoided foreign complications which might have been of a very serious character.

He has continued the policy of President McKinley in the Orient, and our position in China, signalized by our recent commercial treaty with that empire, has never been so high.

He secured the tribunal by which the vexed and perilous question of the Alaskan boundary was finally settled.

Whenever crimes against humanity have been perpetrated which have shocked our people, his protest has been made, and our good offices have been tendered, but always with due regard to international obligations.

Under his guidance we find ourselves at peace with all the world, and never were we more respected or our wishes more regarded by foreign nations.

Pre-eminently successful in regard to our foreign relations, he has been equally fortunate in dealing with domestic questions. The country has known that the public credit and the national currency were absolutely safe in the hands of his administration. In the enforcement of the laws he has shown not only courage, but the wisdom which understands that to permit laws to be violated or disregarded opens the door to anarchy, while the just enforcement of the law is the soundest conservatism. He has held firmly to the fundamental American doctrine that all men must obey the law; that there must be no distinction between rich and poor, between strong and weak, but that justice and equal protection under the law must be secured to every citizen without regard to race, creed, or condition.

His administration has been throughout vigorous and honorable, high-minded and patriotic. We commend it without reservation to the considerate judgment of the American people.

— 1908 —

Once more the Republican Party, in National Convention assembled, submits its cause to the people. This great historic organization, that destroyed slavery, preserved the Union, restored credit, expanded the national domain, established a sound financial system, developed the industries and resources of the country, and gave to the nation her seat of honor in the councils of the world, now meets the new problems of government with the same courage and capacity with which it solved the old.

REPUBLICANISM UNDER ROOSEVELT

In this greatest era of American advancement the Republican party has reached its highest service under the leadership of Theodore Roosevelt. His administration is an epoch in American history. In no other period since national sovereignty was won under Washington, or preserved under Lincoln, has there been such mighty progress in those ideals of government which make for justice, equality and fair dealing among men. The highest aspirations of the American people have found a voice. Their most exalted servant represents the best aims and worthiest purposes of all his countrymen. American manhood has been lifted to a nobler sense of duty and obligation. Conscience and courage in public station and higher standards of right and wrong in private life have become cardinal principles of political faith; capital and labor have been brought into closer relations of confidence and interdependence, and the abuse of wealth, the tyranny of power, and all the evils of privilege and favoritism have been put to scorn by the simple, manly virtues of justice and fair play.

The great accomplishments of President Roosevelt have been, first and foremost, a brave and impartial enforcement of the law, the prosecution of illegal trusts and monopolies, the exposure and punishment of evildoers in the public service; the more effective regulation of the rates and service of the great transportation lines; the complete overthrow of preferences, rebates and discriminations; the arbitration of labor disputes; the amelioration of the condition of wage-workers everywhere; the conservation of the natural resources of the country; the forward step in the improvement of the inland waterways; and always the earnest support and defense of every wholesome safeguard which has made more secure the guarantees of life, liberty and property.

These are the achievements that will make for Theodore Roosevelt his place in history, but more than all else the great things he has done will be an inspiration to those who have yet greater things to do. We declare our unfaltering adherence to the policies thus inaugurated, and pledge their continuance under a Republican administration of the Government.

EQUALITY OF OPPORTUNITY

Under the guidance of Republican principles the American people have become the richest nation in the world. Our wealth to-day exceeds that of England and all her colonies, and that of France and Germany combined. When the Republican Party was born the total wealth of the country was $16,000,000,000. It has leaped to $110,000,000,000 in a generation, while Great Britain has gathered but $60,000,000,000 in five hundred years. The United States now owns one fourth of the world's wealth and makes one-third of all modern manufactured products. In the great necessities of civilization, such as coal, the motive power of all activity; iron, the chief basis of all industry; cotton, the staple foundation of all fabrics; wheat, corn and all the agricultural products that feed mankind, America's supremacy is undisputed. And yet her great natural wealth has been scarcely touched. We have a vast domain of 3,000,000 square miles, literally bursting with latent treasure, still waiting the magic of capital and industry to be converted to the practical uses of mankind; a country rich in soil and climate, in the unharnessed energy of its rivers and in all the varied products of the field, the forest and the factory. With gratitude for God's bounty, with pride in the splendid productiveness of the past and with confidence in the plenty and prosperity of the future, the Republican party declares for the principle that in the development and enjoyment of wealth so great and blessings so benign there shall be equal opportunity for all.

THE REVIVAL OF BUSINESS

Nothing so clearly demonstrates the sound basis upon which our commercial, industrial and agricultural interests are founded, and the necessity of promoting their continued welfare through the operation of Republican policies, as the recent safe passage of the American people through a financial disturbance which, if appearing in the midst of Democratic rule or the menace of it, might have equalled the familiar Democratic panics of the past. We congratulate the people upon this renewed evidence of American supremacy and hail with confidence the signs now manifest of a complete restoration of business prosperity in all lines of trade, commerce and manufacturing.

RECENT REPUBLICAN LEGISLATION

Since the election of William McKinley in 1896, the people of this country have felt anew the wisdom of entrusting to the Republican party, through decisive majorities, the control and direction of national legislation.

The many wise and progressive measures adopted at recent sessions of Congress have demonstrated the patriotic resolve of Republican leadership in the legislative department to keep step in the forward march toward better government.

Notwithstanding the indefensible filibustering of a Democratic minority in the House of Representatives during the last session, many wholesome and progressive laws were enacted, and we especially commend the passage of the emergency currency bill; the appointment of the national monetary commission; the employer's and Government liability laws, the measures for the greater efficiency of the Army and Navy; the widow's pension bill; the child labor law for the District of Columbia; the new statutes for the safety of railroad engineers and firemen, and many other acts conserving the public welfare.

REPUBLICAN PLEDGES FOR THE FUTURE

Tariff

The Republican party declares unequivocally for a revision of the tariff by a special session of Congress immediately following the inauguration of the next President, and commends the steps already taken to this end in the work assigned to the appropriate committees of Congress, which are now investigating the operation and effect of existing schedules.

In all tariff legislation the true principle of protection is best maintained by the imposition of such duties as will equal the difference between the cost of production at home and abroad, together with a reasonable profit to American industries. We favor the establishment of maximum and minimum rates to be administered by the President under limitations fixed in the law, the maximum to be available to meet discriminations by foreign countries against American goods entering their markets, and the minimum to represent the normal measure of protection at home; the aim and purpose of the Republican policy being not only to preserve, without excessive duties, that security against foreign competition to which American manufacturers, farmers and producers are entitled, but also to maintain the high standard of living of the wage-earners of this country, who are the most direct beneficiaries of the protective system. Between the United States and the Philippines we believe in a free interchange of products with such limitations as to sugar and tobacco as will afford adequate protection to domestic interests.

Currency

We approve the emergency measures adopted by the Government during the recent financial disturbance, and especially commend the passage by Congress, at the last session, of the law designed to protect the country from a repetition of such stringency. The Republican party is committed to the development of a permanent currency system, responding to our greater needs; and the appointment of the National Monetary Commission by the present Congress, which will impartially investigate all proposed methods, insures the early realization of this purpose. The present currency laws have fully justified their adoption, but an expanding commerce, a marvelous growth in wealth and population, multiplying the centres of distribution, increasing the demand for the movement of crops in the West and South, and entailing periodic changes in monetary conditions, disclose the need of a more elastic and adaptable system. Such a system must meet the requirements of agriculturists, manufacturers, merchants and business men generally, must be automatic in operation, minimizing the fluctuations of interest rates, and above all, must be in harmony with that Republican doctrine, which insists that every dollar shall be based upon, and as good as, gold.

Postal Savings

We favor the establishment of a postal savings bank system for the convenience of the people and the encouragement of thrift.

Trusts

The Republican party passed the Sherman Antitrust law over Democratic opposition, and enforced it after Democratic dereliction. It has been a wholesome instrument for good in the hands of a wise and fearless administration. But experience has shown that its effectiveness can be strengthened and its real objects better attained by such amendments as will give to the Federal Government greater supervision and control over, and secure greater publicity in, the management of that class of corporations engaged in interstate commerce having power and opportunity to effect monopolies.

Railroads

We approve the enactment of the railroad rate law and the vigorous enforcement by the present administration of the statutes against rebates and discriminations, as a result of which the advantages formerly possessed by the large shipper over the small shipper have substantially disappeared; and in this connection we commend the appropriation by the present Congress to enable the Interstate Commerce Commission to thoroughly investigate, and give public-

ity to, the accounts of interstate railroads. We believe, however, that interstate commerce law should be further amended so as to give railroads the right to to make and publish tariff agreements, subject to the approval of the Commission, but maintaining always the principle of competition between naturally competing lines and avoiding the common control of such lines by any means whatsoever. We favor such national legislation and supervision as will prevent the future over-issue of stocks and bonds by interstate carriers.

Railroad and Government Employees

The enactment in constitutional form at the present session of Congress of the employer's liability law; the passage and enforcement of the safety appliance statutes, as well as the additional protection secured for engineers and firemen; the reduction in the hours of labor of trainmen and railroad telegraphers; the successful exercise of the powers of mediation and arbitration between interstate railroads and their employees, and the law making a beginning in the policy of compensation for injured employees of the Government, are among the most commendable accomplishments of the present administration. But there is further work in this direction yet to be done, and the Republican party pledges its continued devotion to every cause that makes for safety and the betterment of conditions among those whose labor contributes so much to the progress and welfare of the country.

Wage-Earners Generally

The same wise policy which has induced the Republican party to maintain protection to American labor; to establish an eight hour day in the construction of all public works; to increase the list of employees who shall have preferred claims for wages under the bankruptcy laws; to adopt a child labor statute for the District of Columbia; to direct an investigation into the condition of working women and children, and later, of employees of telephone and telegraph companies engaged in interstate business; to appropriate $150,000 at the recent session of Congress in order to secure a thorough inquiry into the causes of catastrophes and loss of life in the mines; and to amend and strengthen the laws prohibiting the importation of contract labor, will be pursued in every legitimate direction within Federal authority to tighten the burdens and increase the opportunity for happiness and advancement of all who toil. The Republican party recognizes the special needs of wage-workers generally, for their well-being means the well-being of all. But more important than all other considerations is that of good citizenship and we especially stand for the needs of every American, whatever his occupation, in his capacity as a self-respecting citizen.

Court Procedure

The Republican party will uphold at all times the authority and integrity of the courts, State and Federal, and will ever insist that their powers to enforce their process and to protect life, liberty and property shall be preserved inviolate. We believe, however, that the rules of procedure in the Federal Courts with respect to the issuance of the writ of injunction should be more accurately defined by statute, and that no injunction or temporary restraining order should be issued without notice, except where irreparable injury would result from delay, in which case a speedy hearing thereafter should be granted.

The American Farmer

Among those whose welfare is as vital to the welfare of the whole country as is that of the wage-earner, is the American farmer. The prosperity of the country rests peculiarly upon the prosperity of agriculture. The Republican party during the last twelve years has accomplished extraordinary work in bringing the resources of the National Government to the aid of the farmer, not only in advancing agriculture itself, but in increasing the conveniences of rural life. Free rural mail delivery has been established; it now reaches millions of our citizens, and we favor its extension until every community in the land receives the full benefits of the postal service. We recognize the social and economical advantages of good country roads, maintained more and more largely at public expense, and less and less at the expense of the abutting owner. In this work we commend the growing practice of State aid, and we approve the efforts of the National Agricultural Department by experiments and otherwise to make clear to the public the best methods of road construction.

Rights of the Negro

The Republican party has been for more than fifty years the consistent friend of the American Negro. It gave him freedom and citizenship. It wrote into the organic law the declarations that proclaim his civil and political rights, and it believes to-day that his noteworthy progress in intelligence, industry and good citizenship has earned the respect and encouragement of the nation. We demand equal justice for all men, without regard to race or color; we declare once more, and without reservation, for the enforcement in letter and spirit of the

Thirteenth, Fourteenth and Fifteenth amendments to the Constitution which were designed for the protection and advancement of the negro, and we condemn all devices that have for their real aim his disfranchisement for reasons of color alone, as unfair, un-American and repugnant to the supreme law of the land.

Natural Resources and Waterways

We indorse the movement inaugurated by the administration for the conservation of natural resources; we approve all measures to prevent the waste of timber; we commend the work now going on for the reclamation of arid lands, and reaffirm the Republican policy of the free distribution of the available areas of the public domain to the landless settler. No obligation of the future is more insistent and none will result in greater blessings to posterity. In line with this splendid undertaking is the further duty, equally imperative, to enter upon a systematic improvement upon a large and comprehensive plan, just to all portions of the country, of the waterways, harbors, and Great Lakes, whose natural adaptability to the increasing traffic of the land is one of the greatest gifts of a benign Providence.

The Army and Navy

The 60th Congress passed many commendable acts increasing the efficiency of the Army and Navy; making the militia of the States an integral part of the national establishment; authorizing joint maneuvers of army and militia; fortifying new naval bases and completing the construction of coaling stations; instituting a female nurse corps for naval hospitals and ships, and adding two new battleships, ten torpedo boat destroyers, three steam colliers, and eight submarines to the strength of the Navy. Although at peace with all the world, and secure in the consciousness that the American people do not desire and will not provoke a war with any other country, we nevertheless declare our unalterable devotion to a policy that will keep this Republic ready at all times to defend her traditional doctrines, and assure her appropriate part in promoting permanent tranquillity among the nations.

Protection of American Citizens Abroad

We commend the vigorous efforts made by the administration to protect American citizens in foreign lands, and pledge ourselves to insist upon the just and equal protection of all our citizens abroad. It is the unquestioned duty of the Government to procure for all our citizens, without distinction, the rights of travel and sojourn in friendly countries, and we declare ourselves in favor of all proper efforts tending to that end.

Extension of Foreign Commerce

Under the administration of the Republican party, the foreign commerce of the United States has experienced a remarkable growth, until it has a present annual valuation of approximately $3,000,000,000, and gives employment to a vast amount of labor and capital which would otherwise be idle. It has inaugurated, through the recent visit of the Secretary of State to South America and Mexico a new era of Pan-American commerce and comity, which is bringing us into closer touch with our twenty sister American republics, having a common historical heritage, a republican form of government, and offering us a limitless field of legitimate commercial expansion.

Arbitration and The Hague Treaties

The conspicuous contributions of American statesmanship to the great cause of international peace so signally advanced in the Hague conferences, are an occasion for just pride and gratification. At the last session of the Senate of the United States eleven Hague conventions were ratified, establishing the rights of neutrals, laws of war on land, restriction of submarine mines, limiting the use of force for the collection of contractual debts, governing the opening of hostilities, extending the application of Geneva principles and, in many ways, lessening the evils of war and promoting the peaceful settlement of international controversies. At the same session twelve arbitration conventions with great nations were confirmed, and extradition, boundary and neutralization treaties of supreme importance were ratified. We indorse such achievements as the highest duty a people can perform and proclaim the obligation of further strengthening the bonds of friendship and good-will with all the nations of the world.

Merchant Marine

We adhere to the Republican doctrine of encouragement to American shipping and urge such legislation as will revive the merchant marine prestige of the country, so essential to national defense, the enlargement of foreign trade and the industrial prosperity of our own people.

Veterans of the Wars

Another Republican policy which must ever be maintained is that of generous provision for those who have fought the country's battles, and for the widows and orphans of those who have fallen. We commend the increase in the widows' pensions, made by the present Congress, and declare for a liberal administration of all pension laws, to the end that the people's gratitude may grow deeper as the memories of heroic sacrifice grow more sacred with the passing years.

Civil Service

We reaffirm our former declarations that the civil service laws, enacted, extended, and enforced by the Republican party, shall continue to be maintained and obeyed.

Public Health

We commend the efforts designed to secure greater efficiency in National Public Health agencies and favor such legislation as will effect this purpose.

Bureau of Mines and Mining

In the interest of the great mineral industries of our country, we earnestly favor the establishment of a Bureau of Mines and Mining.

Cuba, Puerto Rico, the Philippines, and Panama

The American Government, in Republican hands, has freed Cuba, given peace and protection to Puerto Rico and the Philippines under our flag, and begun the construction of the Panama Canal. The present conditions in Cuba vindicate the wisdom of maintaining, between that Republic and this, imperishable bonds of mutual interest, and the hope is now expressed that the Cuban people will soon again be ready to assume complete sovereignty over their land.

In Puerto Rico the Government of the United States is meeting loyal and patriotic support; order and prosperity prevail, and the well-being of the people is in every respect promoted and conserved.

We believe that the native inhabitants of Puerto Rico should be at once collectively made citizens of the United States, and that all others properly qualified under existing laws residing in said island should have the privilege of becoming naturalized.

In the Philippines insurrection has been suppressed, law is established and life and property made secure. Education and practical experience are there advancing the capacity of the people for government, and the policies of McKinley and Roosevelt are leading the inhabitants step by step to an ever-increasing measure of home rule.

Time has justified the selection of the Panama route for the great Isthmian Canal, and events have shown the wisdom of securing authority over the zone through which it is to be built. The work is now progressing with a rapidity far beyond expectation, and already the realization of the hopes of centuries has come within the vision of the near future.

New Mexico and Arizona

We favor the immediate admission of the Territories of New Mexico and Arizona as separate States in the Union.

Centenary of the Birth of Lincoln

February 12, 1909, will be the 100th anniversary of the birth of Abraham Lincoln, an immortal spirit whose fame has brightened with the receding years, and whose name stands among the first of those given to the world by the great Republic. We recommend that this centennial anniversary be celebrated throughout the confines of the nation, by all the people thereof, and especially by the public schools, as an exercise to stir the patriotism of the youth of the land.

DEMOCRATIC INCAPACITY FOR GOVERNMENT

We call the attention of the American people to the fact that none of the great measures here advocated by the Republican party could be enacted, and none of the steps forward here proposed could be taken under a Democratic administration or under one in which party responsibility is divided. The continuance of present policies, therefore, absolutely requires the continuance in power of that party which believes in them and which possesses the capacity to put them into operation.

FUNDAMENTAL DIFFERENCES BETWEEN DEMOCRACY AND REPUBLICANISM

Beyond all platform declarations there are fundamental differences between the Republican party and its chief opponent which make the one worthy and the other unworthy of public trust.

In history, the difference between Democracy and Republicanism is that the one stood for debased currency, the other for honest currency; the one for free silver, the other for sound money; the one for free trade, the other for protection; the one for the contraction of American influence, the other for its expansion; the one has been forced to abandon every position taken on the great issues before the people, the other has held and vindicated all.

In experience, the difference between Democracy and Republicanism is that one means adversity, while the other means prosperity; one means low wages, the other means high; one means doubt and debt, the other means confidence and thrift.

In principle, the difference between Democracy and Republicanism is that one stands for vacillation and timidity in government, the other for strength and purpose; one stands for obstruction, the other for construction; one promises, the other performs, one finds fault, the other finds work.

The present tendencies of the two parties are even more marked by inherent differences. The trend of Democracy is toward socialism, while the Republican party stands for a wise and regulated individualism. Socialism would destroy wealth, Republicanism would prevent its abuse. Socialism would give to each an equal right to take; Republicanism would give to each an equal right to earn. Socialism would offer an equality of possession which would soon leave no one anything to possess, Republicanism would give equality of opportunity which would assure to each his share of a constantly increasing sum of possessions. In line with this tendency the Democratic party of to-day believes in Government ownership, while the Republican party believes in Government regulation. Ultimately Democracy would have the nation own the people, while Republicanism would have the people own the nation.

Upon this platform of principles and purposes, reaffirming our adherence to every Republican doctrine proclaimed since the birth of the party, we go before the country, asking the support not only of those who have acted with us heretofore, but of all our fellow citizens who, regardless of past political differences, unite in the desire to maintain the policies, perpetuate the blessings and make secure the achievements of a greater America.

— 1912 —

The Republican party, assembled by its representatives in National Convention, declares its unchanging faith in government of the people, by the people, for the people. We renew our allegiance to the principles of the Republican party and our devotion to the cause of Republican institutions established by the fathers.

It is appropriate that we should now recall with a sense of veneration and gratitude the name of our first great leader, who was nominated in this city, and whose lofty principles and superb devotion to his country are an inspiration to the party he honored Abraham Lincoln.

In the present state of public affairs we should be inspired by his broad statesmanship and by his tolerant spirit toward men.

The Republican party looks back upon its record with pride and satisfaction, and forward to its new responsibilities with hope and confidence. Its achievements in government constitute the most luminous pages in our history. Our greatest national advance has been made during the years of its ascendancy in public affairs. It has been genuinely and always a party of progress; it has never been either stationary or reactionary. It has gone from the fulfillment of one great pledge to the fulfillment of another in response to the public need and to the popular will.

We believe in our self-controlled representative democracy which is a government of laws, not of men, and in which order is the prerequisite of progress.

The principles of constitutional government, which make provisions for orderly and effective expression of the popular will, for the protection of civil liberty and the rights of man, and for the interpretation of the law by an untrammelled and independent judiciary, have proved themselves capable of sustaining the structure of a government which, after more than a century of development, embraces one hundred millions of people, scattered over a wide and diverse territory, but bound by common purpose, common ideals and common affection to the Constitution of the United States. Under the Constitution and the principles asserted and vitalized by it, the United States has grown to be one of the great civilized and civilizing powers of the earth. It offers a home and an opportunity to the ambitious and the industrious from other lands. Resting upon the broad basis of a people's confidence and a people's support, and managed by the people themselves, the government of the United States will meet the problems of the future as satisfactorily as it has solved those of the past.

The Republican party is now, as always, a party of advanced and constructive statesmanship. It is prepared to go forward with the solution of those new questions, which social, economic and political development have brought into the forefront of the nation's interest. It will strive, not only in the nation but in the several States, to enact the necessary legislation to safeguard the public health; to limit effectively the labor of women and children, and to protect wage earners engaged in dangerous occupations; to enact comprehensive and generous workman's compensation laws in place of the present wasteful and unjust system of employers' liability; and in all possible ways to satisfy the just demand of the people for the study and solution of the complex and constantly changing problems of social welfare.

In dealing with these questions, it is important that the rights of every individual to the freest possible development of his own powers and resources and to the control of his own justly acquired property, so far as those are compatible with the rights of others, shall not be interfered with or destroyed. The social and political structure of the United States rests upon the civil liberty of the individual; and for the protection of that liberty the people have wisely, in the National and State Constitutions, put definite limitations upon themselves and upon their governmental officers and agencies. To enforce these limitations, to secure the orderly and coherent exercise of governmental powers, and to protect the rights of even the humblest and least favored individual are the function of independent Courts of justice.

The Republican party reaffirms its intention to uphold at all times the authority and integrity of the Courts, both State and Federal, and it will ever insist that their powers to enforce their process and to protect life, liberty and property shall be preserved inviolate. An orderly method is provided under our system of government by which the people may, when they choose, alter or amend the constitutional provisions which underlie that government. Until these constitutional provisions are so altered or amended, in orderly fashion, it is the duty of the Courts to see to it that when challenged they are enforced.

That the Courts, both Federal and State, may bear the heavy burden laid upon them to the complete satisfaction of public opinion, we favor legislation to prevent long delays and the tedious and costly appeals which have so often amounted to a denial of justice in civil cases and to a failure to protect the public at large in criminal cases.

Since the responsibility of the judiciary is so great, the standards of judicial action must be always and everywhere above suspicion and reproach. While we regard the recall of judges as unnecessary and unwise, we favor such action as may be necessary to simplify the process by which any judge who is found to be derelict in his duty may be removed from office.

Together with peaceful and orderly development at home, the Republican party earnestly favors all measures for the establishment and protection of the peace of the world and for the development of closer relations between the various nations of the earth. It believes most earnestly in the peaceful settlement of international disputes and in the reference of all justiciable controversies between nations to an International Court of justice.

MONOPOLY AND PRIVILEGE

The Republican party is opposed to special privilege and to monopoly. It placed upon the statutebook the interstate commerce act of 1887, and the important amendments thereto, and the antitrust act of 1890, and it has consistently and successfully enforced the provisions of these laws. It will take no backward step to permit the reestablishment in any degree of conditions which were intolerable.

Experience makes it plain that the business of the country may be carried on without fear or without disturbance and at the same time without resort to practices which are abhorrent to the common sense of justice. The Republican party favors the enactment of legislation supplementary to the existing antitrust act which will define as criminal offenses those specific acts that uniformly mark attempts to restrain and to monopolize trade, to the end that those who honestly intend to obey the law may have a guide for their action and those who aim to violate the law may the more surely be punished. The same certainty should be given to the law prohibiting combinations and monopolies that characterize other provisions of commercial law; in order that no part of the field of business opportunity may be restricted by monopoly or combination, that business success honorably achieved may not be converted into crime, and that the right of every man to acquire commodities, and particularly the necessaries of life, in an open market uninfluenced by the manipulation of trust or combination, may be preserved.

FEDERAL TRADE COMMISSION

In the enforcement and administration of Federal laws governing interstate commerce and enterprises impressed with a public use engaged therein, there is much that may be committed to a Federal trade commission, thus placing in the hands of an administrative board many of the functions now necessarily exercised by the courts. This will promote promptness in the administration of the law and avoid delays and technicalities incident to court procedure.

THE TARIFF

We reaffirm our belief in a protective tariff. The Republican tariff policy has been of the greatest benefit to the country, developing our resources, diversifying our industries, and protecting our workmen against competition with cheaper labor abroad, thus establishing for our wage earners the American standard of living. The protective tariff is so woven into the fabric of our industrial and agricultural life that to substitute for it a tariff for revenue only would destroy many industries and throw millions of our people out of employment. The products of the farm and of the mine should receive the same measure of protection as other products of American labor.

We hold that the import duties should be high enough, while yielding a sufficient revenue, to protect adequately American industries and wages. Some of the existing import duties are too high, and should be reduced. Readjustment should be made from time to time to conform to changing conditions and to reduce excessive rates, but without injury to any American industry. To accomplish this correct information is indispensable. This information can best be obtained by an expert commission, as the large volume of useful facts contained in the recent reports of the Tariff Board has demonstrated.

The pronounced feature of modern industrial life is its enormous diversification. To apply tariff rates justly to these changing conditions requires closer study and more scientific methods than ever before. The Republican party has shown by its creation of a Tariff Board its recognition of this situation, and its determination to be equal to it. We condemn the Democratic party for its failure either to provide funds for the continuance of this board or to make some other provision for securing the information requisite for intelligent tariff legislation. We protest against the Democratic method of legislating on these vitally important subjects without careful investigation.

We condemn the Democratic tariff bills passed by the House of Representatives of the Sixty-second Congress as sectional, as injurious to the public credit, and as destructive to business enterprise.

COST OF LIVING

The steadily increasing cost of living has become a matter not only of national but of worldwide concern. The fact that it is not due to the protective tariff system is evidenced by the existence of similar conditions in countries which have a tariff policy different from our own, as well as by the fact that the cost of living has increased while rates of duty have remained stationary or been reduced.

The Republican party will support a prompt scientific inquiry into the causes which are operative, both in the United States and elsewhere, to increase the cost of living. When the exact facts are known, it will take the necessary steps to remove any abuses that may be found to exist, in order that the cost of the food, clothing and shelter of the people may in no way be unduly or artificially increased.

BANKING AND CURRENCY

The Republican party has always stood for a sound currency and for safe banking methods. It is responsible for the resumption of specie payments and for the establishment of the gold standard. It is committed to the progressive development of our banking and currency systems. Our banking arrangements today need further revision to meet the requirements of current conditions. We need measures which will prevent the recurrence of money panics and financial disturbances and which will promote the prosperity of business and the welfare of labor by producing constant employment. We need better currency facilities for the movement of crops in the West and South. We need banking arrangements under American auspices for the encouragement and better conduct of our foreign trade. In attaining these ends, the independence of individual banks, whether organized under national or State charters, must be carefully protected, and our banking and currency system must be safeguarded from any possibility of domination by sectional, financial, or political interests.

It is of great importance to the social and economic welfare of this country that its farmers have facilities for borrowing easily and cheaply the money they need to increase the productivity of their land. It is as important that financial machinery be provided to supply the demand of farmers for credit as it is that the banking and currency systems be reformed in the interest of general business. Therefore, we recommend and urge an authoritative investigation of agricultural credit societies and corporations in other countries and the passage of State and Federal laws for the establishment and capable supervision of organizations having for their purpose the loaning of funds to farmers.

THE CIVIL SERVICE

We reaffirm our adherence to the principle of appointment to public office based on proved fitness, and tenure during good behavior and efficiency. The Republican party stands committed to the maintenance, extension and enforcement of the Civil Service Law, and it favors the passage of legislation empowering the President to extend the competitive service as far as practicable. We favor legislation to make possible the equitable retirement of disabled and superannuated members of the Civil Service in order that a higher standard of efficiency may be maintained.

We favor the amendment of the Federal Employers' Liability Law so as to extend its provisions to all government employees, as well as to provide a more liberal scale of compensation for injury and death.

CAMPAIGN CONTRIBUTIONS

We favor such additional legislation as may be necessary more effectually to prohibit corporations from contributing funds, directly or indirectly, to campaigns for the nomination or election of the President, the Vice President, Senators, and Representatives in Congress.

We heartily approve the recent Act of Congress requiring the fullest publicity in regard to all campaign contributions, whether made in connection with primaries, conventions, or elections.

CONSERVATION POLICY

We rejoice in the success of the distinctive Republican policy of the conservation of our National resources, for their use by the people without waste and without monopoly. We pledge ourselves to a continuance of such a policy.

We favor such fair and reasonable rules and regulations as will not discourage or interfere with actual bonafide homeseekers, prospectors and miners in the acquisition of public lands under existing laws.

PARCELS POST

In the interest of the general public, and particularly of the agricultural or rural communities, we favor legislation looking to the establishment, under proper regulations, of a parcels post, the postal rates to be graduated under a zone system in proportion to the length of carriage.

PROTECTION OF AMERICAN CITIZENSHIP

We approve the action taken by the President and the Congress to secure with Russia as with other countries, a treaty that will recognize the absolute right of expatriation and that will prevent all discrimination of whatever kind between American citizens, whether nativeborn or aliens, and regardless of race, religion or previous political allegiance. The right of asylum is a precious possession of the people of the United States, and it is to be neither surrendered nor restricted.

THE NAVY

We believe in the maintenance of an adequate navy for the National defense, and we condemn the action of the Democratic House of Representatives in refusing to authorize the construction of additional ships.

MERCHANT MARINE

We believe that one of the country's most urgent needs is a revived merchant marine. There should be American ships, and plenty of them, to make use of the great American InterOceanic canal now nearing completion.

FLOOD PREVENTION IN THE MISSISSIPPI VALLEY

The Mississippi River is the nation's drainage ditch. Its flood waters, gathered from thirty-one States and the Dominion of Canada, constitute an overpowering force which breaks the levees and pours its torrents over many millions of acres of the richest land in the Union, stopping mails, impeding commerce, and causing great loss of life and property. These floods are national in scope, and the disasters they produce seriously affect the general welfare. The States unaided cannot cope with this giant problem; hence, we believe the Federal Government should assume a fair proportion of the burden of its control, so as to prevent the disasters from recurring floods.

RECLAMATION

We favor the continuance of the policy of the government with regard to the reclamation of arid lands; and for the encouragement of the speedy settlement and improvement of such lands we favor an amendment to the law that will reasonably extend the time within which the cost of any reclamation project may be repaid by the landowners under it.

RIVERS AND HARBORS

We favor a liberal and systematic policy for the improvement of our rivers and harbors. Such improvements should be made upon expert information and after a careful comparison of cost and prospective benefits.

ALASKA

We favor a liberal policy toward Alaska to promote the development of the great resources of that district, with such safeguards as will prevent waste and monopoly.

We favor the opening of the coal lands to development through a law leasing the lands on such terms as will invite development and provide fuel for the navy and the commerce of the Pacific Ocean, while retaining title in the United States to prevent monopoly.

PHILIPPINE POLICY

The Philippine policy of the Republican party has been and is inspired by the belief that our duty toward the Filipino people is a national obligation which should remain entirely free from partisan politics.

IMMIGRATION

We pledge the Republican party to the enactment of appropriate laws to give relief from the constantly growing evil of induced or undesirable immigration, which is inimical to the progress and welfare of the people of the United States.

SAFETY AT SEA

We favor the speedy enactment of laws to provide that seamen shall not be compelled to endure involuntary servitude, and that life and property at sea shall be safeguarded by the ample equipment of vessels with lifesaving appliances and with full complements of skilled, ablebodied seamen to operate them.

REPUBLICAN ACCOMPLISHMENT

The approaching completion of the Panama Canal, the establishment of a Bureau of Mines, the institution of postal savings banks, the increased provision made in 1912 for the aged and infirm soldiers and sailors of the Republic and for their widows, and the vigorous administration of laws relating to Pure Foods and Drugs, all mark the successful progress of Republican administration, and are additional evidences of its effectiveness.

ECONOMY AND EFFICIENCY IN GOVERNMENT

We commend the earnest effort of the Republican administration to secure greater economy and increased efficiency in the conduct of government business; extravagant appropriations and the creation of unnecessary offices are an injustice to the taxpayer and a bad example to the citizen.

CIVIC DUTY

We call upon the people to quicken their interest in public affairs, to condemn and punish lynchings and other forms of lawlessness, and to strengthen in all possible ways a respect for law and the observance of it. Indifferent citizenship is an evil against which the law affords no adequate protection and for which legislation can provide no remedy.

ARIZONA AND NEW MEXICO

We congratulate the people of Arizona and New Mexico upon the admission of those States, thus merging in the Union in final and enduring form the last remaining portion of our continental territory.

We ratify in all its parts the platform of 1908 respecting citizenship for the people of Puerto Rico.

REPUBLICAN ADMINISTRATION

We challenge successful criticism of the sixteen years of Republican administration under Presidents McKinley, Roosevelt, and Taft. We heartily reaffirm the endorsement of President McKinley contained in the platforms of 1900 and of 1904, and that of President Roosevelt contained in the Platforms of 1904 and 1908.

We invite the intelligent judgment of the American people upon the administration of William H. Taft. The country has prospered and been at peace under

his Presidency. During the years in which he had the cooperation of a Republican Congress an unexampled amount of constructive legislation was framed and passed in the interest of the people and in obedience to their wish. That legislation is a record on which any administration might appeal with confidence to the favorable judgment of history.

We appeal to the American Electorate upon the record of the Republican party, and upon this declaration of its principles and purposes. We are confident that under the leadership of the candidates here to be nominated our appeal will not be in vain; that the Republican party will meet every just expectation of the people whose servant it is; that under its administration and its laws our nation will continue to advance; that peace and prosperity will abide with the people; and that new glory will be added to the great Republic.

— 1916 —

In 1861 the Republican party stood for the Union. As it stood for the Union of States, it now stands for a united people, true to American ideals, loyal to American traditions, knowing no allegiance except to the Constitution, to the Government, and to the Flag of the United States. We believe in American policies at home and abroad.

PROTECTION OF AMERICAN RIGHTS

We declare that we believe in and will enforce the protection of every American citizen in all the rights secured to him by the Constitution, by treaties and the laws of nations, at home and abroad, by land and by sea. These rights, which in violation of the specific promise of their party made at Baltimore in 1912, the Democratic President and the Democratic Congress have failed to defend, we will unflinchingly maintain.

FOREIGN RELATIONS

We desire peace, the peace of justice and right, and believe in maintaining a strict and honest neutrality between the belligerents in the great war in Europe. We must perform all our duties and insist upon all our rights as neutrals without fear and without favor. We believe that peace and neutrality, as well as the dignity and influence of the United States, cannot be preserved by shifty expedients, by phrasemaking, by performances in language, or by attitudes ever changing in an effort to secure votes or voters. The present Administration has destroyed our influence abroad and humiliated us in our own eyes. The Republican party believes that a firm, consistent, and courageous foreign policy, always maintained by Republican Presidents in accordance with American traditions, is the best, as it is the only true way, to preserve our peace and restore us to our rightful place among the nations.

We believe in the pacific settlement of international disputes, and favor the establishment of a world court for that purpose.

MEXICO

We deeply sympathize with the fifteen million people of Mexico who, for three years have seen their country devastated, their homes destroyed, their fellow citizens murdered and their women outraged, by armed bands of desperadoes led by selfseeking, conscienceless agitators who when temporarily successful in any locality have neither sought nor been able to restore order or establish and maintain peace.

We express our horror and indignation at the outrages which have been and are being perpetrated by these bandits upon American men and women who were or are in Mexico by invitation of the laws and of the government of that country and whose rights to security of person and property are guaranteed by solemn treaty obligations. We denounce the indefensible methods of interference employed by this Administration in the internal affairs of Mexico and refer with shame to its failure to discharge the duty of this country as next friend to Mexico, its duty to other powers who have relied upon us as such friend, and its duty to our citizens in Mexico, in permitting the continuance of such conditions, first by failure to act promptly and firmly, and second, by lending its influence to the continuation of such conditions through recognition of one of the factions responsible for these outrages.

We pledge our aid in restoring order and maintaining peace in Mexico. We promise to our citizens on and near our border, and to those in Mexico, wherever they may be found, adequate and absolute protection in their lives, liberty, and property.

MONROE DOCTRINE

We reaffirm our approval of the Monroe Doctrine, and declare its maintenance to be a policy of this country essential to its present and future peace and safety and to the achievement of its manifest destiny.

LATIN AMERICA

We favor the continuance of Republican policies which will result in drawing more and more closely the commercial, financial and social relations between this country and the countries of Latin America.

PHILIPPINES

We renew our allegiance to the Philippine policy inaugurated by McKinley, approved by Congress, and consistently carried out by Roosevelt and Taft. Even in this short time it has enormously improved the material and social conditions of the Islands, given the Philippine people a constantly increasing participation in their government, and if persisted in will bring still greater benefits in the future.

We accepted the responsibility of the Islands as a duty to civilization and the Filipino people. To leave with our task half done would break our pledges, injure our prestige among nations, and imperil what has already been accomplished.

We condemn the Democratic Administration for its attempt to abandon the Philippines, which was prevented only by the vigorous opposition of Republican members of Congress, aided by a few patriotic Democrats.

RIGHT OF EXPATRIATION

We reiterate the unqualified approval of the action taken in December, 1911, by the President and Congress to secure with Russia, as with other countries, a treaty that will recognize the absolute right of expatriation and prevent all discrimination of what ever kind between American citizens whether nativeborn or alien, and regardless of race, religion or previous political allegiance. We renew the pledge to observe this principle and to maintain the right of asylum, which is neither to be surrendered nor restricted, and we unite in the cherished hope that the war which is now desolating the world may speedily end, with a complete and lasting restoration of brotherhood among the nations of the earth and the assurance of full equal rights, civil and religious, to all men in every land.

PROTECTION OF THE COUNTRY

In order to maintain our peace and make certain the security of our people within our own borders the country must have not only adequate but thorough and complete national defense ready for any emergency. We must have a sufficient and effective Regular Army and a provision for ample reserves, already drilled and disciplined, who can be called at once to the colors when the hour of danger comes.

We must have a Navy so strong and so well proportioned and equipped, so thoroughly ready and prepared, that no enemy can gain command of the sea and effect a landing in force on either our Western or our Eastern coast. To secure these results we must have a coherent continuous policy of national defense, which even in these perilous days the Democratic party has utterly failed to develop, but which we promise to give to the country.

TARIFF

The Republican party stands now, as always, in the fullest sense for the policy of tariff protection to American industries and American labor and does not regard an antidumping provision as an adequate substitute.

Such protection should be reasonable in amount but sufficient to protect adequately American industries and American labor and so adjusted as to prevent undue exactions by monopolies or trusts. It should, moreover, give special attention to securing the industrial independence of the United States as in the case of dyestuffs.

Through wise tariff and industrial legislation our industries can be so organized that they will become not only a commercial bulwark but a powerful aid to national defense.

The Underwood Tariff Act is a complete failure in every respect. Under its administration imports have enormously increased in spite of the fact that intercourse with foreign countries has been largely cut off by reason of the war, while the revenues of which we stand in such dire need have been greatly reduced.

Under the normal conditions which prevailed prior to the war it was clearly demonstrated that this Act deprived the American producer and the American wage earner of that protection which enabled them to meet their foreign competitors, and but for the adventitious conditions created by the war, would long since have paralyzed all forms of American industry and deprived American labor of its just reward.

It has not in the least degree reduced the cost of living, which has constantly advanced from the date of its enactment. The welfare of our people demands its repeal and its substitution by a measure which in peace as well as in war will produce ample revenue and give reasonable protection to all forms of American production in mine, forest, field and factory.

We favor the creation of a tariff commission with complete power to gather and compile information for the use of Congress in all matters relating to the tariff.

BUSINESS

The Republican party has long believed in the rigid supervision and strict regulation of the transportation and of the great corporations of the country. It has put its creed into its deeds, and all really effective laws regulating the railroads and the great industrial corporations are the work of Republican Congresses and Presidents. For this policy of regulation and supervision the Democrats, in a stumbling and piecemeal way, are within the sphere of private enterprise and in direct competition with its own citizens, a policy which is sure to result in waste, great expense to the taxpayer and in an inferior product.

The Republican party firmly believes that all who violate the laws in regulation of business, should be individually punished. But prosecution is very different from persecution, and business success, no matter how honestly attained, is apparently regarded by the Democratic party as in itself a crime. Such doctrines and beliefs choke enterprise and stifle prosperity. The Republican party believes in encouraging American business as it believes in and will seek to advance all American interests.

RURAL CREDITS

We favor an effective system of Rural Credits as opposed to the ineffective law proposed by the present Democratic Administration.

RURAL FREE DELIVERY

We favor the extension of the Rural Free Delivery system and condemn the Democratic Administration for curtailing and crippling it.

MERCHANT MARINE

In view of the policies adopted by all the maritime nations to encourage their shipping interest, and in order to enable us to compete with them for the ocean carrying trade, we favor the payment to ships engaged in the foreign trade of liberal compensation for services actually rendered in carrying the mails, and such further legislation as will build up an adequate American Merchant Marine and give us ships which may be requisitioned by the Government in time of national emergency.

We are utterly opposed to the Government ownership of vessels as proposed by the Democratic party, because Government owned ships, while effectively preventing the development of the American Merchant Marine by private capital, will be entirely unable to provide for the vast volume of American freights and will leave us more helpless than ever in the hard grip of foreign syndicates.

TRANSPORTATION

Interstate and intrastate transportation have become so interwoven that the attempt to apply two and often several sets of laws to its regulation has produced conflicts of authority, embarrassment in operation and inconvenience and expense to the public.

The entire transportation system of the country has become essentially national. We, therefore, favor such action by legislation, or, if necessary, through an amendment to the Constitution of the United States, as will result in placing it under complete Federal control.

ECONOMY AND A NATIONAL BUDGET

The increasing cost of the national Government and the need for the greatest economy of its resources in order to meet the growing demands of the people for Government service call for the severest condemnation of the wasteful appropriations of this Democratic Administration, of its shameless raids on the treasury, and of its opposition to and rejection of President Taft's oftrepeated proposals and earnest efforts to secure economy and efficiency through the establishment of a simple businesslike budget system to which we pledge our support and which we hold to be necessary to effect a real reform in the administration of national finance.

CONSERVATION

We believe in a careful husbandry of all the natural resources of the nation husbandry which means development without waste; use without abuse.

CIVIL SERVICE REFORM

The Civil Service Law has always been sustained by the Republican party, and we renew our repeated declarations that it shall be thoroughly and honestly enforced and extended wherever practicable. The Democratic party has created since March 4, 1913, thirty thousand offices outside of the Civil Service Law at an annual cost of fortyfour million dollars to the taxpayers of the country.

We condemn the gross abuse and the misuse of the law by the present Democratic Administration and pledge ourselves to a reorganization of this service along lines of efficiency and economy.

TERRITORIAL OFFICIALS

Reaffirming the attitude long maintained by the Republican party, we hold that officials appointed to administer the Government of any territory should be bonafide residents of the territory in which their duties are to be performed.

LABOR LAWS

We pledge the Republican party to the faithful enforcement of all Federal laws passed for the protection of labor. We favor vocational education, the enactment and rigid enforcement of a Federal child labor law; the enactment of a generous and comprehensive workmen's compensation law, within the commerce power of Congress, and an accident compensation law covering all Government employees. We favor the collection and collation, under the direction of the Department of Labor, of complete data relating to industrial hazards for the information of Congress, to the end that such legislation may be adopted as may be calculated to secure the safety, conservation and protection of labor from the dangers incident to industry and transportation.

SUFFRAGE

The Republican party, reaffirming its faith in government of the people, by the people, for the people, as a measure of justice to one half the adult people of this country, favors the extension of the suffrage to women, but recognizes the right of each state to settle this question for itself.

CONCLUSION

Such are our principles, such are our "purposes and policies." We close as we began. The times are dangerous and the future is fraught with peril. The great issues of the day have been confused by words and phrases.

The American spirit, which made the country and saved the union, has been forgotten by those charged with the responsibility of power. We appeal to all Americans, whether naturalized or nativeborn, to prove to the world that we are Americans in thought and in deed, with one loyalty, one hope, one aspiration. We call on all Americans to be true to the spirit of America, to the great traditions of their common country, and above all things, to keep the faith.

— 1920 —

The Republican party, assembled in representative national convention, reaffirms its unyielding devotion to the Constitution of the United States, and to the guaranties of civil, political and religious liberty therein contained. It will resist all attempts to overthrow the foundations of the government or to weaken the force of its controlling principles and ideals, whether these attempts be made in the form of international policy or domestic agitation.

For seven years the national government has been controlled by the Democratic party. During that period a war of unparalleled magnitude has shaken the foundations of civilization, decimated the population of Europe, and left in its train economic misery and suffering second only to the war itself.

The outstanding features of the Democratic administration have been complete unpreparedness for war and complete unpreparedness for peace.

UNPREPAREDNESS FOR WAR

Inexcusable failure to make timely preparations is the chief indictment against the Democratic administration in the conduct of the war. Had not our associates protected us, both on land and sea, during the first twelve months of our participation and furnished us to the very day of the armistice with munitions, planes, and artillery, this failure would have been punished with disaster. It directly resulted in unnecessary losses to our gallant troops, in the imperilment of victory itself, and in an enormous waste of public funds, literally poured into the breach created by gross neglect. Today it is reflected in our huge tax burdens and in the high cost of living.

UNPREPAREDNESS FOR PEACE

Peace found the administration as unprepared for peace as war found it unprepared for war. The vital need of the country demanded the early and systematic return of a peace time basis.

This called for vision, leadership, and intelligent planning. All three have been lacking. While the country has been left to shift for itself, the government has continued on a wartime basis. The administration has not demobilized the army of place holders. It continued a method of financing which was indefensible during the period of reconstruction. It has used legislation passed to meet the emergency of war to continue its arbitrary and inquisitorial control over the life of the people in the time of peace, and to carry confusion into industrial life. Under the despot's plea of necessity or superior wisdom, executive usurpation of legislative and judicial function still undermines our institutions. Eighteen months after the armistice, with its wartime powers unabridged, its wartime departments undischarged, its wartime army of place holders still mobilized, the administration still continues to flounder helplessly.

The demonstrated incapacity of the Democratic party has destroyed public confidence, weakened the authority of the government, and produced a feeling of distrust and hesitation so universal as to increase enormously the difficulty of readjustment and to delay the return to normal conditions.

Never has our nation been confronted with graver problems. The people are entitled to know in definite terms how the parties purpose solving these problems. To that end, the Republican party declares its policy and programme to be as follows:

CONSTITUTIONAL GOVERNMENT

We undertake to end executive autocracy and restore to the people their constitutional government.

The policies herein declared will be carried out by the Federal and State governments, each acting within its constitutional powers.

FOREIGN RELATIONS

The foreign policy of the administration has been founded upon no principle and directed by no definite conception of our nation's rights and obligations. It has been humiliating to America and irritating to other nations, with the result that after a period of unexampled sacrifice, our motives are suspected, our moral influence impaired, and our government stands discredited and friendless among the nations of the world.

We favor a liberal and generous foreign policy founded upon definite moral and political principle, characterized by a clear understanding of and a firm adherence to our own rights, and unfailing respect for the rights of others. We should afford full and adequate protection to the life, liberty, property and all international rights of every American citizen, and should require a proper respect for the American flag; but we should be equally careful to manifest a just regard for the rights of other nations. A scrupulous observance of our international engagements when lawfully assumed is essential to our own honor and selfrespect, and the respect of other nations. Subject to a due regard for our international obligations, we should leave our country free to develop its civilization along lines most conducive to the happiness and welfare of its people, and to cast its influence on the side of justice and right should occasion require.

(a) Mexico

The ineffective policy of the present Administration in Mexican matters has been largely responsible for the continued loss of American lives in that country and upon our border; for the enormous loss of American and foreign property; for the lowering of American standards of morality and social relations with Mexicans, and for the bringing of American ideals of justice, national honor and political integrity into contempt and ridicule in Mexico and throughout the world.

The policy of wordy, futile written protests against the acts of Mexican officials, explained the following day by the President himself as being meaningless and not intended to be considered seriously, or enforced, has but added in degree to that contempt, and has earned for us the sneers and jeers of Mexican bandits, and added insult upon insult against our national honor and dignity.

We should not recognize any Mexican government, unless it be a responsible government willing and able to give sufficient guarantees that the lives and property of American citizens are respected and protected; that wrongs will be promptly corrected and just compensation will be made for injury sustained. The Republican party pledges itself to a consistent, firm and effective policy towards Mexico that shall enforce respect for the American flag and that shall protect the rights of American citizens lawfully in Mexico to security of life and enjoyment of property, in accordance with established principles of international law and our treaty rights.

The Republican party is a sincere friend of the Mexican people. In its insistence upon the mainte-nance of order for the protection of American citizens within its borders a great service will be rendered the Mexican people themselves; for a continuation of present conditions means disaster to their interests and patriotic aspirations.

(b) Mandate for Armenia

We condemn President Wilson for asking Congress to empower him to accept a mandate for Armenia. We commend the Republican Senate for refusing the President's request to empower him to accept the mandate for Armenia. The acceptance of such mandate would throw the United States into the very maelstrom of European quarrels. According to the estimate of the Harbord Commission, organized by authority of President Wilson, we would be called upon to send 59,000 American boys to police Armenia and to expend $276,000,000 in the first year and $756,000,000 in five years. This estimate is made upon the basis that we would have only roving bands to fight; but in case of serious trouble with the Turks or with Russia, a force exceeding 200,000 would be necessary.

No more striking illustration can be found of President Wilson's disregard of the lives of American boys or of American interests.

We deeply sympathize with the people of Armenia and stand ready to help them in all proper ways, but the Republican party will oppose now and hereafter the acceptance of a mandate for any country in Europe or Asia.

(c) League of Nations

The Republican party stands for agreement among the nations to preserve the peace of the world. We believe that such an international association must be based upon international justice, and must provide methods which shall maintain the rule of public right by the development of law and the decision of impartial courts, and which shall secure instant and general international conference whenever peace shall be threatened by political action, so that the nations pledged to do and insist upon what is just and fair may exercise their influence and power for the prevention of war.

We believe that all this can be done without the compromise of national independence, without depriving the people of the United States in advance of the right to determine for themselves what is just and fair when the occasion arises, and without involving them as participants and not as peacemakers in a multitude of quarrels, the merits of which they are unable to judge.

The covenant signed by the President at Paris failed signally to accomplish this great purpose, and contains stipulations, not only intolerable for an independent people, but certain to produce the injustice, hostility and controversy among nations which it proposed to prevent.

That covenant repudiated, to a degree wholly unnecessary and unjustifiable, the time honored policies in favor of peace declared by Washington, Jefferson, and Monroe, and pursued by American administrations for more than a century, and it ignored the universal sentiment of America for generations past in favor of international law and arbitration, and it rested the hope of the future upon mere expediency and negotiation.

The unfortunate insistence of the President upon having his own way, without any change and without any regard to the opinions of a majority of the Senate, which shares with him in the treaty making power, and the President's demand that the Treaty should be ratified without any modification, created a situation in which Senators were required to vote upon their consciences and their oaths according to their judgment against the Treaty as it was presented, or submit to the commands of a dictator in a matter where the authority and the responsibility under the Constitution were theirs, and not his.

The Senators performed their duty faithfully. We approve their conduct and honor their courage and fidelity. And we pledge the coming Republican administration to such agreements with the other nations of the world as shall meet the full duty of America to civilization and humanity, in accordance with American ideals, and without surrendering the right of the American people to exercise its judgment and its power in favor of justice and peace.

CONGRESS AND RECONSTRUCTION

Despite the unconstitutional and dictatorial course of the President and the partisan obstruction of the Democratic congressional minority, the Republican majority has enacted a program of constructive legislation which in great part, however, has been nullified by the vindictive vetoes of the President.

The Republican Congress has met the problems presented by the administration's unpreparedness for peace. It has repealed the greater part of the vexatious war legislation. It has enacted a transportation act making possible the rehabilitation of the railroad systems of the country, the operation of which, under the present Democratic administration, has been wasteful, extravagant, and inefficient in the highest degree. The transportation act made provision for the peaceful settlement of wage disputes, partially nullified, however,

by the President's delay in appointing the wage board created by the act. This delay precipitated the outlaw railroad strike.

We stopped the flood of public treasure, recklessly poured into the lap of an inept shipping board, and laid the foundations for the creation of a great merchant marine; we took from the incompetent Democratic administration the administration of the telegraph and telephone lines of the country and returned them to private ownership; we reduced the cost of postage and increased the pay of the postal employees, the poorest paid of all public servants; we provided pensions for superannuated and retired civil servants; and for an increase in pay of soldiers and sailors we reorganized the Army on a peace footing and provided for the maintenance of a powerful and efficient navy.

The Republican Congress established by law a permanent woman's bureau in the Department of Labor; we submitted to the country the constitutional amendment for woman suffrage, and furnished twentynine of the thirtyfive legislatures which have ratified it to date.

Legislation for the relief of the consumers of print paper, for the extension of the powers of the Government under the Food Control Act, for broadening the scope of the War Risk Insurance Act, better provision for the dwindling number of aged veterans of the Civil War and for the better support of the maimed and injured of the great war, and for making practical the Vocational Rehabilitation Act, has been enacted by the Republican Congress.

We passed an oil leasing and water power bill to unlock for the public good the great pent-up resources of the country; we have sought to check the profligacy of the administration, to realize upon the assets of the government and to husband the revenues derived from taxation. The Republicans in Congress have been responsible for cuts in the estimates for government expenditure of nearly $3,000,000,000 since the signing of the armistice.

We enacted a national executive budget law; we strengthened the Federal Reserve Act to permit banks to lend needed assistance to farmers; we authorized financial incorporations to develop export trade; and finally, amended the rules of the Senate and House, which will reform evils in procedure and guarantee more efficient and responsible government.

AGRICULTURE

The farmer is the backbone of the nation. National greatness and economic independence demand a population distributed between industry and the farm, and sharing on equal terms the prosperity which it holds is wholly dependent upon the efforts of both. Neither can prosper at the expense of the other without inviting joint disaster.

The crux of the present agricultural condition lies in prices, labor and credit.

The Republican party believes that this condition can be improved by: practical and adequate farm representation in the appointment of governmental officials and commissions; the right to form cooperative associations for marketing their products, and protection against discrimination; the scientific study of agricultural prices and farm production costs, at home and abroad, with a view to reducing the frequency of abnormal fluctuation; the uncensored publication of such reports; the authorization of associations for the extension of personal credit; a national inquiry on the coordination of rail, water and motor transportation with adequate facilities for receiving, handling and marketing food; the encouragement of our export trade; and end to unnecessary price fixing and ill considered efforts arbitrarily to reduce prices of farm products which invariably result to the disadvantage both of producer and consumer; and the encouragement of the production and importation of fertilizing material and of its extensive use.

The Federal Farm Loan Acts should be so administered as to facilitate the acquisition of farm land by those desiring to become owners and proprietors and thus minimize the evils of farm tenantry, and to furnish such long-time credits as farmers may need to finance adequately their larger and long-time production operations.

INDUSTRIAL RELATIONS

There are two different conceptions of the relations of capital and labor. The one is contractual and emphasizes the diversity of interest of employer and employee. The other is that of copartnership in a common task.

We recognize the justice of collective bargaining as a means of promoting good will, establishing closer and more harmonious relations between employers and employees and realizing the true ends of industrial justice.

The strike or the lockout, as a means of settling industrial disputes, inflicts such loss and suffering on the community as to justify government initiative to reduce its frequency and limit its consequences. We denied the right to strike against the government; but the rights and interests of all government employees must be safeguarded by impartial laws and tribunals.

In public utilities we favor the establishment of an impartial tribunal to make an investigation of the facts and to render decisions to the end that there may be no organized interruption of service necessary to the lives and health and welfare of the people. The decisions of the tribunal to be morally but not legally binding, and an informed public sentiment be relied on to secure their acceptance. The tribunals, however, should refuse to accept jurisdiction except for the purpose of service. For public utilities we favor the type of tribunal provided for in the Transportation Act of 1920.

In private industries we do not advocate the principle of compulsory arbitration, but we favor impartial commissions and better facilities for voluntary mediation, conciliation and arbitration supplemented by the full publicity which will enlist the influence of an aroused public opinion. The government should take the initiative in inviting the establishment of tribunals or commissions for the purpose of voluntary arbitration and of investigation of disputed issues.

We demand the exclusion from interstate commerce of the products of convict labor.

NATIONAL ECONOMY

A Republican Congress reduced the estimates submitted by the Administration almost three billion dollars. Greater economies could have been effected had it not been for the stubborn refusal of the Administration to cooperate with Congress in an economy program. The universal demand for an executive budget is a recognition of the incontrovertible fact that leadership and sincere assistance on the part of the executive departments are essential to effective economy and constructive retrenchment.

The Overman Act invested the President of the United States with all the authority and power necessary to restore the Federal Government to a normal peace basis and to reorganize, retrench and demobilize. The dominant fact is that eighteen months after the armistice, the United States Government is still on a war time basis, and the expenditure program of the Executive reflects war time extravagance rather than rigid peace time economy.

As an example of the failure to retrench which has characterized the post war time Administration we cite the fact that not including the war and navy departments, the executive departments and other establishments at Washington actually record an increase subsequent to the armistice of 2,184 employees. The net decrease in pay roll costs contained in the 1921 demands submitted by the Administration is one percent below that of 1920. The annual expenses of Federal operations can be reduced hundreds of millions of dollars without impairing the efficiency of the public service.

We pledge ourselves to a carefully planned readjustment on a peace time basis and to a policy of rigid economy, to the better co-ordination of departmental activities, to the elimination of unnecessary officials and employees, and to the raising of the standard of individual efficiency.

THE EXECUTIVE BUDGET

We congratulate the Republican Congress on the enactment of a law providing for the establishment of an Executive Budget as a necessary instrument for a sound business administration of the national finances; and we condemn the veto of the President which defeated this great financial reform.

REORGANIZATION OF FEDERAL DEPARTMENTS AND BUREAUS

We advocate a thorough investigation of the present organization of the Federal departments and bureaus, with a view to securing consolidation, a more businesslike distribution of functions, the elimination of duplication, delays and overlapping of work and the establishment of an up to date and efficient administrative organization.

WAR POWERS OF THE PRESIDENT

The President clings tenaciously to his autocratic war time powers. His veto of the resolution declaring peace and his refusal to sign the bill repealing war time legislation, no longer necessary, evidenced his determination not to restore to the Nation and to the State the form of government provided for by the Constitution. This usurpation is intolerable and deserves the severest condemnation.

TAXATION

The burden of taxation imposed upon the American people is staggering; but in presenting a true statement of the situation we must face the fact that, while the character of the taxes can and should be changed, an early reduction of the amount of revenue to be raised is not to be expected. The next Republican Administration will inherit from its Democratic predecessor a floating indebtedness of over three billion dollars the prompt liquidation of which is demanded by sound financial consideration. Moreover, the whole fiscal policy of the Government must be deeply influenced by the necessity of meeting obligations in excess of five billion dollars which mature in 1923. But sound policy equally demands the early accomplishment of that real reduction of the tax burden which may be achieved by substituting simple for complex tax laws and procedure, prompt and certain determination of the tax liability for delay and uncertainty, tax laws which do not, for tax laws which do, excessively mulct the consumer or needlessly repress enterprise and thrift.

We advocate the issuance of a simplified form of income return; authorizing the Treasury Department to make changes in regulations effective only from the date of their approval, empowering the Commissioner of Internal Revenue, with the consent of the taxpayers, to make final and conclusive settlements of tax claims and assessments barring fraud, the creation of a Tax Board consisting of at least three representatives of the taxpaying public and the heads of the principal divisions of the Bureau of Internal Revenue to act as a standing committee on the simplification of forms, procedure and law and to make recommendations to the Congress.

BANKING AND CURRENCY

The fact is that the war to a great extent, was financed by a policy of inflation, through certificate borrowings from the banks, and bonds issued at artificial rates sustained by the low discount rates established by the Federal Reserve Board. The continuance of this policy since the armistice lays the Administration open to severe criticism. Almost up to the present time the practices of the Federal Reserve Board as to credit control have been frankly dominated by the convenience of the Treasury.

The results have been a greatly increased war cost, a serious loss to the millions of people who, in good faith, bought liberty bonds and victory notes at par, and extensive post war speculation followed today by a restricted credit for legitimate industrial expansion and as a matter of public policy, we urge all banks to give credit preference to essential industry.

The Federal Reserve System should be free from political influence, which is quite as important as its independence of domination by financial combinations.

THE HIGH COST OF LIVING

The prime cause of the "High Cost of Living" has been first and foremost, a fifty per cent depreciation in the purchasing power of the dollar, due to a gross expansion of our currency and credit. Reduced production, burdensome taxation, swollen profits, and the increased demand for goods arising from a fictitious but enlarged buying power, have been contributing forces in a greater or less degree. We condemn the unsound fiscal policies of the Democratic Administration which have brought these things to pass, and their attempts to impute the consequences to minor and secondary causes. Much of the injury wrought is irreparable. There is no short way out, and we decline to deceive the people with vain promises or quack remedies. But as the political party that throughout its history has stood for honest money and sound finance, we pledge ourselves to earnest and consistent attack upon the high cost of living, by rigorous avoidance of further inflation in war government borrowing, by courageous and intelligent deflation of overexpanded credit and currency, by encouragement of heightened production of goods and services, by prevention of unreasonable profits, by exercise of public economy and stimulation of private thrift and by revision of war imposed taxes unsuited to peace time economy.

PROFITEERING

We condemn the Democratic Administration for failure impartially to enforce the Antiprofiteering Laws enacted by the Republican Congress.

RAILROADS

We are opposed to government ownership and operation or employee operation of the Railroads. In view of the conditions prevailing in this country, the experience of the last two years, and the conclusion which may fairly be drawn from an observation of the transportation systems of other countries it is clear that adequate transportation service both for the present and future can be furnished more certainly, economically and efficiently through private ownership and operation under proper regulation and control.

There should be no speculative profit in rendering the service of transportation; but in order to do justice to the capital already invested in railway enterprise, to restore railway credit, to induce future investment at a reasonable rate, and to furnish a large facility to meet the requirements of the constantly increasing development and distribution a fair return upon actual value of the railway property used in transportation should be made reasonably sure, and at the same time to provide constant employment to those engaged in transportation service, with fair hours and favorable working conditions, at wages or compensation at least equal to those prevailing in similar lines of industry.

We endorse the Transportation Act of 1920 enacted by the Republican Congress as a most constructive legislative achievement.

WATERWAYS

We declare it to be our policy to encourage and develop water transportation service and facilities in connection with the commerce of the United States.

REGULATION OF INDUSTRY AND COMMERCE

We approve in general the existing Federal Legislation against monopoly and combinations in restraint of trade, but since the known certainty of a law is the safety of all, we advocate such amendment as will provide American business men with better means of determining in advance whether a proposed combination is or is not unlawful. The Federal Trade Commission, under a Democratic Administration, has not accomplished the purpose for which it was created. This commission properly organized and its duties efficiently administered should afford protection to the public and legitimate business interests. There should be no persecution of honest business; but to the extent that circumstances warrant we pledge ourselves to strengthen the law against unfair practices.

We pledge the party to an immediate resumption of trade relations with every nation with which we are at peace.

INTERNATIONAL TRADE AND TARIFF

The uncertain and unsettled condition of international balances, the abnormal economic and trade situation of the world, and the impossibility of forecasting accurately even the near future, preclude the formulation of a definite program to meet conditions a year hence. But the Republican party reaffirms its belief in the protective principles and pledges itself to a revision of the tariff as soon as conditions shall make it necessary for the preservation of the home market for American labor, agriculture and industry.

MERCHANT MARINE

The National defense and our foreign commerce require a merchant marine of the best type of modern ship, flying the American flag, and manned by American seamen, owned by private capital, and operated by private energy. We endorse the sound legislation recently enacted by the Republican Congress that will insure the promotion and maintenance of the American Merchant Marine.

We favor the application of the workmen's compensation act to the Merchant Marine.

We recommend that all ships engaged in coastwise trade and all vessels of the American Merchant Marine shall pass through the Panama Canal without payment of tolls.

IMMIGRATION

The standard of living and the standard of citizenship of a nation are its most precious possessions, and the preservation and the elevation of those standards is the first duty of our government. The immigration policy of the U.S. should be such as to insure that the number of foreigners in the country at any one time shall not exceed that which can be assimilated with reasonable rapidity, and to favor immigrants whose standards are similar to ours.

The selective tests that are at present applied should be improved by requiring a higher physical standard, a more complete exclusion of mental defectives and of criminals, and a more effective inspection applied as near the source of immigration as possible, as well as at the port of entry. Justice to the foreigner and to ourselves demands provision for the guidance, protection and better economic distribution of our alien population. To facilitate government supervision, all aliens should be required to register annually until they become naturalized.

The existing policy of the United States for the practical exclusion of Asiatic immigrants is sound, and should be maintained.

NATURALIZATION

There is urgent need of improvement in our naturalization law. No alien should become a citizen until be has become genuinely American, and adequate tests for determining the alien's fitness for American citizenship should be provided for by law.

We advocate, in addition, the independent naturalization of married women. An American woman, resident in the United States, should not lose her citizenship by marriage to an alien.

FREE SPEECH AND ALIEN AGITATION

We demand that every American citizen shall enjoy the ancient and constitutional right of free speech, free press and free assembly and the no less sacred right of the qualified voted [sic] to be represented by his duly chosen representatives; but no man may advocate resistance to the law, and no man may advocate violent overthrow of the government.

Aliens within the jurisdiction of the United States are not entitled of right to liberty of agitation directed against the government of American institutions.

Every government has the power to exclude and deport those aliens who constitute a real menace to its peaceful existence. But in view of the large numbers of people affected by the immigration acts and in view of the vigorous malpractice of the Departments of Justice and Labor, an adequate public hearing before a competent administrative tribunal should be assured to all.

LYNCHING

We urge Congress to consider the most effective means to end lynching in this country which continues to be a terrible blot on our American civilization.

PUBLIC ROADS AND HIGHWAYS

We favor liberal appropriations in cooperation with the States for the construction of highways, which will bring about a reduction in transportation costs, better marketing of farm products, improvement in rural postal delivery, as well as meet the needs of military defense.

In determining the proportion of Federal aid for road construction among the States, the sums lost in taxation to the respective States by the setting apart of large portions of their area as forest reservations should be considered as a controlling factor.

CONSERVATION

Conservation is a Republican policy. It began with the passage of the Reclamation Act signed by President Roosevelt. The recent passage of the coal, oil and phosphate leasing act by a Republican Congress and the enactment of the waterpower bill fashioned in accordance with the same principle, are consistent landmarks in the development of the conservation of our national resources. We denounce the refusal of the President to sign the waterpower bill, passed after ten years of controversy. The Republican party has taken an especially honorable part in saving our national forests and in the effort to establish a national forest policy. Our most pressing conservation question relates to our forests. We are using our forest resources faster than they are being renewed. The result is to raise unduly the cost of forest products to consumers and especially farmers, who use more than half the lumber produced in America, and in the end to create a timber famine. The Federal Government, the States and private interests must unite in devising means to meet the menace.

RECLAMATION

We favor a fixed and comprehensive policy of reclamation to increase national wealth and production.

We recognize in the development of reclamation through Federal action with its increase of production and taxable wealth a safeguard for the nation.

We commend to Congress a policy to reclaim lands and the establishment of a fixed national policy of development of natural resources in relation to reclamation through the now designated government agencies.

ARMY AND NAVY

We feel the deepest pride in the fine courage, the resolute endurance, the gallant spirit of the officers and men of our army and navy in the World War. They were in all ways worthy of the best traditions of the nation's defenders, and we pledge ourselves to proper maintenance of the military and naval establishments upon which our national security and dignity depend.

THE SERVICE MEN

We hold in imperishable remembrance the valor and the patriotism of the soldiers and sailors of America who fought in the great war for human liberty, and we pledge ourselves to discharge to the fullest the obligations which a grateful nation justly should fulfill, in appreciation of the services rendered by its defenders on sea and on land.

Republicans are not ungrateful. Throughout their history they have shown their gratitude toward the nation's defenders. Liberal legislation for the care of the disabled and infirm and their dependents has ever marked Republican policy toward the soldier and sailor of all the wars in which our country has participated. The present Congress has appropriated generously for the disabled of the World War.

The amounts already applied and authorized for the fiscal year 1920–21 for this purpose reached the stupendous sum of $1,180,571,893. The legislation is significant of the party's purpose in generously caring for the maimed and disabled men of the recent war.

CIVIL SERVICE

We renew our repeated declaration that the civil service law shall be thoroughly and honestly enforced and extended wherever practicable. The recent action of Congress in enacting a comprehensive civil service retirement law and in working out a comprehensive employment and wage policy that will guarantee equal and just treatment to the army of government workers, and in centralizing the administration of the new and progressive employment policy in the hands of the Civil Service Commission is worthy of all praise.

POSTAL SERVICE

We condemn the present administration for its destruction of the efficiency of the postal service, and the telegraph and telephone service when controlled by the government and for its failure to properly compensate employees whose expert knowledge is essential to the proper conduct of the affairs of the postal system. We commend the Republican Congress for the enactment of legislation increasing the pay of postal employees, who up to that time were the poorest paid in the government service.

WOMAN SUFFRAGE

We welcome women into full participation in the affairs of government and the activities of the Republican Party. We earnestly hope that Republican legislatures in states which have not yet acted on the

Suffrage Amendment will ratify the amendment, to the end that all of the women of the nation of voting age may participate in the election of 1920 which is so important to the welfare of our country.

SOCIAL PROGRESS

The supreme duty of the nation is the conservation of human resources through an enlightened measure of social and industrial justice. Although the federal jurisdiction over social problems is limited, they affect the welfare and interest of the nation as a whole. We pledge the Republican party to the solution of these problems through national and state legislation in accordance with the best progressive thought of the country.

EDUCATION AND HEALTH

We endorse the principle of Federal aid to the States for the purpose of vocational and agricultural training.

Wherever Federal money is devoted to education, such education must be so directed as to awaken in the youth the spirit of America and a sense of patriotic duty to the United States.

A thorough system of physical education for all children up to the age of 19, including adequate health supervision and instruction, would remedy conditions revealed by the draft and would add to the economic and industrial strength of the nation. National leadership and stimulation will be necessary to induce the States to adopt a wise system of physical training.

The public health activities of the Federal government are scattered through numerous departments and bureaus, resulting in inefficiency, duplication and extravagance. We advocate a greater centralization of the Federal functions, and in addition urge the better coordination of the work of the Federal, State and local health agencies.

CHILD LABOR

The Republican party stands for a Federal child labor law and for its rigid enforcement. If the present law be found unconstitutional or ineffective, we shall seek other means to enable Congress to prevent the evils of child labor.

WOMEN IN INDUSTRY

Women have special problems of employment which make necessary special study. We commend Congress for the permanent establishment of the Women's Bureau in the United States Department of Labor to serve as a source of information to the States and to Congress.

The principle of equal pay for equal service should be applied throughout all branches of the Federal government in which women are employed.

Federal aid for vocational training should take into consideration the special aptitudes and needs of women workers.

We demand Federal legislation to limit the hours of employment of women engaged in intensive industry, the product of which enters into interstate commerce.

HOUSING

The housing shortage has not only compelled careful study of ways of stimulating building, but it has brought into relief the unsatisfactory character of the housing accommodations of large numbers of the inhabitants of our cities. A nation of home owners is the best guaranty of the maintenance of those principles of liberty, law and order upon which our government is founded. Both National and State governments should encourage in all proper ways the acquiring of homes by our citizens. The United States Government should make available the valuable information on housing and town planning collected during the war. This information should be kept up to date and made currently available.

HAWAII

For Hawaii we recommend Federal assistance in Americanizing and educating their greatly disproportionate foreign population; home rule; and the rehabilitation of the Hawaiian race.

Pointing to its history and relying on its fundamental principles, we declare that the Republican party has the genius, courage and constructive ability to end executive usurpation and restore constitutional government; to fulfill our world obligations without sacrificing our national independence; to raise the national standards of education, health and general welfare; to reestablish a peace time administration and to substitute economy and efficiency for extravagance and chaos; to restore and maintain the national credit; to reform unequal and burdensome taxes; to free business from arbitrary and unnecessary official control; to suppress disloyalty without the denial of justice; to repel the arrogant challenge of any class and to maintain a government of all the people as contrasted with government for some of the people, and finally, to allay unrest, suspicion and strife, and to secure the cooperation and unity of all citizens in the solution of the complex problems of the day; to the end that our country, happy and prosperous, proud of its past, sure of itself and of its institutions, may look forward with confidence to the future.

— 1924 —

We the delegates of the Republican Party in national convention assembled, bow our heads in reverent memory of Warren G. Harding.

We nominated him four years ago to be our candidate; the people of the nation elected him their President. His human qualities gripped the affections of the American people. He was a public servant unswerving in his devotion to duty.

A staunch Republican, he was first of all a true patriot, who gave unstintingly of himself during a trying and critical period of our national life.

His conception and successful direction of the limitation of armaments conference in Washington was an accomplishment which advanced the world along the path toward peace.

As delegates of the Republican Party, we share in the national thanksgiving that in the great emergency created by the death of our great leader there stood forth fully equipped to be his successor one whom we had nominated as Vice President—Calvin Coolidge, who as Vice President and President by his every act has justified the faith and confidence which he has won from the nation.

He has put the public welfare above personal considerations. He has given to the people practical idealism in office. In his every act, he has won without seeking the applause of the people of the country. The constantly accumulating evidence of his integrity, vision and single minded devotion to the needs of the people of this nation strengthens and inspires our confident faith in his continued leadership.

SITUATION IN 1921

When the Republican Administration took control of the government in 1921, there were four and a half million unemployed; industry and commerce were stagnant; agriculture was prostrate; business was depressed; securities of the government were selling below their par values.

Peace was delayed; misunderstanding and friction characterized our relations abroad. There was a lack of faith in the administration of government resulting in a growing feeling of distrust in the very principles upon which our institutions are founded.

To-day industry and commerce are active; public and private credits are sound; we have made peace; we have taken the first step toward disarmament and strengthened our friendship with the world powers, our relations with the rest of the world are on a firmer basis, our position was never better understood, our foreign policy never more definite and consistent. The tasks to which we have put our hands are completed. Time has been too short for the correction of all the ills we received as a heritage from the last democratic administration, and the notable accomplishments under Republican rule warrant us in appealing to the country with entire confidence.

PUBLIC ECONOMY

We demand and the people of the United States have a right to demand rigid economy in government. A policy of strict economy enforced by the Republican Administration since 1921 has made possible a reduction in taxation and has enabled the government to reduce the public debt by $2,500,000,000. This policy vigorously enforced has resulted in a progressive reduction of public expenditures until they are now two billion dollars per annum less than in 1921. The tax burdens of the people have been relieved to the extent of $1,250,000,000 per annum. Government securities have been increased in value more than $3,000,000,000. Deficits have been converted in surpluses. The budget system has been firmly established and the number of federal employees has been reduced more than one hundred thousand. We commend the firm insistence of President Coolidge upon rigid government economy and pledge him our earnest support to this end.

FINANCE AND TAXATION

We believe that the achievement of the Republican Administration in reducing taxation by $1,250,000,000 per annum; reducing of the public debt by $2,432,000,000; installing a budget system; reducing the public expenditures from $5,500,000,000 per annum to approximately $3,400,000,000 per annum, thus reducing the ordinary expenditures of the government to substantially a pre-war basis, and the complete restoration of public credit; the payment or refunding of $7,500,000,000 of public obligations without disturbance of credit or industry—all during the short period of three years—presents a record unsurpassed in the history of public finance.

The assessment of taxes wisely and scientifically collected and the efficient and economical expenditure of the money received by the government are essential to the prosperity of our nation.

Carelessness in levying taxes inevitably breeds extravagance in expenditures. The wisest of taxation rests most rightly on the individual and economic life of the country. The public demand for a sound tax policy is insistent.

Progressive tax reduction should be accomplished through tax reorganization. It should not be confined to less than 4,000,000 of our citizens who pay direct taxes, but is the right of more than 100,000,000 who are daily paying their taxes through their living expenses. Congress has in the main confined its work to tax reduction. The matter of tax reform is still unsettled and is equally essential.

We pledge ourselves to the progressive reduction of taxes of all the people as rapidly as may be done with due regard for the essential expenditures for the government administered with rigid economy and to place our tax system on a sound peace time basis.

We endorse the plan of President Coolidge to call in November a national conference of federal and state officials for the development of the effective methods of lightening the tax burden of our citizens and adjusting questions of taxation as between national and state governments.

We favor the creation by appropriate legislation of a non-partisan federal commission to make a comprehensive study and report upon the tax system of the states and Federal Government with a view to an intelligent reformation of our systems of taxation to a more equitable basis and a proper adjustment of the subjects of taxation as between the national and state governments with justice to the taxpayer and in conformity with the sound economic principles.

REORGANIZATION

We favor a comprehensive reorganization of the executive departments and bureaus along the line of the plan recently submitted by a joint committee of the Congress which has the unqualified support of President Coolidge.

CIVIL SERVICE

Improvement in the enforcement of the merit system both by legislative enactment and executive action since March 4, 1921, has been marked and effective. By executive order the appointment of presidential postmasters has been placed on the merit basis similar to that applying to the classified service.

We favor the classification of postmasters in first, second and third class post offices and the placing of the prohibition enforcement field forces within the classified civil service without necessarily incorporating the present personnel.

FOREIGN DEBTS

In fulfillment of our solemn pledge in the national platform of 1920 we have steadfastly refused to consider the cancellation of foreign debts. Our attitude has not been that of an oppressive creditor seeking immediate return and ignoring existing financial conditions, but has been based on the conviction that a moral obligation such as was incurred should not be disregarded.

We stand for settlements with all debtor countries, similar in character to our debt agreement with Great Britain. That settlement, achieved under a Republican Administration, was the greatest international financial transaction in the history of the world. Under the terms of the agreement the United States now receives an annual return upon four billion six hundred million dollars owing to us by Great Britain with a definite obligation of ultimate payment in full.

The justness of the basis employed has been formally recognized by other debtor nations.

Great nations cannot recognize or admit the principle of repudiation. To do so would undermine the integrity essential for international trade, commerce and credit. Thirty-five per cent of the total foreign debt is now in process of liquidation.

THE TARIFF

We reaffirm our belief in the protective tariff to extend needed protection to our productive industries. We believe in protection as a national policy, with due and equal regard to all sections and to all classes. It is only by adherence to such a policy that the well being of the consumers can be safeguarded that there can be assured to American agriculture, to American labor and to American manufacturers a return to perpetuate American standards of life. A protective tariff is designed to support the high American economic level of life for the average family and to prevent a lowering to the levels of economic life prevailing in other lands.

In the history of the nation the protective tariff system has ever justified itself by restoring confidence, promoting industrial activity and employment, enormously increasing our purchasing power and bringing increased prosperity to all our people.

The tariff protection to our industry works for increased consumption of domestic agricultural products by an employed population instead of one unable to purchase the necessities of life. Without the strict maintenance of the tariff principle our farmers will need always to compete with cheap lands and cheap labor abroad and with lower standards of living.

The enormous value of the protective principle has once more been demonstrated by the Emergency Tariff Act of 1921 and the Tariff Act of 1922.

We assert our belief in the elastic provision adopted by Congress in the Tariff Act of 1922 providing for a method of readjusting the tariff rates and the classifications in order to meet changing economic conditions when such changed conditions are brought to the attention of the President by complaint or application.

We believe that the power to increase or decrease any rate of duty provided in the tariff furnishes a safeguard on the one hand against excessive taxes and on the other hand against too high customs charges.

The wise provisions of this section of the Tariff Act afford ample opportunity for tariff duties to be adjusted after a hearing in order that they may cover the actual differences in the cost of production in the United States and the principal competing countries of the world.

We also believe that the application of this provision of the tariff act will contribute to business stability by making unnecessary general disturbances which are usually incident to general tariff revisions.

FOREIGN RELATIONS

The Republican Party reaffirmed its stand for agreement among the nations to prevent war and preserve peace. As an immediate step in this direction we endorse the permanent court of international justice and favor the adherence of the United States to this tribunal as recommended by President Coolidge. This government has definitely refused membership in the League of Nations or to assume any obligations under the covenant of the league. On this we stand.

While we are unwilling to enter into political commitments which would involve us in the conflict of European politics, it should be the purpose and high privilege of the United States to continue to co-operate with other nations in humanitarian efforts in accordance with our cherished traditions. The basic principles of our foreign policy must be independence without indifference to the rights and necessities of others and cooperation without entangling alliances. The policy overwhelmingly approved by the people has been vindicated since the end of the great war.

America's participation in world affairs under the administration of President Harding and President Coolidge has demonstrated the wisdom and prudence of the national judgment. A most impressive example of the capacity of the United States to serve the cause of the world peace without political affiliations was shown in the effective and beneficent work of the Dawes Commission toward the solution of the perplexing question of German reparations.

The first conference of great powers in Washington called by President Harding accomplished the limitation of armaments and the readjustment of the relations of the powers interested in the far east. The conference resulted in an agreement to reduce armaments, relieved the competitive nations involved from the great burdens of taxation arising from the construction and maintenance of capital battleships; assured a new, broader and better understanding in the far east; brought the assurance of peace in the region of the Pacific and formally adopted the policy of the open door for trade and commerce in the great markets of the Far East.

This historic conference paved the way to avert the danger of renewed hostilities in Europe, and to restore the necessary economic stability. While the military forces of America have been restored to a peace footing, there has been an increase in the land and air forces abroad which constitutes a continual menace to the peace of the world and a bar to the return of prosperity.

We firmly advocate the calling of a conference on the limitation of land forces, the use of submarines and poison gas, as proposed by President Coolidge, when, through the adoption of a permanent reparations plan the conditions in Europe will make negotiations and co-operation opportune and possible.

By treaties of peace, safeguarding our rights and without derogating those of our former associates in arms, the Republican Administration ended the war between this country and Germany and Austria. We have concluded and signed with other nations during the past three years more than fifty treaties and international agreements in the furtherance of peace and good will.

New sanctions and new proofs of permanent accord have marked our relations with all Latin America. The long-standing controversy between Chile and Peru has been advanced toward settlement by its submission to the President of the United States as arbitrator and with the helpful co-operation of this country a treaty has been signed by the representatives of sixteen American republics which will stabilize conditions on the American continent and minimize the opportunities for war.

Our difficulties with Mexico have happily yielded to a most friendly adjustment. Mutual confidence has been restored and a pathway for that friendliness and helpfulness which should exist between this government and the government of our neighboring republic has been marked. Agreements have been entered into for the determination by judicial commissions of the claims of the citizens of each country against the respective governments. We can confidently look forward to more permanent and more stable relations with this republic that joins for so many miles our southern border.

Our policy, now well defined, of giving practical aid to other peoples without assuming political obligations has been conspicuously demonstrated. The ready and generous response of America to the needs of the starving in Russia and the suddenly stricken people of Japan gave evidence of our helpful interest in the welfare of the distressed in other lands.

The work of our representatives in dealing with subjects of such universal concern as the traffic in women and children, the production and distribution of narcotic drugs, the sale of arms and in matters affecting public health and morals, demonstrates that we can effectively do our part for humanity and civilization without forfeiting, limiting or restricting our national freedom of action.

The American people do cherish their independence, but their sense of duty to all mankind will ever prompt them to give their support, service and leadership to every cause which makes for peace and amity among the nations of the world.

AGRICULTURE

In dealing with agriculture the Republican Party recognizes that we are faced with a fundamental national problem, and that the prosperity and welfare of the nation as a whole is dependent upon the prosperity and welfare of our agricultural population.

We recognize our agricultural activities are still struggling with adverse conditions that have brought about distress. We pledge the party to take whatever steps are necessary to bring back a balanced condition between agriculture, industry and labor, which was destroyed by the Democratic Party through an unfortunate administration of legislation passed as war-time measures.

We affirm that under the Republican Administration the problems of the farm have received more serious consideration than ever before both by definite executive action and by congressional action not only in the field of general legislation but also in the enactment of laws to meet emergency situations.

The restoration of general prosperity and the purchasing power of our people through tariff protection has resulted in an increased domestic consumption of food products while the price of many agricultural commodities are above the war price level by reason of direct tariff protection.

Under the leadership of the President at the most critical time, a corporation was organized by private capital making available $100,000,000 to assist the farmers of the northwest.

In realization of the disturbance in the agricultural export market, the result of the financial depression in Europe, and appreciating that the export field would be enormously improved by economic rehabilitation and the resulting increased consuming power, a sympathetic support and direction was given to the work of the American representatives on the European Reparations Commission.

The revival in 1921 of the War Finance Corporation with loans of over $300,000,000 averted in 1921 a complete collapse in the agricultural industry.

We have established new intermediate credit banks for agriculture and increased the capital of the federal farm loan system. Emergency loans have been granted to drought-stricken areas. We have enacted into law the Co-operative Marketing Act, the Grain Futures and Packer Control Acts; given to agriculture direct representation on the Federal Reserve Board and on the Federal Aid Commission. We have greatly strengthened our foreign marketing service for the disposal of our agricultural products.

The crux of the problem from the standpoint of the farmer is the net profit he receives after his outlay. The process of bringing the average prices of what he buys and what he sells closer together can be promptly expedited by reduction in taxes, steady employment in industry and stability in business.

This process can be expedited directly by lower freight rates, by better marketing through cooperative efforts and a more scientific organization of the physical human machinery of distribution and by a greater diversification of farm products.

We promise every assistance in the reorganization of the market system on sounder and more economical lines and where diversification is needed government assistance during the period of transition. Vigorous efforts of this administration toward broadening our exports market will be continued. The Republican Party pledges itself to the development and enactment of measures which will place the agricultural interests of America on a basis of economic equality with other industries to assure its prosperity and success. We favor adequate tariff protection to such of our agriculture products as are threatened by competition. We favor, without putting the government into business, the establishment of a federal system of organization for co-operative marketing of farm products.

HIGHWAYS

The Federal Aid Road Act, adopted by the Republican Congress in 1921 has been of inestimable value to the development of the highway systems of the several states and of the nation. We pledge a continuation of this policy of federal co-operation with the states in highway building.

We favor the construction of roads and trails in our national forests necessary to their protection and utilization. In appropriations, therefore, the taxes which these lands would pay if taxable, should be considered as a controlling factor.

LABOR

The increasing stress of industrial life, the constant and necessary efforts because of world competition to increase production and decrease costs has made it specially incumbent on those in authority to protect labor from undue exactions.

We commend Congress for having recognized this possibility in its prompt adoption of the recommendation of President Coolidge for a constitutional amendment authorizing Congress to legislate on the subject of child labor, and we urge the prompt consideration of that amendment by the legislatures of the various states.

There is no success great enough to justify the employment of women in labor under conditions which will impair their natural functions.

We favor high standards for wage, working and living conditions among the women employed in industry. We pledge a continuance of the successful efforts of the Republican Administration to eliminate the seven-day, twelve-hour-day industry.

We regard with satisfaction the elimination of the twelve-hour day in the steel industry and the agreement eliminating the seven-day work week of alternate thirteen and eleven hours accomplished through the efforts of Presidents Harding and Coolidge.

We declare our faith in the principle of the eight-hour day.

We pledge a continuation of the work of rehabilitating workers in industry as conducted by the federal board for vocational education, and favor adequate appropriations for this purpose.

We favor a broader and better system of vocational education, a more adequate system of federal free employment agencies with facilities for assisting the movements of seasonal and migratory labor, including farm labor, with ample organization for bringing the man and his job together.

RAILROADS

We believe that the demand of the American people for improved railroad service at cheaper rates is justified and that it can be fulfilled by the consolidation of the railroads into a lesser number of connecting systems with the resultant operating economy. The labor board provision should be amended to meet the requirements made evident by experience gained from its actual creation.

Collective bargaining, voluntary mediation and arbitration are the most important steps in maintaining peaceful labor relations. We do not believe in compulsory action at any time. Public opinion must be the final arbiter in any crisis which so vitally affects public welfare as the suspension of transportation. Therefore, the interests of the public require the maintenance of an impartial tribunal which can in any emergency make an investigation of the fact and publish its conclusions. This is accepted as a basis of popular judgment.

GOVERNMENT CONTROL

The prosperity of the American nation rests on the vigor of private initiative which has bred a spirit of independence and self-reliance. The Republican Party stands now, as always, against all attempts to put the government into business.

American industry should not be compelled to struggle against government competition. The right of the government to regulate, supervise and control public utilities and public interests, we believe, should be strengthened, but we are firmly opposed to the nationalization or government ownership of public utilities.

COAL

The price and a constant supply of this essential commodity are of vital interest to the public. The government has no constitutional power to regulate prices, but can bring its influence to bear by the powerful instrument afforded by full publicity. When through industrial conflict, its supply is threatened, the President should have authority to appoint a commission to act as mediators and as a medium for voluntary arbitration. In the event of a strike, the control of distribution must be invoked to prevent profiteering.

MERCHANT MARINE

The Republican Party stands for a strong and permanent merchant marine built by Americans, owned by Americans and manned by Americans to secure the necessary contact with world markets for our surplus agricultural products and manufactures; to protect our shippers and importers from exorbitant ocean freight rates, and to become a powerful arm of our national defense.

That part of the merchant marine now owned by the government should continue to be improved in its economic and efficient management, with reduction of the losses now paid by the government through taxation until it is finally placed on so sound a basis that, with ocean freight rates becoming normal, due to improvement in international affairs, it can be sold to American citizens.

WATERWAYS

Fully realizing the vital importance of transportation in both cost and service to all of our people, we favor the construction of the most feasible waterways from the Great Lakes to the Atlantic seaboard and the Gulf of Mexico, and the improvement and development of rivers, harbors and waterways, inland and coastwise, to the fullest extent justified by the present and potential tonnage available.

We favor a comprehensive survey of the conditions under which the flood waters of the Colorado river may be controlled and utilized for the benefit of the people of the states which border thereon.

The Federal Water Power Act establishes a national water power policy and the way has thereby been opened for the greatest water power development in history under conditions which preserve the initiative of our people, yet protect the public interest.

WORLD WAR VETERANS

The Republican Party pledges a continual and increasing solicitude for all those suffering any disability as a result of service to the United States in time of war. No country and no administration has ever shown a more generous disposition in the care of its disabled, or more thoughtful consideration in providing a sound administration for the solution of the many problems involved in making intended benefits fully, directly and promptly available to the veterans.

The confusion, inefficiency and maladministration existing heretofore since the establishment of this government agency has been cured, and plans are being actively made looking to a further improvement in the operation of the bureau by the passage of new legislation. The basic statute has been so liberalized as to bring within its terms 100,000 additional beneficiaries. The privilege of hospitalization in government hospitals, as recommended by President Coolidge, has been granted to all veterans irrespective of the origin of disability, and over $50,000,000 has been appropriated for hospital construction which will provide sufficient beds to care for all. Appropriations totalling over $1,100,000,000, made by the Republican Congress for the care of the disabled, evidence the unmistakable purpose of the government not to consider costs when the welfare of these men is at stake. No legislation for the benefit of the disabled soldiers proposed during the last four years by veterans' organizations has failed to receive consideration.

We pledge ourselves to meet the problems of the future affecting the care of our wounded and disabled in a spirit of liberality, and with that thoughtful consideration which will enable the government to give to the individual veteran that full measure of care guaranteed by an effective administrative machinery.

CONSERVATION

We believe in the development, effective and efficient, whether of oil, timber, coal or water power resources by this government only as needed and only after the public needs have become a matter of public record, controlled with a scrupulous regard and ever-vigilant safeguards against waste, speculation and monopoly.

The natural resources of the country belong to all the people and are a part of an estate belonging to generations yet unborn. The government policy should be to safeguard, develop and utilize these possessions. The conservation policy of the nation originated with the Republican Party under the inspiration of Theodore Roosevelt.

We hold it a privilege of the Republican Party to build as a memorial to him on the foundation which he laid.

EDUCATION AND RELIEF

The conservation of human resources is one of the most solemn responsibilities of government. This is an obligation which cannot be ignored and which demands that the Federal Government shall, as far as lies in its power, give to the people and the states the benefit of its counsel.

The welfare activities of the government connected with the various departments are already numerous and important, but lack the co-ordination which is essential to effective action. To meet these needs we approve the suggestion for the creation of a Cabinet post of education and relief.

WAR-TIME MOBILIZATION

We believe that in time of war the nation should draft for its defense not only its citizens but also every resource which may contribute to success. The country demands that should the United States ever again be called upon to defend itself by arms the President be empowered to draft such material resources and such service as may be required, and to stabilize the prices of services and essential commodities, whether used in actual warfare or private activities.

COMMERCIAL AVIATION

We advocate the early enactment of such legislation and the taking of such steps by the government as will tend to promote commercial aviation.

ARMY AND NAVY

There must be no further weakening of our regular army and we advocate appropriations sufficient to provide for the training of all members of the National Guard, the citizens' military training camps, the reserve officers' training camps and the reserves who may offer themselves for service. We pledge ourselves for service. We pledge ourselves to round out and maintain the Navy to the full strength provided the United States by the letter and spirit of the Limitation of Armament Conference.

THE NEGRO

We urge the Congress to enact at the earliest possible date a federal anti-lynching law so that the full influence of the Federal Government may be wielded to exterminate this hideous crime. We believe that much of the misunderstanding which now exists can be eliminated by humane and sympathetic study of its causes. The President has recommended the creation of a commission for the investigation of social and economic conditions and the promotion of mutual understanding and confidence.

ORDERLY GOVERNMENT

The Republican Party reaffirms its devotion to orderly government under the guarantees embodied in the Constitution of the United States. We recognize the duty of constant vigilance to preserve at all times a clean and honest government and to bring to the bar of justice every defiler of the public service in or out of office.

Dishonesty and corruption are not political attributes. The recent congressional investigations have exposed instances in both parties of men in public office who are willing to sell official favors and men out of office who are willing to buy them in some cases with money and others with influence.

The sale of influence resulting from the holding of public position or from association while in public office or the use of such influence for private gain or advantage is a perversion of public trust and prejudicial to good government. It should be condemned by public opinion and forbidden by law.

We demand the speedy, fearless and impartial prosecution of all wrongdoers, without regard for political affiliations; but we declare no greater wrong can be committed against the people than the attempt to destroy their trust in the great body of their public servants. Admitting the deep humiliation which all good citizens share that our public life should have harbored some dishonest men, we assert that these undesirable do not represent the standard of our national integrity.

The government at Washington is served to-day by thousands of earnest, conscientious and faithful officials and employees in every department.

It is a grave wrong against these patriotic men and women to strive indiscriminately to besmirch the names of the innocent and undermine the confidence of the people in the government under which they live. It is even a greater wrong when this is done for partisan purposes or for selfish exploitation.

IMMIGRATION

The unprecedented living conditions in Europe following the world war created a condition by which we were threatened with mass immigration that would have seriously disturbed our economic life. The law recently enacted is designed to protect the inhabitants of our country, not only the American citizen, but also the alien already with us who is seeking to secure an economic foothold for himself and family from the competition that would come from unrestricted immigration. The administrative features of the law represent a great constructive advance, and eliminate the hardships suffered by immigrants under emergency statute.

We favor the adoption of methods which will exercise a helpful influence among the foreign born population and provide for the education of the alien in our language, customs, ideals and standards of life. We favor the improvement of naturalization laws.

— 1928 —

The Republican Party in national convention assembled presents to the people of the Nation this platform of its principles, based on a record of its accomplishments, and asks and awaits a new vote of confidence. We reaffirm our devotion to the Constitution of the United States and the principles and institution of the American system of representative government.

THE NATIONAL ADMINISTRATION

We endorse without qualification the record of the Coolidge administration.

The record of the Republican Party is a record of advancement of the nation. Nominees of Republican national conventions have for 52 of the 72 years since the creation of our party been the chief executives of the United States. Under Republican inspiration and largely under Republican executive direction the continent has been bound with steel rails, the oceans and great rivers have been joined by canals, waterways have been deepened and widened for ocean commerce, and with all a high American standard of wage and living has been established.

By unwavering adherence to sound principles, through the wisdom of Republican policies, and the capacity of Republican administrations, the foundations have been laid and the greatness and prosperity of the country firmly established.

Never has the soundness of Republican policies been more amply demonstrated and the Republican genius for administration been better exemplified than during the last five years under the leadership of President Coolidge.

No better guaranty of prosperity and contentment among all our people at home, no more reliable warranty of protection and promotion of American interests abroad can be given than the pledge to maintain and continue the Coolidge policies. This promise we give and will faithfully perform.

Under this Administration the country has been lifted from the depths of a great depression to a level of prosperity. Economy has been raised to the dignity of a principle of government. A standard of character in public service has been established under the chief executive, which has given to the people of the country a feeling of stability and confidence so all have felt encouraged to proceed on new undertakings in trade and commerce. A foreign policy based on the traditional American position and carried on with wisdom and steadfastness has extended American influence throughout the world and everywhere promoted and protected American interests.

The mighty contribution to general well-being which can be made by a government controlled by men of character and courage, whose abilities are equal to their responsibilities, is self-evident, and should not blind us to the consequences which its loss would entail. Under this Administration a high level of wages and living has been established and maintained. The door of opportunity has been opened wide to all. It has given to our people greater comfort and leisure, and the mutual profit has been evident in the increasingly harmonious relations between employers and employees, and the steady rise by promotion of the men in the shops to places at the council tables of the industries. It has also been made evident by the increasing enrollment of our youth in the technical schools and colleges, the increase in savings and life insurance accounts, and by our ability, as a people, to lend the hand of succor not only to those overcome by disasters in our own country but in foreign lands. With all there has been a steady decrease in the burden of Federal taxation, releasing to the people the greatest possible portion of the results of their labor from government exactions.

For the Republican Party we are justified in claiming a major share of the credit for the position which the United States occupies today as the most favored nation on the globe, but it is well to remember that the confidence and prosperity which we enjoy can be shattered, if not destroyed, if this belief in the honesty and sincerity of our government is in any way affected. A continuation of this great public peace of mind now existing, which makes for our material well-being, is only possible by holding fast to the plans and principles which have marked Republican control.

The record of the present Administration is a guaranty of what may be expected of the next. Our words have been made deeds. We offer not promises but accomplishments.

PUBLIC ECONOMY

The citizen and taxpayer has a natural right to be protected from unnecessary and wasteful expenditures. This is a rich but also a growing nation with constantly increasing legitimate demands for public funds. If we are able to spend wisely and meet these requirements, it is first necessary that we save wisely. Spending extravagantly not only deprives men through taxation of the fruits of their labor, but oftentimes means the postponement of vitally important public works. We commend President Coolidge for his establishment of this fundamental principle of sound administration and pledge ourselves to live up to the high standard he has set.

FINANCE AND TAXATION

The record of the United States Treasury under Secretary Mellon stands unrivalled and unsurpassed. The finances of the nation have been managed with sound judgment. The financial policies have yielded immediate and substantial results.

In 1921 the credit of our government was at a low ebb. We were burdened with a huge public debt, a load of war taxes, which in variety and weight exceeded anything in our national life, while vast unfunded intergovernmental debts disorganized the economic life of the debtor nations and seriously affected our own by reason of the serious obstacles which they presented to commercial intercourse. This critical situation was evidenced by a serious disturbance in our own life which made for unemployment.

Today all these major financial problems have been solved.

The Public Debt

In seven years the public debt has been reduced by $6,411,000,000. From March 1921 to September 1928 over eleven billion dollars of securities, bearing high rates of interest, will have been retired or refunded into securities bearing a low rate of interest, while Liberty Bonds, which were selling below par, now command a premium. These operations have resulted in an annual saving in interest charges of not less than

$275,000,000, without which the most recent tax reduction measure would not have been made possible. The Republican Party will continue to reduce our national debt as rapidly as possible and in accordance with the provision of existing laws and the present program.

Tax Reduction

Wise administrative management under Republican control and direction has made possible a reduction of over a billion eight hundred million dollars a year in the tax bill of the American people. Four separate tax reduction measures have been enacted, and millions of those least able to pay have been taken from the tax rolls.

Excessive and uneconomic rates have been radically modified, releasing for industrial and payroll expansion and development great sums of money which formerly were paid in taxes to the Federal government.

Practically all the war taxes have been eliminated and our tax system has been definitely restored to a peace time basis.

We pledge our party to a continuation of these sound policies and to such further reduction of the tax burden as the condition of the Treasury may from time to time permit.

Tariff

We reaffirm our belief in the protective tariff as a fundamental and essential principle of the economic life of this nation. While certain provisions of the present law require revision in the light of changes in the world competitive situation since its enactment, the record of the United States since 1922 clearly shows that the fundamental protective principle of the law has been fully justified. It has stimulated the development of our natural resources, provided fuller employment at higher wages through the promotion of industrial activity, assured thereby the continuance of the farmer's major market, and further raised the standards of living and general comfort and well-being of our people. The great expansion in the wealth of our nation during the past fifty years, and particularly in the past decade, could not have been accomplished without a protective tariff system designed to promote the vital interests of all classes.

Nor have these manifest benefits been restricted to any particular section of the country. They are enjoyed throughout the land either directly or indirectly. Their stimulus has been felt in industries, farming sections, trade circles, and communities in every quarter.

However, we realize that there are certain industries which cannot now successfully compete with foreign producers because of lower foreign wages and a lower cost of living abroad, and we pledge the next Republican Congress to an examination and where necessary a revision of these schedules to the end that American labor in these industries may again command the home market, may maintain its standard of living, and may count upon steady employment in its accustomed field.

Adherence to that policy is essential for the continued prosperity of the country. Under it the standard of living of the American people has been raised to the highest levels ever known. Its example has been eagerly followed by the rest of the world whose experts have repeatedly reported with approval the relationship of this policy to our prosperity, with the resultant emulation of that example by other nations.

A protective tariff is as vital to American agriculture as it is to American manufacturing. The Republican Party believes that the home market, built up under the protective policy, belongs to the American farmer, and it pledges its support of legislation which will give this market to him to the full extent of his ability to supply it. Agriculture derives large benefits not only directly from the protective duties levied on competitive farm products of foreign origin, but also, indirectly, from the increase in the purchasing power of American workmen employed in industries similarly protected. These benefits extend also to persons engaged in trade, transportation, and other activities.

The Tariff Act of 1922 has justified itself in the expansion of our foreign trade during the past five years. Our domestic exports have increased from 3.8 billions of dollars in 1922 to 4.8 billions in 1927. During the same period imports have increased from 3.1 billions to 4.4 billions. Contrary to the prophesies of its critics, the present tariff law has not hampered the natural growth in the exportation of the products of American agriculture, industry, and mining, nor has it restricted the importation of foreign commodities which this country can utilize without jeopardizing its economic structure.

The United States is the largest customer in the world today. If we were not prosperous and able to buy, the rest of the world also would suffer. It is inconceivable that American labor will ever consent to the abolition of protection which would bring the American standard of living down to the level of that in Europe, or that the American farmer could survive if the enormous consuming power of the people in this country were curtailed and its market at home, if not destroyed, at least seriously impaired.

Foreign Debts

In accordance with our settled policy and platform pledges, debt settlement agreements have been negotiated with all of our foreign debtors with the exception of Armenia and Russia. That with France remains as yet unratified. Those with Greece and Austria are before the Congress for necessary authority. If the French Debt Settlement be included, the total amount funded is eleven billion five hundred twenty-two million three hundred fifty-four thousand dollars. We have steadfastly opposed and will continue to oppose cancellation of foreign debts.

We have no desire to be oppressive or grasping, but we hold that obligations justly incurred should be honorably discharged. We know of no authority which would permit public officials, acting as trustees, to shift the burden of the War from the shoulders of foreign taxpayers to those of our own people. We believe that the settlements agreed to are fair to both the debtor nation and to the American taxpayer. Our Debt Commission took into full consideration the economic condition and resources of the debtor nations, and were ever mindful that they must be permitted to preserve and improve their economic position, to bring their budgets into balance, to place their currencies and finances on a sound basis, and to improve the standard of living of their people. Giving full weight to these considerations, we know of no fairer test than ability to pay, justly estimated.

The people can rely on the Republican Party to adhere to a foreign debt policy now definitely established and clearly understood both at home and abroad.

Settlement of War Claims

A satisfactory solution has been found for the question of War Claims. Under the Act, approved by the President on March 10, 1928, a provision was made for the settlement of War Claims of the United States and its citizens against the German, Austrian and Hungarian Governments, and of the claims of the nationals of these governments against the United States; and for the return to its owners of the property seized by the Alien Property Custodian during the War, in accordance with our traditional policy of respect for private property.

FOREIGN POLICIES

We approve the foreign policies of the Administration of President Coolidge. We believe they express the will of the American people in working actively to build up cordial international understanding that will make world peace a permanent reality. We endorse the proposal of the Secretary of State for a multilateral treaty proposed to the principal powers of the world and open to the signatures of all nations, to renounce war as an instrument of national policy and declaring in favor of pacific settlement of international disputes, the first step in outlawing war. The idea has stirred the conscience of mankind and gained widespread approval, both of governments and of the people, and the conclusion of the treaty will be acclaimed as the greatest single step in history toward the conservation of peace.

In the same endeavor to substitute for war the peaceful settlement of international disputes the Administration has concluded arbitration treaties in a form more definite and more inclusive than ever before and plans to negotiate similar treaties with all countries willing in this manner to define their policy peacefully to settle justiciable disputes. In connection with these, we endorse the Resolution of the Sixth Pan American Conference held at Havana, Cuba, in 1928, which called a conference on arbitration and conciliation to meet in Washington during the year and express our earnest hope that such conference will greatly further the principles of international arbitration. We shall continue to demand the same respect and protection for the persons and property of American citizens in foreign countries that we cheerfully accord in this country to the persons and property of aliens.

The commercial treaties which we have negotiated and those still in the process of negotiation are based on strict justice among nations, equal opportunity for trade and commerce on the most-favored-nation principle and are simplified so as to eliminate the danger of misunderstanding. The object and the aim of the United States is to further the cause of peace, of strict justice between nations with due regard for the rights of others in all international dealings. Out of justice grows peace. Justice and consideration have been and will continue to be the inspiration of our nation.

The record of the Administration toward Mexico has been consistently friendly and with equal consistency have we upheld American rights. This firm and at the same time friendly policy has brought recognition of the inviolability of legally acquired rights. This condition has been reached without threat and bluster, through a calm support of the recognized principles of international law with due regard to the rights of a sister sovereign state. The Republican Party will continue to support American rights in Mexico, as elsewhere in

the world, and at the same time to promote and strengthen friendship and confidence.

There has always been, as there always will be, a firm friendship with Canada. American and Canadian interests are in a large measure identical. Our relationship is one of fine mutual understanding and the recent exchange of diplomatic officers between the two countries is worthy of commendation.

The United States has an especial interest in the advancement and progress of all the Latin American countries. The policy of the Republican Party will always be a policy of thorough friendship and co-operation. In the case of Nicaragua, we are engaged in co-operation with the government of that country upon the task of assisting to restore and maintain peace, order and stability, and in no way to infringe upon her sovereign rights. The Marines, now in Nicaragua, are there to protect American lives and property and to aid in carrying out an agreement whereby we have undertaken to do what we can to restore and maintain order and to insure a fair and free election. Our policy absolutely repudiates any idea of conquest or exploitation, and is actuated solely by an earnest and sincere desire to assist a friendly and neighboring state which has appealed for aid in a great emergency. It is the same policy the United States has pursued in other cases in Central America.

The Administration has looked with keen sympathy on the tragic events in China. We have avoided interference in the internal affairs of that unhappy nation, merely keeping sufficient naval and military forces in China to protect the lives of the Americans who are there on legitimate business and in still larger numbers for nobly humanitarian reasons. America has not been stampeded into making reprisals but, on the other hand, has consistently taken the position of leadership among the nations in a policy of wise moderation. We shall always be glad to be of assistance to China when our duty is clear.

The Republican Party maintains the traditional American policy of non-interference in the political affairs of other nations. This government has definitely refused membership in the League of Nations and to assume any obligations under the covenant of the League.

On this we stand.

In accordance, however, with the long established American practice of giving aid and assistance to other peoples, we have most usefully assisted by co-operation in the humanitarian and technical work undertaken by the League, without involving ourselves in European politics by accepting membership.

The Republican Party has always given and will

continue to give its support to the development of American foreign trade, which makes for domestic prosperity. During this Administration extraordinary strides have been made in opening up new markets for American produce and manufacture. Through these foreign contacts a mutually better international understanding has been reached which aids in the maintenance of world peace.

The Republican Party promises a firm and consistent support of American persons and legitimate American interests in all parts of the world. This support will never contravene the rights of other nations. It will always have in mind and support in every way the progressive development of international law, since it is through the operation of just laws, as well as through the growth of friendly understanding, that world peace will be made permanent. To that end the Republican Party pledges itself to aid and assist in the perfection of principles of international law and the settlement of international disputes.

CIVIL SERVICE

The merit system in government service originated with and has been developed by the Republican Party. The great majority of our public service employees are now secured through and maintained in the government service rolls. Steps have already been taken by the Republican Congress to make the service more attractive as to wages and retirement privileges, and we commend what has been done, as a step in the right direction.

AGRICULTURE

The agricultural problem is national in scope and, as such, is recognized by the Republican Party which pledges its strength and energy to the solution of the same. Realizing that many farmers are facing problems more difficult than those which are the portion of many other basic industries, the party is anxious to aid in every way possible. Many of our farmers are still going through readjustments, a relic of the years directly following the great war. All the farmers are being called on to meet new and perplexing conditions created by foreign competition, the complexities of domestic marketing, labor problems, and a steady increase in local and state taxes.

The general depression in a great basic industry inevitably reacts upon the conditions in the country as a whole and cannot be ignored. It is a matter of satisfaction that the desire to help in the correction of agricultural wrongs and conditions is not confined to any one section of our country or any particular group.

The Republican Party and the Republican Administration, particularly during the last five years, have settled many of the most distressing problems as they have arisen, and the achievements in aid of agriculture are properly a part of this record. The Republican Congresses have been most responsive in the matter of agricultural appropriations, not only to meet crop emergencies, but for the extension and development of the activities of the Department of Agriculture.

The protection of the American farmer against foreign farm competition and foreign trade practices has been vigorously carried on by the Department of State. The right of the farmers to engage in collective buying and co-operative selling as provided for by the Capper–Volstead Act of 1922 has been promulgated through the Department of Agriculture and the Department of Justice, which have given most valuable aid and assistance to the heads of the farm organizations. The Treasury Department and the proper committees of Congress have lightened the tax burden on farming communities, and through the Federal Farm Loan System there has been made available to the farmers of the nation one billion eight hundred fifty millions of dollars for loaning purposes at a low rate of interest, and through the Intermediate Credit Banks six hundred fifty-five million dollars of short-term credits have been made available to the farmers. The Post Office Department has systematically and generously extended the Rural Free Delivery routes into even the most sparsely settled communities.

When a shortage of transportation facilities threatened to deprive the farmers of their opportunity to reach waiting markets overseas, the President, appreciative and sensitive of the condition and the possible loss to the communities, ordered the reconditioning of Shipping Board vessels, thus relieving a great emergency.

Last, but not least, the Federal Tariff Commission has at all times shown a willingness under the provisions of the Flexible Tariff Act to aid the farmers when foreign competition, made possible by low wage scales abroad, threatened to deprive our farmers of their domestic markets. Under this Act the President has increased duties on wheat, flour, mill feed, and dairy products. Numerous other farm products are now being investigated by the Tariff Commission.

We promise every assistance in the reorganization of the marketing system on sounder and more economical lines and, where diversification is needed,

Government financial assistance during the period of transition.

The Republican Party pledges itself to the enactment of legislation creating a Federal Farm Board clothed with the necessary powers to promote the establishment of a farm marketing system of farmer-owned-and-controlled stabilization corporations or associations to prevent and control surpluses through orderly distribution.

We favor adequate tariff protection to such of our agricultural products as are affected by foreign competition.

We favor, without putting the Government into business, the establishment of a Federal system of organization for co-operative and orderly marketing of farm products.

The vigorous efforts of this Administration towards broadening our exports market will be continued.

The Republican Party pledges itself to the development and enactment of measures which will place the agricultural interests of America on a basis of economic equality with other industries to insure its prosperity and success.

MINING

The money value of the mineral products of the country is second only to agriculture. We lead the countries of the world in the production of coal, iron, copper and silver. The nation suffers as a whole from any disturbance in the securing of any one of these minerals, and particularly when the coal supply is affected. The mining industry has always been self-sustaining, but we believe that the Government should make every effort to aid the industry by protection by removing any restrictions which may be hampering its development, and by increased technical and economic research investigations which are necessary for its welfare and normal development. The Party is anxious, hopeful, and willing to assist in any feasible plan for the stabilization of the coal mining industry, which will work with justice to the miners, consumers and producers.

HIGHWAYS

Under the Federal Aid Road Act, adopted by the Republican Congress in 1921, and supplemented by generous appropriations each year, road construction has made greater advancement than for many decades previous. Improved highway conditions is a gauge of our rural developments and our commercial activity.

We pledge our support to continued appropriations for this work commensurate with our needs and resources.

We favor the construction of roads and trails in our national forests necessary to their protection and utilization. In appropriations therefor the taxes which these lands would pay if taxable should be considered as a controlling factor.

LABOR

The labor record of the Republican Party stands unchallenged. For 52 of the 72 years of our national existence Republican Administrations have prevailed. Today American labor enjoys the highest wage and the highest standard of living throughout the world. Through the saneness and soundness of Republican rule the American workman is paid a "real wage" which allows comfort for himself and his dependents, and an opportunity and leisure for advancement. It is not surprising that the foreign workman, whose greatest ambition still is to achieve a "living wage," should look with longing towards America as the goal of his desires.

The ability to pay such wages and maintain such a standard comes from the wisdom of the protective legislation which the Republican Party has placed upon the national statute books, the tariff which bars cheap foreign-made goods from the American market and provides continuity of employment for our workmen and fair profits for the manufacturers, and the restriction of immigration which not only prevents the glutting of our labor market, but allows to our newer immigrants a greater opportunity to secure a footing in their upward struggle.

The Party favors freedom in wage contracts, the right of collective bargaining by free and responsible agents of their own choosing, which develops and maintains that purposeful co-operation which gains its chief incentive through voluntary agreement.

We believe that injunctions in labor disputes have in some instances been abused and have given rise to a serious question for legislation.

The Republican Party pledges itself to continue its efforts to maintain this present standard of living and high wage scale.

RAILROADS

Prompt and effective railroad service at the lowest rates which will provide for its maintenance and allow a reasonable return to the investor so they may be encouraged to advance new capital for acquired developments, has long been recognized by the Republican Party as a necessity of national existence.

We believe that the present laws under which our railroads are regulated are soundly based on correct principles, the spirit of which must always be preserved. Because, however, of changes in the public demands, trade conditions and of the character of the competition, which even the greatest railroads are now being called upon to meet, we feel that in the light of this new experience possible modifications or amendments, the need of which is proved, should be considered.

The Republican Party initiated and set in operation the Interstate Commerce Commission. This body has developed a system of railroad control and regulation which has given to the transportation public an opportunity not only to make suggestions for the improvement of railroad service, but to protest against discriminatory rates or schedules. We commend the work which that body is accomplishing under mandate of law in considering these matters and seeking to distribute equitably the burden of transportation between commodities based on their ability to bear the same.

MERCHANT MARINE

The Republican Party stands for the American built, American-owned, and American-operated merchant marine. The enactment of the White Jones Bill is in line with a policy which the party has long advocated.

Under this measure, substantial aid and encouragement are offered for the building in American yards of new and modern ships which will carry the American flag.

The Republican Party does not believe in government ownership or operation, and stands specifically for the sale of the present government vessels to private owners when appropriate arrangements can be made. Pending such a sale, and because private owners are not ready as yet to operate on certain of the essential trade routes, the bill enacted allows the maintenance of these necessary lines under government control till such transfer can be made.

MISSISSIPPI FLOOD RELIEF AND CONTROL

The Mississippi Valley flood in which seven hundred thousand of our fellow citizens were placed in peril of life, and which destroyed hundreds of millions of dollars' worth of property, was met with energetic action by the Republican Administration.

During this disaster the President mobilized every public and private agency under the direction of Secretary Hoover of the Department of Commerce and Dwight Davis, the Secretary of War. Thanks to their joint efforts, a great loss of life was prevented and everything possible was done to rehabilitate the people in their homes and to relieve suffering and distress.

Congress promptly passed legislation authorizing the expenditure of $325,000,000 for the construction of flood control works, which it is believed will prevent the recurrence of such a disaster.

RADIO

We stand for the administration of the radio facilities of the United States under wise and expert government supervision which will

(1) Secure to every home in the nation, whether city or country, the great educational and inspirational values of broadcast programs, adequate in number and varied in character, and
(2) Assign the radio communication channels, regional, continental, and transoceanic, in the best interest of the American business man, the American farmer, and the American public generally.

WATERWAYS

Cheaper transportation for bulk goods from the Midwest agricultural sections to the sea is recognized by the Republican Party as a vital factor for the relief of agriculture. To that end we favor the continued development in inland and in intracoastal waterways as an essential part of our transportation system.

The Republican Administration during the last four years initiated the systematic development of the Mississippi system of inland transportation lanes, and it proposes to carry on this modernization of transportation to speedy completion. Great improvements have been made during this Administration in our harbors, and the party pledges itself to continue these activities for the modernization of our national equipment.

VETERANS

Our country is honored whenever it bestows relief on those who have faithfully served its flag. The Republican Party, appreciative of this solemn obligation and honor, has made its sentiments evident in Congress. Our expenditures for the benefit of all our veterans now aggregate 750 million dollars annually. Increased hospital facilities have been provided, payments in compensation have more than doubled, and in the matter of rehabilitations, pensions, and insurance, generous provision has been made. The administration of laws dealing with the relief of veterans and their dependents has been a difficult task, but every effort has been made to carry service to the veteran and bring about not only a better and generous interpretation of the law, but a sympathetic consideration of the many problems of the veteran. Full and adequate relief for our disabled veterans is our aim, and we commend the action of Congress in further liberalizing the laws applicable to veterans' relief.

PUBLIC UTILITIES

Republican Congresses and Administrations have steadily strengthened the Interstate Commerce Commission. The protection of the public from exactions or burdens in rates for service by reason of monopoly control, and the protection of the smaller organizations from suppression in their own field, has been a fundamental idea in all regulatory enactments. While recognizing that at times Federal regulations might be more effective than State regulations in controlling intrastate utilities, the Party favors and has sustained State regulations, believing that such responsibility in the end will create a force of State public opinion which will be more effective in preventing discriminations and injustices.

CONSERVATION

We believe in the practical application of the conservation principle by the wise development of our natural resources. The measure of development is our national requirement, and avoidance of waste so that future generations may share in this natural wealth. The Republican policy is to prevent monopolies in the control and utilization of natural resources. Under the General Leasing Law, enacted by a Republican Congress, the ownership of the mineral estate remains in the Government, but development occurs through private capital and energy. Important for the operation of this law is the classification and appraisement of public lands according to their mineral content and value. Over five hundred million acres of public land have been thus classified.

To prevent wasteful exploitation of our oil products, President Coolidge appointed an Oil Conservation Board, which is now conducting an inquiry into all phases of petroleum production, in the effort to devise a national policy for the conservation and proper utilization of our oil resources.

The Republican Party has been forehanded in assuring the development of water power in accordance with public interest. A policy of permanent public retention of the power sites on public land and power privileges in domestic and international navigable streams, and one-third of the potential water power resources in the United States on public domain, has been assured by the Federal Water Powers Act, passed by a Republican Congress.

LAW ENFORCEMENT

We reaffirm the American Constitutional Doctrine as announced by George Washington in his "Farewell Address," to wit:

"The Constitution which at any time exists until changed by the explicit and authentic act by the whole people is sacredly obligatory upon all."

We also reaffirm the attitude of the American people toward the Federal Constitution as declared by Abraham Lincoln:

"We are by both duty and inclination bound to stick by that Constitution in all its letter and spirit from beginning to end. I am for the honest enforcement of the Constitution. Our safety, our liberty, depends upon preserving the Constitution of the United States, as our forefathers made it inviolate."

The people through the method provided by the Constitution have written the Eighteenth Amendment into the Constitution. The Republican Party pledges itself and its nominees to the observance and vigorous enforcement of this provision of the Constitution.

HONESTY IN GOVERNMENT

We stand for honesty in government, for the appointment of officials whose integrity cannot be questioned. We deplore the fact that any official has ever fallen from this high standard and that certain American citizens of both parties have so far forgotten their duty as citizens as to traffic in national interests for private gain. We have prosecuted and shall always prosecute any official who subordinates his public duty to his personal interest.

The Government today is made up of thousands of conscientious, earnest, self-sacrificing men and women, whose single thought is service to the nation.

We pledge ourselves to maintain and, if possible, to improve the quality of this great company of Federal employees.

CAMPAIGN EXPENDITURES

Economy, honesty, and decency in the conduct of political campaigns are a necessity if representative government is to be preserved to the people and political parties are to hold the respect of the citizens at large.

The Campaign of 1924 complied with all these requirements. It was a campaign, the expenses of which were carefully budgeted in advance, and, which, at the close, presented a surplus and not a deficit.

There will not be any relaxing of resolute endeavor to keep our elections clean, honest and free from taint of any kind. The improper use of money in governmental and political affairs is a great national evil. One of the most effective remedies for this abuse is publicity in all matters touching campaign contributions and expenditures. The Republican Party, beginning not later than August 1, 1928, and every 30 days thereafter—the last publication being not later than five days before the election—will file with the Committees of the House and Senate a complete account of all contributions, the names of the contributors, the amounts expended, and for what purposes, and will at all times hold its records and books touching such matters open for inspection.

The party further pledges that it will not create, or permit to be created, any deficit which shall exist at the close of the campaign.

RECLAMATION

Federal reclamation of arid lands is a Republican policy, adopted under President Roosevelt, carried forward by succeeding Republican Presidents, and put upon a still higher plane of efficiency and production by President Coolidge. It has increased the wealth of the nation and made the West more prosperous.

An intensive study of the methods and practices of reclamation has been going on for the past four years under the direction of the Department of the Interior in an endeavor to create broader human opportunities and their financial and economic success. The money value of the crops raised on reclamation projects is showing a steady and gratifying increase as well as the number of farms and people who have settled on the lands.

The continuation of a surplus of agricultural products in the selling markets of the world has influenced the Department to a revaluation of plans and projects. It has adopted a ten-year program for the completion of older projects and will hold other suggestions in abeyance until the surveys now under way as to the entire scope of the work are completed.

COMMERCIAL AVIATION

Without governmental grants or subsidies and entirely by private initiative, the nation has made extraordinary advances in the field of commercial aviation. Over 20,000 miles of air mail service privately operated are now being flown daily, and the broadening of this service is an almost weekly event. Because of our close relations with our sister republics on the south and our neighbor on the north, it is fitting our first efforts should be to establish an air communication with Latin-America and Canada.

The achievements of the aviation branches of the Army and Navy are all to the advantage of commercial aviation, and in the Mississippi flood disaster the work performed by civil and military aviators was of inestimable value.

The development of a system of aircraft registration, inspection and control is a credit to the Republican Administration, which, quick to appreciate the importance of this new transportation development, created machinery for its safeguarding.

IMMIGRATION

The Republican Party believes that in the interest of both native and foreign-born wage earners, it is necessary to restrict immigration. Unrestricted immigration would result in widespread unemployment and in the breakdown of the American standard of living. Where, however, the law works undue hardships by depriving the immigrant of the comfort and society of those bound by close family ties, such modification should be adopted as will afford relief.

We commend Congress for correcting defects for humanitarian reasons and for providing an effective system of examining prospective immigrants in their home countries.

NATURALIZATION

The priceless heritage of American citizenship is our greatest gift to our friends of foreign birth. Only those who will be loyal to our institutions, who are here in conformity with our laws, and who are in sympathy with our national traditions, ideals, and principles, should be naturalized.

NAVY

We pledge ourselves to round out and maintain the Navy in all types of combatant ships to the full ratio provided for the United States by the Washington Treaty for the Limitation of Naval Armament and any amendment thereto.

HAWAII–ALASKA

We favor a continuance for the Territory of Hawaii of Federal assistance in harbor improvements, the appropriation of its share of federal funds and the systematic extension of the settlement of public lands by the Hawaiian race.

We endorse the policy of the present Administration with reference to Alaska and favor a continuance of the constructive development of the territory.

WOMEN AND PUBLIC SERVICE

Four years ago at the Republican National Convention in Cleveland women members of the National Committee were welcomed into full association and responsibility in party management. During the four years which have passed they have carried with their men associates an equal share of all responsibilities and their contribution to the success of the 1924 campaign is well recognized.

The Republican Party, which from the first has sought to bring this development about, accepts wholeheartedly equality on the part of women, and in the public service it can present a record of appointments of women in the legal, diplomatic, judicial, treasury and other governmental departments. We earnestly urge on the women that they participate even more generally than now in party management and activity.

NATIONAL DEFENSE

We believe that in time of war the nation should draft for its defense not only its citizens but also every resource which may contribute to success. The country demands that should the United States ever again be

called upon to defend itself by arms, the President be empowered to draft such material resources and such services as may be required, and to stabilize the prices of services and essential commodities, whether utilized in actual warfare or private activity.

OUR INDIAN CITIZENS

National citizenship was conferred upon all native born Indians in the United States by the General Indian Enfranchisement Act of 1924. We favor the creation of a Commission to be appointed by the President including one or more Indian citizens to investigate and report to Congress upon the existing system of the administration of Indian affairs and to report any inconsistencies that may be found to exist between that system and the rights of the Indian citizens of the United States. We also favor the repeal of any law and the termination of any administrative practice which may be inconsistent with Indian citizenship, to the end that the Federal guardianship existing over the persons and properties of Indian tribal communities may not work a prejudice to the personal and property rights of Indian citizens of the United States. The treaty and property rights of the Indians of the United States must be guaranteed to them.

THE NEGRO

We renew our recommendation that the Congress enact at the earliest possible date a Federal Anti-Lynching Law so that the full influence of the Federal Government may be wielded to exterminate this hideous crime.

HOME RULE

We believe in the essential unity of the American people. Sectionalism in any form is destructive of national life. The Federal Government should zealously protect the national and international rights of its citizens. It should be equally zealous to respect and maintain the rights of the States and territories and to upheld the vigor and balance of our dual system of government. The Republican Party has always given its energies to supporting the Government in this direction when any question has arisen.

There are certain other well-defined Federal obligations such as interstate commerce, the development of rivers and harbors, and the guarding and conservation of national resources. The effort, which, however, is being continually made to have the Federal Government move into the field of state activities, has never had, and never will have the support of the Republican Party. In the majority of the cases state citizens and officers are most pressing in their desire to have the Federal Government take over these state functions. This is to be deplored for it weakens the sense of initiative and creates a feeling of dependence which is unhealthy and unfortunate for the whole body politic.

There is a real need of restoring the individual and local sense of principles; there is a real need of restoring the individual and local sense of responsibility and self-reliance; there is a real need for the people once more to grasp the fundamental fact that under our system of government they are expected to solve many problems themselves through their municipal and State governments, and to combat the tendency that is all too common to turn to the Federal Government as the easiest and least burdensome method of lightening their own responsibilities.

— 1932 —

We, the representatives of the Republican Party, in convention assembled, renew our pledge to the principles and traditions of our party and dedicate it anew to the service of the nation.

We meet in a period of widespread distress and of an economic depression that has swept the world. The emergency is second only to that of a great war. The human suffering occasioned may well exceed that of a period of actual conflict.

The supremely important problem that challenges our citizens and government alike is to break the back of the depression, to restore the economic life of the nation and to bring encouragement and relief to the thousands of American families that are sorely afflicted.

The people themselves, by their own courage, their own patient and resolute effort in the readjustments of their own affairs, can and will work out the cure. It is our task as a party, by leadership and a wise determination of policy, to assist that recovery.

To that task we pledge all that our party possesses in capacity, leadership, resourcefulness and ability. Republicans, collectively and individually, in nation and State, hereby enlist in a war which will not end until the promise of American life is once more fulfilled.

LEADERSHIP

For nearly three years the world has endured an economic depression of unparalleled extent and severity.

The patience and courage of our people have been severely tested, but their faith in themselves, in their institutions and in their future remains unshaken. When victory comes, as it will, this generation will hand on to the next a great heritage unimpaired.

This will be due in large measure to the quality of the leadership that this country has had during this crisis. We have had in the White House a leader—wise, courageous, patient, understanding, resourceful, ever present at his post of duty, tireless in his efforts and unswervingly faithful to American principles and ideals.

At the outset of the depression, when no man could foresee its depth and extent, the President succeeded in averting much distress by securing agreement between industry and labor to maintain wages and by stimulating programs of private and governmental construction. Throughout the depression unemployment has been limited by the systematic use of part-time employment as a substitute for the general discharge of employees. Wage scales have not been reduced except under compelling necessity. As a result there have been fewer strikes and less social disturbance than during any similar period of hard times.

The suffering and want occasioned by the great drought of 1930 were mitigated by the prompt mobilization of the resources of the Red Cross and of the government. During the trying winters of 1930–31 and 1931–32 a nation-wide organization to relieve distress was brought into being under the leadership of the President. By the spring of 1931 the possibility of a business upturn in the United States was clearly discernible when, suddenly, a train of events was set in motion in Central Europe which moved forward with extraordinary rapidity and violence, threatening the credit structure of the world and eventually dealing a serious blow to this country.

The President foresaw the danger. He sought to avert it by proposing a suspension of intergovernmental debt payments for one year, with the purpose of relieving the pressure at the point of greatest intensity. But the credit machinery of the nations of Central Europe could not withstand the strain, and the forces of disintegration continued to gain momentum until in September Great Britain was forced to depart from the gold standard. This momentous event, followed by a tremendous raid on the dollar, resulted in a series of bank suspensions in this country, and the hoarding of currency on a large scale.

Again the President acted. Under his leadership the National Credit Association came into being. It mobilized our banking resources, saved scores of banks from failure, helped restore confidence and proved of inestimable value in strengthening the credit structure.

By the time the Congress met, the character of our problems was clearer than ever. In his message to Congress the President outlined a constructive and definite program which in the main has been carried out; other portions may yet be carried out.

The Railroad Credit Corporation was created. The capital of the Federal Land Banks was increased. The Reconstruction Finance Corporation came into being and brought protection to millions of depositors, policy holders and others.

Legislation was enacted enlarging the discount facilities of the Federal Reserve System, and, without reducing the legal reserves of the Federal Reserve Banks, releasing a billion dollars of gold, a formidable protection against raids on the dollar and a greatly enlarged basis for an expansion of credit.

An earlier distribution to depositors in closed banks has been brought about through the action of the Reconstruction Finance Corporation. Above all, the national credit has been placed in an impregnable position by provision for adequate revenue and a program of drastic curtailment of expenditures. All of these measures were designed to lay a foundation for the resumption of business and increased employment.

But delay and the constant introduction and consideration of new and unsound measures has kept the country in a state of uncertainty and fear, and offset much of the good otherwise accomplished.

The President has recently supplemented his original program to provide for distress, to stimulate the revival of business and employment, and to improve the agricultural situation, he recommended extending the authority of the Reconstruction Finance Corporation to enable it:

(a) To make loans to political subdivisions of public bodies or private corporations for the purpose of starting construction of income-producing or self-liquidating projects which will at once increase employment;

(b) To make loans upon security of agricultural commodities so as to insure the carrying of normal stocks of those commodities, and thus stabilize their loan value and price levels;

(c) To make loans to the Federal Farm Board to enable extension of loans to farm cooperatives and loans for export of agricultural commodities to quarters unable to purchase them;

(d) To loan up to $300,000,000 to such States as are unable to meet the calls made on them by their citizens for distress relief.

The President's program contemplates an attack on a broad front, with far-reaching objectives, but entailing no danger to the budget. The Democratic program, on the other hand, contemplates a heavy expenditure of public funds, a budget unbalanced on a large scale, with a doubtful attainment of at best a strictly limited objective.

We strongly endorse the President's program.

UNEMPLOYMENT AND RELIEF

True to American traditions and principles of government, the administration has regarded the relief problem as one of State and local responsibility. The work of local agencies, public and private has been coordinated and enlarged on a nation-wide scale under the leadership of the President.

Sudden and unforeseen emergencies such as the drought have been met by the Red Cross and the Government. The United States Public Health Service has been of inestimable benefit to stricken areas.

There has been magnificent response and action to relieve distress by citizens, organizations and agencies, public and private throughout the country.

PUBLIC ECONOMY

Constructive plans for financial stabilization cannot be completely organized until our national, State and municipal governments not only balance their budgets but curtail their current expenses as well to a level which can be steadily and economically maintained for some years to come.

We urge prompt and drastic reduction of public expenditure and resistance to every appropriation not demonstrably necessary to the performance of government, national or local.

The Republican Party established and will continue to uphold the gold standard and will oppose any measure which will undermine the government's credit or impair the integrity of our national currency. Relief by currency inflation is unsound in principle and dishonest in results. The dollar is impregnable in the marts of the world today and must remain so. An ailing body cannot be cured by quack remedies. This is no time to experiment upon the body politic.

BANKS AND THE BANKING SYSTEM

The efficient functioning of our economic machinery depends in no small measure on the aid rendered to trade and industry by our banking system. There is need of revising the banking laws so as to place our banking structure on a sounder basis generally for all concerned, and for the better protection of the depositing public there should be more stringent supervision and broader powers vested in the supervising authorities. We advocate such a revision.

One of the serious problems affecting our banking system has arisen from the practice of organizing separate corporations by the same interests as banks, but participating in operations which the banks themselves are not permitted legally to undertake. We favor requiring reports of and subjecting to thorough and periodic examination all such affiliates of member banks until adequate information has been acquired on the basis of which this problem may definitely be solved in a permanent manner.

INTERNATIONAL CONFERENCE

We favor the participation by the United States in an international conference to consider matters relating to monetary questions, including the position of silver, exchange problems, and commodity prices, and possible cooperative action concerning them.

HOME LOAN DISCOUNT BANK SYSTEM

The present Republican administration has initiated legislation for the creation of a system of Federally supervised home loan discount banks, designed to serve the home owners of all parts of the country and to encourage home ownership by making possible long term credits for homes on more stable and more favorable terms.

There has arisen in the last few years a disturbing trend away from home ownership. We believe that everything should be done by Governmental agencies, national, State and local, to reverse this tendency; to aid home owners by encouraging better methods of home financing; and to relieve the present inequitable tax burden on the home. In the field of national legislation we pledge that the measures creating a home loan discount system will be pressed in Congress until adopted.

AGRICULTURE

Farm distress in America has its root in the enormous expansion of agricultural production during the war, the deflation of 1919, 1920 and the dislocation of mar-

kets after the war. There followed, under Republican administrations, a long record of legislation in aid of the cooperative organization of farmers and in providing farm credit. The position of agriculture was gradually improved. In 1928 the Republican Party pledged further measures in aid of agriculture, principally tariff protection for agricultural products and the creation of a Federal Farm Board "clothed with the necessary power to promote the establishment of a farm marketing system of farmer-owned and controlled stabilization corporations."

Almost the first official act of President Hoover was the calling of a special session of Congress to redeem these party pledges. They have been redeemed.

The 1930 tariff act increased the rates on agricultural products by 30 per cent, upon industrial products only 12 per cent. That act equalized, so far as legislation can do so, the protection afforded the farmer with the protection afforded industry, and prevented a vast flood of cheap wool, grain, livestock, dairy and other products from entering the American market.

By the agricultural marketing act, the Federal Farm Board was created and armed with broad powers and ample funds. The object of that act, as stated in its preamble, was:

"To promote the effective merchandising of agricultural commodities in interstate and foreign commerce so that . . . agriculture will be placed on the basis of economic equality with other industries . . . by encouraging the organization of producers into effective association for their own control . . . and by promoting the establishment of a farm marketing system of producer owned and producer-controlled cooperative associations."

The Federal Farm Board, created by the agricultural marketing act, has been compelled to conduct its operations during a period in which all commodity prices, industrial as well as agricultural, have fallen to disastrous levels. A period of decreasing demand and of national calamities such as drought and flood has intensified the problem of agriculture.

Nevertheless, after only a little more than two years' efforts, the Federal Farm Board has many achievements of merit to its credit. It has increased the membership of the cooperative farms marketing associations to coordinate efforts of the local associations. By cooperation with other Federal agencies, it has made available to farm marketing associations a large value of credit, which, in the emergency, would not have otherwise been available. Larger quantities of farm products have been handled cooperatively than ever before in the history of the cooperative movement. Grain crops have been sold by the farmer through his association directly upon the world market.

Due to the 1930 tariff act and the agricultural marketing act, it can truthfully be stated that the prices received by the American farmer for his wheat, corn, rye, barley, oats, flaxseed, cattle, butter and many other products, cruelly low though they are, are higher than the prices received by the farmers of any competing nation for the same products.

The Republican Party has also aided the American farmer by relief of the sufferers in the drought-stricken areas, through loans for rehabilitation and through road building to provide employment, by the development of the inland waterway system, by the perishable product act, by the strengthening of the extension system, and by the appropriation of $125,000,000 to recapitalize the Federal land banks and enable them to extend time to worthy borrowers.

The Republican Party pledges itself to the principle of assistance to cooperative marketing associations, owned and controlled by the farmers themselves, through the provisions of the agricultural marketing act, which will be promptly amended or modified as experience shows to be necessary to accomplish the objects set forth in the preamble of that act.

TARIFF AND THE MARKETING ACT

The party pledges itself to make such revision of tariff schedules as economic changes require to maintain the parity of protection to agriculture with other industry.

The American farmer is entitled not only to tariff schedules on his products but to protection from substitutes therefor.

We will support any plan which will help to balance production against demand, and thereby raise agricultural prices, provided it is economically sound and administratively workable without burdensome bureaucracy.

The burden of taxation borne by the owners of farm land constitutes one of the major problems of agriculture.

President Hoover has aptly and truly said, "Taxes upon real property are easiest to enforce and are the least flexible of all taxes. The tendency under pressure of need is to continue these taxes unchanged in times of depression, despite the decrease in the owner's income. Decreasing price and decreasing income results in an increasing burden upon property owners . . . which is now becoming almost unbearable. The tax burden upon real estate is wholly out of proportion to that upon other forms of property and income. There is no farm relief more needed today than tax relief."

The time has come for a reconsideration of our tax systems, Federal, State and local, with a view to developing a better coordination, reducing duplication and relieving unjust burdens. The Republican Party pledges itself to this end.

More than all else, we point to the fact that, in the administration of executive departments, and in every plan of the President for the coordination of national effort and for strengthening our financial structure, for expanding credit, for rebuilding the rural credit system and laying the foundations for better prices, the President has insisted upon the interest of the American farmer.

The fundamental problem of American agriculture is the control of production to such volume as will balance supply with demand. In the solution of this problem the cooperative organization of farmers to plan production, and the tariff, to hold the home market for American farmers, are vital elements. A third element equally as vital is the control of the acreage of land under cultivation, as an aid to the efforts of the farmer to balance production.

We favor a national policy of land utilization which looks to national needs, such as the administration has already begun to formulate. Such a policy must foster reorganization of taxing units in areas beset by tax delinquency and divert lands that are submarginal for crop production to other uses. The national welfare plainly can be served by the acquisition of submarginal lands for watershed protection, grazing, forestry, public parks and game preserves. We favor such acquisition.

THE TARIFF

The Republican Party has always been the staunch supporter of the American system of a protective tariff. It believes that the home market, built up under that policy, the greatest and richest market in the world, belongs first to American agriculture, industry and labor. No pretext can justify the surrender of that market to such competition as would destroy our farms, mines and factories, and lower the standard of living which we have established for our workers.

Because many foreign countries have recently abandoned the gold standard, as a result of which the costs of many commodities produced in such countries have, at least for the time being, fallen materially in terms of American currency, adequate tariff protection is today particularly essential to the welfare of the American people.

The Tariff Commission should promptly investigate individual commodities so affected by currency depreciation and report to the President any increase in duties found necessary to equalize domestic with foreign costs of production.

To fix the duties on some thousands of commodities, subject to highly complex conditions, is necessarily a difficult technical task. It is unavoidable that some of the rates established by legislation should, even at the time of their enactment, be too low or too high. Moreover, a subsequent change in costs or other conditions may render obsolete a rate that was before appropriate. The Republican Party has, therefore, long supported the policy of a flexible tariff, giving power to the President, after investigation by an impartial commission and in accordance with prescribed principles, to modify the rates named by the Congress.

We commend the President's veto of the measure, sponsored by Democratic Congressmen, which would have transferred from the President to Congress the authority to put into effect the findings of the Tariff Commission. Approval of the measure would have returned tariff making to politics and destroyed the progress made during ten years of effort to lift it out of log-rolling methods. We pledge the Republican Party to a policy which will retain the gains made and enlarge the present scope of greater progress.

We favor the extension of the general Republican principle of tariff protection to our natural resource industries, including the products of our farms, forests, mines and oil wells, with compensatory duties on the manufactured and refined products thereof.

VETERANS

Our country is honored whenever it bestows relief on those who have faithfully served its flag. The Republican Party, appreciative of this solemn obligation and honor, has made its sentiments evident in Congress.

Increased hospital facilities have been provided, payments in compensation have more than doubled and in the matter of rehabilitations, pensions and insurance, generous provision has been made.

The administration of laws dealing with the relief of the veterans and their dependents has been a difficult task, but every effort has been made to carry service to the veterans and bring about not only a better and generous interpretation of the law but a sympathetic consideration of the many problems of the veteran.

We believe that every veteran incapacitated in any degree by reason of illness should be cared for and compensated, so far as compensation is possible, by a grateful nation, and that the dependents of those who lost their lives in war or whose death since the war in

which service was rendered is traceable to service causes, should be provided for adequately. Legislation should be in accord with this principle.

Disability from causes subsequent and not attributable to war and the support of dependents of deceased veterans whose death is unconnected with war have been to some measure accepted obligations of the nation as a part of the debt due.

A careful study should be made of existing veterans' legislation with a view to elimination of inequalities and injustices and effecting all possible economies, but without departing from our purpose to provide on a sound basis full and adequate relief for our service disabled men, their widows and orphans.

FOREIGN AFFAIRS

Our relations with foreign nations have been carried on by President Hoover with consistency and firmness, but with mutual understanding and peace with all nations. The world has been overwhelmed with economic strain which has provoked extreme nationalism in every quarter, has overturned many governments, stirred the springs of suspicion and distrust and tried the spirit of international cooperation, but we have held to our own course steadily and successfully.

The party will continue to maintain its attitude of protecting our national interests and policies wherever threatened but at the same time promoting common understanding of the varying needs and aspirations of other nations and going forward in harmony with other peoples without alliances or foreign partnerships.

The facilitation of world intercourse, the freeing of commerce from unnecessary impediments, the settlement of international difficulties by conciliation and the methods of law and the elimination of war as a resort of national policy have been and will be our party program.

FRIENDSHIP AND COMMERCE

We believe in and look forward to the steady enlargement of the principles of equality of treatment between nations great and small, the concessions of sovereignty and self-administration to every nation which is capable of carrying on stable government and conducting sound orderly relationships with other peoples, and the cultivation of trade and intercourse on the basis of uniformity of opportunity of all nations.

In pursuance of these principles, which have steadily gained favor in the world, the administration has asked no special favors in commerce, has protested discriminations whenever they arose, and has steadily cemented this procedure by reciprocal treaties guaranteeing equality for trade and residence.

The historic American plan known as the most-favored-nation principle has been our guiding program, and we believe that policy to be the only one consistent with a full development of international trade, the only one suitable for a country having as wide and diverse a commerce as America, and the one most appropriate for us in view of the great variety of our industrial, agricultural and mineral products and the traditions of our people.

Any other plan involves bargains and partnerships with foreign nations, and as a permanent policy is unsuited to America's position.

Conditions on the Pacific

Events in the Far East, involving the employment of arms on a large scale in a controversy between Japan and China, have caused worldwide concern in the past year and sorely tried the bulwarks erected to insure peace and pacific means for the settlement of international disputes.

The controversy has not only threatened the security of the nations bordering the Pacific but has challenged the maintenance of the policy of the open door in China and the administrative and political integrity of that people, programs which upon American initiation were adopted more than a generation ago and secured by international treaty.

The President and his Secretary of State have maintained throughout the controversy a just balance between Japan and China, taking always a firm position to avoid entanglements in the dispute, but consistently upholding the established international policies and the treaty rights and interests of the United States, and never condoning developments that endangered the obligation of treaties or the peace of the world.

Throughout the controversy our government has acted in harmony with the governments represented in the League of Nations, always making it clear that American policy would be determined at home, but always lending a hand in the common interest of peace and order.

In the application of the principles of the Kellogg pact the American Government has taken the lead, following the principle that a breach of the pact or a threat of infringement thereof was a matter of international concern wherever and however brought about.

As a further step the Secretary of State, upon the instruction of the President, adopted the principle later enlarged upon in his letter to the chairman of the Committee on Foreign Relations of the Senate that this government would not recognize any situation, treaty or agreement brought about between Japan and China by force and in defiance of the covenants of the Kellogg pact.

This principle, associated as it is with the name of President Hoover, was later adopted by the Assembly of the League of Nations at Geneva as a rule for the conduct of all those governments. The principle remains today as an important contribution to international law and a significant moral and material barrier to prevent a nation obtaining the fruits of aggressive warfare. It thus opens a new pathway to peace and order.

We favor enactment by Congress of a measure that will authorize our government to call or participate in an international conference in case of any threat of non-fulfillment of Article 2 of the Treaty of Paris (Kellogg–Briand pact).

Latin-America

The policy of the administration has proved to our neighbors of Latin-America that we have no imperialistic ambitions, but that we wish only to promote the welfare and common interest of the independent nations in the western hemisphere.

We have aided Nicaragua in the solution of its troubles by sending a team of observers, at the request of the Nicaraguan Government, to supervise the coming election. After that they will all be returned to the United States.

In Haiti, in accord with the recommendations of the Forbes commission, appointed by the President, the various services of supervision are being rapidly withdrawn, and only those will be retained which are mandatory under the treaties.

Throughout Latin-America the policy of the government of the United States has been and will, under Republican leadership, continue to be one of frank and friendly understanding.

World Court

The acceptance by America of membership in the World Court has been approved by three successive Republican Presidents and we commend this attitude of supporting in this form the settlement of international disputes by the rule of law. America should join its influence and gain a voice in this institution, which would offer us a safer, more judicial and expeditious instrument for the constantly recurring questions between us and other nations than is now available by arbitration.

Reduction of Armament

Conscious that the limitation of armament will contribute to security against war, and that the financial burdens of military preparation have been shamefully increased throughout the world, the Administration under President Hoover has made steady efforts and marked progress in the direction of proportional reduction of arms by agreement with other nations.

Upon his initiative a treaty between the chief naval powers at London in 1930, following the path marked by the Washington Conference of 1922, established a limitation of all types of fighting ships on a proportionate basis as between the three great naval powers. For the first time, a general limitation of a most costly branch of armament was successfully accomplished.

In the Geneva disarmament conference, now in progress, America is an active participant and a representative delegation of our citizens is laboring for progress in a cause to which this country has been an earnest contributor. This policy will be pursued.

Meanwhile maintenance of our navy on the basis of parity with any nation is a fundamental policy to which the Republican Party is committed. While in the interest of necessary government retrenchment, humanity and relief of the taxpayer we shall continue to exert our full influence upon the nations of the world in the cause of reduction of arms, we do not propose to reduce our navy defenses below that of any other nation.

NATIONAL DEFENSE

Armaments are relative and, therefore, flexible and subject to changes as necessity demands. We believe that in time of war every material resource in the nation should bear its proportionate share of the burdens occasioned by the public need and that it is a duty of government to perfect plans in time of peace whereby this objective may be attained in war.

We support the essential principles of the National Defense Act as amended in 1920 and by the Air Corps Act of 1926, and believe that the army of the United States has, through successive reductions accomplished in the last twelve years, reached an irreducible minimum consistent with the self-reliance, self-respect and security of this country.

WAGES AND WORK

We believe in the principle of high wages.

We favor the principle of the shorter working week and shorter work day—with its application to government as well as to private employment, as rapidly and as constructively as conditions will warrant.

We favor legislation designed to stimulate, encourage and assist in home building.

IMMIGRATION

The restriction of immigration is a Republican policy. Our party formulated and enacted into law the quota system, which for the first time has made possible an adequate control of foreign immigration.

Rigid examination of applicants in foreign countries prevented the coming of criminals and other undesirable classes, while other provisions of the law have enabled the President to suspend immigration of foreign wage-earners who otherwise, directly or indirectly, would have increased unemployment among native-born and legally resident foreign-born wage-earners in this country. As a result, immigration is now less than at any time during the past one hundred years.

We favor the continuance and strict enforcement of our present laws upon this subject.

DEPARTMENT OF LABOR

We commend the constructive work of the United States Department of Labor.

LABOR

Collective bargaining by responsible representatives of employers and employees of their own choice, without the interference of anyone, is recognized and approved.

Legislation, such as laws, prohibiting alien contract labor, peonage labor and the shanghaiing of sailors; the eight-hour law on government contracts and in government employment; provision for railroad safety devices, of methods of conciliation, mediation and arbitration in industrial labor disputes, including the adjustment of railroad disputes; the providing of compensation for injury to government employees (the forerunner of Federal workers' compensation acts), and other laws to aid and protect labor are of

Republican origin, and have had and will continue to have the unswerving support of the party.

EMPLOYMENT

We commend the constructive work of the United States Employment Service in the Department of Labor. This service was enlarged and its activities extended through an appropriation made possible by the President with the cooperation of the Congress. It has done high service for the unemployed in the ranks of civil life and in the ranks of the former soldiers of the World War.

FREEDOM OF SPEECH

Freedom of speech, press and assemblages are fundamental principles upon which our form of government rests. These vital principles should be preserved and protected.

PUBLIC UTILITIES

Supervision, regulation and control of interstate public utilities in the interest of the public is an established policy of the Republican Party, to the credit of which stands the creation of the Interstate Commerce Commission, with its authority to assure reasonable transportation rates, sound railway finance and adequate service.

As proof of the progress made by the Republican Party in government control of public utilities, we cite the reorganization under this administration of the Federal Power Commission, with authority to administer the Federal water power act. We urge legislation to authorize this commission to regulate the charges for electric current when transmitted across State lines.

TRANSPORTATION

The promotion of agriculture, commerce and industry requires coordination of transportation by rail, highway, air and water. All should be subjected to appropriate and constructive regulation.

The public will, of course, select the form of transportation best fitted to its particular service, but the terms of competition fixed by public authority should operate without discrimination, so that all common carriers by rail, highway, air and water shall operate under conditions of equality.

Inland Waterways

The Republican Party recognizes that low-cost transportation for bulk commodities will enable industry to develop in the midst of agriculture in the Mississippi Valley, thereby creating a home market for farm products in that section. With a view to aiding agriculture in the middle west the present administration has pushed forward as rapidly as possible the improvement of the Mississippi waterway system, and we favor the continued vigorous prosecution of these works to the end that agriculture and industry in that great area may enjoy the benefits of these improvements at the earliest possible date.

Railroads

The railroads constitute the backbone of our transportation system and perform an essential service for the country. The railroad industry is our largest employer of labor and the greatest consumer of goods. The restoration of their credit and the maintenance of their ability to render adequate service are of paramount importance to the public, to their many thousands of employees and to savings banks, insurance companies and other similar institutions, to which the savings of the people have been entrusted.

Merchant Marine

We should continue to encourage the further development of the merchant marine under American registry and ownership.

Under the present administration the American merchant fleet has been enlarged and strengthened until it now occupies second place among the merchant marines of the world.

By the gradual retirement of the government from the field of ship operations and marked economies in costs, the United States Shipping Board will require no appropriation for the fiscal year 1933 for ship operations.

St. Lawrence Seaway

The Republican Party stands committed to the development of the Great Lakes–St. Lawrence seaway. Under the direction of President Hoover negotiation of a treaty with Canada for this development is now at a favorable point. Recognizing the inestimable benefits which will accrue to the nation from placing the ports of the Great Lakes on an ocean base, the party reaffirms allegiance to this great project and pledges its best efforts to secure its early completion.

Highways

The Federal policy to cooperate with the States in the building of roads was thoroughly established when the Federal highway act of 1921 was adopted under a Republican Congress. Each year since that time appropriations have been made which have greatly increased the economic value of highway transportation and helped to raise the standards and opportunities of rural life.

We pledge our support to the continuation of this policy in accordance with our needs and resources.

CRIME

We favor the enactment of rigid penal laws that will aid the States in stamping out the activities of gangsters, racketeers and kidnappers. We commend the intensive and effective drive made upon these public enemies by President Hoover and pledge our party to further efforts to the same purpose.

NARCOTICS

The Republican Party pledges itself to continue the present relentless warfare against the illicit narcotic traffic and the spread of the curse of drug addiction among our people. This administration has by treaty greatly strengthened our power to deal with this traffic.

CIVIL SERVICE

The merit system has been amply justified since the organization of the Civil Service by the Republican Party. As a part of our governmental system it is now unassailable. We believe it should remain so.

THE EIGHTEENTH AMENDMENT

The Republican Party has always stood and stands today for obedience to and enforcement of the law as the very foundation of orderly government and civilization. There can be no national security otherwise. The duty of the President of the United States and the officers of the law is clear. The law must be enforced as they find it enacted by the people. To these courses of action we pledge our nominees.

The Republican Party is and always has been the party of the Constitution. Nullification by non-observance by individuals or State action threatens the stability of government.

While the Constitution makers sought a high degree of permanence, they foresaw the need of changes and provided for them. Article V limits the proposals of amendments to two methods: (1) Two-thirds of both houses of Congress may propose amendments or (2) on application of the Legislatures of two-thirds of the States a national convention shall be called by Congress to propose amendments. Thereafter ratification must be had in one of two ways: (1) By the Legislatures of three-fourths of the several States or (2) by conventions held in three-fourths of the several States. Congress is given power to determine the mode of ratification.

Referendums without constitutional sanction cannot furnish a decisive answer. Those who propose them innocently are deluded by false hopes; those who propose them knowingly are deceiving the people.

A nation-wide controversy over the Eighteenth Amendment now distracts attention from the constructive solution of many pressing national problems. The principle of national prohibition as embodied in the amendment was supported and opposed by members of both great political parties. It was submitted to the States by members of Congress of different political faith and ratified by State Legislatures of different political majorities. It was not then and is not now a partisan political question.

Members of the Republican Party hold different opinions with respect to it and no public official or member of the party should be pledged or forced to choose between his party affiliations and his honest convictions upon this question.

We do not favor a submission limited to the issue of retention or repeal, for the American nation never in its history has gone backward, and in this case the progress which has been thus far made must be preserved, while the evils must be eliminated.

We therefore believe that the people should have an opportunity to pass upon a proposed amendment the provision of which, while retaining in the Federal Government power to preserve the gains already made in dealing with the evils inherent in the liquor traffic, shall allow the States to deal with the problem as their citizens may determine, but subject always to the power of the Federal Government to protect those States where prohibition may exist and safeguard our citizens everywhere from the return of the saloon and attendant abuses.

Such an amendment should be promptly submitted to the States by Congress, to be acted upon by State conventions called for that sole purpose in accordance with the provisions of Article V of the Constitution and adequately safeguarded so as to be truly representative.

CONSERVATION

The wise use of all natural resources freed from monopolistic control is a Republican policy, initiated by Theodore Roosevelt. The Roosevelt, Coolidge and Hoover reclamation projects bear witness to the continuation of that policy. Forestry and all other conservation activities have been supported and enlarged.

The conservation of oil is a major problem to the industry and the nation. The administration has sought to bring coordination of effort through the States, the producers and the Federal Government. Progress has been made and the effort will continue.

THE NEGRO

For seventy years the Republican Party has been the friend of the American Negro. Vindication of the rights of the Negro citizen to enjoy the full benefits of life, liberty and the pursuit of happiness is traditional in the Republican Party, and our party stands pledged to maintain equal opportunity and rights for Negro citizens. We do not propose to depart from that tradition nor to alter the spirit or letter of that pledge.

HAWAII

We believe that the existing status of self-government which for many years has been enjoyed by the citizens of the Territory of Hawaii should be maintained, and that officials appointed to administer the government should be bona-fide residents of the Territory.

PUERTO RICO

Puerto Rico being a part of the United States and its inhabitants American citizens, we believe that they are entitled to a good-faith recognition of the spirit and purposes of their organic act.

We, therefore, favor the inclusion of the island in all legislative and administrative measures enacted or adopted by Congress or otherwise for the economic benefit of their fellow-citizens of the mainland.

We also believe that, in so far as possible, all officials appointed to administer the affairs of the island government should be qualified by at least five years of bona-fide residence therein.

ALASKA

We favor the policy of giving to the people of Alaska the widest possible territorial self-government and the selection so far as possible of bona-fide residents for positions in that Territory and the placing of its citizens on an equality with those in the several States.

WELFARE WORK AND CHILDREN

The children of our nation, our future citizens, have had the most solicitous thought of our President. Child welfare and protection has been a major effort of this administration. The organization of the White House Conference on Child Health and Protection is regarded as one of the outstanding accomplishments of this administration.

Welfare work in all its phases has had the support of the President and aid of the administration. The work of organized agencies—local, State and Federal—has been advanced and an increased impetus given by that recognition and help. We approve and pledge a continuation of that policy.

INDIANS

We favor the fullest protection of the property rights of the American Indians and the provision for them of adequate educational facilities.

REORGANIZATION OF GOVERNMENT BUREAUS

Efficiency and economy demand reorganization of government bureaus. The problem is nonpartisan and must be so treated if it is to be solved. As a result of years of study and personal contact with conflicting activities and wasteful duplication of effort, the President is particularly fitted to direct measures to correct the situation. We favor legislation by Congress which will give him the required authority.

DEMOCRATIC FAILURE

The vagaries of the present Democratic House of Representatives offer characteristic and appalling proof of the existing incapacity of that party for leadership in a national crisis. Individualism running amuck has displaced party discipline and has trampled under foot party leadership. A bewildered electorate has viewed the spectacle with profound dismay and deep misgivings.

Goaded to desperation by their confessed failure, the party leaders have resorted to "pork barrel" legislation to obtain a unity of action which could not otherwise be achieved. A Republican President stands resolutely between the helpless citizen and the disaster threatened by such measures; and the people, regardless of party, will demand his continued service.

Many times during his useful life has Herbert Hoover responded to such a call, and his response has never disappointed. He will not disappoint us now.

PARTY GOVERNMENT

The delays and differences which recently hampered efforts to obtain legislation imperatively demanded by prevailing critical conditions strikingly illustrate the menace to self-government brought about by the weakening of party ties and party fealty.

Experience has demonstrated that coherent political parties are indispensable agencies for the prompt and effective operation of the functions of our government under the Constitution.

Only by united party action can consistent, well-planned and wholesome legislative programs be enacted. We believe that the majority of the Congressmen elected in the name of a party have the right and duty to determine the general policies of that party requiring Congressional action, and that Congressmen belonging to that party are, in general, bound to adhere to such policies. Any other course inevitably makes of Congress a body of detached delegates which, instead of representing the collective wisdom of our people, become the confused voices of a heterogeneous group of unrelated local prejudices.

We believe that the time has come when Senators and Representatives of the United States should be impressed with the inflexible truth that their first concern should be the welfare of the United States and the well-being of all of its people, and that stubborn pride of individual opinions is not a virtue, but an obstacle to the orderly and successful achievement of the objects of representative government.

Only by cooperation can self-government succeed. Without it election under a party aegis becomes a false pretense.

We earnestly request that Republicans throughout the Union demand that their representatives in the Congress pledge themselves to these principles, to the end that the insidious influences of party disintegration may not undermine the very foundations of the Republic.

CONCLUSION

In contrast with the Republican policies and record, we contrast those of the Democratic as evidenced by the action of the House of Representatives under Democratic leadership and control, which includes:

1. The issuance of fiat currency.
2. Instructions to the Federal Reserve Board and the Secretary of the Treasury to attempt to manipulate commodity prices.
3. The guarantee of bank deposits.
4. The squandering of the public resources and the unbalancing of the budget through pork-barrel appropriations which bear little relation to distress and would tend through delayed business revival to decrease rather than increase employment.

Generally on economic matters we pledge the Republican Party:

1. To maintain unimpaired the national credit.
2. To defend and preserve a sound currency and an honest dollar.
3. To stand steadfastly by the principle of a balanced budget.
4. To devote ourselves fearlessly and unremittingly to the task of eliminating abuses and extravagance and of drastically cutting the cost of government so as to reduce the heavy burden of taxation.
5. To use all available means consistent with sound financial and economic principles to promote an expansion of credit to stimulate business and relieve unemployment.
6. To make a thorough study of the conditions which permitted the credit and the credit machinery of the country to be made available, without adequate check, for wholesale speculation in securities, resulting in ruinous consequences to millions of our citizens and to the national economy, and to correct those conditions so that they shall not recur.

Recognizing that real relief to unemployment must come through a revival of industrial activity and agriculture, to the promotion of which our every effort must be directed, our party in State and nation undertakes to do all in its power that is humanly possible to see that distress is fully relieved in accordance with American principles and traditions.

No successful solution of the problems before the country today can be expected from a Congress and a President separated by partisan lines or opposed in purposes and principles. Responsibility cannot be placed unless a clear mandate is given by returning to Washington a Congress and a Chief Executive united in principles and program.

The return to power of the Republican Party with that mandate is the duty of every voter who believes in the doctrines of the party and its program as herein stated. Nothing else, we believe, will insure the orderly recovery of the country and that return to prosperous days which every American so ardently desires.

The Republican Party faces the future unafraid!

With courage and confidence in ultimate success, we will strive against the forces that strike at our social and economic ideals, our political institutions.

— 1936 —

America is in peril. The welfare of American men and women and the future of our youth are at stake. We dedicate ourselves to the preservation of their political liberty, their individual opportunity and their character as free citizens, which today for the first time are threatened by government itself.

For three long years the New Deal Administration has dishonored American traditions and flagrantly betrayed the pledges upon which the Democratic Party sought and received public support.

The powers of Congress have been usurped by the President.

The integrity and authority of the Supreme Court have been flouted.

The rights and liberties of American citizens have been violated.

Regulated monopoly has displaced free enterprise.

The New Deal Administration constantly seeks to usurp the rights reserved to the States and to the people.

It has insisted on the passage of laws contrary to the Constitution.

It has intimidated witnesses and interfered with the right of petition.

It has dishonored our country by repudiating its most sacred obligations.

It has been guilty of frightful waste and extravagance, using public funds for partisan political purposes.

It has promoted investigations to harass and intimidate American citizens, at the same time denying investigations into its own improper expenditures.

It has created a vast multitude of new offices, filled them with its favorites, set up a centralized bureaucracy, and sent out swarms of inspectors to harass our people.

It has bred fear and hesitation in commerce and industry, thus discouraging new enterprises, preventing employment and prolonging the depression.

It secretly has made tariff agreements with our foreign competitors, flooding our markets with foreign commodities.

It has coerced and intimidated voters by withholding relief to those opposing its tyrannical policies.

It has destroyed the morale of our people and made them dependent upon government.

Appeals to passion and class prejudice have replaced reason and tolerance.

To a free people, these actions are insufferable. This campaign cannot be waged on the traditional differences between the Republican and Democratic parties. The responsibility of this election transcends all previous political divisions. We invite all Americans, irrespective of party, to join it in defense of American institutions.

CONSTITUTIONAL GOVERNMENT AND FREE ENTERPRISE

We pledge ourselves:

1. To maintain the American system of Constitutional and local self-government, and to resist all attempts to impair the authority of the Supreme Court of the United States, the final protector of the rights of our citizens against the arbitrary encroachments of the legislative and executive branches of government. There can be no individual liberty without an independent judiciary.

2. To preserve the American system of free enterprise, private competition, and equality of opportunity, and to seek its constant betterment in the interests of all.

REEMPLOYMENT

The only permanent solution of the unemployment problem is the absorption of the unemployed by industry and agriculture. To that end, we advocate:

Removal of restrictions on production.
Abandonment of all New Deal policies that raise production costs, increase the cost of living, and thereby restrict buying, reduce volume and prevent reemployment.
Encouragement instead of hindrance to legitimate business.

Withdrawal of government from competition with private payrolls.

Elimination of unnecessary and hampering regulations.

Adoption of such other policies as will furnish a chance for individual enterprise, industrial expansion, and the restoration of jobs.

RELIEF

The necessities of life must be provided for the needy, and hope must be restored pending recovery. The administration of relief is a major failing of the New Deal. It has been faithless to those who must deserve our sympathy. To end confusion, partisanship, waste and incompetence, we pledge:

1. The return of responsibility for relief administration to non-political local agencies familiar with community problems.
2. Federal grants-in-aid to the States and territories while the need exists, upon compliance with these conditions: (a) a fair proportion of the total relief burden to be provided from the revenues of States and local governments; (b) all engaged in relief administration to be selected on the basis of merit and fitness; (c) adequate provision to be made for the encouragement of those persons who are trying to become self-supporting.
3. Undertaking of Federal public works only on their merits and separate from the administration of relief.
4. A prompt determination of the facts concerning relief and unemployment.

SECURITY

Real security will be possible only when our productive capacity is sufficient to furnish a decent standard of living for all American families and to provide a surplus for future needs and contingencies. For the attainment of that ultimate objective, we look to the energy, self-reliance and character of our people, and to our system of free enterprise.

Society has an obligation to promote the security of the people, by affording some measure of protection against involuntary unemployment and dependency in old age. The New Deal policies, while purporting to provide social security, have, in fact, endangered it.

We propose a system of old age security, based upon the following principles:

1. We approve a pay-as-you-go policy, which requires of each generation the support of the aged and the determination of what is just and adequate.
2. Every American citizen over sixty-five should receive the supplementary payment necessary to provide a minimum income sufficient to protect him or her from want.
3. Each state and territory, upon complying with simple and general minimum standards, should receive from the federal government a graduated contribution in proportion to its own, up to a fixed maximum.
4. To make this program consistent with sound fiscal policy the Federal revenues for this purpose must be provided from the proceeds of a direct tax widely distributed. All will be benefited and all should contribute.

We propose to encourage adoption by the states and territories of honest and practical measures for meeting the problems of unemployment insurance.

The unemployment insurance and old age annuity sections of the present Social Security Act are unworkable and deny benefits to about two-thirds of our adult population, including professional men and women and all those engaged in agriculture and domestic service, and the self-employed while imposing heavy tax burdens upon all. The so-called reserve fund estimated at forty-seven billion dollars for old age insurance is no reserve at all, because the fund will contain nothing but the Government's promise to pay, while the taxes collected in the guise of premiums will be wasted by the Government in reckless and extravagant political schemes.

LABOR

The welfare of labor rests upon increased production and the prevention of exploitation. We pledge ourselves to:

Protect the right of labor to organize and to bargain collectively through representatives of its own choosing without interference from any source.

Prevent governmental job holders from exercising autocratic powers over labor.

Support the adoption of state laws and interstate compacts to abolish sweatshops and child labor, and to protect women and children with respect to maximum hours, minimum wages and working conditions. We believe that this can be done within the Constitution as it now stands.

The Encyclopedia of the Republican Party

AGRICULTURE

The farm problem is an economic and social, not a partisan problem, and we propose to treat it accordingly. Following the wreck of the restrictive and coercive A.A.A., the New Deal Administration has taken to itself the principles of the Republican policy of soil conservation and land retirement. This action opens the way for a non-political and permanent solution. Such a solution cannot be had under a New Deal Administration which misuses the program to serve partisan ends, to promote scarcity and to limit by coercive methods the farmer's control over his own farm.

Our paramount object is to protect and foster the family type of farm, traditional in American life, and to promote policies which will bring about an adjustment of agriculture to meet the needs of domestic and foreign markets. As an emergency measure, during the agricultural depression, federal benefits payments or grants-in-aid when administered within the means of the Federal government are consistent with a balanced budget.

We propose:

1. To facilitate economical production and increased consumption on a basis of abundance instead of scarcity.
2. A national land-use program, including the acquisition of abandoned and non-productive farm lands by voluntary sale or lease, subject to approval of the legislative and executive branches of the States concerned, and the devotion of such land to appropriate public use, such as watershed protection and flood prevention, reforestation, recreation, and conservation of wild life.
3. That an agricultural policy be pursued for the protection and restoration of the land resources, designed to bring about such a balance between soil-building and soil-depleting crops as will permanently insure productivity, with reasonable benefits to cooperating farmers on family type farms, but so regulated as to eliminate the New Deal's destructive policy towards the dairy and live-stock industries.
4. To extend experimental aid to farmers developing new crops suited to our soil and climate.
5. To promote the industrial use of farm products by applied science.
6. To protect the American farmer against the importation of all live-stock, dairy, and agricultural products, substitutes thereof, and derivatives therefrom, which will depress American farm prices.
7. To provide effective quarantine against imported live-stock, dairy and other farm products from countries which do not impose health and sanitary regulations fully equal to those required of our own producers.
8. To provide for ample farm credit at rates as low as those enjoyed by other industries, including commodity and live-stock loans, and preference in land loans to the farmer acquiring or refinancing a farm as a home.
9. To provide for decentralized, non-partisan control of the Farm Credit Administration and the election by National Farm Loan Associations of at least one-half of each Board of Directors of the Federal Land Banks, and thereby remove these institutions from politics.
10. To provide in the case of agricultural products of which there are exportable surpluses, the payment of reasonable benefits upon the domestically consumed portion of such crops in order to make the tariff effective. These payments are to be limited to the production level of the family type farm.
11. To encourage and further develop cooperative marketing.
12. To furnish Government assistance in disposing of surpluses in foreign trade by bargaining for foreign markets selectively by countries both as to exports and imports. We strenuously oppose so-called reciprocal treaties which trade off the American farmer.
13. To give every reasonable assistance to producers in areas suffering from temporary disaster, so that they may regain and maintain a self-supporting status.

TARIFF

Nearly sixty percent of all imports into the United States are now free of duty. The other forty percent of imports compete directly with the product of our industry. We would keep on the free list all products not grown or produced in the United States in commercial quantities. As to all commodities that commercially compete with our farms, our forests, our mines, our fisheries, our oil wells, our labor and our industries, sufficient protection should be maintained at all times to defend the American farmer and the American wage earner from the destructive competition emanating from the subsidies of foreign governments and the imports from low-wage and depreciated-currency countries.

We will repeal the present Reciprocal Trade Agreement Law. It is futile and dangerous. Its effect on agriculture and industry has been destructive. Its continuation would work to the detriment of the wage earner and the farmer.

We will restore the principle of the flexible tariff in order to meet changing economic conditions here and abroad and broaden by careful definition the powers of the Tariff Commission in order to extend this policy along non-partisan lines.

We will adjust tariffs with a view to promoting international trade, the stabilization of currencies, and the attainment of a proper balance between agriculture and industry.

We condemn the secret negotiations of reciprocal trade treaties without public hearing or legislative approval.

MONOPOLIES

A private monopoly is indefensible and intolerable. It menaces and, if continued, will utterly destroy constitutional government and the liberty of the citizen.

We favor the vigorous enforcement of the criminal laws, as well as the civil laws, against monopolies and trusts and their officials, and we demand the enactment of such additional legislation as is necessary to make it impossible for private monopoly to exist in the United States.

We will employ the full powers of the government to the end that monopoly shall be eliminated and that free enterprise shall be fully restored and maintained.

REGULATION OF BUSINESS

We recognize the existence of a field within which governmental regulation is desirable and salutary. The authority to regulate should be vested in an independent tribunal acting under clear and specific laws establishing definite standards. Their determinations on law and facts should be subject to review by the Courts. We favor Federal regulation, within the Constitution, of the marketing of securities to protect investors. We favor also Federal regulation of the interstate activities of public utilities.

CIVIL SERVICE

Under the New Deal, official authority has been given to inexperienced and incompetent persons. The Civil Service has been sacrificed to create a national political machine. As a result the Federal Government has never presented such a picture of confusion and inefficiency.

We pledge ourselves to the merit system, virtually destroyed by New Deal spoilsmen. It should be restored, improved and extended.

We will provide such conditions as offer an attractive permanent career in government service to young men and women of ability, irrespective of party affiliations.

GOVERNMENT FINANCE

The New Deal Administration has been characterized by shameful waste, and general financial irresponsibility. It has piled deficit upon deficit. It threatens national bankruptcy and the destruction through inflation of insurance policies and savings bank deposits.

We pledge ourselves to:

Stop the folly of uncontrolled spending.
Balance the budget—not by increasing taxes but by cutting expenditures, drastically and immediately.
Revise the Federal tax system and coordinate it with State and local tax systems.
Use the taxing power for raising revenue and not for punitive or political purposes.

MONEY AND BANKING

We advocate a sound currency to be preserved at all hazards.

The first requisite to a sound and stable currency is a balanced budget.

We oppose further devaluation of the dollar.

We will restore to the Congress the authority lodged with it by the Constitution to coin money and regulate the value thereof by repealing all the laws delegating this authority to the Executive.

We will cooperate with other countries toward stabilization of currencies as soon as we can do so with due regard for our National interests and as soon as other nations have sufficient stability to justify such action.

FOREIGN AFFAIRS

We pledge ourselves to promote and maintain peace by all honorable means not leading to foreign alliances or political commitments.

Obedient to the traditional foreign policy of America and to the repeatedly expressed will of the American people, we pledge that America shall not become a member of the League of Nations nor of the World Court nor shall America take on any entangling alliances in foreign affairs.

We shall promote, as the best means of securing and maintaining peace by the pacific settlement of disputes, the great cause of international arbitration through the establishment of free, independent tribunals, which shall determine such disputes in accordance with law, equity and justice.

NATIONAL DEFENSE

We favor an army and navy, including air forces, adequate for our National Defense.

We will cooperate with other nations in the limitation of armaments and control of traffic in arms.

BILL OF RIGHTS

We pledge ourselves to preserve, protect and defend, against all intimidation and threat, freedom of religion, speech, press and radio; and the right of assembly and petition and immunity from unreasonable searches and seizures.

We offer the abiding security of a government of laws as against the autocratic perils of a government of men.

FURTHERMORE

1. We favor the construction by the Federal Government of head-water storage basins to prevent floods, subject to the approval of the legislative and executive branches of the government of the States whose lands are concerned.

2. We favor equal opportunity for our colored citizens. We pledge our protection of their economic status and personal safety. We will do our best to further their employment in the gainfully occupied life of America, particularly in private industry, agriculture, emergency agencies and the Civil Service.

We condemn the present New Deal policies which would regiment and ultimately eliminate the colored citizen from the country's productive life, and make him solely a ward of the Federal Government.

3. To our Indian population we pledge every effort on the part of the national government to ameliorate living conditions for them.

4. We pledge continuation of the Republican policy of adequate compensation and care for veterans disabled in the service of our country and for their widows, orphans and dependents.

5. We shall use every effort to collect the war debt due us from foreign countries, amounting to $12,000,000—one-third of our national debt. No effort has been made by the present administration even to reopen negotiations.

6. We are opposed to legislation which discriminates against women in Federal and State employment.

CONCLUSION

We assume the obligations and duties imposed upon government by modern conditions. We affirm our unalterable conviction that, in the future as in the past, the fate of the nation will depend, not so much on the wisdom and power of government, as on the character and virtue, self-reliance, industry and thrift of the people and on their willingness to meet the responsibilities essential to the preservation of a free society.

Finally, as our party affirmed in its first Platform in 1856: "Believing that the spirit of our institutions as well as the Constitution of our country guarantees liberty of conscience and equality of rights among our citizens we oppose all legislation tending to impair them," and "we invite the affiliation and cooperation of the men of all parties, however differing from us in other respects, in support of the principles herein declared."

The acceptance of the nomination tendered by the Convention carries with it, as a matter of private honor and public faith, an undertaking by each candidate to be true to the principles and program herein set forth.

— 1940 —

INTRODUCTION

The Republican party, in representative Convention assembled, submits to the people of the United States the following declaration of its principles and purposes:

We state our general objectives in the simple and comprehensive words of the Preamble to the Constitution of the United States.

Those objectives as there stated are these:

> "To form a more perfect Union; establish justice; insure domestic tranquility; provide for the common defense, promote the general welfare and secure the blessings of liberty to ourselves and our posterity."

Meeting within the shadow of Independence Hall where those words were written we solemnly reaffirm them as a perfect statement of the ends for which we as a party propose to plan and to labor.

The record of the Roosevelt Administration is a record of failure to attain any one of those essential objectives.

Instead of leading us into More Perfect Union the Administration has deliberately fanned the flames of class hatred.

Instead of the Establishment of Justice the Administration has sought the subjection of the Judiciary to Executive discipline and domination.

Instead of insuring Domestic Tranquility the Administration has made impossible the normal friendly relation between employers and employees and has even succeeded in alienating both the great divisions of Organized Labor.

Instead of Providing for the Common Defense the Administration, notwithstanding the expenditure of billions of our dollars, has left the Nation unprepared to resist foreign attack.

Instead of promoting the General Welfare the Administration has Domesticated the Deficit, Doubled the Debt, Imposed Taxes where they do the greatest economic harm, and used public money for partisan political advantage.

Instead of the Blessings of Liberty the Administration has imposed upon us a Regime of Regimentation which has deprived the individual of his freedom and has made of America a shackled giant.

Wholly ignoring these great objectives, as solemnly declared by the people of the United States, the New Deal Administration has for seven long years whirled in a turmoil of shifting, contradictory and overlapping administrations and policies. Confusion has reigned supreme. The only steady undeviating characteristic has been the relentless expansion of the power of the Federal government over the everyday life of the farmer, the industrial worker and the business man. The emergency demands organization—not confusion. It demands free and intelligent cooperation—not incompetent domination. It demands a change.

The New Deal Administration has failed America.

It has failed by seducing our people to become continuously dependent upon government, thus weakening their morale and quenching the traditional American spirit.

It has failed by viciously attacking our industrial system and sapping its strength and vigor.

It has failed by attempting to send our Congress home during the world's most tragic hour, so that we might be eased into the war by word of deed during the absence of our elected representatives from Washington.

It has failed by disclosing military details of our equipment to foreign powers over protests by the heads of our armed defense.

It has failed by ignoring the lessons of fact concerning modern, mechanized, armed defense.

In these and countless other ways the New Deal Administration has either deliberately deceived the American people or proved itself incompetent to handle the affairs of our government.

The zero hour is here. America must prepare at once to defend our shores, our homes, our lives and our most cherished ideals.

To establish a first line of defense we must place in official positions men of faith who put America first and who are determined that her governmental and economic system be kept unimpaired.

Our national defense must be so strong that no unfriendly power shall ever set foot on American soil. To assure this strength our national economy, the true basis of America's defense, must be free of unwarranted government interference.

Only a strong and sufficiently prepared America can speak words of reassurance and hope to the liberty-loving peoples of the world.

NATIONAL DEFENSE

The Republican Party is firmly opposed to involving this Nation in foreign war.

We are still suffering from the ill effects of the last World War: a war which cost us a twenty-four billion dollar increase in our national debt, billions of uncollectible foreign debts, and the complete upset of our economic system, in addition to the loss of human life and irreparable damage to the health of thousands of our boys.

The present National Administration has already spent for all purposes more than fifty-four billion dollars; has boosted the national debt and current federal taxes to an all-time high; and yet by the President's own admission we are still wholly unprepared to defend our country, its institutions and our individual liberties in a war that threatens to engulf the whole world; and this in spite of the fact that foreign wars have been in progress for two years or more and that military information concerning these wars and the rearmament programs of the warring nations has been at all times available to the National Administration through its diplomatic and other channels.

The Republican party stands for Americanism, preparedness and peace. We accordingly fasten upon the New Deal full responsibility for our unpreparedness and for the consequent danger of involvement in war.

We declare for the prompt, orderly and realistic building of our national defense to the point at which we shall be able not only to defend the United States, its possessions, and essential outposts from foreign attack, but also efficiently to uphold in war the Monroe Doctrine. To this task the Republican party pledges itself when entrusted with national authority. In the meantime we shall support all necessary and proper defense measures proposed by the Administration in its belated effort to make up for lost time; but we deplore explosive utterances by the President directed at other governments which serve to imperil our peace; and we condemn all executive acts and proceedings which might lead to war without the authorization of the Congress of the United States.

Our sympathies have been profoundly stirred by invasion of unoffending countries and by disaster to nations whose ideals most closely resemble our own. We favor the extension to all peoples fighting for liberty, or whose liberty is threatened, of such aid as shall not be in violation of international law or inconsistent with the requirements of our own national defense.

We believe that the spirit which should animate our entire defensive policy is determination to preserve not our material interests merely, but those liberties which are the priceless heritage of America.

RE-EMPLOYMENT

The New Deal's failure to solve the problem of unemployment and revive opportunity for our youth presents a major challenge to representative government and free enterprise. We propose to recreate opportunity for the youth of America and put our idle millions back to work in private industry, business, and agriculture. We propose to eliminate needless administrative restrictions, thus restoring lost motion to the wheels of individual enterprise.

RELIEF

We shall remove waste, discrimination, and politics from relief—through administration by the States with Federal grants-in-aid on a fair and nonpolitical basis, thus giving the man and woman on relief a larger share of the funds appropriated.

SOCIAL SECURITY

We favor the extension of necessary old age benefits on an ear-marked pay-as-you-go basis to the extent that the revenues raised for this purpose will permit. We favor the extension of the unemployment compensation provisions of the Social Security Act, wherever practicable, to those groups and classes not now included. For such groups as may thus be covered we favor a system of unemployment compensation with experience rating provisions, aimed at protecting the worker in the regularity of his employment and providing adequate compensation for reasonable periods when that regularity of employment is interrupted. The administration should be left with the States with a minimum of Federal control.

LABOR RELATIONS

The Republican party has always protected the American worker.

We shall maintain labor's right of free organization and collective bargaining.

We believe that peace and prosperity at home require harmony, teamwork, and understanding in all relations between worker and employer. When differences arise, they should be settled directly and voluntarily across the table.

Recent disclosures respecting the administration of the National Labor Relations Act require that this Act be amended in fairness to employers and all groups of employees so as to provide true freedom for, and orderliness in self-organization and collective bargaining.

AGRICULTURE

A prosperous and stable agriculture is the foundation of our economic structure. Its preservation is a national and nonpolitical social problem not yet solved, despite many attempts. The farmer is entitled to a profit-price for his products. The Republican party will put into effect such governmental policies, temporary and permanent, as will establish and maintain an equitable balance between labor, industry, and agriculture by expanding industrial and business activity, eliminating unemployment, lowering production costs, thereby creating increased consumer buying power for agricultural products.

Until this balance has been attained, we propose to provide benefit payments, based upon a widely applied, constructive soil conservation program free from government-dominated production control, but administered, as far as practicable, by farmers themselves; to restrict the major benefits of these payments to operators of family-type farms; to continue all present benefit payments until our program becomes operative; and to eliminate the present extensive and costly bureaucratic interference.

We shall provide incentive payments, when necessary, to encourage increased production of agricultural commodities, adaptable to our soil and climate, not now produced in sufficient quantities for our home markets, and will stimulate the use and processing of all farm products in industry as raw materials.

We shall promote a cooperative system of adequate farm credit, at lowest interest rates commensurate with the cost of money, supervised by an independent governmental agency, with ultimate farmer ownership and control; farm commodity loans to facilitate orderly marketing and stabilize farm income; the expansion of sound, farmer-owned and farmer-controlled cooperative associations; and the support of educational and extension programs to achieve more efficient production and marketing.

We shall foster Government refinancing, where necessary, of the heavy Federal farm debt load through an agency segregated from cooperative credit.

We shall promote a national land use program for Federal acquisition, without dislocation of local tax returns, of non-productive farm lands by voluntary sale or lease subject to approval of the States concerned; and the disposition of such lands to appropriate public uses including watershed protection and flood prevention, reforestation, recreation, erosion control, and the conservation of wild life.

We advocate a foreign trade policy which will end one-man tariff making, afford effective protection to farm products, regain our export markets, and assure an American price level for the domestically consumed portion of our export crops.

We favor effective quarantine against imported livestock, dairy, and other farm products from countries which do not impose health and sanitary standards equal to our own domestic standards.

We approve the orderly development of reclamation and irrigation, project by project and as conditions justify.

We promise adequate assistance to rural communities suffering disasters from flood, drought, and other natural causes.

We shall promote stabilization of agricultural income through intelligent management of accumulated surpluses, and through the development of outlets by supplying those in need at home and abroad.

TARIFF AND RECIPROCAL TRADE

We are threatened by unfair competition in world markets and by the invasion of our home markets, espe-cially by the products of state-controlled foreign economies.

We believe in tariff protection for Agriculture, Labor, and Industry, as essential to our American standard of living. The measure of the protection shall be determined by scientific methods with due regard to the interest of the consumer.

We shall explore every possibility of reopening the channels of international trade through negotiations so conducted as to produce genuine reciprocity and expand our exports.

We condemn the manner in which the so-called reciprocal trade agreements of the New Deal have been put into effect without adequate hearings, with undue haste, without proper consideration of our domestic producers, and without Congressional approval. These defects we shall correct.

MONEY

The Congress should reclaim its constitutional powers over money, and withdraw the President's arbitrary authority to manipulate the currency, establish bimetallism, issue irredeemable paper money, and debase the gold and silver coinage. We shall repeal the Thomas Inflation Amendment of 1933 and the (foreign) Silver Purchase Act of 1934, and take all possible steps to preserve the value of the Government's huge holdings of gold and re-introduce gold into circulation.

JOBS AND IDLE MONEY

Believing it possible to keep the securities market clean without paralyzing it, we endorse the principle of truth in securities in the Securities Act. To get billions of idle dollars and a multitude of idle men back to work and to promote national defense, these acts should be revised and the policies of the Commission changed to encourage the flow of private capital into industry.

TAXATION

Public spending has trebled under the New Deal, while tax burdens have doubled. Huge taxes are necessary to pay for New Deal waste and for neglected national defense. We shall revise the tax system and remove those practices which impede recovery and shall apply policies which stimulate enterprise. We shall not use the taxing power as an instrument of punishment or to secure objectives not otherwise obtainable under existing law.

PUBLIC CREDIT

With urgent need for adequate defense, the people are burdened by a direct and contingent debt exceeding fifty billion dollars. Twenty-nine billion of this debt has been created by New Deal borrowings during the past seven years. We pledge ourselves to conserve the public credit for all essential purposes by levying taxation sufficient to cover necessary civil expenditure, a substantial part of the defense cost, and the interest and retirement of the national debt.

PUBLIC SPENDING

Millions of men and women still out of work after seven years of excessive spending refute the New Deal theory that "deficit spending" is the way to prosperity and jobs. Our American system of private enterprise, if permitted to go to work, can rapidly increase the wealth, income, and standard of living of all the people. We solemnly pledge that public expenditures, other than those required for full national defense and relief, shall be cut to levels necessary for the essential services of government.

EQUAL RIGHTS

We favor submission by Congress to the States of an amendment to the Constitution providing for equal rights for men and women.

NEGRO

We pledge that our American citizens of Negro descent shall be given a square deal in the economic and political life of this nation. Discrimination in the civil service, the army, navy, and all other branches of the Government must cease. To enjoy the full benefits of life, liberty and pursuit of happiness universal suffrage must be made effective for the Negro citizen. Mob violence shocks the conscience of the nation and legislation to curb this evil should be enacted.

UN-AMERICAN ACTIVITIES

We vigorously condemn the New Deal encouragement of various groups that seek to change the American form of government by means outside the Constitution. We condemn the appointment of members of such un-American groups to high positions of trust in the national Government. The development of the treacherous so called Fifth Column, as it has operated in war-stricken countries, should be a solemn warning to America. We pledge the Republican Party to get rid of such borers from within.

IMMIGRATION

We favor the strict enforcement of all laws controlling the entry of aliens. The activities of undesirable aliens should be investigated and those who seek to change by force and violence the American form of government should be deported.

VETERANS

We pledge adequate compensation and care for veterans disabled in the service of our country, and for their widows, orphans, and dependents.

INDIANS

We pledge an immediate and final settlement of all Indian claims between the Government and the Indian citizenship of the nation.

HAWAII

Hawaii, sharing the nation's obligations equally with the several States, is entitled to the fullest measure of home rule; and to equality with the several States in the rights of her citizens and in the application of our national laws.

PUERTO RICO

Statehood is a logical aspiration of the people of Puerto Rico who were made citizens of the United States by Congress in 1917; legislation affecting Puerto Rico, in so far as feasible, should be in harmony with the realization of that aspiration.

GOVERNMENT AND BUSINESS

We shall encourage a healthy, confident, and growing private enterprise, confine Government activity to essential public services, and regulate business only so as to protect consumer, employee, and investor and without restricting the production of more and better goods at lower prices.

MONOPOLY

Since the passage of the Sherman Anti-trust Act by the Republican party we have consistently fought to preserve free competition with regulation to prevent abuse. New Deal policy fosters Government monopoly, restricts production, and fixes prices. We shall enforce anti-trust legislation without prejudice or discrimination. We condemn the use or threatened use of criminal indictments to obtain through consent decrees objectives not contemplated by law.

GOVERNMENT COMPETITION

We promise to reduce to the minimum Federal competition with business. We pledge ourselves to establish honest accounting and reporting by every agency of the Federal Government and to continue only those enterprises whose maintenance is clearly in the public interest.

FREE SPEECH

The principles of a free press and free speech, as established by the Constitution, should apply to the radio. Federal regulation of radio is necessary in view of the natural limitations of wave lengths, but this gives no excuse for censorship. We oppose the use of licensing to establish arbitrary controls. Licenses should be revocable only when, after public hearings, due cause for cancellation is shown.

SMALL BUSINESS

The New Deal policy of interference and arbitrary regulation has injured all business, but especially small business. We promise to encourage the small business man by removing unnecessary bureaucratic regulation and interference.

STOCK AND COMMODITY EXCHANGES

We favor regulation of stock and commodity exchanges. They should be accorded the fullest measure of self-control consistent with the discharge of their public trust and the prevention of abuse.

INSURANCE

We condemn the New Deal attempts to destroy the confidence of our people in private insurance institutions. We favor continuance of regulation of insurance by the several States.

GOVERNMENT REORGANIZATION

We shall reestablish in the Federal Civil Service a real merit system on a truly competitive basis and extend it to all non-policy-forming positions.

We pledge ourselves to enact legislation standardizing and simplifying quasi-judicial and administrative agencies to insure adequate notice and hearing, impartiality, adherence to the rules of evidence and full judicial review of all questions of law and fact.

Our greatest protection against totalitarian government is the American system of checks and balances. The constitutional distribution of legislative, executive, and judicial functions is essential to the preservation of this system. We pledge ourselves to make it the basis of all our policies affecting the organization and operation of our Republican form of government.

THIRD TERM

To insure against the overthrow of our American system of government we favor an amendment to the Constitution providing that no person shall be President of the United States for more than two terms.

A PLEDGE OF GOOD FAITH

The acceptance of the nominations made by this Convention carries with it, as a matter of private honor and public faith, an undertaking by each candidate to be true to the principles and program herein set forth.

We earnestly urge all patriotic men and women, regardless of former affiliations, to unite with us in the support of our declaration of principles to the end that "government of the people, by the people and for the people shall not perish from this earth."

— 1944 —

INTRODUCTION

The tragedy of the war is upon our country as we meet to consider the problems of government and our people. We take this opportunity to render homage and enduring gratitude to those brave members of our armed forces who have already made the supreme sacrifice, and to those who stand ready to make the same sacrifice that the American course of life may be secure.

Mindful of this solemn hour and humbly conscious of our heavy responsibilities, the Republican Party in convention assembled presents herewith its principles and makes these covenants with the people of our Nation.

THE WAR AND THE PEACE

We pledge prosecution of the war to total victory against our enemies in full cooperation with the United Nations and all-out support of our Armies and the maintenance of our Navy under the competent and trained direction of our General Staff and Office of Naval Operations without civilian interference and with every civilian resource. At the earliest possible time after the cessation of hostilities we will bring home all members of our armed forces who do not have unexpired enlistments and who do not volunteer for further overseas duty.

We declare our relentless aim to win the war against all our enemies: (1) for our own American security and welfare; (2) to make and keep the Axis powers impotent to renew tyranny and attack; (3) for the attainment of peace and freedom based on justice and security.

We shall seek to achieve such aims through organized international cooperation and not by joining a World State.

We favor responsible participation by the United States in post-war cooperative organization among sovereign nations to prevent military aggression and to attain permanent peace with organized justice in a free world.

Such organization should develop effective cooperative means to direct peace forces to prevent or repel military aggression. Pending this, we pledge continuing collaboration with the United Nations to assure these ultimate objectives.

We believe, however, that peace and security do not depend upon the sanction of force alone, but should prevail by virtue of reciprocal interests and spiritual values recognized in these security agreements. The treaties of peace should be just; the nations which are the victims of aggression should be restored to sovereignty and self-government; and the organized cooperation of the nations should concern itself with basic causes of world disorder. It should promote a world opinion to influence the nations to right conduct, develop international law and maintain an international tribunal to deal with justiciable disputes.

We shall seek, in our relations with other nations, conditions calculated to promote world-wide economic stability, not only for the sake of the world, but also to the end that our own people may enjoy a high level of employment in an increasingly prosperous world.

We shall keep the American people informed concerning all agreements with foreign nations. In all of these undertakings we favor the widest consultation of the gallant men and women in our armed forces who have a special right to speak with authority in behalf of the security and liberty for which they fight. We shall sustain the Constitution of the United States in the attainment of our international aims; and pursuant to the Constitution of the United States any treaty or agreement to attain such aims made on behalf of the United States with any other nation or any association of nations, shall be made only by and with the advice and consent of the Senate of the United States provided two-thirds of the Senators present concur.

We shall at all times protect the essential interests and resources of the United States.

Western Hemisphere Relations

We shall develop Pan-American solidarity. The citizens of our neighboring nations in the Western Hemisphere are, like ourselves, Americans. Cooperation with them shall be achieved through mutual agreement and without interference in the internal affairs of any nation. Our policy should be a genuine Good Neighbor policy, commanding their respect, and not one based on the reckless squandering of American funds by overlapping agencies.

Postwar Preparedness

We favor the maintenance of postwar military forces and establishments of ample strength for the successful defense and the safety of the United States, its possessions and outposts, for the maintenance of the Monroe Doctrine, and for meeting any military commitments determined by Congress. We favor the peacetime maintenance and strengthening of the National Guards under State control with the Federal training and equipment as now provided in the National Defense Act.

DOMESTIC POLICY

We shall devote ourselves to re-establishing liberty at home.

We shall adopt a program to put men to work in peace industry as promptly as possible and with special attention to those who have made sacrifice by serving in the armed forces. We shall take government out of competition with private industry and terminate rationing, price fixing and all other emergency powers. We shall promote the fullest stable employment through private enterprise.

The measures we propose shall avoid federalization of government activities, to the end that our States, schools and cities shall be freed; shall avoid delegation of legislative and judicial power to administrative agencies, to the end that the people's representatives in Congress shall be independent and in full control of legislative policy; and shall avoid, subject to war necessities, detailed regulation of farmers, workers, businessmen and consumers, to the end that the individual shall be free. The remedies we propose shall be based on intelligent cooperation between the Federal Government, the States and local government and the initiative of civic groups—not on the panacea of Federal cash.

Four more years of New Deal policy would centralize all power in the President, and would daily subject every act of every citizen to regulation by his henchmen; and this country could remain a Republic only in name. No problem exists which cannot be solved by American methods. We have no need of either the communistic or the fascist technique.

SECURITY

Our goal is to prevent hardship and poverty in America. That goal is attainable by reason of the productive ability of free American labor, industry and agriculture, if supplemented by a system of social security on sound principles.

We pledge our support of the following:

1. Extension of the existing old-age insurance and unemployment insurance systems to all employees not already covered.
2. The return of the public employment-office system to the States at the earliest possible time, financed as before Pearl Harbor.
3. A careful study of Federal–State programs for maternal and child health, dependent children, and assistance to the blind, with a view to strengthening these programs.
4. The continuation of these and other programs relating to health, and the stimulation by Federal aid of State plans to make medical and hospital service available to those in need without disturbing doctor–patient relationships or socializing medicine.

5. The stimulation of State and local plans to provide decent low-cost housing properly financed by the Federal Housing Administration, or otherwise, when such housing cannot be supplied or financed by private sources.

LABOR

The Republican Party is the historical champion of free labor. Under Republican administrations American manufacturing developed, and American workers attained the most progressive standards of living of any workers in the world. Now the Nation owes those workers a debt of gratitude for their magnificent productive effort in support of the war.

Regardless of the professed friendship of the New Deal for the workingman, the fact remains that under the New Deal American economic life is being destroyed.

The New Deal has usurped selfish and partisan control over the functions of Government agencies where labor relationships are concerned. The continued perversion of the Wagner Act by the New Deal menaces the purposes of the law and threatens to destroy collective bargaining completely and permanently.

The long series of Executive orders and bureaucratic decrees reveal a deliberate purpose to substitute for contractual agreements of employers and employees the political edicts of a New Deal bureaucracy. Labor would thus remain organized only for the convenience of the New Deal in enforcing its orders and inflicting its whims upon labor and industry.

We condemn the conversion of administrative boards, ostensibly set up to settle industrial disputes, into instruments for putting into effect the financial and economic theories of the New Deal.

We condemn the freezing of wage rates at arbitrary levels and the binding of men to their jobs as destructive to the advancement of a free people. We condemn the repeal by Executive order of the laws secured by the Republican Party to abolish "contract labor" and peonage. We condemn the gradual but effective creation of a Labor Front as but one of the New Deal's steps toward a totalitarian state.

We pledge an end to political trickery in the administration of labor laws and the handling of labor disputes; and equal benefits on the basis of equality to all labor in the administration of labor controls and laws, regardless of political affiliation.

The Department of Labor has been emasculated by the New Deal. Labor bureaus, agencies and committees are scattered far and wide, in Washington and throughout the country, and have no semblance of systematic or responsible organization. All governmental labor activities must be placed under the direct authority and responsibility of the Secretary of Labor. Such labor bureaus as are not performing a substantial and definite service in the interest of labor must be abolished.

The Secretary of Labor should be a representative of labor. The office of the Secretary of Labor was created under a Republican President, William Howard Taft. It was intended that a representative of labor should occupy this Cabinet office. The present administration is the first to disregard this intention.

The Republican Party accepts the purposes of the National Labor Relations Act, the Wage and Hour Act, the Social Security Act and all other Federal statutes designed to promote and protect the welfare of American working men and women, and we promise a fair and just administration of these laws.

American well-being is indivisible. Any national program which injures the national economy inevitably injures the wage-earner. The American labor movement and the Republican Party, while continuously striving for the betterment of labor's status, reject the communistic and New Deal concept that a single group can benefit while the general economy suffers.

AGRICULTURE

We commend the American farmers, their wives and families for their magnificent job of wartime production and their contribution to the war effort, without which victory could not be assured. They have accomplished this in spite of labor shortages, a bungled and inexcusable machinery program and confused, unreliable, impractical price and production administration.

Abundant production is the best security against inflation. Governmental policies in war and in peace must be practical and efficient with freedom from regimentation by an impractical Washington bureaucracy in order to assure independence of operation and bountiful production, fair and equitable market prices for farm products, and a sound program for conservation and use of our soil and natural resources. Educational progress and the social and economic stability and well-being of the farm family must be a prime national purpose.

For the establishment of such a program we propose the following:

1. A Department of Agriculture under practical and experienced administration, free from regimenta-

tion and confusing government manipulation and control of farm programs.
2. An American market price to the American farmer and the protection of such price by means of support prices, commodity loans, or a combination thereof, together with such other economic means as will assure an income to agriculture that is fair and equitable in comparison with labor, business and industry. We oppose subsidies as a substitute for fair markets.
3. Disposition of surplus war commodities in an orderly manner without destroying markets or continued production and without benefit to speculative profiteers.
4. The control and disposition of future surpluses by means of (a) new uses developed through constant research, (b) vigorous development of foreign markets, (c) efficient domestic distribution to meet all domestic requirements, and (d) arrangements which will enable farmers to make necessary adjustments in production of any given basic crop only if domestic surpluses should become abnormal and exceed manageable proportions.
5. Intensified research to discover new crops, and new and profitable uses for existing crops.
6. Support of the principle of bona fide farmer-owned and farmer-operated cooperatives.
7. Consolidation of all government farm credit under a non-partisan board.
8. To make life more attractive on the family type farm through development of rural roads, sound extension of rural electrification service to the farm and elimination of basic evils of tenancy wherever they exist.
9. Serious study of and search for a sound program of crop insurance with emphasis upon establishing a self-supporting program.
10. A comprehensive program of soil, forest, water and wildlife conservation and development, and sound irrigation projects, administered as far as possible at State and regional levels.

BUSINESS AND INDUSTRY

We give assurance now to restore peacetime industry at the earliest possible time, using every care to avoid discrimination between different sections of the country, (a) by prompt settlement of war contracts with early payment of government obligations and disposal of surplus inventories, and (b) by disposal of surplus government plants, equipment, and supplies, with due consideration to small buyers and with care to prevent monopoly and injury to existing agriculture and industry.

Small business is the basis of American enterprise. It must be preserved. If protected against discrimination and afforded equality of opportunity throughout the Nation, it will become the most potent factor in providing employment. It must also be aided by changes in taxation, by eliminating excessive and repressive regulation and government competition, by the enforcement of laws against monopoly and unfair competition, and by providing simpler and cheaper methods for obtaining venture capital necessary for growth and expansion.

For the protection of the public, and for the security of millions of holders of policies of insurance in mutual and private companies, we insist upon strict and exclusive regulation and supervision of the business of insurance by the several States where local conditions are best known and where local needs can best be met.

We favor the reestablishment and maintenance, as early as military considerations will permit, of a sound and adequate American Merchant Marine under private ownership and management.

The Republican Party pledges itself to foster the development of such strong privately owned air transportation systems and communications systems as will best serve the interests of the American people.

The Federal Government should plan a program for flood control, inland waterways and other economically justifiable public works, and prepare the necessary plans in advance so that construction may proceed rapidly in emergency and in times of reduced employment. We urge that States and local governments pursue the same policy with reference to highways and other public works within their jurisdiction.

TAXATION AND FINANCE

As soon as the war ends the present rates of taxation on individual incomes, on corporations, and on consumption should be reduced as far as is consistent with the payment of the normal expenditures of government in the postwar period. We reject the theory of restoring prosperity through government spending and deficit financing.

We shall eliminate from the budget all wasteful and unnecessary expenditures and exercise the most rigid economy.

It is essential that Federal and State tax structures be more effectively coordinated to the end that State tax sources be not unduly impaired.

We shall maintain the value of the American dollar and regard the payment of government debt as an obligation of honor which prohibits any policy leading to the depreciation of the currency. We shall reduce that debt as soon as economic conditions make such reduction possible.

Control of the currency must be restored to Congress by repeal of existing legislation which gives the President unnecessary powers over our currency.

FOREIGN TRADE

We assure American farmers, livestock producers, workers and industry that we will establish and maintain a fair protective tariff on competitive products so that the standards of living of our people shall not be impaired through the importation of commodities produced abroad by labor or producers functioning with lower standards than our own.

If the postwar world is to be properly organized, a great extension of world trade will be necessary to repair the wastes of war and build an enduring peace. The Republican Party, always remembering that its primary obligation, which must be fulfilled, is to our own workers, our own farmers and our own industry, pledges that it will join with others in leadership in every cooperative effort to remove unnecessary and destructive barriers to international trade. We will always bear in mind that the domestic market is America's greatest market and that tariffs which protect it against foreign competition should be modified only by reciprocal bilateral trade agreements approved by Congress.

RELIEF AND REHABILITATION

We favor the prompt extension of relief and emergency assistance to the peoples of the liberated countries without duplication and conflict between government agencies.

We favor immediate feeding of the starving children of our Allies and friends in the Nazi-dominated countries and we condemn the New Deal administration for its failure, in the face of humanitarian demands, to make any effort to do this.

We favor assistance by direct credits in reasonable amounts to liberated countries to enable them to buy from this country the goods necessary to revive their economic systems.

BUREAUCRACY

The National Administration has become a sprawling, overlapping bureaucracy. It is undermined by executive abuse of power, confused lines of authority, duplication of effort, inadequate fiscal controls, loose personnel practices and an attitude of arrogance previously unknown in our history.

The times cry out for the restoration of harmony in government, for a balance of legislative and executive responsibility, for efficiency and economy, for pruning and abolishing unnecessary agencies and personnel, for effective fiscal and personnel controls, and for an entirely new spirit in our Federal Government.

We pledge an administration wherein the President, acting in harmony with Congress, will effect these necessary reforms and raise the Federal service to a high level of efficiency and competence.

We insist that limitations must be placed upon spending by government corporations of vast sums never appropriated by Congress but made available by directives, and that their accounts should be subject to audit by the General Accounting Office.

TWO-TERM LIMIT FOR PRESIDENT

We favor an amendment to the Constitution providing that no person shall be President of the United States for more than two terms of four years each.

EQUAL RIGHTS

We favor submission by Congress to the States of an amendment to the Constitution providing for equal rights for men and women. We favor job opportunities in the postwar world open to men and women alike without discrimination in rate of pay because of sex.

VETERANS

The Republican Party has always supported suitable measures to reflect the Nation's gratitude and to discharge its duty toward the veterans of all wars.

We approve, have supported and have aided in the enactment of laws which provide for re-employment of veterans of this war in their old positions, for mustering-out-pay, for pensions for widows and orphans of such veterans killed or disabled, for rehabilitation of disabled veterans, for temporary unemployment benefits, for education and vocational training, and for assisting veterans in acquiring homes and farms and in establishing themselves in business.

We shall be diligent in remedying defects in veterans' legislation and shall insist upon efficient administration of all measures for the veteran's benefit.

RACIAL AND RELIGIOUS INTOLERANCE

We unreservedly condemn the injection into American life of appeals to racial or religious prejudice.

We pledge an immediate Congressional inquiry to ascertain the extent to which mistreatment, segregation and discrimination against Negroes who are in our armed forces are impairing morale and efficiency, and the adoption of corrective legislation.

We pledge the establishment by Federal legislation of a permanent Fair Employment Practice Commission.

ANTI-POLL TAX

The payment of any poll tax should not be a condition of voting in Federal elections and we favor immediate submission of a Constitutional amendment for its abolition.

ANTI-LYNCHING

We favor legislation against lynching and pledge our sincere efforts in behalf of its early enactment.

INDIANS

We pledge an immediate, just and final settlement of all Indian claims between the Government and the Indian citizenship of the Nation. We will take politics out of the administration of Indian affairs.

PROBLEMS OF THE WEST

We favor a comprehensive program of reclamation projects for our arid and semi-arid States, with recognition and full protection of the rights and interests of those States in the use and control of water for present and future irrigation and other beneficial consumptive uses.

We favor (a) exclusion from this country of livestock and fresh and chilled meat from countries harboring foot and mouth disease or Rinderpest; (b) full protection of our fisheries whether by domestic regulation or treaties; (c) consistent with military needs, the prompt return to private ownership of lands acquired for war purposes; (d) withdrawal or acquisition of lands for establishment of national parks, monuments, and wildlife refuges, only after due regard to local problems and under closer controls to be established by the Congress; (e) restoration of the long-established public land policy which provides opportunity of ownership by citizens to promote the highest land use; (f) full development of our forests on the basis of cropping and sustained yield; cooperation with private owners for conservation and fire protection; (g) the prompt reopening of mines which can be operated by miners and workers not subject to military service and which have been closed by bureaucratic denial of labor or material; (h) adequate stockpiling of war minerals and metals for possible future emergencies; (i) continuance, for tax purposes, of adequate depletion allowances on oil, gas and minerals; (j) administration of laws relating to oil and gas on the public domain to encourage exploratory operations to meet the public need; (k) continuance of present Federal laws on mining claims on the public domain, good faith administration thereof, and we state our opposition to the plans of the Secretary of the Interior to substitute a leasing system; and (1) larger representation in the Federal Government of men and women especially familiar with Western problems.

HAWAII

Hawaii, which shares the Nation's obligations equally with the several States, is entitled to the fullest measure of home rule looking toward statehood; and to equality with the several States in the rights of her citizens and in the application of all our national laws.

ALASKA

Alaska is entitled to the fullest measure of home rule looking toward statehood.

PUERTO RICO

Statehood is a logical aspiration of the people of Puerto Rico who were made citizens of the United States by Congress in 1917; legislation affecting Puerto Rico, in so far as feasible, should be in harmony with the realization of that aspiration.

PALESTINE

In order to give refuge to millions of distressed Jewish men, women and children driven from their homes by tyranny, we call for the opening of Palestine to their unrestricted immigration and land ownership, so that in accordance with the full intent and purpose of the Balfour Declaration of 1917 and the Resolution of a Republican Congress in 1922, Palestine may be constituted as a free and democratic Commonwealth. We condemn the failure of the President to insist that the mandatory of Palestine carry out the provision of the Balfour Declaration and of the mandate while he pretends to support them.

FREE PRESS AND RADIO

In times like these, when whole peoples have found themselves shackled by governments which denied the truth, or, worse, dealt in half-truths or withheld the facts from the public, it is imperative to the maintenance of a free America that the press and radio be free and that full and complete information be available to Americans. There must be no censorship except to the extent required by war necessity.

We insistently condemn any tendency to regard the press or the radio as instruments of the Administration and the use of government publicity agencies for partisan ends. We need a new radio law which will define, in clear and unmistakable language, the role of the Federal Communications Commission.

All channels of news must be kept open with equality of access to information at the source. If agreement can be achieved with foreign nations to establish the same principles, it will be a valuable contribution to future peace.

Vital facts must not be withheld.

We want no more Pearl Harbor reports.

GOOD FAITH

The acceptance of the nominations made by this Convention carries with it, as a matter of private honor and public faith, an undertaking by each candidate to be true to the principles and program herein set forth.

CONCLUSION

The essential question at trial in this nation is whether men can organize together in a highly industrialized society, succeed, and still be free. That is the essential question at trial throughout the world today.

In this time of confusion and strife, when moral values are being crushed on every side, we pledge ourselves to uphold with all our strength the Bill of Rights, the Constitution and the law of the land. We so pledge ourselves that the American tradition may stand forever as the beacon light of civilization.

— 1948 —

I

DECLARATION OF PRINCIPLES

To establish and maintain peace, to build a country in which every citizen can earn a good living with the promise of real progress for himself and his family, and to uphold as a beacon light for mankind everywhere, the inspiring American tradition of liberty, opportunity and justice for all—that is the Republican platform.

To this end we propose as a guide to definite action the following principles:

Maximum voluntary cooperation between citizens and minimum dependence on law; never, however, declining courageous recourse to law if necessary.

Our competitive system furnishes vital opportunity for youth and for all enterprising citizens; it makes possible the productive power which is the unique weapon of our national defense; and is the mainspring of material well-being and political freedom.

Government, as the servant of such a system, should take all needed steps to strengthen and develop public health, to promote scientific research, to provide security for the aged, and to promote a stable economy so that men and women need not fear the loss of their jobs or the threat of economic hardships through no fault of their own.

The rights and obligations of workers are commensurate with the rights and obligations of employers and they are interdependent; these rights should be protected against coercion and exploitation from whatever quarter and with due regard for the general welfare of all.

The soil as our basic natural resource must be conserved with increased effectiveness; and farm prices should be supported on a just basis.

Development of the priceless national heritage which is in our West is vital to our nation.

Administration of government must be economical and effective.

Faulty governmental policies share an important responsibility for the present cruelly high cost of living. We pledge prompt action to correct these policies. There must be decent living at decent wages.

Our common defense must be strengthened and unified.

Our foreign policy is dedicated to preserving a free America in a free world of free men. This calls for strengthening the United Nations and primary recognition of America's self-interest in the liberty of other peoples. Prudently conserving our own resources, we shall cooperate on a self-help basis with other peace-loving nations.

Constant and effective insistence on the personal dignity of the individual, and his right to complete justice without regard to race, creed or color, is a fundamental American principle.

We aim always to unite and to strengthen; never to weaken or divide. In such a brotherhood will we Americans get results. Thus we will overcome all obstacles.

II

In the past eighteen months, the Republican Congress, in the face of frequent obstruction from the Executive Branch, made a record of solid achievement. Here are some of the accomplishments of this Republican Congress:

The long trend of extravagant and ill-advised Executive action reversed;

the budget balanced;

taxes reduced;

limitation of Presidential tenure to two terms passed;

assistance to veterans, their widows and orphans provided;

assistance to agriculture and business enacted; elimination of the poll tax as a requisite to soldier voting;

a sensible reform of the labor law, protecting all rights of Labor while safeguarding the entire community against those breakdowns in essential industries which endanger the health and livelihood of all;

a long-range farm program enacted; unification of the armed services launched; a military manpower law enacted; the United Nations fostered; a haven for displaced persons provided; the most far-reaching measures in history adopted to aid the recovery of the free world on a basis of self-help and with prudent regard for our own resources;

and, finally, the development of intelligent plans and party teamwork for the day when the American people entrust the Executive as well as the Legislative branch of our National Government to the Republican Party.

We shall waste few words on the tragic lack of foresight and general inadequacy of those now in charge of the Executive Branch of the National Government; they have lost the confidence of citizens of all parties.

III

Present cruelly high prices are due in large part to the fact that the government has not effectively used the powers it possesses to combat inflation, but has deliberately encouraged higher prices.

We pledge an attack upon the basic causes of inflation, including the following measures:

progressive reduction of the cost of government through elimination of waste;

stimulation of production as the surest way to lower prices;

fiscal policies to provide increased incentives for production and thrift;

a sound currency;

reduction of the public debt.

We pledge further, that in the management of our National Government, we shall achieve

the abolition of overlapping, duplication, extravagance, and excessive centralization;

the more efficient assignment of functions within the government;

and the rooting out of Communism wherever found.

These things are fundamental.

IV

We must, however, do more.

The Constitution gives us the affirmative mandate "to establish justice."

In Lincoln's words: The dogmas of the quiet past are inadequate to the stormy present. The occasion is piled high with difficulty and we must rise with the occasion. As our case is new, so we must think anew and act anew.

The tragic experience of Europe tells us that popular government disappears when it is ineffective and no longer can translate into action the aims and the aspirations of the people.

Therefore, in domestic affairs, we propose:

The maintenance of armed services for air, land and sea, to a degree which will insure our national security; and the achievement of effective unity in the Department of National Defense so as to insure maximum economy in money and manpower, and maximum effectiveness in case of war. We favor sustained effective action to procure sufficient manpower for the services, recognizing the American principle that every citizen has an obligation of service to his country.

An adequate privately operated merchant marine, the continued development of our harbors and waterways, and the expansion of privately operated air transportation and communication systems.

The maintenance of Federal finances in a healthy condition and continuation of the efforts so well started by the Republican Congress to reduce the enormous burden of taxation in order to provide incentives for the creation of new industries and new jobs, and to bring relief from inflation. We favor intelligent integration of Federal–State taxing and spending policies designed to eliminate wasteful duplication, and in order that the State and local governments may be able to assume their separate responsibilities, the Federal government shall as soon as practicable withdraw or reduce those taxes which can be best administered by local governments, with particular consideration of excise and inheritance taxes; and we favor restoring to America a working federalism.

Small business, the bulwark of American enterprise, must be encouraged through aggressive antimonopoly action, elimination of unnecessary controls, protection against discrimination, correction of tax abuses, and limitation of competition by governmental organizations.

Collective bargaining is an obligation as well as a right, applying equally to workers and employers; and the fundamental right to strike is subordinate only to paramount considerations of public health and safety. Government's chief function in this field is to promote good will, encourage cooperation, and where resort is had to intervention, to be impartial, preventing violence and requiring obedience to all law by all parties involved. We pledge continuing study to improve labor-management legislation in the light of experience and changing conditions.

There must be a long-term program in the interest of agriculture and the consumer which should include: An accelerated program of sounder soil conservation; effective protection of reasonable market prices through flexible support prices, commodity loans, marketing agreements, together with such other means as may be necessary, and the development of sound farm credit; encouragement of family-size farms; intensified research to discover new crops, new uses for existing crops, and control of hoof and mouth and other animal diseases and crop pests; support of the principle of bona fide farmer-owned and farmer-operated cooperatives, and sound rural electrification.

We favor progressive development of the Nation's water resources for navigation, flood control and power, with immediate action in critical areas.

We favor conservation of all our natural resources and believe that conservation and stockpiling of strategic and critical raw materials is indispensable to the security of the United States.

We urge the full development of our forests on the basis of cropping and sustained yield with cooperation of States and private owners for conservation and fire protection.

We favor a comprehensive reclamation program for arid and semi-arid areas with full protection of the rights and interests of the States in the use and control of water for irrigation, power development incidental thereto and other beneficial uses; withdrawal or acquisition of lands for public purposes only by Act of Congress and after due consideration of local problems; development of processes for the extraction of oil and other substances from oil shale and coal; adequate representation of the West in the National Administration.

Recognizing the Nation's solemn obligation to all veterans, we propose a realistic and adequate adjustment of benefits on a cost-of-living basis for service-connected disabled veterans and their dependents, and for the widows, orphans and dependents of veterans who died in the service of their country. All disabled veterans should have ample opportunity for suitable, self-sustaining employment. We demand good-faith compliance with veterans preference in Federal service with simplification and codification of the hundreds of piecemeal Federal laws affecting veterans, and efficient and businesslike management of the Veterans Administration. We pledge the highest possible standards of medical care and hospitalization.

Housing can best be supplied and financed by private enterprise; but government can and should encourage the building of better homes at less cost. We recommend Federal aid to the States for local slum clearance and low-rental housing programs only where there is a need that cannot be met either by private enterprise or by the States and localities.

Consistent with the vigorous existence of our competitive economy, we urge: extension of the Federal Old Age and Survivors' Insurance program and increase of the benefits to a more realistic level; strengthening of Federal–State programs designed to provide more adequate hospital facilities, to improve methods of treatment for the mentally ill, to advance maternal and child health and generally to foster a healthy America.

Lynching or any other form of mob violence anywhere is a disgrace to any civilized state, and we favor the prompt enactment of legislation to end this infamy.

One of the basic principles of this Republic is the equality of all individuals in their right to life, liberty, and the pursuit of happiness. This principle is enunciated in the Declaration of Independence and embodied in the Constitution of the United States; it was vindicated on the field of battle and became the cornerstone of this Republic. This right of equal opportunity to work and to advance in life should never be limited in any individual because of race, religion, color, or country of origin. We favor the enactment and just enforcement of such Federal legislation as may be necessary to maintain this right at all times in every part of this Republic.

We favor the abolition of the poll tax as a requisite to voting.

We are opposed to the idea of racial segregation in the armed services of the United States.

V

We pledge a vigorous enforcement of existing laws against Communists and enactment of such new legislation as may be necessary to expose the treasonable activities of Communists and defeat their objective of establishing here a godless dictatorship controlled from abroad.

We favor a revision of the procedure for the election of the President and Vice President which will more exactly reflect the popular vote.

We recommend to Congress the submission of a constitutional amendment providing equal rights for women.

We favor equal pay for equal work regardless of sex.

We propose a well-paid and efficient Federal career service.

We favor the elimination of unnecessary Federal bureaus and of the duplication of the functions of necessary governmental agencies.

We favor equality of educational opportunity for all and the promotion of education and educational facilities.

We favor restoration to the States of their historic rights to the tide and submerged lands, tributary waters, lakes, and streams.

We favor eventual statehood for Hawaii, Alaska and Puerto Rico. We urge development of Alaskan land communications and natural resources. We favor self-government for the residents of the nation's capital.

VI

We dedicate our foreign policy to the preservation of a free America in a free world of free men. With neither malice nor desire for conquest, we shall strive for a just peace with all nations.

America is deeply interested in the stability, security and liberty of other independent peoples. Within the prudent limits of our own economic welfare, we shall cooperate, on a basis of self-help and mutual aid, to assist other peace-loving nations to restore their economic independence and the human rights and fundamental freedoms for which we fought two wars and upon which dependable peace must build. We shall insist on businesslike and efficient administration of all foreign aid.

We welcome and encourage the sturdy progress toward unity in Western Europe.

We shall erect our foreign policy on the basis of friendly firmness which welcomes cooperation but spurns appeasement. We shall pursue a consistent foreign policy which invites steadiness and reliance and which thus avoids the misunderstandings from which wars result. We shall protect the future against the errors of the Democrat Administration, which has too often lacked clarity, competence or consistency in our vital international relationships and has too often abandoned justice.

We believe in collective security against aggression and in behalf of justice and freedom. We shall support the United Nations as the world's best hope in this direction, striving to strengthen it and promote its effective evolution and use. The United Nations should progressively establish international law, be freed of any veto in the peaceful settlement of international disputes, and be provided with the armed forces contemplated by the Charter. We particularly commend the value of regional arrangements as prescribed by the Charter; and we cite the Western Hemispheric Defense Pact as a useful model.

We shall nourish these Pan-American agreements in the new spirit of cooperation which implements the Monroe Doctrine.

We welcome Israel into the family of nations and take pride in the fact that the Republican Party was the first to call for the establishment of a free and independent Jewish Commonwealth. The vacillation of the Democrat Administration on this question has undermined the prestige of the United Nations. Subject to the letter and spirit of the United Nations Charter, we pledge to Israel full recognition, with its boundaries as sanctioned by the United Nations and aid in developing its economy.

We will foster and cherish our historic policy of friendship with China and assert our deep interest in the maintenance of its integrity and freedom.

We shall seek to restore autonomy and self-sufficiency as rapidly as possible in our post-war occupied areas, guarding always against any rebirth of aggression.

We shall relentlessly pursue our aims for the universal limitation and control of arms and implements of war on a basis of reliable disciplines against bad faith.

At all times safeguarding our own industry and agriculture, and under efficient administrative procedures for the legitimate consideration of domestic needs, we shall support the system of reciprocal trade and encourage international commerce.

We pledge that under a Republican Administration all foreign commitments shall be made public and subject to constitutional ratification. We shall say what we mean and mean what we say. In all of these things we shall primarily consult the national security and welfare of our own United States. In all of these things we shall welcome the world's cooperation. But in none of these things shall we surrender our ideals or our free institutions.

We are proud of the part that Republicans have taken in those limited areas of foreign policy in which they have been permitted to participate. We shall invite the Minority Party to join us under the next Republican Administration in stopping partisan politics at the water's edge.

We faithfully dedicate ourselves to peace with justice.

VII

Guided by these principles, with continuing faith in Almighty God; united in the spirit of brotherhood; and using to the full the skills, resources and blessings of liberty with which we are endowed; we, the American people, will courageously advance to meet the challenge of the future.

— 1952 —
PREAMBLE

We maintain that man was not born to be ruled, but that he consented to be governed; and that the reasons that moved him thereto are few and simple. He has voluntarily submitted to government because, only by the establishment of just laws, and the power to enforce those laws, can an orderly life be maintained, full and equal opportunity for all be established, and the blessings of liberty be perpetuated.

We hold that government, and those entrusted with government, should set a high example of honesty, of justice, and unselfish devotion to the public good; that they should labor to maintain tranquility at home and peace and friendship with all the nations of the earth.

We assert that during the last twenty years, leaders of the Government of the United States under successive Democrat Administrations, and especially under this present Administration, have failed to perform these several basic duties; but, on the contrary, that they have evaded them, flouted them, and by a long succession of vicious acts, so undermined the foundations of our Republic as to threaten its existence.

We charge that they have arrogantly deprived our citizens of precious liberties by seizing powers never granted.

We charge that they work unceasingly to achieve their goal of national socialism.

We charge that they have disrupted internal tranquility by fostering class strife for venal political purposes.

We charge that they have choked opportunity and hampered progress by unnecessary and crushing taxation.

They claim prosperity but the appearance of economic health is created by war expenditures, waste and extravagance, planned emergencies, and war crises. They have debauched our money by cutting in half the purchasing power of our dollar.

We charge that they have weakened local self-government which is the cornerstone of the freedom of men.

We charge that they have shielded traitors to the Nation in high places, and that they have created enemies abroad where we should have friends.

We charge that they have violated our liberties by turning loose upon the country a swarm of arrogant bureaucrats and their agents who meddle intolerably in the lives and occupations of our citizens.

We charge that there has been corruption in high places, and that examples of dishonesty and dishonor have shamed the moral standards of the American people.

We charge that they have plunged us into war in Korea without the consent of our citizens through their authorized representatives in the Congress, and have carried on that war without will to victory.

FOREIGN POLICY

The present Administration, in seven years, has squandered the unprecedented power and prestige which were ours at the close of World War II.

In that time, more than 500 million non-Russian people of fifteen different countries have been absorbed into the power sphere of Communist Russia, which proceeds confidently with its plan for world conquest.

We charge that the leaders of the Administration in power lost the peace so dearly earned by World War II.

The moral incentives and hopes for a better world which sustained us through World War II were betrayed, and this has given Communist Russia a mil-

itary and propaganda initiative which, if unstayed, will destroy us.

They abandoned friendly nations such as Latvia, Lithuania, Estonia, Poland and Czechoslovakia to fend for themselves against the Communist aggression which soon swallowed them.

They required the National Government of China to surrender Manchuria with its strategic ports and railroads to the control of Communist Russia. They urged that Communists be taken into the Chinese Government and its military forces. And finally they denied the military aid that had been authorized by Congress and which was crucially needed if China were to be saved. Thus they substituted on our Pacific flank a murderous enemy for an ally and friend.

In all these respects they flouted our peace assuring pledges such as the Atlantic Charter, and did so in favor of despots, who, it was well-known, consider that murder, terror, slavery, concentration camps and the ruthless and brutal denial of human rights are legitimate means to their desired ends.

Tehran, Yalta and Potsdam were the scenes of those tragic blunders with others to follow. The leaders of the Administration in power acted without the knowledge or consent of Congress or of the American people. They traded our overwhelming victory for a new enemy and for new oppression and new wars which were quick to come.

In South Korea, they withdrew our occupation troops in the face of the aggressive, poised for action, Communist military strength on its northern border. They publicly announced that Korea was of no concern to us. Then when the Communist forces acted to take what seemed to have been invited, they committed this Nation to fight back under the most unfavorable conditions. Already the tragic cost is over 110,000 American casualties.

With foresight, the Korean War would never have happened.

In going back into Korea, they evoked the patriotic and sacrificial support of the American people. But by their hampering orders they produced stalemates and ignominious bartering with our enemies, and they offer no hope of victory.

They have effectively ignored many vital areas in the face of a global threat requiring balanced handling.

The people of the other American Republics are resentful of our neglect of their legitimate aspirations and cooperative friendship.

The Middle East and much of Africa seethe with anti-American sentiment.

The peoples of the Far East who are not under Communist control find it difficult to sustain their morale as they contrast Russia's "Asia First" policy with the "Asia Last" policy of those in control of the Administration now in power.

Here at home they have exhibited corruption, incompetence, and disloyalty in public office to such an extent that the very concept of free representative government has been tarnished and has lost its idealistic appeal to those elsewhere who are confronted with the propaganda of Communism.

They profess to be following a defensive policy of "containment" of Russian Communism which has not contained it.

Those in control of the Party in power have, in reality, no foreign policy. They swing erratically from timid appeasement to reckless bluster.

The good in our foreign policies has been accomplished with Republican cooperation, such as the organization of the United Nations, the establishment of the trusteeship principle for dependent peoples, the making of peace with Japan and Germany, and the building of more solid security in Europe. But in the main the Republican Party has been ignored and its participation has not been invited.

The American people must now decide whether to continue in office the Party which has presided over this disastrous reversal of our fortunes and the loss of our hopes for a peaceful world.

The Republican Party offers, in contrast to the performances of those now running our foreign affairs, policies and actions based on enlightened self-interest and animated by courage, self-respect, steadfastness, vision, purpose, competence and spiritual faith.

The supreme goal of our foreign policy will be an honorable and just peace. We dedicate ourselves to wage peace and to win it.

We shall eliminate from the State Department and from every Federal office, all, wherever they may be found, who share responsibility for the needless predicaments and perils in which we find ourselves. We shall also sever from the public payroll the hordes of loafers, incompetents and unnecessary employees who clutter the administration of our foreign affairs. The confusions, overlappings, and extravagance of our agencies abroad hold us up to the ridicule of peoples whose friendship we seek.

We shall substitute a compact and efficient organization where men of proven loyalty and ability shall have responsibility for reaching our objectives. They will reflect a dynamic initiative. Thus we can win the support and confidence which go only to those who demonstrate a capacity to define and get results.

We shall have positive peace-building objectives wherever this will serve the enlightened self-interest of our Nation and help to frustrate the enemy's designs against us.

In Western Europe we shall use our friendly influence, without meddling or imperialistic attitudes, for ending the political and economic divisions which alone prevent that vital area from being strong on its own right.

We shall encourage and aid the development of collective security forces there, as elsewhere, so as to end the Soviet power to intimidate directly or by satellites, and so that the free governments will be sturdy to resist Communist inroads.

In the balanced consideration of our problems, we shall end neglect of the Far East which Stalin has long identified as the road to victory over the West. We shall make it clear that we have no intention to sacrifice the East to gain time for the West.

The Republican Party has consistently advocated a national home for the Jewish people since a Republican Congress declared its support of that objective thirty years ago.

In providing a sanctuary for Jewish people rendered homeless by persecution, the State of Israel appeals to our deepest humanitarian instincts. We shall continue our friendly interest in this constructive and inspiring undertaking.

We shall put our influence at the service of peace between Israel and the Arab States, and we shall cooperate to bring economic and social stability to that area.

Our ties with the sister Republics of the Americas will be strengthened.

The Government of the United States, under Republican leadership, will repudiate all commitments contained in secret understandings such as those of Yalta which aid Communist enslavements. It will be made clear, on the highest authority of the President and the Congress, that United States policy, as one of its peaceful purposes, looks happily forward to the genuine independence of those captive peoples.

We shall again make liberty into a beacon light of hope that will penetrate the dark places. That program will give the Voice of America a real function. It will mark the end of the negative, futile and immoral policy of "containment" which abandons countless human beings to a despotism and godless terrorism, which in turn enables the rulers to forge the captives into a weapon for our destruction.

We shall support the United Nations and loyally help it to become what it was designed to be, a place where differences would be harmonized by honest discussion and a means for collective security under agreed concepts of justice. We shall seek real meaning and value for our regional security treaties, which implies that all parties shall contribute their loyal support and fair shares.

We shall see to it that no treaty or agreement with other countries deprives our citizens of the rights guaranteed them by the Federal Constitution.

We shall always measure our foreign commitments so that they can be borne without endangering the economic health or sound finances of the United States. Stalin said that "the moment for the decisive blow" would be when the free nations were isolated and were in a state of "practical bankruptcy." We shall not allow ourselves to be isolated and economically strangled, and we shall not let ourselves go bankrupt.

Sums available by this test, if competently used, will be more effective than vastly larger sums incompetently spent for vague and endless purposes. We shall not try to buy good will. We shall earn it by sound, constructive, self-respecting policies and actions.

We favor international exchange of students and of agricultural and industrial techniques, and programs for improvement of public health.

We favor the expansion of mutually advantageous world trade. To further this objective we shall press for the elimination of discriminatory practices against our exports, such as preferential tariffs, monetary license restrictions, and other arbitrary devices. Our reciprocal trade agreements will be entered into and maintained on a basis of true reciprocity, and to safeguard our domestic enterprises and the payrolls of our workers against unfair import competition.

The policies we espouse will revive the contagious, liberating influences which are inherent in freedom. They will inevitably set up strains and stresses within the captive world which will make the rulers impotent to continue in their monstrous ways and mark the beginning of their end.

Our Nation will become again the dynamic, moral and spiritual force which was the despair of despots and the hope of the oppressed. As we resume this historic role, we ourselves will come to enjoy again the reality of peace, security and solvency, not the shabby and fleeting counterfeit which is the gift of the Administration in power.

NATIONAL DEFENSE

On the prudent assumption that Communist Russia may not accommodate our own disgracefully lagging program for preparedness, we should develop with utmost speed a force-in-being, as distinguished from paper plans, of such power as to deter sudden attack or promptly and decisively defeat it. This defense against sudden attack requires the quickest possible development of appropriate and completely adequate air power and the simultaneous readiness of coordinated air, land, and sea forces, with all necessary installations, bases, supplies and munitions, including atomic energy weapons in abundance.

Generally, we shall see to it that our military services are adequately supported in all ways required, including manpower, to perform their appropriate tasks in relation to the defense of this country and to meet our treaty obligations.

We shall coordinate our military policy with our foreign policy, always seeking universal limitation and control of armaments on a dependable basis.

We shall review our entire preparedness program and we shall strip it clean of waste, lack of coordination, inertia, and conflict between the services. We shall see that our fighting men in Korea, or wherever they may be, shall not lack the best of weapons or other supplies or services needed for their welfare.

COMMUNISM

By the Administration's appeasement of Communism at home and abroad it has permitted Communists and their fellow travelers to serve in many key agencies and to infiltrate our American life. When such infiltrations became notorious through the revelations of Republicans in Congress, the Executive Department stubbornly refused to deal with it openly and vigorously. It raised the false cry of "red herring" and took other measures to block and discredit investigations. It denied files and information to Congress. It set up boards of its own to keep information secret and to deal lightly with security risks and persons of doubtful loyalty. It only undertook prosecution of the most notorious Communists after public opinion forced action.

The result of these policies is the needless sacrifice of American lives, a crushing cost in dollars for defense, possession by Russia of the atomic bomb, the lowering of the Iron Curtain, and the present threats to world peace. Our people have been mired in fear and distrust and employees of integrity in the Government service have been cruelly maligned by the Administration's tolerance of people of doubtful loyalty.

There are no Communists in the Republican Party. We have always recognized Communism to be a world conspiracy against freedom and religion. We never compromised with Communism and we have fought to expose it and to eliminate it in government and American life.

A Republican President will appoint only persons of unquestioned loyalty. We will overhaul loyalty and security programs. In achieving these purposes a Republican President will cooperate with Congress. We pledge close coordination of our intelligence services for protecting our security. We pledge fair but vigorous enforcement of laws to safeguard our country from subversion and disloyalty. By such policies we will keep the country secure and restore the confidence of the American people in the integrity of our Government.

SMALL BUSINESS IN A FREE ECONOMY

For twenty years the Administration has praised free enterprise while actually wrecking it. Here a little, there a little, year by year, it has sought to curb, regulate, harass, restrain and punish. There is scarcely a phase of our economic and social life today in which government does not attempt to interfere.

Such hostility deadens initiative, discourages invention and experiment, and weakens the self-reliance indispensable to the Nation's vitality. Merciless taxation, the senseless use of controls and ceaseless effort to enter business on its own account, have led the present Government to unrestrained waste and extravagance in spending, irresponsibility in decision and corruption in administration.

The anti-monopoly laws have been employed, not to preserve and foster competition, but to further the political ambitions of the men in power. Wage and price controls have been utilized, not to maintain economic stability, but to reward the friends and punish the enemies of leaders of the Party win power.

Neither small nor large business can flourish in such an atmosphere. The Republican Party will end this hostility to initiative and enterprise.

We will aid small business in every practicable way. We shall remove tax abuses and injurious price and wage controls. Efforts to plan and regulate every phase of small business activity will cease. We will maintain special committees in Congress whose chief function will be to study and review continuously the problems of small business and recommend legislation for their relief. We shall always be mindful of the importance of keeping open the channels of opportunity for young men and women.

We will follow principles of equal enforcement of the anti-monopoly and unfair competition statutes and will simplify their administration to assist the businessman who, in good faith, seeks to remain in compliance. At the same time, we shall relentlessly protect our free enterprise system against monopolistic and unfair trade practices.

We will oppose Federal rent control except in those areas where the expansion of defense production has been accompanied by critical housing shortages. With local cooperation we shall aid slum clearance.

Our goal is a balanced budget, a reduced national debt, an economical administration and a cut in taxes. We believe in combating inflation by encouraging full production of goods and food, and not through a program of restrictions.

TAXATION AND MONETARY POLICY

Only with a sound economy can we properly carry out both the domestic and foreign policies which we advocate. The wanton extravagance and inflationary policies of the Administration in power have cut the value of the dollar in half and imposed the most confiscatory taxes in our history. These policies have made the effective control of Government expenditures impossible. If this Administration is left in power, it will further cheapen the dollar, rob the wage earner, impoverish the farmer and reduce the true value of the savings, pensions, insurance and investments of millions of our people. Further inflation must be and can be prevented. Sound tax and monetary policies are essential to this end. We advocate the following tax policies:

1. Reduction of expenditures by the elimination of waste and extravagance so that the budget will be balanced and a general tax reduction can be made.
2. An immediate study directed toward reallocation of fields of taxation between the Federal, State, and municipal governments so as to allow greater fiscal freedom to the States and municipalities, thus minimizing double taxation and enabling the various divisions of government to meet their obligations more efficiently.
3. A thorough revision and codification of the present hodgepodge of internal revenue laws.
4. Administration of the tax laws free from politics, favoritism and corruption.

We advocate the following monetary policies:

1. A Federal Reserve System exercising its functions in the money and credit system without pressure for political purposes from the Treasury or the White House.

2. To restore a domestic economy, and to use our influence for a world economy, of such stability as will permit the realization of our aim of a dollar on a fully convertible gold basis.

AGRICULTURE

The good earth is the food storehouse for future generations. The tending of the soil is a sacred responsibility. Development of a sound farm program is a high national duty. Any program that will benefit farmers must serve the national welfare. A prosperous agriculture with free and independent farmers is fundamental to the national interest.

We charge the present Administration with seeking to destroy the farmers' freedom. We denounce the Administration's use of tax money and a multitude of Federal agencies to put agriculture under partisan political dictation and to make the farmer dependent upon government. We condemn the Brannan plan which aims to control the farmer and to socialize agriculture. We brand as unscrupulous the Administration's manipulation of grain markets during the 1948 election campaign to drive down farm prices, and its deliberate misrepresentation of laws passed by the Republican 80th Congress, which authorized a long-range farm price support program and provided for adequate grain storage.

We condemn as a fraud on both the farmer and the consumer the Brannan plan scheme to pay direct subsidies from the Federal Treasury in lieu of prices to producers.

We favor a farm program aimed at full parity prices for all farm products in the market place. Our program includes commodity loans on nonperishable products, "on-the-farm" storage, sufficient farm credit, and voluntary self-supporting crop insurance. Where government action on perishable commodities is desirable, we recommend locally controlled marketing agreements and other voluntary methods.

Our program should include commodity loans on all nonperishable products supported at the level necessary to maintain a balanced production. We do not believe in restrictions on the American farmers' ability to produce.

We favor a bipartisan Federal Agricultural Commission with power to review the policies and administration of our farm programs and to make recommendations.

We support a constructive and expanded soil conservation program administered through locally controlled local districts, and which shall emphasize that

payments shall be made for practices and improvements of a permanent nature.

Flood control programs should include the application of sound land use, reforestation and water-management practices on each watershed. These, so far as feasible, should be decentralized and locally controlled to insure economy and effective soil conservation.

We recommend expanded agricultural research and education to promote new crops and uses, new markets, both foreign and domestic, more trustworthy crop and market estimates, a realistic trade program for agriculture aimed at restoring foreign markets and developing new outlets at home. Promotion of world trade must be on a basis of fair competition.

We support the principle of bona fide farmer-owned, farmer-operated co-operatives and urge the further development of rural electrification and communication, with federally assisted production of power and facilities for distribution when these are not adequately available through private enterprise at fair rates.

We insist that an adequate supply of manpower on the farm is necessary to our national welfare and security and shall do those things required to assure this result.

The Republican Party will create conditions providing for farm prosperity and stability, safeguarding the farmers' independence and opening opportunities for young people in rural communities. We will do those things necessary to simplify and make efficient the operation of the Department of Agriculture, prevent that Department from assuming powers neither intended nor delegated by Congress, and to place the administration of farm programs as closely as possible to State and local levels.

LABOR

The Republican Party believes that regular and adequate income for the employee together with uninterrupted production of goods and services, through the medium of private enterprise, are essential to a sound national economy. This can only be obtained in an era of industrial peace.

With the above in mind, we favor the retention of the Taft–Hartley Act, which guarantees:

To the Working Man:

The right to quit his job at any time.
The right to take part in legal union activities.
The right to remain in his union so long as he pays his dues.

The right to protection against unfair practices by either employer or union officials.

The right to political activity of his own choice and freedom to contribute thereto.

The right to a job without first joining a union.

The right to a secret ballot in any election concerned with his livelihood.

The right to protection from personal financial responsibility in damage cases against his union.

To the Labor Union:

The right to establish "union shop" contracts by agreement with management.

The right to strike.

The right to free collective bargaining.

The right to protection from rival unions during the life of union contracts.

The right to assurance from employers that they will bargain only with certified unions as a protection against unfair labor practices.

We urge the adoption of such amendments to the Taft–Hartley Act as time and experience show to be desirable, and which further protect the rights of labor, management and the public.

We condemn the President's seizure of plants and industries to force the settlement of labor disputes by claims of inherent Constitutional powers.

NATURAL RESOURCES

We vigorously advocate a full and orderly program for the development and conservation of our natural resources.

We deplore the policies of the present Administration which allow special premiums to foreign producers of minerals available in the United States. We favor reasonable depletion allowances, defense procurement policies, synthetic fuels research, and public land policies, including good-faith administration of our mining laws, which will encourage exploration and development of our mineral resources consistent with our growing industrial and defense needs.

We favor stockpiling of strategic and critical raw materials and special premium incentives for their domestic exploration and development.

We favor restoration to the States of their rights to all lands and resources beneath navigable inland and offshore waters within their historic boundaries.

We favor protection of our fisheries by domestic regulation and treaties, including safeguards against unfair foreign competition.

PUBLIC WORKS AND WATER POLICY

The Federal Government and State and local governments should continuously plan programs of economically justifiable public works.

We favor continuous and comprehensive investigations of our water resources and orderly execution of programs approved by the Congress. Authorized water projects should go forward progressively with immediate priority for those with defense significance, those in critical flood and water-shortage areas, and those substantially completed.

We favor greater local participation in the operation and control, and eventual local ownership, of federally sponsored, reimbursable water projects.

We vigorously oppose the efforts of this national Administration, in California and elsewhere, to undermine State control over water use, to acquire paramount water rights without just compensation, and to establish all-powerful Federal socialistic valley authorities.

PUBLIC LANDS

We favor restoration of the traditional Republican public land policy, which provided opportunity for ownership by citizens to promote the highest land use. We favor an impartial study of tax-free Federal lands and their uses to determine their effects on the economic and fiscal structures of our States and local communities.

In the management of public lands and forests we pledge the elimination of arbitrary bureaucratic practices. To this end we favor legislation to define the rights and privileges of grazers and other cooperators and users, to provide the protection of independent judicial review against administrative invasions of those rights and privileges, and to protect the public against corrupt or monopolistic exploitation and bureaucratic favoritism.

VETERANS

We believe that active duty in the Armed Forces of the United States of America during a state of war or national emergency constitutes a special service to our Nation, and entitles those who have so served to aid and compensation in return for this service.

Consequently we propose:

That the aid and compensation given to veterans of previous wars be extended to veterans of the Korean conflict;

That compensation be fairly and adequately adjusted to meet changes in the cost of living;

That aid be given to veterans, particularly disabled veterans, to obtain suitable employment, by providing training and education, and through strict compliance with veterans' preference laws in Federal service;

That the Veterans' Administration be maintained as a single, independent agency in full charge of all veterans' affairs, and that the Veterans' Administration manage veterans' affairs in an efficient, prompt and uniform manner;

That the Veterans' Administration should be equipped to provide and maintain medical and hospital care of the highest possible standard for all eligible veterans.

SOCIAL SECURITY

Inflation has already cut in half the purchasing power of the retirement and other benefits under the Federal Old Age and Survivors Insurance system. Sixty million persons are covered under the system and four and one-half million are now receiving benefits.

The best assurance of preserving the benefits for which the worker has paid is to stop the inflation which causes the tragic loss of purchasing power, and that we propose to do.

We favor amendment of the Old Age and Survivors Insurance system to provide coverage for those justly entitled to it but who are now excluded.

We shall work to achieve a simple, more effective and more economical method of administration.

We shall make a thorough study of universal pay-as-we-go pension plans.

HEALTH

We recognize that the health of our people as well as their proper medical care cannot be maintained if subject to Federal bureaucratic dictation. There should be a division of responsibility between government, the physician, the voluntary hospital, and voluntary health insurance. We are opposed to Federal compulsory health insurance with its crushing cost, wasteful inefficiency, bureaucratic dead weight, and debased standards of medical care. We shall support those health activities by government which stimulate the development of adequate hospital services without Federal interference in local administration. We favor support of scientific research. We pledge our continuous encouragement of improved methods of assuring health protection.

EDUCATION

The tradition of popular education, tax-supported and free to all, is strong with our people. The responsibility for sustaining this system of popular education has always rested upon the local communities and the States. We subscribe fully to this principle.

CIVIL RIGHTS

We condemn bigots who inject class, racial and religious prejudice into public and political matters. Bigotry is un-American and a danger to the Republic.

We deplore the duplicity and insincerity of the Party in power in racial and religious matters. Although they have been in office as a Majority Party for many years, they have not kept nor do they intend to keep their promises.

The Republican Party will not mislead, exploit or attempt to confuse minority groups for political purposes. All American citizens are entitled to full, impartial enforcement of Federal laws relating to their civil rights.

We believe that it is the primary responsibility of each State to order and control its own domestic institutions, and this power, reserved to the States, is essential to the maintenance of our Federal Republic. However, we believe that the Federal Government should take supplemental action within its constitutional jurisdiction to oppose discrimination against race, religion or national origin.

We will prove our good faith by:

Appointing qualified persons, without distinction of race, religion or national origin, to responsible positions in the Government.

Federal action toward the elimination of lynching.

Federal action toward the elimination of poll taxes as a prerequisite to voting.

Appropriate action to end segregation in the District of Columbia.

Enacting Federal legislation to further just and equitable treatment in the area of discriminatory employment practices. Federal action should not duplicate State efforts to end such practices; should not set up another huge bureaucracy.

CENSORSHIP

We pledge not to infringe by censorship or gag order the right of a free people to know what their Government is doing.

EQUAL RIGHTS

We recommend to Congress the submission of a Constitutional Amendment providing equal rights for men and women.

We favor legislation assuring equal pay for equal work regardless of sex.

STATEHOOD

We favor immediate statehood for Hawaii.

We favor statehood for Alaska under an equitable enabling act.

We favor eventual statehood for Puerto Rico.

DISTRICT OF COLUMBIA

We favor self-government and national suffrage for the residents of the Nation's Capital.

INDIAN AFFAIRS

All Indians are citizens of the United States and no longer should be denied full enjoyment of their rights of citizenship.

We shall eliminate the existing shameful waste by the Bureau of Indian Affairs which has obstructed the accomplishment of our national responsibility for improving the condition of our Indian friends. We pledge to undertake programs to provide the Indians with equal opportunities for education, health protection and economic development.

The next Republican Administration will welcome the advice and counsel of Indian leaders in selecting the Indian Commissioner.

CIVIL SERVICE

We condemn the flagrant violations of the Civil Service merit system by the Party in power.

We favor a personnel program for the Federal career service comparable to the best practices of progressive private employers. Federal employees shall be selected under a strengthened and extended merit system. Civil servants of ability and integrity shall receive proper recognition, with merit the sole test for promotion.

DELIVERY OF MAIL

We pledge a more efficient and frequent mail delivery service.

GOVERNMENT REORGANIZATION

We pledge a thorough reorganization of the Federal Government in accordance with the principles set forth in the report of the Hoover Commission which was established by the Republican 80th Congress.

We denounce the duplicity in submitting to Congress for approval, reorganization plans which were represented as being in accordance with the principles of the Hoover Commission recommendations, but which in fact were actually intended to further partisan political purposes of the Administration in power.

CORRUPTION

The present Administration's sordid record of corruption has shocked and sickened the American people. Its leaders have forfeited any right to public faith by the way they transact the Federal Government's business.

Fraud, bribery, graft, favoritism and influence peddling have come to light. Immorality and unethical behavior have been found to exist among some who were entrusted with high policy-making positions, and there have been disclosures of close alliances between the present Government and underworld characters.

Republicans exposed cases of questionable and criminal conduct and relentlessly pressed for full investigations into the cancer-like spread of corruption in the Administration. These investigations uncovered a double standard in Federal tax law enforcement—lenient treatment to political favorites including even some gangsters and crooks, but harassment and threats of prosecution for many honest taxpayers over minor discrepancies.

Besides tax fixes and scandals in the Internal Revenue Bureau, investigations have disclosed links between high officials and crime, favoritism and influence in the RFC, profiteering in grain, sale of postmasterships, tanker-ship deals in the Maritime Commission, ballot-box stuffing and thievery, and bribes and pay-offs in contract awards by officials in agencies exercising extraordinary powers and disbursing billions of dollars.

Under public pressure, the Administration took reluctant steps to clean house. But it was so eager to cover up and block more revelations that its clean-up drive launched with much fanfare ended in a farce.

The Republican Party pledges to put an end to corruption, to oust the crooks and grafters, to administer tax laws fairly and impartially, and to restore honest government to the people.

REPUBLICAN 80TH CONGRESS

The Republican Party does not rest its case upon promises alone. We have a record of performance which was grossly defamed by the Party in power. The Republican 80th Congress launched the program to stop Communism; unified the armed services; authorized a 70-group Air Force which the President blocked; enacted a national service law; balanced the budget; accumulated an eight-billion-dollar surplus; reduced taxes, with 70 per cent of the tax savings to those with incomes under $5,000; freed 7,400,000 wage earners in the lower brackets from having to pay any further income tax at all, allowed married couples to divide their incomes for tax purposes, and granted an additional $600 exemption to those over 65 years of age and to the blind; enacted the Taft–Hartley law for equitable labor–management relations; passed the first long-range agriculture program; increased social security benefits; and carried out every single pledge they made to the voters in the 1946 election.

CONCLUSION

Upon this statement of truths and this pledge of performance, the Republican Party stands confident that it expresses the hopes of the citizens of America and certain that it points out with integrity a road upon which free men may march into a new and better day in which shall be fulfilled the decent aspirations of our people for peace, for solvency and for the fulfillment of our best welfare, under the guidance of Divine Providence.

— 1956 —

DECLARATION OF FAITH

America's trust is in the merciful providence of God, in whose image every man is created . . . the source of every man's dignity and freedom.

In this trust our Republic was founded. We give devoted homage to the Founding Fathers. They not only proclaimed that the freedom and rights of men came from the Creator and not from the State, but they provided safeguards to those freedoms.

Our Government was created by the people for all the people, and it must serve no less a purpose.

The Republican Party was formed 100 years ago to preserve the Nation's devotion to these ideals.

On its Centennial, the Republican Party again calls to the minds of all Americans the great truth first spoken by Abraham Lincoln: "The legitimate object of Government is to do for a community of people whatever they need to have done but cannot do at all, or cannot so well do, for themselves in their separate and individual capacities. But in all that people can individually do as well for themselves, Government ought not to interfere."

Our great President Dwight D. Eisenhower has counseled us further: "In all those things which deal with people, be liberal, be human. In all those things which deal with people's money, or their economy, or their form of government, be conservative."

While jealously guarding the free institutions and preserving the principles upon which our Republic was founded and has flourished, the purpose of the Republican Party is to establish and maintain a peaceful world and build at home a dynamic prosperity in which every citizen fairly shares.

We shall ever build anew, that our children and their children, without distinction because of race, creed or color, may know the blessings of our free land.

We believe that basic to governmental integrity are unimpeachable ethical standards and irreproachable personal conduct by all people in government. We shall continue our insistence on honesty as an indispensable requirement of public service. We shall continue to root out corruption whenever and wherever it appears.

We are proud of and shall continue our farreaching and sound advances in matters of basic human needs—expansion of social security, broadened coverage in unemployment insurance, improved housing, and better health protection for all our people. We are determined that our Government remain warmly responsive to the urgent social and economic problems of our people.

To these beliefs we commit ourselves as we present this record and declare our goals for the future.

Nearly four years ago when the people of this Nation entrusted their Government to President Eisenhower and the Republican Party, we were locked in a costly and stalemated war. Now we have an honorable peace, which has stopped the bitter toll in casualties and resources, ended depressing wartime restraints, curbed the runaway inflation and unleashed the boundless energy of our people to forge forward on the road to progress.

In four years we have achieved the highest economic level with the most widely shared benefits that the world has ever seen. We of the Republican Party have fostered this prosperity and are dedicated to its expansion and to the preservation of the climate in which it has thrived.

We are proud of our part in bringing into a position

of unique authority in the world one who symbolizes, as can no other man, the hopes of all peoples for peace, liberty and justice. One leader in the world today towers above all others and inspires the trust, admiration, confidence and good will of all the peoples of every nation—Dwight D. Eisenhower. Under his leadership, the Republican Administration has carried out foreign policies which have enabled our people to enjoy in peace the blessings of liberty. We shall continue to work unceasingly for a just and enduring peace in a world freed of tyranny.

Every honorable means at our command has been exercised to alleviate the grievances and causes of armed conflict among nations. The advance of Communism and its enslavement of people has been checked, and, at key points, thrown back. Austria, Iran and Guatemala have been liberated from Kremlin control. Forces of freedom are at work in the nations still enslaved by Communist imperialism.

We firmly believe in the right of peoples everywhere to determine their form of government, their leaders, their destiny, in peace. Where needed, in order to promote peace and freedom throughout the world, we shall within the prudent limits of our resources, assist friendly countries in their determined efforts to strengthen their economies.

We hold high hopes for useful service to mankind in the power of the atom. We shall generously assist the International Atomic Energy Agency, now evolving from President Eisenhower's "Atoms for Peace" proposal, in an effort to find ways to dedicate man's genius not to his death, but to his life.

We maintain that no treaty or international agreement can deprive any of our citizens of Constitutional rights. We shall see to it that no treaty or agreement with other countries attempts to deprive our citizens of the rights guaranteed them by the Federal Constitution.

President Eisenhower has given the world bold proposals for mutual arms reduction and protection against aggression through flying sentinels in an "open sky."

We support this and his further offer of United States participation in an international fund for economic development financed from the savings brought by true disarmament. We approve his determined resistance to disarmament without effective inspection.

We work and pray for the day when the domination of any people from any source will have ended, and when there will be liberation and true freedom for the hundreds of millions of individuals now held in subjugation. We shall continue to dedicate our best efforts to this lofty purpose.

We shall continue vigorously to support the United Nations.

We shall continue to oppose the seating of Communist China in the United Nations.

We shall maintain our powerful military strength as a deterrent to aggression and as a guardian of the peace. We shall maintain it ready, balanced and technologically advanced for these objectives only.

Good times in America have reached a breadth and depth never before known by any nation. Moreover, it is a prosperity of a nation at peace, not at war. We shall continue to encourage the good business and sound employee relationships which have made possible for the first time in our history a productive capacity of more than $400 billion a year. Nearly 67 million people have full-time jobs, with real wages and personal income at record highs.

The farmers of America are at last able to look to the future with a confidence based on expanding peacetime markets instead of on politically contrived formulas foredoomed to fail except in a wartime economy. The objective is to insure that agriculture shares fairly and fully in our record prosperity without needless Federal meddlings and domination.

Restoration of integrity in Government has been an essential element to the achievement of our unparalleled good times. We will faithfully preserve the sound financial management which already has reduced annual spending $14 billion below the budgets planned by our Democratic predecessors and made possible in 1954 a $7.4 billion tax cut, the largest one-year tax reduction in history.

We will ever fight the demoralizing influence of inflation as a national way of life. We are proud to have fulfilled our 1952 pledge to halt the skyrocketing cost of living that in the previous 13 years had cut the value of the dollar by half, and robbed millions of the full value of their wages, savings, insurance, pensions and social security.

We have balanced the budget. We believe and will continue to prove that thrift, prudence and a sensible respect for living within income applies as surely to the management of our Government's budget as it does to the family budget.

We hold that the major world issue today is whether Government shall be the servant or the master of men. We hold that the Bill of Rights is the sacred foundation of personal liberty. That men are created equal needs no affirmation, but they must have equality of opportunity and protection of their civil rights under the law.

We hold that the strict division of powers and the primary responsibility of State and local governments must be maintained, and that the centralization of powers in the national Government leads to expansion of the mastery of our lives.

We hold that the protection of the freedom of men requires that budgets be balanced, waste in Government eliminated, and taxes reduced.

In these and all other areas of proper Government concern, we pledge our best thought and whole energy to a continuation of our prized peace, prosperity and progress.

For our guidance in fulfilling this responsibility, President Eisenhower has given us a statement of principles that is neither partisan nor prejudiced, but warmly American:

The individual is of supreme importance.
The spirit of our people is the strength of our Nation.
America does not prosper unless all Americans prosper.
Government must have a heart as well as a head.
Courage in principle, cooperation in practice make freedom positive.
To stay free, we must stay strong.
Under God, we espouse the cause of freedom and justice and peace for all peoples.

Embracing these guides to positive, constructive action, and in their rich spirit, we ask the support of the American people for the election of a Republican Congress and the re-election of the Nation's devoted and dedicated leader Dwight D. Eisenhower.

DECLARATION OF DETERMINATION

In the interest of complete public understanding, elaboration of Republican aspirations and achievements is desirable in the areas of broadest public concern.

DYNAMIC ECONOMY–FREE LABOR

Taxation and Fiscal Policy

The Republican Party takes pride in calling attention to the outstanding fiscal achievements of the Eisenhower Administration, several of which are mentioned in the foreword to these resolutions.

In order to progress further in correcting the unfortunate results of unwise financial management during 20 years of Democrat Administrations, we pledge to pursue the following objectives:

Further reductions in Government spending as recommended in the Hoover Commission Report,

without weakening the support of a superior defense program or depreciating the quality of essential services of Government to our people.
Continued balancing of the budget, to assure the financial strength of the country which is so vital to the struggle of the free world in its battle against Communism; and to maintain the purchasing power of a sound dollar, and the value of savings, pensions and insurance.
Gradual reduction of the national debt.

Then, insofar as consistent with a balanced budget, we pledge to work toward these additional objectives:

Further reductions in taxes with particular consideration for low- and middle-income families.
Initiation of a sound policy of tax reductions which will encourage small independent businesses to modernize and progress.
Continual study of additional ways to correct inequities in the effect of various taxes.
Consistent with the Republican Administration's accomplishment in stemming the inflation—which under five Democrat Administrations had cut the value of the dollar in half, and so had robbed the wage earner and millions of thrifty citizens who had savings, pensions and insurance—we endorse the present policy of freedom for the Federal Reserve System to combat both inflation and deflation by wise fiscal policy.

The Republican Party believes that sound money, which retains its buying power, is an essential foundation for new jobs, a higher standard of living, protection of savings, a secure national defense, and the general economic growth of the country.

Business and Economic Policy

The Republican Party has as a primary concern the continued advancement of the well-being of the individual. This can be attained only in an economy that, as today, is sound, free and creative, ever building new wealth and new jobs for all the people.

We believe in good business for all business, small, medium and large. We believe that competition in a free economy opens unrivaled opportunity and brings the greatest good to the greatest number.

The sound economic policies of the Eisenhower Administration have created an atmosphere of confidence in which good businesses flourish and can plan for growth to create new job opportunities for our expanding population.

We have eliminated a host of needless controls.

To meet the immense demands of our expanding

economy, we have initiated the largest highway, air and maritime programs in history, each soundly financed.

We shall continue to advocate the maintenance and expansion of a strong, efficient, privately owned and operated and soundly financed system of transportation that will serve all of the needs of our Nation under Federal regulatory policies that will enable each carrier to realize its inherent economic advantages and its full competitive capabilities.

We recognize the United States' world leadership in aviation, and we shall continue to encourage its technical development and vigorous expansion. Our goal is to support and sponsor air services and to make available to our citizens the safest and most comprehensive air transportation. We favor adequate funds and expeditious action in improving air safety, and highest efficiency in the control of air traffic.

We stand for forward-looking programs, created to replace our war-built merchant fleet with the most advanced types in design, with increased speed. Adaptation of new propulsion power units, including nuclear, must be sponsored and achieved.

We should proceed with the prompt construction of the Atomic Powered Peace Ship in order that we may demonstrate to the world, in this as in other fields, the peaceful uses of the atom.

Our steadily rising prosperity is constantly reflecting the confidence of our citizens in the policies of our Republican Administration.

Small Business

We pledge the continuation and improvement of our drive to aid small business. Every constrictive potential avenue of improvement—both legislative and executive—has been explored in our search for ways in which to widen opportunities for this important segment of America's economy.

Beginning with our creation of the very successful Small Business Administration, and continuing through the recently completed studies and recommendations of the Cabinet Committee on Small Business, which we strongly endorse, we have focused our attention on positive measures to help small businesses get started and grow.

Small business can look forward to expanded participation in Federal procurement, valuable financing, and technical aids, a continuously vigorous enforcement of antitrust laws, important cuts in the burdens of paper work, and certain tax reductions as budgetary requirements permit.

Small business now is receiving approximately one-third, dollarwise, of all defense contracts. We recom-

mend a further review of procurement procedures for all defense departments and agencies with a view to facilitating and extending such participation for the further benefit of small business.

We favor loans at reasonable rates of interest to small businesses which have records of permanency but who are in temporary need and which are unable to obtain credit in commercial channels. We recommend an extension at the earliest opportunity of the Small Business Administration which is now scheduled to expire in mid 1957.

We also propose:

Additional technical research in problems of development and distribution for the benefit of small business;

Legislation to enable closer Federal scrutiny of mergers which have significant or potential monopolistic connotations;

Procedural changes in the antitrust laws to facilitate their enforcement;

Simplification of wage reporting by employers for purposes of social security records and income tax withholding;

Continuance of the vigorous SEC policies which are providing maximum protection to the investor and maximum opportunity for the financing of small business without costly red tape.

Labor

Under the Republican Administration, as our country has prospered, so have its people. This is as it should be, for as President Eisenhower said: "Labor is the United States. The men and women, who with their minds, their hearts and hands, create the wealth that is shared in this country—they are America."

The Eisenhower Administration has brought to our people the highest employment, the highest wages and the highest standard of living ever enjoyed by any nation. Today there are nearly 67 million men and women at work in the United States, 4 million more than in 1952. Wages have increased substantially over the past $3\frac{1}{2}$ years; but, more important, the American wage earner today can buy more than ever before for himself and his family because his pay check has not been eaten away by rising taxes and soaring prices.

The record of performance of the Republican Administration on behalf of our working men and women goes still further. The Federal minimum wage has been raised for more than 2 million workers. Social Security has been extended to an additional 10 million workers and the benefits raised for 6.5 million. The protection of unemployment insurance has been brought to 4 million additional workers. There have been increased workmen's compensation benefits for longshoremen and harbor workers, increased retirement benefits for railroad employees, and wage increases and improved welfare and pension plans for Federal employees.

In addition, the Eisenhower Administration has enforced more vigorously and effectively than ever before, the laws which protect the working standards of our people.

Workers have benefited by the progress which has been made in carrying out the programs and principles set forth in the 1952 Republican platform. All workers have gained and unions have grown in strength and responsibility, and have increased their membership by 2 millions.

Furthermore, the process of free collective bargaining has been strengthened by the insistence of this Administration that labor and management settle their differences at the bargaining table without the intervention of the Government. This policy has brought to our country an unprecedented period of labor–management peace and understanding.

We applaud the effective, unhindered, collective bargaining which brought an early end to the 1956 steel strike, in contrast to the six months' upheaval, Presidential seizure of the steel industry and ultimate Supreme Court intervention under the last Democrat Administration.

The Eisenhower Administration will continue to fight for dynamic and progressive programs which, among other things, will:

Stimulate improved job safety of our workers, through assistance to the States, employees and employers;

Continue and further perfect its programs of assistance to the millions of workers with special employment problems, such as older workers, handicapped workers, members of minority groups, and migratory workers;

Strengthen and improve the Federal–State Employment Service and improve the effectiveness of the unemployment insurance system;

Protect by law the assets of employee welfare and benefit plans so that workers who are the beneficiaries can be assured of their rightful benefits;

Assure equal pay for equal work regardless of sex;

Clarify and strengthen the eight-hour laws for the benefit of workers who are subject to Federal wage standards on Federal and Federally assisted construction, and maintain and continue the vigorous administration of the Federal prevailing minimum wage law for public supply contracts;

Extend the protection of the Federal minimum wage laws to as many more workers as is possible and practicable;

Continue to fight for the elimination of discrimination in employment because of race, creed, color, national origin, ancestry or sex;

Provide assistance to improve the economic conditions of areas faced with persistent and substantial unemployment;

Revise and improve the Taft–Hartley Act so as to protect more effectively the rights of labor unions, management, the individual worker, and the public. The protection of the right of workers to organize into unions and to bargain collectively is the firm and permanent policy of the Eisenhower Administration. In 1954, 1955 and again in 1956, President Eisenhower recommended constructive amendments to this Act. The Democrats in Congress have consistently blocked these needed changes by parliamentary maneuvers. The Republican Party pledges itself to overhaul and improve the Taft–Hartley Act along the lines of these recommendations.

HUMAN WELFARE AND ADVANCEMENT

Health, Education and Welfare

The Republican Party believes that the physical, mental, and spiritual, well-being of the people is as important as their economic health. It will continue to support this conviction with vigorous action.

Republican action created the Department of Health, Education and Welfare as the first new Federal department in 40 years, to raise the continuing consideration of these problems for the first time to the highest council of Government, the President's Cabinet.

Through the White House Conference on Education, our Republican Administration initiated the most comprehensive Community–State–Federal attempt ever made to solve the pressing problems of primary and secondary education.

Four thousand communities, studying their school populations and their physical and financial resources, encouraged our Republican Administration to urge a five-year program of Federal assistance in building schools to relieve a critical classroom shortage.

The Republican Party will renew its efforts to enact a program based on sound principles of need and designed to encourage increased State and local efforts to build more classrooms.

Our Administration also proposed for the first time in history, a thorough nation-wide analysis of rapidly growing problems in education beyond the high schools.

The Republican Party is determined to press all such actions that will help insure that every child has the educational opportunity to advance to his own greatest capacity.

We have fully resolved to continue our steady gains in man's unending struggle against disease and disability.

We have supported the distribution of free vaccine to protect millions of children against dreaded polio.

Republican leadership has enlarged Federal assistance for construction of hospitals, emphasizing low-cost care of chronic diseases and the special problems of older persons, and increased Federal aid for medical care of the needy.

We have asked the largest increase in research funds ever sought in one year to intensify attacks on cancer, mental illness, heart disease and other dread diseases.

We demand once again, despite the reluctance of the Democrat 84th Congress, Federal assistance to help build facilities to train more physicians and scientists.

We have encouraged a notable expansion and improvement of voluntary health insurance, and urge that reinsurance and pooling arrangements be authorized to speed this progress.

We have strengthened the Food and Drug Administration, and we have increased the vocational rehabilitation program to enable a larger number of the disabled to return to satisfying activity.

We have supported measures that have made more housing available than ever before in history, reduced urban slums in local–Federal partnership, stimulated record home ownership, and authorized additional low-rent public housing.

We initiated the first flood insurance program in history under Government sponsorship in cooperation with private enterprise.

We shall continue to seek extension and perfection of a sound social security system.

We pledge close cooperation with State, local and private agencies to reduce the ghastly toll of fatalities on the Nation's highways.

RURAL AMERICA'S RECOVERY— AGRICULTURE

The men and women operating the farms and ranches of America have confidence in President Eisenhower and the Republican farm program. Our farmers have earned the respect and appreciation of our entire nation for their energy, resourcefulness, efficiency, and ability.

Agriculture, our basic industry, must remain free and prosperous. The Republican Party will continue to move boldly to help the farmer obtain his full share of the rewards of good business and good Government. It is committed to a program for agriculture which creates the widest possible markets and highest attainable income for our farm and ranch families. This program must be versatile and flexible to meet effectively the impact of rapidly changing conditions. It does not envision making farmers dependent upon direct governmental payments for their incomes. Our objective is markets which return full parity to our farm and ranch people when they sell their products. There is no simple, easy answer to farm problems. Our approach as ever is a many-sided, versatile and positive program to help all farmers and ranchers.

Farm legislation, developed under the Democrat Administration to stimulate production in wartime, carried a built-in mechanism for the accumulation of price-depressing surpluses in peacetime. Under laws sponsored by the Republican Administration, almost $7 billion in price-depressing surplus farm products have been moved into use, and the rate of movement is being accelerated.

Agriculture is successfully making the transition from wartime to peacetime markets, with less disruption than at any time after a great war. We are gratified by the improvement this year in farm prices and income as a result of our policies.

Our Republican Administration fostered a constructive Soil Bank Program further to reduce surpluses and to permit improvement of our soil, water and timber resources. The Democrat Party tactics of obstruction and delay have prevented our farm families from receiving the full benefits of this program in 1956.

However, by aggressive action, we now have the Soil Bank in operation, and in 3 months, half a million farmers have contracted to shift more than 10 million acres from producing more surpluses to a soil reserve for the future. For this they already have earned $225 million.

This program is a sound aid to removing the burdens of surpluses which Democrat programs placed on farmers. It is now moving into full operation.

Benefits of Social Security have been extended to farm families. Programs of loans and grants for farm families hit by flood and drought have been made operative.

Tax laws were improved to help farmers with respect to livestock, farm equipment, and conservation practices. We initiated action to refund to the farmers $60 million annually in taxes on gasoline used in machinery on the farm.

Cooperation between the U.S. Department of Agriculture, the State Departments of Agriculture and land grant colleges and universities is at an all-time high. This Republican Administration has increased support for agricultural research and education to the highest level in history. New records of assistance to farm and ranch families in soil and water conservation were attained in every year of this Republican Administration.

Convinced that the Government should ever be the farmer's helper, never his master, the Republican Party is pledged:

To establish an effective, new research program, fully and completely implemented to find and vigorously promote new uses for farm crops;

To move our agriculture commodities into use at home and abroad, and to use every appropriate and effective means to improve marketing, so that farmers can produce and sell their products to increase their income and enjoy an improving level of living;

To encourage the improvement of quality in farm products through agricultural research, education and price support differentials, thus increasing market acceptance both at home and abroad;

To further help and cooperate with the several States as co-equals with the Federal Government to provide needed research, education, service and regulatory programs;

To develop farm programs that are fair to all farmers;

To work toward full freedom instead of toward more regimentation, developing voluntary rather than oppressive farm programs;

To encourage agricultural producers in their efforts to seek solutions to their own production and price problems;

To provide price supports as in the Agricultural Act of 1954 that protect farmers, rather than price their products out of the market;

To continue our commodity loan and marketing agreement programs as effective marketing tools;

To make every effort to develop a more accurate measurement of farm parity;

To safeguard our precious soil and water resources for generations yet unborn;

To encourage voluntary self-supporting federal crop insurance;

To bring sympathetic and understanding relief promptly to farm and ranch families hard hit with problems of drought, flood or other natural disaster, or economic disaster, and to maintain the integrity of these programs by terminating them when the emergency is over;

To assist the young people of American farms and ranches in their development as future farmers and homemakers;

To continue and expand the Republican-sponsored school milk program, to encourage further use of the school lunch program now benefiting 11 million children, and to foster improved nutritional levels;

To provide constructive assistance by effective purchase and donation to ease temporary market surpluses, especially for the producers of perishable farm products;

To give full support to farmer-owned and farmer-operated cooperatives;

To encourage and assist adequate private and cooperative sources of credit, to provide supplemental credit through the Farmers Home Administration where needed, with an understanding of both the human and economic problems of farmers and ranchers;

To expand rural electrification through REA loans for generation and transmission, and to expand rural communication facilities;

To continue the improvement of rural mail delivery to farm families;

To promote fully the Republican-sponsored Rural-Development Program to broaden the operation and increase the income of low-income farm families and help tenant farmers;

To work with farmers, ranchers and others to carry forward the Great Plains program to achieve wise use of lands in the area subject to wind erosion, so that the people of this region can enjoy a higher standard of living; and in summation:

To keep agriculture strong, free, attuned to peace and not war, to stand ready with a reserve capacity at all times as a part of our defense, based on sound agricultural economy.

We are an expanding nation. Our needs for farm products will continue to grow. Farm prices are improving and farm income is climbing.

Our farm and ranch people are confident of the future, despite efforts to frighten them into accepting economic nostrums and political panaceas. Record numbers of farms are owned by those who operate them.

The Republican Party is pledged to work for improved farm prices and farm income. We will seek that improvement boldly, in ways that protect the family farm. Our objective is a prosperous, expanding and free agriculture. We are dedicated to creating the opportunity for farmers to earn a high per-family income in a world at peace.

FEDERAL GOVERNMENT INTEGRITY

The Republican Party is wholeheartedly com-mitted to maintaining a Federal Government that is clean, honorable and increasingly efficient. It proudly affirms that it has achieved this kind of Government and dedicated it to the service of all the people.

Our many economic and social advances of the past four years are the result of our faithful adherence to our 1952 pledge to reverse a 20-year Democratic philosophy calling for more and more power in Washington.

We have left no stone unturned to remove from Government the irresponsible and those whose employment was not clearly consistent with national security.

We believe that working for the Government is not a right but a privilege. Based on that principle we will continue a security program to make certain that all people employed by our Government are of unquestioned loyalty and trustworthiness. The Republican Party will, realistically and in conformity with constitutional safeguards for the individual, continue to protect our national security by enforcing our laws fairly, vigorously, and with certainty. We will act through the new division established to this end in the Department of Justice, and by close coordination among the intelligence services.

We promise unwavering vigilance against corruption and waste, and shall continue so to manage the public business as to warrant our people's full confidence in the integrity of their Government.

We condemn illegal lobbying for any cause and improper use of money in political activities, including the use of funds collected by compulsion for political purposes contrary to the personal desires of the individual.

Efficiency and Economy in Government

We pledge to continue our far-reaching program for improving the efficiency and the effectiveness of the Federal Government in accordance with the principles set forth in the report of the Hoover Commission.

We are unalterably opposed to unwarranted growth of centralized Federal power. We shall carry forward the worthy effort of the Kestnbaum Com-mission on Intergovernmental Affairs to clarify Federal relationships and strengthen State and local government.

We shall continue to dispense with Federal activities wrongfully competing with private enterprise, and take other sound measures to reduce the cost of Government.

GOVERNMENTAL AFFAIRS

Postal Service

In the last four years, under direction from President Eisenhower to improve the postal service and reduce costs, we have modernized and revitalized the postal establishment from top to bottom, inside and out. We have undertaken and substantially completed the largest reorganization ever to take place in any unit of business or government:

We have provided more than 1200 badly needed new post office buildings, and are adding two more every day. We are using the very latest types of industrial equipment where practicable; and, through a program of research and engineering, we are inventing new mechanical and electronic devices to speed the movement of mail by eliminating tedious old-fashioned methods.

We have improved service across the country in hundreds of ways. We have extended city carrier service to millions of new homes in thousands of urban and suburban communities which have grown and spread under the favorable economic conditions brought about by the Eisenhower Administration.

We have re-inspired the morale of our half million employees through new programs of promotion based on ability, job training and safety, and through our sponsorship of increased pay and fringe benefits.

We have adopted the most modern methods of transportation, accounting and cost control, and other operating procedures; through them we have saved many millions of dollars a year for the taxpayers while advancing the delivery of billions of letters by a day or more—all this while reducing the enormous deficit of the Department from its all time high of almost three-quarters of a billion dollars in 1952 to less than half that amount in 1955.

We pledge to continue our efforts, blocked by the Democratic leadership of the 84th Congress, for a financially sound, more nearly self-sustaining postal service—with the users of the mails paying a greater share of the costs instead of the taxpayers bearing the burden of huge postal deficits.

We pledge to continue and to complete this vitally needed program of modernization of buildings, equipment, methods and service, so that the American people will receive the kind of mail delivery they deserve—the speediest and best that American ingenuity, technology and modern business management can provide.

Civil Service

We will vigorously promote, as we have in the past, a non-political career service under the merit system which will attract and retain able servants of the people. Many gains in this field, notably pay increases and a host of new benefits, have been achieved in their behalf in less than four years.

The Republican Party will continue to fight for eagerly desired new advances for Government employees, and realistic reappraisement and adjustment of benefits for our retired civil service personnel.

Statehood for Alaska and Hawaii

We pledge immediate statehood for Alaska, recognizing the fact that adequate provision for defense requirements must be made.

We pledge immediate statehood for Hawaii.

Puerto Rico

We shall continue to encourage the Commonwealth of Puerto Rico in its political growth and economic development in accordance with the wishes of its people and the fundamental principle of self-determination.

Indian Affairs

We shall continue to pursue our enlightened policies which are now producing exceptional advances in the long struggle to help the American Indian gain the material and social advantages of his birthright and citizenship, while maintaining to the fullest extent the cultural integrity of the various tribal groups.

We commend the present Administration for its progressive programs which have achieved such striking progress in preparing our Indian citizens for participation in normal community life. Health, educational and employment opportunities for Indians have been greatly expanded beyond any previous level, and we favor still further extensions of these programs.

We favor most sympathetic and constructive execution of the Federal trusteeship over Indian affairs, always in full consultation with Indians in the management of their interests and the expansion of their rights of self-government in local and tribal affairs.

We urge the prompt adjudication or settlement of pending Indian claims.

District of Columbia

We favor self-government, national suffrage and representation in the Congress of the United States for residents of the District of Columbia.

Equal Rights

We recommend to Congress the submission of a constitutional amendment providing equal rights for men and women.

EQUAL OPPORTUNITY AND JUSTICE

Civil Rights

The Republican Party points to an impressive record of accomplishment in the field of civil rights and commits itself anew to advancing the rights of all our people regardless of race, creed, color or national origin.

In the area of exclusive Federal jurisdiction, more progress has been made in this field under the present Republican Administration than in any similar period in the last 80 years.

The many Negroes who have been appointed to high public positions have played a significant part in the progress of this Administration.

Segregation has been ended in the District of Columbia Government and in the District public facilities including public schools, restaurants, theaters and playgrounds. The Eisenhower Administration has eliminated discrimination in all Federal employment.

Great progress has been made in eliminating employment discrimination on the part of those who do business with the Federal Government and secure Federal contracts. This Administration has impartially enforced Federal civil rights statutes, and we pledge that we will continue to do so. We support the enactment of the civil rights program already presented by the President to the Second Session of the 84th Congress.

The regulatory agencies under this Administration have moved vigorously to end discrimination in interstate commerce. Segregation in the active Armed Forces of the United States has been ended. For the first time in our history there is no segregation in veterans' hospitals and among civilians on naval bases. This is an impressive record. We pledge ourselves to continued progress in this field.

The Republican Party has unequivocally recognized that the supreme law of the land is embodied in the Constitution, which guarantees to all people the blessings of liberty, due process and equal protection of the laws. It confers upon all native-born and naturalized citizens not only citizenship in the State where the individual resides but citizenship of the United States as well. This is an unqualified right, regardless of race, creed or color.

The Republican Party accepts the decision of the U.S. Supreme Court that racial discrimination in publicly supported schools must be progressively eliminated. We concur in the conclusion of the Supreme Court that its decision directing school desegregation should be accomplished with "all deliberate speed" locally through Federal District Courts. The implementation order of the Supreme Court recognizes the complex and acutely emotional problems created by its decision in certain sections of our country where racial patterns have been developed in accordance with prior and longstanding decisions of the same tribunal.

We believe that true progress can be attained through intelligent study, understanding, education and good will. Use of force or violence by any group or agency will tend only to worsen the many problems inherent in the situation. This progress must be encouraged and the work of the courts supported in every legal manner by all branches of the Federal Government to the end that the constitutional ideal of equality before the law, regardless of race, creed or color, will be steadily achieved.

Immigration

The Republican Party supports an immigration policy which is in keeping with the traditions of America in providing a haven for oppressed peoples, and which is based on equality of treatment, freedom from implications of discrimination between racial, nationality and religious groups, and flexible enough to conform to changing needs and conditions.

We believe that such a policy serves our self-interest, reflects our responsibility for world leadership and develops maximum cooperation with other nations in resolving problems in this area.

We support the President's program submitted to the 84th Congress to carry out needed modifications in existing law and to take such further steps as may be necessary to carry out our traditional policy.

In that concept, this Republican Administration spon-

sored the Refugee Relief Act to provide asylum for thousands of refugees, expellees and displaced persons, and undertook in the face of Democrat opposition to correct the inequities in existing law and to bring our immigration policies in line with the dynamic needs of the country and principles of equity and justice.

We believe also that the Congress should consider the extension of the Refugee Relief Act of 1953 in resolving this difficult refugee problem which resulted from world conflict. To all this we give our whole-hearted support.

Human Freedom and Peace

Under the leadership of President Eisenhower, the United States has advanced foreign policies which enable our people to enjoy the blessings of liberty and peace.

The changes in the international scene have been so great that it is easy to forget the conditions we inherited in 1953.

Peace, so hardly won in 1945, had again been lost. The Korean War, with its tragic toll of more than an eighth of a million American casualties, seemed destined to go on indefinitely. Its material costs and accompanying inflation were undermining our economy.

Freedom was under assault, and despotism was on the march. Armed conflict continued in the Far East, and tensions mounted elsewhere.

The threat of global war increased daily.

International Communism which, in 1945, ruled the 200 million people in the Soviet Union and Baltic States, was conquering so that, by 1952, it dominated more than 700 million people in 15 once-independent nations.

Today

Now, we are at peace. The Korean War has been ended. The Communist aggressors have been denied their goals.

The threat of global war has receded.

The advance of Communism has been checked, and, at key points, thrown back. The once monolithic structure of International Communism, denied the stimulant of successive conquests, has shown hesitancy both internally and abroad.

The Far East

The Korean War was brought to a close when the Communist rulers were made to realize that they could not win.

The United States has made a Collective Defense Treaty with the Republic of Korea which will exclude, for the future, the Communist miscalculation as to announced American interests and intentions which led to the original aggression.

The United States has made a security Treaty with the Republic of China covering Formosa and the Pescadores; and the Congress, by virtually unanimous action; has authorized the President to employ the armed forces of the United States to defend this area. As a result, the Chinese Communists have not attempted to implement their announced intention to take Formosa by force.

In Indochina the Republics of Vietnam and Cambodia and Laos are now free and independent nations. The Republic of Vietnam, with the United States assistance, has denied the Communists the gains which they expected from the withdrawal of French forces.

The security of Southeast Asia has now been bolstered by the collective defense system of SEATO, and its peoples encouraged by the declarations in the Pacific Charter of the principles of equal rights and self-determination of peoples.

The Middle East and Southeast Asia

The Middle East has been strengthened by the defensive unity of the four "northern tier" countries—Turkey, Iraq, Iran and Pakistan—which hold gateways to the vast oil resources upon which depend the industry and military strength of the free world. This was made possible by the liberation of Iran from the grip of the Communist Tudeh Party. Iran has again made its oil reserves available to the world under an equitable settlement negotiated by the United States.

We have maintained, and will maintain, friendly relations with all nations in this vital area, seeking to mediate differences among them, and encouraging their legitimate national aspirations.

Europe

In Western Europe, the scene has been transformed. The Federal Republic of Germany, which until 1953 was denied sovereignty and the opportunity to join the North Atlantic Treaty Organization, has now had full sovereignty restored by the Treaties of 1954, and has become a member of NATO despite the intense opposition of the Soviet Union.

NATO itself has been strengthened by developing reliance upon new weapons and retaliatory power, thus assisting the NATO countries increasingly to attain both economic welfare and adequate military defense.

On our initiative, the political aspects of NATO are being developed. Instead of being merely a military alliance, NATO will provide a means for coordinating the policies of the member states on vital matters, such as the reunification of Germany, the liberation of the satellites, and general policies in relation to the Soviet Union.

Austria has been liberated. The freedom treaty, blocked since 1947 by the Soviet Union, was signed in 1955. For the first time since the end of World War II, Red Army forces in Europe evacuated occupied lands.

The emotion-charged dispute between Italy and Yugoslavia about Trieste was settled with the active participation of the United States. The City of Trieste was restored to Italian sovereignty, and United States and British forces withdrawn.

The Spanish base negotiations, which had long languished, were successfully concluded, and close working relations in this important respect established between the United States and Spain.

The Americas

Our good neighbor policy continues to prove its wisdom. The American Republics have taken effective steps against the cancer of Communism. At the Caracas Conference of March, 1954, they agreed that if International Communism gained control of the political institutions of any American republic, this would endanger them all, and would call for collective measures to remove the danger. This new Doctrine, first proposed by the United States, extends into modern times the principles of the Monroe Doctrine.

A first fruit of the Caracas Doctrine was the expulsion of the Communist regime ruling Guatemala. Today, Guatemala is liberated from Kremlin control. The Organization of American States has grown in vigor. It has acted promptly and effectively to settle hemispheric disputes. In Costa Rica, for the first time in history, international aerial inspection was employed to maintain peace. The Panama Conference was probably the most successful in the long history of the Organization of American States in its promotion of good will, understanding and friendship.

Relations With Soviet Russia

Far-reaching steps have been taken to eliminate the danger of a third world war. President Eisenhower led the way at Geneva. There he impressed the Soviet leaders and the world with the dedication of the United States to peace, but also with its determination not to purchase peace at the price of freedom.

That Summit Conference set new forces into motion. The Soviet rulers professed to renounce the use of violence, which Stalin had made basic in the Communist doctrine. Then followed a repudiation of Stalin, the growth of doctrinal disputes within the Communist Party, and a discrediting of Party authority and its evil power. Forces of liberalism within the Soviet Bloc challenge the brutal and atheistic doctrines of Soviet Communism. For the first time, we see positive evidence that forces of freedom and liberation will inevitably prevail if the free nations maintain their strength, unity and resolution.

The Future

We re-dedicate ourselves to the pursuit of a just peace and the defense of human liberty and national independence.

We shall continue vigorously to support the United Nations.

We shall continue our cooperation with our sister states of the Americas for the strengthening of our security, economic and social ties with them.

We shall continue to support the collective security system begun in 1947 and steadily developed on a bipartisan basis. That system has joined the United States with 42 other nations in common defense of freedom. It has created a deterrent to war which cannot be nullified by Soviet veto.

Where needed, we shall help friendly countries maintain such local forces and economic strength as provide a first bulwark against Communist aggression or subversion. We shall reinforce that defense by a military capacity which, operating in accordance with the United Nations Charter, could so punish aggression that it ceases to be a profitable pursuit.

We will continue efforts with friends and allies to assist the underdeveloped areas of the free world in their efforts to attain greater freedom, independence and self-determination, and to raise their standards of living.

We recognize the existence of a major threat to international peace in the Near East. We support a policy of impartial friendship for the peoples of the Arab states and Israel to promote a peaceful settlement of the causes of tension in that area, including the human problem of the Palestine–Arab refugees.

Progress toward a just settlement of the tragic conflict between the Jewish State and the Arab nations in Palestine was upset by the Soviet Bloc sale of arms to Arab countries. But prospects of peace have now been reinforced by the mission to Palestine of the United Nations Secretary General upon the initiative of the United States.

We regard the preservation of Israel as an important tenet of American foreign policy. We are determined that the integrity of an independent Jewish State shall be maintained. We shall support the independence of Israel against armed aggression. The best hope for peace in the Middle East lies in the United Nations. We pledge our continued efforts to eliminate the obstacles to a lasting peace in this area.

We shall continue to seek the reunification of Germany in freedom, and the liberation of the satellite states—Poland, Czechoslovakia, Hungary, Rumania, Bulgaria, Latvia, Lithuania, Estonia and other, once-free countries now behind the Iron Curtain. The Republican Party stands firmly with the peoples of these countries in their just quest for freedom. We are confident that our peaceful policies, resolutely pursued, will finally restore freedom and national independence to oppressed peoples and nations.

We continue to oppose the seating of Communist China in the United Nations, thus upholding international morality. To seat a Communist China which defies, by word and deed, the principles of the United Nations Charter would be to betray the letter, violate the spirit and subvert the purposes of that charter. It would betray our friend and ally, the Republic of China. We will continue our determined efforts to free the remaining Americans held prisoner by Communist China.

Recognizing economic health as an indispensable basis of military strength and world peace, we shall strive to foster abroad and to practice at home, policies to encourage productivity and profitable trade.

Barriers which impede international trade and the flow of capital should be reduced on a gradual, selective and reciprocal basis, with full recognition of the necessity to safeguard domestic enterprises, agriculture and labor against unfair import competition. We proudly point out that the Republican Party was primarily responsible for initiating the escape clause and peril point provisions of law to make effective the necessary safeguards for American agriculture, labor and business. We pledge faithful and expeditious administration of these provisions.

We are against any trade with the Communist world that would threaten the security of the United States and our allies.

We recognize that no single nation can alone defend the liberty of all nations threatened by Communist aggression or subversion. Mutual security means effective mutual cooperation. Poverty and unrest in less developed countries make them the target for international communism. We must help them achieve the economic growth and stability necessary to attain and preserve their independence.

Technical and economic assistance programs are effective countermeasures to Soviet economic offensives and propaganda. They provide the best way to create the political and social stability essential to lasting peace.

We will strive to bring about conditions that will end the injustices of nations divided against their will, of nations held subject to foreign domination, of peoples deprived of the right of self-government.

We reaffirm the principle of freedom for all peoples, and look forward to the eventual end of colonialism.

We will overlook no opportunity that, with prudence, can be taken to bring about a progressive elimination of the barriers that interfere with the free flow of news, information and ideas, and the exchange of persons between the free peoples and the captive peoples of the world. We favor the continuance and development of the "exchange-of-persons" programs between free nations.

We approve appropriate action to oppose the imposition by foreign governments of discrimination against United States citizens, based on their religion or race.

We shall continue the bipartisan development of foreign policies. We hold this necessary if those policies are to have continuity, and be regarded by other free nations as dependable.

The Republican Party pledges itself to continue the dynamic, courageous, sound and patriotic policies which have protected and promoted the interests of the United States during the past four years.

In a world fraught with peril, peace can be won and preserved only by vigilance and inspired leadership. In such a world, we believe it is essential that the vast experience of our proven leader, President Dwight D. Eisenhower, continues to guide our country in the achievement and maintenance of a just, honorable and durable peace.

BULWARK FOR THE FREE WORLD— OUR NATIONAL DEFENSE

The military strength of the United States has been a key factor in the preservation of world peace during the past four years. We are determined to maintain that strength so long as our security and the peace of the world require it.

This Administration, within six months after President Eisenhower's inauguration, ended the war in Korea by concluding an honorable armistice. The lesson of that war and our lack of preparedness which brought it about will not be forgotten. Such mistakes must not be repeated.

As we maintain and strengthen the security of this Nation, we shall, consistent with this Administration's dedication to peace, strive for the acceptance of realistic proposals for disarmament and the humanitarian control of weapons of mass destruction.

Our country's defense posture is today a visible and powerful deterrent against attack by any enemy, from any quarter, at any time.

We have the strongest striking force in the world— in the air—on the sea—and a magnificent supporting land force in our Army and Marine Corps. Such visible and powerful deterrents must continue to include:

A) A jet-powered, long-range strategic air force, and a tactical air force of the fastest and very latest type aircraft, with a striking capability superior to any other;
B) The most effective guided and ballistic missiles;
C) A modern navy, with a powerful naval aircraft arm prepared to keep the sea lanes open to meet any assignment;
D) An army whose mobility and unit fire-power are without equal;
E) Bases, strategically dispersed at home and around the world, essential to all these operations.

We will maintain and improve the effective strength and state of readiness of all these armed forces.

To achieve this objective, we must depend upon attracting to, and retaining in our military services vigorous and well-trained manpower, and upon continuously maintaining in reserve, an enthusiastic and well-informed group of men and women. This will require incentives that will make armed service careers attractive and rewarding. A substantial start has been made toward bolstering the rewards and benefits that accompany a military career. We must continue to provide them.

In order that American youth in our armed services shall be provided with the most modern weapons, we have supported and will continue to support an effective and well-directed program of research and development, staffed by men of the highest caliber and ability in this field. There is no substitute for the best where the lives of our men and the defense of our Nation are concerned.

We fully appreciate the importance of scientific knowledge and its application particularly in the military field.

We pledge ourselves to stimulate and encourage the education of our young people in the sciences with a determination to maintain our technological leadership.

In this age of weapons of inconceivable destructiveness, we must not neglect the protection of the civilian population by all known means, while, at the same time, preparing our armed forces for every eventuality.

We wholeheartedly agree with President Eisenhower that our military defense must be backed by a strong civil defense, and that an effective civil defense is an important deterrent against attack upon our country, and an indispensable reliance should our Nation ever be attacked.

We support his proposals for strengthening civil defense, mindful that it has become an effective Government arm to deal with natural disasters.

We shall continue to carry forward, vigorously and effectively, the valued services of the Federal Bureau of Investigation, as well as all other Government intelligence agencies, so as to insure that we are protected at all times against subversive activities. We will never relax our determined efforts to keep our Government, and our people, safely guarded against all enemies from within.

We agree and assert that civilian authority and control over our defense structure and program must be maintained at all times. We believe, without qualification, that in our present Commander-in-Chief, Dwight D. Eisenhower, this Nation possesses a leader equipped by training, temperament, and experience in war and in peace, for both that personal example and that direction of our national defense in which the American people will continue to have confidence, and in which the peoples of all the free world will find an increasing sense of security and of an opportunity for peace.

VETERANS

We believe that active duty in the Armed Forces during a state of war or national emergency is the highest call of citizenship constituting a special service to our Nation and entitles those who have served to positive assistance to alleviate the injuries, hardships and handicaps imposed by their service.

In recognizing this principle under previous Republican Administrations we established the Veterans Administration. This Republican Administration increased compensation and pension benefits for veterans and survivors to provide more adequate levels and to off-set cost-of-living increases that occurred during the most recent Democratic Administration.

We have also improved quality of hospital service and have established a long-range program for continued improvement of such service. We have strength-

ened and extended survivors' benefits, thus affording greater security for all veterans in the interest of equity and justice.

In advancing this Republican program we pledge:

That compensation for injuries and disease arising out of service be fairly and generously provided for all disabled veterans and for their dependents or survivors;

That a pension program for disabled war veterans in need and for their widows and orphans in need be maintained as long as necessary to assure them adequate income;

That all veterans be given equal and adequate opportunity for readjustment following service, including unemployment compensation when needed, but placing emphasis on obtaining suitable employment for veterans, particularly those disabled, by using appropriate facilities of government and by assuring that Federal employment preference and re-employment rights, to which the veteran is entitled, are received;

That the Veterans Administration be continued as a single independent agency providing veterans services;

That the service-disabled continue to receive first-priority medical services of the highest standard and that non–service disabled war veterans in need receive hospital care to the extent that beds are available.

GUARDING AND IMPROVING OUR RESOURCES

One of the brightest areas of achievement and progress under the Eisenhower Administration has been in resource conservation and development and in sound, long-range public works programming.

Policies of sound conservation and wise development originally advanced half a century ago under that pre-eminent Republican conservation team of President Theodore Roosevelt and Gifford Pinchot and amplified by succeeding Republican Administrations have been pursued by the Eisenhower Administration. While meeting the essential development needs of the people, this Administration has conserved and safeguarded our natural resources for the greatest good of all, now and in the future.

Our National Parks, National Forests and wildlife refuges are now more adequately financed, better protected and more extensive than ever before. Long-range improvement programs, such as Mission 66 for the National Parks system, are now under way, and studies are nearing completion for a comparable program for the National Forests. These forward-looking programs will be aggressively continued.

Our Republican Administration has modernized and vitalized our mining laws by the first major revision in more than 30 years.

Recreation, Parks and Wildlife

Achievements: Reversed the 15-year trend of neglect of our National Parks by launching the 10-year, $785 million Mission 66 parks improvement program. Has nearly completed field surveys for a comparable forest improvement program. Obtained passage of the so-called "Week-end Miner Bill." Added more than 400,000 acres to our National Parks system, and 90,000 acres to wildlife refuges. Has undertaken well-conceived measures to protect reserved areas of all types and to provide increased staffs and operating funds for public recreation agencies.

We favor full recognition of recreation as an important public use of our National Forests and public domain lands.

We favor a comprehensive study of the effect upon wildlife of the drainage of our wetlands.

We favor recognition, by the States, of wildlife and recreation management and conservation as a beneficial use of water.

We subscribe to the general objectives of groups seeking to guard the beauty of our land and to promote clean, attractive surroundings throughout America.

We recognize the need for maintaining isolated wilderness areas to provide opportunity for future generations to experience some of the wilderness living through which the traditional American spirit of hardihood was developed.

Public Land and Forest Resources

Achievements: Approved conservation programs of many types, including improvement of western grazing lands through reseeding programs, water spreading systems, and encouragement of soil and moisture-conservation practices by range users. Returned to the States their submerged lands and resources of their coasts, out to their historical boundaries—an area comprising about one tenth of the area off the Continental Shelf and about 17 per cent of the mineral resources. Initiated leasing of the Federally owned 83 per cent of the Continental Shelf which is expected ultimately to bring from 6 to 8 billion dollars into the Treasury and already has brought in over 250 million

dollars. Enacted new legislation to encourage multiple use of the public domain.

We commend the Eisenhower Administration for its administration of our public lands and for elimination of bureaucratic abuses. We recommend continuing study and evaluation of the advisability of returning unused or inadequately used public lands.

We commend the Administration for expanding forest research and access road construction.

We shall continue to improve timber conservation practices, recreational facilities, grazing management, and watershed protection of our national forests and our public domain.

Minerals

Recognizing that a vigorous and efficient mineral industry is essential to the long-term development of the United States, and to its defense, we believe the Federal Government should foster a long-term policy for the development and prudent use of domestic mineral resources, and to assure access to necessary sources abroad, without dangerously weakening the market for domestic production of defense-essential materials.

We favor reasonable depletion allowances. We favor freedom of mineral producers from unnecessary governmental regulation; expansion of government minerals exploration and research, and establishment of minerals stockpile objectives which will reduce, and, where possible, eliminate foreseeable wartime shortages.

Achievements: St. Lawrence Seaway and power projects, Colorado River Storage Project, Great Lakes connecting channels, small watershed protection and flood prevention under local control, Mississippi Gulf level canal, extension of water-pollution control program, survey of power potential of Passamaquoddy Bay tides, expansion of small project development for flood control, navigation and reclamation; extension to all 48 States of water facilities act, accelerated research on saline water conversion, authorized planning surveys and construction of more than 200 navigation, flood-control, beach erosion, rivers and harbors, reclamation, and watershed projects throughout the nation, advanced partnership water resource developments in a number of states.

Water Resources

Water resource development legislation enacted under the Eisenhower Administration already has ushered in one of the greatest water resource development programs this Nation has ever seen, a soundly-conceived construction program that will continue throughout this Century and beyond.

We recognize that the burgeoning growth of our nation requires a combination of Federal, State and local water and power development—a real partnership of effort by all interested parties. In no other way can the nation meet the huge and accelerated demands for increasing generating capacity and uses of water, both by urban and agricultural areas. We also are aware that water demands have been accentuated by the ravages of drought, creating emergency conditions in many sections of our country. We commend the Eisenhower Administration for encouraging state and local governments, public agencies, and regulated private enterprise, to participate actively in comprehensive water and power development. In such partnership we are leading the way with great Federal developments such as the Upper Colorado Project and with partnership projects of great importance, some of which have been shelved by the Democratic 84th Congress.

In the marketing of federally produced power we support preference to public bodies and cooperatives under the historic policy of the Congress.

We will continue to press for co-operative solution of all problems of water supply and distribution, reclamation, pollution, flood control, and saline-water conversion.

We pledge legislative support to the arid and semi-arid states in preserving the integrity of their water laws and customs as developed out of the necessities of these regions. We affirm the historic policy of Congress recognizing State water rights, as repeatedly expressed in Federal law over the past 90 years.

We pledge an expansion in research and planning of water resource development programs, looking to the future when it may be necessary to re-distribute water from water-surplus areas to water-deficient areas.

Fisheries

Achievements: Accelerated research and administrative action to rehabilitate our long-neglected fishing industry. Approval of measures for additional conservation and propagation of fish. Development of the comprehensive program for fisheries management and assistance adopted by the Congress.

We favor continuation of the Eisenhower program to rehabilitate our long-neglected domestic fishing industry.

We advocate protective treaties insuring the United States commercial-fisheries industry against unfair foreign competition.

The Republican Party is acutely aware that a foundation stone of the nation's strength is its wealth of natural resources and the high development of its physical assets. They are the basis of our great progress in 180 years of freedom and of our nation's military and economic might.

We pledge that we will continue the policies of sound conservation and wise development instituted by this Administration to insure that our resources are managed as a beneficial trust for all the people.

FOR A BRIGHTER TOMORROW

Atomic Energy

The Republican Party pledges continuous, vigorous development of Atomic Energy:

> for the defense of our own country and to deter aggression, and
> for the promotion of world peace and the enhancement of our knowledge of basic science and its application to industry, agriculture and the healing arts.

From the passage of the first Atomic Energy Act in 1946 to the beginning of this Republican Administration, a stalemate had existed, and only an arms race with the prospect of eventual catastrophe faced the nations of the world.

President Eisenhower has inaugurated and led a strong program for developing the peaceful atom—a program which has captured the imagination of men and women everywhere with its widespread, positive achievements.

The Government and private enterprise are working together on a number of large-scale projects designed to develop substantial quantities of electric power from atomic sources. The first power reactor will be completed next year. More and more private funds are being invested as the Government monopoly is relaxed.

In relaxing its monopoly, Government can stimulate private enterprise to go ahead by taking recognition of the tremendous risks involved and the complexity of the many technical problems that will arise, and assist in those ways that will make advances possible.

The Atomic Energy Commission also is encouraging a vigorous rural electrification program by cooperatives.

Every day, radioactive isotopes are brought more and more into use on farms, in clinics and hospitals, and in industry. The use of isotopes already has resulted in annual savings of hundreds of millions of dollars and the nuclear age has only begun.

It is to the benefit of the United States, as well as to all nations everywhere, that the uses of atomic energy be explored and shared. The Republican Party pledges that it will continue this imaginative, world-embracing program. We shall continue to chart our course so as to fortify the security of the free nations and to further the prosperity and progress of all people everywhere.

DECLARATION OF DEDICATION

With utmost confidence in the future and with justifiable pride in our achievements, the Republican Party warmly greets the dawn of our second century of service in the cause of unity and progress in the nation.

As the Party of the Young and in glowing appreciation of his dynamic leadership and inspiration, we respectfully dedicate this Platform of the Party of the Future to our distinguished President Dwight D. Eisenhower, and to the Youth of America.

— 1960 —
PREAMBLE

The United States is living in an age of profoundest revolution. The lives of men and of nations are undergoing such transformations as history has rarely recorded. The birth of new nations, the impact of new machines, the threat of new weapons, the stirring of new ideas, the ascent into a new dimension of the universe—everywhere the accent falls on the new.

At such a time of world upheaval, great perils match great opportunities—and hopes, as well as fears, rise in all areas of human life. Such a force as nuclear power symbolizes the greatness of the choice before the United States and mankind. The energy of the atom could bring devastation to humanity. Or it could be made to serve men's hopes for peace and progress—to make for all peoples a more healthy and secure and prosperous life than man has ever known.

One fact darkens the reasonable hopes of free men: the growing vigor and thrust of Communist imperialism. Everywhere across the earth, this force challenges us to prove our strength and wisdom, our capacity for sacrifice, our faith in ourselves and in our institutions.

Free men look to us for leadership and support, which we dedicate ourselves to give out of the abundance of our national strength.

The fate of the world will be deeply affected, perhaps determined, by the quality of American leadership. American leadership means both how we govern ourselves and how we help to influence others. We

deliberate the choice of national leadership and policy, mindful that in some measure our proposals involve the fate of mankind.

The leadership of the United States must be responsible and mature; its promises must be rational and practical, soberly pledged and faithfully undertaken. Its purposes and its aspirations must ascend to that high ground of right and freedom upon which mankind may dwell and progress in decent security.

We are impressed, but not dismayed, by the revolutionary turbulence that is wracking the world. In the midst of violence and change, we draw strength and confidence from the changeless principles of our free Constitution. Free men are invincible when the power and courage, the patience and the fortitude latent in them are drawn forth by reasonable appeal.

In this Republican Platform we offer to the United States our program—our call to service, our pledge of leadership, our proposal of measures in the public interest. We call upon God, in whose hand is every blessing, to favor our deliberations with wisdom, our nation with endurance, and troubled mankind everywhere with a righteous peace.

FOREIGN POLICY

The Republican Party asserts that the sovereign purpose of our foreign policy is to secure the free institutions of our nation against every peril, to hearten and fortify the love of freedom everywhere in the world, and to achieve a just peace for all of anxious humanity.

The pre-eminence of this Republic requires of us a vigorous, resolute foreign policy—inflexible against every tyrannical encroachment, and mighty in its advance toward our own affirmative goals.

The Government of the United States, under the administration of President Eisenhower and Vice President Nixon, has demonstrated that firmness in the face of threatened aggression is the most dependable safeguard of peace. We now reaffirm our determination to defend the security and the freedom of our country, to honor our commitments to our allies at whatever cost or sacrifice, and never to submit to force or threats. Our determination to stand fast has forestalled aggression before Berlin, in the Formosa Straits, and in Lebanon. Since 1954 no free nation has fallen victim behind the Iron Curtain. We mean to adhere to the policy of firmness that has served us so well.

We are unalterably committed to maintaining the security, freedom and solidarity of the Western Hemisphere. We support President Eisenhower's reaffirmation of the Monroe Doctrine in all its vitality.

Faithful to our treaty commitments, we shall join the Republics of the Americas against any intervention in our hemisphere, and in refusing to tolerate the establishment in this hemisphere of any government dominated by the foreign rule of Communism.

In the Middle East, we shall continue to support the integrity and independence of all the states of that area including Israel and the Arab States.

With specific reference to Israel and the Arab Nations we urge them to undertake negotiations for a mutually acceptable settlement of the causes of tension between them. We pledge continued efforts:

To eliminate the obstacles to a lasting peace in the area, including the human problem of the Arab refugees.

To seek an end to transit and trade restrictions, blockades and boycotts.

To secure freedom of navigation in international waterways, the cessation of discrimination against Americans on the basis of religious beliefs, and an end to the wasteful and dangerous arms race and to the threat of an arms imbalance in the area.

Recognition of Communist China and its admission to the United Nations have been firmly opposed by the Republican Administration. We will continue in this opposition because of compelling evidence that to do otherwise would weaken the cause of freedom and endanger the future of the free peoples of Asia and the world. The brutal suppression of the human rights and the religious traditions of the Tibetan people is an unhappy evidence of the need to persist in our policy.

The countries of the free world have been benefited, reinforced and drawn closer together by the vigor of American support of the United Nations, and by our participation in such regional organizations as NATO, SEATO, CENTO, the Organization of American States and other collective security alliances. We assert our intention steadfastly to uphold the action and principles of these bodies.

We believe military assistance to our allies under the mutual security program should be continued with all the vigor and funds needed to maintain the strength of our alliances at levels essential to our common safety.

The firm diplomacy of the Eisenhower–Nixon Administration has been supported by a military power superior to any in the history of our nation or in the world. As long as world tensions menace us with war, we are resolved to maintain an armed power exceeded by no other.

Under Republican administration, the Government has developed original and constructive programs in many fields—open skies, atoms for peace, cultural and technical exchanges, the peaceful uses of outer space and Antarctica—to make known to men everywhere our desire to advance the cause of peace. We mean, as a Party, to continue in the same course.

We recognize and freely acknowledge the support given to these principles and policies by all Americans, irrespective of party. Standing as they do above partisan challenge, such principles and policies will, we earnestly hope, continue to have bipartisan support.

We established a new independent agency, the United States Information Agency, fully recognizing the tremendous importance of the struggle for men's minds. Today, our information program throughout the world is a greatly improved medium for explaining our policies and actions to audiences overseas, answering Communist propaganda, and projecting a true image of American life.

This is the Republican record. We rededicate ourselves to the principles that have animated it; and we pledge ourselves to persist in those principles, and to apply them to the problems, the occasions, and the opportunities to be faced by the new Administration.

We confront today the global offensive of Communism, increasingly aggressive and violent in its enterprises. The agency of that offensive is Soviet policy, aimed at the subversion of the world.

Recently we have noted Soviet Union pretexts to intervene in the affairs of newly independent countries, accompanied by threats of the use of nuclear weapons. Such interventions constitute a form of subversion against the sovereignty of these new nations and a direct challenge to the United Nations.

The immediate strategy of the Soviet imperialists is to destroy the world's confidence in America's desire for peace, to threaten with violence our mutual security arrangements, and to sever the bonds of amity and respect among the free nations. To nullify the Soviet conspiracy is our greatest task. The United States faces this challenge and resolves to meet it with courage and confidence.

To this end we will continue to support and strengthen the United Nations as an instrument for peace, for international cooperation, and for the advancement of the fundamental freedoms and humane interests of mankind.

Under the United Nations we will work for the peaceful settlement of international disputes and the extension of the rule of law in the world.

And, in furtherance of President Eisenhower's proposals for the peaceful use of space, we suggest that the United Nations take the initiative to develop a body of law applicable thereto.

Through all the calculated shifts of Soviet tactics and mood, the Eisenhower–Nixon Administration has demonstrated its willingness to negotiate in earnest with the Soviet Union to arrive at just settlements for the reduction of world tensions. We pledge the new Administration to continue in the same course.

We are similarly ready to negotiate and to institute realistic methods and safeguards for disarmament, and for the suspension of nuclear tests. We advocate an early agreement by all nations to forego nuclear tests in the atmosphere, and the suspension of other tests as verification techniques permit. We support the President in any decision he may make to re-evaluate the question of resumption of underground nuclear explosions testing, if the Geneva Conference fails to produce a satisfactory agreement. We have deep concern about the mounting nuclear arms race. This concern leads us to seek disarmament and nuclear agreements. And an equal concern to protect all peoples from nuclear danger, leads us to insist that such agreements have adequate safeguards.

We recognize that firm political and military policies, while imperative for our security, cannot in themselves build peace in the world.

In Latin America, Asia, Africa and the Middle East, peoples of ancient and recent independence, have shown their determination to improve their standards of living, and to enjoy an equality with the rest of mankind in the enjoyment of the fruits of civilization. This determination has become a primary fact of their political life. We declare ourselves to be in sympathy with their aspirations.

We have already created unprecedented dimensions of diplomacy for these purposes. We recognize that upon our support of well-conceived programs of economic cooperation among nations rest the best hopes of hundreds of millions of friendly people for a decent future for themselves and their children. Our mutual security program of economic help and technical assistance; the Development Loan Fund, the Inter-American Bank, the International Development Association and the Food for Peace Program, which create the conditions for progress in less-developed countries; our leadership in international efforts to help children, eliminate pestilence and disease and aid refugees—these are programs wise in concept and generous in purpose. We mean to continue in support of them.

Now we propose to further evolution of our programs for assistance to and cooperation with other nations, suitable to the emerging needs of the future.

We will encourage the countries of Latin America, Africa, the Middle East and Asia, to initiate appropriate regional groupings to work out plans for economic and educational development. We anticipate that the United Nations Special Fund would be of assistance in developing such plans. The United States would offer its cooperation in planning, and the provision of technical personnel for this purpose. Agreeable to the developing nations, we would join with them in inviting countries with advanced economies to share with us a proportionate part of the capital and technical aid required. We would emphasize the increasing use of private capital and government loans, rather than outright grants, as a means of fostering independence and mutual respect. The President's recent initiative of a joint partnership program for Latin America opens the way to this approach.

We would propose that such groupings adopt means to attain viable economies following such examples as the European Common Market. And if from these institutions, there should follow stronger economic and political unions, we would welcome them with our support.

Despite the counterdrive of international Communism, relentless against individual freedom and subversive of the sovereignty of nations, a powerful drive for freedom has swept the world since World War II and many heroic episodes in the Communist countries have demonstrated anew that freedom will not die.

The Republican Party reaffirms its determination to use every peaceful means to help the captive nations toward their independence, and thus their freedom to live and worship according to conscience. We do not condone the subjugation of the peoples of Hungary, Poland, East Germany, Czechoslovakia, Rumania, Albania, Bulgaria, Latvia, Lithuania, Estonia, and other once-free nations. We are not shaken in our hope and belief that once again they will rule themselves.

Our time surges with change and challenge, peril and great opportunities. It calls us to great tasks and efforts—for free men can hope to guard freedom only if they prove capable of historic acts of wisdom and courage.

Dwight David Eisenhower stands today throughout the world as the greatest champion of peace and justice and good.

The Republican Party brings to the days ahead trained, experienced, mature and courageous leadership.

Our Party was born for freedom's sake. It is still the Party of full freedom in our country. As in Lincoln's time, our Party and its leaders will meet the challenges and opportunities of our time and keep our country the best and enduring hope of freedom for the world.

NATIONAL DEFENSE

The future of freedom depends heavily upon America's military might and that of her allies. Under the Eisenhower–Nixon Administration, our military might has been forged into a power second to none. This strength, tailored to serve the needs of national policy, has deterred and must continue to deter aggression and encourage the growth of freedom in the world. This is the only sure way to a world at peace.

We have checked aggression. We ended the war in Korea. We have joined with free nations in creating strong defenses. Swift technological change and the warning signs of Soviet aggressiveness make clear that intensified and courageous efforts are necessary, for the new problems of the 1960's will of course demand new efforts on the part of our entire nation. The Republican Party is pledged to making certain that our arms, and our will to use them, remain superior to all threats. We have, and will continue to have, the defenses we need to protect our freedom.

The strategic imperatives of our national defense policy are these:

- A second-strike capability, that is, a nuclear retaliatory power that can survive surprise attack, strike back, and destroy any possible enemy.
- Highly mobile and versatile forces, including forces deployed to deter or check local aggressions and "brush fire wars" which might bring on all-out nuclear war.
- National determination to employ all necessary military capabilities so as to render any level of aggression unprofitable. Deterrence of war since Korea, specifically, has been the result of our firm statement that we will never again permit a potential aggressor to set the ground rules for his aggression; that we will respond to aggression with the full means and weapons best suited to the situation.

Maintenance of these imperatives requires these actions:

- Unremitting modernization of our retaliatory forces, continued development of the manned bomber well into the missile age, with necessary numbers of these bombers protected through dispersal and airborne alert.
- Development and production of new strategic weapons, such as the Polaris submarine and ballistic missile. Never again will they be neglected, as intercontinental missile development was neglected between the end of World War II and 1953.
- Accelerate as necessary development of hardening, mobility, dispersal, and production programs for long-range missiles and the speedy perfection of new and advanced generations of missiles and anti-missile missiles.
- Intensified development of active civil defense to enable our people to protect themselves against the deadly hazards of atomic attack, particularly fallout; and to develop a new program to build a reserve of storable food, adequate to the needs of the population after an atomic attack.
- Constant intelligence operations regarding Communist military preparations to prevent another Pearl Harbor.
- A military establishment organized in accord with a national strategy which enables the unified commands in Europe, the Pacific, and this continent to continue to respond promptly to any kind of aggression.
- Strengthening of the military might of the free-world nations in such ways as to encourage them to assume increasing responsibility for regional security.
- Continuation of the "long pull" preparedness policies which, as inaugurated under the Eisenhower–Nixon Administration, have avoided the perilous peaks and slumps of defense spending and planning which marked earlier administrations.

There is no price ceiling on America's security. The United States can and must provide whatever is necessary to insure its own security and that of the free world and to provide any necessary increased expenditures to meet new situations, to guarantee the opportunity to fulfill the hopes of men of good will everywhere. To provide more would be wasteful. To provide less would be catastrophic. Our defense posture must remain steadfast, confident, and superior to all potential foes.

ECONOMIC GROWTH AND BUSINESS

To provide the means to a better life for individual Americans and to strengthen the forces of freedom in the world, we count on the proved productivity of our free economy.

Despite the lamentations of the opposition in viewing the economic scene today, the plain fact is that our 500-billion-dollar economy finds more Americans at work, earning more, spending more, saving more, investing more, building more than ever before in history. The well-being of our people, by virtually every yardstick, has greatly advanced under this Republican Administration.

But we can and must do better. We must raise employment to even higher levels and utilize even more fully our expanding, overall capacity to produce. We must quicken the pace of our economic growth to prove the power of American free enterprise to meet growing and urgent demands: to sustain our military posture, to provide jobs for a growing labor force in a time of rapid technological change, to improve living standards, to serve all the needs of an expanding population.

We therefore accord high priority to vigorous economic growth and recognize that its mainspring lies in the private sector of the economy. We must continue to foster a healthy climate in that sector. We reject the concept of artificial growth forced by massive new federal spending and loose money policies. The only effective way to accelerate economic growth is to increase the traditional strengths of our free economy—initiative and investment, productivity and efficiency. To that end we favor. . . .

Broadly based tax reform to foster job-making and growth-making investment for modernization and expansion, including realistic incentive depreciation schedules.

Use of the full powers of government to prevent the scourges of depression and inflation.

Elimination of featherbedding practices by labor and business.

Maintenance of a stable dollar as an indispensable means to progress.

Relating wage and other payments in production to productivity—except when necessary to correct inequities—in order to help us stay competitive at home and abroad.

Spurring the economy by advancing the successful Eisenhower–Nixon program fostering new and small business, by continued active enforcement of the anti-trust laws, by protecting consumers and investors against the hazard and economic waste of fraudulent and criminal practices in the market place, and by keeping the federal government from unjustly competing with private enterprise upon which Americans mainly depend for their livelihood.

Continued improvement of our vital transportation network, carrying forward rapidly the vast Eisenhower–Nixon national highway program and promoting safe, efficient, competitive and integrated transport by air, road, rail and water under equitable, impartial and minimal regulation directed to those ends.

Carrying forward, under the Trade Agreements Act, the policy of gradual selective—and truly reciprocal—reduction of unjustifiable barriers to trade among free nations. We advocate effective administration of the Act's escape clause and peril point provisions to safeguard American jobs and domestic industries against serious injury. In support of our national trade policy we should continue the Eisenhower–Nixon program of using this government's negotiating powers to open markets abroad and to eliminate remaining discrimination against our goods. We should also encourage the development of fair labor standards in exporting countries in the interest of fair competition in international trade. We should, too, expand the Administration's export drive, encourage tourists to come from abroad, and protect U.S. investors against arbitrary confiscations and expropriations by foreign governments. Through these and other constructive policies, we will better our international balance of payments.

Discharge by government of responsibility for those activities which the private sector cannot do or cannot so well do, such as constructive federal local action to aid areas of chronic high unemployment, a sensible farm policy, development and wise use of natural resources, suitable support of education and research, and equality of job opportunity for all Americans.

Action on these fronts, designed to release the strongest productive force in human affairs—the spirit of individual enterprise—can contribute greatly to our goal of a steady, strongly growing economy.

LABOR

America's growth cannot be compartmentalized. Labor and management cannot prosper without each other. They cannot ignore their mutual public obligation.

Industrial harmony, expressing these mutual interests, can best be achieved in a climate of free collective bargaining, with minimal government intervention except by mediation and conciliation.

Even in dealing with emergency situations imperiling the national safety, ways of solution must be found to enhance and not impede the processes of free collective bargaining—carefully considered ways that are in keeping with the policies of national labor relations legislation and with the need to strengthen the hand of the President in dealing with such emergencies.

In the same spirit, Republican leadership will continue to encourage discussions, away from the bargaining table, between labor and management to consider the mutual interest of all Americans in maintaining industrial peace.

Republican policy firmly supports the right of employers and unions freely to enter into agreements providing for the union shop and other forms of union security as authorized by the Labor–Management Relations Act of 1947 (the Taft–Hartley Act).

Republican-sponsored legislation has supported the right of union members to full participation in the affairs of their union and their right to freedom from racketeering and gangster interference whether by labor or management in labor–management relations.

Republican action has given to millions of American working men and women new or expanded protection and benefits, such as:

Increased federal minimum wage;

Extended coverage of unemployment insurance and the payment of additional temporary benefits provided in 1958–59;

Improvement of veterans' re-employment rights;

Extension of federal workman's compensation coverage and increase of benefits;

Legislative assurance of safety standards for longshore and harbor workers and for the transportation of migratory workers;

An increase of railroad workers' retirement and disability benefits.

Seven past years of accomplishments, however, are but a base to build upon in fostering, promoting and improving the welfare of America's working men and women, both organized and unorganized. We pledge, therefore, action on these constructive lines:

Diligent administration of the amended Labor-Management Relations Act of 1947 (Taft–Hartley Act) and the Labor–Management Reporting and Disclosure Act of 1959 (Landrum–Griffin Act) with recommendations for improvements which experience shows are needed to make them more effective or remove any inequities.

Correction of defects in the Welfare and Pension Plans Disclosure Act to protect employees' and beneficiaries' interests.

Upward revision in amount and extended coverage of the minimum wage to several million more workers.

Strengthening the unemployment insurance system and extension of its benefits.

Improvement of the eight-hour laws relating to hours and overtime compensation on federal and federally assisted construction, and continued vigorous enforcement and improvement of minimum wage laws for federal supply and construction contracts.

Continued improvement of manpower skills and training to meet a new era of challenges, including action programs to aid older workers, women, youth, and the physically handicapped.

Encouragement of training programs by labor, industry and government to aid in finding new jobs for persons dislocated by automation or other economic changes.

Improvement of job opportunities and working conditions of migratory farm workers.

Assurance of equal pay for equal work regardless of sex; encouragement of programs to insure on-the-job safety, and encouragement of the States to improve their labor standards legislation, and to improve veterans' employment rights and benefits.

Encouragement abroad of free democratic institutions, higher living standards and higher wages through such agencies as the International Labor Organization, and cooperation with the free trade union movement in strengthening free labor throughout the world.

AGRICULTURE

Americans are the best-fed and the best-clothed people in the world. Our challenge fortunately is one of dealing with abundance, not overcoming shortage. The fullness of our fields, forests and grazing lands is an important advantage in our struggle against worldwide tyranny and our crusade against poverty. Our farmers have provided us with a powerful weapon in the ideological and economic struggle in which we are now engaged.

Yet, far too many of our farm families, the source of this strength, have not received a fair return for their labors. For too long, Democratic-controlled Congresses have stalemated progress by clinging to obsolete programs conceived for different times and different problems.

Promises of specific levels of price support or a single type of program for all agriculture are cruel deceptions based upon the pessimistic pretense that only with rigid controls can farm families be aided. The Republican Party will provide within the framework of individual freedom a greater bargaining power to assure an equitable return for the work and capital supplied by farmers.

The Republican Party pledges itself to develop new

programs to improve and stabilize farm family income. It recognizes two main challenges: the immediate one of utilizing income-depressing surpluses, and the long-range one of steady balanced growth and development with a minimum of federal interference and control.

To utilize immediately surpluses in an orderly manner, with a minimum impact on domestic and foreign markets, we pledge:

Intensification of the Food for Peace program, including new cooperative efforts among food surplus nations to assist the hungry peoples in less favored areas of the world.

Payment-in-kind, out of existing surpluses, as part of our land retirement program.

Creation of a Strategic Food Reserve properly dispersed in forms which can be preserved for long periods against the contingency of grave national emergency.

Strengthened efforts to distribute surpluses to schools and low-income and needy citizens of our own country.

A reorganization of the Commodity Credit Corporation's inventory management operations to reduce competition with the marketings of farmers.

To assure steady balanced growth and agricultural progress, we pledge:

A crash research program to develop industrial and other uses of farm products.

Use of price supports at levels best fitted to specific commodities, in order to widen markets, ease production controls, and help achieve increased farm family income.

Acceleration of production adjustments, including a large-scale land conservation reserve program on a voluntary and equitable rental basis, with full consideration of the impact on local communities.

Continued progress in the wise use and conservation of water and soil resources.

Use of marketing agreements and orders, and other marketing devices, when approved by producers, to assist in the orderly marketing of crops, thus enabling farmers to strengthen their bargaining power.

Stepped-up research to reduce production costs and to cut distribution costs.

Strengthening of the educational programs of the U.S. Department of Agriculture and the Land Grant institutions.

Improvement of credit facilities for financing the capital needs of modern farming.

Encouragement of farmer-owned-and-operated cooperatives including rural electric and telephone facilities.

Expansion of the Rural Development Program to help low-income farm families not only through better farming methods, but also through opportunities for vocational training, more effective employment services, and creation of job opportunities through encouragement of local industrialization.

Continuation and further improvement of the Great Plains Program.

Legislative action for programs now scheduled to expire for the school milk program, wool, and sugar, including increased sugar acreage to domestic areas.

Free movement in interstate commerce of agricultural commodities meeting federal health standards.

To prevent dumping of agricultural imports upon domestic markets.

To assure the American farmer a more direct voice in his own destiny, we pledge:

To select an official committee of farmers and ranchers, on a regional basis, broadly representative of American agriculture, whose function will be to recommend to the President guidelines for improving the operation of government farm programs.

NATURAL RESOURCES

A strong and growing economy requires vigorous and persistent attention to wise conservation and sound development of all our resources. Teamwork between federal, state and private entities is essential and should be continued. It has resulted in sustained conservation and resource development programs on a scale unmatched in our history.

The past seven years of Republican leadership have seen the development of more power capacity, flood control, irrigation, fish and wildlife projects, recreational facilities, and associated multipurpose benefits than during any previous administration in history. The proof is visible in the forests and waters of the land and in Republican initiation of and support for the Upper Watershed Program and the Small Reclamation Projects Act. It is clear, also, in the results of continuing administration-encouraged forest management practices which have brought, for the first time, a favorable balance between the growth and cutting of America's trees.

Our objective is for further growth, greater strength, and increased utilization in each great area of resource use and development.

We pledge:

Use of the community watershed as the basic natural unit through which water resource, soil, and forest management programs may best be developed, with interstate compacts encouraged to handle regional aspects without federal domination.

Development of new water resource projects throughout the nation.

Support of the historic policy of Congress in preserving the integrity of the several States to govern water rights.

Continued federal support for Republican-initiated research and demonstration projects which will supply fresh water from salt and brackish water sources.

Necessary measures for preservation of our domestic fisheries.

Continued forestry conservation with appropriate sustained-yield harvesting, thus increasing jobs for people and increasing revenue.

To observe the "preference clause" in marketing federal power.

Support of the basic principles of reclamation.

Recognition of urban and industrial demands by making available to states and local governments, federal lands not needed for national programs.

Full use and preservation of our great outdoors are pledged in:

Completion of the "Mission 66" for the improvement of National Park areas as well as sponsorship of a new "Mission 76" program to encourage establishment and rehabilitation of local, state, and regional parks, to provide adequate recreational facilities for our expanding population.

Continued support of the effort to keep our great out-of-doors beautiful, green, and clean.

Establishment of a citizens board of conservation, resource and land management experts to inventory those federal lands now set aside for a particular purpose; to study the future needs of the nation for parks, seashores, and wildlife and other recreational areas; and to study the possibility of restoring lands not needed for a federal program.

Minerals, metals, fuels, also call for carefully considered actions in view of the repeated failure of Democratic-controlled Congresses to enact any long-range minerals legislation. Republicans, therefore, pledge:

Long-range minerals and fuels planning and programming, including increased coal research.

Assistance to mining industries in bridging the gap between peak defense demands and anticipated peacetime demands.

Continued support for federal financial assistance and incentives under our tax laws to encourage exploration for domestic sources of minerals and metals, with reasonable depletion allowances.

To preserve our fish and wildlife heritage, we pledge:

Legislation to authorize exchange of lands between state and federal governments to adapt programs to changing uses and habits.

Vigorous implementation of long-range programs for fish and wildlife.

GOVERNMENT FINANCE

To build a better America with broad national purposes such as high employment, vigorous and steady economic growth, and a dependable currency, responsible management of our federal finances is essential. Even more important, a sound economy is vital to national security. While leading Democrats charge us with a "budget balancing" mentality, their taunts really reflect their frustration over the people's recognition that as a nation we must live within our means. Government that is careless with the money of its citizens is careless with their future.

Because we are concerned about the well-being of people, we are concerned about protecting the value of their money. To this end, we Republicans believe that:

Every government expenditure must be tested by its contribution to the general welfare, not to any narrow interest group.

Except in times of war or economic adversity, expenditures should be covered by revenues.

We must work persistently to reduce, not to increase, the national debt, which imposes a heavy economic burden on every citizen.

Our tax structure should be improved to provide greater incentives to economic progress, to make it fair and equitable, and to maintain and deserve public acceptance.

We must resist assaults upon the independence of the Federal Reserve System; we must strengthen, not weaken, the ability of the Federal Reserve System and the Treasury Department to exercise effective control over money and credit in order better to combat both deflation and inflation that retard economic growth and shrink people's savings and earnings.

In order of priority, federal revenues should be used: first, to meet the needs of national security; second, to fulfill the legitimate and urgent needs of the nation that cannot be met by the States, local governments or private action; third, to pay down on the national debt in good times; finally, to improve our tax structure.

National security and other essential needs will continue to make enormous demands upon public revenues. It is therefore imperative that we weigh carefully each demand for a new federal expenditure. The federal government should undertake not the most things nor the least things, but the right things.

Achieving this vital purpose demands:

That Congress, in acting on new spending bills, have figures before it showing the cumulative effect of its actions on the total budget.

That spending commitments for future years be clearly listed in each budget, so that the effect of built-in expenditure programs may be recognized and evaluated.

That the President be empowered to veto individual items in authorization and appropriation bills.

That increasing efforts be made to extend business-like methods to government operations, particularly in purchasing and supply activities, and in personnel.

GOVERNMENT ADMINISTRATION

The challenges of our time test the very organization of democracy. They put on trial the capacity of free government to act quickly, wisely, resolutely. To meet these challenges:

The President must continue to be able to reorganize and streamline executive operations to keep the executive branch capable of responding effectively to rapidly changing conditions in both foreign and domestic fields. The Eisenhower–Nixon Administration did so by creating a new Department of Health, Education and Welfare, by establishing the National Aeronautics and Space Agency and the Federal Aviation Agency, and by reorganizations of the Defense Department.

Two top positions should be established to assist the President in, (1) the entire field of National Security and International Affairs, and, (2) Governmental Planning and Management, particularly in domestic affairs.

We must undertake further reorganization of the Defense Department to achieve the most effective unification of defense planning and command.

Improved conflict-of-interest laws should be enacted for vigilant protection of the public interest and to remove deterrents to governmental service by our most able citizens.

The federal government must constantly strengthen its career service and must be truly progressive as an employer. Government employment must be a vocation deserving of high public respect. Common sense demands continued improvements in employment, training and promotion practices based on merit, effective procedures for dealing with employment grievances, and salaries which are comparable to those offered by private employers.

As already practiced by the Republican membership, responsible Policy Committees should be elected by each party in each house of Congress. This would provide a mechanism for meetings of party Congressional leaders with the President when circumstances demand.

Needed federal judgeships, appointed on the basis of the highest qualifications and without limitation to a single political party, should be created to expedite administration of justice in federal courts.

The remarkable growth of the Post Office since 1952 to serve an additional 9 million urban and 1.5 million farm families must be continued. The Post Office must be continually improved and placed on a self-sustaining basis. Progressive Republican policies of the past seven years have resulted in reduced costs, decentralization of postal operations, liberal pay, fringe benefits, improved working conditions, streamlined management, and improved service.

Vigorous state and local governments are a vital part of our federal union. The federal government should leave to state and local governments those programs and problems which they can best handle and tax sources adequate to finance them. We must continue to improve liaison between federal, state and local governments. We believe that the federal government, when appropriate, should render significant assistance in dealing with our urgent problems of urban growth and change. No vast new bureaucracy is needed to achieve this objective.

We favor a change in the Electoral College system to give every voter a fair voice in presidential elections.

We condemn bigotry, smear and other unfair tactics in political campaigns. We favor realistic and effective safeguards against diverting nonpolitical funds to partisan political purposes.

Republicans will continue to work for Congressional representation and self-government for the District of Columbia and also support the constitutional amendment granting suffrage in national elections.

We support the right of the Puerto Rican people to achieve statehood, whenever they freely so determine. We support the right of the people of the Virgin Islands to an elected Governor, national representation and suffrage, looking toward eventual statehood, when qualified. We also support the right of the people of Guam to an elected Governor and national representation. These pledges are meaningful from the Republican leadership under which Alaska and Hawaii have newly entered the Union.

Congress should submit a constitutional amendment providing equal rights for women.

EDUCATION

The rapid pace of international developments serves to reemphasize dramatically the challenge which generations of Americans will face in the years ahead. We are reminded daily of the crucial importance of strengthening our system of education to prepare our youth for understanding and shaping the powerful emerging forces of the modern world and to permit the fullest possible development of individual capacities and potentialities.

We express our gratefulness and we praise the countless thousands of teachers who have devoted themselves in an inspired way towards the development of our greatest heritage—our own children—the youth of the country.

Education is not a luxury, nor a gift to be bestowed upon ourselves and our children. Education is an investment; our schools cannot become second best. Each person possesses the right to education—it is his birthright in a free Republic.

Primary responsibility for education must remain with the local community and state. The federal government should assist selectively in strengthening education without interfering with full local control of schools. One objective of such federal assistance should be to help equalize educational opportunities. Under the Eisenhower–Nixon Administration, the federal government will spend more than a billion dollars in 1960 to strengthen American education.

We commend the objective of the Republican Administration in sponsoring the National Defense Education Act to stimulate improvement of study and teaching in selected fields at the local level.

Toward the goal of fullest possible educational opportunity for every American, we pledge these actions:

Federal support to the primary and secondary schools by a program of federal aid for school construction—pacing it to the real needs of individual school districts in states and territories, and requiring state approval and participation.

Stimulation of actions designed to update and strengthen vocational education for both youth and adults.

Support of efforts to make adequate library facilities available to all our citizens.

Continued support of programs to strengthen basic research in education; to discover the best methods for helping handicapped, retarded, and gifted children to realize their highest potential.

The federal government can also play a part in stimulating higher education. Constructive action would include:

The federal program to assist in construction of college housing.

Extension of the federal student loan program and graduate fellowship program.

Consideration of means through tax laws to help offset tuition costs,

Continued support of the East–West Center for cultural and technical interchange in Hawaii for the purpose of strengthening our relationship with the peoples of the Pacific world.

Federal matching grants to help states finance the cost of state surveys and inventories of the status and needs of their school systems.

Provision should be made for continuous attention to education at all levels by the creation of a permanent, top-level commission to advise the President and the Secretary of Health, Education and Welfare, constantly striving to focus the interest of each citizen on the quality of our education at every level, from primary through postgraduate, and for every age group from children to adults.

We are aware of the fact that there is a temporary shortage of classrooms for our elementary and secondary schools in a limited number of states. But this shortage, due to the vigilant action of state legislatures and local school boards, is not increasing, but is decreasing.

We shall use our full efforts in all the states of the

Union to have these legislatures and school boards augment their present efforts to the end that this temporary shortage may be eliminated and that every child in this country shall have the opportunity to obtain a good education. The respective states as a permanent program can shoulder this long-standing and cherished responsibility easier than can the federal government with its heavy indebtedness.

We believe moreover that any large plan of federal aid to education, such as direct contributions to or grants for teachers' salaries can only lead ultimately to federal domination and control of our schools to which we are unalterably opposed.

In the words of President Eisenhower, "Education best fulfills its high purpose when responsibility for education is kept close to the people it serves—when it is rooted in the homes, nurtured in the community and sustained by a rich variety of public, private and individual resources. The bond linking home and school and community—the responsiveness of each to the needs of the others—is a precious asset of American education."

SCIENCE AND TECHNOLOGY

Much of America's future depends upon the inquisitive mind, freely searching nature for ways to conquer disease, poverty and grinding physical demands, and for knowledge of space and the atom.

We Republicans express our profound gratitude to the great scientists and engineers of our country, both in and out of government, for the remarkable progress they have made. Reliable evidence indicates, all areas of scientific knowledge considered, that our country has been, is, and under our system of free inquiry, will continue to be the greatest arsenal and reservoir of effective scientific knowledge in the world.

We pledge our continued leadership in every field of science and technology, earth bound as well as spacial, to assure a citadel of liberty from which the fruits of freedom may be carried to all people.

Our continuing and great national need is for basic research—a wellspring of knowledge and progress. Government must continue to take a responsible role in science to assure that worthwhile endeavors of national significance are not retarded by practical limitations of private and local support. This demands from all Americans the intellectual leadership and understanding so necessary for these creative endeavors and an equal understanding by our scientists and technicians of the needs and hopes of mankind.

We believe the federal roles in research to be in the area of (1) basic research which industry cannot be rea-sonably expected to pursue, and (2) applied research in fields of prime national concern such as national defense, exploration and use of space, public health, and better common use of all natural resources, both human and physical. We endorse the contracting by government agencies for research and urge allowance for reasonable charges for overhead and management in connection therewith.

The vigor of American science and technology may best be inspired by:

An environment of freedom and public understanding in which intellectual achievement and scientific research may flourish.

A decentralization of research into as many centers of creativity as possible.

The encouragement of colleges and universities, private enterprise, and foundations as a growing source of new ideas and new applications.

Opportunity for scientists and engineers, in and out of government, to pursue their search with utmost aggressiveness.

Continuation of the advisory committee to represent the views of the scientific community to the President and of the Federal Council for Science and Technology to foster coordination in planning and execution.

Continued expansion of the Eisenhower–Nixon Atoms-for-Peace program and a constant striving, backed by scientific advice, for international agreement for peaceful and cooperative exploration and use of space.

HUMAN NEEDS

The ultimate objective of our free society and of an ever-growing economy is to enable the individual to pursue a life of dignity and to develop his own capacities to his maximum potential.

Government's primary role is to help provide the environment within which the individual can seek his own goals. In some areas this requires federal action to supplement individual, local and state initiative. The Republican Party has acted and will act decisively, compassionately, and with deep human understanding in approaching such problems as those of the aged, the infirm, the mentally ill, and the needy.

This is demonstrated by the significant increase in social security coverage and benefits as a result of recommendations made by the Eisenhower–Nixon Administration. As a result of these recommendations and normal growth, 14 million persons are receiving benefits today compared to five million in 1952, and benefit payments total $10.3 billion as compared to $2.5 billion in 1952. In addition, there have been increases in payments to those on public assistance, both for their basic needs and for their health and medical care; and a broad expansion in our federal–state program for restoring disabled persons to useful lives—an expansion which has accomplished the rehabilitation of over half a million persons during this Administration.

New needs, however, are constantly arising in our highly complex, interdependent, and urbanized society.

Older Citizens

To meet the needs of the aging, we pledge:

Expansion of coverage, and liberalization of selected social security benefits on a basis which would maintain the fiscal integrity of the system.

Support of federal–state grant programs to improve health, welfare and rehabilitation services for the handicapped older persons and to improve standards of nursing home care and care and treatment facilities for the chronically and mentally ill.

Federal leadership to encourage policies that will make retirement at a fixed age voluntary and not compulsory.

Support of programs that will persuade and encourage the nation to utilize fully the skills, wisdom and experience of older citizens.

Prompt consideration of recommendations by the White House Conference on Aging called by the President for January, 1961.

Health Aid

Development of a health program that will provide the aged needing it, on a sound fiscal basis and through a contributory system, protection against burdensome costs of health care. Such a program should:

Provide the beneficiaries with the option of purchasing private health insurance—a vital distinction between our approach and Democratic proposals in that it would encourage commercial carriers and voluntary insurance organizations to continue their efforts to develop sound coverage plans for the senior population.

Protect the personal relationship of patient and physician.

Include state participation.

For the needs which individuals of all age groups cannot meet by themselves, we propose:

Removing the arbitrary 50-year age requirement under the disability insurance program while amending the law also to provide incentives for rehabilitated persons to return to useful work.

A single, federal assistance grant to each state for aid to needy persons rather than dividing such grants into specific categories.

A strengthened federal–state program to rehabilitate the estimated 200,000 persons who annually could become independent after proper medical services and occupational training.

A new federal–state program, for handicapped persons completely dependent on others, to help them meet their needs for personal care.

Juvenile Delinquency

The federal government can and should help state and local communities combat juvenile delinquency by inaugurating a grant program for research, demonstration, and training projects and by placing greater emphasis on strengthening family life in all welfare programs for which it shares responsibility.

Veterans

We believe that military service in the defense of our Republic against aggressors who have sought to destroy the freedom and dignity of man imposes upon the nation a special responsibility to those who have served. To meet this responsibility, we pledge:

Continuance of the Veterans Administration as an independent agency.

The highest possible standard of medical care with increasing emphasis on rehabilitation.

Indian Affairs

As recently as 1953, thirty per cent of Indian school-age children were unable to obtain an education. Through Republican efforts, this fall, for the first time in history, every eligible Indian child will be able to attend an elementary school. Having accomplished this, we will now accelerate our efforts to open up both secondary and higher education opportunities for every qualified Indian youth.

As a result of a stepped-up health program there has been a marked decrease in death rates from tuberculosis and in the infant mortality rate. Also substantial progress has been made in the modernization of health facilities. We pledge continued progress in this area.

We are opposed to precipitous termination of the federal Indian trusteeship responsibility, and pledge not to support any termination plan for any tribe which has not approved such action.

Housing

Despite noteworthy accomplishments, stubborn and deep-seated problems stand in the way of achieving the national objective of a decent home in a suitable environment for every American. Recognizing that the federal government must help provide the economic climate and incentives which make this objective obtainable, the Republican Party will vigorously support the following steps, all designed to supplement and not supplant private initiative.

Continued effort to clear slums, and promote rebuilding, rehabilitation, and conservation of our cities.

New programs to stimulate development of specialized types of housing, such as those for the elderly and for nursing homes.

A program of research and demonstration aimed at finding ways to reduce housing costs, including support of efforts to modernize and improve local building codes.

Adequate authority for the federal housing agencies to assist the flow of mortgage credit into private housing, with emphasis on homes for middle- and lower-income families and including assistance in urban residential areas.

A stepped-up program to assist in urban planning, designed to assure far-sighted and wise use of land and to coordinate mass transportation and other vital facilities in our metropolitan areas.

Health

There has been a five-fold increase in government-assisted medical research during the last six years. We pledge:

Continued federal support for a sound research program aimed at both the prevention and cure of diseases, and intensified efforts to secure prompt and effective application of the results of research. This will include emphasis on mental illness.

Support of international health research programs.

We face serious personnel shortages in the health and medical fields. We pledge:

Federal help in new programs to build schools of medicine, dentistry, and public health and nursing, and financial aid to students in those fields.

We are confronted with major problems in the field of environmental health. We pledge:

Strengthened federal enforcement powers in combatting water pollution and additional resources for research and demonstration projects. Federal grants for the construction of waste disposal plants should be made only when they make an identifiable contribution to clearing up polluted streams.

Federal authority to identify, after appropriate hearings, air pollution problems and to recommend proposed solutions.

Additional resources for research and training in the field of radiological medicine.

Protection of Consumers

In safeguarding the health of the nation the Eisenhower–Nixon Administration's initiative has resulted in doubling the resources of the Food and Drug Administration and in giving it new legal weapons. More progress has been made during this period in protecting consumers against harmful food, drugs, and cosmetics than in any other time in our history. We will continue to give strong support to this consumer-protection program.

CIVIL RIGHTS

This nation was created to give expression, validity and purpose to our spiritual heritage—the supreme worth of the individual. In such a nation—a nation dedicated to the proposition that all men are created equal—racial discrimination has no place. It can hardly be reconciled with a Constitution that guarantees equal protection under law to all persons. In a deeper sense, too, it is immoral and unjust. As to those matters within reach of political action and leadership, we pledge ourselves unreservedly to its eradication.

Equality under law promises more than the equal right to vote and transcends mere relief from discrimination by government. It becomes a reality only when all persons have equal opportunity, without distinction of race, religion, color or national origin, to acquire the essentials of life—housing, education and employment. The Republican Party—the party of Abraham Lincoln from its very beginning has striven to make this promise a reality. It is today, as it was then, unequivocally dedicated to making the greatest amount of progress toward the objective.

We recognize that discrimination is not a problem localized in one area of the country, but rather a problem that must be faced by North and South alike. Nor is discrimination confined to the discrimination against Negroes. Discrimination in many, if not all, areas of the country on the basis of creed or national origin is equally insidious. Further we recognize that in many communities in which a century of custom and tradition must be overcome heartening and commendable progress has been made.

The Republican Party is proud of the civil rights record of the Eisenhower Administration. More progress has been made during the past eight years than in the preceding 80 years. We acted promptly to end discrimination in our nation's capital. Vigorous executive action was taken to complete swiftly the desegregation of the armed forces, veterans' hospitals, navy yards, and other federal establishments.

We supported the position of the Negro school children before the Supreme Court. We believe the Supreme Court school decision should be carried out in accordance with the mandate of the Court.

Although the Democratic-controlled Congress watered them down, the Republican Administration's recommendations resulted in significant and effective civil rights legislation in both 1957 and 1960—the first civil rights statutes to be passed in more than 80 years.

Hundreds of Negroes have already been registered to vote as a result of Department of Justice action, some in counties where Negroes did not vote before. The new law will soon make it possible for thousands and thousands of Negroes previously disenfranchised to vote.

By executive order, a committee for the elimination of discrimination in government employment has been reestablished with broadened authority. Today, nearly one-fourth of all federal employees are Negro.

The President's Committee on Government Contracts, under the chairmanship of Vice President Nixon, has become an impressive force for the elimination of discriminatory employment practices of private companies that do business with the government.

Other important achievements include initial steps toward the elimination of segregation in federally aided housing; the establishment of the Civil Rights Division of the Department of Justice, which enforces federal civil rights laws; and the appointment of the bipartisan Civil Rights Commission, which has prepared a significant report that lays the groundwork for further legislative action and progress.

The Republican record is a record of progress, not merely promises. Nevertheless, we recognize that much remains to be done.

Each of the following pledges is practical and within realistic reach of accomplishment. They are serious—not cynical—pledges made to result in maximum progress.

1. *Voting*. We pledge:

Continued vigorous enforcement of the civil rights laws to guarantee the right to vote to all citizens in all areas of the country.
Legislation to provide that the completion of six primary grades in a state accredited school is conclusive evidence of literacy for voting purposes.

2. *Public Schools*. We pledge:

The Department of Justice will continue its vigorous support of court orders for school desegregation. Desegregation suits now pending involve at least 39 school districts. Those suits and others already concluded will affect most major cities in which school segregation is being practiced.
It will use the new authority provided by the Civil Rights Act of 1960 to prevent obstruction of court orders.
We will propose legislation to authorize the Attorney General to bring actions for school desegregation in the name of the United States in appropriate cases, as when economic coercion or threat of physical harm is used to deter persons from going to court to establish their rights.
Our continuing support of the President's proposal to extend federal aid and technical assistance to schools which in good faith attempted to desegregate.
We oppose the pretense of fixing a target date 3 years from now for the mere submission of plans for school desegregation. Slow-moving school districts would construe it as a three-year moratorium during which progress would cease, postponing until 1963 the legal process to enforce compliance. We believe that each of the pending court actions should proceed as the Supreme Court has directed and that in no district should there be any such delay.

3. *Employment*. We pledge:

Continued support for legislation to establish a Commission on Equal Job Opportunity to make permanent and to expand with legislative backing the excellent work being performed by the President's Committee on Government Contracts.
Appropriate legislation to end the discriminatory membership practices of some labor union locals, unless such practices are eradicated promptly by the labor unions themselves.
Use of the full-scale review of existing state laws,

and of prior proposals for federal legislation, to eliminate discrimination in employment now being conducted by the Civil Rights Commission, for guidance in our objective of developing a federal–state program in the employment area.

Special consideration of training programs aimed at developing the skills of those now working in marginal agricultural employment so that they can obtain employment in industry, notably in the new industries moving into the South.

4. *Housing*. We pledge:

Action to prohibit discrimination in housing constructed with the aid of federal subsidies.

5. *Public Facilities and Services*. We pledge:

Removal of any vestige of discrimination in the operation of federal facilities or procedures which may at any time be found.

Opposition to the use of federal funds for the construction of segregated community facilities.

Action to ensure that public transportation and other government-authorized services shall be free from segregation.

6. *Legislative Procedure*. We pledge:

Our best efforts to change present Rule 22 of the Senate and other appropriate Congressional procedures that often make unattainable proper legislative implementation of constitutional guarantees.

We reaffirm the constitutional right to peaceable assembly to protest discrimination in private business establishments. We applaud the action of the businessmen who have abandoned discriminatory practices in retail establishments, and we urge others to follow their example.

Finally we recognize that civil rights is a responsibility not only of states and localities; it is a national problem and a national responsibility. The federal government should take the initiative in promoting intergroup conferences among those who, in their communities, are earnestly seeking solutions of the complex problems of desegregation—to the end that closed channels of communication may be opened, tensions eased, and a cooperative solution of local problems may be sought.

In summary, we pledge the full use of the power, resources and leadership of the federal government to eliminate discrimination based on race, color, religion or national origin and to encourage understanding and good will among all races and creeds.

IMMIGRATION

Immigration has historically been a great factor in the growth of the United States, not only in numbers but in the enrichment of ideas that immigrants have brought with them. This Republican Administration has given refuge to over 32,000 victims of Communist tyranny from Hungary, ended needless delay in processing applications for naturalization, and has urged other enlightened legislation to liberalize existing restrictions.

Immigration has been reduced to the point where it does not provide the stimulus to growth that it should, nor are we fulfilling our obligation as a haven for the oppressed. Republican conscience and Republican policy require that:

The annual number of immigrants we accept be at least doubled.

Obsolete immigration laws be amended by abandoning the outdated 1920 census data as a base and substituting the 1960 census.

The guidelines of our immigration policy be based upon judgment of the individual merit of each applicant for admission and citizenship.

CONCLUSION

We have set forth the program of the Republican Party for the government of the United States. We have written a Party document, as is our duty, but we have tried to refrain from writing a merely partisan document. We have no wish to exaggerate differences between ourselves and the Democratic Party; nor can we, in conscience, obscure the differences that do exist. We believe that the Republican program is based upon a sounder understanding of the action and scope of government. There are many things a free government cannot do for its people as well as they can do them for themselves. There are some things no government should promise or attempt to do. The functions of government are so great as to bear no needless enlargement. We limit our proposals and our pledges to those areas for which the government of a great republic can reasonably be made responsible. To the best of our ability we have avoided advocating measures that would go against the grain of a free people.

The history and composition of the Republican Party make it the natural instrument for eradicating the injustice and discrimination in this country. We Republicans are fortunate in being able to contend against these evils, without having to contend against each other for the principle.

We believe that we see, so far as men can see through the obscurity of time and trouble, the prudent course for the nation in its hour of trial. The Soviet Union has created another of the new situations of peril which has been the Communist record from the beginning and will continue to be until our strategy for victory has succeeded. The speed of technological change makes it imperative that we measure the new situations by their special requirements and accelerate as appropriate our efforts in every direction, economic and military and political, to deal with them.

As rapidly as we perfect the new generations of weapons we must arm ourselves effectively and without delay. In this respect the nation stands now at one of the new points of departure. We must never allow our technology, particularly in nuclear and propulsion fields, to lag for any reason until such time as we have dependable and honest safeguards of inspection and control. We must take steps at once to secure our position in this regard and at the same time we must intensify our efforts to develop better safeguards in the field of disarmament.

The free nations of the world must ever be rallied to the cause and be encouraged to join together in more effective alliances and unions strong enough to meet all challenges and sustain the common effort. It is urgent that we innovate to keep the initiative for our free cause.

We offer toil and sweat, to ward off blood and tears. We advocate an immovable resistance against every Communist aggression. We argue for a military might commensurate with our universal tasks. We end by declaring our faith in the Republic and in its people, and in the deathless principles of right from which it draws its moral force.

— 1964 —

SECTION ONE

For a Free People

Humanity is tormented once again by an age-old issue—is man to live in dignity and freedom under God or be enslaved—are men in government to serve, or are they to master, their fellow men?

It befalls us now to resolve this issue anew—perhaps this time for centuries to come. Nor can we evade the issue here at home. Even in this Constitutional Republic, for two centuries the beacon of liberty the world over, individual freedom retreats under the mounting assault of expanding centralized power. Fiscal and economic excesses, too long indulged, already have eroded and threatened the greatest experiment in self-government mankind has known.

We Republicans claim no monopoly of love of freedom. But we challenge as unwise the course the Democrats have charted; we challenge as dangerous the steps they plan along the way; and we deplore as self-defeating and harmful many of the moves already taken.

Dominant in their council are leaders whose words extol human liberty, but whose deeds have persistently delimited the scope of liberty and sapped its vitality. Year after year, in the name of benevolence, these leaders have sought the enlargement of Federal power. Year after year, in the guise of concern for others, they have lavishly expended the resources of their fellow citizens. And year after year freedom, diversity and individual, local and state responsibility have given way to regimentation, conformity and subservience to central power.

We Republicans hold that a leadership so misguided weakens liberty in America and the world. We hold that the glittering enticements so invitingly proffered the people, at their own expense, will inevitably bring disillusionment and cruel disappointment in place of promised happiness.

Such leaders are Federal extremists—impulsive in the use of national power, improvident in the management of public funds, thoughtless as to the long-term effects of their acts on individual freedom and creative, competitive enterprise. Men so recklessly disposed cannot be safely entrusted with authority over their fellow citizens.

To Republicans, liberty is still today man's most precious possession. For every citizen, and for the generations to come, we Republicans vow that it shall be preserved.

In substantiation of this belief the Republican Party submits this platform. To the American people it is our solemn bond.

To Stay Free

The shape of the future is our paramount concern. Much of today's moral decline and drift—much of the prevailing preoccupation with physical and material comforts of life—much of today's crass political appeals to the appetites of the citizenry—can be traced to a leadership grown demagogic and materialistic through indifference to national ideals founded in devoutly held religious faith. The Republican Party seeks not to renounce this heritage of faith and high purpose; rather, we are determined to reaffirm and reapply it. So doing, these will be our guides:

1. Every person has the right to govern himself, to fix his own goals, and to make his own way with a minimum of governmental interference.
2. It is for government to foster and maintain an environment of freedom encouraging every individual to develop to the fullest his God-given powers of mind, heart and body; and, beyond this, government should undertake only needful things, rightly of public concern, which the citizen cannot himself accomplish.

    We Republicans hold that these two principles must regain their primacy in our government's relations, not only with the American people, but also with nations and peoples everywhere in the world.
3. Within our Republic the Federal Government should act only in areas where it has Constitutional authority to act, and then only in respect to proven needs where individuals and local or state governments will not or cannot adequately perform. Great power, whether governmental or private, political or economic, must be so checked, balanced and restrained and, where necessary, so dispersed as to prevent it from becoming a threat to freedom any place in the land.
4. It is a high mission of government to help assure equal opportunity for all, affording every citizen an equal chance at the starting line but never determining who is to win or lose. But government must also reflect the nation's compassionate concern for those who are unable, through no fault of their own, to provide adequately for themselves.
5. Government must be restrained in its demands upon and its use of the resources of the people, remembering that it is not the creator but the steward of the wealth it uses; that its goals must ever discipline its means; and that service to all the people, never to selfish or partisan ends, must be the abiding purpose of men entrusted with public power.

Deeds Not Words

The future we pledge, then, for freedom, by faithful adherence to these guides. Let the people compare these guides with those of the Democratic Party, then test, not the words of the two Parties, but their performance during the past four years of Democratic control.

Let the people ask:

Is the Republic stronger today or wiser than when the present Administration took office four years ago?

Is its guardianship of freedom more respected at home and throughout the world?

For these four years the leaders of the Democratic Party have been entrusted with the nation's executive power and overwhelmingly in control of the Congress. The question must be asked: Have these leaders successfully advanced the purposes of this mightiest nation mankind has known?

Tragically, in each instance, the answer must be "no." Let the Democratic Party stand accused.

SECTION TWO

Failures of Foreign Policy

This Democratic Administration has been, from its beginning, not the master but the prisoner of major events. The will and dependability of its leadership, even for the defense of the free world, have come to be questioned in every area of the globe.

Disregard of Allies

This Administration has neglected to consult with America's allies on critical matters at critical times, leading to lack of confidence, lack of respect and disintegrating alliances.

It has permitted an erosion of NATO force and unity, alienating most of its member nations by negotiating with the common foe behind their backs. It has offered concessions to the Communists while according our allies little understanding, patience, or cooperation.

This Administration has created discord and distrust by failing to develop a nuclear policy for NATO.

It has provoked crises of confidence with our oldest friends, including England and France, by bungling such major projects as Skybolt and NATO's nuclear needs.

It has allowed other great alliances—SEATO and CENTO—also to deteriorate, by failing to provide the leadership required for their revitalization and by neglecting their cooperation in keeping the peace.

Weakness Before Communism

This Administration has sought accommodations with Communism without adequate safeguards and compensating gains for freedom. It has alienated proven allies by opening a "hot line" first with a sworn enemy rather than with a proven friend, and in general pursued a risky path such as began at Munich a quarter century ago.

It has misled the American people and forfeited a priceless opportunity to win concessions for freedom by mishandling sales of farm commodities to Communists. At first it disavowed any intent to subsidize prices or use credit; later it demanded such authority and forced the Democrats in Congress to acquiesce. At first it hinted at concessions for freedom in return for wheat sold to Russia; later it obtained no concessions at all. At first it pledged not to breach restraints on trade with Communist countries in other parts of the world; later it stimulated such trade itself, and thus it encouraged trade with Cuba by America's oldest friends.

This Administration has collaborated with Indonesian imperialism by helping it to acquire territory belonging to the Netherlands and control over the Papuan people.

It has abetted further Communist takeover in Laos, weakly accepted Communist violations of the Geneva Agreement, which the present Administration perpetrated, and increased Soviet influence in Southeast Asia.

It has encouraged an increase of aggression in South Vietnam by appearing to set limits on America's willingness to act—and then, in the deepening struggle, it has sacrificed the lives of American and allied fighting men by denial of modern equipment.

This Administration has permitted the shooting down of American pilots, the mistreatment of American citizens, and the destruction of American property to become hallmarks of Communist arrogance.

It has stood by as a wire barricade in Berlin became a wall of shame, defacing that great city, humiliating every American, and disgracing free men everywhere.

It has turned its back on the captive peoples of Eastern Europe, abandoning their cause in the United Nations and in the official utterances of our government.

This Administration has forever blackened our nation's honor at the Bay of Pigs, bungling the invasion plan and leaving brave men on Cuban beaches to be shot down. Later the forsaken survivors were ransomed, and Communism was allowed to march deeper into Latin America.

It has turned a deaf ear to pleas from throughout the Western Hemisphere for decisive American leadership to seal off subversion from the Soviet base just off our shore.

It has increased the long-term troubles for America by retreating from its pledge to obtain on-the-spot proof of the withdrawal of Soviet offensive weapons from Cuba.

It left vacant for many critical months the high posts of ambassador in Panama and with the Organization of American States, and thus it failed to anticipate and forestall the anti-American violence that burst forth in Panama.

Undermining the United Nations

This Administration has failed to provide forceful, effective leadership in the United Nations.

It has weakened the power and influence of this world organization by failing to demand basic improvements in its procedures to guard against its becoming merely a forum of anti-Western insult and abuse.

It has refused to insist upon enforcement of the United Nations' rules governing financial support though such enforcement is supported by an advisory opinion of the International Court of Justice.

It has shouldered virtually the full costs of the United Nations' occupation of the Congo, only to have the ousted leadership asked back when United Nations forces had withdrawn.

Forsaking America's Interests

This Administration has subsidized various forms of socialism throughout the world, to the jeopardy of individual freedom and private enterprise.

It has proved itself inept and weak in international trade negotiations, allowing the loss of opportunities historically open to American enterprise and bargaining away markets indispensable to the prosperity of American farms.

Failure of National Security Planning

Losing a Critical Lead

This Administration has delayed research and development in advanced weapons systems and thus confronted the American people with a fearsome possibility that Soviet advances, in the decade of the 1970's, may surpass America's present lead. Its misuse of "cost effectiveness" has stifled the creativity of the nation's military, scientific and industrial communities.

It has failed to originate a single new major strategic weapons system after inheriting from a Republican Administration the most powerful military force of all time. It has concealed a lack of qualitative advance for the 1970's by speaking of a quantitative strength which by then will be obsolete. It has not demonstrated the foresight necessary to prepare a strategic strength which in future years will deter war.

It has endangered security by downgrading efforts to prepare defenses against enemy ballistic missiles. It has retarded our own military development for near and outer space, while the enemy's development moves on.

Invitations to Disaster

This Administration has adopted policies which will lead to a potentially fatal parity of power with Communism instead of continued military superiority for the United States.

It has permitted disarmament negotiations to proceed without adequate consideration of military judgment—a procedure which tends to bring about, in effect, a unilateral curtailment of American arms rendered the more dangerous by the Administration's discounting known Soviet advances in nuclear weaponry.

It has failed to take minimum safeguards against possible consequences of the limited nuclear test ban treaty, including advanced underground tests where permissible and full readiness to test elsewhere should the need arise.

Distortions and Blackouts

This Administration has adopted the policies of news management and unjustifiable secrecy, in the guise of guarding the nation's security; it has shown a contempt of the right of the people to know the truth.

This Administration, while claiming major defense savings, has in fact raised defense spending by billions of dollars a year, and yet has shortchanged critical areas.

Undermining Morale

This Administration has weakened the bonds of confidence and understanding between civilian leaders and the nation's top military professionals. It has bypassed seasoned military judgment in vital national security policy decisions.

It has permitted non-military considerations, political as well as spurious economic arguments, to reverse professional judgment on major weapons and equipment such as the controversial TFX, the X-22, and the nuclear carrier.

In sum, both in military and foreign affairs, the Democratic record all the world around is one of disappointment and reverses for freedom.

And this record is no better at home.

Failures at Home

Inability to Create Jobs

This Administration has failed to honor its pledges to assure good jobs, full prosperity and a rapidly growing economy for all the American people:

- failing to reduce unemployment to four percent, falling far short of its announced goal every single month of its tenure in office; and
- despite glowing promises, allowing a disheartening increase in long-term and youth unemployment.

This Administration has failed to apply Republican-initiated retraining programs where most needed, particularly where they could afford new economic opportunities to Negro citizens. It has preferred, instead, divisive political proposals.

It has demonstrated its inability to measure up to the challenge of automation which, wisely guided, will enrich the lives of all people. Administration approaches have been negative and unproductive, as for example the proposed penalties upon the use of overtime. Such penalties would serve only to spread existing unemployment and injure those who create jobs.

It has failed to perform its responsibility under Republican amendments to the Manpower Training Act. It has neglected, for example, the basic requirement of developing a dictionary of labor skills which are locally, regionally and nationally in short supply, even though many thousands of jobs are unfilled today for lack of qualified applicants.

Failing the Poor

This Administration has refused to take practical free enterprise measures to help the poor. Under the last Republican Administration, the percentage of poor in the country dropped encouragingly from 28 percent to 21 percent. By contrast, the present Administration, despite a massive increase in the Federal bureaucracy, has managed a mere two percentage point reduction.

This Administration has proposed a so-called war on poverty which characteristically overlaps, and often contradicts, the 42 existing Federal poverty programs. It would dangerously centralize Federal controls and bypass effective state, local and private programs.

It has demonstrated little concern for the acute problems created for the poor by inflation. Consumer prices have increased in the past three and a half years by almost 5 percent, amounting in effect to a 5 percent national sales tax on the purchases of a family living on fixed income.

Under housing and urban renewal programs, notably in the Nation's Capital, it has created new slums by forcing the poor from their homes to, make room for luxury apartments, while neglecting the vital need for adequate relocation assistance.

Retarding Enterprises

This Administration has violently thrust Federal power into the free market in such areas as steel prices, thus establishing precedents which in future years could critically wound free enterprise in the United States.

It has so discouraged private enterprise that the annual increase in the number of businesses has plummeted from the Republican level of 70,000 a year to 47,000 a year.

It has allowed the rate of business failures to rise higher under its leadership than in any period since depression days.

It has aggravated the problems of small business by multiplying Federal record-keeping requirements and has hurt thousands of small businessmen by forcing up their costs.

This Administration has curtailed, through such agencies as the National Labor Relations Board, the simple, basic right of Americans voluntarily to go into or to go out of business.

It has failed to stimulate new housing and attract more private capital into the field. In the past three years it has fallen short by 1,500,000 units of meeting its pledge of 2,000,000 new homes each year.

It has sought to weaken the patent system which is so largely responsible for America's progress in technology, medicine and science.

It has required private electric power companies to submit to unreasonable Federal controls as a condition to the utilization of rights-of-way over public lands. It has sought to advance, without Congressional authorization, a vastly expensive nationwide electrical transmission grid.

Betrayal of the Farmer

This Administration has refused, incredibly, to honor the clear mandate of American wheat farmers, in the largest farm referendum ever held, to free them of rigid Federal control and to restore their birthright to make their own management decisions.

It has strangled the Republican rural development program with red tape and neglected its most essential ingredient, local initiative.

It has broken its major promises to farm people, dropping the parity ratio to its lowest level since 1939. It has dumped surplus stocks so as to lower farm income and increase the vicious cost-price squeeze on the farmer.

It has evidenced hostility toward American livestock producers by proposals to establish mandatory marketing quotas on all livestock, to fine and imprison dairy farmers failing to maintain Federally-acceptable records, and to establish a subsidized grazing cropland conversion program. It has allowed imports of beef and other meat products to rise to an all-time high during a slump in cattle prices which was aggravated by government grain sales.

Neglect of Natural Resources

This Administration has delayed the expeditious handling of oil shale patent applications and the early development of a domestic oil shale industry.

It has allowed the deterioration of the domestic mining and petroleum industries including displacement of domestic markets by foreign imports. It has failed to protect the American fishing industry and has retreated from policies providing equitable sharing of international fishing grounds.

Fiscal Irresponsibility

This Administration has misled the American people by such budget manipulations as crowding spending into the previous fiscal year, presenting a proposal to sell off $2.3 billion in government assets as a cut in spending, and using bookkeeping devices to make expenditures seem smaller than they actually are.

It has, despite pledges of economy, burdened this nation with four unbalanced budgets in a row, creating deficits totaling $26 billion, with still more debt to come, reflecting a rate of sustained deficit spending unmatched in peacetime.

It has failed to establish sensible priorities for Federal funds. In consequence, it has undertaken needlessly expensive crash programs, as for example accelerating a trip to the moon, to the neglect of other critical needs such as research into health and the increasingly serious problems of air and water pollution and urban crowding.

This Administration has continued to endanger retirement under Social Security for millions of citizens; it has attempted to overload the system with costly, unrelated programs which ignore the dangers of overly regressive taxation and the unfairness of forcing the poor to finance such programs for the rich.

It has demanded the elimination of a substantial portion of personal income tax deductions for charitable and church contributions, for real property taxes paid by home owners, and for interest payments. The elimination of these deductions would impose great hardship upon millions of our citizens and discourage the growth of some of the finest organizations in America.

This Administration has impeded investigations of suspected wrongdoing which might implicate public officials in the highest offices in the land. It has thus aroused justifiable resentment against those who use the high road of public service as the low road to illicitly acquired wealth.

It has permitted the quality and morale of the postal system to deteriorate and drastically restricted its services. It has made the Post Office almost inaccessible to millions of working people, reduced the once admired Parcel Post System to a national laughing stock—and yet it is intimated that Americans may soon have to pay 8¢ for a first-class postage stamp.

It has resisted personal income tax credits for education, always preferring the route leading to Federal control over our schools. Some leading Democrats have even campaigned politically in favor of such tax credits while voting against them in Congress.

Contrary to the intent of the Manpower Training Act, it has sought to extend Department of Labor influence over vocational education.

Discord and Discontent

This Administration has exploited interracial tensions by extravagant campaign promises, without fulfillment, playing on the just aspirations of the minority groups, encouraging disorderly and lawless elements, and ineffectually administering the laws.

It has subjected career civil servants and part-time Federal employees, including employees of the Agriculture Department, to political pressures harmful to the integrity of the entire Federal service. It has weakened veterans' preference in Federal jobs.

It has made Federal intervention, even on the, Presidential level, a standard operating practice in labor disputes, thus menacing the entire system of free collective bargaining.

It has resorted to police state tactics, using the great power of Federal Departments and agencies, to compel compliance with Administration desires, notably in the steel price dispute. The Department of Justice, in particular, has been used improperly to achieve partisan political, economic, and legislative goals. This abuse of power should be the subject of a Congressional investigation.

Weakening Responsibility

This administration has moved, through such undertakings as its so-called war on poverty, accelerated public works and the New Communities Program in the 1964 housing proposal, to establish new Federal offices duplicating existing agencies, bypassing the state capitals, thrusting aside local government, and siphoning off to Washington the administration of private citizen and community affairs.

It has undermined the Federally assisted, State-operated medical and hospital assistance program, while using—and abusing—Federal authority to force a compulsory hospital program upon the people and the Congress.

This enumeration is necessarily incomplete. It does not exhaust the catalog of misdeeds and failures of the present Administration. And let the nation realize that the full impact of these many ill-conceived and ill-fated activities of the Democratic Administration is yet to come.

SECTION THREE

The Republican Alternative

We Republicans are not content to record Democratic misdeeds and failures. We now offer policies and programs new in conception and dynamic in operation. These we urge to recapture initiative for freedom at home and abroad and to rebuild our strength at home.

Nor is this a new role. Republican Presidents from Abraham Lincoln to Dwight D. Eisenhower stand as witness that Republican leadership is steadfast in principle, clear in purpose and committed to progress. The many achievements of the Eisenhower Administration in strengthening peace abroad and the well-being of all at home have been unmatched in recent times. A new Republican Administration will stand proudly on this record.

We do not submit, in the platform, extravagant promises to be cynically cast aside after election day. Rather, we offer examples of Republican initiatives in areas of overriding concern to the whole nation—North, South, East and West—which befit a truly national party. In the interest of brevity, we do not repeat the commitments of the 1960 Republican Platform, "Building a Better America," and the 1962 "Declaration of Republican Principle and Policy." We incorporate into this Platform as pledges renewed those commitments which are relevant to the problems of 1964.

These, then, will be our guides, and these our additional pledges, in meeting the nation's needs.

Faith in the Individual

1. We Republicans shall first rely on the individual's right and capacity to advance his own economic well-being, to control the fruits of his efforts and to plan his own and his family's future; and, where government is rightly involved, we shall assist the individual in surmounting urgent problems beyond his own power and responsibility to control. For instance, we pledge:

- enlargement of employment opportunities for urban and rural citizens, with emphasis on training programs to equip them with needed skills; improved job information and placement services; and research and extension services channeled toward helping rural people improve their opportunities;
- tax credits and other methods of assistance to help needy senior citizens meet the costs of medical and hospital insurance;
- a strong, sound system of Social Security, with improved benefits to our people;
- continued Federal support for a sound research pro-

gram aimed at both the prevention and cure of diseases, and intensified efforts to secure prompt and effective application of the results of research. This will include emphasis on mental illness, drug addiction, alcoholism, cancer, heart disease and other diseases of increasing incidence;

- revision of the Social Security laws to allow higher earnings, without loss of benefits, by our elderly people;
- full coverage of all medical and hospital costs for the needy elderly people, financed by general revenues through broader implementation of Federal–State plans, rather than the compulsory Democratic scheme covering only a small percentage of such costs, for everyone regardless of need;
- adoption and implementation of a fair and adequate program for providing necessary supplemental farm labor for producing and harvesting agricultural commodities;
- tax credits for those burdened by the expenses of college education;
- vocational rehabilitation, through cooperation between government—Federal and State—and industry, for the mentally and physically handicapped, the chronically unemployed and the poverty-stricken;
- incentives for employers to hire teenagers, including broadening of temporary exemptions under the minimum wage law;
- to repeal the Administration's wheat certificate "bread-tax" on consumers, so burdensome to low-income families and overwhelmingly rejected by farmers;
- revision of present non-service-connected pension programs to provide increased benefits for low-income pensioners, with emphasis on rehabilitation, nursing homes and World War I veterans;
- re-evaluation of the armed forces' manpower procurement programs with the goal of replacing involuntary inductions as soon as possible by an efficient voluntary system, offering real career incentives;
- enactment of legislation, despite Democratic opposition, to curb the flow through the mails of obscene materials which has flourished into a multimillion dollar obscenity racket;
- support of a Constitutional amendment permitting those individuals and groups who choose to do so to exercise their religion freely in public places, provided religious exercises are not prepared or prescribed by the state or political subdivision thereof and no person's participation therein is coerced, thus preserving the traditional separation of church and state;

- full implementation and faithful execution of the Civil Rights Act of 1964, and all other civil rights statutes, to assure equal rights and opportunities guaranteed by the Constitution to every citizen;
- improvements of civil rights statutes adequate to the changing needs of our times;
- such additional administrative or legislative actions as may be required to end the denial, for whatever unlawful reason, of the right to vote;
- immigration legislation seeking to re-unite families and continuation of the "Fair Share" Refugee Program;
- continued opposition to discrimination based on race, creed, national origin or sex. We recognize that the elimination of any such discrimination is a matter of heart, conscience, and education, as well as of equal rights under law.

In all such programs, where Federal initiative is properly involved to relieve or prevent misfortune or meet overpowering need, it will be the Republican way to move promptly and energetically, and wherever possible to provide assistance of a kind enabling the individual to gain or regain the capability to make his own way and to have a fair chance to achieve his own goals. In all matters relating to human rights it will be the Republican way fully to implement all applicable laws and never to lose sight of the intense need for advancing peaceful progress in human relations in our land. The Party of Abraham Lincoln will proudly and faithfully live up to its heritage of equal rights and equal opportunities for all.

In furtherance of our faith in the individual, we also pledge prudent, responsible management of the government's fiscal affairs to protect the individual against the evils of spendthrift government—protecting most of all the needy and fixed-income families against the cruelest tax, inflation—and protecting every citizen against the high taxes forced by excessive spending, in order that each individual may keep more of his earnings for his own and his family's use. For instance, we pledge:

- a reduction of not less than five billion dollars in the present level of Federal spending;
- an end to chronic deficit financing, proudly reaffirming our belief in a balanced budget;
- further reduction in individual and corporate tax rates as fiscal discipline is restored;
- repayments on the public debt;
- maintenance of an administrative, legislative and regulatory climate encouraging job-building enterprise to help assure every individual a real chance for a good job;

- wise, firm and responsible conduct of the nation's foreign affairs, backed by military forces kept modern, strong and ready, thereby assuring every individual of a future promising peace.

In all such matters it will be the Republican way so to conduct the affairs of government as to give the individual citizen the maximum assurance of a peaceful and prosperous future, freed of the discouragement and hardship produced by wasteful and ineffectual government.

In furtherance of our faith in the individual, we also pledge the maximum restraint of Federal intrusions into matters more productively left to the individual. For instance, we pledge:

- to continue Republican sponsorship of practical Federal–State–local programs which will effectively treat the needs of the poor, while resisting direct Federal handouts that erode away individual self-reliance and self-respect and perpetuate dependency;
- to continue the advancement of education on all levels, through such programs as selective aid to higher education, strengthened State and local tax resources, including tax credits for college education, while resisting the Democratic efforts which endanger local control of schools;
- to help assure equal opportunity and a good education for all, while opposing Federally-sponsored "inverse discrimination," whether by the shifting of jobs, or the abandonment of neighborhood schools, for reasons of race;
- to provide our farmers, who have contributed so much to the strength of our nation, with the maximum opportunity to exercise their own management decisions on their own farms, while resisting all efforts to impose upon them further Federal controls;
- to establish realistic priorities for the concentration of Federal spending in the most productive and creative areas, such as education, job training, vocational rehabilitation, educational research, oceanography, and the wise development and use of natural resources in the water as well as on land, while resisting Democratic efforts to spend wastefully and indiscriminately;
- to open avenues of peaceful progress in solving racial controversies while discouraging lawlessness and violence.

In all such matters, it will be the Republican way to assure the individual of maximum freedom as government meets its proper responsibilities, while resisting the Democratic obsession to impose from above, uniform and rigid schemes for meeting varied and complex human problems.

Faith in the Competitive System

2. We Republicans shall vigorously protect the dynamo of economic growth—free, competitive enterprise—that has made America the envy of the world. For instance, we pledge:

- removal of the wartime Federal excise taxes, favored by the Democratic Administration, on pens, pencils, jewelry, cosmetics, luggage, handbags, wallets and toiletries;
- assistance to small business by simplifying Federal and State tax and regulatory requirements, fostering the availability of longer-term credit at fair terms and equity capital for small firms, encouraging strong State programs to foster small business, establishing more effective measures to assure a sharing by small business in Federal procurement, and promoting wider export opportunities;
- an end to power-grabbing regulatory actions, such as the reach by the Federal Trade Commission for injunctive powers and the ceaseless pressing by the White House, the Food and Drug Administration and Federal Trade Commission to dominate consumer decisions in the market place;
- returning the consumer to the driver's seat as the chief regulator and chief beneficiary of a free economy, by resisting excessive concentration of power, whether public or private;
- a drastic reduction in burdensome Federal paperwork and overlapping regulations, which weigh heavily on small businessmen struggling to compete and to provide jobs;
- a determined drive, through tough, realistic negotiations, to remove the many discriminatory and restrictive trade practices of foreign nations;
- greater emphasis on overseas sales of surplus farm commodities to friendly countries through long-term credits repayable in dollars under the Republican Food for Peace program;
- dedication to freedom of expression for all news media, to the right of access by such media to public proceedings, and to the independence of radio, television and other news-gathering media from excessive government control;
- improvement, and full and fair enforcement, of the anti-trust statutes, coupled with long-overdue clarification of Federal policies and interpretations relating thereto in order to strengthen competition and protect the consumer and small business;
- constant opposition to any form of unregulated monopoly, whether business or labor;
- meaningful safeguards against irreparable injuries to any domestic industries by disruptive surges of

imports, such as in the case of beef and other meat products, textiles, oil, glass, coal, lumber and steel;

- enactment of law, such as the Democratic Administration vetoed in the 88th Congress, requiring that labels of imported items clearly disclose their foreign origin;
- to completely reorganize the National Labor Relations Board to assure impartial protection of the rights of the public, employees and employers, ending the defiance of Congress by the present Board;
- the redevelopment of an atmosphere of confidence throughout the government and across the nation, in which vigorous competition can flourish.

In all such matters it will be the Republican way to support, not harass—to encourage, not restrain—to build confidence, not threaten—to provide stability, not unrest—to speed genuine growth, not conjure up statistical fantasies and to assure that all actions of government apply fairly to every element of the nation's economy.

In furtherance of our faith in the competitive system, we also pledge:

- a continual re-examination and reduction of government competition with private business, consistent with the recommendations of the second Hoover Commission;
- elimination of excessive bureaucracy;
- full protection of the integrity of the career governmental services, military and civilian, coupled with adequate pay scales;
- maximum reliance upon subordinate levels of government and individual citizens to meet the nation's needs, in place of establishing even more Federal agencies to burden the people.

In all such matters relating to Federal administration it will be the Republican way to provide maximum service for each tax dollar expended, watchfully superintend the size and scope of Federal activities, and assure an administration always fair, efficient and cooperatively disposed toward every element of our competitive system.

Faith in Limited Government

3. We Republicans shall insist that the Federal Government have effective but limited powers, that it be frugal and efficient, and that it fully meet its Constitutional responsibilities to all the American people. For instance, we pledge:

- restoration of collective bargaining responsibility to labor and management, minimizing third-party

intervention and preventing any agency of government from becoming an advocate for any private economic interest;

- development of truly voluntary commodity programs for commercial agriculture, including payments in kind out of government-owned surpluses, diversion of unneeded land to conservation uses, price supports free of political manipulation in order to stimulate and attain fair market prices, together with adequate credit facilities and continued support of farm-owned-and-operated cooperatives including rural electric and telephone facilities, while resisting all efforts to make the farmer dependent, for his economic survival, upon either compensatory payments by the Federal Government or upon the whim of the Secretary of Agriculture;
- full cooperation of all governmental levels and private enterprise in advancing the balanced use of the nation's natural resources to provide for man's multiple needs;
- continuing review of public-land laws and policies to assure maximum opportunity for all beneficial uses of the public lands; including the development of mineral resources;
- comprehensive water-resource planning and development, including projects for our growing cities, expanded research in desalinization of water, and continued support of multi-purpose reclamation projects;
- support of sustained yield management of our forests and expanded research for control of forest insects, disease, and forest fires;
- protection of traditional domestic fishing grounds and other actions, including tax incentives, to encourage modernization of fishing vessels, and improve processing and marketing practices;
- continued tax support to encourage exploration and development of domestic sources of minerals and metals, with reasonable depletion allowances;
- stabilization of present oil programs, private development of atomic power, increased coal research and expansion of coal exports;
- a replanning of the present space program to provide for a more orderly, yet aggressively pursued, step-by-step development, remaining alert to the danger of over diversion of skilled personnel in critical shortage from other vital areas such as health, industry, education and science.

In furtherance of our faith in limited, frugal and efficient government we also pledge:

- credit against Federal taxes for specified State and local taxes paid, and a transfer to the States of excise and other Federal tax sources, to reinforce the fiscal strength of State and local governments so that they may better meet rising school costs and other pressing urban and suburban problems such as transportation, housing, water systems and juvenile delinquency;

- emphasis upon channeling more private capital into sound urban development projects and private housing;
- critical re-examination and major overhaul of all Federal grant-in-aid programs with a view to channeling such programs through the States, discontinuing those no longer required and adjusting others in a determined effort to restore the unique balance and creative energy of the traditional American system of government;
- revitalization of municipal and county governments throughout America by encouraging them, and private citizens as well, to develop new solutions of their major concerns through a streamlining and modernizing of State and local processes of government, and by a renewed consciousness of their ability to reach these solutions, not through Federal action, but through their own capabilities;
- support of a Constitutional amendment, as well as legislation, enabling States having bicameral legislatures to apportion one House on bases of their choosing, including factors other than population;
- complete reform of the tax structure, to include simplification as well as lower rates to strengthen individual and business incentives;
- effective budgetary reform, improved Congressional appropriation procedures, and full implementation of the anti-deficiency statute;
- a wide-ranging reform of other Congressional procedures, including the provision of adequate professional staff assistance for the minority membership on Congressional Committees, to insure that the power and prestige of Congress remain adequate to the needs of the times;
- high priority for the solution of the nation's balance of payment difficulties to assure unquestioned confidence in the dollar, maintenance of the competitiveness of American products in domestic and foreign markets, expansion of exports, stimulation of foreign tourism in the United States, greater foreign sharing of mutual security burdens abroad, a drastic reorganization and redirection of the entire foreign aid effort, gradual reductions in overseas U.S. forces as manpower can be replaced by increased firepower; and strengthening of the international monetary system without sacrifice of our freedom of policy making.

In all such matters it will be the Republican way to achieve not feigned but genuine savings, allowing a reduction of the public debt and additional tax reductions while meeting the proper responsibilities of government. We pledge an especially determined effort to help strengthen the ability of State and local governments to meet the broad range of needs facing the nation's urban and suburban communities.

SECTION FOUR

Freedom Abroad

The Republican commitment to individual freedom applies no less abroad.

America must advance freedom throughout the world as a vital condition of orderly human progress, universal justice, and the security of the American people.

The supreme challenge to this policy is an atheistic imperialism—Communism.

Our nation's leadership must be judged by—indeed, American independence and even survival are dependent upon—the stand it takes toward Communism.

That stand must be: victory for freedom. There can be no peace, there can be no security, until this goal is won.

As long as Communist leaders remain ideologically fixed upon ruling the world, there can be no lesser goal. This is the supreme test of America's foreign policy. It must not be defaulted. In the balance is human liberty everyplace on earth.

Reducing the Risks of War

A dynamic strategy aimed at victory—pressing always for initiatives for freedom, rejecting always appeasement and withdrawal—reduces the risk of nuclear war. It is a nation's vacillation, not firmness, that tempts an aggressor into war. It is accommodation, not opposition, that encourages a hostile nation to remain hostile and to remain aggressive.

The road to peace is a road not of fawning amiability but of strength and respect. Republicans judge foreign policy by its success in advancing freedom and justice, not by its effect on international prestige polls.

In making foreign policy, these will be our guidelines:

Trusting Ourselves and Our Friends

1. Secrecy in foreign policy must be at a minimum, public understanding at a maximum. Our own citi-

zens, rather than those of other nations, should be accorded primary trust.

2. Consultation with our allies should take precedence over direct negotiations with Communist powers. The bypassing of our allies has contributed greatly to the shattering of free world unity and to the loss of free world continuity in opposing Communism.

Communism's Course

3. We reject the notion that Communism has abandoned its goal of world domination, or that fat and well-fed Communists are less dangerous than lean and hungry ones. We also reject the notion that the United States should take sides in the Sino-Soviet rift.

Republican foreign policy starts with the assumption that Communism is the enemy of this nation in every sense until it can prove that its enmity has been abandoned.

4. We hold that trade with Communist countries should not be directed toward the enhancement of their power and influence but could only be justified if it would serve to diminish their power.

5. We are opposed to the recognition of Red China. We oppose its admission into the United Nations. We steadfastly support free China.

6. In negotiations with Communists, Republicans will probe tirelessly for reasonable, practicable and trustworthy agreements. However, we will never abandon insistence on advantages for the free world.

7. Republicans will continue to work for the realization of the Open Skies policy proposed in 1955 by President Eisenhower. Only open societies offer real hope of confidence among nations.

Communism's Captives

8. Republicans reaffirm their long-standing commitment to a course leading to eventual liberation of the Communist-dominated nations of Eastern Europe, Asia and Latin America, including the peoples of Hungary, Poland, East Germany, Czechoslovakia, Rumania, Albania, Bulgaria, Latvia, Lithuania, Estonia, Armenia, Ukraine, Yugoslavia, and its Serbian, Croatian and Slovene peoples, Cuba, mainland China, and many others. We condemn the persecution of minorities, such as the Jews, within Communist borders.

The United Nations

9. Republicans support the United Nations. However, we will never rest in our efforts to revitalize its original purpose.

We will press for a change in the method of voting in the General Assembly and in the specialized agencies that will reflect population disparities among the member states and recognize differing abilities and willingness to meet the obligations of the Charter. We will insist upon General Assembly acceptance of the International Court of Justice advisory opinion, upholding denial of the votes of member nations which refuse to meet properly levied assessments, so that the United Nations will more accurately reflect the power realities of the world. Further to assure the carrying out of these recommendations and to correct the above abuses, we urge the calling of an amending convention of the United Nations by the year 1967.

Republicans will never surrender to any international group the responsibility of the United States for its sovereignty, its own security, and the leadership of the free world.

NATO: The Great Shield

10. Republicans regard NATO as indispensable for the prevention of war and the protection of freedom. NATO's unity and vitality have alarmingly deteriorated under the present Administration. It is a keystone of Republican foreign policy to revitalize the alliance.

To hasten its restoration, Republican leadership will move immediately to establish an international commission, comprised of individuals of high competence in NATO affairs, whether in or out of government, to explore and recommend effective new ways to strengthen alliance participation and fulfillment.

Freedom's Further Demands

11. To our nation's associates in SEATO and CENTO, Republicans pledge reciprocal dedication of purpose and revitalized interest. These great alliances, with NATO, must be returned to the forefront of foreign policy planning. A strengthened alliance system is equally necessary in the Western Hemisphere.

This will remain our constant purpose: Republicans will labor tirelessly with free men everywhere and in every circumstance toward the defeat of Communism and victory for freedom.

The Geography of Freedom

12. In diverse regions of the world, Republicans will make clear to any hostile nation that the United States will increase the costs and risks of aggression to make them outweigh hopes for gain. It was just such a com-

munication and determination by the Eisenhower Republican Administration that produced the 1953 Korean Armistice. The same strategy can win victory for freedom and stop further aggression in Southeast Asia.

We will move decisively to assure victory in South Vietnam. While confining the conflict as closely as possible, America must move to end the fighting in a reasonable time and provide guarantees against further aggression. We must make it clear to the Communist world that, when conflict is forced with America, it will end only in victory for freedom.

We will demand that the Berlin Wall be taken down prior to the resumption of any negotiations with the Soviet Union on the status of forces in, or treaties affecting, Germany.

We will reassure our German friends that the United States will not accept any plan for the future of Germany which lacks firm assurance of a free election on reunification.

We will urge the immediate implementation of the Caracas Declaration of Solidarity against international Communist intervention endorsed in 1954 by the Organization of American States during the Eisenhower Administration, which Declaration, in accordance with the historic Monroe Doctrine, our nation's official policy since 1823, opposes domination of any of our neighbor-nations by any power outside this Hemisphere.

We will vigorously press our OAS partners to join the United States in restoring a free and independent government in Cuba, stopping the spread of Sino-Soviet subversion, forcing the withdrawal of the foreign military presence now in Latin America, and preventing future intrusions. We Republicans will recognize a Cuban government in exile; we will support its efforts to regain the independence of its homeland; we will assist Cuban freedom fighters in carrying on guerrilla warfare against the Communist regime; we will work for an economic boycott by all nations of the free world in trade with Cuba; and we will encourage free elections in Cuba after liberty and stability are restored.

We will consider raising the economic participation of the Republic of Panama in the operation of the Panama Canal and assure the safety of Americans in the area. We will reaffirm this nation's treaty rights and study the feasibility of a substitute, sea-level canal at an appropriate location including the feasibility of nuclear excavation.

Republicans will make clear to all Communists now supporting or planning to support guerrilla and subversive activities, that henceforth there will be no privileged sanctuaries to protect those who disrupt the peace of the world. We will make clear that blockade, interception of logistical support, and diplomatic and economic pressure are appropriate United States counters to deliberate breaches of the peace.

We will make clear to all Communist leaders everywhere that aggressive actions, including those in the German air corridors, will be grounds for re-evaluation of any and all trade or diplomatic relations currently to Communism's advantage.

We will take the cold war offensive on all fronts, including, for example, a reinvigorated USIA. It will broadcast not our weaknesses but our strengths. It will mount a psychological warfare attack on behalf of freedom and against Communist doctrine and imperialism.

Republicans will recast foreign aid programs. We will see that all will serve the cause of freedom. We will see that none bolster and sustain anti-American regimes; we will increase the use of private capital on a partnership basis with foreign nationals, as a means of fostering independence and mutual respect but we assert that property of American Nationals must not be expropriated by any foreign government without prompt and adequate compensation as contemplated by international law.

Respecting the Middle East, and in addition to our reaffirmed pledges of 1960 concerning this area, we will so direct our economic and military assistance as to help maintain stability in this region and prevent an imbalance of arms.

Finally, we will improve the efficiency and coordination of the foreign service, and provide adequate allowance for foreign service personnel.

The Development of Freedom

13. Freedom's wealth must never support freedom's decline, always its growth. America's tax revenues derived from free enterprise sources must never be employed in support of socialism. America must assist young and underdeveloped nations. In the process, however, we must not sacrifice the trust of old friends.

Our assistance, also, must be conditional upon self-help and progress toward the development of free institutions. We favor the establishment in underdeveloped nations of an economic and political climate that will encourage the investment of local capital and attract the investment of foreign capital.

Freedom's Shield—and Sword

Finally, Republicans pledge to keep the nation's sword sharp, ready, and dependable.

We will maintain a superior, not merely equal, military capability as long as the Communist drive for world domination continues. It will be a capability of balanced force, superior in all its arms, maintaining flexibility for effective performance in the rapidly changing science of war.

Republicans will never unilaterally disarm America.

We will demand that any arms reduction plan worthy of consideration guarantee reliable inspection. We will demand that any such plan assure this nation of sufficient strength, step by step, to forestall and defend against possible violations.

We will take every step necessary to carry forward the vital military research and development programs. We will pursue these programs as absolutely necessary to assure our nation of superior strength in the 1970's.

We will revitalize research and development programs needed to enable the nation to develop advanced new weapons systems, strategic as well as tactical.

We will include the fields of anti-submarine warfare, astronautics and aeronautics, special guerrilla forces, and such other defense systems required to keep America ready for any threat.

We will fully implement such safeguards as our security requires under the limited nuclear test ban treaty. We will conduct advanced tests in permissible areas, maintain facilities to test elsewhere in case of violations, and develop to the fullest our ability to detect Communist transgressions. Additionally, we will regularly review the status of nuclear weaponry under the limited nuclear test ban to assure this nation's protection. We shall also provide sensible, continuing reviews of the treaty itself.

We will end "second-best" weapons policies. We will end the false economies which place price ahead of the performance upon which American lives may depend. Republicans will bring an end once again to the "peak and valley" defense planning, so costly in morale and strength as well as in dollars. We will prepare a practical civil defense program.

We will restore the morale of our armed forces by upgrading military professionalism, and we will allow professional dissent while insuring that strong and sound civilian authority controls objective decision-making.

We will return the joint Chiefs of Staff to their lawful status as the President's principal military advisors. We will insure that an effective planning and operations staff is restored to the National Security Council.

We will reconsecrate this nation to human liberty, assuring the freedom of our people, and rallying mankind to a new crusade for freedom all around the world.

We Republicans, with the help of Almighty God, will keep those who would bury America aware that this nation has the strength and also the will to defend its every interest. Those interests, we shall make clear, include the preservation and expansion of freedom—and ultimately its victory—everyplace on earth.

We do not offer the easy way. We offer dedication and perseverance, leading to victory. This is our Platform. This is the Republican way.

— 1968 —

PREAMBLE, PURPOSES AND PLEDGES

Twice before, our Party gave the people of America leadership at a time of crisis—leadership which won us peace in place of war, unity in place of discord, compassion in place of bitterness.

A century ago, Abraham Lincoln gave that leadership. From it came one nation, consecrated to liberty and justice for all.

Fifteen years ago, Dwight D. Eisenhower gave that leadership. It brought the end of a war, eight years of peace, enhanced respect in the world, orderly progress at home, and trust of our people in their leaders and in themselves.

Today, we are in turmoil.

Tens of thousands of young men have died or been wounded in Vietnam.

Many young people are losing faith in our society.

Our inner cities have become centers of despair.

Millions of Americans are caught in the cycle of poverty—poor education, unemployment or serious under-employment, and the inability to afford decent housing.

Inflation has eroded confidence in the dollar at home and abroad. It has severely cut into the incomes of all families, the jobless, the farmers, the retired and those living on fixed incomes and pensions.

Today's Americans are uncertain about the future, and frustrated about the recent past.

America urgently needs new leadership—leadership courageous and understanding—leadership that will recapture control of events, mastering them rather than permitting them to master us, thus restoring our confidence in ourselves and in our future.

Our need is new leadership which will develop imaginative new approaches assuring full opportunity to all our citizens—leadership which will face and resolve the basic problems of our country.

Our Convention in 1968 can spark a "Republican Resurgence" under men and women willing to face the realities of the world in which we live.

We must urgently dedicate our efforts toward restoration of peace both at home and abroad.

We must bring about a national commitment to rebuild our urban and rural slum areas.

We must enable family farm enterprise to participate fully in the nation's prosperity.

We must bring about quality education for all.

We must assure every individual an opportunity for satisfying and rewarding employment.

We must attack the root causes of poverty and eradicate racism, hatred and violence.

We must give all citizens the opportunity to influence and shape the events of our time.

We must give increasing attention to the views of the young and recognize their key role in our present as well as the future.

We must mobilize the resources, talents and energy of public and private sectors to reach these goals, utilizing the unique strength and initiative of state and local governments.

We must re-establish fiscal responsibility and put an end to increases in the cost of living.

We must reaffirm our commitment to Lincoln's challenge of one hundred six years ago. To Congress he wrote: "The dogmas of the quiet past are inadequate to the stormy present. The occasion is piled high with difficulty and we must rise with the occasion. As our case is new, so we must think anew and act anew. We must disenthrall ourselves and then we shall save our country."

In this, our stormy present, let us rededicate ourselves to Lincoln's thesis. Let the people know our commitment to provide the dynamic leadership which they rightly expect of this Party—the Party not of empty promises, but of performance—the Party not of wastefulness, but of responsibility—the Party not of war, but the Party whose Administrations have been characterized by peace—the Republican Party.

To these ends, we solemnly pledge to every American that we shall think anew and act anew.

DOMESTIC POLICY

A peaceful, reunified America, with opportunity and orderly progress for all—these are our overriding domestic goals.

Clearly we must think anew about the relationship of man and his government, of man and his fellow-man. We must act anew to enlarge the opportunity and autonomy of the individual—and the range of his choice.

Republican leadership welcomes challenge.

We eagerly anticipate new achievement.

A new, vital partnership of government at all levels will be a prime Republican objective. We will broaden the base of decision-making. We will create a new mix of private responsibility and public participation in the solution of social problems.

There is so much which urgently needs to be done.

In many areas poverty and its attendant ills afflict large numbers of Americans. Distrust and fear plague us all. Our inner cities teem with poor, crowded in slums. Many rural areas are run down and barren of challenge or opportunity. Minorities among us—particularly the black community, the Mexican-American, the American Indian—suffer disproportionately.

Americans critically need—and are eager for—new and dynamic leadership. We offer that leadership—a leadership to eradicate bitterness and discrimination—responsible, compassionate leadership that will keep its word—leadership every citizen can count on to move this nation forward again, confident, reunited, and sure of purpose.

Crisis of the Cities

For today and tomorrow, there must be—and we pledge—a vigorous effort, nation-wide, to transform the blighted areas of cities into centers of opportunity and progress, culture and talent.

For tomorrow, new cities must be developed—and smaller cities with room to grow, expanded—to house and serve another 100 million Americans by the turn of the century.

The need is critical. Millions of our people are suffering cruelly from expanding metropolitan blight—congestion, crime, polluted air and water, poor housing, inadequate educational, economic and recreational opportunities. This continuing decay of urban centers—the deepening misery and limited opportunity of citizens living there—is intolerable in America. We promise effective, sustainable action enlisting new energies by the private sector and by governments at all levels. We pledge:

Presidential leadership which will buttress state and local government;

Vigorous federal support to innovative state programs, using new policy techniques such as urban development corporations, to help rebuild our cities;

Energetic, positive leadership to enforce statutory and constitutional protections to eliminate discrimination;

Concern for the unique problems of citizens long disadvantaged in our total society by race, color, national origin, creed, or sex;

A greater involvement of vast private enterprise resources in the improvement of urban life. induced by tax and other incentives;

New technological and administrative approaches through flexible federal programs enabling and encouraging communities to solve their own problems;

A complete overhaul and restructuring of the competing and overlapping jumble of federal programs to enable state and local governments to focus on priority objectives.

These principles as urgently apply to rural poverty and decay. There must be a marked improvement of economic and educational opportunities to relieve widespread distress. Success with urban problems in fact requires acceleration of rural development in order to stem the flow of people from the countryside to the city.

Air and water pollution, already acute in many areas, require vigorous state and federal action, regional planning, and maximum cooperation among neighboring cities, counties and states. We will encourage this planning and cooperation and also spur industrial participation by means of economic incentives.

Skyrocketing building costs and interest rates have crippled home building and threaten a housing crisis in the nation, endangering the prospect of a decent home and a suitable living environment for every family. We will vigorously implement the Republican-conceived home ownership program for lower-income families and also the Republican-sponsored rent certificate program. Economic incentives will be developed to attract private industry and capital to the low-cost housing market. By reducing interest rates through responsible fiscal and monetary policy we will lower the costs of home ownership, and new technologies and programs will be developed to stimulate low-cost methods of housing rehabilitation. Local communities will be encouraged to adopt uniform, modern building codes, research in cost-cutting technology through private enterprise will be accelerated, and innovative state and local programs will be supported. We will also stimulate the investment of "sweat equity" by home owners.

Our metropolitan transportation systems—the lifelines of our cities—have become tangled webs of congestion which not only create vast citizen inconvenience, discontent and economic inefficiency, but also tend to barricade inner city people against job opportunities in suburban areas. We will encourage priority attention by private enterprise and all levels of government to sound planning and the rapid development of improved mass transportation systems. Additionally, in the location of federal buildings and installations and the awarding of federal contracts, account will be taken of such factors as traffic congestion, housing, and the effect on community development.

Americans are acutely aware that none of these objectives can be achieved unless order through law and justice is maintained in our cities. Fire and looting, causing millions of dollars of property damage, have brought great suffering to home owners and small businessmen, particularly in black communities least able to absorb catastrophic losses. The Republican Party strongly advocates measures to alleviate and remove the frustrations that contribute to riots. We simultaneously support decisive action to quell civil disorder, relying primarily on state and local governments to deal with these conditions.

America has adequate peaceful and lawful means for achieving even fundamental social change if the people wish it. We will not tolerate violence!

Crime

Lawlessness is crumbling the foundations of American society.

Republicans believe that respect for the law is the cornerstone of a free and well-ordered society. We pledge vigorous and even-handed administration of justice and enforcement of the law. We must re-establish the principle that men are accountable for what they do, that criminals are responsible for their crimes, that while the youth's environment may help to explain the man's crime, it does not excuse that crime.

We call on public officials at the federal, state and local levels to enforce our laws with firmness and fairness. We recognize that respect for law and order flows naturally from a just society; while demanding protection of the public peace and safety, we pledge a relentless attack on economic and social injustice in every form.

The present Administration has:

Ignored the danger signals of our rising crime rates until very recently and even now has proposed only narrow measures hopelessly inadequate to the need;

Failed to implement most of the recommendations of the President's own Crime Commission;

Opposed legislative measures that would assist law enforcement officials in bringing law-breakers to justice;

Refused to sanction the use of either the court supervised wiretapping authority to combat organized crime or the revised rules of evidence, both made available by Congress;

Failed to deal effectively with threats to the nation's internal security by not prosecuting identified subversives.

By contrast, Republican leadership in Congress has:

Provided funds for programs administered by state and local governments to control juvenile delinquency and crime;

Created a National Institute of Law Enforcement and Criminal Justice to conduct crime research and facilitate the expansion of police training programs;

Secured enactment of laws enabling law enforcement officials to obtain and use evidence needed to prosecute criminals, while at the same time protecting the rights and privacy of all citizens;

Secured new laws aimed at "loan-sharking," the intimidation of witnesses, and obstruction of investigations;

Established disability as well as survivorship benefits for local police officers wounded or killed in pursuit of federal lawbreakers.

For the future, we pledge an all-out, federal–state–local crusade against crime, including:

Leadership by an Attorney General who will restore stature and respect to that office;

Continued support of legislation to strengthen state and local law enforcement and preserve the primacy of state responsibility in this area;

Full support of the F.B.I. and all law enforcement agencies of the federal government;

Improved federal cooperation with state and local law enforcement agencies;

Better coordination of the federal law enforcement, crime control, and criminal justice systems;

A vigorous nation-wide drive against trafficking in narcotics and dangerous drugs, including special emphasis on the first steps toward addiction—the use of marijuana and such drugs as LSD;

Total commitment to a federal program to deter, apprehend, prosecute, convict and punish the overlords of organized crime in America, including full implementation of the Congressional mandate that court-supervised wiretapping and electronic surveillance tools be used against the mobsters and racketeers;

Increased public protection against racketeer infiltration into legitimate business;

Increased research into the causes and prevention of crime, juvenile delinquency, and drug addiction;

Creation of a Federal Corrections Service to consolidate the fragmented and overlapping federal efforts and to assist state and local corrections systems;

A new approach to the problem of chronic offenders, including adequate staffing of the corrections system and improvement of rehabilitative techniques;

Modernization of the federal judicial system to promote swift, sure justice;

Enactment of legislation to control indiscriminate availability of firearms, safeguarding the right of responsible citizens to collect, own and use firearms for legitimate purposes, retaining primary responsibility at the state level, with such federal laws as necessary to better enable the states to meet their responsibilities.

Youth

More than any other nation, America reflects the strength and creative energy of youth. In every productive enterprise, the vigor, imagination and skills of our young people have contributed immeasurably to progress.

Our youth today are endowed with greater knowledge and maturity than any such generation of the past. Their political restlessness reflects their urgent hope to achieve a meaningful participation in public affairs commensurate with their contributions as responsible citizens.

In recognition of the abilities of these citizens, their desire to participate, and their service in the nation's defense, we believe that lower age groups should be accorded the right to vote. We believe that states which have not yet acted should reevaluate their positions with respect to 18-year-old voting, and that each such state should decide this matter for itself. We urge the states to act now.

For greater equity we will further revise Selective Service policies and reduce the number of years during which a young man can be considered for the draft, thereby providing some certainty to those liable for military service. When military manpower needs can be appreciably reduced, we will place the Selective Service System on standby and substitute a voluntary force obtained through adequate pay and career incentives.

We encourage responsible young men and women to join actively in the political process to help shape the future of the nation. We invite them to join our Republican effort to assure the new direction and the new leadership which this nation so urgently needs and rightfully expects.

Education

The birthplace of American opportunity has been in the classrooms of our schools and colleges. From early childhood through the college years, American schools must offer programs of education sufficiently flexible to meet the needs of all Americans—the advantaged, the average, the disadvantaged and the handicapped alike. To help our educators meet this need we will establish a National Commission to Study the Quality and Relevance of American Education.

To treat the special problems of children from impoverished families, we advocate expanded, better programs for preschool children. We will encourage state, local or private programs of teacher training. The development and increased use of better teaching methods and modern instruction techniques such as educational television and voluntary bilingual education will continue to have our support.

To help assure excellence and equality of educational opportunity, we will urge the states to present plans for federal assistance which would include state distribution of such aid to non–public school children and include non–public school representatives in the planning process. Where state conditions prevent use of funds for non–public school children, a public agency should be designated to administer federal funds.

Greater vocational education in high school and post–high school years is required for a new technological and service-oriented economy. Young people need expansion of post–high school technical institutes to enable them to acquire satisfactory skills for meaningful employment. For youths unable to obtain such training, we propose an industry youth program, coupled with a flexible approach to minimum wage laws for young entry-level workers during their training periods.

The rapidly mounting enrollments and costs of colleges and universities deprive many qualified young people of the opportunity to obtain a quality college education. To help colleges and universities provide this opportunity, we favor grant and loan programs for expansion of their facilities. We will also support a flexible student aid program of grants, loans and work opportunities, provided by federal and state governments and private organizations. We continue to favor tax credits for those burdened with the costs of higher education, and also tax deductions to encourage savings for this purpose. No young American should be denied a quality education because he cannot afford it or find work to meet its costs.

HUMAN DEVELOPMENT

The inability of the poor to cope meaningfully with their environment is compounded by problems which blunt opportunity—inadequate income, inferior education, inadequate health care, slum housing, limited job opportunities, discrimination, and crime.

Full opportunity requires a coordinated attack on the total problem through community human development programs. Federal revenue sharing would help provide the resources to develop such coordinated programs.

Jobs

The nation must look to an expanding free enterprise system to provide jobs. Republican policies and programs will encourage this expansion.

To qualify for jobs with permanence and promise, many disadvantaged citizens need special assistance and job training. We will enact the Republican-proposed Human Investment Act, offering tax credits to employers, to encourage such training and upgrading.

A complete overhaul of the nation's job programs is urgent. There are some 70 federally funded job training programs, with some cities having as many as 30 operating side by side. Some of these programs are ineffective and should be eliminated. We will simplify the federal effort and also encourage states and localities to establish single-headed manpower systems, to correlate all such federal activities and gear them to local conditions and needs. Local business advisory boards will assist in the design of such programs to fit training to employment needs. To help the unemployed find work we will also inaugurate a national job Opportunity Data Bank to report the number, nature and location of unfilled jobs and to match the individuals with the jobs.

The Poor

Welfare and poverty programs will be drastically revised to liberate the poor from the debilitating dependence which erodes self-respect and discourages family unity and responsibility. We will modify the rigid welfare requirements that stifle work motivation and support locally operated children's day-care centers to free the parents to accept work.

Burdensome administrative procedures will be simplified, and existing programs will be revised so that they will encourage and protect strong family units.

This nation must not blink the harsh fact—or the special demands it places upon us—that the incidence of poverty is consistently greater among Negroes, Mexican-Americans, Indians and other minority groupings than in the population generally.

An essential element of economic betterment is the opportunity for self-determination—to develop or acquire and manage one's own business enterprise. This opportunity is bleak for most residents of impoverished areas. We endorse the concept of state and community development corporations. These will provide capital, technical assistance and insurance for the establishment and renewal of businesses in depressed urban and rural areas. We favor efforts to enable residents of such areas to become owners and managers of businesses and, through such agencies as a Domestic Development Bank, to exercise economic leadership in their communities.

Additionally, we support action by states, with federal reinsurance, to help provide insurance coverage for homes and small businesses against damage and fire caused by riots.

We favor maximum reliance on community leaders utilizing the regular channels of government to provide needed public services. One approach is the Republican-sponsored Community Service Corps which would augment cooperation and communication between community residents and the police.

In programs for the socially and economically disadvantaged we favor participation by representatives of those to be served. The failure so to encourage creative and responsible participation from among the poor has been the greatest among the host of failures of the War on Poverty.

Recent studies indicate that many Americans suffer from malnutrition despite six separate federal food distribution programs. Here again, fragmentation of federal effort hinders accomplishment. We pledge a unified federal food distribution program, as well as active cooperation with the states and innovative private enterprise, to help provide the hungry poor sufficient food for a balanced diet.

A new Republican Administration will strive for fairness for all consumers, including additional information and protection programs as necessary, state and local consumer education, vigorous enforcement of the numerous protection laws already enacted, and active encouragement of the many consumer-protection initiatives and organizations of private enterprise.

Health

The inflation produced by the Johnson–Humphrey Administration has struck hardest in the area of health care. Hospital costs are rising 16 percent a year—four times the national average of price increases.

We pledge to encourage the broadening of private health insurance plans, many of which cover hospital care only, and to review the operation of government hospital care programs in order to encourage more patients to utilize nonhospital facilities. Expansion of the number of doctors, nurses, and supporting staff to relieve shortages and spread the availability of health care services will have our support. We will foster the construction of additional hospitals and encourage regional hospital and health planning for the maximum development of facilities for medical and nursing care. We will also press for enactment of Republican-sponsored programs for financing of hospital modernization. New diagnostic methods and also preventive care to assure early detection of physical impairments, thus fostering good health and avoiding illnesses requiring hospitalization, will have our support.

Additionally, we will work with states and local communities to help assure improved services to the mentally ill within a community setting and will intensify research to develop better treatment methods. We will encourage extension of private health insurance to cover mental illness.

While believing no American should be denied adequate medical treatment, we will be diligent in protecting the traditional patient–doctor relationship and the integrity of the medical practitioner.

We are especially concerned with the difficult circumstances of thousands of handicapped citizens who daily encounter architectural barriers which they are physically unable to surmount. We will support programs to reduce and where possible to eliminate such barriers in the construction of federal buildings.

The Elderly

Elderly Americans desire and deserve independence, dignity, and the opportunity for continued useful participation. We will strengthen the Social Security system and provide automatic cost-of-living adjustments under Social Security and the Railroad Retirement Act. An increase in earnings permitted to Social Security recipients without loss of benefits, provision for post–age 65 contributions to Social Security with deferment of benefits, and an increase in benefits to widows will also be provided. The age for universal Social

Security coverage will be gradually reduced from 72 to 65 and the former 100-percent income tax deduction will be restored for medical and drug expenses for people over 65. Additionally, we will take steps to help improve and extend private pension plans.

Veterans

The Republican Party pledges vigorous efforts to assure jobs for returning Vietnam war veterans, as well as other assistance to enable them and their families to establish living conditions befitting their brave service. We pledge a rehabilitation allowance for paraplegics to afford them the means to live outside a hospital environment. Adequate medical and hospital care will be maintained for all veterans with service-connected disabilities and veterans in need, and timely revisions of compensation programs will be enacted for service-connected death and disability to help assure an adequate standard of living for all disabled veterans and their survivors. We will see that every veteran is accorded the right to be interred in a national cemetery as near as possible to his home, and pledge to maintain all veterans' programs in an independent Veterans Administration.

Indian Affairs

The plight of American Indians and Eskimos is a national disgrace. Contradictory government policies have led to intolerable deprivation for these citizens. We dedicate ourselves to the promotion of policies responsive to their needs and desires and will seek the full participation of these people and their leaders in the formulation of such policies.

Inequality of jobs, of education, of housing and of health blight their lives today. We believe the Indian and Eskimo must have an equal opportunity to participate fully in American society. Moreover, the uniqueness and beauty of these native cultures must be recognized and allowed to flourish.

THE INDIVIDUAL AND GOVERNMENT

In recent years an increasingly impersonal national government has tended to submerge the individual. An entrenched, burgeoning bureaucracy has increasingly usurped powers, unauthorized by Congress. Decentralization of power, as well as strict Congressional oversight of administrative and regulatory agency compliance with the letter and spirit of the law, are urgently needed to preserve personal liberty,

improve efficiency, and provide a swifter response to human problems.

Many states and localities are eager to revitalize their own administrative machinery, procedures, and personnel practices. Moreover, there is growing interstate cooperation in such fields as education, elimination of air and water pollution, utilization of airports, highways and mass transportation. We pledge full federal cooperation with these efforts, including revision of the system of providing federal funds and reestablishment of the authority of state governments in coordinating and administering the federal programs. Additionally, we propose the sharing of federal revenues with state governments. We are particularly determined to revise the grant-in-aid system and substitute block grants wherever possible. It is also important that state and local governments retain the historic right to raise funds by issuing tax-exempt securities.

The strengthening of citizen influence on government requires a number of improvements in political areas. For instance, we propose to reform the electoral college system, establish a nation-wide, uniform voting period for Presidential elections, and recommend that the states remove unreasonable requirements, residence and otherwise, for voting in Presidential elections. We specifically favor representation in Congress for the District of Columbia. We will work to establish a system of self-government for the District of Columbia which will take into account the interests of the private citizens thereof, and those of the federal government.

We will support the efforts of the Puerto Rican people to achieve statehood when they freely request such status by a general election, and we share the hopes and aspirations of the people of the Virgin Islands who will be closely consulted on proposed gubernatorial appointments.

We favor a new Election Reform Act that will apply clear, reasonable restraints to political spending and fund-raising, whether by business, labor or individuals, ensure timely publication of the financial facts in campaigns, and provide a tax deduction for small contributions.

We will prevent the solicitation of federal workers for political contributions and assure comparability of federal salaries with private enterprise pay. The increasing government intrusion into the privacy of its employees and of citizens in general is intolerable. All such snooping, meddling, and pressure by the federal government on its employees and other citizens will be stopped and such employees, whether or not union members, will be provided a prompt and fair method of settling their grievances. Further, we pledge to protect federal employees in the exercise of their right freely and without fear of penalty or reprisal to form, join or assist any employee organization or to refrain from any such activities.

Congress itself must be reorganized and modernized in order to function efficiently as a co-equal branch of government. Democrats in control of Congress have opposed Republican efforts for Congressional reform and killed legislation embodying the recommendations of a special bipartisan committee. We will again press for enactment of this measure.

We are particularly concerned over the huge and mounting postal deficit and the evidence, recently stressed by the President's Commission on Postal Organization, of costly and inefficient practices in the postal establishment. We pledge full consideration of the Commission's recommendations for improvements in the nation's postal service. We believe the Post Office Department must attract and retain the best qualified and most capable employees and offer them improved opportunities for advancement and better working conditions and incentives. We favor extension of the merit principle to postmasters and rural carriers.

Public confidence in an independent judiciary is absolutely essential to the maintenance of law and order. We advocate application of the highest standards in making appointments to the courts, and we pledge a determined effort to rebuild and enhance public respect for the Supreme Court and all other courts in the United States.

A HEALTHY ECONOMY

The dynamism of our economy is produced by millions of individuals who have the incentive to participate in decision-making that advances themselves and society as a whole. Government can reinforce these incentives, but its overinvolvement in individual decisions distorts the system and intrudes inefficiency and waste.

Under the Johnson–Humphrey Administration we have had economic mismanagement of the highest order. Inflation robs our pay checks at a present rate of $4\frac{1}{2}$ percent per year. In the past three years the real purchasing power of the average wage and salary worker has actually declined. Crippling interest rates, some the highest in a century, prevent millions of Americans from buying homes and small businessmen, farmers and other citizens from obtaining the loans they need. Americans must work longer today than ever before to pay their taxes.

New Republican leadership can and will restore fiscal integrity and sound monetary policies, encourage sustained economic vitality, and avoid such economic distortions as wage and price controls. We favor strengthened Congressional control over federal expenditures by scheduled Congressional reviews of, or reasonable time limits on, unobligated appropriations. By responsibly applying federal expenditure controls to priority needs, we can in time live both within our means and up to our aspirations. Such funds as become available with the termination of the Vietnam war and upon recovery from its impact on our national defense will be applied in a balanced way to critical domestic needs and to reduce the heavy tax burden. Our objective is not an endless expansion of federal programs and expenditures financed by heavier taxation. The imperative need for tax reform and simplification will have our priority attention. We will also improve the management of the national debt, reduce its heavy interest burden, and seek amendment of the law to make reasonable price stability an explicit objective of government policy.

The Executive Branch needs urgently to be made a more efficient and economical instrument of public policy. Low-priority activities must be eliminated and conflicting missions and functions simplified. We pledge to establish a new Efficiency Commission to root out the unnecessary and overlapping, as well as a Presidential Office of Executive Management to assure a vigorous follow-through.

A new Republican Administration will undertake an intensive program to aid small business, including economic incentives and technical assistance, with increased emphasis in rural and urban poverty areas.

In addition to vigorous enforcement of the antitrust statutes, we pledge a thorough analysis of the structure and operation of these laws at home and abroad in the light of changes in the economy, in order to update our antitrust policy and enable it to serve us well in the future.

We are determined to eliminate and prevent improper federal competition with private enterprise.

Labor

Organized labor has contributed greatly to the economic strength of our country and the well being of its members. The Republican Party vigorously endorses its key role in our national life.

We support an equitable minimum wage for American workers—one providing fair wages without unduly increasing unemployment among those on the lowest rung of the economic ladder—and will improve the Fair Labor Standards Act, with its important protections for employees.

The forty-hour week adopted 30 years ago needs reexamination to determine whether or not a shorter work week, without loss of wages, would produce more jobs, increase productivity and stabilize prices.

We strongly believe that the protection of individual liberty is the cornerstone of sound labor policy. Today, basic rights of some workers, guaranteed by law, are inadequately guarded against abuse. We will assure these rights through vigorous enforcement of present laws, including the Taft–Hartley Act and the Landrum–Griffin Act, and the addition of new protections where needed. We will be vigilant to prevent any administrative agency entrusted with labor-law enforcement from defying the letter and spirit of these laws.

Healthy private enterprise demands responsibility by government, management and labor to avoid the imposition of excessive costs or prices and to share with the consumer the benefits of increased productivity. It also demands responsibility in free collective bargaining, not only by labor and management, but also by those in government concerned with these sensitive relationships.

We will bar government-coerced strike settlements that cynically disregard the public interest and accelerate inflation. We will again reduce government intervention in labor-management disputes to a minimum, keep government participation in channels defined by the Congress, and prevent back-door intervention in the administration of labor laws.

Repeated Administration promises to recommend legislation dealing with crippling economic strikes have never been honored. Instead, settlements forced or influenced by government and overriding the interests of the parties and the public have shattered the Administration's own wage and price guidelines and contributed to inflation.

Effective methods for dealing with labor disputes involving the national interest must be developed. Permanent, long-range solutions of the problems of national emergency disputes, public employee strikes and crippling work stoppages are imperative. These solutions cannot be wisely formulated in the heat of emergency. We pledge an intensive effort to develop practical, acceptable solutions that conform fully to the public interest.

Transportation

Healthy economic growth demands a balanced, competitive transportation system in which each mode of transportation—train, truck, barge, bus and aircraft—is efficiently utilized. The Administration's failure to evolve a coordinated transportation policy now results in outrageous delays at major airports and in glacial progress in developing high-speed train transportation linking our major population centers.

The nation's air transport system performs excellently, but under increasingly adverse conditions. Airways and airport congestion has become acute. New and additional equipment, modern facilities including the use of computers, and additional personnel must be provided without further delay. We pledge expert evaluation of these matters in developing a national air transportation system.

We will make the Department of Transportation the agency Congress intended it to be—effective in promoting coordination and preserving competition among carriers. We promise equitable treatment of all modes of transportation in order to assure the public better service, greater safety, and the most modern facilities. We will also explore a trust fund approach to transportation, similar to the fund developed for the Eisenhower interstate highway system, and perhaps in this way speed the development of modern mass transportation systems and additional airports.

RESOURCES AND SCIENCE

Agriculture

During seven and a half years of Democrat Administrations and Democrat Congresses the farmer has been the forgotten man in our nation's economy. The cost-price squeeze has steadily worsened, driving more than four and a half million people from the farms, many to already congested urban areas. Over eight hundred thousand individual farm units have gone out of existence.

During the eight years of the Eisenhower Administration, the farm parity ratio averaged 85. Under Democratic rule, the parity ratio has consistently been under 80 and averaged only 74 for all of 1967. It has now fallen to 73. Actions by the Administration, in line with its apparent cheap food policy, have held down prices received by farmers.

Government payments to farmers, from taxes paid by consumers, have far from offset this loss.

Inflationary policies of the Administration and its Congress have contributed greatly to increased costs of production. Using 1958 as a base year with an index of 100, prices paid by farmers in 1967 had risen to a weighted index of 117, whereas the prices they received were at a weighted index of only 104. From the 1958 index of 100, interest was up to 259, taxes 178, labor costs 146, and farm machinery 130.

The cost–price squeeze has been accompanied by a dangerous increase in farm debt—up nearly $24 billion in the last seven years. In 1967 alone, net debt per farm increased $1,337 while net income per farm went down $605. While net farm equity has increased, it is due mainly to inflated land values. Without adequate net income to pay off indebtedness, the farm owner has no choice but to liquidate some of his equity or go out of business. Farm tenants are even worse off, since they have no comparable investment for inflation to increase in value as their indebtedness increases.

The Republican Party is committed to the concept that a sound agricultural economy is imperative to the national interest. Prosperity, opportunity, abundance, and efficiency in agriculture benefit every American. To promote the development of American agriculture, we pledge:

Farm policies and programs which will enable producers to receive fair prices in relation to the prices they must pay for other products;

Sympathetic consideration of proposals to encourage farmers, especially small producers, to develop their bargaining position;

Sound economic policies which will brake inflation and reduce the high interest rates;

A truly two-way export-import policy which protects American agriculture from unfair foreign competition while increasing our overseas commodity dollar sales to the rapidly expanding world population;

Reorganization of the management of the Commodity Credit Corporation's inventory operations so that the Corporation will no longer compete with the marketings of farmers;

Improved programs for distribution of food and milk to schools and low-income citizens;

A strengthened program to export our food and farm technology in keeping with the Republican-initiated Food for Peace program;

Assistance to farm cooperatives including rural electric and telephone cooperatives, consistent with prudent development of our nation's resources and rural needs;

Greater emphasis on research for industrial uses of agricultural products, new markets, and new methods for cost-cutting in production and marketing techniques;

Revitalization of rural America through programs emphasizing vocational training, economic incentives for industrial development, and the development of human resources;

Improvement of credit programs to help finance the heavy capital needs of modern farming, recognizing the severe credit problems of young farm families seeking to enter into successful farming;

A more direct voice for the American farmer in shaping his own destiny.

Natural Resources

In the tradition of Theodore Roosevelt, the Republican Party promises sound conservation and development of natural resources in cooperative government and private programs.

An expanding population and increasing material wealth require new public concern for the quality of our environment. Our nation must pursue its activities in harmony with the environment. As we develop our natural resources we must be mindful of our priceless heritage of natural beauty.

A national minerals and fuels policy is essential to maintain production needed for our nation's economy and security. Present economic incentives, including depletion allowances, to encourage the discovery and development of vital minerals and fuels must be continued. We must recognize the increasing demand for minerals and fuels by our economy, help ensure an economically stable industry, maintain a favorable balance of trade and balance of payments, and encourage research to promote the wise use of these resources.

Federal laws applicable to public lands and related resources will be updated and a public land-use policy formulated. We will manage such lands to ensure their multiple use as economic resources and recreational areas. Additionally, we will work in cooperation with cities and states in acquiring and developing green space—convenient outdoor recreation and conservation areas. We support the creation of additional national parks, wilderness areas, monuments and outdoor recreation areas at appropriate sites, as well as their continuing improvement, to make them of maximum utility and enjoyment to the public.

Improved forestry practices, including protection and improvement of watershed lands, will have our vigorous support. We will also improve water resource information, including an acceleration of river basin commission inventory studies. The reclaiming of land by irrigation and the development of flood control programs will have high priority in these studies. We will support additional multi-purpose water projects for reclamation, flood control, and recreation based on accurate cost-benefit estimates.

We also support efforts to increase our total fresh water supply by further research in weather modification, and in better methods of desalinization of salt and brackish waters.

The United States has dropped to sixth among the fishing nations of the world. We pledge a reversal of present policies and the adoption of a progressive national fisheries policy, which will make it possible for the first time to utilize fully the vast ocean reservoir of protein. We pledge a more energetic control of pollution, encouragement of an increase in fishery resources, and will also press for international agreements assuring multi-national conservation.

We pledge a far more vigorous and systematic program to expand knowledge about the unexplored storehouses of the sea and polar regions. We must undertake a comprehensive polar plan and an oceanographic program to develop these abundant resources for the continued strength of the United States and the betterment of all mankind.

Science

In science and technology the nation must maintain leadership against increasingly challenging competition from abroad. Crucial to this leadership is growth in the supply of gifted, skilled scientists and engineers. Government encouragement in this critical area should be stable and related to a more rational and selective scheme of priorities.

Vigorous effort must be directed toward increasing the application of science and technology, including the social sciences, to the solution of such pressing human problems as housing, transportation, education, environmental pollution, law enforcement, and job training. We support a strong program of research in the sciences, with protection for the independence and integrity of participating individuals and institutions. An increase in the number of centers of scientific creativity and excellence, geographically dispersed, and active cooperation with other nations in meaningful scientific undertakings will also have our support.

We regret that the Administration's budgetary mismanagement has forced sharp reductions in the space program. The Republican Party shares the sense of urgency manifested by the scientific community concerning the exploration of outer space. We recognize that the peaceful applications of space probes in communications, health, weather, and technological advances have been beneficial to every citizen. We regard the ability to launch and deploy advanced spacecraft as a military necessity. We deplore the failure of the Johnson–Humphrey Administration to emphasize the military uses of space for America's defense.

FOREIGN POLICY

Our nation urgently needs a foreign policy that realistically leads toward peace. This policy can come only from resolute, new leadership, leadership that can and will think anew and act anew—a leadership not bound by mistakes of the past.

Our best hope for enduring peace lies in comprehensive international cooperation. We will consult with nations that share our purposes. We will press for their greater participation in man's common concerns and encourage regional approaches to defense, economic development, and peaceful adjustment of disputes.

We will seek to develop law among nations and strengthen agencies to effectuate that law and cooperatively solve common problems. We will assist the United Nations to become the keystone of such agencies, and its members will be pressed to honor all charter obligations, including specifically its financial provisions. Worldwide resort to the International Court of Justice as a final arbiter of legal disputes among nations will have our vigorous encouragement, subject to limitations imposed by the U.S. Senate in accepting the Court's jurisdiction.

The world abounds with problems susceptible of cooperative solution—poverty, hunger, denial of human rights, economic development, scientific and technological backwardness. The worldwide population explosion in particular, with its attendant grave problems, looms as a menace to all mankind and will have our priority attention. In all such areas we pledge to expand and strengthen international cooperation.

A more selective use of our economic strength has become imperative. We believe foreign aid is a necessary ingredient in the betterment of less developed countries. Our aid, however, must be positioned realistically in our national priorities. Only those nations which urgently require America's help and clearly evince a desire to help themselves will receive such assistance as can be diverted from our pressing needs. In providing aid, more emphasis will be given to technical assistance. We will encourage multilateral agencies so that other nations will help share the burden. The administration of all aid programs will be revised and improved to prevent waste, inefficiency and corruption. We will vigorously encourage maximum participation by private enterprise.

No longer will foreign aid activities range free of our foreign policy. Nations hostile to this country will receive no assistance from the United States. We will not provide aid of any kind to countries which aid and abet the war efforts of North Vietnam.

Only when Communist nations prove by actual deeds that they genuinely seek world peace and will live in harmony with the rest of the world, will we support expansion of East–West trade. We will strictly administer the Export Control Act, taking special care to deny export licenses for strategic goods.

In the development and execution of the nation's foreign policy, our career Foreign Service officers play a critical role. We strongly support the Foreign Service and will strengthen it by improving its efficiency and administration and providing adequate allowances for its personnel.

The principles of the 1965 Immigration Act—nondiscrimination against national origins, reunification of families, and selective support for the American labor market—have our unreserved backing. We will refine this new law to make our immigration policy still more equitable and non-discriminatory.

The Republican Party abhors the activities of those who have violated passport regulations contrary to the best interests of our nation and also the present policy of reissuing passports to such violators. We pledge to tighten passport administration so as to bar such violators from passport privileges.

The balance of payments crisis must be ended, and the international position of the dollar strengthened. We propose to do this, not by peremptory efforts to limit American travel abroad or by self-defeating restraints on overseas investments, but by restraint in Federal spending and realistic monetary policies, by adjusting overseas commitments, by stimulating exports, by encouraging more foreign travel to the United States and, as specific conditions require, by extending tax treatment to our own exports and imports comparable to such treatment applied by foreign countries. Ending inflation is the first step toward solving the payments crisis.

It remains the policy of the Republican Party to work toward freer trade among all nations of the free world. But artificial obstacles to such trade are a serious concern. We promise hardheaded bargaining to lower the non-tariff barriers against American exports and to develop a code of fair competition, including international fair labor standards, between the United States and its principal trading partners.

A sudden influx of imports can endanger many industries. These problems, differing in each industry, must be considered case by case. Our guideline will be fairness for both producers and workers, without foreclosing imports.

Thousands of jobs have been lost to foreign producers because of discriminatory and unfair trade practices.

The State Department must give closest attention to the development of agreements with exporting nations to bring about fair competition. Imports should not be permitted to capture excessive portions of the American market but should, through international agreements, be able to participate in the growth of consumption.

Should such efforts fail, specific countermeasures will have to be applied until fair competition is reestablished. Tax reforms will also be required to preserve the competitiveness of American goods.

The basis for determining the value of imports and exports must be modified to reflect true dollar value.

Not the least important aspect of this problem is the relative obsolescence of machinery in this country. An equitable tax write-off is necessary to strengthen our industrial competitiveness in the world.

We also favor the broadening of governmental assistance to industries, producers and workers seriously affected by imports—assistance denied by the Johnson–Humphrey Administration's excessively stringent application of the Trade Expansion Act of 1962.

Ties of history and geography link us closely to Latin America. Closer economic and cultural cooperation of the United States and the Latin American countries is imperative in a broad attack on the chronic problems of poverty, inadequate economic growth and consequent poor education throughout the hemisphere. We will encourage in Latin America the progress of economic integration to improve opportunity for industrialization and economic diversification.

The principles of the Monroe Doctrine, affirmed at Caracas 14 years ago by all the independent nations of this hemisphere, have been discarded by Democrat Administrations. We hold that they should be reaffirmed and should guide the collective policy of the Americas. Nor have we forgotten in this context, the Cuban people who still cruelly suffer under Communist tyranny.

In cooperation with other nations, we will encourage the less developed nations of Asia and Africa peacefully to improve their standards of living, working with stronger regional organizations where indicated and desired.

In the tinderbox of the Middle East, we will pursue a stable peace through recognition by all nations of each other's right to assured boundaries, freedom of navigation through international waters, and independent existence free from the threat of aggression. We will seek an end to the arms race through international agreement and the stationing of peace-keeping forces of the United Nations in areas of severe tension, as we encourage peace-table talks among adversaries.

Nevertheless, the Soviets persist in building an imbalance of military forces in this region. The fact of a growing menace to Israel is undeniable. Her forces must be kept at a commensurate strength both for her protection and to help keep the peace of the area. The United States, therefore, will provide countervailing help to Israel, such as supersonic fighters, as necessary for these purposes. To replace the ancient rivalries of this region with new hope and opportunity, we vigorously support a well-conceived plan of regional development, including the bold nuclear desalinization and irrigation proposal of former President Eisenhower.

Our relations with Western Europe, so critical to our own progress and security, have been needlessly and dangerously impaired. They must be restored, and NATO revitalized and strengthened. We continue to pursue the goal of a Germany reunified in freedom.

The peoples of the captive nations of Eastern Europe will one day regain their freedom and independence. We will strive to speed this day by encouraging the greater political freedom actively sought by several of these nations. On occasions when a liberalization of trade in nonstrategic goods with the captive nations can have this effect, it will have our support.

We do not intend to conduct foreign policy in such manner as to make the United States a world policeman. However, we will not condone aggression, or so-called "wars of national liberation," or naively discount the continuing threats of Moscow and Peking. Nor can we fail to condemn the Soviet Union for its continuing anti-Semitic actions, its efforts to eradicate all religions, and its oppression of minorities generally. Improved relations with Communist nations can come only when they cease to endanger other states by force or threat. Under existing conditions, we cannot favor recognition of Communist China or its admission to the United Nations.

We encourage international limitations of armaments, provided all major powers are proportionately restrained and trustworthy guarantees are provided against violations.

VIETNAM

The Administration's Vietnam policy has failed—militarily, politically, diplomatically, and with relation to our own people.

We condemn the Administration's breach of faith with the American people respecting our heavy involvement in Vietnam. Every citizen bitterly recalls the Democrat campaign oratory of 1964: "We are not about to send American boys 9–10,000 miles away from home to do what Asian boys ought to be doing for themselves." The Administration's failure to honor its own words has led millions of Americans to question its credibility.

The entire nation has been profoundly concerned by hastily extemporized, undeclared land wars which embroil massive U.S. armed forces thousands of miles from our shores. It is time to realize that not every international conflict is susceptible of solution by American ground forces.

Militarily, the Administration's piecemeal commitment of men and material has wasted our massive military superiority and frittered away our options. The result has been a prolonged war of attrition. Throughout this period the Administration has been slow in training and equipping South Vietnamese units both for fighting the war and for defending their country after the war is over.

Politically, the Administration has failed to recognize the entirely novel aspects of this war. The over-emphasis on its old-style, conventional aspects has blinded the Administration to the fact that the issue is not control of territory but the security and loyalty of the population. The enemy's primary emphasis has been to disrupt orderly government.

The Administration has paid inadequate attention to the political framework on which a successful outcome ultimately depends. Not only has the Administration failed to encourage assumption of responsibility by the Vietnamese, but their sense of responsibility has been in fact undermined by our approach to pacification. An added factor has been a lack of security for the civilian population.

At home, the Administration has failed to share with the people the full implication of our challenge and of our commitments.

To resolve our Vietnam dilemma, America obiously requires new leadership—one capable of thinking and acting anew, not one hostage to the many mistakes of the past. The Republican Party offers such leadership.

We pledge to adopt a strategy relevant to the real problems of the war, concentrating on the security of the population, on developing a greater sense of nation-hood, and on strengthening the local forces. It will be a strategy permitting a progressive de-Americanization of the war, both military and civilian.

We will see to it that our gallant American servicemen are fully supported with the highest-quality equipment, and will avoid actions that unnecessarily jeopardize their lives.

We will pursue a course that will enable and induce the South Vietnamese to assume increasing responsibility.

The war has been conducted without a coherent program for peace.

We pledge a program for peace in Vietnam—neither peace at any price nor a camouflaged surrender of legitimate United States or allied interests—but a positive program that will offer a fair and equitable settlement to all, based on the principle of self-determination, our national interests and the cause of long-range world peace.

We will sincerely and vigorously pursue peace negotiations as long as they offer any reasonable prospect for a just peace. We pledge to develop a clear and purposeful negotiating position.

We will return to one of the cardinal principles of the last Republican Administration: that American interests are best served by cooperative multilateral action with our allies rather than by unilateral U.S. action.

Our pride in the nation's armed forces in Southeast Asia and elsewhere in the world is beyond expression.

In all our history none have fought more bravely or more devotedly than our sons in this unwanted war in Vietnam.

They deserve—and they and their loved ones have—our total support, our encouragement, and our prayers.

NATIONAL DEFENSE

Grave errors, many now irretrievable, have characterized the direction of our nation's defense.

A singular notion—that salvation for America lies in standing still—has pervaded the entire effort. Not retention of American superiority but parity with the Soviet Union has been made the controlling doctrine in many critical areas. We have frittered away superior military capabilities, enabling the Soviets to narrow their defense gap, in some areas to outstrip us, and to move to cancel our lead entirely by the early Seventies. In a host of areas, advanced military research and development have been inhibited and stagnated by inexpert, cost-oriented administrators imbued with a euphoric concept of Soviet designs. A strange Administration preference for such second-best weaponry as the costly Navy Flll-B(TFX) has deprived our armed forces of more advanced weapons systems. Improvements in our submarines have been long delayed as the Soviets have proceeded apace with their own. Our anti-submarine warfare capabilities have been left seriously inadequate, new fighter planes held up, and new strategic weaponry left on the drawing boards.

This mismanagement has dangerously weakened the ability of the United States to meet future crises with great power and decisiveness. All the world was respectful of America's decisive strategic advantage over the Soviets achieved during the Eisenhower Administration. This superiority proved its worth in the Cuban missile crisis six years ago. But now we have had an augury of things to come—a shameful, humiliating episode, the seizure of the USS *Pueblo* and its crew, with devastating injury to America's prestige everywhere in the world.

We pledge to include the following in a comprehensive program to restore the pre-eminence of U.S. military strength:

Improve our deterrent capability through an ocean strategy which extends the Polaris–Poseidon concept and accelerates submarine technology;

Redirect and stimulate military strength to encourage major innovations rather than merely respond belatedly to Communist advances;

Strengthen intelligence gathering and evaluation by the various military services;

Use the defense dollar more effectively through simplication of the cumbersome, overcentralized administration of the Defense Department, expanded competitive bidding on defense contracts, and improved safeguards against excessive profits;

Reinvigorate the nation's most important security planning organization—the National Security Council—to prevent future haphazard diplomatic and military ventures, integrate the nation's foreign and military policies and programs, and enable our nation once again to anticipate and prevent crises rather than hastily contriving counter-measures after they arise.

Our merchant marine, too, has been allowed to deteriorate. Now there are grave doubts that it is capable of adequate response to emergency security needs.

The United States has drifted from first place to sixth place in the world in the size of its merchant fleet. By contrast, the Russian fleet has been rapidly expanding and will attain a dominant position by 1970. Deliveries of new ships are now eight to one in Russia's favor.

For reasons of security, as well as of economics, the decline of our merchant marine must be reversed. We therefore pledge a vigorous and realistic ship replacement program to meet the changing pattern of our foreign commerce. We will also expand industry–government maritime research and development, emphasizing nuclear propulsion, and simplify and revise construction and operating subsidy procedures.

Finally, we pledge to assemble the nation's best diplomatic, military and scientific minds for an exhaustive reassessment of America's worldwide commitments and military preparedness. We are determined to assure our nation of the strength required in future years to deter war and to prevail should it occur.

CONCLUSION

We believe that the principles and programs we have here presented will find acceptance with the American people. We believe they will command the victory.

There are points of emphasis which we deem important.

The accent is on freedom. Our Party historically has been the Party of freedom. We are the only barricade against those who, through excessive government power, would overwhelm and destroy man's liberty. If liberty fails, all else is dross.

Beyond freedom we emphasize trust and credibility. We have pledged only what we honestly believe we can perform. In a world where broken promises become a way of life, we submit that a nation progresses not on promises broken but on pledges kept.

We have also accented the moral nature of the crisis which confronts us. At the core of that crisis is the life, the liberty, and the happiness of man. If life can be taken with impunity, if liberty is subtly leeched away, if the pursuit of happiness becomes empty and futile, then indeed are the moral foundations in danger.

We have placed high store on our basic theme. The dogmas of the quiet past simply will not do for the restless present. The case is new. We must most urgently think anew and act anew. This is an era of rapid, indeed violent change. Clearly we must disenthrall ourselves. Only then can we save this great Republic.

We rededicate ourselves to this Republic—this one nation, under God, indivisible, with liberty and justice for all.

— 1972 —

PREAMBLE

This year our Republican Party has greater reason than ever before for pride in its stewardship.

When our accomplishments are weighed—when our opponents' philosophy, programs and candidates are assessed—we believe the American people will rally eagerly to the leadership which since January 1969 has brought them a better life in a better land in a safer world.

This political contest of 1972 is a singular one. No Americans before have had a clearer option. The choice is between going forward from dramatic achievements to predictable new achievements, or turning back toward a nightmarish time in which the torch of free America was virtually snuffed out in a storm of violence and protest.

It is so easy to forget how frightful it was.

There was Vietnam—so bloody, so costly, so bitterly divisive—a war in which more than a half million of America's sons had been committed to battle—a war, it seemed, neither to be won nor lost, but only to be endlessly fought—a war emotionally so tormenting as almost to obliterate America's other worldly concerns.

And yet, as our eyes were fixed on the carnage in Asia, in Europe our alliance had weakened. The Western will was dividing and ebbing. The isolation of the People's Republic of China with one-fourth of the world's population, went endlessly on.

At home our horrified people watched our cities burn, crime burgeon, campuses dissolve into chaos. A mishmash of social experimentalism, producing such fiscal extravaganzas as the abortive war on poverty, combined with war pressures to drive up taxes and balloon the cost of living. Working men and women found their living standards fixed or falling, the victim of inflation. Nationwide, welfare skyrocketed out of control.

The history of our country may record other crises more costly in material goods, but none so demoralizing to the American people. To millions of Americans it seemed we had lost our way.

So it was when our Republican Party came to power.

Now, four years later, a new leadership with new policies and new programs has restored reason and order and hope. No longer buffeted by internal violence and division, we are on course in calmer seas with a sure, steady hand at the helm. A new spirit, buoyant and confident, is on the rise in our land, nourished by the changes we have made. In the past four years:

We have turned toward concord among all Americans;

We have turned toward reason and order;

We have turned toward government responding sensitively to the people's hopes and needs;

We have turned toward innovative solutions to the nation's most pressing problems;

We have turned toward new paths for social progress—from welfare rolls to payrolls; from wanton pollution to vigorous environmental protection;

We have moved far toward peace: withdrawal of our fighting men from Vietnam, constructive new relationships with the Soviet Union and the People's Republic of China, the nuclear arms race checked, the Mid-East crisis dampened, our alliances revitalized.

So once again the foreign policy of the United States is on a realistic footing, promising us a nation secure in a full generation of peace, promising the end of conscription, promising a further allocation of resources to domestic needs.

It is a saga of exhilarating progress.

We have come far in so short a time. Yet, much remains to be done.

Discontents, frustrations and concerns still stir in the minds and hearts of many of our people, especially the young. As long as America falls short of being truly peaceful, truly prosperous, truly secure, truly just for all, her task is not done.

Our encouragement is in the fact that things as they are, are far better than things that recently were. Our resolve is that things to come can be, and will be, better still.

Looking to tomorrow, to President Nixon's second term and on into the third century of this Republic, we of the Republican Party see a quarter-billion Americans peaceful and prospering as never before, humane as never before, their nation strong and just as never before.

It is toward this bright tomorrow that we are determined to move, in concert with millions of discerning Democrats and concerned Independents who will not, and cannot, take part in the convulsive leftward lurch of the national Democratic Party.

The election of 1972 requires of the voters a momentous decision—one that will determine the kind of nation that is to be on its 200th birthday four years hence. In this year we must choose between strength and weakness for our country in the years to come. This year we must choose between negotiating and begging with adversary nations. This year we must choose between an expanding economy in which workers will prosper and a hand-out economy in which the idle live at ease. This year we must choose between running our own lives and letting others in a distant bureaucracy run them. This year we must choose between responsible fiscal policy and fiscal folly.

This year the choice is between moderate goals historically sought by both major parties and far-out goals of the far left. The contest is not between the two great parties Americans have known in previous years. For in this year 1972 the national Democratic Party has been seized by a radical clique which scorns our nation's past and would blight her future.

We invite our troubled friends of other political affiliations to join with us in a new coalition for progress. Together let us reject the New Left prescription for folly and build surely on the solid achievements of President Nixon's first term.

Four years ago we said, in Abraham Lincoln's words, that Americans must think anew and act anew. This we have done, under gifted leadership. The many advances already made, the shining prospects so clearly ahead, are presented in this Platform for 1972 and beyond.

May every American measure our deeds and words thoughtfully and objectively, and may our opponents' claims be equally appraised. Once this is done and judgment rendered on election day, we will confidently carry forward the task of doing for America what her people need and want and deserve.

TOWARD A FULL GENERATION OF PEACE

Foreign Policy

When Richard Nixon became President, our country was still clinging to foreign policies fashioned for the era immediately following World War II. The world has changed dramatically in the 1960's, but our foreign policies had not.

America was hopelessly enmeshed in Vietnam. In all parts of the globe our alliances were frayed. With the principal Communist powers our relations showed little prospect of improvement. Trade and monetary problems were grave. Periodic crises had become the way of international economic life.

The nation's frustrations had fostered a dangerous spirit of isolationism among our people. America's influence in the world had waned.

In only four years we have fashioned foreign policies based on a new spirit of effective negotiation with our adversaries, and a new sense of real partnership with our allies. Clearly, the prospects for lasting peace are greater today than at any time since World War II.

New Era of Diplomacy

Not all consequences of our new foreign policy are yet visible, precisely because one of its great purposes is to anticipate crises and avoid them rather than merely respond. Its full impact will be realized over many years, but already there are vivid manifestations of its success:

Before this Administration, a Presidential visit to Peking would have been unthinkable. Yet our President has gone there to open a candid airing of differences so that they will not lead some day to war. All over the world tensions have eased as, after a generation of hostility, the strongest of nations and the most populous of nations have started discoursing again.

During the 1960's, Presidential visits to Moscow were twice arranged and twice cancelled. Now our President has conferred, in the Soviet Union, with Soviet leaders, and has hammered out agreements to make this world a much safer place. Our President's quest for peace has taken him to 20 other countries, including precedent shattering visits to Rumania, Yugoslavia and Poland.

Around the globe America's alliances have been renewed and strengthened. A new spirit of partnership shows results in our NATO partners' expenditures for the common defense—up by some $2 billion in two years.

Historians may well regard these years as a golden age of American diplomacy. Never before has our country negotiated with so many nations on so wide a range of subjects—and never with greater success. In the last four years we have concluded agreements:

To limit nuclear weapons.

To ban nuclear weapons from the world's seabeds.

To reduce the risk of an accidental nuclear war.

To end the threat of biological and toxin warfare.

To terminate American responsibility for the administration of Okinawa.

To end the recurrent crises over Berlin.

To provide for U.S.–Soviet cooperation in health and space research.

To reduce the possibility of dangerous incidents at sea.

To improve emergency communications between the White House and the Kremlin.

To exercise restraint in situations threatening conflict.

To realign the world's currencies.

To reduce barriers to American exports.

To combat the international drug traffic.

To protect the international environment.

To expand cultural relations with peoples of Eastern Europe.

To settle boundary disputes with Mexico.

To restore the water quality of the Great Lakes in cooperation with Canada.

In Vietnam, too, our new policies have been dramatically effective.

In the 1960's, our nation was plunged into another major war—for the fourth time in this century, the third time in a single generation.

More than a half-million Americans were fighting in Vietnam in January 1969. Fatalities reached 562 in a single week. There was no plan for bringing Americans home; no hope for an end of the war.

In four years, we have marched toward peace and away from war. Our forces in Vietnam have been cut by 93 per cent. No longer do we have a single ground combat unit there. Casualties are down by 95 per cent. Our young draftees are no longer sent there without their consent.

Through it all, we have not abandoned an ally to aggression, not turned our back on their brave defense against brutal invasion, not consigned them to the bloodbath that would follow Communist conquest. By helping South Vietnam build a capability to withstand aggression, we have laid the foundation for a just peace and a durable peace in Southeast Asia.

From one sector of the globe to another, a sure and strong America, in partnership with other nations, has once again resumed her historic mission—the building of lasting peace.

The Nixon Doctrine

When President Nixon came into office, America's foremost problem was the bloody, costly, divisive involvement in Vietnam. But there was an even more profound task—to redefine the international role of the United States in light of new realities around the globe and new attitudes at home. Precisely and clearly, the President stated a new concept of a positive American role. This—the Nixon Doctrine—is monumentally important to every American and to all other people in the world.

The theme of this Doctrine is that America will remain fully involved in world affairs, and yet do this in ways that will elicit greater effort by other nations and the sustaining support of our people.

For decades, our nation's leaders regarded virtually every problem of local defense or economic development anyplace in the world as an exclusive American responsibility. The Nixon Doctrine recognizes that continuing defense and development are impossible unless the concerned nations shoulder the principal burden.

Yet, strong economic and military assistance programs remain essential. Without these, we are denied a middle course—the course between abruptly leaving allies to struggle alone against economic stagnation or aggression, or intervening massively ourselves. We cannot move from the overinvolvement of the Sixties to the selective involvement of the Seventies if we do not assist our friends to make the transition with us.

In the Nixon Doctrine, therefore, we define our interests and commitments realistically and clearly; we offer, not an abdication of leadership, but more rational and responsible leadership.

We pledge that, under Republican leadership, the United States will remain a leader in international affairs. We will continue to shape our involvement abroad to national objectives and realities in order to sustain a strong, effective American role in the world.

Over time we hope this role will eventually lead the peace-loving nations to undertake an exhaustive, coordinated analysis of the root causes of war and the most promising paths of peace, so that those causes may in time be removed and the prospects for enduring peace strengthened year by year.

Peace in the 1970's

We stand with our President for his strategy for Peace—a strategy of national strength, a new sense of international partnership, a willingness to negotiate international differences.

We will strengthen our relationships with our allies, recognizing them as full-fledged partners in securing the peace and promoting the common well-being.

With our adversaries, we will continue to negotiate in order to improve our security, reduce tension, and extend the realm of cooperation. Especially important is continued negotiation to maintain the momentum established by the Strategic Arms Limitation agreements to limit offensive and defensive nuclear weapons systems and further to reduce the danger of nuclear conflict. In addition, we will encourage increased trade for the benefit of our consumers, businessmen, workers, and farmers.

Along with NATO allies, we will seek agreement with the Warsaw Pact nations on a mutual and balanced reduction of military forces in Europe.

We will press for expansion of contacts with the people of Eastern Europe and the People's Republic of China, so long isolated from most of the world.

We will continue to seek a settlement of the Vietnam war which will permit the people of Southeast Asia to live in peace under political arrangements of their own choosing. We take specific note of the remaining major obstacle to settlement—Hanoi's demand that the United States overthrow the Saigon government and impose a Communist-dominated government on the South Vietnamese. We stand unequivocally at the side of the President in his effort to negotiate honorable terms, and in his refusal to accept terms which would dishonor this country.

We commend his refusal to perform this act of betrayal—and we most emphatically say the President of the United States should not go begging to Hanoi. We believe that the President's proposal to withdraw remaining American forces from Vietnam four months after an internationally supervised ceasefire has gone into effect throughout Indochina and all prisoners have been returned is as generous an offer as can be made by anyone—by anyone, that is, who is not bemused with surrender—by anyone who seeks, not a fleeting peace at whatever cost, but a real peace that will be both just and lasting.

We will keep faith with American prisoners of war held by the enemy, and we will keep faith, too, with their families here at home who have demonstrated remarkable courage and fortitude over long periods of uncertainty. We will never agree to leave the fate of our men unclear, dependent upon a cruel enemy's whim. On the contrary—we insist that, before all American forces are withdrawn from Vietnam, American prisoners must be returned and a full accounting made of the missing in action and of those who have died in enemy hands.

We pledge that upon repatriation our returned prisoners will be received in a manner befitting their valor and sacrifice.

We applaud the Administration's program to assure each returned prisoner the finest medical care, personal counseling, social services and career orientation. This around-the-clock personal service will ease their reintegration into American life.

North Vietnam's violation of the Geneva Convention in its treatment of our prisoners of war has called forth condemnation from leaders around the world—but not by our political opposition at home. We denounce the enemy's flagrant breach of international law and common decency. We will continue to demand full implementation of the rights of the prisoners.

If North Vietnam continues obdurately to reject peace by negotiation, we shall nevertheless achieve peace for our country through the successful program of Vietnamization, phasing out our involvement as our ally strengthens his defense against aggression.

In the Middle East, we initiated arrangements leading to a cease-fire which has prevailed for two years. We pledge every effort to transform the cease-fire into lasting peace.

Since World War II, our country has played the major role in the international effort to assist the developing countries of the world. Reform of our foreign assistance program, to induce a greater international sharing of the aid effort, is long overdue. The reforms proposed by the President have been approved only in part. We call for further reforms to make our aid more effective and protect the taxpayer's interests.

We stand for an equitable, non-discriminatory immigration policy, reaffirming our support of the principles of the 1965 Immigration Act—non-discrimination against national origins, reunification of families, and the selective admission of the specially talented. The immigration process must be just and orderly, and we will increase our efforts to halt the illegal entry of aliens into the United States.

We also pledge to strengthen the agencies of international cooperation. We will help multilateral organizations focus on international issues affecting the quality of life—for example the peaceful uses of nuclear energy and the protection of man's cultural heritage and freedom of communication, as well as drug abuse, pollution, overpopulation, exploitation of the oceans and seabeds, aircraft hijacking and international crime. We will seek to improve the performance of the United Nations, including more objective leadership. We support a more equitable sharing of the costs of international organizations and have serious concerns over the delinquency of many UN members in meeting their financial obligations.

Our country, which from its beginnings has proclaimed that all men are endowed with certain rights, cannot be indifferent to the denial of human rights anywhere in the world. We deplore oppression and persecution, the inevitable hallmarks of despotic systems of rule. We will continue to strive to bring them to an end, both to reestablish the right of self-determination and to encourage where and when possible the political freedom of subjugated peoples everywhere in the world.

We firmly support the right of all persons to emigrate from any country, and we have consistently upheld that doctrine. We are fully aware of and share the concern of many citizens for the plight of Soviet Jews with regard to their freedoms and emigration. This view, together with our commitment to the principles of the Universal Declaration of Human Rights of the United Nations, was made known to Soviet leaders during the President's discussions in Moscow.

The Middle East

We support the right of Israel and its courageous people to survive and prosper in peace. We have sought a stable peace for the Middle East and helped to obtain a cease-fire which contained the tragic conflict. We will help in any way possible to bring Israel and the Arab states to the conference table, where they may negotiate a lasting peace. We will continue to act to prevent the development of a military imbalance which would imperil peace in the region and elsewhere by providing Israel with support essential for her security, including aircraft, training and modern and sophisticated military equipment, and also by helping friendly Arab governments and peoples, including support for their efforts to diminish their dependence on outside powers. We support programs of economic assistance to Israel pursued by President Nixon that have helped her achieve a nine per cent annual economic growth rate. This and the special refugee assistance ordered by the President have also helped to provide resettlement for the thousands of immigrants seeking refuge in Israel.

We will maintain our technical forces in Europe and the Mediterranean area at adequate strength and high levels of efficiency. The irresponsible proposals of our political opposition to slash the defense forces of the United States, specifically, by cutting the strength of our fleet, by reducing our aircraft carriers from 16 to six and by unilateral withdrawals from Europe, would increase the threat of war in the Middle East and gravely menace Israel. We flatly reject these dangerous proposals.

With a settlement fair to all nations of the Middle East, there would be an opportunity for their peoples to look ahead to shared opportunities rather than backward to rancorous animosities. In a new environment of cooperation, Israel will be able to contribute much to economic renaissance in the Mid-East crossroads of the world.

The Atlantic Community

We place high priority on the strengthening of the North Atlantic Alliance. One of the President's first initiatives was to visit Western European capitals to reinvigorate the NATO alliance and indicate its importance in U.S. foreign policy.

Right now, with plaintive cries of "come home America" echoing a new isolationism, the Republican Party states its firm belief that no nation can be an island or a fortress unto itself. Now, more than ever, there is need for interdependence among proven friends and old allies.

The North Atlantic Alliance remains the strongest most successful peacetime association ever formed among a group of free nations. The continued strengthening of the Alliance will remain an important element in the foreign policies of the second Nixon Administration.

Japan

During the 1960's a number of economic and political issues developed in our country's relations with Japan, our major ally in Asia. To resolve these, President Nixon terminated our responsibility for the administration of Okinawa and initiated action to reduce our trade deficit with Japan. We are consulting closely to harmonize our two countries' separate efforts to normalize relations with Peking. In these ways we have shifted our vital alliance with Japan to a more sustainable basis for the long term, recognizing that the maintenance of United States–Japanese friendship advances the interests of both countries.

The Soviet Union

Over many years our relations with the Soviet Union have oscillated between superficial improvements and new crises. False hopes have been repeatedly followed by disillusioned confrontation. In the closing months of 1968, our relations with the Soviet Union deteriorated steadily, forcing the cancellation of a scheduled Presidential visit to Moscow and immobilizing projected negotiations on strategic arms limitation.

President Nixon immediately began the difficult task of building a new relationship—one based on a realistic acceptance of the profound differences in the values and systems of our two nations. He moved decisively on key issues—such as the Berlin problem and strategic arms limitation—so that progress in one area would add momentum to progress in other areas. The success of these efforts was demonstrated at the summit in Moscow. Agreements were reached on new areas of cooperation—public health, environmental control, space exploration and trade. The first historic agreements limiting strategic arms were signed last May 26 in Moscow, and the Soviet Union subscribed to a broad declaration of principles governing our relations.

We pledge to build upon these promising beginnings in reorienting relations between the world's strongest nuclear powers to establish a truly lasting peace.

China

In the 1960's it seemed beyond possibility that the United States could dispel the ingrained hostility and confrontation with the China mainland. President Nixon's visit to the People's Republic of China was, therefore, an historic milestone in his effort to transform our era from one of confrontation to one of negotiation. While profound differences remain between the United States and China, at least a generation of hostility has been replaced by frank discussions. In February 1972 rules of international conduct were agreed upon which should make the Pacific region a more peaceful area now and in the future. Both the People's Republic and the United States affirmed the usefulness of promoting trade and cultural exchanges as ways of improving understanding between our two peoples.

All this is being done without affecting our mutual defense treaty or our continued diplomatic relations with our valued friend and ally on Taiwan, the Republic of China.

Latin America

Our common long-range interests, as well as history and geography, give the relations among nations of the Western Hemisphere a special importance. We will foster a more mature partnership among the nations of this hemisphere, with a wider sharing of ideas and responsibility, a broader understanding of diversities, and firm commitment to the common pursuit of economic progress and social justice.

We believe the continuing campaign by Cuba to foment violence and support subversion in other countries makes it ineligible for readmission to the community of American states. We look forward to the day when changes in Cuba's policies will justify its reentry into the American community—and to the day when the Cuban people achieve again their freedom and their true independence.

Africa

Our ties with Africa are rooted in the heritage of many Americans and in our historic commitment to self-determination. We respect the hard-earned sovereignty of Africa's new states and will continue to do our utmost to make a meaningful contribution to their development. We have no illusions that the United States can singlehandedly solve the seemingly intractable problems of apartheid and minority rule, but we can and will encourage non-violent, evolutionary change by supporting international efforts peacefully to resolve the problems of southern Africa and by maintaining our contacts with all races on the Continent.

DEFENSE

We believe in keeping America strong.

In times past, both major parties shared that belief.

Today this view is under attack by militants newly in control of the Democratic Party. To the alarm of free nations everywhere, the New Democratic Left now would undercut our defenses and have America retreat into virtual isolation, leaving us weak in a world still not free of aggression and threats of aggression. We categorically reject this slash-now, beg-later, approach to defense policy.

Only a strong America can safely negotiate with adversaries. Only a strong America can fashion partnerships for peace.

President Nixon has given the American people their best opportunity in this century to achieve lasting peace. The foundations are well laid. By adhering to a defense policy based on strength at home, partnership abroad and a willingness to negotiate everywhere, we hold that lasting peace is now achievable.

We will surely fail if we go crawling to the conference table. Military weakness is not the path to peace; it is invitation to war.

A Modern, Well-Equipped Force

We believe that the first prerequisite of national security is a modern, well-equipped armed force.

From 1965 to 1969 the Vietnam war so absorbed the resources of the Defense Department that maintenance, modernization, and research and development fell into neglect. In the late 1960's the Soviet Union outspent the United States by billions of dollars for force modernization, facing the United States with the dangerous prospect that its forces would soon be qualitatively inferior. Our Reserve Forces and the National Guard had become a dumping ground for cast-off arms and equipment. The military posture of our country became seriously undermined.

To assure our strength and counter the mounting Soviet threat, President Nixon directed:

The most significant ship construction and modernization program since World War II;

The development of new types of tactical aircraft such as the F-155, a lightweight fighter, and a fighter plane for close support of ground troops;

Improvements in our strategic bomber force and development of the new B-1 strategic bomber;

Development of a new Trident submarine and undersea missile system;

Greatly increasing the capability of existing strategic missiles through multiple warheads;

Strengthening of strategic defenses, including initial deployment of an anti-ballistic missile system;

The largest research and development budget in history to insure continued technological superiority;

Equipping of the National Guard and Reserves with the most modern and sophisticated weapons;

Improved command and control communications systems.

We draw a sharp distinction between prudent reductions in defense spending and the meat-ax slashes with which some Americans are now beguiled by the political opposition. Specifically, we oppose plans to stop the Minuteman III and Poseidon programs, reduce the strategic bomber force by some 60 per cent, cancel the B-I bomber, reduce aircraft carriers from 16 to 6, reduce tactical air wings by a third, and unilaterally reduce U.S. forces in Europe by half.

These slashes are worse than misguided; they are dangerous.

They would torpedo negotiations on arms and troop reductions, create a crisis of confidence with our allies, damage our own industrial and technological capacity, destabilize Europe and the Middle East, and directly endanger the nation's security.

A New Partnership

The Nixon Doctrine has led to a new military strategy of realistic deterrence. Its essence is the sharing of the responsibilities and the burdens of defense. The strategy is based on the efficient utilization of the total force available—our own and our allies', and our civilian reserve elements as well as our regular forces.

For years our country shouldered the responsibility for the defense of other nations. There were fears that we were attempting to be the policeman of the world. Our country found it necessary to maintain a military force of 3.5 million persons, more than a million overseas at 2,270 installations.

A new partnership is emerging between the United States and other nations of the free world. Other countries are assuming a much greater responsibility for the common defense. Twice in the last two years our European allies have agreed to substantial increases in their support for NATO forces. In Asia we have been heartened by the efforts of the Koreans, Vietnamese, Thais, Nationalist Chinese, Australians, New Zealanders and others who have sought improvements in their own forces.

We have been able to reduce our military forces by more than one million men and women. We have cut by half the number deployed overseas, reduced overseas installations by more than 10 per cent, and sharply reduced the economic burden of defense spending from the Vietnam high. All this has been done by virtue of our new security posture, without impairing our own or our allies' security.

We pledge to press on toward a lasting peace. To that end we declare ourselves unalterably opposed to a unilateral slash of our military power, and we reject a whimpering "come back America" retreat into isolationism.

An All-Volunteer Armed Force

We wholeheartedly support an all-volunteer armed force and are proud of our historic initiatives of bring it to pass.

Four years ago, the President pledged to work toward an early end of the draft. That promise has been kept. Today we approach a zero draft that will enlarge the personal freedom of millions of young Americans.

Prior to 1969, annual draft calls exceeded 300,000. The Selective Service System was inequitable in operation, and its rules caused prolonged uncertainty for young men awaiting call. Since 1969, the Selective Service System has been thoroughly reorganized, and local draft boards are more representative than ever before. Today draftees are called by random selection of the youngest first, so that the maximum length of vulnerability is no longer seven years but one year only. Youth advisory committees are in operation all across the country.

Of critical importance, we are nearing the elimination of draft calls altogether. In every year since 1968, draft calls have been reduced. Monthly draft calls are now down to a few thousand, and no draftees are sent involuntarily to Vietnam. We expect to achieve our goal by July 1973. Then, for the first time in a quarter-century, we hope and expect that young Americans of all ages will be free from conscription.

Our political opponents have talked for years of their concern for young people. It is our Republican Administration that has taken the strong, effective action required to end the draft, with its many hardships and uncertainties for the youth of America.

Improvements in Service Life

We believe that the men and women in the uniformed services deserve the gratitude and respect of all Americans and are entitled to better treatment than they received in the past.

For years most servicemen have been underpaid, harassed with restrictions, and afforded few opportunities for self-development. Construction of military housing was allowed to fall badly behind.

Since 1968 improvements in service life have been many and major:

The largest pay raises in military history have been enacted. While increases have been in all grades, the largest have gone to new recruits whose base pay will have risen more than 300 per cent by the end of this year.

Construction of new housing for military personnel and their families has increased sixfold since January 1969.

Without sacrificing discipline, needlessly harsh, irksome and demeaning practices of the past have been abandoned.

An effective program against dangerous drugs has been initiated.

Educational and training opportunities have been expanded.

Major strides have been made toward wiping out the last vestiges of racial discrimination.

We regard these tasks as never completed, but we are well on the way and pledge ourselves to press forward assuring all men and women in the armed forces rewarding careers.

Better Defense Management

In the 1960's, the Department of Defense became administratively top-heavy and inefficient. The acquisition of new weapons systems was handled with inadequate attention to cost or performance, and there was little recognition of the human dimensions of the Department. Morale was low.

Our improvements have been many and substantial. Healthy decentralization has taken place. The methods of acquiring new weapons systems have been reformed by such procedures as "fly before you buy," the use of prototypes and the elimination of frills. Service personnel and civilian employees are now treated as the most important asset of the Department.

We have sharply reduced defense spending. In 1968, 45 per cent of the Federal budget was spent for defense and 32 per cent for human resources. In the 1973 budget the proportions were reversed—45 per cent for human resources, 32 per cent for defense. The 1973 defense budget imposes the smallest economic burden on the country of any defense budget in more than 20 years, consuming only 6.4 per cent of the estimated Gross National Product.

Arms Limitation

We believe in limiting arms—not unilaterally, but by mutual agreement and with adequate safeguards.

When the Nixon Administration began, the Soviet Union was rapidly building its strategic armaments, and any effort to negotiate limitations on such weapons seemed hopeless. The Soviet buildup threatened the efficacy of our strategic deterrent.

The Nixon years have achieved a great breakthrough in the long-term effort to curb major armaments by international agreement and given new momentum to arms limitations generally. Of greatest importance were agreements with the Soviet leaders to limit offensive and defensive nuclear weapons. The SALT accords established mutually agreed restraints between the United States and the Soviet Union and reduced tensions throughout the world.

With approval of the SALT agreements by the Congress, negotiations will be resumed to place further restrictions on nuclear weapons, and talks will begin on mutual, balanced force reductions in Europe.

We believe it is imperative that these negotiations go forward under President Nixon's continuing leadership. We pledge him our full support.

For the Future

We will continue the sound military policies laid down by the President—policies which guard our interests but do not dissipate our resources in vain efforts to police the world. As stated by the President:

> We will maintain a nuclear deterrent adequate to meet any threat to the security of the United States or of our allies.
> We will help other nations develop the capability of defending themselves.
> We will faithfully honor all of our treaty commitments.
> We will act to defend our interests whenever and wherever they are threatened.
> But where our vital interests or treaty commitments are not involved our role will be limited.

We are proud of the men and women who wear our country's uniform, especially of those who have borne the burden of fighting a difficult and unpopular war. Here and now we reject all proposals to grant amnesty to those who have broken the law by evading military service. We reject the claim that those who fled are more deserving, or obeyed a higher morality, than those next in line who served in their places.

In carrying out our defense policies, we pledge to maintain at all times the level of military strength required to deter conflict, to honor our commitments to our allies, and to protect our people and vital interests against all foreign threats. We will not let America become a second-class power, dependent for survival on the good will of adversaries.

We will continue to pursue arms control agreements—but we recognize that this can be successful only if we maintain sufficient strength and will fail if we allow ourselves to slip into inferiority.

A NEW PROSPERITY

Jobs, Inflation and the Economy

The goal of our Party is prosperity, widely shared, sustainable in peace.

We stand for full employment—jobs for everyone willing and able to work in an economy freed of inflation, its vigor not dependent upon war or massive military spending.

Under the President's leadership our country is once again moving toward these peacetime goals. We have checked the inflation which had started to skyrocket when our Administration took office, making the difficult transition from inflation toward price stability and from war toward peace. We have brought about a rapid rise in both employment and in real income, and laid the basis for a continuing decline in the rate of unemployment.

All Americans painfully recall the grave economic troubles we faced in January 1969. The Federal budget in fiscal 1968 had a deficit of more than $25 billion even though the economy was operating at capacity. Predictably, consumer prices soared by an annual rate of 6.6 per cent in the first quarter of 1969. "Jawboning" of labor and business had utterly failed. The inevitable tax increase had come too late. The kaleidoscope of "Great Society" programs added to the inflationary fires. Our international competitive position slumped from a trade surplus of $7 billion in 1964 to $800 million in 1968. Foreign confidence in the value of the dollar plummeted.

Strategies and Achievements

Our Administration took these problems head on, accepting the unpopular tasks of holding down the budget, extending the temporary tax surcharge, and checking inflation. We welcomed the challenge of reorienting the economy from war to peace, as the more than two and one-half million Americans serving the military or working in defense-related industries had to be assimilated into the peacetime work force.

At the same time, we kept the inflation fight and defense employment cuts from triggering a recession.

The struggle to restore the health of our nation's economy required a variety of measures. Most important, the Administration developed and applied sound economic and monetary policies which provided the fundamental thrust against inflation.

To supplement these basic policies, Inflation Alerts were published; a new National Commission on Productivity enlisted labor, business and public leaders against inflation and in raising real incomes through increased output per worker; proposed price increases in lumber, petroleum, steel and other commodities were modified. A new Construction Industry Stabilization Committee, with the cooperation of unions and management, braked the dangerously sky-rocketing costs in the construction industry.

Positive results from these efforts were swift and substantial. The rate of inflation, more than 6 per cent in early 1969, declined to less than 4 per cent in early 1971.

Even so, the economic damage inflicted by past excesses had cut so deeply as to make a timely recovery impossible, forcing the temporary use of wage and price controls.

These controls were extraordinary measures, not needed in a healthy free economy, but needed temporarily to recapture lost stability.

Our mix of policies has worked. The nation's economic growth is once again strong and steady.

The rate of increase of consumer prices is now down to 2.7 per cent.

On the employment front, expenditures for manpower programs were increased from $2.3 billion to a planned $5.1 billion; new enrollees receiving training or employment under these programs were increased by more than half a million; computerized job banks were established in all cities; more than a million young people received jobs this summer through Federal programs, 50 per cent more than last year; engineers, scientists and technicians displaced by defense reductions were given assistance under the nation-wide Technology Mobilization and Reemployment program; 13 additional weeks of unemployment compensation were authorized; and a Special Revenue Sharing Program for Manpower was proposed to train more people for more jobs—a program still shelved by the opposition Congress.

Civilian employment increased at an annual rate of about 2.4 million from August 1971 to July 1972. Almost four and one-half million new civilian jobs have been added since President Nixon took office, and total employment is at its highest level in history.

The total productive output of this country increased at an annual rate of 9.4 per cent in the second quarter of 1972, the highest in many years.

Workers' real weekly take-home pay—the real value left after taxes and inflation—is increasing at an annual rate of 4.5 per cent, compared to less than one per cent from 1960 to 1970. For the first time in six years real spendable income is going up, while the rate of inflation has been cut in half.

Time lost from strikes is at the lowest level in many years.

The rate of unemployment has been reduced from 6.1 per cent to 5.5 per cent, lower than the average from 1961 through 1964 before the Vietnam buildup began, and is being steadily driven down.

In negotiation with other countries we have revalued the dollar relative to other currencies, helping to increase sales at home and abroad and increasing the number of jobs. We have initiated a reform of the international monetary and trading system and made clear our determination that this reform must lead to a strong United States position in the balance of trade and payments.

The Road Ahead

We will continue to pursue sound economic policies that will eliminate inflation, further cut unemployment, raise real incomes, and strengthen our international economic position.

We will fight for responsible Federal budgets to help assure steady expansion of the economy without inflation.

We will support the independent Federal Reserve Board in a policy of non-inflationary monetary expansion.

We have already removed some temporary controls on wages and prices and will remove them all once the economic distortions spawned in the late 1960's are repaired. We are determined to return to an unfettered economy at the earliest possible moment.

We reaffirm our support for the basic principles of capitalism which underlie the private enterprise system of the United States. At a time when a small but dominant faction of the opposition Party is pressing for radical economic schemes which so often have failed around the world, we hold that nothing has done more to help the American people achieve their unmatched standard of living than the free-enterprise system.

It is our conviction that government of itself cannot produce the benefits to individuals that flow from our unique combination of labor, management and capital.

We will continue to promote steady expansion of the whole economy as the best route to a long-term solution of unemployment.

We will devote every effort to raising productivity, primarily to raise living standards but also to hold down costs and prices and to increase the ability of American producers and workers to compete in world markets.

In economic policy decisions, including tax revisions, we will emphasize incentives to work, innovate and invest; and research and development will have our full support.

We are determined to improve Federal manpower programs to reduce unemployment and increase productivity by providing better information on job openings and more relevant job training. Additionally, we reaffirm our commitment to removing barriers to a full life for the mentally and physically handicapped, especially the barriers to rewarding employment. We commit ourselves to the full educational opportunities and the humane care, treatment and rehabilitation services necessary for the handicapped to become fully integrated into the social and economic mainstream.

We will press on for greater competition in our economy. The energetic antitrust program of the past four years demonstrates our commitment to free competition as our basic policy. The Antitrust Division has moved decisively to invalidate those conglomerate mergers which stifle competition and discourage economic concentration. The 87 antitrust cases filed in fiscal year 1972 broke the previous one-year record of more than a decade ago, during another Republican Administration.

We will pursue the start we have made for reform of the international monetary and trading system, insisting on fair and equal treatment.

Since the 1930's it has been illegal for United States citizens to own gold. We believe it is time to reconsider that policy. The right of American citizens to buy, hold, or sell gold should be reestablished as soon as this is feasible. Review of the present policy should, of course, take account of our basic objective of achieving a strengthened world monetary system.

Taxes and Government Spending

We pledge to spread the tax burden equitably, to spend the Federal revenues prudently, to guard against waste in spending, to eliminate unnecessary programs, and to make sure that each dollar spent for essential government services buys a dollar's worth of value.

Federal deficit spending beyond the balance of the full employment budget is one sure way to refuel inflation, and the prime source of such spending is the United States Congress. Because of its present procedures and particularly because of its present political leadership, Congress is not handling Federal fiscal policies in a responsible manner. The Congress now permits its legislative committees—instead of its fiscal committees—to decide, independently of each other, how much should be devoted to individual programs. Total Federal spending is thus haphazard and uncontrolled. We pledge vigorous efforts to reform the Congressional budgeting process.

As an immediate first step, we believe the Nation needs a rigid spending ceiling on Federal outlays each fiscal year—a ceiling controlling both the executive branch and the Congress—as President Nixon strongly recommended when he submitted his fiscal 1973 budget. Should the total of all appropriations exceed the ceiling, some or all of them would be reduced by executive action to bring the total within the ceiling.

Our tax system needs continual, timely reform. Early in this Administration we achieved the first comprehensive tax reform since 1954. The record shows that as a result of the Tax Reform Act of 1969 and the Revenue Act of 1971:

9.5 million low-income Americans are removed from the Federal income tax rolls.

Persons in the lowest income tax bracket will pay 82 per cent less this year than they would have paid, had the 1969 and 1971 tax reforms not been enacted; those in the $10,000 to $15,000 income range will pay 13 per cent less, and those with incomes above $100,000 will pay about 7 per cent more.

This year the tax reduction for a family of four earning $7,500 a year will be $270.

In this fiscal year individual taxpayers will pay $22 billion less in Federal income taxes than they would have paid if the old tax rates and structures were still in force.

The tax disadvantage of single taxpayers is sharply reduced and we urge further changes to assure full equality.

Working parents can now deduct more of their costs for the care of their children during working hours.

The seven per cent automobile excise tax is repealed, saving the new-car buyer an average of $200 and creating more jobs in that part of the economy.

This is sound tax reform, the kind that more equitably spreads the tax burden and avoids incentive-destroying tax levels which would cripple the economy and put people out of work.

We reject the deceitful tax "reform" cynically represented as one that would soak the rich, but in fact one that would sharply raise the taxes of millions of families in middle-income brackets as well. We reject as well the lavish spending promised by the opposition Party which would more than double the present budget of the United States Government. This, too, would cause runaway inflation or force heavy increases in personal taxes.

Taxes and government spending are inseparable. Only if the taxpayers' money is prudently managed can taxes be kept at reasonable levels.

When our Administration took office, Federal spending had been mounting at an average annual rate of 17 per cent—a rate we have cut almost in half. We urge the Congress to serve all Americans by cooperating with the President in his efforts to curb increases in Federal spending—increases which will ordain more taxes or more inflation.

Since 1969 we have eliminated over $5 billion of spending on unneeded domestic and defense programs. This large saving would have been larger still, had Congress passed the Federal Economy Act of 1970 which would have discontinued other programs. We pledge to continue our efforts to purge the Government of these wasteful activities.

Tax reform must continue. During the next session of Congress we pledge:

To pursue such policies as Revenue Sharing that will allow property tax relief;

Further tax reform to ensure that the tax burden is fairly shared;

A simplified tax system to make it easier for all of us to pay no more and no less than we rightly owe;

Prudent fiscal management, including the elimination of unnecessary or obsolete programs, to keep the tax burden to a minimum.

International Economic Policy

In tandem with our foreign policy innovations, we have transformed our international economic policy into a dynamic instrument to advance the interests of farmers, workers, businessmen and consumers. These efforts are designed to make the products of American workers and farmers more competitive in the world. Within the last year we achieved the Smithsonian Agreements which revalued our currency, making our exports more competitive with those of our major trading partners, and we pledge continuing negotiations further to reform the international monetary system. We also established negotiations to expand foreign market access for products produced by United States workers, with further comprehensive negotiations committed for 1973.

As part of our effort to begin a new era of negotiations, we are expanding trade opportunities and the jobs related to them for American workers and businessmen. The President's Summit negotiations, for example, yielded an agreement for the Soviet purchase, over a three-year period, of a minimum of $750 million in United States grains—the largest long-term commercial trade purchase agreement ever made between two nations. This amounts to a 17 per cent increase in grain exports by United States farmers. A U.S.–Soviet Commercial Commission has been established, and negotiations are now under way as both countries seek a general expansion of trade.

As we create a more open world market for American exports, we are not unmindful of dangers to American workers and industries from severe and rapid dislocation by changing patterns of trade. We have several agreements to protect these workers and industries—for example, for steel, beef, textiles and shoes. These actions, highly important to key American industries, were taken in ways that avoided retaliation by our trading partners and the resultant loss of American jobs.

As part of this adjustment process, we pledge improvement of the assistance offered by government to facilitate readjustment on the part of workers, businessmen and affected communities.

In making the world trading system a fairer one, we have vigorously enforced anti-dumping and countervailing duty laws to make them meaningful deterrents to foreign producers who would compete unfairly.

The growth of multinational corporations poses both new problems and new opportunities in trade and investment areas. We pledge to ensure that international investment problems are dealt with fairly and effectively—including consideration of effects on jobs, expropriation and treatment of investors, as well as equitable principles of taxation.

At the same time that we seek a better environment for American exports, we must improve our productivity and competitiveness. We must have a strong domestic economy with increased investment in new plants and equipment and an advancing technology.

We pledge increased efforts to promote export opportunities, including coordination of tax policy and improved export financing techniques, designed to make America more competitive in exporting. Of critical importance will be new legislative proposals to equip American negotiators with the tools for constructing an open and fair world trading system.

We deplore the practice of locating plants in foreign countries solely to take advantage of low wage rates in order to produce goods primarily for sale in the United States. We will take action to discourage such unfair and disruptive practices that result in the loss of American jobs.

Small Business

Small business, so vital to our economic system, is free enterprise in its purest sense. It holds forth opportunity to the individual, regardless of race or color, to fulfill the American dream. The seedbed of innovation and invention, it is the starting point of many of the country's large businesses, and today its role in our increasingly technological economy is crucial. We pledge to sustain and expand that role.

We have translated this philosophy into many beneficial actions. Primarily through the Small Business Administration, we have delivered financial assistance to small business at a dramatically increasing rate. Today small business is receiving double the SBA funds it was receiving when our Administration took office. During the 1970–72 fiscal years the Agency loaned small business $3.3 billion—40 per cent of the total amount loaned in the entire 19-year history of the Small Business Administration.

Financial help to minorities has been more than tripled, and now more than 17 per cent of the SBA dollar goes to minority businesses. Procurement of Federal contracts for small business has surged above $12 billion.

In his first year in office, the President established a Task Force to discover ways in which the prospects of the small businessman could be improved.

The findings, reported to Congress, were followed by legislative proposals to give small business tax and interest advantages, to provide incentives for more participation of small business, to make venture capital and long-term credit easier to obtain, and to open the doors for disadvantaged minorities to go into business for themselves. Some of these measures have been signed into law. Others are still in the hands of the indifferent opposition in control of Congress.

The results of our efforts have been significant. Today small business is once again gaining ground. Incorporations are at a record level and the number of business failures is dropping. The current new growth of small businesses is about 100,000 units a year. For tomorrow, the challenges are many. We will:

Continue to fill the capital gap in the small business community by increasing SBA financing to upwards of $3 billion next year.

Provide more incentives for the private sector to join the SBA in direct action programs, such as lease guarantees, revolving lines of credit, and other sophisticated financial techniques, such as factoring and mortgage financing.

Increase SBA's Community Development program so that growth-minded communities can help themselves by building industrial parks and shopping centers.

Continue the rejuvenation of the Small Business Investment Company (SBIC) program, leading to greater availability of venture capital for new business enterprises.

See that a fair share of all Federal dollars spent on goods and services goes to small business.

Create established secondary financial markets for SBA loans, affording ready liquidity for financial institutions and opening up more financial resources to small firms.

Through tax incentives, encourage the start-up of more new businesses, and work for a tax system that more fairly applies to small business.

Establish special programs that will permit small firms to comply with consumer, environmental, and other new government regulations without undue financial burden.

IMPROVING THE QUALITY OF LIFE

Health Care

Our goal is to enable every American to secure quality health care at reasonable cost. We pledge a balanced approach—one that takes into account the problems of providing sufficient medical personnel and facilities.

Last year President Nixon proposed one of the most all-inclusive health programs in our history. But the opposition Congress has dragged its feet and most of this program has yet to be enacted into law.

To increase the supply of medical services, we will continue to support programs to help our schools graduate more physicians, dentists, nurses, and allied health personnel, with special emphasis on family practitioners and others who deliver primary medical care.

We will also encourage the use of such allied personnel as doctors' assistants, foster new area health education centers, channel more services into geographic areas which now are medically deprived, and improve the availability of emergency medical care.

We note with pride that the President has already signed the most comprehensive health manpower legislation ever enacted.

To improve efficiency in providing health and medical care, we have developed and will continue to encourage a pluralistic approach to the delivery of quality health care, including innovative experiments such as health maintenance organizations. We also support efforts to develop ambulatory medical care services to reduce hospitalization and keep costs down.

To reduce the cost of health care, we stress our efforts to curb inflation in the economy; we will also expand the supply of medical services and encourage greater cost consciousness in hospitalization and medical care. In doing this we realize the importance of the doctor-patient relationship and the necessity of insuring that individuals have freedom of choice of health providers.

To assure access to basic medical care for all our people, we support a program financed by employers, employees and the Federal Government to provide comprehensive health insurance coverage, including insurance against the cost of long-term and catastrophic illnesses and accidents and renal failure which necessitates dialysis, at a cost which all Americans can afford. The National Health Insurance Partnership plan and the Family Health Insurance Plan proposed by the President meet these specifications. They would build on existing private health insurance systems, not destroy them.

We oppose nationalized compulsory health insurance. This approach would at least triple in taxes the amount the average citizen now pays for health and would deny families the right to choose the kind of care they prefer. Ultimately it would lower the overall quality of health care for all Americans.

We believe that the most effective way of improving health in the long run is by emphasis on preventive measures.

The serious physical fitness problem in our country requires urgent attention. The President recently reorganized the Council on Physical Fitness and Sports to increase the leadership of representatives of medicine, physical education, sports associations and school administrations. The Republican Party urges intensification of these efforts, particularly in the Nation's school systems, to encourage widespread participation in effective physical fitness programs.

We have initiated this Nation's first all-out assault against cancer. Led by the new National Cancer Institute, the drive to eliminate this cruel killer will involve Federal spending of nearly $430 million in fiscal year 1973, almost twice the funding of just two years ago.

We have also launched a major new attack on sickle cell anemia, a serious blood disorder afflicting many black Americans, and developed a comprehensive program to deal with the menace of lead-based paint poisoning, including the screening of approximately 1,500,000 Americans.

We support expanded medical research to find cures for the major diseases of the heart, blood vessels, lungs and kidneys—diseases which now account for over half the deaths in the United States.

We have significantly advanced efforts to combat mental retardation and established a national goal to cut its incidence in half by the year 2000.

We continue to support the concept of comprehensive community mental health centers. In this fiscal year $135 million—almost three times the 1970 level—will be devoted to the staffing of 422 community mental health centers serving a population of 56 million people. We have intensified research on methods of treating mental problems, increasing our outlays from

$76 million in 1969 to approximately $96 million for 1973. We continue to urge extension of private health insurance to cover mental illness.

We have also improved consumer protection, health education and accident prevention programs. And in Moscow this year, President Nixon reached an agreement with the Soviet Union on health research which may yield substantial benefits in many fields in the years ahead.

Education

We take pride in our leadership these last four years in lifting both quality and equality in American education—from preschool to graduate school—working toward higher standards than ever before.

Our two most pressing needs in the 1970's are the provision of quality education for all children, an equitable financing of steadily rising costs. We pledge our best efforts to deal effectively with both.

Months ago President Nixon sent Congress a two-part comprehensive proposal on school busing. The first is the Student Transportation Moratorium Act of 1972—legislation to halt immediately all further court-ordered busing and give Congress time to devise permanent new arrangements for assuring desegregated, quality education.

The details of such arrangements are spelled out in a companion bill, the Equal Educational Opportunities Act. This measure would:

Provide $2.5 billion in Federal aid funds to help promote quality education while preserving neighborhood schools;

Accord equal educational opportunities to all children;

Include an educational bill of rights for Spanish-speaking people, American Indians, and others who face special language problems in schools;

Offer, for the first time, a real chance for good schooling for the hundreds of thousands of children who live in urban centers;

Assure that the people's elected representatives in Congress play their proper role in developing specific methods for protecting the rights guaranteed by the 14th amendment, rather than leaving this task to judges appointed for life.

We are committed to guaranteeing equality of educational opportunity and to completing the process of ending de jure school segregation.

At the same time, we are irrevocably opposed to busing for racial balance. Such busing fails its stated objective—improved learning opportunities—while it achieves results no one wants—division within communities and hostility between classes and races. We regard it as unnecessary, counterproductive and wrong.

We favor better education for all children, not more transportation for some children. We favor the neighborhood school concept. We favor the decisive actions the President has proposed to support these ends. If it is necessary to accomplish these purposes, we would favor consideration of an appropriate amendment to the Constitution.

In the field of school finance, we favor a coordinated effort among all levels of government to break the pattern of excessive reliance on local property taxes to pay educational costs.

Our Nation's intellectual resources are remarkable for their strength and public availability. American intellectuals have at least two important historical roles of which we are deeply conscious. One is to inform the public, the other is to assist government by thoughtful criticism and consultation. We affirm our confidence in these functions and especially in the free play of ideas and discourse which they imply.

We cherish the Nation's universities as centers of learning, as conserves of our culture, and as analysts of our society and its institutions. We will continue to strive to assure their economic well-being. The financial aid we have given and will continue to give in the form of funds for scholarships, research, building programs and new teaching methods must never be used as a device for imposing political controls on our schools.

We believe that universities should be centers of excellence—that they should recruit faculty on the basis of ability to teach and admit students on the basis of ability to learn. Yet, excellence can be too narrowly confined—abilities overlooked, and social conformity mistaken for educational preparation.

We pledge continued support of collegiate and university efforts to insure that no group in our society—racial, economic, sexual or regional—is denied access to the opportunities of higher education.

Our efforts to remedy ancient neglect of disadvantaged groups will continue in universities as well as in society at large, but we distinguish between such efforts and quotas. We believe the imposition of arbitrary quotas in the hiring of faculties or the enrollment of students has no place in our universities; we believe quotas strike at the excellence of the university.

We recognize that the public should have access to the most rational and most effective kinds of education. Vocational training should be available to both young and old. We emphasize the importance of continuing education, of trades and technologies, and of all the honorable vocations which provide the society with its basic necessities. Such training must complement our more traditional forms of education; it will relieve the pressures on our universities and help us adapt to the rapid pace of technological change. Perhaps most important, it will help to restore a public sense of importance to these essential jobs and trades.

Moreover, we believe our educational system should not instruct in a vacuum, unmindful that the students ultimately will engage in a career. Our institutions of learning, from earliest years to graduate schools, can perform a vital function by coupling an awareness of the world of work to the delivery of fundamental education. We believe this kind of career education, blended into our school curricula, can help to prevent the aimlessness and frustration now experienced by large numbers of young people who leave the education system unable to cope with today's complex society.

In recognizing the fundamental necessity for quality education of all children, including the exceptional child, we recommend research and assistance in programs directed to the problems of dyslectic and hyperkinetic children who represent an estimated ten per cent of the school population.

By every measure, our record in the field of education is exceptionally strong. The United States Office of Education is operating this year under its highest budget ever—$5.1 billion. Federal aid to elementary and secondary education has increased 60 per cent over the past four years. Federal aid for college students has more than tripled.

We are proud of these accomplishments. We pledge to carry them forward in a manner consistent with our conviction that the Federal Government should assist but never control the educational process. But we also believe that the output of results, not the input of dollars, is the best yardstick of effectiveness in education. When this Administration took office in 1969, it found American schools deficient at many points. Our reform initiatives have included:

An Office of Child Development to coordinate all Federal programs targeted on the first five years of life and to make the Head Start Program work better;

A Right to Read Program, aimed at massive gains in reading ability among Americans of all ages;

A Career Education curriculum which will help to prepare students for the world of work;

A National Institute of Education to be a center for research on the learning process; and

A proposed National Foundation for Higher Education.

We have also proposed grant and loan programs to support a national commitment that no qualified student should be barred from college by lack of money. The Education Amendment of 1972 embodied substantial portions of that proposal and marked the nation's most far-reaching commitment to make higher education available to all.

Our nonpublic schools, both church-oriented and nonsectarian, have been our special concern. The President has emphasized the indispensable role these schools play in our educational system—from the standpoints of the large numbers of pupils they serve, the competition and diversity they help to maintain in American education, and the values they help to teach—and he has stated his determination to help halt the accelerating trend of nonpublic school closures.

We believe that means which are consistent with the Constitution can be devised for channeling public financial aid to support the education of all children in schools of their parents' choice, nonpublic as well as public. One way to provide such aid appears to be through the granting of income tax credits.

For the future, we also pledge Special Revenue Sharing for Education, continued work to develop and implement the Career Education concept, and continued efforts to establish a student financial aid system to bring together higher education within the reach of any qualified person.

Welfare Reform

The nation's welfare system is a mess. It simply must be reformed.

This system, essentially unchanged since the 1930's has turned into a human and fiscal nightmare. It penalizes the poor. It provides discriminatory benefits. It kills any incentives its victims might have to work their way out of the morass.

Among its victims are the taxpayers. Since 1961 the Federal cost of welfare has skyrocketed over 10 times—from slightly over $1 billion then to more than $11 billion now. State and local costs add to this gigantic expenditure. And here are things we are paying for:

The present system drains work incentive from the employed poor, as they see welfare families making as much or more on the dole.

Its discriminatory benefits continue to ensnare the needy, aged, blind and disabled in a web of inefficient rules and economic contradictions.

It continues to break up poor families, since a father's presence makes his family ineligible for benefits in many States. Its dehumanizing

lifestyle thus threatens to envelop yet another "welfare generation."

Its injustices and costs threaten to alienate taxpayer support for welfare programs of any kind.

Perhaps nowhere else is there a greater contrast in policy and philosophy than between the Administration's remedy for the welfare ills and the financial orgy proposed by our political opposition.

President Nixon proposed to change our welfare system "to provide each person with a means of escape from welfare into dignity." His goals were these:

A decent level of payment to genuinely needy welfare recipients regardless of where they live.

Incentives not to loaf, but to work.

Requiring all adults who apply for welfare to register for work and job training and to accept work or training. The only exceptions would be the aged, blind and disabled and mothers of preschool children.

Expanding job training and child care facilities so that recipients can accept employment.

Temporary supplements to the incomes of the working poor to enable them to support their families while continuing to work.

Uniform Federal payment standards for all welfare recipients.

In companion actions, our efforts to improve the nutrition of poor people resulted in basic reforms in the Food Stamp Program. The number of recipients increased from some three million to 13 million, and now 8.4 million needy children participate in the School Lunch Program, almost three times the number that participated in 1968.

Now, nearly 10,000 nutrition aides work in low-income communities. In 1968 there were none.

Since 1969, we have increased the Federal support for family planning threefold. We will continue to support expanded family planning programs and will foster research in this area so that more parents will be better able to plan the number and spacing of their children should they wish to do so. Under no circumstances will we allow any of these programs to become compulsory or infringe upon the religious conviction or personal freedom of any individual.

We all feel compassion for those who through no fault of their own cannot adequately care for themselves. We all want to help these men, women and children achieve a decent standard of living and become self-supporting.

We continue to insist, however, that there are too many people on this country's welfare rolls who should not be there. With effective cooperation from the Congress, we pledge to stop these abuses.

We flatly oppose programs or policies which embrace the principle of a government-guaranteed income. We reject as unconscionable the idea that all citizens have the right to be supported by the government, regardless of their ability or desire to support themselves and their families.

We pledge to continue to push strongly for sound welfare reform until meaningful and helpful change is enacted into law by the Congress.

LAW ENFORCEMENT

We have solid evidence that our unrelenting war on crime is being won. The American people know that once again the thrust of justice in our society will be to protect the law-abiding citizenry against the criminal, rather than absolve the criminal of the consequences of his own desperate acts.

Serious crimes rose only one per cent during the first quarter of this year—down from six per cent last year and 13 per cent the year before. From 1960 to 1968 major crime went up 122 per cent.

The fact is, in the first quarter of 1972, 80 of our 155 largest cities had an actual decline in reported crime.

In our Nation's Capital, our anti-crime programs have been fully implemented. Through such measures as increased police, street lighting, a Narcotics Treatment Administration, court reform and special prosecuting units for major offenders, we have steadily dropped the crime rate since November 1969. By the first quarter of this year, the serious crime rate was down to half its all-time high.

When our Administration took office, a mood of lawlessness was spreading rapidly, undermining the legal and moral foundations of our society. We moved at once to stop violence in America. We have:

Greatly increased Federal aid to State and local law enforcement agencies across the country, with more than $1.5 billion spent on 50,000 crime fighting projects.

Augmented Justice Department funding fourfold and provided more marshals, more judges, more narcotics agents, more Assistant United States Attorneys in the field.

Raised the Law Enforcement Assistance Administration budget tenfold, earmarking $575 million of the $850 million for 1973 to upgrade State and local police and courts through revenue sharing.

Added 600 new Special Agents to the FBI.

Raised Federal spending on juvenile delinquency from $15 million to more than $180 million and proposed legislation to launch a series of model youth services.

Appointed Attorneys General with a keen sense of the rights of both defendants and victims, and determination to enforce the laws.

Appointed judges whose respect for the rights of the accused is balanced by an appreciation of the legitimate needs of law enforcement.

Added to the Supreme Court distinguished lawyers of firm judicial temperament and fidelity to the Constitution.

Even more fundamentally, we have established a renewed climate of respect for law and law enforcement. Now those responsible for enforcing the law know they have the full backing of their Government.

We recognize that programs involving work release, study release and half-way houses have contributed substantially to the rehabilitation of offenders and we support these programs. We further support training programs for the staffs in our correctional institutions and will continue to see that minority group staff members are recruited to work in these institutions.

The Fight Against Organized Crime

To most of us, organized criminal activity seems remote and unreal—yet syndicates supply the narcotics pushed on our youth, corrupt local officials terrify legitimate businesses and fence goods stolen from our homes. This Administration strongly supported the Organized Crime Control Act of 1970, and under our Strike Force concept we have combined Federal enforcement agencies to wage a concerted assault on organized crime. We have expanded the number of these strike forces and set a high priority for a new campaign against the syndicates.

Last year we obtained indictments against more than 2,600 members or associates of organized crime syndicates—more than triple the number indicted in 1968.

At last we have the lawless elements in our society on the run.

The Republican Party intends to keep them running.

Rehabilitation of Offenders

We have given the rehabilitation of criminal offenders more constructive, top-level attention than it has received at any time in our Nation's history. In November 1969, the President ordered a ten-year improvement program in prison facilities, correctional systems and rehabilitation methods and procedures.

We believe the correctional system not only should punish, but also should educate and rehabilitate. We are determined to press ahead with reform of the system to make it more effective against crime.

Almost a decade of inadequate Federal support of law enforcement has left deep scars in our society, but now a new mood pervades the country. Civil disorders and campus violence are no longer considered inevitable. Today, we see a new respect for law and order.

Our goal is justice—for everyone.

We pledge a tireless campaign against crime to restore safety to our streets, and security to law-abiding citizens who have a right to enjoy their homes and communities free from fear.

We pledge to:

Continue our vigorous support of local police and law enforcement agencies, as well as Federal law enforcement agencies.

Seek comprehensive procedural and substantive reform of the Federal Criminal Code.

Accelerate the drive against organized crime.

Increase the funding of the Federal judiciary to help clear away the logjam in the courts which obstructs the administration of justice.

Push forward in prison reform and the rehabilitation of offenders.

Intensify efforts to prevent criminal access to all weapons, including special emphasis on cheap, readily obtainable handguns, retaining primary responsibility at the State level, with such Federal law as necessary to enable the States to meet their responsibilities.

Safeguard the right of responsible citizens to collect, own and use firearms for legitimate purposes, including hunting, target shooting and self-defense. We will strongly support efforts of all law enforcement agencies to apprehend and prosecute to the limit of the law all those who use firearms in the commission of crimes.

Drug Abuse

The permissiveness of the 1960's left no legacy more insidious than drug abuse. In that decade narcotics became widely available, most tragically among our young people. The use of drugs became endowed with a sheen of false glamour identified with social protest.

By the time our Nation awakened to this cancerous social ill, it found no major combat weapons available.

Soon after we took office, our research disclosed there were perhaps hundreds of thousands of heroin users in the United States. Their cravings multiplied violence and crime. We found many more were abusing other drugs, such as amphetamines and barbiturates. Marijuana had become commonplace. All this was spurred by criminals using modern methods of mass distribution against outnumbered authorities lacking adequate countermeasures.

We quickly launched a massive assault against drug abuse.

We intercepted the supply of dangerous drugs at points of entry and impeded their internal distribution. The budget for international narcotics control was raised from $5 million to over $50 million. Narcotics control coordinators were appointed in 59 United States embassies overseas to work directly with foreign governments in stopping drug traffic. We have narcotics action agreements with over 20 countries. Turkey has announced a total ban on opium production and, with our cooperation, France has seized major heroin laboratories and drugs.

To inhibit the distribution of heroin in our own country, we increased the law enforcement budget for drug control more than 10 times—from $20 million to $244 million.

We are disrupting major narcotics distribution in wholesale networks through the combined efforts of the Bureau of Narcotics and Dangerous Drugs, Customs operations at our borders, and a specially credited unit of over 400 Internal Revenue agents who conduct systematic tax investigations of targeted middle and upper echelon traffickers, smugglers, and financiers. Last January we established the Office of Drug Abuse Law Enforcement to disrupt street and mid-level heroin traffickers.

We established the "Heroin Hot Line"—a nationwide toll free phone number (800/368-5363)—to give the public a single number for reporting information on heroin pushers.

Last year we added 2,000 more Federal narcotics agents, and the Bureau of Narcotics and Dangerous Drugs has trained over 170,000 State and local personel.

And we are getting results. This past year four times as much heroin was seized as in the year this Administration took office. Since 1969, the number of drug-related arrests has nearly doubled.

For drug abuse prevention and treatment we increased the budget from $46 million to over $485 million.

The demand for illicit drugs is being reduced through a massive effort directed by a newly created office in the White House. Federally funded drug treatment and rehabilitation programs were more than doubled last fiscal year, and Federal programs now have the capacity to treat more than 60,000 drug abusers a year.

To alert the public, particularly the youth, to the dangers of drugs, we established a National Clearinghouse for Drug Abuse Information in 1970 as well as a $3.5 million Drug Education and Training Program.

We realize that the problem of drug abuse cannot be quickly solved, but we have launched a massive effort where practically none existed before. Nor will we relax this campaign:

We pledge to seek further international agreements to restrict the production and movement of dangerous drugs.

We pledge to expand our programs of education, rehabilitation, training and treatment. We will do more than ever before to conduct research into the complex psychological regions of disappointment and alienation which have led many young people to turn desperately toward drugs.

We firmly oppose efforts to make drugs easily available. We equally oppose the legalization of marijuana. We intend to solve problems, not create bigger ones by legalizing drugs of unknown physical impact.

We pledge the most intensive law enforcement war ever waged. We are determined to drive the pushers of dangerous drugs from the streets, schools and neighborhoods of America.

Agriculture and Rural Life

Our agriculture has become the economic marvel of the world. Our American farmers and ranchers have tripled per worker production in the last 20 years, while non-farm industries have increased theirs a little over half.

Yet when we took office three and a half years ago, the farm community was being shockingly short-changed for its remarkable achievements.

Inflation was driving up both the cost of farming and the cost of living—indeed, driving up all prices except the prices of products the farmers were taking to market. Overall farm income was down. Farm exports were low. Bureaucratic planting regulations were oppressive. All across the country family farms were failing.

Our moves to deal with these problems have been numerous and effective.

The rate of inflation has been curbed without forcing down prices for commodities, even as we have stepped up our drive against rising food costs in the cities.

Net farm income has soared to a record high of more than $18 billion. During these Republican years average net farm income has been over $2 billion a year higher than during the last two Administrations. For the same period average income per farm is up more than 40 percent.

And farm exports now stand at a record $8 billion, sharply up from the $5.7 billion when we took office.

Operating loans to help young farmers have reached the highest levels in history. Administration-backed legislation has given farmers much greater freedom to plant what they choose, and we have given assistance to cooperatives to strengthen the farmers' bargaining positions.

Rural development has been energetically carried forward, and small towns and rural areas have been helped to adjust and grow. The loan programs of the Farmers Home Administration for farm and rural people have been dramatically increased. Electric and telephone service in rural areas has been substantially expanded, a Rural Telephone Bank has been enacted, and the Farm Credit Administration has been streamlined. The total national investment in rural development has almost tripled. Heading the Department of Agriculture have been leaders who understand and forcefully speak out for the farming people of America.

Farmers are benefiting markedly from our successful efforts to expand exports—notably a $750 million sale of United States grains to the Soviet Union, with prospects of much more. Last year we negotiated a similar sale amounting to $135 million.

For the future, we pledge to intensify our efforts to:

Achieve a $10 billion annual export market by opening new foreign markets, while continuing to fight for fair treatment for American farm products in our traditional markets;

Follow sound economic policies to brake inflation and reduce interest rates;

Expand activities to assist farmers in bargaining for fair prices and reasonable terms in a rapidly changing marketing system;

Keep farm prices in the private sector, not subject to price controls;

Support family farms as the preferred method of organizing agricultural production, and protect them from the unfair competition of farming by tax-loss corporations and non-farm enterprises;

Reform Federal estate tax laws, which often force the precipitate sale of family farms to help pay the tax, in such ways as to help support the continuance of family farms as institutions of great importance to the American way of life;

Provide greater credit, technical assistance, soil and water conservaton aid, environmental enhancement, economic stimulus and sympathetic leadership to America's rural area and communities.

Concentrate research on new uses of agricultural products;

Continue assistance to farm cooperatives, including rural electric and telephone cooperatives, in their efforts to improve their members;

Develop land and water policy that takes account of the many uses to which these resources may be put;

Establish realistic environmental standards which safeguard wise resource use, while avoiding undue burdens on farmers;

Use forums of national leaders to create a better understanding by all citizens, those in the cities and suburbs as well as those in small towns, of the difficult problems confronting farm and ranch families in a modern agriculture.

We will not relax our efforts to increase net farm income, to narrow the spread between farm and non-farm income levels, and to pursue commodity programs that will enable farmers and ranchers to receive fair prices for what they produce.

Community Development

For more than a quarter century the Federal Government has sought to assist in the conservation and rebuilding of our urban centers. Yet, after the spending of billions of dollars and the commitment of billions more to future years, we now know that many existing programs are unsuited to the complex problems of the 1970's. Programs cast in the mold of the "big government" philosophy of the 1930's are simply incapable of meeting the challenge of today.

Our Party stands, therefore, for major reform of Federal community development programs and the development of a new philosophy to cope with urban ills.

Republican urban strategy rejects throwing good money after bad money. Instead, through fundamental fiscal, management and program reforms, we have created a new Federal partnership through which State, county and municipal governments can best cope with specific problems such as education, crime, drug abuse, transportation, pollution and housing.

We believe the urban problems of today fall into these categories:

The fiscal crises of State, county and municipal governments;

The need for a better quality and greater availability of urban services;

The continual requirement of physical development;

The need for better locally designed, locally implemented, locally controlled solutions to the problems of individual urban areas.

In the last category—the importance of grass roots planning and participation—our Republican Party has made its most important contribution to solving urban problems.

We hold that government planners should be guided by the people through their locally elected representatives. We believe that real solutions require the full participation of the private sector.

To help ease the fiscal crises of State, county and municipal governments, we pledge increased Federal assistance—assistance we have more than doubled in the past four years. And, as stressed elsewhere in this Platform, we remain committed to General Revenue Sharing, which could reduce the oppressive property tax.

Our proposals for Special Revenue Sharing for Urban Development, transportation, manpower and law enforcement—all still bottled up by the opposition Congress—are designed to make our towns and cities places where Americans can once again live and work without physical or environmental hazard. Urban areas are already benefiting from major funding increases which we fought for in the Law Enforcement Assistance Administration programs and in our $10 billion mass transit program.

Urban areas are also benefiting from our new Legacy of Parks program, which is bringing recreation opportunities closer to where people live.

We are committed also to the physical development of urban areas. We have quadrupled subsidized housing starts for low- and moderate-income families since 1969, and effected substantial increases for construction of municipal waste treatment facilities.

We strongly oppose the use of housing or community development programs to impose arbitrary housing patterns on unwilling communities. Neither do we favor dispersing large numbers of people away from their homes and neighborhoods against their will. We do believe in providing communities, with their full consent, guidance and cooperation with the means and incentives to increase the quantity and quality of housing in conjunction with providing increased access to jobs for their low-income citizens.

We also pledge to carry forward our policy on encouraging the development of new towns in order to afford all Americans a wider range of residential choices. Additionally, our Special Revenue Sharing for Urban and Rural Community Development, together with General Revenue Sharing and nationwide welfare reform, are basic building blocks for a balanced policy of national growth, leading to better lives for all Americans, whether they dwell in cities, suburbs or rural areas.

Our Party recognizes counties as viable units of regional government with a major role in modernizing and restructuring local services, eliminating duplication and increasing local cooperation. We urge Federal and State governments, in implementing national goals and programs, to utilize the valuable resources of counties as area-wide, general-purpose governments.

Housing

Our Republican Administration has made more and better housing available to more of our citizens than ever before.

We are building two-and-a-third million new homes a year—65 per cent more than the average in the eight years of the two previous Administrations. Progress has not been in numbers alone; housing quality has also risen to an all-time high—far above that of any other country.

We will maintain and increase this pattern of growth. We are determined to attain the goal of a decent home for every American.

Significant numbers of Americans still lack the means for decent housing, and in such cases where special need exists we will continue to apply public resources to help people acquire better apartments and homes.

We further pledge:

Continued housing production for low- and moderate-income families, which has sharply increased since President Nixon took office;

Improvement of housing subsidy programs and expansion of mortgage credit activities of Federal housing agencies as necessary to keep Americans the best-housed people in the world;

Continued development of technological and management innovations to lower housing costs—a program begun by Operation Breakthrough, which is assisting in the development of new methods for more economical production of low-cost, high-quality homes.

We urge prompt action by State, county and municipal governments to seek solutions to the serious problems caused by abandoned buildings in urban areas.

Transportation

When President Nixon took office a crisis in transportation was imminent, as indicated by declining mass transportation service, mounting highway deaths, congested urban streets, long delays at airports and airport terminals, deterioration of passenger train service, and a dwindling Merchant Marine. Within two years the President had proposed and signed into law:

A $10 billion, 12-year program—the Urban Mass Transportation Act of 1970—to infuse new life into mass transportation systems and help relieve urban congestion;

A major 10-year program involving $280 million annually for airport development projects as well as an additional $250 million annually to expand airways systems and facilities;

The Rail Passenger Service Act of 1970 to streamline and improve the Nation's passenger train service;

New research and development projects, including automatic people movers, improved Metroliner and Turbo-trains, quieter aircraft jet engines, air pollution reduction for mass transportation vehicles, and experimental safety automobiles. We strongly support these research and development initiatives of the Department of Transportation.

Four years ago we called attention to the decline of our Merchant Marine due to previous neglect and apathy. We promised a vigorous ship replacement program to meet the changing pattern of our foreign commerce. We also pledged to expand maritime research and development and the simplification and revision of construction and operating subsidy procedures.

By the enactment of the Merchant Marine Act of 1970, we have reversed the long decline of our Merchant Marine. We reaffirm our goals set forth in 1968 and anticipate the future development of a merchant fleet that will give us defensive mobility in time of emergency as well as economic strength in time of peace.

To reduce traffic and highway deaths, the National Highway Traffic Safety Administration has been reorganized and expanded, with dramatic results. In 1971, the number of traffic deaths per hundred million miles driven was the lowest in history.

To help restore decision-making to the people, we have proposed a new Single Urban Fund providing almost $2 billion a year by 1975 to State and metropolitan areas to assist local authorities in solving their own transportation problems in their own way.

Our proposal for Special Revenue Sharing for Transportation would also help governments close to the people meet local needs and provide greater freedom to achieve a proper balance among the Nation's major transportation modes.

To revitalize the surface freight transportation industry, we have recommended measures to modernize railway equipment and operations and to update regulatory practices. These measures, on which Congress still dawdles, would help curb inflation by saving the public billions of dollars a year in freight costs. Their enactment would also expand employment and improve our balance of trade.

The Nation's transportation needs are expected to double in the next 20 years. Our Party will continue to pursue policies and programs that will meet these needs and keep the country well ahead of rapidly changing transportation demands.

Environment

In January 1969, we found the Federal Government woefully unprepared to deal with the rapidly advancing environmental crisis. Our response was swift and substantial.

First, new decision-making organizations were set in place—the first Council on Environmental Quality, the Environmental Protection Agency, the National Oceanic and Atmospheric Administration. We also proposed a new Department of Natural Resources, but Congress has failed to act. We also created a National Industrial Pollution Control Council to enlist the private sector more actively against environmental decay, and Presidential Federal Property Review Board was appointed to ferret out Federal property for transfer to local park and recreational uses.

Second, we gave top priority in the Federal Budget to environmental improvements. This fiscal year approximately $2.4 billion will be expended for major environmental programs—three times more than was being spent when President Nixon took office.

Third, sweeping environmental messages were sent to Congress in 1970, 1971 and 1972 covering air quality, water quality, toxic waste substances, ocean dumping, noise, solid waste management, land use, parklands and many other environmental concerns. Almost all of these proposals still languish in the opposition Congress.

Although the President cannot move until and unless Congress passes laws in many of these areas, he nevertheless can act—and has acted forcefully—on many fronts:

He has directed the Federal Government to practice ecological leadership by using low-lead gasoline and recycled paper. He has cracked down on flagrant polluters, greatly increasing prosecutions and making the first use of Federal authority to shut down major industries during an air pollution crisis. The fragile and unique Everglades were saved from a jetport. Pesticide abuses were curtailed.

Strict new clean-air standards were set, and in many urban centers the air is improving. Regulations were issued to make one grade of lead-free and phosphorous-free gasoline available throughout the Nation by July 1, 1974, and a phased reduction was required in the lead content of regular and premium gasolines. Auto makers were required to design air pollution control systems to assure that vehicles comply with Federal emission standards throughout their usual life.

Additionally, the President launched the Legacy of Parks program to convert underutilized Federal properties to park and recreational use, with special emphasis on new parks in or near urban areas. More than 140 areas have already been made available to States, counties and municipalities for such use, including priceless stretches of ocean beach. Moreover, nearly two million acres of land have been purchased by Federal, State and local governments for recreation and for historical and natural preservation purposes.

A system of recreational trails for hiking, bicycling and horseback riding will help meet the pressing recreational needs of our increasingly urbanized society. Many State, county and municipal governments are developing bicycle, hiking, and horseback trails with our active assistance through various Federal programs. We pledge our continued commitment to seeking out practical ways for more and safer bicycling opportunities within our cities and metropolitan areas.

We have also provided effective leadership in international environmental activity. The President has negotiated the Great Lakes Water Quality Agreement with Canada and a Cooperative Agreement on Environmental Protection with the Soviet Union.

The United Nations Conference on the Human Environment in Stockholm adopted our government's initiatives for the creation of an international fund for the environment, a continuing United Nations agency for environmental problems, and the control of ocean dumping. Our President has led the effort for a ten-year moratorium on commercial whaling everywhere in the world.

We call upon the Congress to act promptly on the President's environmental proposals still stalled there—more than 20 in all. These include:

Legislation to control, and in some cases prohibit, the dumping of wastes into the oceans, estuaries and the Great Lakes;

A Federal Noise Control Act to reduce and regulate unwanted sound from aircraft, construction, and transportation equipment;

Authority to control hundreds of chemical substances newly marketed each year;

Legislation to encourage the States to step up pressing decisions on how best to use land. Both environmentally critical areas such as wetlands and growth-inducing developments such as airports would have particular scrutiny;

A proposal to provide for early identification and

protection of endangered wildlife species. This would, for the first time, make the taking of endangered species a Federal offense;

Establishment of recreational areas near metropolitan centers such as the Gateway National Recreational Area in New York and New Jersey and the Golden Gate National Recreation Area in and around San Francisco Bay.

The nostalgic notion of turning the clock back to a simpler time may be appealing but is neither practical nor desirable. We are not going to abandon the automobile, but we are going to have a clean-burning engine.

We are not going to give up electric lighting and modern industry, but we do expect cleanly produced electric power to run them.

We are not going to be able to do without containers for our foods and materials, but we can improve them and make them reusable or biodegradable.

We pledge a workable balance between a growing economy and environmental protection. We will resolve the conflicts sensibly within that framework.

We commit ourselves to comprehensive pollution control laws, vigorous implementation of those laws and rigorous research into the technological problems of pollution control. The beginnings we have made in these first years of the 1970's are evidence of our determination to follow through.

We intend to leave the children of America a legacy of clean air, clean water, vast open spaces and easily accessible parks.

Natural Resources and Energy

Wilderness areas, forests, fish and wildlife are precious natural resources. We have proposed 36 new wilderness areas, adding another 3.6 million acres to the National Wilderness Preservation System. We have made tough new proposals to protect endangered species of wildlife.

Public lands provide us with natural beauty, wilderness and great recreational opportunities as well as minerals, timber, food and fiber. We pledge to develop and manage these lands in a balanced way, both to protect the irreplaceable environment and to maximize the benefits of their use to our society. We will continue these conservation efforts in the years ahead.

We recognize and commend the humane societies and the animal welfare societies in their work to protect animals.

Water supplies are not a boundless resource. The Republican Party is committed to developing additional water supplies by desalinization, the discovery of new groundwater stocks, recycling and wiser and more efficient use of the waters we have.

We will continue the development of flood control, navigation improvement and reclamation projects based on valid cost-benefit estimates, including full consideration of environmental concerns.

No modern nation can thrive without meeting its energy needs, and our needs are vast and growing. Last year we proposed a broad range of actions to facilitate research and development for clean energy, provide energy resources on Federal lands, assure a timely supply of nuclear fuels, use energy more efficiently, balance environmental and energy needs and better organize Federal efforts.

The National Minerals Policy Act of 1970 encourages development of domestic resources by private enterprise. A program to tap our vast shale resources has been initiated consistent with the National Environmental Policy Act of 1969.

We need a Department of Natural Resources to continue to develop a national, integrated energy policy and to administer and implement that policy as the United States approaches the 21st Century. Energy sources so vitally important to the welfare of our Nation are becoming increasingly interchangeable. There is nothing inherently incompatible between an adequate energy supply and a healthy environment.

Indeed, vast quantities of energy are needed to do the work necessary to clean up our air and streams. Without sufficient supplies of power we will not be able to attain our goals of reducing unemployment and poverty and enhancing the American standard of living.

Responsible government must consider both the short-term and the long-term aspects of our energy supplies. Avoidance of brown-outs and power disruptions now and in the future call for sound policies supporting incentives that will encourage the exploration for, and development of, our fossil fuels. Such policies will buy us time to develop the sophisticated and complex technologies needed to utilize the exotic energy sources of the future.

National security and the importance of a favorable balance of trade and balance of payments dictate that we must not permit our Nation to become overly dependent on foreign sources of energy. Since more than half our Nation's domestic fossil resources now lie under Federal lands, high priority must be given to the governmental steps necessary to the development of these resources by private industry.

A liquid-metal fast-breeder reactor demonstration plant will be built with the financial support of the Atomic Energy Commission, the electric power industry and the Tennessee Valley Authority.

We will accelerate research on harnessing thermonuclear energy and continue to provide leadership in the production of energy from the sun and geothermal steam. We recognize the serious problem of assuring adequate electric generating capacity in the Nation, and pledge to meet this need without doing violence to our environment.

Oceans

The oceans are a vast, largely untapped reservoir of resources, a source of food, minerals, recreation and pleasure, with great potential for economic development. For their maintenance we must:

Encourage the development of coastal zone management systems by the States, in cooperation with the Federal Government, to preserve the coastal environment while allowing for its prudent social and economic development;

Protect the oceans from pollution through the creation of binding domestic and international legal and institutional arrangements;

Foster arrangements to develop the untapped mineral resources of the seas in an equitable and environmentally sound manner;

Establish domestic and international institutions for the management of the ocean fisheries. Fishing in international waters, a way of life for many Americans, must be maintained without harassment on the high seas or unreasonable restrictions;

Protect and conserve marine mammals and other marine species to ensure their abundance and especially to protect species whose survival is endangered;

Maintain a national capability in ocean science and technology and, through the United Nations Conference on the Law of the Sea, work to codify an international legal framework for the peaceful conduct of ocean activities.

Science and Technology

Basic and applied scientific research and development are indispensable to our national security, our international competitive position, and virtually every aspect of the domestic economy. We have initiated a new research and development strategy which emphasizes a public-private partnership in searching out new ideas and technologies to create new jobs, new internationally competitive industries and new solutions for complex domestic problems.

In support of this strategy we have increased Federal efforts in civilian research and development by 65 per cent—from $3.3 billion to $5.4 billion—and expanded research in drug abuse, law enforcement, health care, home building, motor vehicle safety, energy and child development as well as many other fields.

We will place special emphasis on these areas in which breakthroughs are urgently needed:

Abundant, clean energy sources;
Safe, fast and pollution-free transportation;
Improved emergency health care;
Reduction of loss of life, health and property in natural disasters;
Rehabilitation of alcoholics and addicts to dangerous drugs.

Additionally, we urge the fair and energetic enforcement of all fire-prevention laws and applaud the work of the National Commission on Fire Prevention and Control. We encourage accelerated research on methods of fire prevention and suppression, including studies on flammable fabrics, hazardous materials, fire equipment and training procedures.

The space program is yielding impressive dividends in earth-oriented applications of space technology—advances in medicine, industrial techniques and consumer products that would still be unknown had we not developed the technology to reach the moon. We will press ahead with the space shuttle program to replace today's expendable launch vehicles and provide low-cost access to space for a wide variety of missions, including those related to earth resources. We pledge to continue to extend our knowledge of the most distant frontiers in space.

We will also extend our exploration of the seabed and the sea. We will seek food for the hungry, power for future technologies, new medicines for the sick and new treatments of water for arid regions of the world.

The quantities of metals and minerals needed to maintain our economic health and living standards are so huge as to require the re-use of all recoverable commodities from solid waste materials. We pledge a vigorous program of research and development in order to seek out more economical methods to recover and recycle such commodities, including the processing of municipal solid wastes.

We pledge to extend the communications frontier, and to foster the development of orbiting satellite systems that will make possible wholly new, world-wide educational and entertainment programs.

We recognize that the productivity of our Nation's research and development efforts can be enhanced through cooperative international projects. The signing of the Moscow agreements for cooperation in space, environment, health and science and technology has opened a new era in international relations. A similar agreement between the United States and Polish Governments will permit expansion of programs such as the jointly funded Copernicus Astronomical Center and Krakow Children's Hospital.

Finally, we pledge expanded efforts to aid unemployed scientists and engineers. We are determined to see that such on-going efforts as the Technology Mobilization and Reemployment Program are effective.

The Individual and Government

Even though many urgently needed Administration proposals have been long delayed or stopped by the opposition Congress, we have kept our 1968 promise to make government more accountable and more responsive to the citizen. One such proposal is General Revenue Sharing with State and local governments—a means of returning to the people powers which for 40 years have grown increasingly centralized in the remote Washington bureaucracy. Another is consolidation of scores of categorical grant programs into six Special Revenue Sharing programs which would make available some $12 billion annually in broad policy fields for States and localities to apply in their own ways to their own needs. Yet another is our proposal to modernize the Executive Branch of the Federal Government by combining six Cabinet departments and several independent agencies into four new departments. So far, the opposition-controlled Congress has blocked or ignored all of these proposals.

In addition, we have:

Improved domestic policy formulation and implementation by the new Domestic Council and Office of Management and Budget within the Executive Office of the President;

Established stronger liaison between the Federal Government and the States, counties and municipalities by a new Office of Intergovernmental Relations, headed by the Vice President;

Overhauled the fragmented and poorly coordinated Federal agencies concerned with drug abuse and the environment;

Utilized voluntary citizen effort through the formation of the ACTION agency in government and the National Center for Voluntary Action outside of government;

Proposed reorganization of the Federal regulatory agencies and appointed distinguished people to those agencies;

Assured more open government, ending abuse of document classification and providing fuller information to the public.

We pledge continuing reform and revitalization of government to assure a better response to individual needs.

We express deep concern for the flood victims of tropical Storm Agnes, the worst natural disaster in terms of property damage in our Nation's history. Past laws were totally inadequate to meet this crisis, and we commend the President's leadership in urgently recommending the newly enacted $1.8 billion flood relief measure, greatly expanding and enlarging the present program. We pledge to reevaluate and enlarge the national flood disaster insurance program so that it will be adequate for future emergencies.

We will continue to press for the enactment of General and Special Revenue Sharing and to pursue further initiatives both to decentralize governmental activities and to transfer more such activities to the private sector.

We will continue to defend the citizen's right to privacy in our increasingly interdependent society. We oppose computerized national databanks and all other "Big Brother" schemes which endanger individual rights.

We reaffirm our view that voluntary prayer should be freely permitted in public places—particularly, by school children while attending public schools—providing that such prayers are not prepared or prescribed by the state or any of its political subdivisions and that no person's participation is coerced, thus preserving the traditional separation of church and state.

We remain committed to a comprehensive program of human rights, social betterment and political participation for the people of the District of Columbia. We will build on our strong record in this area—a record which includes cutting the District of Columbia crime rate in half, aggressive support for a balanced transportation system in metropolitan Washington, initiation of a Bicentennial program and celebration in the national capital region, and support for the first Congressional Delegate in nearly a century. We support voting representation for the District of Columbia in the United States Congress and will work for a system of self-government for the city which takes fair account of the needs and interests of both the Federal Government and the citizens of the District of Columbia.

The Republican Party adheres to the principle of self-determination for Puerto Rico. We will welcome and support statehood for Puerto Rico if that status should be the free choice of its people in a referendum vote.

Additionally, we will pursue negotiations with the Congress of Micronesia on the future political status of the Trust Territories of the Pacific Islands to meet the mutual interests of both parties. We favor extending the right of electing the territorial Governor to the people of American Samoa, and will take complementary steps to increase local self-government in American Samoa. We vigorously support such action as is necessary to permit American citizens resident in Guam,

Puerto Rico and the Virgin Islands to vote for President and Vice President in national elections. We support full voting rights in committees for the Delegates to Congress from Guam and the Virgin Islands.

In our territorial policy we seek a maximum degree of local self-sufficiency and self-government, while encouraging greater inclusion in Federal services and programs and greater participation in national decision-making.

Volunteerism

In our free system, the people are not only the source of our social problems but also the main source of solutions. Volunteerism, therefore, an indispensable national resource, is basic to our Republican philosophy. We applaud the Administration's efforts to encourage volunteerism by all Americans and commend the millions of volunteers who are working in communities and states across the country on myriad projects. We favor further implementation of voluntary action programs throughout the fifty States to assist public and private agencies in working to assure quality life for all human beings.

Arts and Humanities

The United States is experiencing a cultural renaissance of inspiring dimension. Scores of millions of our people are now supporting and participating in the arts and humanities in quest of a richer life of the mind and the spirit. Our national culture, no longer the preserve of the elite, is becoming a people's heritage of importance to the whole world.

We believe, with the President, that "the Federal Government has a vital role as catalyst, innovator, and supporter of public and private efforts for cultural development."

We have supported a three-year extension of the National Foundation on the Arts and the Humanities, and increased the funding of its two endowments by more than four times the level of three years ago. The State Arts Councils, which operate in all 50 States and the five special jurisdictions, have also been strengthened.

The Arts Endowment has raised its support for the Nation's museums, orchestras, theatre, dance, opera companies and film centers and encouraged the creativity of individual artists and writers. In addition, the new Federal Expansion Arts Program has been sharply increased.

We have encouraged Federal agencies to use the arts in their programs, sponsored an annual Design Assembly for Federal administrators, requested the National Endowment for the Arts to recommend a program for upgrading the design of Federal buildings, and moved to set new standards of excellence in all design endeavors of the Federal Government.

Moreover, the National Endowment for the Humanities, now greatly enlarged, is fostering improved teaching and scholarship in history, literature, philosophy and ethics. The Endowment also supports programs to raise levels of scholarship and teaching in Afro-American, American Indian and Mexican-American studies, has broadened its fellowship programs to include junior college teachers, and stresses adult or continuing education, including educational television and film series. We have also expanded the funding of public broadcasting.

For the future, we pledge continuance of our vigorous support of the arts and humanities.

A BETTER FUTURE FOR ALL

Children

We believe, with the President, that the first five years of life are crucial to a child's development, and further, that every child should have the opportunity to reach his full potential as an individual.

We have, therefore, established the Office of Child Development, which has taken a comprehensive approach to the development of young children, combining programs dealing with their physical, social and educational needs and development.

We have undertaken a wide variety of demonstration programs to assure our children, particularly poor children, a good start in life—for example, the Parent and Child Center program for infant care, Home Start to strengthen the environment of the preschool child, and Health Start to explore new delivery systems of health care for young children.

We have redirected Head Start to perform valuable full-day child care and early education services, and more than 380,000 preschool children are now in the program. We have doubled funds for early childhood demonstration programs which will develop new tools and new teaching techniques to serve children who suffer from deafness, blindness and other handicaps.

So that no child will be denied the opportunity for a productive life because of inability to read effectively, we have established the Right to Read Program.

To add impetus to the entire educational effort, our newly-created National Institute of Education ensures that broad research and experimentation will develop the best educational opportunities for all children. Additionally, we have taken steps to help ensure that children receive proper care while their parents are at work.

Moreover, as stated elsewhere in this Platform, we have broadened nutritional assistance to poor children by nearly tripling participation in the Food Stamp Program, more than doubling the number of needy children in the school lunch program, operating a summer feeding program for three million young people, increasing the breakfast program fivefold, and doubling Federal support for child nutritional programs. We are improving medical care for poor children through more vigorous treatment procedures under Medicaid and more effectively targeting maternal and child health services to low-income mothers. We will continue to seek out new means to reach and teach children in their crucial early years.

Youth

We believe that what our youth most want and need is not special treatment as a group apart, but just the opposite—the opportunity for full participation by exercising the rights and responsibilities of adults.

In 1970 the President approved legislation which gave the vote to more than 11 million 18- to 20-year-olds. The 26th Amendment, which places this important new right in the Constitution, has our enthusiastic backing.

Our Administration has already made the draft a far less arbitrary factor in young men's lives. Now we near the point where we can end conscription altogether and achieve our goal of an all-volunteer armed force.

Our total war on drug abuse has had special benefits for youth, hardest hit by this menace. Last year we held the first White House Conference ever held by and for young people themselves. The Administration gave the Conference's more than 300 recommendations a searching review, and last spring the President returned a detailed response and action report to the conferees.

The anarchy which swept major campuses in the late 1960's penalized no one more severely than the young people themselves. The recent calm on campus is, we believe, in part the result of the President's leadership in winding down the war in Vietnam, reducing the draft, and taking a strong stand against lawlessness, but our view is that colleges themselves are responsible for maintaining a campus climate that will preserve academic freedom.

We have proposed legislation to ensure that no qualified student is denied a higher education by lack of funds, and have also moved to meet the often-overlooked concerns of the two-thirds of the college-age young not in school. We have developed a new job-oriented, career-education concept, expanded Federal manpower programs and provided a record number of summer job opportunities for young men and women.

To engage youthful idealism and energies more effectively, we have created the new ACTION volunteer service agency, bringing together the Peace Corps, VISTA, and other volunteer programs; and we encouraged the establishment of the independent National Center for Voluntary Action.

We stand for lowering the legal age of majority in all jurisdictions to 18; and we will seek to broaden the involvement of young people in every phase of the political process—as voters, party workers and leaders, candidates and elected officials, and participants in government at municipal, State and Federal levels.

We will continue to build on these solid achievements in keeping with our conviction that these young people should have the opportunity to participate fully in the affairs of our society.

Equal Rights for Women

The Republican Party recognizes the great contributions women have made to our society as homemakers and mothers, as contributors to the community through volunteer work, and as members of the labor force in careers outside the home. We fully endorse the principle of equal rights, equal opportunities and equal responsibilities for women, and believe that progress in these areas is needed to achieve the full realization of the potentials of American women both in the home and outside the home.

We reaffirm the President's pledge earlier this year: "The Administration will . . . continue its strong efforts to open equal opportunities for women, recognizing clearly that women are often denied such opportunities today. While every woman may not want a career outside the home, every woman should have the freedom to choose whatever career she wishes—and an equal chance to pursue it."

This Administration has done more than any before it to help women of America achieve equality of opportunity.

Because of its efforts, more top-level and middle-management positions in the Federal Government are held by women than ever before. The President has appointed a woman as his special assistant in the White House, specifically charged with the recruitment of women for policy making jobs in the United States Government. Women have also been named to high positions in the Civil Service Commission and the Department of Labor to ensure equal opportunities for employment and advancement at all levels of the Federal service.

In addition we have:

Significantly increased resources devoted to enforcement of the Fair Labor Standards Act, providing equal pay for equal work;

Required all firms doing business with the Government to have affirmative action plans for the hiring and promotion of women;

Requested Congress to expand the jurisdiction of the Commission on Civil Rights to cover sex discrimination;

Recommended and supported passage of Title IX of the Higher Education Act opposing discrimination against women in educational institutions;

Supported the Equal Employment Opportunity Act of 1972 giving the Equal Employment Opportunity Commission enforcement power in sex discrimination cases;

Continued our support of the Equal Rights Amendment to the Constitution, our Party being the first national party to back this Amendment.

Other factors beyond outright employer discrimination—the lack of child care facilities, for example—can limit job opportunities for women. For lower- and middle-income families, the President supported and signed into law a new tax provision which makes many child care expenses deductible for working parents. Part of the President's recent welfare reform proposal would provide comprehensive day care services so that women on welfare can work.

We believe the primary responsibility for a child's care and upbringing lies with the family. However, we recognize that for economic and many other reasons many parents require assistance in the care of their children.

To help meet this need, we favor the development of publicly or privately run, voluntary, comprehensive, quality day care services, locally controlled but federally assisted, with the requirement that the recipients of these services will pay their fair share of the costs according to their ability.

We oppose ill-considered proposals, incapable of being administered effectively, which would heavily engage the Federal Government in this area.

To continue progress for women's rights, we will work toward:

Ratification of the Equal Rights Amendment;

Appointment of women to highest-level positions in the Federal Government, including the Cabinet and Supreme Court;

Equal pay for equal work;

Elimination of discrimination against women at all levels in Federal Government;

Elimination of discrimination against women in the criminal justice system, in sentencing, rehabilitation and prison facilities;

Increased opportunities for the part-time employment of women, and expanded training programs for women who want to reenter the labor force;

Elimination of economic discrimination against women in credit, mortgage, insurance, property, rental and finance contracts.

We pledge vigorous enforcement of all Federal statutes and executive orders barring job discrimination on the basis of sex.

We are proud of the contributions made by women to better government. We regard the active involvement of women at all levels of the political process, from precinct to national status, as of great importance to our country. The Republican Party welcomes and encourages their maximum participation.

Older Americans

We believe our Nation must develop a new awareness of the attitudes and needs of our older citizens. Elderly Americans are far too often forgotten Americans, relegated to lives of idleness and isolation by a society bemused with the concerns of other groups. We are distressed by the tendency of many Americans to ignore the heartbreak and hardship resulting from the generation gap which separates so many of our people from those who have reached the age of retirement. We deplore what is tantamount to cruel discrimination—age discrimination in employment, and the discrimination of neglect and indifference, perhaps the cruelest of all.

We commit ourselves to helping older Americans achieve greater self-reliance and greater opportunities for direct participation in the activities of our society. We believe that the later years should be, not isolated years, not years of dependency, but years of fulfillment and dignity. We believe our older people are not to be regarded as a burden but rather should be valuable participants in our society. We believe their judgment, their experience, and their talents are immensely valuable to our country.

Because we so believe, we are seeking and have sought in many ways to help older Americans, for example:

Federal programs of direct benefit to older Americans have increased more than $16 billion these past four years;

As part of this, social security benefits are more than 50 per cent higher than they were four years ago, the largest increase in the history of social security;

Social security benefits have become inflation proof by making them rise automatically to match cost-of-living increases, a protection long advocated by the Republican Party;

We have upgraded nursing homes.

Expenditures under the Older Americans Act have gone up 800 per cent since President Nixon took office, with a strong emphasis on programs enabling older Americans to live dignified, independent lives in their own homes.

The valuable counsel of older people has been sought directly through the White House Conference on Aging. The President has appointed high-level advisers on the problems of the aging to his personal staff.

We have urged upon the opposition Congress—again, typically to no avail—numerous additional programs of benefit to the elderly. We will continue pressing for these new initiatives:

Increase the amount of money a person can earn without losing social security benefits;

Increase widow, widower, and delayed retirement benefits;

Improve the effectiveness of Medicare, including elimination of the monthly premium required under Part B of Medicare—the equivalent of more than a three per cent social security increase;

Strengthen private pension plans through tax deductions to encourage their expansion, improved vesting, and protection of the investments in these funds;

Reform our tax system so that persons 65 or over will receive increased tax-free income;

Encourage volunteer service activities for older Americans, such as the Retired Senior Volunteer Program and the Foster Grandparents Program;

Give special attention to bringing full government services within the reach of the elderly in rural areas who are often unable to share fully in their deserved benefits because of geographic inaccessibility;

Upgrade other Federal activities important to the elderly including programs for nutrition, housing and nursing homes, transportation, consumer protection, and elimination of age discrimination in government and private employment.

We encourage constructive efforts which will help older citizens to be better informed about existing programs and services designed to meet their needs, and we pledge to cut away excessive Federal red tape to make it easier for older Americans to receive the benefits to which they are entitled.

Working Men and Women

The skill, industry and productivity of American workers are the driving force of our free economy. The Nation's labor unions, comprised of millions of working people, have advanced the well-being not only of their members but also of our entire free-enterprise system. We of the Republican Party reaffirm our strong endorsement of Organized Labor's key role in our national life.

We salute the statesmanship of the labor union movement. Time and time again, at crucial moments, it has voiced its outspoken support for a firm and effective foreign policy and for keeping the Armed Forces of the United States modern and strong.

The American labor movement and the Republican Party have always worked against the spread of totalitarian forms of government. Together we can continue to preserve in America the best system of government ever devised for human happiness and fulfillment.

We are for the right of American workers and their families to enjoy and to retain to the greatest possible extent the rewards of their own labor.

We regard collective bargaining as the cornerstone of the Nation's labor relations policy. The government's role is not to encroach upon this process but rather to aid the differing parties to make collective bargaining more effective both for themselves and for the public. In furtherance of that concept, we will continue to develop procedures whereby the imagination, ingenuity and knowledge of labor and management can more effectively seek solutions for such problems as structural adjustment and productivity.

In the construction industry, for example, we will build on a new joint effort between government and all parts of the industry to solve such problems as seasonality and varying peaks of demand to ensure a stable growth in the number of skilled craftsmen.

We call upon management and labor to devote their best efforts to finding better ways to conduct labor–management relations so the good of all the people can be advanced without strikes or lockouts.

We will continue to search for realistic and fair solutions to emergency labor disputes, guided by two basic principles; first, that the health and safety of the people of the United States should always be paramount; and second, that collective bargaining should be kept as free as possible from government interference.

For mine health and safety, we have implemented the most comprehensive legislation in the Nation's history, resulting in a major reduction in mine-related accidents. We pledge continued advancement of the health and safety of workers.

We will continue to press for improved pension vesting and other statutory protections to assure that Americans will not lose their hard-earned retirement income.

We pledge further modernization of the Federal Civil Service System, including emphasis on executive development. We rededicate ourselves to promotion on merit, equal opportunity, and the setting of clear incentives for higher productivity. We will give continuing close attention to the evolving labor–management relationship in the Federal service.

We pledge realistic programs of education and training so that all Americans able to do so can make their own way, on their own ability, receiving an equal and fair chance to advance themselves. We flatly oppose the notion that the hard-earned tax dollars of American workers should be used to support those who can work but choose not to, and who believe that the world owes them a living free from any responsibility or care.

We are proud of our many other solid achievements on behalf of America's working people—for example:

- Nearly five million additional workers brought under the coverage of the unemployment insurance system, and eligibility deadlines twice extended;
- Funding for more than 166,000 jobs under the Emergency Employment Act;
- Expansion of vocational education and manpower training programs;
- Use of the long-neglected Trade Expansion Act to help workers who lose their jobs because of imports. We strongly favor vigorous competition by American business in the world market but in ways that do not displace American jobs;
- Negotiation of long-needed limitations on imports of man-made fibers, textiles and other products, thus protecting American jobs.

We share the desire of all Americans for continued prosperity in peacetime. We will work closely with labor and management toward our mutual goal of assuring a job for every man and woman seeking the dignity of work.

Ending Discrimination

From its beginning, our Party has led the way for equal rights and equal opportunity. This great tradition has been carried forward by the Nixon Administration.

Through our efforts de jure segregation is virtually ended. We pledge continuation of these efforts until no American schoolchild suffers educational deprivation because of the color of his skin or the language he speaks and all school children are receiving high-quality education. In pursuit of this goal, we have proposed $2.5 billion of Federal aid to school districts to improve educational opportunities and build facilities for disadvantaged children. Further to assure minority progress, we have provided more support to predominantly black colleges than ever before—twice the amount being spent when President Nixon took office.

Additionally, we have strengthened Federal enforcement of equal opportunity laws. Spending for civil rights enforcement has been increased from $75 million to $602 million—concrete evidence of our commitment to equal justice for all. The President also supported and signed into law the Equal Employment Opportunity Act of 1972, which makes the Equal Employment Opportunity Commission a much more powerful body.

Working closely with leaders of construction unions, we have initiated 50 "home-town" plans which call for more than 35,000 additional minority hirings in the building trades during the next four years. We will continue to search out new employment opportunities for minorities in other fields as well. We believe such new jobs can and should be created without displacing those already at work. We will give special consideration to minority Americans who live and make their way in the rural regions of our country—Americans too often bypassed in the advances of the general society.

We have made unprecedented progress in strengthening minority participation in American business. We created the Office of Minority Business Enterprise in March 1969 to coordinate the Federal programs assisting members of minority groups who seek to establish or expand businesses. We have more than tripled Federal loans, guarantees and grants to minority-owned businesses. More minority Americans are now in our Nation's economic mainstream than at any other time in our history, and we pledge every effort to expand these gains.

Minority businesses now receive 16 per cent of the Small Business Administration dollar—more than double the proportion in 1968. Many Minority Enterprise Small Business Investment Companies have been licensed since 1969 to provide venture capital for minority enterprises. More than $200 million is now available through this program, and we have requested additional funding.

In late 1970, we initiated a combined Government–private program to increase minority bank deposits. This year our goal of $100 million has been reached four times over.

We pledge to carry forward our efforts to place minority citizens in responsible positions—efforts we feel are already well under way. During the last four years the percentage of minority Federal employees has risen to a record high of almost 20 per cent and, perhaps more important, the quality of jobs for minority Americans has improved. We have recruited more minority citizens for top managerial posts in Civil Service than ever before. We will see that our progress in this area will continue and grow.

In 1970 President Nixon approved strong new amendments to the Voting Rights Act of 1965, and we pledge continued vigilance to ensure that the rights affirmed by this act are upheld.

The cultural diversity of America's heritage groups has always been a source of strength for our society and our Party. We reaffirm our commitment to the basic American values which have made this Nation the land of opportunity for these groups, originating from all sectors of the world, from Asia to Africa to Europe to Latin America. We will continue our Party's open-door policy and work to assure all minorities full opportunity for participation in the political process. We pledge vigorous support of the Bilingual Act and the Ethnic Studies Heritage Act.

Spanish-Speaking Americans

In recognition of the significant contributions to our country by our proud and independent Spanish-speaking citizens, we have developed a comprehensive program to help achieve equal opportunity.

During the last four years Spanish-speaking Americans have achieved a greater role in national affairs. More than thirty have been appointed to high Federal positions.

To provide the same learning opportunities enjoyed by other American children, we have increased bilingual education programs almost sixfold since 1969. We initiated a 16-point employment program to help Spanish-speaking workers, created the National Economic Development Association to promote Spanish-speaking business development and expanded economic development opportunities in Spanish-speaking communities.

We will work for the use of bilingual staffs in localities where this language capability is desirable for effective health care.

Indians, Alaska Natives, and Hawaiians

President Nixon has evolved a totally new Indian policy which we fully support. The opposition Congress, by inaction on most of the President's proposals, has thwarted Indian rights and opportunities.

We commend the Department of the Interior for its stalwart defense of Indian land and water rights, and we urge the Congress to join in support of that effort. We further request Congress to permit Indian tribal governments to assume control over the programs of the Departments of Interior and Health, Education and Welfare in their homelands, to assure Indians a role in determining how funds can best be used for their children's schools, to expand Indian economic development opportunity, to triple the funds for Indian credit and create a new Assistant Secretary of the Interior for Indian and Territorial Affairs.

These reforms, all urged by the President, have been ignored by the Congress. We—with the Indian people—are impatiently waiting.

Knowing the Indians' love for their land and recognizing the many wrongs committed in years past, the President has restored Blue Lake in New Mexico to the Taos Pueblo and the Mt. Adams area in Washington to the Yakima Nation. We are seeking to protect Indian water rights in Pyramid Lake by bringing suit in the Supreme Court.

We are fully aware of the severe problems facing the Menominee Indians in seeking to have Federal recognition restored to their tribe and promise a complete and sympathetic examination of their pleas.

We have increased the Bureau of Indian Affairs' budget by 214 percent, nearly doubled funds for Indian health, and are arranging with tribal leaders for the allocation of Bureau funds in accordance with priorities set by the tribal governments themselves.

We pledge continued attention to the needs of off-reservation Indians and have launched demonstration projects at Indian centers in nine major cities. We are determined that the first Americans will not be the forgotten Americans, and that their rights will be respected.

We will continue the policy of Indian preference in hiring and promotion and apply it to all levels, including management and supervisory positions in those agencies with programs affecting Indian peoples.

The standard of living of Indian Americans is still far below that of any of the peoples of the United States. This intolerable level of existence should be alleviated by the enactment of new legislation designed to further Indian self-determination without termination and to close this economic gap and raise the Indian standard of life to that of the rest of America. We favor the development of such legislation in the 93rd Congress.

At the President's recommendation, the Congress voted an Alaska Native Claims Settlement which confirms the titles of the Eskimos, Indians and Aleuts to 40 million acres and compensates them with a generous cash settlement.

We will also preserve and continue to protect the Hawaiian Homes Commission Act which provides land already set aside for Hawaiians for homes and the opportunity to preserve their culture.

Our achievements for human dignity and opportunity are specific and real, not idle promises. They have brought tremendous progress to many thousands of minority citizens and made our society more just for all.

We will press on with our fight against social injustice and discrimination, building upon the achievements already made. Knowing that none of us can reap the fullest blessings of liberty until all of us can, we reaffirm our commitment to the upward struggle for universal freedom led by Abraham Lincoln a century ago.

Consumers

The American consumer has a right to product safety; clearly specified qualities and values, honest descriptions and guarantees, fair credit procedures, and due recourse for fraud and deception. We are addressing these concerns forcefully, with executive action and legislative and legal initiatives.

The issues involved in this accelerating awareness on the part of consumers lie close to the heart of the dynamic American market: Good products at fair prices made it great; the same things will keep it great.

Enlightened business management is as interested in consumer protection and consumer education as are consumers themselves. In a marketplace as competitive and diverse as ours, a company's future depends on the reputation of its products. One safety error can wipe out an established firm overnight.

Unavoidably, the remoteness of business manage-ment from the retail counter tends to hamper consumers in resolving quality and performance questions. Technical innovations make it harder for the consumer to evaluate new products. Legal complexities often deny efficient remedies for deception or product failure.

To assist consumers and business, President Nixon established the first Office of Consumer Affairs in the White House and made its Director a member of his personal staff and of the Cost of Living Council. We have also proposed a Buyer's Bill of Rights, including:

Federal authority for the regulation of hazardous consumer products;

Requirement of full disclosure of the terms of warranties and guarantees in language all can understand.

We support the establishment of an independent Consumer Protection Agency to present the consumer's case in proceedings before Federal agencies and also a consumer product safety agency in the Department of Health, Education and Welfare. We oppose punitive proposals which are more anti-business than pro-consumer.

We pledge vigorous enforcement of all consumer protection laws and to foster more consumer education as a vital necessity in a marketplace ever increasing in variety and complexity.

Veterans

We regard our Nation's veterans precisely as our President does:

"Americans have long known that those who defended the great values of our Nation in wartime are of great value to the Nation when the war is over. It is traditional that the American veteran has been helped by his Nation so that he can create his own 'peace story,' a story of prosperity, independence and dignity.

"Veterans benefit programs have therefore become more than a recognition for services performed in the past; they have become an investment in the future of the veteran and of his country."

Under Republican leadership, far more for our veterans is being done than ever before:

G.I. Bill education benefits have been increased more than 35 per cent. Vietnam-era veterans have the highest assistance levels in history to help them pursue educational opportunities.

Major cost-of-living adjustments have been made in compensation and pension payments.

Medical services are the best in the history of the Veterans Administration and now include a strong new drug treatment and rehabilitation program.

Disability benefits have been increased.

G.I. home loan benefits have been expanded and improved.

The total Administration commitment is massive—$12.4 billion for this fiscal year. This is the largest Veterans Administration budget in history, and the third largest of all Federal agencies and departments.

We are giving the highest priority to the employment problems of Vietnam veterans. In 1971 we initiated a comprehensive program which recently placed more than one million Vietnam-era veterans in jobs, training and education programs.

For the future, we pledge:

Continuation of the Veterans Administration as a strong, independent agency;

Continuation of an independent system of Veterans Administration health care facilities to provide America's veterans with the best medical care available, including appropriate attention to the problems of the ex-serviceman afflicted with drug and alcohol problems;

Continuing attention to the needs of the Vietnam-era veteran, with special emphasis on employment opportunities, education and housing.

Continuation of our efforts to raise G.I. Bill education benefits to a level commensurate with post–World War II benefits in adjusted dollars;

Continued effort for a better coordinated national policy on cemeteries and burial benefits for veterans.

We will not fail our obligation to the Nation's 29 million veterans and will stand ever watchful of their needs and rights.

CONCLUSION

The record is clear.

More than any President, Richard Nixon has achieved major changes in policy and direction in our government. He has restored faith—faith that our system will indeed reflect the will of the people—faith that there will be a new era of peace and human progress at home and around the world.

To be sure there is unfinished business on the agenda of our ever-restless Nation. We have great concern for those who have not participated more fully in the general prosperity. The twin evils of crime and drug abuse are still to be conquered. Peace in the world is not yet won.

But Republican leadership has restored stability and sanity to our land once again. We have vigorously attacked every major problem.

Once again our direction is peace; once again our determination is national strength; once again we are prospering; once again, on a host of fronts, we are making progress.

Now we look to tomorrow.

We pledge ourselves to go forward at an accelerated pace—with a determination and zeal unmatched before.

In four years we mark the 200th anniversary of the freest, most productive, most benevolent Nation of all human history. In four years we celebrate one of man's highest achievements—two hundred years as a constitutional republic founded on the noble concept that every person is a sovereign being, possessed of dignity and inalienable rights.

Almost two centuries ago, the Founding Fathers envisioned a Nation of free people, at peace with themselves and the world—each with equal opportunity to pursue happiness in his own way. Much of that dream has come true; much is still to be fulfilled.

We, the Republican Party, pledge ourselves to go forward, hand-in-hand with every citizen, to solve those problems that yet stand in the way of realizing that more perfect union, the dream of the Founding Fathers—a dream enhanced by the free and generous gift of people working together, not in shifting alliances of separated minorities, but in unison of spirit and purpose. We cannot favor, nor can we respect, the notion of group isolation in our United States of America. We must not divide and weaken ourselves by attitudes or policies which would segregate our citizens into separate racial, ethnic, economic, religious or social groups. It is the striving of all of us—our striving together as Americans—that will move our Nation continually onward to our Founders' dream.

Building on the foundations of peace in the world, and reason and prosperity at home, our Republican Party pledges a new era of progress for man—progress toward more freedom, toward greater protection of individual rights, toward more security from want and fear, toward greater fulfillment and happiness for all.

We pledge to the American people that the 200th anniversary of this Nation in 1976 will be more than a celebration of two centuries of unequaled success; we pledge it also to be the beginning of the third and greatest century for all of our countrymen and, we pray, for all people in the world.

— 1976 —

PREAMBLE

To you, an American citizen:

You are about to read the 1976 Republican Platform. We hope you will also find time to read the Democrats' Platform. Compare. You will see basic differences in how the two parties propose to represent you.

"The Platform is the Party's contract with the people." This is what it says on the cover of the official printing of the Democrat Platform. So it should be. The Democrats' Platform repeats the same thing on every page: more government, more spending, more inflation. Compare. This Republican Platform says exactly the opposite, less government, less spending, less inflation. In other words, we want you to retain more of your own money, money that represents the worth of your labors, to use as you see fit for the necessities and conveniences of life.

No matter how many statements to the contrary that Mr. Carter makes, he is firmly attached to a contract with you to increase vastly the powers of government. Is bigger government in Washington really what you want?

Make no mistake: you cannot have bigger programs in Washington and less government by Washington. You must choose.

What is the cost of these added or expanded programs? The Democrats' Platform is deliberately vague. When they tell you, as they do time after time, that they will "expand federal support," you are left to guess the cost. The price tag of five major Democrat Platform promises could add as much as $100 billion to the annual cost of government. But the Democrats' Platform proposes over 60 new or expanded spending programs and the expansion or creation of some 22 Washington agencies, offices or bureaus. In fact, the total of all Democrat proposals can be as high as $200 billion a year. While this must be a rough estimate, it does give you a clue to the magnitude and direction of these commitments. The Democrats' Platform can increase federal spending by 50 percent. If a Democrat Congress passes the Democrat Platform and it is signed by a Democrat President, what happens then? The Democrats could raise your taxes by 50 percent to pay for the new programs. Or the Democrats could not raise taxes and the result would be runaway inflation. Of course, contract or no contract, the Democrats may not honor their promises. Are you prepared to risk it?

In stark contrast to the Democrats' Platform, we offer you a responsive and moderate alternative based on these principles:

We believe that liberty can be measured by how much freedom you have to make your own decisions—even your own mistakes. Government must step in when your liberties impinge on your neighbor's. Government must protect your constitutional rights. Government must deal with other governments and protect you from aggressors. Government must assure equal opportunity. And government must be compassionate in caring for those citizens who are unable to care for themselves.

Our federal system of local–state–national government is designed to sort out on what level these actions should be taken. Those concerns of a national character that do not respect state boundaries—such as air and water pollution or the national transportation system or efforts to safeguard your civil liberties—must, of course, be handled on the national level.

As a general rule, however, we believe that government action should be taken first by the government that resides as close to you as possible. Governments tend to become less responsive to your needs the farther away they are from you. Thus, we prefer local and state government to national government, and decentralized national government wherever possible.

We also believe that you, often acting through voluntary organizations, should have the opportunity to solve many of the social problems of your community. This spirit of freely helping others is uniquely American and should be encouraged in every way by government.

Every dollar spent by government is a dollar earned by you. Government must always ask: Are your dollars being wisely spent? Can we afford it? Is it not better for the country to leave your dollars in your pocket?

Your elected officials, their appointees, and government workers are expected to perform their public acts with honesty, openness, diligence, and special integrity. At the heart of our system must be confidence that these people are always working for you.

We believe that your initiative and energy create jobs, our standard of living and the underlying economic strength of the country. Government must work for the goal of justice and the elimination of unfair practices, but no government has yet designed a more productive economic system or one which benefits as many people.

The beauty of our land is our legacy to our children. It must be protected by us so that they can pass it on intact to their children.

The United States must always stand for peace and liberty in the world and the rights of the individual.

We must form sturdy partnerships with our allies for the preservation of freedom. We must be ever willing to negotiate differences, but equally mindful that there are American ideals that cannot be compromised. Given that there are other nations with potentially hostile designs, we recognize that we can reach our goals only while maintaining a superior national defense.

We support these principles because they are right, knowing full well that they will not be easy to achieve. Acting with restraint is most difficult when confronted by an opposition Congress that is determined to promise everything to everybody. And this is what the Democrat Congress has been doing. A document, such as this Platform, which refuses to knuckle under to special interest groups, will be accused of being "uncaring." Yet it is exactly because we do care about your basic freedom to manage your own life with a minimum of government interference, because we do care about encouraging permanent and meaningful jobs, because we do care about your getting paid in sound dollars, because we do care about resisting the use of your tax dollars for wasteful or unproven programs—it is for these reasons that we are proposing only actions that the nation can afford and are opposing excessive tinkering with an economic system that works better than any other in the world.

Our great American Republic was founded on the principle: "One nation under God, with liberty and justice for all." This bicentennial year marks the anniversary of the greatest secular experiment in history: That of seeking to determine that a people are truly capable of self-government. It was our "Declaration" which put the world and posterity on notice "that Men are . . . endowed by their Creator with certain unalienable Rights" and that those rights must not be taken from those to whom God has given them.

Recently, Peggy Pinder, a 23-year-old student from Grinnell, Iowa, who is a delegate to this convention, said that she joined our party "because Republicans understand the place of government in the people's lives better than the Democrats. Republicans try to find ways to take care of needs through the private sector first while it seems automatic for Democrats to take care of them through the governmental system."

The perception of Peggy Pinder governs this Platform. Aren't these the principles that you want your elected representatives to have?

JOBS AND INFLATION

We believe it is of paramount importance that the American people understand that the number one destroyer of jobs is inflation. We wish to stress that the number one cause of inflation is the government's expansion of the nation's supply of money and credit needed to pay for deficit spending. It is above all else deficit spending by the federal government which erodes the purchasing power of the dollar. Most Republicans in Congress seem to understand this fundamental cause-and-effect relationship and their support in sustaining over 40 Presidential vetoes in the past two years has prevented over $13 billion in federal spending. It is clear that most of the Democrats do not understand this vital principle, or, if they do, they simply don't care.

Inflation is the direct responsibility of a spendthrift Democrat-controlled Congress that has been unwilling to discipline itself to live within our means. The temptation to spend and deficit-spend for political reasons has simply been too great for most of our elected politicians to resist. Individuals, families, companies and most local and state governments must live within a budget. Why not Congress?

Republicans hope every American realizes that if we are permanently to eliminate high unemployment, it is essential to protect the integrity of our money. That means putting an end to deficit spending. The danger, sooner or later, is runaway inflation.

Wage and price controls are not the solution to inflation. They attempt to treat only the symptom—rising prices—not the cause. Historically, controls have always been a dismal failure, and in the end they create only shortages, black markets and higher prices. For these reasons the Republican Party strongly opposes any reimposition of such controls, on a standby basis or otherwise.

Unfortunately, the Democrat-controlled Congress now persists in attempting to obtain control over our nation's money creation policies by taking away the independence of the Federal Reserve Board. The same people who have so massively expanded government spending should not be allowed politically to dominate our monetary policy. The independence of the Federal Reserve System must be preserved.

Massive, federally funded public employment programs, such as the Humphrey–Hawkins Bill currently embraced by the new National Platform of the Democratic Party will cost billions and can only be financed either through very large tax increases or through ever increasing levels of deficit spending. Although such government "make work" programs usually provide a temporary stimulus to the economy, "quick-fix" solutions of this sort—like all narcotics—lead to addiction, larger and larger doses, and ultimately the destruction of far more jobs than they create. Sound job creation can only be accomplished in the private sector of the economy. Americans must not be fooled into accepting government as the employer of last resort.

Nor should we sit idly by while 2.5 million American jobs are threatened by imports of textile products. We encourage the renewal of the GATT Multifiber Arrangement and the signing of other necessary bilateral agreements to protect our domestic textile industry.

In order to be able to provide more jobs, businesses must be able to expand; yet in order to build and expand, they must be profitable and able to borrow funds (savings) that someone else has been willing to part with on a temporary basis. In the long run, inflation discourages thrift, encourages debt and destroys the incentive to save which is the mainspring of capital formation. When our government—through deficit spending and debasement of the currency—destroys the incentive to save and to invest, it destroys the very wellspring of American productivity. Obviously, when production falls, the number of jobs declines.

The American people are beginning to understand that no government can ever add real wealth (purchasing power) to an economy by simply turning on the printing presses or by creating credit out of thin air. All government can do is confiscate and redistribute wealth. No nation can spend its way into prosperity; a nation can only spend its way into bankruptcy.

TAXES AND GOVERNMENT SPENDING

The Republican Party recognizes that tax policies and spending policies are inseparable. If government spending is not controlled, taxes will inevitably rise either directly or through inflation. By failing to tie spending directly to income, the Democrat-controlled Congress has not kept faith with the American people. Every American knows he cannot continually live beyond his means.

The Republican Party advocates a legislative policy to obtain a balanced federal budget and reduced tax rates. While the best tax reform is tax reduction, we recognize the need for structural tax adjustments to help the working men and women of our nation. To that end, we recommend tax credits for college tuition, postsecondary technical training and child care expenses incurred by working parents.

Over the past two decades of Democrat control of the Congress, our tax laws have become a nightmare of complexity and unfair tax preferences, virtually

destroying the credibility of the system. Simplification should be a major goal of tax reform.

We support economic and tax policies to insure the necessary job-producing expansion of our economy. These include hastening capital recovery through new systems of accelerated depreciation, removing the tax burden on equity financing to encourage more capital investment, ending the unfair double taxation of dividends, and supporting proposals to enhance the ability of our working and other citizens to own "a piece of the action" through stock ownership. When balanced by expenditure reductions, the personal exemption should be raised to $1,000.

AGRICULTURE AND RURAL DEVELOPMENT

The bounty of our farms is so plentiful that we may tend to forget what an amazing production achievement this really is. Each American farmer and rancher produces enough food to feed over 56 people—a three-fold increase in productivity in 20 years.

Rural America must be maintained as a rewarding place to live. To accomplish this, our rural areas are entitled to services comparable to their urban neighbors, such as water and sewer systems, improved electricity and telephone service, adequate transportation, available and adequate financial credit, and employment opportunities which will allow small farmers to supplement their incomes.

Farm exports have continued to expand under the policies of this Republican Administration from a low of $6 billion in 1968, the last Democrat year, to $22 billion in 1975. These exports are not giveaway programs; most are earning dollars from the marketplaces of the world, establishing a favorable balance of trade and a higher standard of living for all. Through our farm exports we fight the problem of world hunger, especially with the humanitarian Food for Peace Program (Public Law 480) of the Eisenhower Administration and the Republican-controlled Congress of 1954.

Republican farm policy has permitted farmers to use their crop land fully. We are at last moving toward making effective use of our superb resources. Net farm income from 1972 through 1975 averaged $26 billion, more than double the average of the 1960's. Government should not dictate to the productive men and women who work the land. To assure this, we support the continuation of the central principles of the Agricultural Act of 1973, with adjustments of target prices and loan levels to reflect increased production costs.

We oppose government-controlled grain reserves,

just as we oppose federal regulations that are unrealistic in farm practices, such as those imposed by the Occupational Safety and Health Administration (OSHA) and the Environmental Protection Agency (EPA).

We urge prompt action by Congress in amending the Grain Inspection Act to strengthen the present inspection system and restore its integrity.

We firmly believe that when the nation asks our farmers to go all out to produce as much as possible for world-wide markets, the government should guarantee them unfettered access to those markets. Our farmers should not be singled out by export controls. Also, when a foreign nation subsidizes its farm exports, our farmers deserve protection against such unfair practices. The federal government should assure that foreign imported commodities are equal in quality to our domestic commodities. Nations from whom we buy commodities should not be allowed to circumvent import restriction laws, such as the Meat Import Quota Act of 1964.

We recognize the importance of the multilateral trade negotiations now in progress and urge our representatives to obtain the most beneficial agreements for our farmers and the nation's economy.

In order to assure the consumers of America an uninterrupted source of food, it is necessary to pass labor relations legislation which is responsive to the welfare of workers and to the particular needs of food production. Such legislation should recognize the need to prevent work stoppages during the critical harvest periods.

We must help farmers protect themselves from drought, flood and other natural disasters through a system of all-risk crop insurance through federal government reinsurance of private insurance companies combined with the existing disaster payment program.

As in 1972, we urge prompt passage of the Republican-sponsored legislation now pending in Congress which will increase the estate tax exemption to $200,000, allow valuation of farm property on a current use basis and provide for extension of the time of payment in the case of farms and small businesses. This overdue estate and gift tax legislation must be approved this year. We favor a liberalized marital deduction and oppose capital gains tax at death.

Innovations in agriculture need to be encouraged by expanding research programs including new pest and predator control measures, and utilization of crops as a new energy resource. If we expect our farmers to produce an abundant food supply, they must have all the energy they need to produce, market and process their crops and livestock.

We continue to support farmer cooperatives, including rural electric and telephone cooperatives, in their efforts to improve services to their members. We support the Capper–Volstead Act.

We believe that non-farm corporations and tax-loss farming should be prevented from unfairly competing against family farms, which we support as the preferred method of farm organization.

Since farmers are practicing conservationists, they should not be burdened with unrealistic environmental regulations. We are concerned about regulations issued by the Army Corps of Engineers that will regulate all "routine" agricultural and forestry activities on "all" our waters and wetland, and support legislation to exempt routine farming operations from these requirements. The adjudication of water rights should be a matter of state determination.

SMALL BUSINESS

Small business, so vital to our economic system, is free enterprise in its purest sense. It holds forth opportunity to the individual, regardless of race or sex, to fulfill the American dream. Small businesses are the base of our economy and its main source of strength. Some 9.6 million small firms generate 55 percent of our private employment or the livelihood of over 100 million Americans. Yet while small businesses have a unique place in our society, they also have unique problems that government must address. Therefore, we recommend that the Small Business Administration (SBA):

Assure adequate financing to those credit worthy firms that cannot now obtain funds through conventional channels;

Include the proper mix of loan programs to meet the needs of the many different types of firms that constitute the American small business community;

Serve as an aggressive advocate for small business and provide procurement, management and technological assistance.

For survival, small businesses must have relief from the overwhelming burden placed on them by many regulatory bodies. Paperwork proliferation has grown out of control, and small business is not equipped to deal with this aggravation.

The present tax structure does not allow small firms to generate enough capital to grow and create jobs. Estate taxes need liberalization to benefit the family business in the same manner as the family farm.

Encouraging investment in small businesses through more equitable tax treatment remains the best and least expensive method of creating productive employment.

The Republican Party, recognizing that small and independent business is the backbone of the American competitive system, pledges itself to strengthen this vital institution.

ANTITRUST

The Republican Party believes in and endorses the concept that the American economy is traditionally dependent upon fair competition in the marketplace. To assure fair competition, antitrust laws must treat all segments of the economy equally.

Vigorous and equitable enforcement of antitrust laws heightens competition and enables consumers to obtain the lowest possible price in the marketplace.

BUREAUCRATIC OVERREGULATION

We believe that the extent of federal regulation and bureaucratic interference in the lives of the American people must be reduced. The programs and activities of the federal government should be required to meet strict tests of their usefulness and effectiveness.

In particular, we consider essential an analysis of the extensive growth of laws and regulations governing production processes and conditions and standards for consumer products, so as to determine whether the services and benefits the American people receive are worth the price they are paying for these services in higher taxes and consumer prices.

We are intensely aware of the need to protect our environment and provide safe working conditions in American industry, while at the same time preventing the loss of jobs and the closing of small businesses through unrealistic or overrigorous government regulations. We support a balanced approach that considers the requirements of a growing economy and provides jobs for American workers.

The average businessman and employer is being overwhelmed by government-required paperwork. We support legislation to control and reduce the burden of federal paperwork, particularly that generated by the Internal Revenue Service and the Census Bureau.

GOVERNMENT THAT WORKS

We believe that Americans are fed up with and frustrated by national government that makes great promises and fails to deliver. We are! We think that Democrat Congresses—in control for 40 out of the last 44 years—are the grand masters of this practice. We think that a national government grown so big that the left hand doesn't know what the right hand is doing has caused the condition we are in.

What we now have is a government organization that doesn't make any sense. It has not developed by design. It just grew—by whim, bureaucratic fighting, and the caving in of Democrat Congresses to special-interest demands. So today we find that nine federal departments and twenty independent agencies are involved in education; seven departments and eight agencies in health; federal recreation areas are administered by six agencies in three departments; and so forth.

What we need is a top-to-bottom overhaul. Two high-level presidential commissions under two Presidents—one a Democrat, one a Republican—have investigated and come up with the same answer: There must be functional realignment of government, instead of the current arrangement by subject areas or constituencies.

We want federal domestic departments to reflect the major purposes of government, such as natural resources, human resources, community development and economic affairs. Unfortunately, the Democrat Congress has refused to address this problem. Now we insist that attention must be paid.

Too often in the past, we have been content with organizational or procedural solutions to complex economic and social regulatory problems. We should no longer accept rhetoric as a substitute for concrete results. The President has proposed to Congress the Agenda for Government Reform Act, which would guarantee the systematic re-examination and reform of all federal regulatory activities within the next four years. This legislation requires Congress and the President to agree to undertake an exhaustive reassessment of the combined effects of all government regulations, and it requires them to adhere to a disciplined timetable to assure annual results. The American people deserve no less. Every agency of government must be made efficient, and every government regulation should be subjected to cost–benefit analysis. The Occupational Safety and Health Administration (OSHA) is a typical example of a well-intentioned regulatory effort which has imposed large costs but has not solved our problems.

The beauty of America's original concept of government was its diversity, the belief that different purposes are best served by governments at different levels. In our lifetime, however, Democrat Congresses have allowed this system to become warped and over-nationalized. As powers have flowed to Washington, the ability to attend to our problems has often dried up in our communities and states. This trend must be reversed. Local government is simply accountable to the people, and local people are perfectly capable of making decisions.

We reaffirm the long-standing principle of the Republican Party that the best government is the one closest to the people. It is less costly, more accountable, and more responsive to the people's needs. Our confidence in the people of this nation was demonstrated by initiating the Revenue Sharing Program. To date, $30 billion of federal tax dollars have been returned to the states and localities. This program is administered with fewer than 100 people and a computer. Revenue Sharing is an effort to reverse the trend toward centralization. Revenue Sharing must continue without unwarranted federal strictures and regulations.

As a further step in this direction, the Republicans in Congress promoted the new concept of federal block grants to localities for much greater flexibility. Under block grants, federal funds can be tailored by the states and localities to the wishes of each community. There are now two block grant programs—in community development and employment training. Block grant programs should be extended to replace many existing categorical health, education, child nutrition and social services programs. The Democrat Congress stands guilty of failing to enact these vital reforms. Our ultimate goal is to restore taxing and spending to the local level.

The Republican Party has always believed that the proper role of government is to do only those things which individuals cannot do for themselves. We encourage individual initiative and oppose the trend of ever expanding government programs which is destroying the volunteer spirit in America. We firmly believe that community involvement is essential to the development of effective solutions to the problems confronting our country.

While we oppose a uniform national primary, we encourage the concept of regional presidential primaries, which would group those states which voluntarily agree to have presidential primaries in a geographic area on a common date.

We encourage full participation in our electoral process. We further recognize the sanctity and value of the ballot. In that regard, we oppose "federal post card registration." The possibilities of fraud are inherent in registration by mail. Such possibilities could not only cheapen our ballot, but in fact threaten the entire electoral process.

Control of the United States Congress by the Democrat Party for 40 of the past 44 years has resulted in a system dominated by powerful individuals and riddled with corruption. Recent events have demonstrated an unwillingness and inability by the Democrat Party to cleanse itself. Selective morality has been the order of the day. Positive Republican initiatives have languished in Democrat-controlled Congressional Committees while business as usual has continued in Washington. The American people demand and deserve reform of the United States Congress. We offer these proposals of far-reaching reform:

Repeal of legislation which permits automatic increases in the salaries of Members of Congress, congressional staffs, and official expense allowances. Public accountability demands that Members publicly vote on increases of the expenses of their office. Members' salary increases should not become effective until a new Congress is elected.

Elimination of proxy voting which allows Members to record votes in Committee without being present for the actual deliberations or vote on a measure.

Elimination of Democrat Caucus rules which allow a Party to bind its Members' votes on legislation. Each Member of Congress represents his constituency and must be free to vote in accordance with the dictates of his constituency and individual conscience.

A complete audit by the General Accounting Office of all congressional allowances and appropriate disciplinary measures for those who have violated the public trust.

Full public disclosure of financial interests by Members and divestiture of those interests which present conflicts of interest.

Changes in the House rules which would allow a House majority to require the House Ethics Committee to conduct an investigation into alleged misconduct by any Member of Congress if the Committee refuses to act on its own.

Quarterly publication of names, titles and salaries of all Congressional employees.

Improved lobby disclosure legislation so that the people will know how much money is being spent to influence public officials.

Citizens are demanding the end to the rapid and wasteful increase in the size of Washington government. All steps must be taken to insure that unnecessary federal agencies and programs are eliminated and that Congress carefully scrutinize the total budget of each agency. If it is determined that sunset laws and zero-based budgeting can accomplish these ends, then they will have our support. Washington programs must be made as cost-effective as those in the states and localities. Among the many serious complaints that we wish to register on behalf of the American people is the poor operation of the United States Postal Service.

We note the low respect the public has for Congress—a Democrat-controlled institution—and wonder how the Democrats can possibly honor their pledge to reform government when they have utterly failed to reform Congress.

A SAFE AND JUST SOCIETY

Every American has a right to be protected from criminals. Violence has no place in our land. A society that excuses crime will eventually fall victim to it. The American people have been subjected to an intolerable wave of violent crime.

The victim of a crime should be treated with compassion and justice. The attacker must be kept from harming others. Emphasis must be on protecting the innocent and punishing the guilty. Prevention of crime is its best deterrent and should be stressed.

Fighting crime is—and should be—primarily a local responsibility. We support the continuation of the federal help given through the Law Enforcement Assistance Administration (LEAA) to law enforcement officials in our states, counties and municipalities. Each state should have the power to decide whether it wishes to impose the death penalty for certain crimes. All localities are urged to tighten their bail practices and to review their sentencing and parole procedures.

The federal criminal code should include automatic and mandatory minimum sentences for persons committing offenses under federal jurisdiction that involve the use of a dangerous weapon; that involve exceptionally serious crimes, such as trafficking in hard drugs, kidnapping and aircraft hijacking; and that involve injuries committed by repeat offenders.

The work presently being done to tighten the antiobscenity provisions of the criminal code has our full support. Since the jurisdiction of the federal government in this field is limited to interstate commerce and the mails, we urge state and local governments to assume a major role in limiting the distribution and availability of obscene materials.

We support the right of citizens to keep and bear arms. We oppose federal registration of firearms. Mandatory sentences for crimes committed with a lethal weapon are the only effective solution to this problem.

Sure and swift justice demands additional judges, United States Attorneys and other court workers. The Democrat Congress has created no new federal judgeships since 1970; we deplore this example of playing politics with the justice system.

Drug abuse is not simply a health problem, but also a very real law enforcement concern and a problem of worldwide dimension. Controlling drug abuse calls for the ratification of the existing international treaty on synthetic drugs, increased emphasis on preventing the diversion of amphetamines and barbiturates into illegal markets, and intensive effort to keep drugs out of this country. Heroin continues to come across our borders. Drug enforcement agents and international cooperation must cut off this supply. We say: Treat the addicts, but, at the same time, remove the pushers from the street and give them mandatory sentences.

Juveniles now account for almost half the arrests for serious crimes—murder, rape, robbery and aggravated assault. The cost of school violence and vandalism is estimated at $600 million annually, about what is spent on textbooks. Primary responsibility for raising our children, instilling proper values and thus preventing juvenile delinquency lies with the family, not the government. Yet when families fail, local law enforcement authorities must respond. Law enforcement block grant funds can be used by states in correcting and preventing juvenile delinquency. The LEAA should promote additional research in this area.

The structure of the family must be strengthened. All enterprises have to be encouraged to find *more* jobs for young people. A youth differential must be included in the minimum wage law. Citizen action should let the television industry know that we want it to curb violence in programming because of its effect on our youth.

The criminal justice system must be more vigilant in preventing rape, eliminating discrimination against the victim and dealing with the offenders.

States should recognize that antiquated and overcrowded prisons are not conducive to rehabilitation. A high priority of prison reform should be to help the young first-time offender. There should be adequate separation of young adult offenders, more relevant prison industries, better counseling, community-based alternatives and more help in getting a job for the offender who has served his or her time.

Terrorism—both domestic and international—must be stopped. Not only must the strongest steps be taken in the United States, but collective action must come from all nations. Deterring every form of hijacking calls for sanctions against countries that aid terrorists. The world community should take appropriate action to deal with terrorist organizations. We applaud the daring rescue by Israel of innocent civilian hostages who were kidnapped by terrorists. While we regret that loss of life was involved, the courageous manner in which the hostages were freed speaks eloquently to our abhorrence of world bandits.

THE RIGHT TO PRIVACY

Liberty depends in great measure on the privacy that each American retains.

We are alarmed by Washington's growing collection of information. The number of federal data banks is now estimated at between 800 and 900 and more than 50 agencies are involved. We question the need for all these computers to be storing the records of our lives. Safeguards must protect us against this information being misused or disclosed. Major changes, for example, are needed to maintain the confidentiality of tax returns and Social Security records.

Recent Supreme Court decisions have held that an individual has no constitutional right to the privacy of records held in banks or other depository institutions and that they can be readily obtained by law enforcement agencies without a person's consent or knowledge. Law enforcement authorities must be able to pursue criminal violators, yet at the same time, there should be reasonable controls imposed to protect the privacy of law-abiding citizens. We support legislation, now pending, to assure this protection.

Too many government records, on the other hand, are unnecessarily classified. Congress and the Executive should devise a more reasonable system for classifying and handling government information.

The President's achievements in protecting privacy are unequalled by past administrations and must be built upon in the future. We particularly note changes in federal record-keeping systems, the appointment of the Commission on the CIA, the reorganization of the intelligence community and restriction of White House access to income tax returns.

THE AMERICAN FAMILY

Families must continue to be the foundation of our nation.

Families—not government programs—are the best way to make sure our children are properly nurtured, our elderly are cared for, our cultural and spiritual heritages are perpetuated, our laws are observed and our values are preserved.

If families fail in these vitally important tasks, there is little the government, no matter how well intentioned, can do to remedy the results. Schools cannot educate children adequately if families are not supportive of the learning process. Law enforcement authorities are nearly helpless to curb juvenile delinquency without family cooperation in teaching young people respect for property and laws. Neither medicine nor school feeding programs can replace the family's ability to provide the basis for good health. Isolation from meaningful family contact makes it virtually impossible for the elderly to avoid loneliness or dependence. The values of hard work and responsibility start with the family.

As modern life brings changes in our society, it also puts stresses on families trying to adjust to new realities while maintaining cherished values. Economic uncertainty, unemployment, housing difficulties, women's and men's concerns with their changing and often conflicting roles, high divorce rates, threatened neighborhoods and schools, and public scandal all create a hostile atmosphere that erodes family structures and family values. Thus it is imperative that our government's programs, actions, officials and social welfare institutions never be allowed to jeopardize the family. We fear the government may be powerful enough to destroy our families; we know that it is not powerful enough to replace them.

Because of our concern for family values, we affirm our beliefs, stated elsewhere in this Platform, in many elements that will make our country a more hospitable environment for family life—neighborhood schools; educational systems that include and are responsive to parents' concerns; estate tax changes to establish more realistic exemptions which will minimize disruption of already bereaved families; a position on abortion that values human life; a welfare policy to encourage rather than discourage families to stay together and seek economic independence; a tax system that assists rather than penalizes families with elderly members, children in day care or children in college; economic and employment policies that stop the shrinkage of our dollars and stimulate the creation of jobs so that families can plan for their economic security.

EDUCATION

Our children deserve quality education.

We believe that segregated schools are morally wrong and unconstitutional. However, we oppose forced busing to achieve racial balances in our schools. We believe there are educational advantages for children in attending schools in their own neighborhoods and that the Democrat-controlled Congress has failed to enact legislation to protect this concept. The racial composition of many schools results from decisions by people about where they choose to live. If Congress continues to fail to act, we would favor consideration of an amendment to the Constitution forbidding the assignment of children to schools on the basis of race.

Our approach is to work to eradicate the root causes of segregated schools, such as housing discrimination and gerrymandered school districts. We must get on with the education of all our children.

Throughout our history, the education of our children has been a community responsibility. But now federal categorical grant programs pressure local school districts into substituting Washington-dictated priorities for their own. Local school administrators and school boards are being turned into bookkeepers for the federal government. Red tape and restrictive regulations stifle imagination and creativity. We are deeply concerned about the decline in the performance of our schools and the decline in public confidence in them.

We favor consideration of tax credits for parents making elementary and secondary school tuition payments.

Local communities wishing to conduct nonsectarian prayers in their public schools should be able to do so. We favor a constitutional amendment to achieve this end.

We propose consolidating federal categorical grant programs into block grants and turning the money over to the states to use in accordance with their own needs and priorities and with minimum bureaucratic controls. A single program must preserve the funding that is directed at the needs of such special groups as the handicapped and the disadvantaged.

Responsibility for education, particularly on the elementary and secondary levels, belongs to local communities and parents. Intrusion by the federal government must be avoided. Bureaucratic control of schools by Washington has the potential for destruction of our educational system by taking more and more decisions away from parents and local school authorities. Financial dependence on the federal government inevitably leads to greater centralization of authority. We believe, therefore, that a study should be authorized concerning funding of elementary and secondary education, coupled with a study regarding return to the states of equivalent revenue to compensate for any loss in present levels of federal funding.

Unless steps are taken immediately, soaring prices will restrict a college education to the rich and those poor enough to qualify now for government aid. Federal higher education policy should continue to focus on financial aid for needy individuals, but because the financial ability to go to college is fast slipping out of the grasp of middle-income families, more realistic eligibility guidelines for student aid are essential.

Government interference in the management of colleges and universities must be stopped. Federal support to assist in meeting the grave financial problems of higher education should be forthcoming, but such funds should never be used as devices for imposing added controls.

Diversity in education has great value. Public schools and non-public schools should share in education funds on a constitutionally acceptable basis. Private colleges and universities should be assisted to maintain healthy competition and to enrich diversity. The cost of expanding public campuses can be kept down if existing private institutions are helped to accommodate our student population.

We favor continued special federal support for vocational education.

HEALTH

Every American should have access to quality health care at an affordable price.

The possibility of an extended illness in a family is a frightening prospect, but, if it does happen, a person should at least be protected from having it wipe out lifetime savings. Catastrophic expenses incurred from major illnesses and accidents affect only a small percentage of Americans each year, but for those people, the financial burden can be devastating. We support extension of catastrophic illness protection to all who cannot obtain it. We should utilize our private health insurance system to assure adequate protection for those who do not have it. Such an approach will eliminate the red tape and high bureaucratic costs inevitable in a comprehensive national program.

The Republican Party opposes compulsory national health insurance.

Americans should know that the Democrat Platform, which offers a government-operated and financed "comprehensive national health insurance system with universal and mandatory coverage," will increase federal government spending by more than $70 billion in its first full year. Such a plan could require a personal income tax increase of approximately 20 percent. We oppose this huge, new health insurance tax. Moreover, we do not believe that the federal government can administer effectively the Democrats' cradle-to-grave proposal.

The most effective, efficient and economical method to improve health care and extend its availability to all is to build on the present health delivery and insurance system, which covers nine out of every ten Americans.

A coordinated effort should be mounted immediately to contain the rapid increase in health care costs by all available means, such as development of healthier life styles through education, improved preventive care, better distribution of medical manpower, emphasis on out-of-hospital services and elimination of wasteful duplication of medical services.

We oppose excessive intrusions from Washington in the delivery of health care. We believe in preserving the privacy that should exist between a patient and a physician, particularly in regard to the confidentiality of medical records.

Federal health programs should be consolidated into a single grant to each state, where possible, thereby allowing much greater flexibility in setting local priorities. Our rural areas, for example, have different health care delivery needs than our cities. Federal laws and regulations should respect these differences and make it possible to respond differently to differing needs. Fraud in Medicare and Medicaid programs should be exposed and eliminated.

We need a comprehensive and equitable approach to the subject of mental health. Such a program should focus on the prevention, treatment and care of mental illness. It should cover all aspects of the interrelationships between emotional illness and other developmental disabilities that seek to remove us from the dark ages in these areas.

Alcoholism and drug abuse, growing problems in America today, should receive the utmost attention.

While we support valid medical and biological research efforts which can produce life-saving results, we oppose any research on live fetuses. We are also opposed to any legislation which sanctions ending the life of any patient.

CHILD NUTRITION

Every child should have enough to eat. Good nutrition is a prerequisite of a healthy life. We must focus our resources on feeding needy children. The present school lunch programs provide a 20 percent subsidy to underwrite the meals of children from middle- and upper-income families.

The existing 15 child nutrition programs should be consolidated into one program, administered by the states, and concentrated on those children truly in need. Other federal programs should insure that low-income people will be able to purchase a nutritionally adequate food supply.

EQUAL RIGHTS AND ENDING DISCRIMINATION

Roadblocks must be removed that may prevent Americans from realizing their full potential in society. Unfair discrimination is a burden that intolerably weighs morally, economically and politically upon a free nation.

While working to eradicate discriminatory practices, every citizen should be encouraged to take pride in and foster the cultural heritage that has been passed on from previous generations. Almost every American traces ancestry from another country; this cultural diversity gives strength to our national heritage.

There must be vigorous enforcement of laws to assure equal treatment in job recruitment, hiring, promotion, pay, credit, mortgage access and housing. The way to end discrimination, however, is not by resurrecting the much discredited quota system and attempting to cloak it in an aura of new respectability. Rather, we must provide alternative means of assisting the victims of past discrimination to realize their full worth as American citizens.

Wiping out past discrimination requires continued emphasis on providing educational opportunities for minority citizens, increasing direct and guaranteed loans to minority business enterprises, and affording qualified minority persons equal opportunities for government positions at all levels.

Women

Women, who comprise a numerical majority of the population, have been denied a just portion of our nation's rights and opportunities. We reaffirm our pledge to work to eliminate discrimination in all areas for reasons of race, color, national origin, age, creed or sex and to enforce vigorously laws guaranteeing women equal rights.

The Republican Party reaffirms its support for ratification of the Equal Rights Amendment. Our Party was the first national party to endorse the E.R.A. in 1940.

We continue to believe its ratification is essential to insure equal rights for all Americans. In our 1972 Platform, the Republican Party recognized the great contributions women have made to society as homemakers and mothers, as contributors to the community through volunteer work, and as members of the labor force in careers. The Platform stated then, and repeats now, that the Republican Party "fully endorses the principle of equal rights, equal opportunities and equal responsibilities for women." The Equal Rights Amendment is the embodiment of this principle and therefore we support its swift ratification.

The question of abortion is one of the most difficult and controversial of our time. It is undoubtedly a moral and personal issue but it also involves complex questions relating to medical science and criminal justice. There are those in our Party who favor complete support for the Supreme Court decision which permits abortion demand. There are others who share sincere convictions that the Supreme Court's decision must be changed by a constitutional amendment prohibiting all abortions. Others have yet to take a position, or they have assumed a stance somewhere in between polar positions.

We protest the Supreme Court's intrusion into the family structure through its denial of the parents' obligation and right to guide their minor children. The Republican Party favors a continuance of the public dialogue on abortion and supports the efforts of those who seek enactment of a constitutional amendment to restore protection of the right to life for unborn children.

The Social Security System, our federal tax laws, and unemployment and disability programs currently discriminate against women and often work against married couples as well. These inequities must be corrected. We recognize that special support must be given to the increasing number of women who have assumed responsibility as the heads of households while also being wage earners. Programs for job training, counseling and other services should be established to help them attain their dual role in society.

We reiterate the pledges elsewhere in this platform of support for child care assistance, part-time and flexible-time work that enables men and women to combine employment and family responsibilities, estate tax reform, small business assistance for women, rape prevention and elimination of discriminatory housing practices.

Ethnic Americans

Ethnic Americans have enriched this nation with their hard work, self-reliance and respect for the rights and needs of others. Ethnic groups reaching our shores at various times have given our country its unique identity and strength among the nations of the world. We recognize and value the contributions of Ethnic Americans to our free and democratic society.

Hispanic-Americans

When language is a cause for discrimination, there must be an intensive educational effort to enable Spanish-speaking students to become fully proficient in English while maintaining their own language and cultural heritage. Hispanic-Americans must not be treated as second-class citizens in schools, employment or any other aspect of life just because English is not their first language. Hispanic-Americans truly believe that individual integrity must be paramount; what they want most from government and politics is the opportunity to participate fully. The Republican Party has and always will offer this opportunity.

Indians and Alaska Natives

We have a unique commitment to Native Americans; we pledge to continue to honor our trust relationship with them, and we reaffirm our federal Indian policy of self-determination without termination. This means moving smoothly and quickly away from federal domination to elective participation and communication by Indians in the political process and in the planning, content and administration of federal programs. We shall pursue our joint effort with Indian leaders to assist in the orderly development of Indian and native-owned resources and to continue to attack the severe health, education and unemployment problems which exist among Indians and Alaska Natives.

Puerto Rico, the District of Columbia and the Territories

The principle of self-determination also governs our positions on Puerto Rico and the District of Columbia as it has in past platforms. We again support statehood for Puerto Rico, if that is the people's choice in a referendum, with full recognition within the concept of a multicultural society of the citizens' right to retain their Spanish language and traditions; and support giving the District of Columbia voting representation in the United States Senate and House of Representatives and full home rule over those matters that are purely local.

We will continue to negotiate with the Congress of Micronesia on the future political status of the Trust Territories of the Pacific Islands to meet the mutual interests of both parties. We support a plebiscite by the people of American Samoa on whether they wish to elect a territorial governor. We favor whatever action is necessary to permit American citizens resident in Guam, Puerto Rico and the Virgin Islands to vote for President and Vice President in national elections. With regard to Guam and the Virgin Islands, we urge an increased degree of self-sufficiency and support maximum broadening of self-government.

Responsibilities

Finally, the most basic principle of all: Achievement and preservation of human rights in our society is based on the willing acceptance by millions of Americans of their responsibilities as free citizens. Instead of viewing government programs with ever increasing expectations, we must readily assume the obligations of wage-earners, taxpayers and supporters of our government and laws. This is often forgotten, and so it is appropriate to remind ourselves in this Platform that this is why our society works.

HANDICAPPED CITIZENS

Handicapped persons must be admitted into the mainstream of our society.

Too often the handicapped population of the nation—over 30 million men, women and children—has been denied the rights taken for granted by other citizens. Time after time, the paths are closed to the handicapped in education, employment, transportation, health care, housing, recreation, insurance, polling booths and due process of law. National involvement is necessary to correct discrimination in these areas. Individual incentive alone cannot do it.

We pledge continued attention to the problems caused by barriers in architecture, communication, transportation and attitudes. In addition, we realize that to deny education and employment simply because of an existing disability runs counter to our accepted belief in the free enterprise system and forces the handicapped to be overly dependent on others. Similarly, the denial of equal access to credit and to acquisition of venture capital on the basis of a handicap or other disability conflicts with Republican philosophy. We advocate the elimination of needless barriers for all handicapped persons.

WORKING AMERICANS

Free collective bargaining remains the best way to insure that American workers receive a fair price for their labors.

The special problems of collective bargaining in state and local government should be addressed at those levels. Washington should not impose its standards on local governments. While we oppose strikes by public employees, we recognize that states have the right to permit them if they choose.

Union membership as a condition of employment has been regulated by state law under Section 14 (b) of the Taft–Hartley Act. This basic right should continue to be determined by the states. We oppose strikes by federal employees, the unionization of our military forces and the legalization of common-situs picketing.

Employees of the federal government should not engage in partisan politics. The Civil Service System must remain non-partisan and non-political. The Hatch Act now protects federal employees; we insist that it be uniformly administered.

Among the rights that are the entitlement of every American worker is the right to join a union—large, small or independent; the right to be protected against racial discrimination and misuse of dues; the right to union elections that are fair and democratic; and the right to be assured of ultimately receiving his or her promised pension benefits.

Safe and healthful working conditions are goals of utmost importance. We should expect the Occupational Safety and Health Administration to help employers, particularly in small businesses, comply with the law, and we will support legislation providing on-site consultation.

There should be considerable concern over the presence of several million illegal aliens in the country who fill jobs that otherwise would be available to American workers. We support increased efforts to deal more effectively with this problem and favor legislation prohibiting employers from knowingly hiring illegal aliens. The Democrat leaders in Congress have systematically killed every attempt to debate this legislation in recent years.

Increased part-time and flexible-hour work should be encouraged wherever feasible. In keeping with our belief in family life, we want to expand more opportunities for men and women to combine family responsibilities and employment.

WELFARE REFORM

The work of all Americans contributes to the strength of our nation, and all who are able to contribute should be encouraged to do so.

In every society there will be some who cannot work, often through no fault of their own. The measure of a country's compassion is how it treats the least fortunate.

We appreciate the magnificent variety of private charitable institutions which have developed in the United States.

The Democrat-controlled Congress has produced a jumble of degrading, dehumanizing, wasteful, overlapping and inefficient programs failing to assist the needy poor. A systematic and complete overhaul of the welfare system should be initiated immediately.

The following goals should govern the reform of the welfare system:

1. Provide adequate living standards for the truly needy;
2. End welfare fraud and prevent it in the future with emphasis on removing ineligible recipients from the welfare rolls, tightening food stamp eligibility requirements, and ending aid to illegal aliens and the voluntarily unemployed;
3. Strengthen work requirements, particularly directed at the productive involvement of ablebodied persons in useful community work projects;
4. Provide educational and vocational incentives to allow recipients to become self-supporting;
5. Better coordinate federal efforts with local and state social welfare agencies and strengthen local and state administrative functions.

We oppose federalizing the welfare system; local levels of government are most aware of the needs of their communities. Consideration should be given to a range of options in financing the programs to assure that state and local responsibilities are met. We also oppose the guaranteed annual income concept or any programs that reduce the incentive to work.

Those features of the present law, particularly the food stamp program, that draw into assistance programs people who are capable of paying for their own needs should be corrected. The humanitarian purpose of such programs must not be corrupted by eligibility loopholes. Food stamp program reforms proposed by Republicans in Congress would accomplish the twin goals of directing resources to those most in need and streamlining administration.

We must never forget that unemployment compensation is insurance, not a welfare program. It should be redesigned to assure that working is always more beneficial than collecting unemployment benefits. The benefits should help most the hard-core unemployed. Major efforts must be encouraged through the private sector to speed up the process of finding jobs for those temporarily out of work.

OLDER AMERICANS

Older Americans constitute one of our most valuable resources.

Families should be supported in trying to take care of their elderly. Too often government laws and policies contribute to the deterioration of family life. Our tax laws, for example, permit a contribution to a charitable institution that might care for an elderly parent, but offer little or no incentive to provide care in the home. If an elderly parent relinquishes certain assets and enters a nursing home, the parent may qualify for full Medicaid coverage, but if parents live with their children, any Supplemental Security income benefit for which they are eligible may be reduced. Incentives must be written into law to encourage families to care for their older members.

Along with loneliness and ill health, older Americans are deeply threatened by inflation. The costs of the basic necessities of life—food, shelter, clothing, health care—have risen so drastically as to reduce the ability of many older persons to subsist with any measure of dignity. In addition to our program for protecting against excessive costs of long-term illness, nothing will be as beneficial to the elderly as the effect of this Platform's proposals on curbing inflation.

The Social Security benefits are of inestimable importance to the well-being and financial peace of mind of most older Americans. We will not let the Social Security system fail. We will work to make the Social Security system actuarily sound. The Social Security program must not be turned into a welfare system, based on need rather than contributions. The cost to employers for Social Security contributions must not be raised to the point where they will be unable to afford contributions to employees' private pension programs. We will work for an increase in the earned income ceiling or its elimination so that, as people live longer, there will not be the present penalty on work. We will also seek to correct those provisions of the system that now discriminate against women and married couples.

Such programs as Foster Grandparents and Senior Companions, which provide income exempt from Social Security limitations, should be continued and extended to encourage senior citizens to continue to be active and involved in society. Appropriate domiciliary care programs should be developed to enable senior citizens to receive such care without losing other benefits to which they may be entitled.

We favor the abolition of arbitrary age levels for mandatory retirement.

The Medicare program must be improved to help

control inflation in health care costs triggered by present regulations.

Other areas of concern to the elderly that need increased attention are home and outpatient care, adequate transportation, nutrition, day care and homemaker care as an alternative to costly institutional treatment.

A nation should be judged by its ability to help make all the years of life as productive and gainful as possible. This nation still has a job to do.

VETERANS

The nation must never forget its appreciation and obligation to those who have served in the armed forces.

Because they bear the heaviest burdens of war, we owe special honor and compensation to disabled veterans and survivors of the war dead.

We are firmly committed to maintaining and improving our Veterans Administration hospital system.

Younger veterans, especially those who served in the Vietnam conflict, deserve education and job and housing loan benefits equivalent to those of World War II and the Korean conflict. Because of our deep and continuing concern for those still listed as Prisoners of War or Missing in Action in Vietnam, the Foreign Policy section of this Republican Platform calls for top-priority actions.

And we must continue to provide for our veterans at their death a final resting place for their remains in a national cemetery and the costs of transportation thereto.

A NATIONAL URBAN STRATEGY

The decay and decline of communities in this country is not just a physical and economic crisis, but is traceable to the decline of a real "sense of community" in our society. Community development cannot be achieved merely by throwing dollars and mortar at our community problems; what must be developed is a new sense of mutual concern and responsibility among all members of a community for its improvement.

We recognize the family, the neighborhood and the private volunteer sector to be the most basic and vital units within our communities and we recognize their central role in revitalizing our communities. We propose a strategy for urban revitalization that both treats our urban areas as social organisms and recognizes that the family is the basic building block in these organisms.

Effectively helping our cities now requires a coordinated National Urban Policy. The cornerstone of this policy must be to curb inflation. This policy must be based on the principle that the levels of government closest to the cities' problems are best able to respond. Thus federal and state assistance to cities and counties should give the greatest flexibility to those directly on the scene, the local elected officials. Such a policy should replace the welter of confusing and often conflicting federal categorical grant programs—the approach of the Democrat Congress—with block grant programs that allow cities and counties to set their own priorities.

Without an urban policy, the Democrat-controlled Congress has created a hodgepodge of programs which have all but destroyed our once vital cities. At the same time, urban crime rates have skyrocketed and the quality and promise of metropolitan education systems have plummeted. All this has happened during the years that the number of federal urban programs has increased almost tenfold: from 45 in 1946 to 435 in 1968; and expenditures have increased 3000 percent; from $1 billion to $30 billion.

The Republican programs of revenue sharing and block grants for community development and manpower have already helped our cities and counties immensely. We favor extension of revenue sharing and the orderly conversion of categorical grants into block grants. When federal assistance programs for general purpose local governments are administered through the states, there should be direct pass-through and effective roles for cities and counties in the planning, allocation and use of the funds.

Federal, state and local government resources combined are not enough to solve our urban problems. The private sector must be the major participant. Economic development is the best way to involve business and industry. Government support should emphasize capital formation and technical assistance for small and minority businesses.

We can bring about a new birth of freedom by following the example of those individuals, organizations and community leaders who have successfully solved specific undesirable conditions and problems through private efforts. Government officials should be aware of these successes in developing new approaches to public problems.

Financial institutions should be encouraged to participate in the financial requirements of urban development. Each institution should recognize its responsibility in promoting and maintaining economic growth and stability in the central cities.

Our urban policies should encourage families and

businesses to improve their neighborhoods by means of participation in neighborhood self-help groups, improving and rehabilitating their homes and businesses, and investing in and managing local businesses. We support the revision of federal business assistance programs to encourage joint efforts by local merchants' associations.

We need a comprehensive approach to plan, develop and implement a variety of programs which take into account the many diverse needs of each neighborhood. The establishment of a National Neighborhood Policy will signal a commitment to the improvement of the quality of our life in our neighborhoods.

We call for an expansion of the President's Committee on Urban Development and Neighborhood Revitalization to include representatives of elected state and local officials and the private sector.

Taken together, the thrust of the proposals in this section and in such related areas as housing, transportation, safety and taxes should contribute significantly to making our cities again pleasant places to live. The Republican National Urban Strategy has been formed in the realization that when the bell tolls for the cities it tolls for all of America.

HOUSING

In the United States today we are the best-housed nation in the history of world civilization. This accomplishment was achieved by a private enterprise system using free market concepts.

All of our citizens should be given the opportunity to live in decent, affordable housing.

We believe that we should continue to pursue the primary goal of expanding housing opportunities for all Americans and we should pursue the companion goal of reducing the degree of direct federal involvement in housing.

To most Americans the American dream is a home of their own. The time has come to face some hard realities, primarily that the greatest impediment to decent and affordable housing is inflation. It logically follows that one effective housing program would be simply to elect a Republican Congress which would balance the federal budget.

To meet the housing needs of this country there must be a continuous, stable and adequate flow of funds for the purpose of real estate mortgages at realistic interest rates.

To continue to encourage home ownership, which now encompasses 64 percent of our families, we support the deductibility of interest on home mortgages and property taxes.

We favor the concept of federal revenue sharing and block grants to reduce the excessive burden of the property tax in financial local government.

We are concerned with the excessive reliance of financing welfare and public school costs primarily by the property tax.

We support inflation-impact studies on governmental regulations, which are inflating housing costs.

Current economic problems and environmental concerns must be balanced in each community by a policy of "Sensible Growth."

We oppose discrimination in housing, whether by individuals or by institutional financing policies.

We urge continued incentives to support the development of low- and moderate-income housing in order to assure the availability of adequate shelter for the less fortunate.

Rehabilitation and preservation of existing housing stock should be given high priority in federal housing policy.

We urge the continuation of the self-help restoration of housing, such as urban homesteading, which is providing housing for low-income families.

TRANSPORTATION

The federal government has a special responsibility to foster those elements of our national transportation system that are essential to foreign and interstate commerce and national defense. In other transportation systems that primarily support local needs, the federal government's responsibility is to encourage the greatest possible decision-making and flexibility on the part of state and local governments to spend funds in ways that make the best sense for each community. Thus all levels of government have an important role in providing a balanced and coordinated transportation network.

In keeping with national transportation goals, the Railroad Revitalization and Regulatory Reform Act of 1976 has begun the task of removing regulatory constraints of the Interstate Commerce Commission on America's ailing railroads. Now we should carefully assess the need to remove many of the regulatory constraints imposed on the nation's airlines and motor carriers. Consumers pay too high a price for the artificial fare and rate structures imposed by federal regulations.

The great Interstate Highway System, initiated by President Eisenhower, has brought new freedom of travel to every American and must be completed and maintained. Our road network should always stress safety through better design as well as bridge maintenance and replacement.

We must also have a safe and efficient aviation system capable of responding to the air transportation needs of the future and of reducing exposure to aircraft noise. This includes airport development, navigational and safety facilities, and the design and adequate staffing of advanced air traffic control systems. In airplane use as in other modes of transportation, the impact on the physical environment must always be a basic consideration in federal decisions and such decisions should also include appraisals of impact on the economy. We deplore unfair treatment of United States airlines under foreign landing regulations.

Research must be continued to find safe, more fuel-efficient automobile engines and airplanes; safer, faster rail service; and more convenient, less expensive urban transportation. Tax policies should be considered which would stimulate the development and installation of new energy sources in transportation, such as railroad electrification.

The disorganization of a Democratic-controlled Congress frustrates the coordination of transportation policy. Currently there are more than 50 congressional subcommittees with independent jurisdiction in the transportation field. This hopelessly disjointed and disorganized approach must be reformed.

In keeping with the local goal setting in transportation, the Republican Party applauds the system under which state and local governments can divert funds from interstate highway mileage not essential to interstate commerce or national defense to other, more pressing community needs, such as urban mass transit.

We support the concept of a surface transportation block grant which would include the various highway and mass transit programs now in existence. This will provide local elected officials maximum flexibility in selecting and implementing the balanced transportation systems best suited to each locality. It will encompass both capital and operating subsidies for urban mass transit. It will eliminate red tape and overregulation. We regret that the Democrat-controlled Congress has not adopted such reform.

ENERGY

In 1973, Americans were shocked to discover that a plentiful supply of energy could no longer be assumed. Unfortunately, the Democrat majority in Congress still has not responded to this clear and urgent warning. The United States is now consuming more imported oil than it was three years ago and our dependence on foreign sources has continued to increase to the point where we now import more than 40 percent of our oil.

One fact should now be clear: We must reduce sharply our dependence on other nations for energy and strive to achieve energy independence at the earliest possible date. We cannot allow the economic destiny and international policy of the United States to be dictated by the sovereign powers that control major portions of the world's petroleum supplies.

Our approach toward energy self-sufficiency must involve both expansion of energy supply and improvement of energy efficiency. It must include elements that insure increased conservation at all levels of our society. It must also provide incentive for the exploration and development of domestic gas, oil, coal and uranium, and for expanded research and development in the use of solar, geothermal, co-generation, solid waste, wind, water, and other sources of energy.

We must use our non-renewable resources wisely while we develop alternative supplies for the future. Our standard of living is directly tied to a continued supply of energy resources. Without an adequate supply of energy, our entire economy will crumble.

Unwise government intervention in the marketplace has caused shortage of supply, unrealistic prices and increased dependence on foreign sources. We must immediately eliminate price controls on oil and newly discovered natural gas in order to increase supply, and to provide the capital that is needed to finance further exploration and development of domestic hydrocarbon reserves.

Fair and realistic market prices will encourage sensible conservation efforts and establish priorities in the use of our resources, which over the long run will provide a secure supply at reasonable prices for all.

The nation's clear and present need is for vast amounts of new capital to finance exploration, discovery, refining, and delivery of currently usable forms of energy, including the use of coal as well as discovery and development of new sources. At this critical time, the Democrats have characteristically resorted to political demagoguery seeking short-term political gain at the expense of the long-term national interest. They object to the petroleum industry making any profit. The petroleum industry is an important segment of our economy and is entitled to reasonable profits to permit further exploration and development.

At the height of the energy crisis, the Republican Administration proposed a strong, balanced energy package directed at both expansion of supply and conservation of energy. The response from the Democrats in Congress was to inhibit expanded production through artificially set price and allocation controls, thereby preventing market forces from working to make energy expansion economically feasible.

Now, the Democrats propose to dismember the American oil industry. We vigorously oppose such divestiture of oil companies—a move which would surely result in higher energy costs, inefficiency and undercapitalization of the industry. Democrats have also proposed that the federal government compete with industry in energy development by creating a national oil company. We totally oppose this expensive, inefficient and wasteful intrusion into an area which is best handled by private enterprise.

The Democrats are playing politics with energy. If they are permitted to continue, we will pay a heavy price in lost energy and lost jobs during the decades ahead.

Immediate removal of counter-productive bureaucratic red tape will eliminate hindrances to the exploration and development of hydrocarbons and other energy resources. We will accelerate development of oil shale reserves, Alaskan petroleum and the leasing of the Outer Continental Shelf, always within the context of preserving the fullest possible protection for the environment. We will reduce complexity and delays involved in siting, licensing and the regulatory procedures affecting power generation facilities and refineries.

Coal, America's most abundant energy resource, is of inestimable value to the American people. It can provide the energy needed to bridge the gap between oil and gas and nuclear and other sources of energy. The uncertainties of governmental regulation regarding the mining, transportation and use of coal must be removed and a policy established which will assure that governmental restraints, other than proper environmental controls, do not prevent the use of coal. Mined lands must be returned to beneficial use.

Uranium offers the best intermediate solution to America's energy crisis. We support accelerated use of nuclear energy processes that have been proven safe. Government research on the use of nuclear energy will be expanded to include perfecting a long-term solution to the problems of nuclear waste.

Among alternative future energy sources, fusion, with its unique potential for supplying unlimited clean energy and the promise of new methods of natural resource recovery, warrants continued emphasis in our national energy research program, and we support measures to assure adequate capital investment in the development of new energy sources.

ENVIRONMENT AND NATURAL RESOURCES

A clean and healthy natural environment is the rightful heritage of every American. In order to preserve this heritage, we will provide for proper development of resources, safeguards for clean air and water, and protection and enhancement of our recreation and scenic areas.

As our environmental sophistication grows, we must more clearly define the role of the federal government in environmental protection.

We believe that it is a national responsibility to support scientific and technological research and development to identify environmental problems and arrive at solutions.

We are in complete accord with the recent Supreme Court decision on air pollution that allows the level of government closest to the problem and the solution to establish and apply appropriate air quality standards.

We are proud of the progress that the current Republican Administration has made toward bringing pollution of water, land and air under control. We will meet the challenges that remain by stepping up efforts to perfect our understanding of pollutants and the means for reducing their effects. Moreover, as the nation develops new energy sources and technologies, we must insure that they meet safe environmental standards.

We renew our commitments to the development of additional water supplies by desalinization, and to more efficient use and re-use of waters currently available.

We are determined to preserve land use planning as a unique responsibility of state and local government.

We take particular pride in the expanded use of the National Park system in recent years, and will provide for continued improvement of the national parks and historic sites.

We support establishment of a Presidential panel, including representatives of environmental groups, industry, the scientific community and the public to assist in the development of national priorities on environmental and energy issues. This panel will hear and consider alternative policy recommendations set forth by all of the interested groups, and then develop solutions that represent the overall public interest on environmental and energy matters.

One of this nation's greatest assets has been our abundant natural resources which have made possible our strong economic and strategic role in the world. We still have a wealth of resources, but they are not of infinite quantity. We must recognize that our material blessings stem from what we grow in the soil, take from the sea, or extract from the ground. We have a responsibility to future generations to conserve our non-renewable natural resources. Consistent with our needs, conservation should remain our national policy.

The vast land holdings of the federal government—

approximately one-third of our nation's area—are the lands from which much of our future production of minerals must come. Public lands must be maintained for multiple use management where such uses are compatible. Public land areas should not be closed to exploration for minerals or for mining without an overriding national interest.

We believe Americans want their resources developed properly, their environment kept clean and their recreational and scenic areas kept intact. We support appropriate measures to achieve these goals.

We also believe that Americans are realistic and recognize that the emphasis on environmental concerns must be brought into balance with the needs for industrial and economic growth so that we can continue to provide jobs for an ever-growing work force.

The United States possesses the most productive softwood forests in the world, as well as extensive hardwood forests. Demands for housing, fuel, paper, chemicals and a multitude of other such needs require that these renewable resources be managed wisely on both public and private forest lands—not only to meet these needs but also to provide for soil conservation, wildlife habitats and recreation.

Recognizing that timber is a uniquely renewable resource, we will use all scientifically sound means to maximize sustained yield, including clear-cutting and replanting where appropriate. We urge the Congress to strengthen the National Forest Service so that it can realize its potential in becoming an effective participant in the reforestation program.

We will support broader use of resource recovery and recycling processes through removal of economic disincentives caused by unnecessary government regulation.

One of the important issues at stake in the United Nations Law of the Sea Conference is access to the mineral resources in and beneath the sea. Technology, developed by United States industry, is at hand which can unlock resources of petroleum, manganese, nickel, cobalt, copper and other minerals. We will safeguard the national interest in development and use of these resources.

SCIENCE AND TECHNOLOGY

Every aspect of our domestic economy and well-being, our international competitive position, and national security is related to our past and present leadership in basic and applied research and the development of our technology. But there can be no complacency about our continued commitment to maintain this leadership position. In the past, most of these accomplishments have been achieved through a unique partner-

ship between government and industry. This must continue and be expanded in the future.

Because our society is so dependent upon the advancement of science and the development of technology, it is one of the areas where there must be central federal policy. We support a national science policy that will foster the public–private partnership to insure that we maintain our leadership role.

The national space program plays a pioneer role in exploring the mysteries of our universe and we support its expansion.

We recognize that only when our technology is fully distributed can it be assimilated and used to increase our productivity and our standard of living. We will continue to encourage young Americans to study science and engineering.

Finally, we support new initiatives to utilize better the recoverable commodities from solid waste materials. We can no longer afford the luxury of a throwaway world. Recycling offers environmental benefits, economic expansion, resource conservation and energy savings. We support a policy which will reward recycling and economic incentives which will encourage its expansion.

ARTS AND HUMANITIES

The arts and humanities offer an opportunity for every American to become a participant in activities that add fullness, expression, challenge and joy to our daily lives. We Republicans consider the preservation of the rich cultural heritages of our various ethnic groups as a priority goal.

During our bicentennial year we have celebrated our anniversary with cultural activities as varied and colorful as our cultural heritage. The Republican Party is proud of its record of support to the arts and humanities during the last eight years. We are committed to steadily increase our support through the National Endowments for the nation's museums, theaters, orchestras, dance, opera and film centers as well as for individual artists and writers.

This upward trend in funding for the National Arts and Humanities Endowments deserves to continue. But Washington's presence should never dominate; it must remain limited to supporting and stimulating the artistic and cultural lives of each community.

We favor continued federal assistance to public broadcasting which provides us with creative educational and cultural alternatives. We recognize that public broadcasting is supported mainly through private sector contributions and commend this policy as the best insurance against political interference.

In 1976, we have seen vivid evidence that America's history lives through the nation. We support the continued commemoration throughout the bicentennial era by all Americans of those significant events between 1776 and 1789 which contributed to the creation of this nation. We support the efforts of both the public and private sectors, working in partnership, for the historic sites and buildings.

We propose safeguarding the rights of performing artists in the copyright laws, providing tax relief to artists who contribute their own talents and art works for public enjoyment, and encouraging the use of one percent of the cost of government buildings for art works.

Much of the support of the arts and humanities comes from private philanthropy. This generosity should be encouraged by government policies that facilitate charitable donations.

FISCAL RESPONSIBILITY

As Republicans, we are proud that in this Platform we have urged tax reductions rather than increased government spending. With firm restraint on federal spending this Platform pledges that its proposals for tax changes—reductions, structural adjustments, differentials, simplifications and job producing incentives—can all be achieved within the balanced federal budgets we also demand as vital to the interests of all Americans. Without such spending restraint, we cannot responsibly cut back taxes. We reaffirm our determination that any net reduction of revenues must be offset by reduced government spending.

FOREIGN POLICY, NATIONAL DEFENSE AND INTERNATIONAL ECONOMIC POLICY

Prologue

The foreign policy of the United States defines the relationships we seek with the world as a whole, with friends and with adversaries. Our policy must be firmly rooted in principle and must clearly express our goals. Our principles cannot be subject to passing whim; they must be true, strong, consistent and enduring.

We pledge a realistic and principled foreign policy designed to meet the needs of the nation in the years ahead. The policies we pursue will require an informed consensus; the basis of that consensus will be the American people, whose most cherished desire is to live in freedom and peace, secure from war or threat of war.

The United States is a world power with worldwide interests and responsibilities. We pledge the continuation of efforts to revitalize our traditional alliances and to maintain close consultation with our friends. International cooperation and collaboration are required because we can achieve neither our own most important objectives nor even our own security in the type of "splendid isolation" which is urged upon us by so many strident voices. The regrettable emergence of neo-isolationism often expressed in Congress and elsewhere is detrimental, we believe, to a sound foreign policy.

The branches of government can and should work together as the necessary prerequisite for a sound foreign policy. We lament the reckless intrusion of one branch into the clear constitutional prerogative of another. Confronted by so many challenges and so many crises, the United States must again speak with one voice, united in spirit and in fact. We reject partisan and ideological quarrels across party lines and urge Democrats to join with us to lay the foundations of a true bipartisan spirit. Let us speak for this country with one voice, so that our policies will not be misunderstood by our allies or our potential adversaries.

Effective policy must rest on premises which are understood and shared, and must be defined in terms of priorities. As the world has changed in a dynamic fashion, so too have our priorities and goals, and so too have the methods of debating and discussing our objectives. When we assumed executive office eight years ago, we found the national security and foreign policy machinery in shambles. Last-minute reactions to crises were the practice. The National Security Council, so effective under President Eisenhower, had fallen into disuse. As an important first step, the National Security Council machinery was streamlined to cope with the problems of the moment and long-range planning. This restored process allows once again the exhaustive consideration of all the options from which a President must choose. Far from stifling internal debate and dissent as had been the practice in the past, Republican leadership now invites and stimulates evaluation of complex issues in an orderly decision-making process.

Republican leadership has also taken steps to report comprehensively its foreign policy and national security objectives. An annual "State of the World" message, designed to increase communication with the people and with Congress, has become a permanent part of Presidential practice.

A strong and effective program of global public

diplomacy is a vital component of United States foreign policy. In an era of instant communications, the world is infinitely and forever smaller, and we must have the capacity to communicate to the world—to inform, to explain and to guard against accidental or willful distortion of United States policies.

Interdependence has become a fact of international life, linking our actions and policies with those of the world at large. The United States should reach out to other nations to enrich that interdependence. Republican leadership has demonstrated that recognition of the ties that bind us to our friends will serve our mutual interests in a creative fashion and will enhance the chances for world peace.

Morality in Foreign Policy

The goal of Republican foreign policy is the achievement of liberty under law and a just and lasting peace in the world. The principles by which we act to achieve peace and to protect the interests of the United States must merit the restored confidence of our people.

We recognize and commend that great beacon of human courage and morality, Alexander Solzhenitsyn, for his compelling message that we must face the world with no illusions about the nature of tyranny. Ours will be a foreign policy that keeps this ever in mind.

Ours will be a foreign policy which recognizes that in international negotiations we must make no undue concessions; that in pursuing detente we must not grant unilateral favors with only the hope of getting future favors in return.

Agreements that are negotiated, such as the one signed in Helsinki, must not take from those who do not have freedom the hope of one day gaining it.

Finally, we are firmly committed to a foreign policy in which secret agreements, hidden from our people, will have no part.

Honestly, openly, and with firm conviction, we shall go forward as a united people to forge a lasting peace in the world based upon our deep belief in the rights of man, the rule of law and guidance by the hand of God.

National Defense

A superior national defense is the fundamental condition for a secure America and for peace and freedom for the world. Military strength is the path to peace. A sound foreign policy must be rooted in a superior defense capability, and both must be perceived as a deterrent to aggression and supportive of our national interests.

The American people expect that their leaders will assure a national defense posture second to none. They know that planning for our national security must be a joint effort by the President and Congress. It cannot be the subject of partisan disputes. It should not be held hostage to domestic political adventurism.

A minimum guarantee to preserve freedom and insure against blackmail and threats in the face of growing Soviet military power requires a period of sustained growth in our defense effort. In constant dollars, the present defense budget will no more than match the defense budget of 1964, the year before a Democrat Administration involved America so deeply in the Vietnam War. In 1975 Soviet defense programs exceeded ours in investment by 85 percent, and exceeded ours in operating costs by 25 percent, and exceeded ours in research and development by 66 percent. The issue is whether our forces will be adequate to future challenges. We say they must be.

We must always achieve maximum value for each defense dollar spent. Along with the elimination of the draft and the creation, under a Republican President, of all-volunteer armed services, we have reduced the personnel requirements for support functions without affecting our basic posture. Today there are fewer Americans in the uniformed services than at any time since the fall of 1950. Substantial economies have been made in weapons procurement and we will continue to act in a prudent manner with our defense appropriations.

Our national defense effort will include the continuation of the major modernization program for our strategic missile and bomber forces, the development of a new intercontinental ballistic missile, a new missile launching submarine force and a modern bomber—the B-1—capable of penetrating the most sophisticated air defenses of the 1980's. These elements will comprise a deterrent of the first order.

We will increase our army to 16 divisions, reinforce our program of producing new tanks and other armored vehicles, and support the development of new, highly accurate precision weapons.

Our Navy, the guarantor of freedom of the seas, must have a major shipbuilding program, with an adequate balance between nuclear and non-nuclear ships. The composition of the fleet must be based on a realistic assessment of the threat we face, and must assure that no adversary will gain naval superiority.

An important modernization program for our tactical air forces is under way. We will require new fighters and interceptor aircraft for the Air Force, Navy and Marines. As a necessary component of our long-range strategy, we will produce and deploy the B-1 bomber in a timely manner, allowing us to retain air superiority.

Consistent with our total force policy, we will maintain strong reserve components.

Our investments in military research and development are of great importance to our future defense capabilities. We must not lose the vital momentum.

With increasing complexity of weapons, lead times for weapons systems are often as long as a decade, requiring careful planning and prudent financial decisions. An outstanding example of this process is the development and deployment of the cruise missile, which incorporates pinpoint precision by means of sophisticated guidance systems and is an exceptionally economical weapon to produce.

Security assistance programs are important to our allies and we will continue to strengthen their efforts at self-defense. The improvement of their capabilities can help to ensure that the world balance is not tipped against us and can also serve to lessen chances for direct U.S. involvement in remote conflicts.

As a vital component of our over-all national security posture, the United States must have the best intelligence system in the world. The effectiveness of the intelligence community must be restored, consonant with the reforms instituted by President Ford. We favor the creation of an independent oversight function by Congress and we will withstand partisan efforts to turn any part of our intelligence system into a political football. We will take every precaution to prevent the breakdown of security controls on sensitive intelligence information endangering the lives of United States officials abroad, or affecting the ability of the President to act expeditiously whenever legitimate foreign policy and defense needs require it.

NATO and Europe

Fundamental to a stable, secure world is the continuation of our traditional alliances. The North Atlantic Treaty Organization (NATO) now approaching the end of its third decade, remains healthy and vigorous.

The threat to our mutual security by a totalitarian power bent on expansion brought 15 nations together. The expression of our collective will to resist resulted in the creation and maintenance of a military deterrent which, while not without occasional strains, has served our vital interests well. Today that threat continues.

We have succeeded in extending our cooperation within NATO and have taken bold new steps in economic cooperation with our partners. Faced with a serious crisis in the energy field following the imposition of the oil boycott, we demonstrated that it was possible to coordinate our joint activities with the other NATO nations.

The economic strength of Western Europe has increased to the point where our NATO partners can now assume a larger share of the common defense; in response to our urging, our allies are demonstrating a greater willingness to do so. This is not the time to recommend a unilateral reduction of American military forces in Europe. We will, however, pursue the balanced reduction of forces in both Western and Eastern Europe, based on agreements which do not jeopardize the security of the Alliance. With our Alliance partners, we affirm that a strong NATO defense, based on a United States military presence, is vital to the defense of Western Europe.

Some of our NATO allies have experienced rapid and dynamic changes. We are encouraged by developments in the Iberian peninsula, where both Portugal and Spain now face more promising futures. Early consideration should be given to Spain's accession to NATO.

At the same time we would view with concern any political developments elsewhere in Europe which are destabilizing to NATO interests. We support the rights of all nations to choose their leaders. Democracy and freedom are best served by ensuring that those fundamental rights are preserved and extended for future generations to choose in freedom.

The difficult problem of Cyprus, which separates our friends in Greece and Turkey, should be addressed and resolved by those two countries. The eastern flank of NATO requires restored cooperation there and, eventually, friendly relations between the two countries.

Republican leadership has strengthened this nation's good relations with the European Economic Community (EEC) in an age of increasing competition and potential irritations. We will maintain and strengthen the excellent relations we have achieved with the EEC.

In the final analysis, the NATO Alliance will be as effective as our will and determination, as well as that of our allies, to support it. The function of collective security is to deter wars and, if necessary, to fight and win those wars not successfully deterred. Our vigilance is especially required during periods of prolonged relaxation of tensions with our adversaries because we cannot permit ourselves to accept words and promises as a substitute for deeds. We are determined that the NATO Alliance shall not be lulled into a false sense of security. It can and must respond vigorously when called upon to act.

Asia and the Pacific

The United States has vital interests in the entire Pacific Basin and those interests lie foremost in Asian tranquility and stability.

The experience of ending direct American involvement in a difficult and costly war initiated during Democrat Administrations has taught us a great deal about how we ought to define our interests in this part of the world. The United States is indisputably a Pacific power. We have sought to express our interests in the area through strengthening existing friendly ties and creating new ones.

Japan will remain the main pillar of our Asian policy. We have helped to provide the framework, over the course of thirty years, for the development of the Japanese economy, which has risen to second place among free world nations. This nation, without natural resources, has maximized its greatest resource, the Japanese people, to achieve one of the world's most significant economic advances. We will continue our policy of close consultation and cooperation with this valued friend. We have succeeded in establishing an exceptional relationship with Japan. Our long-range goals of stability and economic cooperation are identical, forming the essential strength of a relationship which both countries seek actively to deepen.

With respect to the Republic of Korea, a nation with which we have had traditionally close ties and whose economy has grown rapidly in recent years, we shall continue our policy of military and economic assistance. United States troops will be maintained in Korea so long as there exists the possibility of renewed aggression from North Korea. Time has not dimmed our memories of the sudden assault against South Korea. We reaffirm the commitment of the United States to the territorial integrity and the sovereignty of the Republic of Korea. Simultaneously we encourage the governments of South Korea and North Korea to institute domestic policy initiatives leading to the extension of basic human rights.

When Republicans assumed executive office in 1969, we were confronted with a war in Vietnam involving more than 500,000 United States troops, and to which we had committed billions of dollars and our national honor and prestige. It was in the spirit of bipartisan support for Presidential foreign policy initiatives, inaugurated in the postwar era by Senator Arthur Vandenberg, that most Republicans supported the United States commitment to assist South Vietnam resist Communist-sponsored aggression. The human cost to us was great; more than 55,000 Americans died in that conflict, and more than 300,000 were wounded.

A policy of patient, persistent and principled negotiations extricated the United States from that ill-fated war with the expectation that peace would prevail. The refusal of the Democrat-controlled Congress to give support to Presidential requests for military aid to the beleaguered nations of South Vietnam, Cambodia and Laos, coupled with sustained military assaults by the Communists in gross violation of the Paris Peace Accords, brought about the collapse of those nations and the subjugation of their people to totalitarian rule.

We recognize that there is a wide divergence of opinion concerning Vietnam, but we pledge that American troops will never again be committed for the purpose of our own defense, or the defense of those to whom we are committed by treaty or other solemn agreements, without the clear purpose of achieving our stated diplomatic and military objectives.

We must achieve the return of all Americans who may be held in Southeast Asia, and a full accounting for those listed as Missing in Action. We strongly urge continued consultation between the President and the National League of Families of American Prisoners and Missing in Southeast Asia. This country owes at least this much to all of these courageous people who have anguished so long over this matter. To this end, and to underscore our top-priority commitment to the families of these POWs and MIAs, we recommend, among other actions, the establishment of a Presidential representative.

We condemn the inhumane and criminal retributions which have taken place in Cambodia, where mass executions and forced resettlements have been imposed on innocent civilians.

The important economic developments taking place in Singapore, Indonesia, Malaysia, the Philippines and other Asian countries, will lead to much improved living standards for the people there.

We reaffirm our friendship with these nations. Equally, our relationships with Australia and New Zealand are historic and important to us; they have never been better and provide a firm base on which to build.

United States–Chinese Relations

A development of significance for the future of Asia and for the world came to fruition in 1972 as our communications were restored with the People's Republic of China. This event has allowed us to initiate dialogue with the leaders of a quarter of the earth's population, and trade channels with the People's Republic have been opened, leading to benefits for each side.

The People's Republic of China can and will play an increasingly important role in world affairs. We shall seek to engage the People's Republic of China in an expanded network of contacts and trade. Such a process cannot realistically proceed at a forced or incautious pace; the measured but steady growth of our relations best serves our interests. We do not ignore the profound differences in our respective philosophies, governmental institutions, policies and views on individual liberty, and we are hopeful that basic human rights will be extended to the Chinese people. What is truly fundamental is that we have established regular working channels with the People's Republic of China and that this process can form an important contribution to world peace.

Our friendly relations with one great power should not be considered as a challenge to any other nation, large or small. The United States government, while engaged in a normalization of relations with the People's Republic of China, will continue to support the freedom and independence of our friend and ally, the Republic of China, and its 16 million people. The United States will fulfill and keep its commitments, such as the mutual defense treaty, with the Republic of China.

The Americas

The relations of the United States with the Americas are of vital and immediate importance. How we conduct our affairs with our neighbors to the North and South will continue to be a priority.

In the recent past our attention has at times been diverted to more distant parts of the world. There can be no sensible alternative to close relationships and understandings among the nations of the hemisphere.

It is true for a series of new departures in our relations with Canada. Canada is our most important trading partner, and we are hers. We, as Americans, feel a deep affinity for our Canadian friends, and we have much at stake in the development of closer relationships based on mutual understanding and complete equality.

To our neighbors in Mexico, Central America and South America, we also say that we wish the opportunity to expand our dialogue. The needs of our friends are great, but this must not serve as an obstacle for a concerted effort to work together more closely. The United States has taken steps to adjust tariffs so as to maximize access to our markets. We recognize that our neighbors place no value on complex and cumbersome aid schemes; they see self-help, modernization, and expanded trade as the main sources of economic progress. We will work with them to define specific steps that we can take to help them achieve greater economic strength, and to advance our mutual interests.

By continuing its policies of exporting subversion and violence, Cuba remains outside the inter-American family of nations. We condemn attempts by the Cuban dictatorship to intervene in the affairs of other nations; and, as long as such conduct continues, it shall remain ineligible for admission to the Organization of American States.

We shall continue to share the aspirations of the Cuban people to regain their liberty. We insist that decent and humane conditions be maintained in the treatment of political prisoners in the Cuban jails, and we will seek arrangements to allow international entities, such as the International Red Cross, to investigate and monitor the conditions in those jails.

The present Panama Canal Treaty provides that the United States has jurisdictional rights in the Canal Zone as "if it were the sovereign." The United States intends that the Panama Canal be preserved as an international waterway for the ships of all nations. This secure access is enhanced by a relationship which commands the respect of Americans and Panamanians and benefits the people of both countries. In any talks with Panama, however, the United States negotiators should in no way *cede, dilute, forfeit, negotiate or transfer any rights, power, authority, jurisdiction, territory or property that are necessary for the protection* and *security of the United States and the entire Western Hemisphere.*

We reaffirm our faith in the ability of the Organization of American States, which remains a valuable means of inter-American consultation.

The Middle East

The preservation of peace and stability in the Middle East is a paramount concern. The efforts of two Republican Administrations, summoning diplomatic and political skills, have been directed toward reduction of tension and toward avoiding flashpoints which could serve as an excuse for yet another round of conflict between Israel and the Arab countries.

Our commitment to Israel is fundamental and enduring. We have honored and will continue to honor that commitment in every way—politically, economically and providing the military aid that Israel requires to remain strong enough to deter any potential aggression. Forty percent of all United States aid that Israel has received since its creation in 1948 has come in the last two fiscal years, as a result of Republican initiatives. Our policy must remain one of decisive support for the security and integrity of Israel.

An equally important component of our commitment to Israel lies in continuing our efforts to secure a just and durable peace for all nations in that complex region. Our efforts have succeeded, for the first time since the creation of the state of Israel, in moving toward a negotiated peace settlement which would serve the interests and the security of all nations in the Middle East. Peace in the Middle East now requires face-to-face direct negotiations between the states involved with the recognition of safe, secure and defensible borders for Israel.

At the same time, Republic Administrations have succeeded in reestablishing communications with the Arab countries, and have made extensive progress in our diplomatic and commercial relations with the more moderate Arab nations.

As a consequence of the Middle East conflict of 1973, the petroleum producing states imposed an embargo on the export of oil to most of the advanced industrial countries. We have succeeded in creating numerous cooperative mechanisms to protect ourselves, working in concert with our allies, against any future embargoes. The United States would view any attempt to reimpose an embargo as an essentially hostile act. We will oppose discriminatory practices, including boycotts of any type.

Because we have such fundamental interests in the Middle East, it will be our policy to continue our efforts to maintain the balance of power in the Mediterranean region. Our adversaries must recognize that we will not permit a weakening of our defenses or any attempt to disturb valued Alliance relationships in the Eastern Mediterranean.

We shall continue to support peace initiatives in the civil war in Lebanon; United States envoys engaged in precisely such an initiative were murdered, and we express our sorrow for their untimely deaths and for all other dedicated government employees who have been slain elsewhere while in service to their country. In Lebanon, we stand ready to provide food and medical and other humanitarian assistance.

Africa

The United States has always supported the process of self-determination in Africa. Our friendship for the African countries is expressed in support for continued peaceful economic development, expansion of trade, humanitarian relief efforts and our belief that the entire continent should be free from outside military intervention. Millions of Americans recognize their historical and cultural ties with Africa and express their desire that United States policy toward Africa is a matter of great importance.

We support all forces which promote negotiated settlements and racial peace. We shall continue to deplore all violence and terrorism and to urge all concerned that the rights of tribal, ethnic and racial minorities be guaranteed through workable safeguards. Our policy is to strengthen the force of moderation recognizing that solutions to African problems will not come quickly. The peoples of Africa can coexist in security,

work together in freedom and harmony, and strive together to secure their prosperity. We hope that the Organization of African Unity will be able to achieve mature and stable relationships within Africa and abroad.

The interests of peace and security in Africa are best served by the absence of arms and greater concentration on peaceful development. We reserve the right to maintain the balance by extending our support to nations facing a threat from Soviet-supplied states and from Soviet weapons.

United States–Soviet Relations

American foreign policy must be based upon a realistic assessment of the Communist challenge in the world. It is clear that the perimeters of freedom continue to shrink throughout the world in the face of the Communist challenge. Since 1917, totalitarian Communism has managed through brute force, not through the free electoral process, to bring an increasingly substantial portion of the world's land area and peoples under its domination. To illustrate, most recently South Vietnam, Cambodia, and Laos have fallen under the control of Communist dictatorships, and in that part of the world the Communist pressure mounts against Thailand, the Republic of China, and the Republic of Korea. In Africa, Communist Cuba forces, brazenly assisted by the Soviet Union, have recently imposed a Communist dictatorship upon the people of Angola. Other countries in Africa and throughout the world generally await similar fates. These are the realities of world power in our time. The United States is thoroughly justified in having based its foreign policy upon these realities.

Thirty years ago relations between the United States and the Soviet Union were in a phase of great difficulty, leading to the tensions of the Cold War era. Although there have been changes in this crucial superpower relationship, there remain fundamental and profound differences between us. Republican Presidents, while acknowledging the depth of the gulf which separates our free society from the Soviet society, have sought methodically to isolate and develop those areas of our relations which would serve to lessen tension and reduce the chance of unwanted conflict.

In a world beset by countless opportunities for discord and armed conflict, the relationship between the United States and the Soviet Union is critically important; on it rest the hopes of the world for peace. We offer a policy that maintains our fundamental strength and demonstrates our steadfast determination to prevent aggressive use of Soviet power.

The role of a responsible, participating Congress in maintaining this diplomatic and military posture is critical to success. The United States must remain a loyal and dependable ally, and must be prepared to carry out commitments and to demonstrate a willingness to act. Resistance to open aggression, such as the Soviet-sponsored Cuban intervention in Angola, must not be allowed to become the subject of a partisan debate, nor can it be allowed to become an unchallenged and established pattern of international behavior, lest our credibility and deterrent strength be greatly diminished.

Soviet military power has grown rapidly in recent years, and while we shall prevent a military imbalance or a sudden shift in the global balance of power, we shall also diligently explore with the Soviet Union new ways to reduce tensions and to arrive at mutually beneficial and self-enforcing agreements in all fields of international activity. Important steps have been taken to limit strategic nuclear arms. The Vladivostok Agreement of November 1974 placed a ceiling on the strategic forces of both the United States and the Soviet Union. Further negotiations in arms control are continuing. We shall not agree for the sake of agreement; on the contrary, we will make sure that any agreements yield fundamental benefits to our national security.

As an example of hard-headed bargaining our success in concluding agreements limiting the size of peaceful nuclear explosions and nuclear weapons tests will, for the first time, permit the United States to conduct on-site inspections in the Soviet Union itself. This important step can now be measured in practical terms. All such agreements must stand the test of verification. An agreement that does not provide this safeguard is worse than no agreement at all.

We support the consolidation of joint efforts with our allies to verify that our policies regarding the transfer of technology to the Soviet Union and its allies are in concert and that consultation will be designed to preclude the sale of those technology-intensive products to the Soviet Union by the United States and our allies which will directly or indirectly jeopardize our national security.

Our trade in non-strategic areas creates jobs here at home, substantially improves our balance-of-payments position, and can contribute to an improved political climate in the world. The overseas sale of our agricultural products benefits American farmers and consumers. To guard against any sudden shift in domestic prices as the consequence of unannounced purchases, we have instituted strict reporting procedures and other treaty safeguards. We shall not permit concessional sales of agricultural products to the Soviet Union, nor shall we permit the Soviet Union or others to determine our agricultural export policies by irregular and unpredictable purchases.

The United States and the Soviet Union remain ideological competitors. We do not shrink from such a challenge; rather, we welcome the opportunity to demonstrate that our way of life is inherently preferable to regimentation and government-enforced orthodoxy. We shall expect the Soviet Union to implement the United Nations Declaration on Human Rights and the Helsinki Agreements, which guarantee conditions for the free interchange of information and the right to emigrate, including emigration of Soviet Jews, Christians, Moslems and others who wish to join relatives abroad. In this spirit we shall expect the immediate end of all forms of harassment, including imprisonment and military service, aimed at preventing such emigration. America must take a firm stand to bring about liberalization of emigration policy in countries which limit or prohibit free emigration. Governments which enjoy the confidence of their people need have no fear of cultural, intellectual or press freedom.

Our support for the people of Central and Eastern Europe to achieve self-determination will continue. Their ability to choose their future is of great importance to peace and stability. We favor increasing contacts between Eastern and Western Europe and support the increasing economic ties of all the countries of Europe. We strongly support the continuation of the Voice of America, Radio Free Europe and Radio Liberty with adequate appropriations. Strict reciprocity must govern our diplomatic relations with the Soviet Union. We express our concern for the safety of our diplomatic representatives in the Soviet Union, and we insist that practices such as microwave transmissions directed at the United States Embassy be terminated immediately.

Thus our relations with the Soviet Union will be guided by solid principles. We will maintain our strategic and conventional forces; we will oppose the development of Soviet power for unilateral advantages or political and territorial expansion; we will never tolerate a shift against us in the strategic balance; and will remain firm in the face of pressure, while at the same time expressing our willingness to work on the basis of strict reciprocity toward new agreements which will help achieve peace and stability.

International Cooperation

Strong support for international cooperation in all fields has been a hallmark of United States international policy for many decades. Two Republican

Administrations have strengthened agencies of international cooperation not only because of our humanitarian concern for others, but also because it serves United States interests to be a conscientious member of the world community.

The political character of the United Nations has become complex. With 144 sovereign members, the U.N. experiences problems associated with a large, sometimes cumbersome and diverse body. We seek to accommodate to these changes in the spirit of friendly concern, but when the United Nations becomes arrayed against the vital interests of any of its member states—on ideological or other narrow grounds—the very principles of the organization are threatened. The United States does not wish to dictate to the U.N., yet we do have every right to expect and insist that scrupulous care be given to the rights of all members. Steamroller techniques for advancing discriminatory actions will be opposed. Actions such as the malicious attempt to depict Zionism as a form of racism are inconsistent with the objectives of the United Nations and are repugnant to the United States. The United States will continue to be a firm supporter and defender of any nation subjected to such outrageous assaults. We will not accept ideological abuses of the United States.

In the many areas of international cooperation which benefit the average American—elimination of terrorism, peacekeeping, non-proliferation of nuclear weapons, termination of the international drug trade, and orderly use of ocean resources—we pledge to build new international structures of cooperation. At the same time, we shall seek to insure that the cost of such new structures, as well as the cost of existing structures, is more equitably shared among participating nations. In the continued tradition of American concern for the quality of human life everywhere, we shall give vigorous support to the non-political work of the specialized agencies of the United Nations which deal with such areas as nutrition and disaster relief for the world's poor and disadvantaged.

The United States should withdraw promptly from the International Labor Organization if that body fails to stop its increasing politicization.

Eight years ago we pledged to eliminate waste and to make more business-like the administration of the United States foreign aid programs. We have endeavored to fulfill these pledges. Our foreign economic assistance programs are now being operated efficiently with emphasis on helping others to help themselves, on food production and rural development, on health programs and sound population planning assistance, and on development of human resources.

We have sought to encourage others, including the oil producing countries, to assume a larger share of the burden of assistance. We shall continue our efforts to secure adequate sources of financing for economic projects in emerging countries.

The world's oceans, with their vast resources, must become areas of extended cooperation. We favor a successful conclusion to the Law of the Sea Conference provided it will suitably protect legitimate national interests, freedom of the seas and responsible use of the seas. We are determined to maintain the right of free and unmolested passage for ships of all nations on the high seas and in international waterways.

We favor an extension of the territorial sea from three to twelve miles, and we favor in principle the creation of a 200-mile economic zone in which coastal states would have exclusive rights to explore and develop natural resources.

We strongly condemn illegal corporate payments made at home and abroad. To eliminate illegal payments to foreign officials by American corporations, we support passage of President Ford's proposed legislation and the OECD Declaration on Investment setting forth reasonable guidelines for business conduct.

The growth of civilian nuclear technology, and the rising demand for nuclear power as an alternative to increasingly costly fossil fuel resources, combine to require our recognition of the potential dangers associated with such developments. All nations must work to assure that agreements and treaties currently governing nuclear technology and nuclear exports are carefully monitored. We shall work to devise new multilateral policies governing the export of sensitive nuclear technologies.

International Economic Policy

The tumultuous events of the past several years in the world economy were an enormous challenge to our creativity and to our capacity for leadership. We have emerged from this difficult period in a new position in the world, and we have directed and guided a sound recovery.

To assure the permanence of our own prosperity, we must work with others, demonstrating our leadership and the vitality of our economy. Together with the industrial democracies, we must ensure steady, non-inflationary growth, based on expanded international cooperation.

The Republican Administration will cooperate fully in strengthening the international trade and monetary system, which provides the foundation for our prosperity and that of all nations. We shall bargain hard to remove barriers to an open economic system, and we shall oppose new restrictions to trade. We shall continue to represent vigorously our nation's economic interest in the trade negotiations taking place in Geneva, guard against protectionism, and insist that the principles of fair trade be scrupulously observed. When industries and jobs are adversely affected by foreign competition, adjustment assistance under the Trade Act of 1974 is made available. This Act must be under continuous review to ascertain that it reflects changing circumstances.

The Republican Party believes that cooperation in the energy field is indispensable to international stability. Most of the industrial democracies and the less-developed countries are increasingly dependent on imported oil, which causes them to be politically, economically and strategically vulnerable. Through the establishment of the International Energy Agency, steps have been taken to expand consumer cooperation. We shall also continue the dialogue with the oil producing countries.

We shall continue to work closely with the less-developed countries to promote their economic growth. Those countries will be encouraged to enter into mutually beneficial trade relationships with us that contribute to world peace. To achieve this, we must strengthen the confidence of the major industrial countries as they take part in discussions with less-developed countries. There is no reason for us to be defensive; our combined assets can be used in a coordinated strategy to make our influence effective. We will not yield to threats or confrontational politics.

While we shall support a global increase of investment in natural resources of all types, we shall also oppose the replacement of the free market mechanism by cartels, price-fixing arrangements or commodity agreements. We shall continue policies designed to assure free market consumers abroad that the United States will remain a dependable supplier of agricultural commodities.

CONCLUSION

The American people can be proud of our nation's achievements in foreign policy over the past eight years.

We are at peace.

We are strong.

We re-emphasize the importance of our ties with the nations of the Americas.

Our relations with allies in the Atlantic community and with Japan have never been closer.

Significant progress has been made toward a just and durable settlement in the Middle East.

We have sought negotiation rather than confrontation with our adversaries, while maintaining our strategic deterrent.

The world economic recovery, led by the United States, is producing sustainable growth.

In this year of our nation's bicentennial, the American people have confidence in themselves and are optimistic about the future.

We, the Republican Party, proudly submit our record and our Platform to you.

— 1980 —

A PREAMBLE

The Republican Party convenes, presents this platform, and selects its nominees at a time of crisis. America is adrift. Our country moves agonizingly, aimlessly, almost helplessly into one of the most dangerous and disorderly periods in history.

At home, our economy careens, whiplashed from one extreme to another. Earlier this year, inflation skyrocketed to its highest levels in more than a century; weeks later, the economy plummeted, suffering its steepest slide on record. Prices escalate at more than 10 percent a year. More than eight million people seek employment. Manufacturing plants lie idle across the country. The hopes and aspirations of our people are being smothered.

Overseas, conditions already perilous deteriorate. The Soviet Union for the first time is acquiring the means to obliterate or cripple our land-based missile system and blackmail us into submission. Marxist tyrannies spread more rapidly through the Third World and Latin America. Our alliances are frayed in Europe and elsewhere. Our energy supplies become even more dependent on uncertain foreign suppliers. In the ultimate humiliation, militant terrorists in Iran continue to toy with the lives of Americans.

These events are not isolated, or unrelated. They are signposts. They mark a continuing downward spiral in economic vitality and international influence. Should the trend continue, the 1980s promise to be our most dangerous years since World War II. History could record, if we let the drift go on, that the American experiment, so marvelously successful for 200 years, came strangely, needlessly, tragically to a dismal end early in our third century.

By far the most galling aspect of it all is that the chief architects of our decline—Democratic politicians—are without program or ideas to reverse it. Divided, leaderless, unseeing, uncomprehending, they plod on with listless offerings of pale imitations of the same policies they have pursued so long, knowing full well their futility. The Carter Administration is the unhappy and inevitable consequence of decades of increasingly outmoded Democratic domination of our national life. Over the past four years it has repeatedly demonstrated that it has no basic goals other than the perpetuation of its own rule and no guiding principle other than the fleeting insights provided by the latest opinion poll. Policies announced one day are disavowed or ignored the next, sowing confusion among Americans at home and havoc among our friends abroad.

Republicans, Democrats, and Independents have been watching and reading these signs. They have been watching incredulously as disaster after disaster unfolds. They now have had enough. They are rising up in 1980 to say that this confusion must end; this drift must end; we must pull ourselves together as a people before we slide irretrievably into the abyss.

It doesn't have to be this way; it doesn't have to stay this way. We, the Republican Party, hold ourselves forth as the Party best able to arrest and reverse the decline. We offer new ideas and candidates, from the top of our ticket to the bottom, who can bring to local and national leadership firm, steady hands and confidence and eagerness. We have unparalleled unity within our own ranks, especially between our Presidential nominee and our congressional membership. Most important, we go forth to the people with ideas and programs for the future that are as powerful and compelling as they are fresh. Together, we offer a new beginning for America.

Our foremost goal here at home is simple: economic growth and full employment without inflation. Sweeping change in economic policy in America is needed so that Mr. Carter's promise of hard times and austerity—his one promise well kept—can be replaced with Republican policies that promise economic growth and job creation. It is our belief that the stagflation of recent years not only has consigned millions of citizens to hardship but also has bottled up the enormous ingenuity and creative powers of our people. Those energies will not be released by the sterile policies of the past: we specifically reject the Carter doctrine that inflation can be reduced only by throwing people out of work. Prosperity will not be regained simply by government fiat. Rather, we must offer broad new incentives to labor and capital to stimulate a great outpouring of private goods and services and to create an abundance of jobs. From America's grassroots to the White House we will stand united as a party behind a bold program of tax rate reductions, spending restraints, and regulatory reforms that will inject new life into the economic bloodstream of this country.

Overseas, our goal is equally simple and direct: to preserve a world at peace by keeping America strong. This philosophy once occupied a hallowed place in American diplomacy, but it was casually, even cavalierly dismissed at the outset by the Carter Administration—and the results have been shattering. Never before in modern history has the United States endured as many humiliations, insults, and defeats as it has during the past four years: our ambassadors murdered, our embassies burned, our warnings ignored, our diplomacy scorned, our diplomats kidnapped. The Carter Administration has shown that it neither understands totalitarianism nor appreciates the way tyrants take advantage of weakness. The brutal invasion of Afghanistan promises to be only the forerunner of much more serious threats to the West—and to world peace—should the Carter Administration somehow cling to power.

Republicans are united in a belief that America's international humiliation and decline can be reversed only by strong Presidential leadership and a consistent, far-sighted foreign policy, supported by a major upgrading of our military forces, a strengthening of our commitments to our allies, and a resolve that our national interests be vigorously protected. Ultimately, those who practice strength and firmness truly guard the peace.

This platform addresses many concerns of our Party. We seek to restore the family, the neighborhood, the community, and the workplace as vital alternatives in our national life to ever-expanding federal power.

We affirm our deep commitment to the fulfillment of the hopes and aspirations of all Americans—blacks and whites, women and men, the young and old, rural and urban.

For too many years, the political debate in America has been conducted in terms set by the Democrats. They believe that every time new problems arise beyond the power of men and women as individuals to solve, it becomes the duty of government to solve them, as if there were never any alternative. Republicans disagree and have always taken the side of the individual, whose freedoms are threatened by the big government that Democratic idea has spawned. Our case for the individual is stronger than ever. A defense of the individual against government was never more needed. And we will continue to mount it.

But we will redefine and broaden the debate by transcending the narrow terms of government and the individual; those are not the only two realities in America. Our society consists of more than that; so should the political debate. We will reemphasize those vital communities like the family, the neighborhood, the workplace, and others which are found at the center of society, between government and the individual. We will restore and strengthen their ability to solve problems in the places where people spend their daily lives and can turn to each other for support and help.

We seek energy independence through economic policies that free up our energy production and encourage conservation. We seek improvements in health care, education, housing, and opportunities for youth. We seek new avenues for the needy to break out of the tragic cycle of dependency. All of these goals—and many others—we confidently expect to achieve through a rebirth of liberty and resurgence of private initiatives, for we believe that at the root of most of our troubles today is the misguided and discredited philosophy of an all-powerful government, ceaselessly striving to subsidize, manipulate, and control individuals. But it is the individual, not the government, who reigns at the center of our Republican philosophy.

To those Democrats who say Americans must be content to passively accept the gradual but inexorable decline of America, we answer: The American people have hardly begun to marshal their talents and resources or realize the accomplishments and dreams that only freedom can inspire.

To those Democrats who say we face an "age of limits," we ask: Who knows the limit to what Americans can do when their capacity for work, creativity, optimism, and faith is enhanced and supported by strong and responsive political leadership and ideals.

To those who, with Mr. Carter, say the American people suffer from a national "malaise," we respond: The only malaise in this country is found in the leadership of the Democratic Party, in the White House and in Congress. Its symptoms are an incompetence to lead, a refusal to change, and a reluctance to act. This malaise has become epidemic in Washington. Its cure is government led by Republicans who share the values of the majority of Americans.

Republicans pledge a restoration of balance in American society. But society cannot be balanced by the actions of government or of individuals alone. Balance is found at society's vital center, where we find the family and the neighborhood and the workplace.

America will not, however, achieve any of these goals on its present course nor under its present leadership. The uncharted course of Mr. Carter will lead surely to catastrophe. By reversing our economic decline, by reversing our international decline, we can and will resurrect our dreams.

And so, in this 1980 Republican Platform, we call out to the American people: With God's help, let us now, together, make America great again; let us now, together, make a new beginning.

FREE INDIVIDUALS IN A FREE SOCIETY

It has long been a fundamental conviction of the Republican Party that government should foster in our society a climate of maximum individual liberty and freedom of choice. Properly informed, our people as individuals or acting through instruments of popular consultation can make the right decisions affecting personal or general welfare, free of pervasive and heavy-handed intrusion by the central government into the decision-making process. This tenet is the genius of representative democracy.

Republicans also treasure the ethnic, cultural, and regional diversity of our people. This diversity fosters a dynamism in American society that is the envy of the world.

Taxes

Elsewhere in this platform we discuss the benefits, for society as a whole, of reduced taxation, particularly in terms of economic growth. But we believe it is essential to cut personal tax rates out of fairness to the individual.

Presently, the aggregate burden of taxation is so great that the average American spends a substantial part of every year, in effect, working for government.

Substantial tax rate reductions are needed to offset the massive tax increases facing the working men and women of this country. Over the next four years, federal taxes are projected to increase by over $500 billion due to the Carter Administration's policies. American families are already paying taxes at higher rates than ever in our history; as a result of these Carter policies, the rates will go even higher. The direct and indirect burden of federal taxes alone, imposed on the average family earning $20,000, has risen to $5,451—over 27 percent of the family's gross income. During the Carter term, the federal tax alone on this family will have risen $2,000.

The Republican Party believes balancing the budget is essential but opposes the Democrats' attempt to do so through higher taxes. We believe that an essential aspect of balancing the budget is spending restraint by the federal government and higher economic growth, not higher tax burdens on working men and women.

Policies of the Democratic Party are taxing work, savings, investment, productivity, and the rewards for human ingenuity. These same tax policies subsidize debt, unemployment, and consumption. The present structure of the personal income tax system is designed to broaden the gap between effort and reward.

Therefore, the Republican Party supports across-the-board reductions in personal income tax rates, phased in over three years, which will reduce tax rates from the range of 14 to 70 percent to a range of from 10 to 50 percent.

For most Americans, these reduced tax rates will slow the rate at which taxes rise. This will assure workers and savers greater rewards for greater effort by lowering the rate at which added earnings would be taxed.

These reductions have been before the Congress for three years in the Roth–Kemp legislation. The proposal will not only provide relief for all American taxpayers, but also promote non-inflationary economic growth by restoring the incentive to save, invest, and produce. These restored incentives will in turn increase investment and help reinvigorate American business and industry, leading to the creation of more jobs. In fact, Governor Reagan and Congressional Republicans have already taken the first step. Working together, they have boldly offered the American people a 10 percent tax rate cut for 1981, which will stimulate growth in our economy, and a simplification and liberalization of depreciation schedules to create more jobs.

Once tax rates are reduced, Republicans will move to end tax bracket creep caused by inflation. We support tax indexing to protect taxpayers from the automatic tax increases caused when cost-of-living wage increases move them into higher tax brackets.

Tax rate reductions will generate increases in economic growth, output, and income which will ultimately generate increased revenues. The greater justification for these cuts, however, lies in the right of the individual to keep and use the money they earn.

Improving the Welfare System

The measure of a country's compassion is how it treats the least fortunate. In every society there will be some who cannot work, often through no fault of their own.

Yet current federal government efforts to help them have become counter-productive, perpetuating and aggravating the very conditions of dependence they seek to relieve. The Democratic Congress has produced a jumble of degrading, dehumanizing, wasteful, over-lapping, and inefficient programs that invite waste and fraud but inadequately assist the needy poor.

Poverty is defined not by income statistics alone, but by an individual's true situation and prospects. For two generations, especially since the mid-1960s, the Democrats have deliberately perpetuated a status of federally subsidized poverty and manipulated dependency for millions of Americans. This is especially so for blacks and Hispanics, many of whom remain pawns of the bureaucracy, trapped outside the social and economic mainstream of American life.

For those on welfare, our nation's tax policies provide a penalty for getting a job. This is especially so for those whose new income from a job is either equal to, or marginally greater than, the amount received on welfare. In these cases, due to taxes, the individual's earned income is actually less than welfare benefits. This is the "poverty trap" which will continue to hold millions of Americans as long as they continue to be punished for working.

The Carter Administration and the Democratic Party continue to foster that dependency. Our nation's welfare problems will not be solved merely by providing increased benefits. Public service jobs are not a substitute for employable skills, nor can increases in the food stamp program by themselves provide for individual dignity. By fostering dependency and discouraging self-reliance, the Democratic Party has created a welfare constituency dependent on its continual subsidies.

The Carter Administration has proposed, and its allies in the House of Representatives actually voted for, legislation to nationalize welfare, which would have cost additional billions and made billions more dependent upon public assistance. The Democrats have presided over—and must take the blame for—the most monstrous expansion and abuse of the food stamp program to date. They have been either unable or unwilling to attack the welfare fraud that diverts resources away from the truly poor. They have sacrificed the needy to the greedy, and sent the welfare bills to the taxpayers.

We categorically reject the notion of a guaranteed annual income, no matter how it may be disguised, which would destroy the fiber of our economy and doom the poor to perpetual dependence.

As a party we commit ourselves to a welfare policy that is truly reflective of our people's true sense of compassion and charity as well as an appreciation of every individual's need for dignity and self-respect. We pledge a system that will:

- provide adequate living standards for the truly needy;
- end welfare fraud by removing ineligibles from the welfare rolls, tightening food stamp eligibility requirements, and ending aid to illegal aliens and the voluntarily unemployed;
- strengthen work incentives, particularly directed at the productive involvement of able-bodied persons in useful community work projects;
- provide educational and vocational incentives to allow recipients to become self-supporting; and
- better coordinate federal efforts with local and state social welfare agencies and strengthen local and state administrative functions.

We oppose federalizing the welfare system; local levels of government are most aware of the needs in their communities. We support a block grant program that will help return control of welfare programs to the states. Decisions about who gets welfare, and how much, can be better made on the local level.

Those features of the present law, particularly the food stamp program, that draw into assistance programs people who are capable of paying for their own needs should be corrected. The humanitarian purpose of such programs must not be corrupted by eligibility loopholes. Food stamp program reforms proposed by Republicans in Congress would accomplish the twin goals of directing resources to those most in need and streamlining administration.

Through long association with government programs, the word "welfare" has come to be perceived almost exclusively as tax-supported aid to the needy. But in its most inclusive sense—and as Americans understood it from the beginning of the Republic—such aid also encompasses those charitable works performed by private citizens, families, and social, ethnic, and religious organizations. Policies of the federal government leading to high taxes, rising inflation, and bureaucratic empire-building have made it difficult and often impossible for such individuals and groups to exercise their charitable instincts. We believe that government policies that fight inflation, reduce tax rates, and end bureaucratic excesses can help make private effort by the American people once again a major force in those works of charity which are the true signs of a progressive and humane society.

Veterans

Republicans recognize the very special sacrifice of those who have served in our nation's armed forces.

Individual rights and societal values are only as strong as a nation's commitment to defend them. Because of this our country must never forget its appreciation of and obligation to our veterans.

Today the veteran population numbers 30 million. This is the largest veteran population in our nation's history. We recognize the major sacrifices they have made for their fellow Americans.

We will maintain the integrity of the Veterans Administration. We will seek to keep it separate and distinct from other federal agencies as the single agency for the administration of all veterans' programs. In particular we feel it is of vital importance to continue and expand the health programs provided to veterans through the Veterans Administration hospitals. Here we see the need for increased access to care, especially for older veterans.

We further advocate continued and expanded health care for our Vietnam veterans and consider it vital for the Veterans Administration to continue its programs for the rehabilitation of the disabled as well as its job training efforts. We are committed to providing timely and adequate adjustments in compensation for service-disabled veterans and the survivors of those who died as a result of their service. We are also committed to maintaining the pension program for those who have served during a period of war, for those who were disabled and impoverished, and for their widows and orphans.

We will support measures to provide for every veteran at death a final resting place for his remains in a national cemetery, and for costs of transportation thereto.

Veterans preference in federal employment in all departments and agencies will be continued and strictly enforced.

Retired military benefits deserve more than the cursory attention given them by a Department of Defense otherwise interested in on-going programs. We believe that such benefits should be administered by the Veterans Administration.

Private Property

The widespread distribution of private property ownership is the cornerstone of American liberty. Without it neither our free enterprise system nor our republican form of government could long endure.

Under Democratic rule, the federal government has become an aggressive enemy of the human right to private property ownership. It has dissipated savings through depreciation of the dollar, enforced price controls on private exchange of goods, attempted to enforce severe land use controls, and mistreated hundreds of thousands of national park and forest inholders.

The next Republican Administration will reverse this baneful trend. It will not only protect the cherished human right of property ownership, but will also work to help millions of Americans—particularly those from disadvantaged groups—to share in the ownership of the wealth of their nation.

Transportation—Personal Mobility

Americans enjoy greater personal mobility than any other people on earth, largely as a result of the availability of automobiles and our modern highway system. Republicans reject the elitist notion that Americans must be forced out of their cars. Instead, we vigorously support the right of personal mobility and freedom as exemplified by the automobile and our modern highway system. While recognizing the importance of fuel efficiency and alternate modes of transportation, we quickly acknowledge that for millions of Americans there is no substitute on the horizon for the automobile. We reaffirm our support for a healthy domestic automobile industry, complete with continued support for the highway trust fund, which is the fairest method yet devised for financing America's highway system.

Republicans recognize the need for further improvement in highway safety. Projections indicate that highway fatalities may exceed 60,000 per year in the coming decades. Republicans support accelerated cost-effective efforts to improve highway, automobile, and individual driver safety.

Privacy

The essence of freedom is the right of law-abiding individuals to life, liberty, and the pursuit of happiness without undue governmental intervention. Yet government in recent years, particularly at the federal level, has overwhelmed citizens with demands for personal information and has accumulated vast amounts of such data through the IRS, Social Security Administration, the Bureau of the Census, and other agencies. Under certain limited circumstances, such information can serve legitimate societal interests, but there must be protection against abuse.

Republicans share the concerns of our citizens as to the nature, use, and final disposition of the volume of personal information being collected. We are alarmed by Washington's growing collection and dissemination of such data. There must be protection against its misuse or disclosure.

The Republican Party commits itself to guaranteeing an individual's right of privacy. We support efforts of state governments to ensure individual privacy.

Black Americans

For millions of black Americans, the past four years have been a long trail of broken promises and broken dreams. The Carter Administration entered office with a pledge to all minorities of a brighter economic future. Today there are more black Americans unemployed than on the day Mr. Carter became President. The unemployment rate of black teenagers is once again rising sharply. And the median income of black families has declined to less than 60 percent of white family income.

Republicans will not make idle promises to blacks and other minorities; we are beyond the day when any American can live off rhetoric or political platitudes.

Our Party specifically rejects the philosophy of the Carter Administration that unemployment is the answer to inflation. We abhor the notion that our cities should become battle grounds in the fight against inflation and that the jobs of black Americans should be sacrificed in an attempt to counterbalance the inflationary excesses of government. Nor are we prepared to accept the practice of turning the poor into permanent wards of the state, trading their political support for continued financial assistance.

Our fundamental answer to the economic problems of black Americans is the same answer we make to all Americans—full employment without inflation through economic growth. First and foremost, we are committed to a policy of economic expansion through tax-rate reductions, spending restraint, regulatory reform and other incentives.

As the Party of Lincoln, we remain equally and steadfastly committed to the equality of rights for all citizens, regardless of race. Although this nation has not yet eliminated all vestiges of racism over the years, we are heartened by the progress that has been made, we are proud of the role that our Party has played, and we are dedicated to standing shoulder to shoulder with black Americans in that cause.

Elsewhere in this platform, we set forth a number of specific proposals that will also serve to improve the quality of life for blacks. During the next four years we are committed to policies that will:

- encourage local governments to designate specific enterprise zones within depressed areas that will promote new jobs, new and expanded businesses and new economic vitality;

- open new opportunities for black men and women to begin small businesses of their own by, among other steps, removing excessive regulations, disincentives for venture capital and other barriers erected by the government;
- bring strong, effective enforcement of federal civil rights statutes, especially those dealing with threats to physical safety and security which have recently been increasing; and
- ensure that the federal government follows a nondiscriminatory system of appointments up and down the line, with a careful eye for qualified minority aspirants.

Hispanic-Americans

Hispanics are rapidly becoming the largest minority in the country and are one of the major pillars in our cultural, social, and economic life. Diverse in character, proud in heritage, they are greatly enriching the American melting pot.

Hispanics seek only the full rights of citizenship—in education, in law enforcement, in housing—and an equal opportunity to achieve economic security. Unfortunately, those desires have not always been fulfilled; as in so many other areas, the Carter Administration has been long on rhetoric and short on action in its approach to the Hispanic community.

We pledge to pursue policies that will help to make the opportunities of American life a reality for Hispanics. The economic policies enunciated in this platform will, we believe, create new jobs for Hispanic teenagers and adults and will also open up new business opportunities for them. We also believe there should be local educational programs which enable those who grew up learning another language such as Spanish to become proficient in English while also maintaining their own language and cultural heritage. Neither Hispanics nor any other American citizen should be barred from education or employment opportunities because English is not their first language.

The Handicapped

The Republican Party strongly believes that handicapped persons must be admitted into the mainstream of American society. It endorses efforts to enable our handicapped population to enjoy a useful and productive life.

Too often in the past, barriers have been raised to their education, employment, transportation, health care, housing, recreation, and insurance. We support a concerted national effort to eliminate discrimination in all

these areas. Specifically we support tax incentives for the removal of architectural and transportation barriers. We pledge continued efforts to improve communications for the handicapped and to promote a healthy, constructive attitude toward them in our society.

Women's Rights

We acknowledge the legitimate efforts of those who support or oppose ratification of the Equal Rights Amendment.

We reaffirm our Party's historic commitment to equal rights and equality for women.

We support equal rights and equal opportunities for women, without taking away traditional rights of women such as exemption from the military draft. We support the enforcement of all equal opportunity laws and urge the elimination of discrimination against women. We oppose any move which would give the federal government more power over families.

Ratification of the Equal Rights Amendment is now in the hands of state legislatures, and the issues of the time extension and rescission are in the courts. The states have a constitutional right to accept or reject a constitutional amendment without federal interference or pressure. At the direction of the White House, federal departments launched pressure against states which refused to ratify ERA. Regardless of one's position on ERA, we demand that this practice cease.

At this time, women of America comprise 53 percent of the population and over 42 percent of the work force. By 1990, we anticipate that 51 percent of the population will be women, and there will be approximately 57 million in the work force. Therefore, the following urgent problems must be resolved:

- total integration of the work force (not separate but equal) is necessary to bring women equality in pay;
- girls and young women must be given improved early career counseling and job training to widen the opportunities for them in the world of work;
- women's worth in the society and in the jobs they hold, at home or in the workplace, must be reevaluated to improve the conditions of women workers concentrated in low-status, low-paying jobs;
- equal opportunity for credit and other assistance must be assured to women in small businesses; and one of the most critical problems in our nation today is that of inadequate child care for the working mother. As champions of the free enterprise system, of the individual, and of the idea that the best solutions to most problems rest at the community level, Republicans must find ways to meet this, the working woman's

need. The scope of this problem is fully realized only when it is understood that many female heads of households are at the poverty level and that they have a very large percentage of the nation's children.

The important secret about old age in America today is that it is primarily a woman's issue, and those over 65 are the fastest growing segment of the population. With current population trends, by the year 2020, 15.5 percent of our population will be over 65; by 2035, women in this age group will outnumber men by 13 million.

In 1980, 42 percent of women between 55 and 64 are in the work force. Half of the 6 million elderly women who live alone have incomes of $3,700 or less, and black women in that category have a median income of $2,600. How do they survive with the present rate of inflation? The lower salaries they earned as working women are now reflected in lower retirement benefits, if they have any at all. The Social Security system is still biased against women, and nonexistent pension plans combine with that to produce a bereft elderly woman. The Republican Party must not and will not let this continue.

We reaffirm our belief in the traditional role and values of the family in our society. The damage being done today to the family takes its greatest toll on the woman. Whether it be through divorce, widowhood, economic problems, or the suffering of children, the impact is greatest on women. The importance of support for the mother and homemaker in maintaining the values of this country cannot be over-emphasized.

In other sections of this platform, we call for greater equity in the tax treatment of working spouses. We deplore this marriage tax which penalizes married two-worker families. We call for a reduction in the estate tax burden, which creates hardships for widows and minor children. We also pledge to address any remaining inequities in the treatment of women under the Social Security system.

Women know better than anyone the decline in the quality of life that is occurring in America today. The peril to the United States and especially to women must be stressed. Women understand domestic, consumer, economic issues more deeply because they usually manage the households and have the responsibility for them. With this responsibility must also come greater opportunity for achievement and total equality toward solution of problems.

Equal Rights

The truths we hold and the values we share affirm that no individual should be victimized by unfair discrimination because of race, sex, advanced age, physical handicap, difference of national origin or religion, or economic circumstance. However, equal opportunity should not be jeopardized by bureaucratic regulations and decisions which rely on quotas, ratios, and numerical requirements to exclude some individuals in favor of others, thereby rendering such regulations and decisions inherently discriminatory.

We pledge vigorous enforcement of laws to assure equal treatment in job recruitment, hiring promotion, pay, credit, mortgage access and housing.

Millions of Americans who trace their heritage to the nations of Eastern, Central, and Southern Europe have for too long seen their values neglected. The time has come to go beyond the ritual election-year praise given to Ethnic Americans. We must make them an integral part of government. We must make recognition of their values an integral part of government policy. The Republican Party will take positive steps to see to it that these Americans, along with others too long neglected, have the opportunity to share the power, as well as the burdens of our society. The same holds true of our Asian-American citizens from the cultures of the Orient.

As a party we also recognize our commitment to Native Americans. We pledge to continue to honor our trusted relationship with them and we reaffirm our federal policy of self-determination. We support the assumption by Indians, Aleuts, and Eskimos themselves of the decisions and planning which will affect their lives and the end of undue federal influence on those plans and decisions.

Puerto Rico has been a territory of the United States since 1898. The Republican Party vigorously supports the right of the United States citizens of Puerto Rico to be admitted into the Union as a fully sovereign state after they freely so determine. We believe that the statehood alternative is the only logical solution to the problem of inequality of the United States citizens of Puerto Rico within the framework of the federal constitution, with full recognition within the concept of a multicultural society of the citizens' right to retain their Spanish language and traditions. Therefore we pledge to support the enactment of the necessary legislation to allow the people of Puerto Rico to exercise their right to apply for admission into the Union at the earliest possible date after the presidential election of 1980.

We also pledge that such decision of the people of Puerto Rico will be implemented through the approval of an admission bill. This bill will provide for the island's smooth transition from its territorial fiscal system to that of a member of the Union. This enactment will enable the new state of Puerto Rico to stand economically on an equal footing with the rest of the states and to assume gradually its fiscal responsibilities as a state.

We continue to favor whatever action may be necessary to permit American citizens resident in the United States territories of the Virgin Islands and Guam to vote for President and Vice President in national elections.

Abortion

There can be no doubt that the question of abortion, despite the complex nature of its various issues, is ultimately concerned with equality of rights under the law. While we recognize differing views on this question among Americans in general—and in our own Party—we affirm our support of a constitutional amendment to restore protection of the right to life for unborn children. We also support the Congressional efforts to restrict the use of taxpayers' dollars for abortion.

We protest the Supreme Court's intrusion into the family structure through its denial of the parents' obligation and right to guide their minor children.

STRONG FAMILIES

The family is the foundation of our social order. It is the school of democracy. Its daily lessons—cooperation, tolerance, mutual concern, responsibility, industry—are fundamental to the order and progress of our Republic. But the Democrats have shunted the family aside. They have given its power to the bureaucracy, its jurisdiction to the courts, and its resources to government grantors. For the first time in our history, there is real concern that the family may not survive.

Government may be strong enough to destroy families, but it can never replace them.

Unlike the Democrats, we do not advocate new federal bureaucracies with ominous power to shape a national family order. Rather, we insist that all domestic policies, from child care and schooling to Social Security and the tax code, must be formulated with the family in mind.

Education

Next to religious training and the home, education is the most important means by which families hand down to each new generation their ideals and beliefs. It is a pillar of a free society. But today, parents are losing control of their children's schooling. The Democratic Congress and its counterparts in many states have launched one fad after another, building huge new bureaucracies to misspend our taxes. The result has been a shocking drop in student performance, lack of basics in the classroom, forced busing, teacher strikes, manipulative and sometimes amoral indoctrination.

The Republican Party is determined to restore common sense and quality to education for the sake of all students, especially those for whom learning is the highway to equal opportunity. Because federal assistance should help local school districts, not tie them up in red tape, we will strive to replace the crazy quilt of wasteful programs with a system of block grants that will restore decision making to local officials responsible to voters and parents. We recognize the need to preserve within the structure of block grants, special educational opportunities for the handicapped, the disadvantaged, and other needy students attending public and private non-profit elementary and secondary schools.

We hail the teachers of America. Their dedication to our children is often taken for granted, and they are frequently underpaid for long hours and selfless service, especially in comparison with other public employees.

We understand and sympathize with the plight of America's public school teachers, who so frequently find their time and attention diverted from their teaching responsibilities to the task of complying with federal reporting requirements. America has a great stake in maintaining standards of high quality in public education. The Republican Party recognizes that the achievement of those standards is possible only to the extent that teachers are allowed the time and freedom to teach. To that end, the Republican Party supports deregulation by the federal government of public education, and encourages the elimination of the federal Department of Education.

We further sympathize with the right of qualified teachers to be employed by any school district wishing to hire them, without the necessity of their becoming enrolled with any bargaining agency or group. We oppose any federal action, including any action on the part of the Department of Education to establish "agency shops" in public schools.

We support Republican initiatives in the Congress to restore the right of individuals to participate in voluntary, non-denominational prayer in schools and other public facilities. We applaud the action of the Senate in passing such legislation.

Our goal is quality education for all of America's children, with a special commitment to those who must overcome handicap, deprivation, or discrimination. That is why we condemn the forced busing of school children to achieve arbitrary racial quotas. Busing has been a prescription for disaster, blighting whole communities across the land with its divisive impact. It has failed to improve the quality of education, while diverting funds from programs that could make the difference between success and failure for the poor, the disabled, and minority children.

We must halt forced busing and get on with the education of all our children, focusing on the real causes of their problems, especially lack of economic opportunity.

Federal education policy must be based on the primacy of parental rights and responsibility. Toward that end, we reaffirm our support for a system of educational assistance based on tax credits that will in part compensate parents for their financial sacrifices in paying tuition at the elementary, secondary, and post-secondary level. This is a matter of fairness, especially for low-income families, most of whom would be free for the first time to choose for their children those schools which best correspond to their own cultural and moral values. In this way, the schools will be strengthened by the families' involvement, and the families' strengths will be reinforced by supportive cultural institutions.

We are dismayed that the Carter Administration cruelly reneged on promises made during the 1976 campaign. Wielding the threat of his veto, Mr. Carter led the fight against Republican attempts to make tuition tax credits a reality.

Next year, a Republican White House will assist, not sabotage, congressional efforts to enact tuition tax relief into law.

We will halt the unconstitutional regulatory vendetta launched by Mr. Carter's IRS Commissioner against independent schools.

We will hold the federal bureaucracy accountable for its harassment of colleges and universities and will clear away the tangle of regulation that has unconscionably driven up their expenses and tuitions. We will respect the rights of state and local authorities in the management of their school systems.

The commitment of the American people to provide educational opportunities for all has resulted in a tremendous expansion of schools at all levels. And the more we reduce the federal proportion of taxation, the more resources will be left to sustain and develop state and local institutions.

Health

Our country's unequalled system of medical care, bringing greater benefits to more people than any-

where else on earth, is a splendid example of how Americans have taken care of their own needs with private institutions.

Significant as these achievements are, we must not be complacent. Health care costs continue to rise, farther and faster than they should, and threaten to spiral beyond the reach of many families. The causes are the Democratic Congress' inflationary spending and excessive and expensive regulations.

Republicans unequivocally oppose socialized medicine, in whatever guise it is presented by the Democratic Party. We reject the creation of a national health service and all proposals for compulsory national health insurance.

Our country has made spectacular gains in health care in recent decades. Most families are now covered by private insurance, Medicare, or in the case of the poor, the entirely free services under Medicaid.

Republicans recognize that many health care problems can be solved if government will work closely with the private sector to find remedies that will enhance our current system of excellent care. We applaud, as an example, the voluntary effort which has been undertaken by our nation's hospitals to control costs. The results have been encouraging. More remains to be done.

What ails American medicine is government meddling and the strait-jacket of federal programs. The prescription for good health care is deregulation and an emphasis upon consumer rights and patient choice.

As consumers of health care, individual Americans and their families should be able to make their own choices about health care protection. We propose to assist them in so doing through tax and financial incentives. These could enable them to choose their own health coverage, including protection from the catastrophic costs of major long-term illness, without compulsory regimentation.

Americans should be protected against financial disaster brought on by medical expense. We recognize both the need to provide assistance in many cases and the responsibility of citizens to provide for their own needs. By using tax incentives and reforming federal medical assistance programs, government and the private sector can jointly develop compassionate and innovative means to provide financial relief when it is most needed.

We endorse alternatives to institutional care. Not only is it costly but it also separates individuals from the supportive environment of family and friends. This is especially important for the elderly and those requiring long-term care. We advocate the reform of Medicare to encourage home-based care whenever feasible. In addition, we encourage the development of innovative alternate health care delivery systems and other out-patient services at the local level.

We must maintain our commitment to the aged and to the poor by providing quality care through Medicare and Medicaid. These programs need the careful, detailed reevaluation they have never received from the Democrats, who have characteristically neglected their financial stability. We believe that the needs of those who depend upon their programs, particularly the elderly, can be better served, especially when a Republican Administration cracks down on fraud and abuse so that program monies can be directed toward those truly in need. In the case of Medicaid, we will aid the states in restoring its financial integrity and its local direction.

We welcome the long-overdue emphasis on preventive health care and physical fitness that is making Americans more aware than ever of their personal responsibility for good health. Today's enthusiasm and emphasis on staying well holds the promise of dramatically improved health and well-being in the decades ahead. Additionally, health professionals as well as individuals have long recognized that preventing illness or injury is much less expensive than treating it. Therefore, preventive medicine, combined with good personal health habits and health education, can make a major impact on the cost of health care. Employers and employees, unions and business associations, families, schools, and neighborhood groups all have important parts in what is becoming a national crusade for better living.

Youth

The Republican Party recognizes that young people want the opportunity to exercise the rights and responsibilities of adults.

The Republican agenda for making educational and employment opportunities available to our youth has been addressed in detail in other sections of this platform.

Republicans are committed to the enactment of a youth differential in the minimum wage and other vitally needed incentives for the creation of jobs for our young.

In addition, we reaffirm our commitment to broaden the involvement of young people in all phases of the political process—as voters, party workers and leaders, candidates and elected officials, and participants in government at all levels.

We pledge, as we have elsewhere in this platform,

efforts to create an environment which will enable our nation's youth:

- to live in a society which is safe and free;
- to pursue personal, educational, and vocational goals to the utmost of their abilities;
- to experience the support, encouragement, and strength that comes from maintenance of the family and its values; and
- to know the stimulus of challenge, renewal through encouragement, provision of opportunities, and the growth that comes from responsible participation in numerous aspects of our society.

Older Americans

Inflation is called "the cruelest tax." It strikes most cruelly at the elderly, especially those on fixed incomes. It strikes viciously at the sick and the infirm, and those who are alone in the world.

Inflation has robbed our elderly of dignity and security. An entire generation of responsible and productive citizens who toiled and saved a full working life to build up a retirement nest egg now finds that it cannot survive on its savings. Today's inflation rates dwarf yesterday's interest rates, and the pensions and annuities of our elderly citizens cannot keep up with the rising cost of living. Millions of once-proud and independent elderly Americans face a future of welfare dependency and despair.

We propose to assist families, and individuals of all ages, to meet the needs of the elderly, primarily through vigorous private initiative. Only a comprehensive reduction in tax rates will enable families to save for retirement income, and to protect that income from ravaging inflation. Only new tax exemptions and incentives can make it possible for many families to afford to care for their older members at home.

Present laws can create obstacles to older Americans' remaining in the family home. Federal programs for the elderly, such as Medicare and Supplemental Security Income, must address, humanely and generously, the special circumstances of those who choose to stay with their families rather than enter a nursing home or other institution.

Social Security is one of this nation's most vital commitments to our senior citizens. We commit the Republican Party to first save, and then strengthen, this fundamental contract between our government and its productive citizens.

Republicans consider older Americans a community asset, not a national problem. We are committed to using the sadly wasted talents of the aged throughout our society, which sorely needs their experience and wisdom. To that end, and as a matter of basic fairness, we proudly reaffirm our opposition to mandatory retirement and our long-standing Republican commitment to end the Democrats' earnings limitation upon Social Security benefits. In addition, the Republican Party is strongly opposed to the taxation of the Social Security benefits and we pledge to oppose any attempts to tax these benefits.

Republicans have resisted Democratic electioneering schemes to spend away the Social Security trust funds for political purposes. Now the bill has come due, and the workers of America are staggering under their new tax burdens. This must stop.

Precisely because Social Security is a precious lifeline for millions of the elderly, orphaned, and disabled, we insist that its financing be sound and stable. We will preserve Social Security for its original purpose.

The problems of Social Security financing are only an aspect of the overriding problems of the economy which Democratic mismanagement has produced. There is but one answer, the comprehensive tax rate reduction to which Republicans are committed. To save Social Security, we have no choice but to redirect our economy toward growth. To meet this country's commitments to Social Security recipients, present and future, we need more people at work, earning more money, thereby paying more into the trust funds. That same growth can balance the federal budget with lower taxes, over time reducing inflation, which falls so cruelly on senior citizens whose income is fixed by the size of their public or private pension.

We pledge to clean up the much-abused disability system. We will also expand eligibility for Individual Retirement Accounts to enable more persons to plan for their retirement years.

The Welfare System

The Republican agenda for welfare reform has been discussed in a previous section, but we think it important to stress that central to it is the preservation of the families the system is designed to serve. The current system does not do this. Neither would guaranteed annual income schemes. By supplanting parental responsibility and by denying children parental guidance and economic support, they encourage and reward the fragmentation of families. This is unconscionable. The values and strengths of the family provide a vital element in breaking the bonds of poverty.

Ultimately, the Republican Party supports the orderly, wholesale transfer of all welfare functions to the states along with the tax sources to finance them.

The Family Economy

It is increasingly common for both husbands and wives to work outside the home. Often, it occurs out of economic necessity, and it creates major difficulties for families with children, especially those of pre-school age. On one hand, they are striving to improve the economic well-being of their family; on the other, they are concerned about the physical and emotional well-being of their children. This dilemma is further aggravated in instances of single parenthood due to death or divorce.

Recognizing these problems, we pledge to increase the availability of non-institutional child care. We see a special role for local, private organizations in meeting this need.

We disapprove of the bias in the federal tax system against working spouses, whose combined incomes are taxed at a proportionately higher rate than if they were single. We deplore this "marriage tax" and call for equity in the tax treatment of families.

We applaud our society's increasing awareness of the role of homemakers in the economy, not apart from the work force but as a very special part of it: the part that combines the labor of a full-time job, the skills of a profession, and the commitment of the most dedicated volunteer. Recognizing that homemaking is as important as any other profession, we endorse expanded eligibility for Individual Retirement Accounts for homemakers and will explore other ways to advance their standing and security.

Family Protection

In view of the continuing efforts of the present Administration to define and influence the family through such federally funded conferences as the White House Conference on Families, we express our support for legislation protecting and defending the traditional American family against the ongoing erosion of its base in our society.

Handicapped People

Republicans will seek every effective means to enable families more easily to assist their handicapped members and to provide for their education and special medical and therapeutic needs. In the case of handicapped children particularly, flexibility must be maintained in programs of public assistance so that, whenever possible, these youngsters may remain at home rather than in institutions.

Targeted tax relief can make it possible for parents to keep such a child at home without foregoing essential professional assistance. Similarly, tax incentives can assist those outside the home, in the neighborhood and the workplace, who undertake to train, hire, or house the handicapped.

SECURE AND PROSPEROUS NEIGHBORHOODS

The quality of American neighborhoods is the ultimate test of the success or failure of government policies for the cities, for housing, and for law enforcement.

Obsessed with the demands of special interest groups and preoccupied with the design of expensive "comprehensive" programs, the Democrats in Congress and the Administration have lost sight of that simple but important criterion. They have proposed more social and fiscal tinkering with our cities and towns.

Republicans will address the real problems that face Americans in their neighborhoods day by day—deterioration and urban blight, dangerous streets and violent crime that make millions of Americans, especially senior citizens, fearful in their own neighborhoods and prisoners in their own homes.

In the summer of 1980, Americans suffer a rising national unemployment rate, now at nearly 8 percent, and double-digit inflation and interest rates. As Republicans meet in Detroit, the policies of the Carter Administration and the Democratic Congress have pushed the economy into recession and have resulted in unemployment approaching 20 percent in our host city.

The people of Detroit have worked long and hard to revitalize their city and the evidence of its rebirth is impressive. Their efforts have been severely set back by Carter Administration policies outside of this or any city's control. The grim evidence is manifested in jobs lost as a direct consequence of bankrupt economic policies which have fostered this recession. Republicans will address and resolve the real problems of today's economy, problems that destroy jobs and deny even the hope of home ownership to millions of American families. We are, moreover, committed to nurturing the spirit of self-help and cooperation through which so many neighborhoods have revitalized themselves and served their residents.

Neighborhood Self-Help

The American ethic of neighbor helping neighbor has been an essential factor in the building of our nation. Republicans are committed to the preservation of this great tradition.

To help non-governmental community programs aid in serving the needs of poor, disabled, or other disadvantaged, we support permitting taxpayers to deduct charitable contributions from their federal income tax whether they itemize or not.

In contrast, the Democrats' assault against Meals-on-Wheels highlights their insensitivity to the neighborly spirit that motivates so many Americans. For over 25 years, voluntary Meals-on-Wheels organizations have been feeding needy homebound citizens—usually the elderly—with funding from local private charitable sources. Promising for the first time to "help" these neighborhood volunteer efforts in 1978, the Democratic Congress and Administration instead used the carrot of federal funding and the stick of federal regulation to crowd out private ventures.

Government must never elbow aside private institutions—schools, churches, volunteer groups, labor and professional associations—in meeting the social needs in our neighborhoods and communities.

Neighborhood Revitalization

The city is the focus for the lives of millions of Americans. Its neighborhoods are places of familiarity, of belonging, of tradition and continuity. They are arenas for civic action and creative self-help. The human scale of the neighborhood encourages citizens to exercise leadership, to invest their talents, energies, and resources, to work together to create a better life for their families.

Republican economic programs will create conditions for rebirth of citizen activity in neighborhoods and cities across the land. In a Republican economic climate, America's cities can once again produce, build, and grow.

A Republican Administration will focus its efforts to revitalize neighborhoods in five areas. We will:

- cut taxes, increase incentives to save, restore sound money, and stimulate capital investment to create jobs;
- create and apply new tax incentives for employees and employers alike to stimulate economic growth and reduce red tape for business ventures. Local government will be invited to designate specific depressed areas as job and enterprise zones;
- encourage our cities to undertake neighborhood revitalization and preservation programs in cooperation with the three essential local interests: local government, neighborhood property owners and residents, and local financial institutions;
- replace the categorical aid programs with block

grant or revenue sharing programs and, where appropriate, transfer the programs, along with the tax sources to pay for them, back to the state and local governments; and

- remain fully committed to the fair enforcement of all federal civil rights statutes and continue minority business enterprise and similar programs begun by Republican Administrations but bungled by over-regulation and duplication during the Carter Administration.

Republican programs will revitalize the inner cities. New jobs will be created. The federal government's role will be substantially reduced. The individual citizen will reclaim his or her independence.

The revitalization of American cities will proceed from the revitalization of the neighborhoods. Cities and neighborhoods are no more nor less than the people who inhabit them. Their strengths and weaknesses provide their character. If they are to grow, it is the people who must seize the initiative and lead.

Housing and Homeownership

Our citizens must have a real opportunity to live in decent, affordable housing. Due to the disastrous policies of the Carter Administration and the Democratic Congress, however, the goal of homeownership and all that aspiration entails is now in jeopardy. These irrational policies have been catastrophic to the housing industry. The highest home mortgage interest rates in the history of the United States have depressed housing starts to the lowest level since World War II. Democratic policies guarantee shortages in owner-occupied and rental housing.

As many as 1.4 million people who depend upon homebuilding for work may lose their jobs in this recession. Many already have. In addition to the toll taken on millions of American families, intolerable pressures will build on state, local, and federal budgets as tax revenues decline and expenditures increase to aid the unemployed.

We support financing and tax incentives to encourage the construction of rental housing as an essential addition to our housing inventory.

Prospective first-time home buyers simply cannot afford to buy. The affordability of housing has become a crisis. The high rates of inflation have driven mortgage payments, house prices, and down-payment requirements beyond the means of close to 80 percent of young American families. In order to assist the record number of young families who wish to become home buyers, we propose to implement a young fam-

ily housing initiative, which would include several elements such as: urban homesteading, savings and tax reforms, and innovative alternate mortgage instruments to help meet monthly payment requirements without federal subsidies. To assist older homeowners, again without federal subsidy, we urge more extensive availability of the reverse annuity mortgage which allows older homeowners to withdraw the substantial equity they have built up in their homes and thus supplement their retirement income. In order to slow increases in housing costs, regulations which artificially limit housing production and raise housing costs must be eliminated.

We favor expansion of the Republican-sponsored urban homesteading program as a means of restoring abandoned housing. This innovative program is locally administered, returns property to the tax rolls, and develops new ownership and stability within our neighborhoods.

The collapse of new home production and the distress of the housing finance system are closely related. The stop-and-go economic policies of the past year have created extreme volatility in financial markets which have made it impossible for thrift institutions to supply housing credit at a reasonable cost.

A set of policies aimed at higher and more stable levels of housing production will simultaneously reduce housing costs and unemployment in the economy. To assure a stable and continuous flow of funds for home mortgage financing, we pledge to allow responsible use of mortgage revenue bonds. We will work to change the tax laws to encourage savings so that young families will be able to afford their dreams.

Specifically, we will support legislation to lower tax rates on savings in order to increase funds available for housing. This will help particularly to make homeownership an accessible dream for younger families, encouraging them not to despair of ever having a home of their own, but to begin working and saving for it now. We oppose any attempt to end the income tax deductability of mortgage interest and property taxes.

Republicans will also end the mismanagement and waste that has characterized the Department of Housing and Urban Development during the Carter Administration. As presently structured, HUD programs present local governments and developers with a maze of bureaucracy, complicated applications, and inflexible requirements, often unsuited to local needs. Such programs often infringe upon the right of local government to retain jurisdiction over their own zoning laws and building codes. As a result, their cost is so high that relatively few of the needy are ultimately housed or helped. Republicans will replace many of HUD's categorical programs with decentralized block grants to provide more efficient and responsive housing assistance to the elderly, the handicapped, and the poor. In remaining programs, particular emphasis should be given to rehabilitation and preservation of existing housing stock as a priority in federal housing policy.

Crime

Safety and security are vital to the health and well-being of people in their neighborhoods and communities. Republicans are committed to ensuring that neighborhoods will be safe places in which families and individuals can live, and we support and encourage community crime fighting efforts such as neighborhood crime watch and court monitoring programs.

First, we believe that Republican economic proposals, more particularly those proposals which strengthen society and smaller communities discussed elsewhere in this document, will go a long way toward stabilizing American society.

Second, we support a vigorous and effective effort on the part of law enforcement agencies. Although we recognize the vital role of federal law enforcement agencies, we realize that the most effective weapons against crime are state and local agencies. Just as vital to efforts to stem crime is the fair but firm and speedy application of criminal penalties. The existence and application of strong penalties are effective disincentives to criminal actions. Yet these disincentives will only be as strong as our court system's willingness to use them.

We believe that the death penalty serves as an effective deterrent to capital crime and should be applied by the federal government and by states which approve it as an appropriate penalty for certain major crimes.

We believe the right of citizens to keep and bear arms must be preserved. Accordingly, we oppose federal registration of firearms. Mandatory sentences for commission of armed felonies are the most effective means to deter abuse of this right. We therefore support Congressional initiatives to remove those provisions of the Gun Control Act of 1968 that do not significantly impact on crime but serve rather to restrain the law-abiding citizen in his legitimate use of firearms.

In recent years, a murderous epidemic of drug abuse has swept our country. Mr. Carter, through his policies and his personnel, has demonstrated little interest in stopping its ravages. Republicans consider drug abuse an intolerable threat to our society, especially to the young. We pledge a government that will take seriously its responsibility to curb illegal drug traffic. We will first and most urgently restore the ability of the FBI to act effectively in this area. Republican government will work with local law enforcement agencies to apprehend and firmly punish drug pushers and drug smugglers, with mandatory sentences where appropriate. We support efforts to crack down on the sale and advertising of drug paraphernalia. Private, non-profit drug abuse rehabilitation agencies have taken the lead in fighting drug abuse, and they deserve greater cooperation and flexibility from federal, state, and local agencies and grant programs. We pledge the enactment of legislation to ban the utilization of federal funds by grantees of the Legal Services Corporation to render their services in cases involving the pushing or smuggling of drugs as well as in cases of repeat offenders. We commend the religious leaders, community activists, parents, and local officials who are working with fervor and dedication to protect young Americans from the drug plague.

Urban Transportation

The complex problems of mobility, congestion, and energy resources demand creative solutions if we are to improve the living conditions of our urban areas. Many urban centers of our nation need dependable and affordable mass transit systems. The first line of responsibility must lie with the local governments. They must be given the latitude to design and implement the transportation system best suited to their singular circumstances. Republicans believe we should encourage effective competition among diverse modes of transportation. The role of the federal government should be one of giving financial and technical support to local authorities, through surface transportation block grants. Because of the long planning and construction times inherent in bus, rail, and other mass transit systems, a consistent and dependable source of revenue should be established.

Mass transportation offers the prospect for significant energy conservation. In addition, both management and labor agree that ease of access to the workplace is an important factor in employment decisions and industrial plant locations. Lack of adequate access is a major reason why businesses have moved out of crowded urban areas, resulting in lower tax bases for cities. To encourage existing businesses to remain in urban centers and to attract new businesses to urban areas, it is vital that adequate public and private transportation facilities be provided.

Rural Transportation

Republicans recognize the importance of transportation in the rural areas of America.

Public transit is becoming more significant to rural areas as the costs of energy rise. While public transit will not replace the importance of private vehicles in rural America, it can serve as a vital adjunct to transportation in the neighborhoods throughout rural America.

JOBS AND THE WORKPLACE

We propose to put Americans back to work again by restoring real growth without inflation to the United States economy. Republican programs and initiatives detailed in this platform will create millions of additional new jobs in the American workplace. As a result of Mr. Carter's recession, more than 8 million Americans are now out of work.

Sweeping change in America's economic policy is needed. We must replace the Carter Administration's promise of hard times and austerity—one promise which has been kept—with Republican policies that restore economic growth and create more jobs.

The Democratic Congress and the Carter Administration are espousing programs that candidate Carter in 1976 said were inhumane: using recession, unemployment, high interest rates, and high taxes to fight inflation. The Democrats are now trying to stop inflation with a recession, a bankrupt policy which is throwing millions of Americans out of work. They say Americans must tighten their belts, abandon their dreams, and accept higher taxes, less take-home pay, fewer jobs, and no growth in the national economy.

We categorically reject this approach. Inflation is too much money chasing too few goods. Shutting down our nation's factories and throwing millions of people out of work leads only to shortages and higher prices.

We believe inflation can only be controlled by monetary and spending restraint, combined with sharp reductions in the tax and regulatory barriers to savings, investments, production, and jobs.

The Need for Growth and Its Impact on Workers

The Republican Party believes nothing is more important to our nation's defense and social well-being than economic growth.

Since 1973, the U.S. economy has grown in real terms at a rate of only 1.9 percent a year. This is barely half of the 3.7 percent annual growth rate we experienced between 1950 and 1973 and well below the 4.6 percent growth rate we enjoyed between 1961 and 1969. If our economy continues to grow at our current rate of less than 2 percent a year, our Gross National Product (GNP) will barely reach $3 trillion by 1990.

But if we can regain the growth we experienced during the economic boom of the 1960s, our GNP will reach nearly $4 trillion by the end of the decade, nearly one-third higher.

With this kind of economic growth, incomes would be substantially higher and jobs would be plentiful. Federal revenues would be high enough to provide for a balanced budget, adequate funding of health, education and social spending, and unquestioned military preeminence, with enough left over to reduce payroll and income taxes on American workers and retirees. Economic growth would generate price stability as the expanding economy eliminated budget deficits and avoided pressure on the Federal Reserve to create more money. And the social gains from economic growth would be enormous. Faster growth, higher incomes, and plentiful jobs are exactly what the unemployed, the underprivileged, and minorities have been seeking for many years.

All working men and women of America have much to gain from economic growth and a healthy business environment. It enhances their bargaining position by fostering competition among potential employers to provide more attractive working conditions, better retirement and health benefits, higher wages and salaries, and generally improving job security. A stagnant economy, which Democratic policies have brought about, decreases competition among business for workers, discourages improved employee benefits, reduces income levels, and dramatically increases unemployment.

Savings, Productivity, and Jobs

Savings and investment are the keys to economic growth. Only that part of national income which goes into savings and which is not consumed by government deficits is available to finance real economic growth.

Americans now save less than any other people in the Western world because inflation and the high rates of taxation imposed by the Carter Administration and the Democratic Congress have destroyed their ability and incentive to save and invest. This has strangled economic growth, choked off private initiative, pushed up prices, and retarded productivity and job creation.

The sharp drop in the growth of American productivity is the main reason why Americans' average real weekly earnings are no more than they were 19 years ago. This problem has worsened to the point that workers earn 8 percent less in real purchasing power as the Carter term comes to a close than they did when it began.

The 25 years of Democratic domination of the Congress have cost us a generation of lost opportunities.

The Carter Administration in particular has opposed every Republican effort to restore the health of the economy through lower taxes and work efforts, savings, and the modernization of America's productive machinery.

Republicans are committed to an economic policy based on lower tax rates and a reduced rate of government spending.

Therefore, the Republican Party pledges to:

- reduce tax rates on individuals and businesses to increase incentives for all Americans and to encourage more savings, investment, output and productivity, and more jobs for Americans;
- provide special incentives for savings by lowering the tax rates on savings and investment income;
- revitalize our productive capacities by simplifying and accelerating tax depreciation schedules for facilities, structures, equipment, and vehicles;
- limit government spending to a fixed and smaller percentage of the Gross National Product; and
- balance the budget without tax increases at these lower levels of taxation and spending.

We also oppose Carter proposals to impose withholding on dividend and interest income. They would serve as a disincentive to save and invest and create needless paperwork burdens for government, business, industry, and the private citizen. They would literally rob the saver of the benefits of interest compounding and automatic dividend reinvestment programs.

Unless taxes are reduced and federal spending is restrained, our nation's economy faces continued inflation, recession, and economic stagnation. Tax rate reductions and spending restraint will restore the savings and investment needed to create new jobs, increase living standards, and restore our competitive position in the world.

Employment Safety-Net

To those individuals who have lost their jobs because of the Carter recession we pledge to insure that they receive their rightfully earned unemployment compensation benefits.

The Republican Party recognizes the need to provide workers who have lost their jobs because of technological obsolescence or imports the opportunity to adjust to changing economic conditions. In particular,

we will seek ways to assist workers threatened by foreign competition.

The Democratic Administration's inability to ensure fairness and equity between our nation and some of our trading partners has resulted in massive unemployment in many core industries. As we meet in Detroit, this Party takes special notice that among the hardest hit have been the automotive workers whose jobs are now targeted by aggressive foreign competition. Much of this problem is a result of the present Administration's inability to negotiate foreign trade agreements which do not jeopardize American jobs. We will take steps to ensure competitiveness of our domestic industries to protect American jobs. But for workers who have already lost their jobs, we will provide assistance, incentives for job retraining and placement, and job search and relocation allowances. Toward this end, we will pursue specific tax and regulatory changes to revitalize America's troubled basic industries. We will also seek the aid of private individuals, businesses, and non-profit organizations to formulate creative new self-supporting answers to training and placement problems as well as nongovernmental sources of temporary financial support.

The Republican Party believes that protectionist tariffs and quotas are detrimental to our economic wellbeing. Nevertheless, we insist that our trading partners offer our nation the same level of equity, access, and fairness that we have shown them. The mutual benefits of trade require that it be conducted in the spirit of reciprocity. The Republican Party will consider appropriate measures necessary to restore equal and fair competition between ourselves and our trading partners.

The international exchange of goods and services must take place under free and unfettered conditions of market entry.

Training and Skills

Unemployment is a growing problem for millions of Americans, but it is an unparalleled disaster for minority Americans. As this country's economic growth has slowed over the past decade, unemployment has become more intractable. The gravity of the crisis is so severe that as we entered the present recession, unemployment was over 6 percent for the entire labor force but it was 33 percent for minority youth. In addition, the black unemployment rate was 10.8 percent and youth between the ages of 16 and 24 continued to account for about one-half of the total unemployed.

Despite the almost $100 billion spent on well intended public sector employment and training programs, the structural unemployment problem continues to fester among minorities and young people. In addition to providing a growth climate for job creation, specific and targeted programs must be developed to alleviate these problems.

Since four out of every five jobs are in the private sector, the success of federal employment efforts is dependent on private sector participation. It must be recognized as the ultimate location for unsubsidized jobs, as the provider of means to attain this end, and as an active participant in the formulation of employment and training policies on the local and national level. Throughout America, the private and independent sectors have repeatedly helped in the creation of minority business through donated counseling and consulting services. They have encouraged equal opportunity hiring practices within their own industries and have built non-profit, self-supporting training centers where the products produced during training are sold to support the programs.

A coordinated approach needs to be developed which maximizes the use of existing community resources, offers adequate incentives to the private sector, focuses on both large and small business, and minimizes red tape.

In recognizing the seriousness of the youth employment problem, Republicans also realize that a job alone will do very little to move a disadvantaged young person beyond the poverty line. Republicans support the creation of comprehensive programs for disadvantaged youth which would offer pre-employment training, educational instruction, job placement, and retention services. Second, Republicans support efforts to establish and maintain programs which seek to match the needs of the private sector and our young people as efficiently and effectively as possible. We also support expansion of proven skill training practices, such as apprenticeship, as well as private schools and trade schools. These methods can provide quality training and point toward the acquisition of specific job skills leading to specific employment goals.

We will encourage and foster the growth of new organizations operated by public–private partnerships to help forge a closer link between the schools and private employers. These institutions can afford in-school and out-of-school disadvantaged youth with the opportunity to upgrade basic skills, acquire work habits and orientation to work, and move directly from successful completion of the program to private unsubsidized jobs.

We believe that present laws create additional barriers for unemployed youth. One of the keys to resolving the youth unemployment problem is to reduce the cost to private employers for hiring young people who lack the necessary skills and experience to become immediately productive. Unfortunately, current government policy makes it too expensive for employers to hire unskilled youths. We urge a reduction of payroll tax rates, a youth differential for the minimum wage, and alleviation of other costs of employment until a young person can be a productive employee.

Small Business

Small business is the backbone of the American economy, with unique strengths and problems which must be recognized and addressed. For more than half of all American workers, the workplace is a small business. Small business is family business both in the sense that many of them are owned and operated by single families, and also because most American families rely not only on the goods and services, but on the jobs produced there for their livelihood and standard of living.

Republicans have demonstrated their sensitivity to the problems of the small business community. The Carter Administration held a conference to learn what Republicans have long known. In the Congress, we have been working to pass legislation to solve small business problems and achieve the very goals later identified by that conference. A 1978 initiative by the late Representative Bill Steiger reduced the capital gains tax rates which were destroying capital formation in America. Under the leadership of Republicans in Congress, efforts to simplify and liberalize the restrictive depreciation schedule are a top priority. Another proposal long advocated by our Party is the drive to encourage the entrepreneur by reform of the regulatory laws which stifle the very life of business through fines, threats, and harassment. Republicans realize the immediate necessity of reducing the regulatory burden to give small business a fighting chance against the federal agencies. We believe that wherever feasible, small business should be exempt from regulations and, where exemption is not feasible, small business should be subject to a less onerous tier of regulation. We have offered legislation to reimburse small businessmen who successfully challenge the federal government in court. Republicans believe the number one priority for small business in America is the achievement of lower business and personal tax rates for small businessmen and women and we intend to work to secure them.

All of these initiatives will receive immediate attention from a Republican Administration and Congress.

Without such changes as these, the small entrepreneur, who takes the risks which help make the economy grow and provides over 90 percent of all new jobs annually, will be an endangered species.

By fostering small business growth, we are promoting permanent private sector solutions to the unemployment problem. We will continue to provide for small business needs by enacting a substantial increase in the surtax exemption. The heavy estate tax burden imposed on the American people is threatening the life savings of millions of our families, forcing spouses and children to sell their homes, businesses, and family farms to pay the estate taxes. To encourage continuity of family ownership, we will seek to ease this tax burden on all Americans and abolish excessive inheritance taxes to allow families to retain and pass on their small businesses and family farms.

We will reform the patent laws to facilitate innovation and we will further this goal by encouraging a greater share of federal research and development be done by small business. Finally, we will reform those tax laws which make it more profitable to break up a small business or merge it into a conglomerate, than to allow it to grow and develop as an independent business.

Fairness to the Worker

The Republican Party is committed to full employment without inflation. We will seek to provide more jobs, increase the standard of living, and ensure equitable treatment on the job for all American workers by stimulating economic growth.

We reaffirm our commitment to the fundamental principle of fairness in labor relations, including the legal right of unions to organize workers and to represent them through collective bargaining consistent with state laws and free from unnecessary government involvement. We applaud the mutual efforts of labor and management to improve the quality of work life.

Wage demands today often represent the attempt of working men and women to catch up with government-caused inflation and high tax rates. With the blessing of the Democrat's majority in Congress, the Council on Wage and Price Stability has put a de facto ceiling of 7 to 8.5 percent on workers' wages, while the Administration devalues their paychecks at a rate of 13 to 15 percent. The government, not the worker, is the principle cause of inflation.

We recognize the need for governmental oversight of the health and safety of the workplace without interfering in the economic well-being of employers or the job security of workers.

The Republican Party reaffirms its long-standing support for the right of states to enact "Right-to-Work" laws under section 14(b) of the Taft–Hartley Act.

The political freedom of every worker must be protected. Therefore the Republican Party strongly supports protections against the practice of using compulsory dues and fees for partisan political purposes.

Fairness to the Consumer

The Republican Party shares the concerns of consumers that there be full disclosure and fairness in the marketplace. We recognize that government regulation and taxes add significantly to costs of goods and services to the consumer, reducing the standard of living for all Americans. For example, safety and environmental standards, some of which are counterproductive, increase the average price of a new car by over $700. Compliance with those regulations alone costs motorists as much as $12 billion a year.

Fairness to the consumer, like fairness to the employer and the worker, requires that government perform certain limited functions and enforce certain safeguards to ensure that equity, free competition, and safety exist in the free market economy. However, government action is not itself the solution to consumer problems; in fact, it has become in large measure a part of the problem. By consistent enforcement of law and enhancement of fair competition, government can and should help the consumer.

An informed consumer making economic choices and decisions in the marketplace is the best regulator of the free enterprise system. Consumers are also taxpayers, workers, investors, shoppers, farmers, and producers. The Republican Party recognizes the need for consumer protection but feels that such protection will not be enhanced by the creation of a new consumer protection bureaucracy. Just as there can be no single monolithic consumer viewpoint, so the Republican Party opposes the funding of special self-proclaimed advocates to represent consumer interests in federal agency proceedings.

Fairness to the Employer

The Republican Party declares war on government overregulation. We pledge to cut down on federal paperwork, cut out excessive regulation, and cut back the bloated bureaucracy.

In addressing these problems we recognize that overregulation is particularly harmful to America's small businesses whose survival is often threatened by the excessive costs of complying with government rules and handling federal paperwork.

While we recognize the role of the federal government in establishing certain minimum standards designed to improve the quality of life in America, we reaffirm our conviction that these standards can best be attained through innovative efforts of American business without the federal government mandating the methods of attainment.

The extraordinary growth of government, particularly since the middle 1960s, has brought mounting costs to society which, in turn, have added to inflationary pressures, reduced productivity, discouraged new investment, destroyed jobs, and increased bureaucratic intrusion into everyday life.

Regulatory costs are now running in excess of $100 billion each year, or about $1,800 for every American family. Federal paperwork annually costs businesses from $25 to $32 billion. According to official figures, it takes individuals and business firms over 143 million man-hours to complete 4,400 different federal forms each year. Government regulation produces many indirect, immeasurable costs as well and has led to increased bureaucratization of industry. Regulation also restricts personal choices, tends to undermine America's democratic public institutions, and threatens to destroy the private, competitive free market economy it was originally designed to protect.

Government Reform

In the face of a crisis of overregulation, the Carter Administration and the Democrats who control Congress have failed to recognize the problems facing workers, employers, and consumers and seem unable to come to grips with the underlying causes. While belatedly supporting transportation deregulation programs initiated by previous Republican Administrations, they have embarked on ambitious new schemes to tighten Washington's hold on energy and education. They have ignored or sidetracked Republican proposals to eliminate wasteful and outmoded spending programs and regulations. They have combined to push through more legislation and create additional programs which expand the size and power of the federal bureaucracy at the expense of ordinary taxpayers, consumers and businesses. In contradiction to 1976 Carter campaign promises to cut back on regulation, the number of pages in the *Federal Register* devoted to new rules and regulations has increased from 57,072 in 1976 to 77,497 in 1979 and will approach 90,000 by the end of 1980.

The result of Democratic rule in both the White House and the Congress is that government power has grown unchecked. Excessive regulation remains a major component of our nation's spiraling inflation and continues to stifle private initiative, individual freedom, and state and local government automony.

The Republican Party pledges itself to a comprehensive program of government reform. We propose to enact a temporary moratorium on all new federal regulations that diminish the supply of goods and services and add significantly to inflation. Such a moratorium will be consistent with the goal of achieving a safe and healthy working environment. We shall work to reduce substantially the regulatory and paperwork burdens on small businesses.

We encourage management and labor to form joint safety and health committees to make the workplace a better place to produce goods and services. At the same time we believe that the arbitrary and high-handed tactics used by OSHA bureaucrats must end. OSHA should concentrate its resources on encouraging voluntary compliance by employers and monitoring situations where close federal supervision is needed and serious hazards are most likely to occur. OSHA should be required to consult with, advise, and assist businesses in coping with the regulatory burden before imposing any penalty for non-compliance. Small businesses and employers with good safety records should be exempt from safety inspections, and penalties should be increased for those with consistently poor performance.

AGRICULTURE

In no American workplace is there to be found greater productivity, cooperation, neighborly concern, creative use of applied science, information and relevant research, honesty, perseverance, hard work, and independence than on the farm and ranch.

The Republican Party takes pride in the ability of American farmers to provide abundant, high-quality, and nutritious food and fiber for all our citizens including those most in need and to millions throughout the world, and at the same time to supply the largest single component in our export balance of trade.

Crisis in Agriculture

Four years of the Carter Administration and 25 consecutive years of a Congress controlled by Democrats have brought farmers and ranchers to the brink of disaster and the hardest times they have known since the Great Depression. In the last four years, more than 100,000 family farms have failed as farm income has plummeted. Even the present Administration's own figures show a decrease in real net farm income of some 40 percent in the last year alone—from $33 billion in 1979 to less than $22 billion projected for 1980.

The Democratic Party and the Carter Administration have abused their authority and failed in their responsibility to provide sound agricultural policies. Republicans pledge to make life in rural America prosperous again. We will:

- increase net farm income by supporting and refining programs to bring profitable farm prices with the goal of surpassing parity levels in a market-oriented agricultural economy;
- control inflation by adopting sound fiscal and monetary policies and by eliminating excessive and unnecessary federal regulations;
- expand markets at home by effectively utilizing the advantages of the energy potential for farm, forestry, and other biomass products. We encourage the continued innovative efforts in developing alcohol and other renewable energy sources and equipment for both on-farm and commercial use;
- aggressively expand markets abroad by effectively using the Eisenhower Food for Peace program and revolving credit incentives, working to remove foreign restraints on American products and encouraging the development of dependable new markets in developing countries;
- assure a priority allocation of fuel for U.S. agriculture, including food and fiber production, transportation, and processing; and
- combine efforts to encourage the renewable resource timber production capability of privately owned forests and woodlands with a federal program committed to multiple-use (timber, recreation, wildlife, watershed and/or range management) where federal land has not been designated as wilderness.

Rural America

Attention to the quality of life in our rural areas is a vital necessity because rural Americans impart a special strength to the national character. It is our goal to assure that all rural citizens—whether they are farmers or not—have the same consideration in matters of economic development, in energy, credit and transportation availability, and in employment opportunities which are given to those who live in towns and cities. The opportunity for non-farm jobs enhances the ability of people to live and work in rural America in the decade ahead, and our dedication to a prosperous and energetic rural America is part and parcel of our commitment to make America great again.

Expand Export Markets

Agriculture's contribution to the U.S. trade balance makes it especially fitting that an aggressive market development program to establish dependable new markets for farm exports will be a vital part of the policies to restore profitability to American agriculture. Republicans will ensure that:

- international trade is conducted on the basis of fair and effective competition and that all imported agricultural products meet the same standards of quality that are required of American producers;
- the General Agreement on Tariffs and Trade becomes a meaningful vehicle for handling agricultural trade problems and grievances;
- an aggressive agricultural market development program and the streamlining of the export marketing system is given top national priority;
- government-to-government sales of agricultural commodities be eliminated, except as specifically provided by law;
- the future of U.S. agricultural commodities is protected from the economic evils of predatory dumping by other producing nations and that the domestic production of these commodities, so important to the survival of individuals and small rural communities is preserved; and
- the important and productive potential of the commercial seafood industry is given encouragement.

Farmer-Held Reserves

We support farmer-owned grain reserves, should they become necessary, and adamantly oppose government-controlled reserves.

Grain Embargo

We believe that agricultural embargoes are only symbolic and are ineffective tools of foreign policy. We oppose singling out American farmers to bear the brunt of Carter's ill-conceived, ineffective, and improperly implemented grain embargo. The Carter grain embargo should be terminated immediately.

Excessive Regulation of Agriculture

The crushing burden of excessive federal regulation such as many of those imposed on farmers, ranchers, foresters, and commercial fishermen by OSHA, EPA, the departments of Agriculture, Labor, Justice, Interior, and other government entities are unrealistic and unnecessary.

We pledge a sensible approach to reduce excessive federal regulation that is draining the profitability from farming, ranching, and commercial fishing. Especially high on the agenda for changes in policy under Republican leadership are such regulatory issues as the Interior Department's ineffective predator control policies, EPA and FDA's excessive adherence to "zero risk" policies relative to the use of pesticides, herbicides, antibiotics, food additives, preservatives, and the like.

Soil and Water Conservation

We believe the strong soil and water conservation stewardship to which farmers, ranchers, watermen, and rural Americans are devoted is exemplary, and encourage appropriate local, state, and federal programs to give conservation practices vitality. Voluntary participation with adequate incentives is essential to the effective conservation of our soil and water resources.

Water Policy

The conservation and development of the nation's water resources are vital requisites for rebuilding America's national strength. The natural abundance of water can no longer be taken for granted. The impending crisis in water could be far more serious than our energy problems unless we act now. A dynamic water policy, which addresses our national diversity in climate, geography, and patterns of land ownership, and includes all requirements across the spectrum of water use, including reclamation policy, will be a priority of the Republican Administration working with the advice and counsel of state and local interests. We must develop a partnership between the federal and state governments which will not destroy traditional state supremacy in water law. Further, there must be cooperation between the Executive Branch and Congress in developing and implementing that policy. Lack of such partnership has resulted in four years of bitter confrontation between the states and the obstructive policies of the Democratic Administration. The Congress has been frustrated in its efforts to conserve and develop our water resources. Working together, the states and the federal government can meet the impending water crisis through innovative and alternative approaches to such problems as cleaning our lakes and rivers, reducing toxic pollution, developing multiple-use projects, and achieving a workable balance between the many competing demands on our water resources.

Agricultural Labor

Comprehensive labor legislation, which will be fair to American workers and encourage better relations with our neighbors in Mexico and Canada with whom we wish to establish a working North American Accord, is an essential endeavor. We deplore disruptive work stoppages which interrupt the supply of food to consumers.

Taxation

Federal estate and gift taxes have a particularly pernicious effect on family farms. Young farmers who inherit farm property are often forced to sell off part of the family farm to pay taxes. Once these taxes are paid, young farmers often must begin their careers deeply in debt. Our tax laws must be reformed to encourage rather than discourage family farming and ranching.

We deplore the imposition of present excessive estate and gift taxes on family farms. We support the use of lower, productivity-based valuation when farms are transferred within the family. Further, we believe that no spouse should pay estate taxes on farm property inherited from a husband or wife. We support the Republican tax cut proposal which provides accelerated depreciation and expanded investment tax credits to farm vehicles, equipment, and structures. Finally, we support legislation which would remove tax advantages foreign investors realize on the sale of U.S. forests, farmland, and other real estate.

Rural Transportation

It is essential to the well-being and security of our nation that an adequate rural transportation system be restored as a vital link between rural areas and their markets, both domestic and export. Overall, we pledge to eliminate those rules and regulations which are restrictive to the free flow of commerce and trade of agricultural products and encourage an environment that will enhance the private development and improvement of all modes of transportation to move agricultural production swiftly, safely, and economically. Recognizing the inherent advantages of each mode of transportation, the Republican Party will work to encourage and allow those advantages to be utilized on a balanced and equitable basis.

We believe the federal 55-miles-per-hour speed limit is counterproductive and contributes to higher costs of goods and services to all communities, particularly in rural America. The most effective, no-cost federal assistance program available would be for each state to set its own speed limit.

A Strong USDA

We pledge an Administration dedicated to restoring profitability to agriculture. A top priority will be the selection of a qualified and effective Secretary and policy staff who will speak up for American farmers and a President who will listen.

America's preeminence in agriculture is rooted in a system of agricultural research, extension, and teaching—unique and unequalled in the world. Land Grant Universities focus on problems of national, regional, and local concern. Cooperative extension, operating in every county of the United States and its territories, brings the results of USDA and Land Grant University research to farmers and ranchers, rural women, consumers, agribusiness, and to youth through 4-H programs.

Food Safety

The Republican Party favors a legislative effort to revise and modernize our food safety laws, providing guidelines for risk assessment, benefit assessment, peer review, and regulatory flexibility which are consistent with other government health and safety policies.

Cooperatives

We believe farmer cooperatives and rural electric and telephone cooperatives provide essential benefits to farmers and the rural Americans they serve, and we support exclusive jurisdiction of USDA in the effective administration of the Capper–Volstead Act.

We Republicans pledge ourselves to work with farmers, ranchers, and our friends and neighbors to make America great again.

THE NATION

Though a relatively young nation among those of western civilization we are possessed of one of the oldest institutions of government extant. Steeped in the Judeo-Christian ethic and in Anglo-Saxon theories of law and right, our legal and political institutions have evolved over many generations to form a stable system that serves free men and women well. It governs a people of multifarious heritage dispersed across a great continent of marked geographical contrasts. It presides over a diverse economy that in its collective whole is the largest, most powerful and most resilient in the world. In the two centuries of its life, though it has from time to time been sorely tested by constitutional, economic, and social crises, it has stood and not been found wanting. Its timeless strength, coupled with and reinforced by the faith and good will, the wisdom and confidence of the people from whom it derives its powers, has preserved us as a nation of enormous vitality.

The intent of the Founders, embraced and reflected by succeeding generations of Americans, was that the central government should perform only those functions which are necessary concomitants of nationality, preserve order, and do for people only those things which they cannot do for themselves. The durability of our system lies in its flexibility and its accommodation to diversity and changing circumstance. It is notable as much for what it permits as for what it proscribes. Government must ever be the servant of the nation, not its master.

Big Government

Under the guise of providing for the common good, Democratic Party domination of the body politic over the last 47 years has produced a central government of vastly expanded size, scope, and rigidity. Confidence in government, especially big government, has been the chief casualty of too many promises made and broken, too many commitments unkept. It is time for change—time to de-emphasize big bureaucracies—time to shift the focus of national politics from expanding government's power to that of restoring the strength of smaller communities such as the family, neighborhood, and the workplace.

Government's power to take and tax, to regulate and require has already reached extravagant proportions. As government's power continues to grow, the "consent of the governed" will diminish. Republicans support an end to the growth of the federal government and pledge to return the decision-making process to the smaller communities of society.

The emergence of policies and programs which will revitalize the free enterprise system and reverse the trend toward regulation is essential. To sustain the implementation of such policy, it is necessary to raise the public awareness and understanding that our free enterprise system is the source of all income, government and private, and raise the individual's awareness of his or her vested interest in its growth and vitality.

The Republican Party believes that it is important to develop a growing constituency which recognizes its direct relationship to the health and success of free enterprise, and realizes the negative impact of excessive regulation. Education and involvement in the system are the best means to accomplish this. To this end, we will actively pursue new and expanding opportunities for all Americans to become more directly involved in our free enterprise system.

Government Reorganization

The Republican Party reaffirms its belief in the decentralization of the federal government and in the traditional American principle that the best government is the one closest to the people. There, it is less costly, more accountable, and more responsive to people's needs. Against the prevailing trend toward increased centralization of government under the Democrats, Republicans succeeded in the 1970s in initiating large-scale revenue sharing and block grant programs to disperse the power of the federal government and share it with the states and localities.

Our states and localities have the talent, wisdom, and determination to respond to the variety of demands made upon them. Block grants and revenue sharing provide local governments with the means and the flexibility to solve their own problems in ways most appropriate for each locale. Unlike categorical grants, they do not lock states and localities into priorities and needs perceived by Washington. They are also more efficient because block grants and revenue sharing relieve both local government and the federal government from the costly and complicated process of program application, implementation, and review associated with the categorical grant system.

We pledge to continue to redouble our efforts to return power to the state and local governments. The regionalization of government encouraged by federal policies diminishes the responsiveness of state and local governments and impairs the power of the people to control their destiny.

While Republican efforts have been focused on sharing revenues and the powers that go with it, the Carter Administration has been preoccupied with the reorganization and consolidation of central authority. As a result, we have the Departments of Energy and Education, for example, but no more oil and gas, or learning, to show for it.

When we mistakenly rely on government to solve all our problems we ignore the abilities of people to solve their own problems. We pledge to renew the dispersion of power from the federal government to the states and localities. But this will not be enough. We pledge to extend the process so that power can be transferred as well to non-governmental institutions.

Government Reform

We favor the establishment of a commission of distinguished citizens to recommend ways of organizing and reducing the size and scope of the Executive Branch. Federal departments, agencies, and bureaus should be consolidated where possible to end waste and improve the delivery of essential services. Republicans pledge to eliminate bureaucratic red tape and reduce government paperwork. Agencies should be made to justify every official form and filing requirement. Where possible, we favor deregulation, especially in the energy, transportation, and communications industries. We believe that the marketplace, rather than the bureaucrats, should regulate management decisions.

The unremitting delegation of authority to the rule-makers by successive Democratic Congresses and the abuse of that authority has led to our current crisis of overregulation. For that reason, we support use of the Congressional veto, sunset laws, and strict budgetary control of the bureaucracies as a means of eliminating unnecessary spending and regulations. Agencies should be required to review existing regulations and eliminate those that are outmoded, duplicative, or contradictory. They must conduct cost–benefit analyses of major proposed regulations to determine their impact on the economy, on public health and safety, on state and local government, and on competition. We recommend legislation which would eliminate the present presumption of validity in favor of federal regulations. We also support legislation to require the federal government to provide restitution to those who have been wrongfully injured by agency actions. We oppose the use of tax monies of intervenors in the rule-making process.

We recognize that there are dangers inherent in the rapid growth of the federal bureaucracy, especially the arbitrary nature of its discretionary power and the abuses of procedural safeguards. Accordingly, we pledge to work for fundamental changes in the federal Administrative Procedures Act in order to give citizens the same constitutional protections before a government agency that they have in a courtroom. Among these reforms are requirements that agencies publish in the *Federal Register* all rules and statements of policy before they are adopted, that a person be guaranteed written notice and the opportunity to submit facts and arguments in any adjudicatory proceeding, that an agency decision be consistent with prior decisions unless otherwise provided by law, and that a person may seek judicial review without first exhausting his or her administrative remedies. At the same time we urge the Congress to strengthen its oversight to ensure that the agencies comply with the deadlines, report filing and other requirements mandated by law.

We propose to repeal federal restrictions and rewrite

federal standards which hinder minorities from finding employment, starting their own businesses, gaining valuable work experience, or enjoying the fruits of their own labors.

Because there are too many federal employees in comparison to private sector employees, there should be no further increase in the number of civilian federal employees if that would increase the ratio of federal employees to private sector employees over the present ratio.

Election Reform

The Republican Party has consistently encouraged full participation in our electoral process and is disturbed by the steady decline in voter participation in the United States in recent years. We believe that the increased voter turnout during the past year in Republican campaigns is due to dissatisfaction with Democratic officials and their failure to heed popular demands to cut taxes, restrain spending, curb inflation, and drastically reduce regulation.

Republicans support public policies that will promote electoral participation without compromising ballot-box security. We strongly oppose national postcard voter registration schemes because they are an open invitation to fraud.

Republicans support public policies that encourage political activity by individual citizens. We support the repeal of those restrictive campaign spending limitations that tend to create obstacles to local grassroots participation in federal elections. We also oppose the proposed financing of congressional campaigns with taxpayers' dollars as an effort by the Democratic Party to protect its incumbent members of Congress with a tax subsidy. We prefer the present system of having the states and party rules determine the presidential nominating process to the concept of a uniform national primary which would only add to the already high costs of, and excessive federal intrusion into, presidential campaigns.

We support the critical roles of competitive political parties in the recruitment of candidates, the conduct of campaigns, and the development of broad-based public policy responsive to the people. We urge Congress and state legislatures to frame their regulations of campaign finance, their nominating systems, and other election laws to strengthen rather than weaken parties.

Arts and Humanities

Recent Republican Administrations led the way in bringing together private support and governmental encouragement to effect a tremendous expansion of artistic and scholarly endeavor. The Carter Administration has crudely politicized these programs, lowering their standards of excellence and increasing federal control over them.

The Republican Party will restore the sound economy which is absolutely necessary for the arts and humanities to flourish. We will restore, as well, the integrity of federal programs in this area. Most important, to ensure the continued primacy of private funding for the arts, we reiterate our support of broader tax incentives for contributions to charitable and cultural organizations.

Transportation

America's transportation system must be designed to meet the requirements of the people, not to dictate what those requirements should be. Essential to any industrialized country is a transportation system which provides efficient and reliable service for both the movement of people and freight, urban and rural, domestic and foreign. Our nation has one of the finest transportation systems in the world but there is a danger that it will be unable to meet the future needs of a growing America.

Present levels of public and private investment will not preserve the existing system. For example, highways are deteriorating twice as fast as they are being rebuilt and inadequate rehabilitation will soon cost users more in reduced service levels than the cost of adequate rehabilitation.

The demand for transportation will grow dramatically in the next two decades with people-miles travelled increasing by over 50 percent and freight tonmiles more than doubling.

Government overregulation is inhibiting the return on investment necessary to attract capital for future growth and job creation.

A maze of federal agencies, Congressional committees, and conflicting policies is driving up costs and retarding innovation.

A lackluster energy policy, impeding production of oil, coal, and other forms of energy is endangering transportation's ability to keep up with demand.

Consequently, the role of government in transportation must be redefined. The forces of the free market must be brought to bear to promote competition, reduce costs, and improve the return on investment to stimulate capital formation in the private sector. The role of government must change from one of overbearing regulation to one of providing incentives for technological and innovative developments, while assuring through anti-trust enforcement that neither predatory competitive pricing nor price gouging of captive customers will occur.

Increased emphasis must be placed on the importance of having a well-balanced national transportation system where highways, passenger vehicles, buses, trucks, rail, water, pipelines, and air transportation each provide those services which they do best, while offering the widest range of reasonable choices for both passenger and freight movement. A sound transportation system is a prerequisite for the vision of America that Republicans embrace—a prosperous, growing nation where dreams can still come true.

Energy

Energy is the lifeblood of our economy. Without adequate energy supplies now and in the future, the jobs of American men and women, the security of their lives, and their ability to provide for their families will be threatened and their standard of living will be lowered. Every American is painfully aware that our national energy situation has deteriorated badly over the past four years of Democratic control. Gasoline prices have more than doubled. Our oil import bill has risen 96 percent. Our energy supplies have become increasingly vulnerable because U.S. oil production outside of Alaska is now 23 percent below 1973 levels. The threat of sudden shortages, curtailments, and gas lines has become a recurring reality.

This steady deterioration has not only compounded our economic problems of inflation, recession, and dollar weakness, but even more importantly, it has infected our confidence as a nation. Energy shortages, spiralling costs, and increasing insecurity are beginning to darken our basic hopes and expectations for the future.

The National Association for the Advancement of Colored People has very accurately focused on the effects that a no-growth energy policy will have on the opportunities of America's black people and other minorities. The NAACP said that "a pessimistic attitude toward energy supplies for the future . . . cannot satisfy the fundamental requirement of a society of expanding economic opportunity."

In commenting on the Carter energy proposals the Association said, "We cannot accept the notion that our people are best served by a policy based upon the inevitability of energy shortage and the need for government to allocate an ever diminishing supply among competing interests. . . . The plan reflects the absence of a black perspective in its development."

Three and one-half years ago, President Carter declared energy the "moral equivalent of war" and sent Congress 109 recommendations for action, including the creation of a new Department of Energy. Since then, the federal budget for government's energy bureaucracy has grown to about $10 billion per year and more than 20,000 pages of new energy regulations and guidelines have been issued. But these have not fostered the production of a single extra unit of energy.

The Democratic Congress has joined in the stampede, taking action on 304 energy bills since 1977. As a result, the federal bureaucracy is busy from coast to coast allocating gasoline, setting building temperatures, printing rationing coupons, and readying standby plans to ban weekend boating, close factories, and pass out "no drive day" stickers to American motorists—all the time saying, "we must make do with less." Never before in the history of American government has so much been done at such great expense with such dismal results.

Republicans believe this disappointing cycle of shrinking energy prospects and expanding government regulation and meddling is wholly unnecessary. We believe that the proven American values of individual enterprise can solve our energy problems. This optimism stands in stark contrast to the grim predictions of the Democrats who have controlled Congress for the last 25 years.

They seem to believe not only that we are a nation without resources, but also that we have lost our resourcefulness. Republicans believe in the common sense of the American people rather than a complex web of government controls and interventions that threaten America's ability to grow. We are committed to an alternative strategy of aggressively boosting the nation's energy supplies; stimulating new energy technology and more efficient energy use; restoring maximum feasible choice and freedom in the marketplace for energy consumers and producers alike; and eliminating energy shortages and disruptions as a roadblock to renewed national economic growth, rising living standards, and a reawakening of the hopes and dreams of the American people for a better and more abundant future.

We believe the United States must proceed on a steady and orderly path toward energy self-sufficiency. But in the interim, our pressing need for insurance against supply disruption should not be made hostage to the whims of foreign governments, as is presently the case under the Carter Administration. We believe it is necessary to resume rapid filling of strategic oil reserves to planned levels of 500 million barrels in the short term and ultimately to the one billion barrel level, and to insure that non-contiguous areas of the United States have their fair share of emergency oil reserves stored within their respective boundaries, as authorized by the Energy Policy and Conservation Act of 1975.

In order to increase domestic production of energy, Republicans advocate the decontrol of the price at the wellhead of oil and gas. We believe that the so-called windfall profits tax (which is unrelated to profit), should be repealed as it applies to small-volume royalty owners, new oil, stripper wells, tertiary-recovery, and heavy crude oil, and that the phase-out of the tax on old oil should be accelerated. This tax legislation should be amended to include a plowback provision. We will seek decontrol of prices on all oil products and an end to government authority to allocate petroleum supplies except in national emergency. We also believe that market restrictions on the use of natural gas should be eliminated.

Coal, our most abundant energy resource, can bridge the gap between our other present energy sources and the renewable energy sources of the future. The coal industry has been virtually ignored by the Carter Administration and the Democratic Congress. In 1977, President Carter promised to double coal production by 1985. Instead, because of obstructionist actions of the Administration, coal production has increased by only 11 percent to date and future prospects are dim. Today, thousands of coal miners are out of work and without hope for the future.

Republicans support a comprehensive program of regulatory reform, improved incentives, and revision of cumbersome and overly stringent Clean Air Act regulations. This program will speed conversion of utility, industrial, and large commercial oil-burning boilers to coal to the greatest extent feasible, thus substantially cutting our dependence on foreign oil. This program must begin immediately on a priority basis and be completed at the earliest date possible.

To effectively utilize this vast resource, our coal transportation systems must be upgraded and the government controls on them relaxed. Government regulation regarding the mining and use of coal must be simplified. We will propose a policy which will assure that governmental restraints, other than necessary and reasonable environmental controls, do not prevent the use of coal. We also reaffirm that mined lands must be returned to beneficial use and that states, in accordance with past Congressional mandate, have the primary responsibility to implement rules concerning the mining of coal which are adapted to the states' unique characteristics.

Coal, gas, and nuclear fission offer the best intermediate solutions to America's energy needs. We support accelerated use of nuclear energy through technologies that have been proven efficient and safe. The safe operation, as well as design, of nuclear generating plants will have our highest priority to assure the continued availability of this important energy source. The design and operation of these plants can be guaranteed in less than the 10-to-12-year lead time now required to license and build them. We believe that the licensing process can and should be streamlined through consolidation of the present process and the use of standardized reactor designs.

The Three Mile Island incident suggests the need for certain reforms, such as in the area of operator training, but illustrates that properly designed and operated nuclear plants do not endanger public health or safety. We further encourage the research, development, and demonstration of the breeder reactor with its potential for safely contributing to our nation's future energy supplies.

Nuclear power development requires sound plans for nuclear waste disposal and storage and reprocessing of spent fuel. Technical solutions to these problems exist, and decisive federal action to choose and implement solutions is essential. The Democratic controlled Congress and Administration have failed to address the spent fuel problem. A Republican Congress and Administration will immediately begin to implement plans for regional away-from-reactor storage of spent fuel with the goal of implementation of a program no later than 1984.

Republicans are committed to the rapid development of permanent storage facilities for nuclear wastes. Since waste disposal is a national responsibility, no state should bear an unacceptable share of this responsibility.

Republicans will also move toward reprocessing of spent fuel.

Republicans will continue to support the development of new technologies to develop liquid, gaseous, and solid hydrocarbons which can be derived from coal, oil shale, and tar sands. The decontrol of oil and gas prices will eliminate any necessity for government support for a synthetic fuel industry except possibly for limited demonstration projects. Clean air, water, waste disposal, mine reclamation, and leasing rules must be made rational and final to accelerate private investment.

Gasohol is an important, immediately available source of energy that is helping to extend our petroleum reserves. We encourage development of a domestic gasohol industry.

We also believe the government must continue supporting productive research to speed the development of renewable energy technology, including solar energy, geothermal, wind, nuclear fusion, alcohol synthesis, and biomass, to provide the next generation of energy sources.

Conservation clearly plays a vital role in the consideration and formulation of national energy policy. Republicans reject, however, the position of the Democrats which is to conserve through government fiat. Republicans understand that free markets based on the collective priorities and judgments of individual consumers will efficiently allocate the energy supplies to their most highly valued uses. We also believe that the role of government is best performed by structuring creative cost-effective incentives to achieve energy efficiency and conservation.

We reject unequivocally punitive gasoline and other energy taxes designed to artificially suppress energy consumption.

Much inefficient energy use results from government subsidization of imported oil and holding the price of natural gas substantially below its market value. When the price of energy is held artificially low, there is no incentive for conservation. This kind of energy consumption stems not from the excesses of the public, but the foolish policy distortions of government. Every BTU of genuine energy "waste" in our economy would rapidly disappear if we immediately and completely dismantle all remaining energy price controls and subsidies.

A Republican policy of decontrol, development of our domestic energy resources, and incentives for new supply and conservation technologies will substantially reduce our dependence on imported oil. We reject the Carter Administration's incessant excuse that the high price of imported oil and OPEC are the primary cause of inflation and recession at home and a weak dollar and declining balance of payments abroad. The fastest way to bring international oil prices under control is to stop printing so recklessly the dollar in which those prices are denominated. Fully 60 percent of the world oil price increase since 1973 represents the depreciation of our dollars rather than an increase in the real price of oil.

Virtually all major environmental legislation in the past decade reflected a bipartisan concern over the need to maintain a clean and healthful environment.

While the new environmental policies have resulted in improving air quality, cleaner waters, and more careful analysis of toxic chemicals, the price paid has far exceeded the direct and necessary cost of designing and installing new control technology. In the energy area, the increased complexity of regulations, together with continual changes in the standards imposed,

have brought about tremendous delays in the planning and construction of new facilities ranging from electric power plants to oil refineries, pipelines, and synthetic fuel plants.

Republicans believe that an effective balance between energy and environmental goals can be achieved. We can ensure that government requirements are firmly grounded on the best scientific evidence available, that they are enforced evenhandedly and predictably, and that the process of their development and enforcement has finality.

Republicans condemn the Democrats' withdrawal of a massive amount of the most promising federal lands from prospective energy development, including the rich potential of our Outer Continental Shelf. It has been estimated that by the end of the 1980s resources from government-controlled acreage could yield over two million barrels of oil per day and four trillion cubic feet of gas per year, the equivalent of nearly all of our imports from OPEC countries. It is clear that restrictive leasing policies have driven us further to depend on OPEC by severely impairing the exploration for, and development of, domestic oil, gas, and coal resources, thereby aggravating our balance of trade deficit and making our country less secure. Republicans will move toward making available all suitable federal lands for multiple use purposes including exploration and production of energy resources.

Republicans believe that in order to address our energy problem we must maximize our domestic energy production capability. In the short term, therefore, the nation must move forward on all fronts simultaneously, including oil and gas, coal, and nuclear. In the longer term, renewable resources must be brought significantly on line to replace conventional sources. Finally, in conjunction with this all-out production initiative, we must strive to maximize conservation and the efficient use of energy.

The return to the traditions that gave vitality and strength to this nation is urgent.

The free world—indeed western civilization—needs a strong United States. That strength requires a prospering economy. That economy will be secure with a vigorous domestic energy industry. That vigor can only be achieved in an atmosphere of freedom—one that encourages individual initiatives and personal resourcefulness.

Environment

The Republican Party reaffirms its long standing commitment to the conservation and wise management of America's renewable natural resources.

We believe that a healthy environment is essential to the present and future well-being of our people, and to sustainable national growth.

The nature of environmental pollution is such that a government role is necessary to insure its control and the proper protection of public health. Much progress has been made in achieving the goals of clean air, clean water, and control of toxic wastes. At the same time, we believe that it is imperative that environmental laws and regulations be reviewed, and where necessary, reformed to ensure that the benefits achieved justify the costs imposed. Too often, current regulations are so rigid and narrow that even individual innovations that improve the environment cannot be implemented. We believe, in particular, that regulatory procedures must be reformed to expedite decision making. Endless delay harms both the environment and the economy.

We strongly affirm that environmental protection must not become a cover for a "no-growth" policy and a shrinking economy. Our economy can continue to grow in an acceptable environment.

We believe that agricultural policy should give emphasis to the stewardship of the nation's soil and water resources. The permanent loss of productive farm land is a growing problem and we encourage states and local communities to adopt policies that help maintain and protect productive agricultural land as a national asset.

Immigration and Refugee Policy

Residency in the United States is one of the most precious and valued of conditions. The traditional hospitality of the American people has been severely tested by recent events, but it remains the strongest in the world. Republicans are proud that our people have opened their arms and hearts to strangers from abroad and we favor an immigration and refugee policy which is consistent with this tradition. We believe that to the fullest extent possible those immigrants should be admitted who will make a positive contribution to America and who are willing to accept the fundamental American values and way of life. At the same time, United States immigration and refugee policy must reflect the interests of the nation's political and economic well-being. Immigration into this country must not be determined solely by foreign governments or even by the millions of people around the world who wish to come to America. The federal government has a duty to adopt immigration laws and follow enforcement procedures which will fairly and effectively implement the immigration policy desired by American people.

The immediate adoption of this policy is essential to an orderly approach to the great problem of oppressed people seeking entry, so that the deserving can be accepted in America without adding to their hardships.

The refugee problem is an international problem and every effort should be made to coordinate plans for absorbing refugee populations with regional bodies, such as the Organization of American States and the Association of Southeast Asian Nations, on a global basis.

The Judiciary

Under Mr. Carter, many appointments to federal judgeships have been particularly disappointing. By his partisan nominations, he has violated his explicit campaign promise of 1976 and has blatantly disregarded the public interest. We pledge to reverse that deplorable trend, through the appointment of women and men who respect and reflect the values of the American people, and whose judicial philosophy is characterized by the highest regard for protecting the rights of law-abiding citizens, and is consistent with the belief in the decentralization of the federal government and efforts to return decision-making power to state and local elected officials.

We will work for the appointment of judges at all levels of the judiciary who respect traditional family values and the sanctity of innocent human life.

Taxes and Government Spending

Elsewhere in this platform, we have pledged for the sake of individual freedom and economic growth to cut personal income tax rates for all. Republicans believe that these tax rate reductions should be complemented by firm limitations on the growth of federal spending as provided by the Roth–Kemp Bill. The Republican Party therefore, pledges to place limits on federal spending as a percent of the Gross National Product. It is now over 21 percent. We pledge to reduce it. If federal spending is reduced as tax cuts are phased in, there will be sufficient budget surpluses to fund the tax cuts, and allow for reasonable growth in necessary program spending.

By increasing economic growth, tax rate reduction will reduce the need for government spending on unemployment, welfare, and public jobs programs. However, the Republican Party will also halt excessive government spending by eliminating waste, fraud, and duplication.

We believe that the Congressional budget process has failed to control federal spending. Indeed, because of its big spending bias, the budget process has actually contributed to higher levels of social spending, has prevented necessary growth in defense spending, and has been used to frustrate every Republican attempt to lower tax rates to promote economic growth.

The immediate burden of reducing federal spending rests on the shoulders of the President and the Congress. We believe a Republican Congress can balance the budget and reduce spending through legislative actions, eliminating the necessity for a Constitutional amendment to compel it. However, if necessary, the Republican Party will seek to adopt a Constitutional amendment to limit federal spending and balance the budget, except in time of national emergency as determined by a two-thirds vote of Congress.

Government Lending

Not only has the Democratic Congress failed to control spending, but in the last 10 years federal credit assistance programs have soared out of control.

Many federal loan guarantees and related credit programs are off-budget. As a result, no one knows the nature and extent of our obligations or the effect such practices have on our economy. The best estimate is that outstanding federal credit is now close to $600 billion.

Runaway government lending can be just as dangerous as runaway federal spending.

The Republican Party will establish a workable federal credit policy that will bring order to the reckless lending practices of the past.

Inflation

We consider inflation and its impact on jobs to be the greatest domestic threat facing our nation today. Mr. Carter must go! For what he has done to the dollar; for what he has done to the life savings of millions of Americans; for what he has done to retirees seeking a secure old age; for what he has done to young families aspiring to a home, an education for their children, and a rising living standard, Mr. Carter must not have another four years in office.

In his three and one-half years in office, Mr. Carter has presented and supported policies which carried inflation from 4.8 percent in 1976 to a peak of 18 percent during 1980.

He has fostered a 50 percent increase in federal spending, an increase of more than $200 billion, boosting spending in an era of scarce resources, and driving up prices.

He has through both inaction and deliberate policy permitted or forced tax increases of more than 70 percent, more than $250 billion, directly increasing the cost of living and the costs of hiring and producing. This has crippled living standards, productivity, and

our ability to compete in the world. It has led to reduced output, scarcity, and higher prices.

He has imposed burdensome regulations and controls on production which have reduced the availability of domestic goods and energy resources, increased our dependence on imports, particularly in the energy area, driven down the value of the dollar, and driven up prices.

He has permitted continuing federal budget deficits and increased federal borrowing, forcing higher interest rates and inflationary money creation, increasing prices.

The inflation policies of the Carter Administration have been inconsistent, counterproductive, and tragically inept. Mr. Carter has blamed everyone from OPEC to the American people themselves for his crisis of inflation—everyone, that is, but his own Administration and its policies which have been the true cause of inflation.

Inflation is too much money chasing too few goods. Much can be done to increase the growth of real output. But ultimately price stability requires a non-inflationary rate of growth of the money supply in line with the real growth of the economy. If the supply of dollars rapidly outstrips the quantity of goods, year in, year out, inflation is inevitable.

Ultimately, inflation is a decline in the value of the dollar, the monetary standard, in terms of the goods it can buy. Until the decade of the 1970s, monetary policy was automatically linked to the overriding objective of maintaining a stable dollar value. The severing of the dollar's link with real commodities in the 1960s and 1970s, in order to pursue economic goals other than dollar stability, has unleashed hyper-inflationary forces at home and monetary disorder abroad, without bringing any of the desired economic benefits. One of the most urgent tasks in the period ahead will be the restoration of a dependable monetary standard—that is, an end to inflation.

Lower tax rates, less spending, and a balanced budget are the keys to maintaining real growth and full employment as we end inflation by putting our monetary policy back on track. Monetary and fiscal policy must each play its part if we are to achieve our joint goals of full employment and price stability.

Unfortunately, Mr. Carter and the Democratic Congress seek to derail our nation's money creation policies by taking away the independence of the Federal Reserve Board. The same people who have so massively expanded government spending should not be allowed politically to dominate our monetary policy. The independence of the Federal Reserve System must be preserved.

The Republican Party believes inflation can be controlled only by fiscal and monetary restraint, combined with sharp reductions in the tax and regulatory disincentives for savings, investments, and productivity. Therefore, the Republican Party opposes the imposition of wage and price controls and credit controls.

Controls will not stop inflation, as past experience has shown. Wage and price controls will only result in shortages, inequities, black markets, and ultimately higher prices. We reject this short-sighted and misguided approach.

PEACE AND FREEDOM

At the start of the 1980s, the United States faces the most serious challenge to its survival in the two centuries of its existence. Our ability to meet this challenge demands a foreign policy firmly rooted in principle. Our economic and social welfare in the 1980s may depend as much on our foreign and defense policy as it does on domestic policy. The Republican Party reasserts that it is the solemn purpose of our foreign policy to secure the people and free institutions of our nation against every peril; to hearten and fortify the love of freedom everywhere in the world; and to achieve a secure environment in the world in which freedom, democracy, and justice may flourish.

For three and one-half years, the Carter Administration has been without a coherent strategic concept to guide foreign policy, oblivious to the scope and magnitude of the threat posed to our security, and devoid of competence to provide leadership and direction to the free world. The Administration's conduct of foreign policy has undermined our friends abroad, and led our most dangerous adversaries to miscalculate the willingness of the American people to resist aggression. Republicans support a policy of peace through strength; weakness provokes aggression.

For three and one-half years the Carter Administration has given us a foreign policy not of constancy and credibility, but of chaos, confusion, and failure. It has produced an image of our country as a vacillating and reactive nation, unable to define its place in the world, the goals it seeks, or the means to pursue them. Despite the Administration's rhetoric, the most flagrant offenders of human rights including the Soviet Union, Vietnam, and Cuba have been the beneficiaries of Administration good will, while nations friendly to the United States have suffered the loss of U.S. commercial access and economic and military assistance.

The threat to the United States and its allies is not only a military one. We face a threat from international terrorism. Our access to energy and raw material resources is challenged by civil unrest, Soviet-sponsored subversion, and economic combinations in restraint of free trade. Our first line of defense, our network of friendly nations and alliances, has been undermined by the inept conduct of foreign affairs.

American policy since World War II has rested upon the pillars of collective security, military and technological superiority, and economic strength, and upon the perception by our adversaries that the United States possesses the will to use its power where necessary to protect its freedom. These tenets have enabled a commonwealth of free and independent nations to enjoy the benefits and confidence that come from expanding economic interchange in peace and bilateral and multilateral support in time of war. The entire structure of peace was guaranteed by American and allied military power sufficient to deter conflict, or to prevail in conflict if deterrence should fail.

The Administration's neglect of America's defense posture in the face of overwhelming evidence of a threatening military buildup is without parallel since the 1930s. The scope and magnitude of the growth of Soviet military power threatens American interest at every level, from the nuclear threat to our survival, to our ability to protect the lives and property of American citizens abroad.

Despite clear danger signals indicating that Soviet nuclear power would overtake that of the United States by the early 1980s, threatening the survival of the United States and making possible, for the first time in post-war history, political coercion and defeat, the Administration reduced the size and capability of our nuclear forces.

Despite clear danger signals indicating that the Soviet Union was using Cuban, East German, and now Nicaraguan, as well as its own, military forces to extend its power to Africa, Asia, and the Western Hemisphere, the Administration often undermined the very governments under attack. As a result, a clear and present danger threatens the energy and raw material lifelines of the Western world.

Despite clear danger signals indicating that the Soviet Union was augmenting its military threat to the nations of Western Europe, American defense programs such as the enhanced radiation warhead and cruise missiles, which could have offset that buildup, were cancelled or delayed—to the dismay of allies who depend upon American military power for their security.

The evidence of the Soviet threat to American security has never been more stark and unambiguous, nor has any President ever been more oblivious to this threat and its potential consequences.

The entire Western world faces complex and multidimensional threats to its access to energy and raw material resources. The growth of Soviet military power poses a direct threat to the petroleum resources of the Persian Gulf now that its military forces deployed in Afghanistan are less than 300 miles from the Straits of Hormuz, through which half the free world's energy supplies flow.

Soviet efforts to gain bases in areas astride the major sea lanes of the world have been successful due to their use of military power, either directly or indirectly through Cuban and other Soviet bloc forces. Since the Carter Administration took office in 1977, the Soviets or their clients have taken over Afghanistan, Cambodia, Ethiopia, and South Yemen, and have solidified their grasp on a host of other nations in the developing world. The Soviet noose is now being drawn around southern Africa, the West's most abundant single source of critical raw materials.

The failure of the United States to respond to direct threats to its security has left American citizens vulnerable to terrorist assaults as well. American diplomatic personnel have been subject to seizure and assault by terrorists throughout the world without drawing a meaningful Administration response.

No failure of the Administration has been so catastrophic as its failure of leadership. Mired in incompetence, bereft of strategic vision and purpose, the President's failure to shoulder the burden of leadership in the Western alliance has placed America in danger without parallel since December 7, 1941. The United States cannot abdicate that role without inducing a diplomatic and eventually a military catastrophy.

Republicans realize that if the challenges of the 1980s are not met, we will continue to lose the respect of the world, our honor, and in the end, our freedom. Republicans pledge to meet these challenges with confidence and strength. We pledge to restore to the United States and its people a government with conviction in our cause, a government that will restore to our great nation its self-respect, its self-confidence, and its national pride.

NATIONAL SECURITY

Defense Budget Trends

In the late 1960s, the Republicans returned to the White House, inheriting a war in Southeast Asia. Because of this war, they also inherited a Fiscal Year (FY) 1968 defense budget which, if calculated in constant 1981 dollars to account for inflation, had risen to over $194 billion from $148 billion in FY 1961, the last Eisenhower year. By the beginning of the second Nixon Administration, U.S. forces were totally disengaged from Southeast Asia. The FY 1974 defense budget had dropped back to $139 billion, and the country had reaped its desired "peace dividend" of an over $50 billion reduction in annual defense spending. During this period, between 1969 and 1973, the Democrats who controlled Congress, led by Senators Mondale and Muskie, cut almost $45 billion from Nixon defense requests. Until 1975, Congress continued to ignore long-range defense needs, and made severe cuts in Republican defense proposals. The Ford Administration, however, succeeded in reversing this trend. From a low point of $134 billion in FY 75, the FY 76 defense budget rose, in response to President Ford's request, to $139 billion; and in FY 77 it rose again to $147 billion.

Despite the growing sentiment for a stronger defense, candidate Carter ran on a promise of massive cuts in U.S. defense spending, one promise he has kept. In his first three years in the White House, Mr. Carter reduced defense spending by over $38 billion from President Ford's last Five Year Defense Plan. Now, in his last year in office, faced with the total collapse of his foreign policy, and with his policy advisers and their assumptions disgraced, he has finally proposed an increase beyond the rate of inflation in defense spending. But this growth for 1981 will be less than 1 percent.

We deplore Mr. Carter's personal attempts to rewrite history on defense budgets. His tough speeches before military audiences cannot hide his continuing opposition to Congressional defense increases. The four chiefs of the armed services have each characterized the Carter defense program as "inadequate" to meet the military threat posed to the United States. We associate ourselves with the characterization by Democratic Congressional leaders of the President's behavior on defense as "hypocritical." We would go further; it is disgraceful.

Mr. Carter cut back, cancelled, or delayed every strategic initiative proposed by President Ford. He cancelled production of the Minuteman missile and the B-1 bomber. He delayed all cruise missiles, the MX missile, the Trident submarine and the Trident II missile. He did this while the Soviet Union deployed the Backfire bomber and designed two additional bombers equal in capability to the B-1, and while it deployed four new large ICBMs and developed four others.

Mr. Carter postponed production and deployment of enhanced radiation (neutron) warheads while the

Soviet Union deployed the SS-20 mobile missile and the Backfire bomber against Western Europe. He cut President Ford's proposed shipbuilding plan in half. He vetoed a nuclear aircraft carrier. He did this while the Soviet Union pursued an aggressive shipbuilding program capable of giving them worldwide naval supremacy in the 1980s unless current trends are reversed immediately. Mr. Carter opposed efforts to correct the terribly inadequate pay rates for our military personnel and stood by as the alarming exodus of trained and skilled personnel from the services quickened. At the same time, the Soviet Union increased its military manpower to a level of 4.8 million, more than double that of the U.S.

Recovery from the Carter Administration's neglect will require effort, but Americans know that effort is the unavoidable precondition to peace and economic prosperity. The Soviet Union is now devoting over $50 billion more to defense annually than the United States, achieving military superiority as a result. We have depleted our capital and must now devote the resources essential to catching up. The Secretary of Defense has stated that even if we were to maintain a constant increase in our spending of 5 percent in real terms, it would require 40 years for us to catch up.

Republicans commit themselves to an immediate increase in defense spending to be applied judiciously to critically needed programs. We will build toward a sustained defense expenditure sufficient to close the gap with the Soviets, and ultimately reach the position of military superiority that the American people demand.

Defense Strategy

More is required than reversing our military decline alone. We have seen in recent years how an Administration, possessed of dwindling but still substantial strength, has stood paralyzed in the face of an inexorable march of Soviet or Soviet-sponsored aggression. To be effective in preserving our interests, we must pursue a comprehensive military strategy which guides both the design and employment of our forces. Such a strategy must proceed from a sober analysis of the diverse threats before us.

Republicans approve and endorse a national strategy of peace through strength as set forth in House Concurrent Resolution 306. We urge speedy approval of this legislation by both the U.S. House of Representatives and the U.S. Senate as a means of making clear to the world that the United States has not forgotten that the price of peace is eternal vigilance against tyranny. Therefore we commend to all Americans the text of House Concurrent Resolution

306, which reads as follows: The foreign policy of the United States should reflect a national strategy of peace through strength. The general principles and goals of this strategy would be:

- to inspire, focus, and unite the national will and determination to achieve peace and freedom;
- to achieve overall military and technological superiority over the Soviet Union;
- to create a strategic and civil defense which would protect the American people against nuclear war at least as well as the Soviet population is protected;
- to accept no arms control agreement which in any way jeopardizes the security of the United States or its allies, or which locks the United States into a position of military inferiority;
- to reestablish effective security and intelligence capabilities;
- to pursue positive non-military means to roll back the growth of Communism;
- to help our allies and other non-Communist countries defend themselves against Communist aggression; and
- to maintain a strong economy and protect our overseas sources of energy and other vital raw materials.

Our strategy must encompass the levels of force required to deter each level of foreseeable attack and to prevail in conflict in the event deterrence fails. The detailed analysis that must form the intellectual basis for the elaboration of such a strategy will be the first priority of a Republican Administration. It must be based upon the following principles.

Nuclear Forces

Nuclear weapons are the ultimate military guarantor of American security and that of our allies. Yet since 1977, the United States has moved from essential equivalence to inferiority in strategic nuclear form with the Soviet Union. This decline has resulted from Mr. Carter's cancellation or delay of strategic initiatives like the B-1 bomber, the MX missile, and the Trident II submarine missile programs and from his decisions to close the Minuteman production line and forego production of enhanced radiation weapons.

As the disparity between American and Soviet strategic nuclear forces grows over the next three years, most U.S. land-based missiles, heavy bombers, and submarines in port will become vulnerable to a Soviet first-strike. Such a situation invites diplomatic blackmail and coercion of the United States by the Soviet Union during the coming decade.

An administration that can defend its interest only

by threatening the mass extermination of civilians, as Mr. Carter implied in 1979, dooms itself to strategic, and eventually geopolitical, paralysis. Such a strategy is simply not credible and, therefore, is ineffectual. Yet the declining survivability of the U.S. ICBM force in the early 1980s will make this condition unavoidable unless prompt measures are taken. Our objective must be to assure the survivability of U.S. forces possessing an unquestioned, prompt, hard-target counterforce capability sufficient to disarm Soviet military targets in a second-strike. We reject the mutual-assured-destruction (MAD) strategy of the Carter Administration which limits the President during crises to a Hobson's choice between mass mutual suicide and surrender. We propose, instead, a credible strategy which will deter a Soviet attack by the clear capability of our forces to survive and ultimately to destroy Soviet military targets.

In order to counter the problem of ICBM vulnerability, we will propose a number of initiatives to provide the necessary survivability of the ICBM force in as timely and effective a manner as possible. In addition, we will proceed with:

- the earliest possible deployment of the MX missile in a prudent survival configuration;
- accelerated development and deployment of a new manned strategic penetrating bomber that will exploit the $5.5 billion already invested in the B-1, while employing the most advanced technology available;
- deployment of an air defense system comprised of dedicated modern interceptor aircraft and early warning support systems;
- acceleration of development and deployment of strategic cruise missiles deployed on aircraft, on land, and on ships and submarines;
- modernization of the military command and control system to assure the responsiveness of U.S. strategic nuclear forces to Presidential command in peace or war; and
- vigorous research and development of an effective anti-ballistic missile system, such as is already at hand in the Soviet Union, as well as more modern ABM technologies.

For more than 20 years, commencing in the mid-1950s, the United States has maintained tactical nuclear weapons in Europe for the purpose of assuring against deep penetrations into the West by the Soviet forces. Since 1977, however, the Administration has allowed our former superiority to erode to the point where we now face a more than three-to-one disadvantage.

A Republican Administration will strive for early modernization of our theater nuclear forces so that a seamless web of deterrence can be maintained against all levels of attack, and our credibility with our European allies is restored. In consultation with them we will proceed with deployments in Europe of medium-range cruise missiles, ballistic missiles, enhanced radiation warheads, and the modernization of nuclear artillery.

Conventional Forces

The greatest single result of our loss of nuclear parity has been the manifest increase in the willingness of the Soviet Union to take risks at the conventional level. Emboldened by the Carter Administration's failure to challenge their use of surrogate Cuban forces in Africa and the later Soviet presence in Angola, Ethiopia, and South Yemen, the Soviets, for the first time in post-war history, employed their own army units outside of the Soviet bloc in a brutal invasion on Afghanistan. The invasion presents chilling evidence of the mounting threat and raises fundamental questions with respect to United States strategy.

We believe it is not feasible at this time, and in the long term would be unworkable, to deploy massive U.S. ground forces to such areas as the Persian Gulf on a permanent basis as we do in Europe and elsewhere. A more effective strategy must be built on the dual pillars of maintaining a limited full-time presence in the area as a credible interdiction force, combined with the clear capability to reinforce this presence rapidly with the forces necessary to prevail in battle. In addition, the strategy must envision military action elsewhere at points of Soviet vulnerability—an expression of the classic doctrine of global maneuver.

The forces essential to the support of such a strategy must include a much-improved Navy, the force most suitable for maintaining U.S. presence in threatened areas and protecting sea lines of communication. In addition, we will require a substantial improvement in the air and sea mobility forces and improved access to regional installations. A Republican Administration will propose their substantial improvement, to include the establishment of a permanent fleet in the Indian Ocean. We will also improve contingency planning for the use and expansion of our commercial maritime fleet, and a new rational approach to emergency use of our civil aircraft fleet.

The budget cuts imposed by Mr. Carter on the Army and his restoration of the supremacy of systems analysis in the Pentagon have resulted in slowdowns, deferrals and cost increases in nine vitally needed Army procurement programs in armor, firepower, air defense, and helicopters. These critical and long-delayed modernization programs must be restored to economical production rates and must be speeded into the field. Of equal importance is the need to bring our stocks of ammunition, spare parts and supplies—now at woefully inadequate levels—to a standard that will enable us to sustain our forces in conflict.

In addition to the strategic programs needed for our Air Force, we pledge to restore tactical aircraft development and procurement to economical levels and to speed the achievement of 26 modernized wings of aircraft able to conduct missions at night, in all weather conditions, and against the most sophisticated adversary.

We pledge to increase substantially our intra- and inter-theater airlift capability and to increase our aerial tanker fleet through procurement and speedy modernization.

Of all the services, the Navy and Marines have suffered most from Mr. Carter's cuts. Their share of the defense budget has shrunk from 40 to 33 percent during the Carter Administration. Mr. Carter slashed President Ford's 157-ship, five-year construction program to 83. He has slowed the Trident submarine and requested only one attack submarine each year in spite of a Soviet three-to-one advantage. He vetoed the Fiscal Year 79 Defense Authorization Bill because it included an aircraft carrier which a year later Congress forced him to accept. For the fourth straight year he has requested fewer than half the number of 325 aircraft needed annually to stay even with peacetime attrition and modernization requirements. He has requested fewer than one-third of the amphibious ships needed just to keep the current level of capability for the Marines, and he has opposed Marine tactical aircraft and helicopter modernization.

The current Chief of Naval Operations has testified that, "We are trying to meet a three-ocean requirement with a one-and-a-half ocean Navy." Republicans pledge to reverse Mr. Carter's dismantling of U.S. Naval and Marine forces. We will restore our fleet to 600 ships at a rate equal to or exceeding that planned by President Ford. We will build more aircraft carriers, submarines and amphibious ships. We will restore Naval and Marine aircraft procurement to economical rates enabling rapid modernization of the current forces, and expansion to meet the requirements of additional aircraft carriers.

Defense Manpower and the Draft

The Republican Party is not prepared to accept a peacetime draft at this time. Under Mr. Carter, the all-volunteer force has not been given a fair chance to succeed. The unconscionable mismanagement and neglect of personnel policy by the Carter Administration has made a shambles of the all-volunteer force concept.

Perhaps the most compelling vulnerability of our forces results from the dramatic exodus of the core of highly skilled men and women who form the backbone of our military strength. This loss is the direct result of neglect by the Commander-in-Chief.

The sustained malign neglect of our military manpower is nothing short of a national scandal. This Administration's active assault on military benefits and military retirement has been accompanied by an enforced pay-cap set at half the inflation rate. The average military family has lost between 14 percent and 25 percent in purchasing power over the past seven years.

Officers and skilled enlisted personnel are leaving in droves, and 250,000 of our servicemen qualify for public assistance. Many of our career people earn less than the minimum wage. The services are currently short 70,000 senior enlisted personnel. This scandal is the direct result of Mr. Carter's willful downgrading of the military and inept mismanagement of personnel policy. As a top priority, the Republican Party pledges to end this national disgrace.

We pledge to restore a national attitude of pride and gratitude for the service of our men and women in the armed forces. We will act immediately to correct the great inequities in pay and benefits of career military personnel. Specifically, we support immediate action to:

- provide for an increase in military pay targeted in particular toward the career grades now experiencing the greatest attrition;
- increase enlistment and reenlistment bonuses;
- improve continuation bonuses for aviators;
- increase per diem travel allowances;
- increase the allowance for moving mobile homes;
- provide family separation allowances for junior personnel; and
- expand benefit entitlement under the CHAMPUS program.

A Republican Administration will index military pay and allowances to protect military personnel from absorbing the burden of inflation. We pledge that the profession of arms will be restored to its rightful place as a preeminent expression of patriotism in America.

In order to attract recruits of high ability, a Republican Administration will act to reintroduce G.I. Bill benefits for those completing two years active service. We will press for enactment of legislation denying federal funds to any educational institution that impedes access of military recruiters to their students.

We regard as a serious loss the decision of many of our finest institutions of higher learning to discontinue their military officer training programs. The leadership of our armed forces must include the best trained minds in our nation. Republicans call upon our colleges and universities to shoulder their responsibilities in the defense of freedom. We will investigate legislative inducements toward this end. We will not consider a peacetime draft unless a well-managed, Congressionally funded, full-scale effort to improve the all-volunteer force does not meet expectations.

Reserve Forces

The armed forces of the U.S. are today critically dependent upon our nation's Reserve components for both combat arms and combat support. The Army Reserve and National Guard provide one-third of the Army's combat divisions, 80 percent of its independent combat brigades, one-half of its artillery battalions, and one-third of its special forces groups. The Navy Reserve provides 90 percent of the Navy's ocean mine sweeping and two-thirds of its mobile construction battalions. The Air Force Reserve and Air National Guard provide all of our strategic interceptors, 60 percent of our tactical airlift, and one-third of our tactical fighters. Reserve and National Guard units may be mobilized for even the smallest of conflicts and many such units today are expected to deploy immediately with the active duty units they support.

Today, however, the reserves are ill equipped, underpaid, and undermanned by several hundred thousand personnel. Proper equipment, realistic, challenging training, and greater full-time support must be made available. We must ensure that all Americans take note of the proud and vital role played by the Reserve and National Guard components of the armed forces of the United States.

Readiness and Industrial Preparedness

History records that readiness for war is the surest means of preventing it. Lack of preparedness is the most dangerously provocative course we can take. Yet funding requests for sufficient fuel, spare parts, ammunition, and supplies for U.S. war reserves have been cut each year for the past four years from the minimum quantities the armed services have stated they need. This has left the U.S. Armed Forces at their lowest state of preparedness since 1950, seriously compromising their ability to sustain a military conflict.

Crippling shortages of spare parts, fuel, and ammunition compromise the ability of the armed forces to sustain a major military conflict. Some critical types of ammunition could not support combat operations for more than a week although we are committed to holding a 90-day inventory of major ammunition types. In addition, critical facilities such as airfields, ammunition depots, maintenance installations, and living quarters for our troops are in serious disrepair. The backlog of deferred maintenance and the underfunded purchase of vital combat consumables is so vast that years of effort will be required to rebuild U.S. forces to the required level of readiness.

The problem of maintaining the day-to-day combat readiness of U.S. armed forces is compounded by the reduced ability of American industry to respond to wartime contingencies. Reduced acquisition of equipment for the modernization of the armed forces and the Carter Administration's failure to maintain combat readiness have eroded the incentive of American industry to maintain capacity adequate to potential defense requirements.

Republicans pledge to make the combat readiness of U.S. armed forces and the preparedness of the industrial base a top priority.

Research and Development

Research and development (R&D) provides a critical means by which our nation can cope with threats to our security. In the past, the United States' qualitative and technological superiority provided a foundation for our military superiority. Yet we are now on the verge of losing this advantage to the Soviet Union because of Mr. Carter's opposition to real increases in the R&D effort. Delays imposed on the R&D process now allow 7 to 10 years or more to elapse between the time when a new weapon system is proposed and when it becomes available.

The Soviet Union now invests nearly twice as much in military research and development as does the United States. This disparity in effort threatens American technological superiority in the mid-1980s and could result in Soviet breakthroughs in advanced weapon systems.

Republicans pledge to revitalize America's military research and development efforts, from basic research through the deployment of weapons and support systems, to assure that our vital security needs will be met for the balance of the century. We will seek increased funding to guarantee American superiority in this critical area and to enable us to deal with possible breakthroughs in anti-missile defense, anti-satellite killers, high-energy directed systems, and the military and civilian exploitation of space.

America's technological advantage has always depended upon its interaction with our civilian science and technology sector. The economic policy of the Carter Administration has severely encumbered private research and development efforts, thereby depriving both our civil and military sectors of the fruits of scientific innovation.

Underfunding of beneficial government-sponsored research efforts in basic and applied scientific research has disrupted the benefits of years of effective effort. In particular, America's preeminence in the exploration of space is threatened by the failure of the Carter Administration to fund fully the Space Shuttle program (with its acknowledged benefits for both the civil and military applications) as well as advanced exploration programs. Republicans pledge to support a vigorous space research program.

Management and Organization

The Republican Party pledges to reform the defense programming and budgeting management system established by the Carter Administration. The ill-informed, capricious intrusions of the Office of Management and Budget, and the Department of Defense Office of Program Analysis and Evaluation have brought defense planning full circle to the worst faults of the McNamara years. Orderly planning by the military services has become impossible. Waste, inefficiency, and paralysis have been the hallmarks of Carter Administration defense planning and budgeting. This has resulted in huge cost overruns and in protracted delays in placing advanced systems in the field.

National Intelligence

At a time of increasing danger, the U.S. intelligence community has lost much of its ability to supply the President, senior U.S. officials, and the Congress with accurate and timely analyses concerning fundamental threats to our nation's security. Morale and public confidence have been eroded and American citizens and friendly foreign intelligence services have become increasingly reluctant to cooperate with U.S. agencies. As a result of such problems, the U.S. intelligence community has incorrectly assessed critical foreign developments, as in Iran, and has, above all, underestimated the size and purpose of the Soviet Union's military efforts.

We believe that a strong national consensus has emerged on the need to make our intelligence community a reliable and productive instrument of national policy once again. In pursuing its objectives, the Soviet Union and its surrogates operate by a far different set of rules than does the United States. We do not favor countering their efforts by mirroring their tactics. However, the United States requires a realistic assessment of the threats it faces, and it must have the best intelligence capability in the world. Republicans pledge this for the United States.

A Republican Administration will seek to improve U.S. intelligence capabilities for technical and clandestine collection, cogent analysis, coordinated counterintelligence and covert action.

We will reestablish the President's Foreign Intelligence Advisory Board, abolished by the Carter Administration, as a permanent non-partisan body of distinguished Americans to perform a constant audit of national intelligence research and performance. We will propose methods of providing alternative intelligence estimates in order to improve the quality of the estimates by constructive competition.

Republicans will undertake an urgent effort to rebuild the intelligence agencies, and to give full support to their knowledgeable and dedicated staffs. We will propose legislation to enable intelligence officers and their agents to operate safely and efficiently abroad.

We will support legislation to invoke criminal sanctions against anyone who discloses the identities of U.S. intelligence officers abroad or who makes unauthorized disclosures of U.S. intelligence sources and methods.

We will support amendments to the Freedom of Information Act and the Privacy Act to permit meaningful background checks on individuals being considered for sensitive positions and to reduce costly and capricious requests to the intelligence agencies.

We will provide our government with the capability to help influence international events vital to our national security interests, a capability which only the United States among the major powers has denied itself.

A Republican Administration will seek adequate safeguards to ensure that past abuses will not recur, but we will seek the repeal of ill-considered restrictions sponsored by Democrats, which have debilitated U.S. intelligence capabilities while easing the intelligence collection and subversion efforts of our adversaries.

Terrorism

In the decade of the seventies, all civilized nations were shaken by a wave of widespread, international terrorist attacks. Time and again, nations and individuals have been subjected to extortion and murder at the hands of extremists who reject the rule of law, civil order, and the sanctity of individual human rights. Terrorism has been elevated to the level of overt national policy as authorities in Iran, encouraged by the Soviet Union, have held 53 Americans captive for more than eight months. Comprehensive support of international terrorist organizations has been a central, though generally covert, element of Soviet foreign policy.

Republicans believe that this tragic history contains lessons that must serve as the basis for a determined international effort to end this era of terrorism. We believe that certain principles have emerged from incidents in which states have defeated terrorist attacks, and we believe the United States should take the lead in a multilateral drive to eliminate the terrorist threat. A first requirement is the establishment of a military capability to deal promptly and effectively with any terrorist acts. We cannot afford, as in the abortive Iranian rescue mission, to allow months to pass while we prepare responses.

The United States must provide the leadership to forge an international consensus that firmness and refusal to concede are ultimately the only effective deterrents to terrorism. The United States should take the lead in combating international terrorism. We must recognize and be prepared to deal with the reality of expanded Soviet sponsorship of international terrorist movements. Development of an effective anti-terrorist military capability and establishment of a Congressional and Executive capability to oversee our internal security efforts will no longer be neglected.

The Role of Arms Control in Defense Policy

The Republican approach to arms control has been markedly different from that of the Democratic Party. It has been based on three fundamental premises:

- first, before arms control negotiations may be undertaken, the security of the United States must be assured by the funding and deployment of strong military forces sufficient to deter conflict at any level or to prevail in battle should aggression occur;
- second, negotiations must be conducted on the basis of strict reciprocity of benefits—unilateral restraint by the U.S. has failed to bring reductions by the Soviet Union; and
- third, arms control negotiations, once entered, represent an important political and military undertaking that cannot be divorced from the broader political and military behavior of the parties.

A Republican Administration will pursue arms control solely on the principles outlined above.

During the past three and one-half years, the Carter Administration's policy has been diametrically opposed to these principles. First, by its willful cancellation or delay of essential strategic military programs such as the B-1, the MX missile, and the Trident sub-

marine, it has seriously damaged the credibility and effectiveness of the U.S. deterrent force. Second, by not insisting upon corresponding concessions from the Soviet Union it has, in effect, practiced unilateral disarmament and removed any incentives for the Soviets to negotiate for what they could obviously achieve by waiting. The Republican Party rejects the fundamentally flawed SALT II treaty negotiated by the Carter Administration.

The Republican Party deplores the attempts of the Carter Administration to cover up Soviet non-compliance with arms control agreements including the now overwhelming evidence of blatant Soviet violation of the Biological Warfare Convention by secret production of biological agents at Sverdlovsk.

In our platform four years ago, we stated that, "The growth of civilian nuclear technology and the rising demand for nuclear power as an alternative to increasingly costly fossil fuel resources, combine to require our recognition of the potential dangers associated with such development." We called for the formation of new multilateral arrangements to control the export of sensitive nuclear technologies. Unfortunately, the Carter Administration has failed to provide the leadership and creative diplomacy essential to forging effective international safeguards and cooperation in this vital area. In particular we oppose and deplore the pending delivery to India of nuclear material which can be directed to the manufacture of weapons.

The Republican Party reaffirms its commitment to the early establishment of effective multilateral arrangements for the safe management and monitoring of all transfers and uses of nuclear materials in the international market.

FOREIGN POLICY

U.S.–Soviet Relations

The premier challenge facing the United States, its allies, and the entire globe is to check the Soviet Union's global ambitions. This challenge must be met, for the present danger is greater than ever before in the 200-year history of the United States. The Soviet Union is still accelerating its drive for military superiority and is intensifying its military pressure and its ideological combat against the industrial democracies and the vulnerable developing nations of the world.

Republicans believe that the United States can only negotiate with the Soviet Union from a position of unquestioned principle and unquestioned strength.

Unlike Mr. Carter we see nothing "inordinate" in our nation's historic judgment about the goals, tactics, and dangers of Soviet communism. Unlike the Carter Administration, we were not surprised by the brutal Soviet invasion of Afghanistan or by other Soviet violations of major international agreements regulating international behavior, human rights, and the use of military force. And, unlike the Carter Administration, we will not base our policies toward the Soviet Union on naive expectations, unilateral concessions, futile rhetoric, and insignificant maneuvers.

As the Soviet Union continues in its expansionist course, the potential for dangerous confrontations has increased. Republicans will strive to resolve critical issues through peaceful negotiations, but we recognize that negotiations conducted from a position of military weakness can result only in further damage to American interests.

A Republican Administration will continue to seek to negotiate arms reductions in Soviet strategic weapons, in Soviet bloc force levels in Central Europe, and in other areas that may be amenable to reductions or limitations. We will pursue hard bargaining for equitable, verifiable, and enforceable agreements. We will accept no agreement for the sake of having an agreement, and will accept no agreements that do not fundamentally enhance our national security.

Republicans oppose the transfer of high technology to the Soviet Union and its Eastern European satellites such as has been done in the past, permitting development of sophisticated military hardware which threatens the United States and our allies. The Carter Administration has encouraged the most extensive raid on American technology by the Soviet bloc since World War II. The Soviet Union has gained invaluable scientific expertise in electronics, computer sciences, manufacturing techniques, mining, transportation, aviation, agriculture, and a host of other disciplines. This has contributed to the ability of the Soviet Union to divert investment and manpower from their civilian economy to their armed forces. The fruits of Soviet access to American technology will improve the performance of the Soviet military establishment for years to come. The matter is compounded by the practice of subsidized financing of much of the Soviet bloc's acquisition of American technology through U.S. financial institutions.

Republicans pledge to stop the flow of technology to the Soviet Union that could contribute, directly or indirectly, to the growth of their military power. This objective will be pursued by a Republican Administration with our allies and other friendly nations as well. We will ensure that the Soviet Union fully understands that it will be expected to fulfill all of the commercial and diplomatic obligations it has undertaken in its international agreements.

We oppose Mr. Carter's singling out of the American farmer to bear the brunt of his failed foreign policy by imposition of a partial and incompetently managed grain embargo. Because of his failure to obtain cooperation from other grain exporting countries, the embargo has been a travesty and a substitute for policy. We call for the immediate lifting of this embargo.

We reaffirm our commitment to press the Soviet Union to implement the United Nations Declaration on Human Rights and the Helsinki Agreements which guarantee rights such as the free interchange of information and the right to emigrate. A Republican Administration will press the Soviet Union to end its harassment and imprisonment of those who speak in opposition to official policy, who seek to worship according to their religious beliefs, or who represent diverse ethnic minorities and nationalities.

Republicans deplore growing anti-Semitism in the Soviet Union and the mistreatment of "refuseniks" by Soviet authorities. The decline in exit visas to Soviet Jews and others seeking religious freedom and the promulgation of ever more rigorous conditions inhibiting their emigration is a fundamental affront to human rights and the U.N. Charter. Republicans will make the subject of emigration from the Soviet Union a central issue in Soviet–American relations. Human rights in the Soviet Union will not be ignored as it has been during the Carter Administration. As a party to the Helsinki Conference Final Act, a Republican Administration will insist on full Soviet compliance with the humanitarian provisions of the agreement.

Republicans pledge our continued support for the people of Cuba and the captive nations of Central and Eastern Europe in their hope to achieve self-determination. We stand firmly for the independence of Yugoslavia. We support self-determination and genuine independence for new captive nations of Africa and Latin America threatened by the growing domination of Soviet power.

A Republican Administration will end the sustained Carter policy of misleading the American people about Soviet policies and behavior. We will spare no efforts to publicize to the world the fundamental differences in the two systems and will strengthen such means as the International Communication Agency, the Voice of America, Radio Free Europe, and Radio Liberty actively to articulate U.S. values and policies, and to highlight the weaknesses of totalitarianism.

We pledge to end the Carter cover-up of Soviet violations of SALT I and II, to end the cover-up of Soviet violation of the Biological Warfare Convention, and to end the cover-up of Soviet use of gas and chemical weapons in Afghanistan and elsewhere.

NATO and Western Europe

Since its inception three decades ago, the North Atlantic Treaty Organization has expressed the collective will of free nations to resist totalitarian aggression. As a cornerstone of the Western Alliance, NATO has stood on the firm foundations of American strategic strength, joint Allied defense efforts, and cooperative diplomacy based on shared interest and close consultations. The Republican Party recognizes that NATO serves the vital interests of the entire Western world and over the years we have continued to give the Alliance our undiminished and bipartisan support.

Republicans deplore the current drift toward neutralism in Western Europe. We recognize that NATO and our Western Allies today face the greatest array of threats in their history, both from within and from without. Through its inept policies, the Carter Administration has substantially contributed to the evident erosion of Alliance security and confidence in the U.S. A Republican Administration, as one of its highest priorities and in close concert with our NATO partners, will therefore ensure that the United States leads a concerted effort to rebuild a strong, confident Alliance fully prepared to meet the threats and the challenges of the 1980s.

The chief external threat to NATO is that of developing Soviet military superiority. In a period of supposed "detente," the NATO nations have too often cut back or delayed essential defense programs and too often placed excessive hopes in arms control negotiations, while the Soviet-dominated Warsaw Pact has been transformed into the world's most powerful offensive military force.

Three-and-a-half years of Carter Administration policies have resulted in an increased threat to vital Alliance security interests. Mr. Carter's unilateral cancellations, reductions, and long delays in the B-1, Trident, MX, cruise-missile, and shipbuilding programs have increased the vulnerability of the U.S. strategic triad and have contributed to a developing strategic imbalance which undermines the foundation of Western deterrent and defense capabilities. His fundamentally flawed SALT II treaty would have codified Western inferiority. His reversals on the development and deployment of the "enhanced radiation" or neutron weapon, his treatment of future theater nuclear force modernization negotiations, and his manner of

dealing with terrorist actions directed against Americans abroad, further undermined Alliance solidarity and security.

These Carter Administration inconsistencies have caused disunity in the Alliance. We have seen confusion in the fields of trade, fiscal, and energy policies. The lack of close coordination regarding Iran, the Middle East, Afghanistan, the Olympic boycott, nuclear proliferation, East–West trade, human rights, North–South issues, and a host of other international issues affecting Alliance interests, has reinforced Allied concerns. Republicans are concerned that these Carter Administration actions have increased Allied temptation to conduct independent diplomacy and to seek accommodation in the face of pressure from the Soviet Union. In this regard, we categorically reject unilateral moratoria on the deployment by the U.S. and NATO of theater nuclear weapons. Further, Republicans will oppose arms control agreements that interfere with the transfer of military technology to our allies.

In pledging renewed United States leadership, cooperation, and consultation, Republicans assert their expectation that each of the allies will bear a fair share of the common defense effort and that they will work closely together in support of common Alliance goals. Defense budgets, weapons acquisition, force readiness, and diplomatic coordination need to be substantially increased and improved. Within Europe as well as in areas beyond Europe which affect the shared vital interests of the Alliance, we will seek to increase our cooperative efforts, including increased planning for joint actions to meet common threats.

The Republican Party recognizes the vital importance of countries defending the flanks of NATO. We will search for an early resolution of problems that currently inhibit the effective participation of all the nations of NATO's southern flank and we call for the integration of Spain into the North Atlantic Alliance.

Middle East, Persian Gulf

In the past three years, the nations of the Middle East and Persian Gulf have suffered an unprecedented level of political, economic, and military turmoil. The Soviet Union has been prompt in turning these sources of instability to its advantage and is now in an excellent position to exploit the chaos in Iran and to foment similar upheavals in other countries in the region. Today, the countries of the Middle East and Persian Gulf are encircled as never before by Soviet advisers and troops based in the Horn of Africa, South Yemen, and Afghanistan. Moreover, the Soviets have close political and military ties with other states in the region.

The Soviet goal is clear—to use subversion and the threat of military intervention to establish a controlling influence over the regions' resource-rich states, and thereby to gain decisive political and economic leverage over Western and Third World nations vulnerable to economic coercion. The first signs of Soviet success in this undertaking are already evidenced in the recent proposal by European countries to associate the Palestinian Liberation Organization in the West Bank autonomy talks.

Republicans believe that the restoration of order and stability to the region must be premised upon an understanding of the interrelationship between Soviet and radical Palestinian goals, the fundamental requirements of stable economic development and marketing of the area's resources, and the growing ferment among Islamic radical groups. Republicans believe that a wise and credible United States policy must make clear that our foremost concern is for the long-term peaceful development of all states in the region, not purely a self-serving exploitation of its resources. Our goal is to bring a just and lasting peace to the Arab–Israeli conflict.

With respect to an ultimate peace settlement, Republicans reject any call for involvement of the PLO as not in keeping with the long-term interests of either Israel or the Palestinian Arabs. The imputation of legitimacy to organizations not yet willing to acknowledge the fundamental right to existence of the State of Israel is wrong. Repeated indications, even when subsequently denied, of the Carter Administration's involvement with the PLO have done serious harm to the credibility of U.S. policy in the Middle East and have encouraged the PLO's position of intransigence. We believe the establishment of a Palestinian State on the West Bank would be destabilizing and harmful to the peace process.

Our long- and short-term policies for the area must be developed in consultation with our NATO allies, Israel, Egypt, and other friends in the area, and we will spare no effort in seeking their consultation throughout the policy process, not merely demanding their acquiescence to our plans.

The sovereignty, security, and integrity of the State of Israel is a moral imperative and serves the strategic interests of the United States. Republicans reaffirm our fundamental and enduring commitment to this principle. We will continue to honor our nation's commitment through political, economic, diplomatic, and military aid. We fully recognize the strategic importance of Israel and the deterrent role of its armed forces in the Middle East and East–West military equations.

Republicans recognize that a just and durable peace for all nations of the region is the best guarantee of continued stability and is vital to deterring further Soviet inroads. Peace between Israel and its neighbors requires direct negotiations among the states involved. Accordingly, a Republican Administration will encourage the peace process now in progress between Egypt and Israel, will seek to broaden it, and will welcome those Arab nations willing to live in peace with Israel. We are encouraged by the support given to the Middle East peace process by Sudan and Oman and the progress brought about by the strong and effective leadership of their governments.

We applaud the vision and courage of Egyptian President Anwar Sadat and we pledge to build our relationship with Egypt in cultural affairs, economic development, and military cooperation.

Republicans recognize that the Carter Administration's vacillations have left friend and foe alike unsure as to United States policies. While reemphasizing our commitment to Israel, a Republican Administration will pursue close ties and friendship with moderate Arab states. We will initiate the economic and military framework for assuring long-term stability both in the internal development of regional states and an orderly marketplace for the area's resources. We will make clear that any reimposition of an oil embargo would be viewed as a hostile act. We will oppose discriminatory practices, including boycotts, and we will discourage arms sales which contribute to regional instability.

Republicans believe that Jerusalem should remain an undivided city with continued free and unimpeded access to all holy places by people of all faiths.

The Americas

Latin America is an area of primary interest for the United States. Yet, the Carter Administration's policies have encouraged a precipitous decline in United States relations with virtually every country in the region. The nations of South and Central America have been battered by the Carter Administration's economic and diplomatic sanctions linked to its undifferentiated charges of human rights violations.

In the Caribbean and Central America, the Carter Administration stands by while Castro's totalitarian Cuba, financed, directed, and supplied by the Soviet Union, aggressively trains, arms, and supports forces of warfare and revolution throughout the Western hemisphere. Yet the Carter Administration has steadily denied these threats and in many cases has actively worked to undermine governments and parties opposed to the expansion of Soviet power. This must end.

We deplore the Marxist Sandinista takeover of Nicaragua and the Marxist attempts to destabilize El Salvador, Guatemala, and Honduras. We do not support United States assistance to any Marxist government in this hemisphere and we oppose the Carter Administration aid program for the government of Nicaragua. However, we will support the efforts of the Nicaraguan people to establish a free and independent government.

Republicans deplore the dangerous and incomprehensible Carter Administration policies toward Cuba. The Administration has done nothing about the Soviet combat brigade stationed there, or about the transfer of new Soviet offensive weapons to Cuba in the form of modern MIG aircraft and submarines. It has done nothing about the Soviet pilots flying air defense missions in Cuba or about the extensive improvements to Soviet military bases, particularly the submarine facilities in Cienfuegos, and the expanded Soviet intelligence facilities near Havana. Republicans recognize the importance of our relations within this hemisphere and pledge a strong new United States policy in the Americas. We will stand firm with countries seeking to develop their societies while combating the subversion and violence exported by Cuba and Moscow. We will return to the fundamental principle of treating a friend as a friend and self-proclaimed enemies as enemies, without apology. We will make it clear to the Soviet Union and Cuba that their subversion and their buildup of offensive military forces is unacceptable.

Republicans recognize the special importance of Puerto Rico and the United States Virgin Islands in the defense of freedom in the Caribbean. We believe that Puerto Rico's admission to the Union would demonstrate our common purpose in the face of growing Soviet and Cuban pressure in that area.

Republicans recognize the fundamental importance of Mexico and restoration of good working relations with that country will be of highest priority. A new Republican Administration will immediately begin high-level, comprehensive negotiations, seeking solutions to common problems on the basis of mutual interest and recognizing that each country has unique contributions to make in resolving practical problems.

Republicans pledge to reestablish close and cooperative relations with the nations of Central and South America and repair the diplomatic damage done by the Carter Administration. We pledge understanding and assistance in the efforts of these nations, and their neighbors, to deal seriously with serious domestic problems.

We pledge to ensure that the Panama Canal remains open, secure, and free of hostile control.

The reservations and understandings to the Panama Canal treaties, including those assuring the United States of primary responsibility for protecting and defending the Canal, are an integral part of those treaties and we will hold Panama to strict interpretation of the language of the treaties, clearly established by the legislative history of Senate adoption of amendments, reservations, and understandings at the time of Senate approval of the treaties.

We would remind the American taxpayers that President Carter gave repeated assurances that the Panama Canal treaties would not cost the American taxpayers "one thin dime" and we emphasize the fact that implementing the Panama Canal treaties will cost them $4.2 billion.

We will work closely with Canada as our most important trading partner in the hemisphere. We will foster the deep affinity that exists between our two nations and our policies will be based on mutual understanding and complete equality.

We will seek a North American Accord designed to foster close cooperation and mutual benefit between the United States, Canada, and Mexico.

A new Republican Administration will, in close cooperation with its neighbors, seek to work together to build prosperity and to strengthen common efforts to combat externally produced revolution and violence.

Asia and the Pacific

The United States is and must remain a Pacific power. It is in our vital interest to maintain U.S. guaranteed stability in the area. Republicans recognize the dangerous shifts in power that have accelerated under the current Democratic Administration. The balance on the Korean peninsula has shifted dangerously toward the North. Soviet naval forces in Asia and the Pacific have steadily increased and are now at least equal to U.S. Naval forces there. Unilateral cancellation by the United States of the mutual defense pact with Taiwan and the abrupt announcement of withdrawal of U.S. ground forces from Korea, have led countries throughout the region to question the value of alliance with the United States.

A new Republican Administration will restore a strong American role in Asia and the Pacific. We will make it clear that any military action which threatens the independence of America's allies and friends will bring a response sufficient to make its cost prohibitive to potential adversaries.

Japan will continue to be a pillar of American policy in Asia. Republicans recognize the mutual interests and special relationships that exist between the two countries in their commitment to democracy and in trade, defense, and cultural matters. A new Republican Administration will work closely with the Japanese government to resolve outstanding trade and energy problems on an equitable basis. We strongly support a substantially increased Japanese national defense effort and reaffirm that our long-range objectives of military security and a balancing of the expanded Soviet military presence in the region are of mutual interest.

Republicans recognize the unique danger presented to our ally, South Korea. We will encourage continued efforts to expand political participation and individual liberties within the country, but will recognize the special problems brought on by subversion and potential aggression from the North. We will maintain American ground and air forces in South Korea, and will not reduce our presence further. Our treaty commitments to South Korea will be restated in unequivocal terms and we will reestablish the process of close consultations between our governments.

We reaffirm our special and historic relationships with the Philippines, Singapore, Malaysia, Indonesia, Thailand, New Zealand, and Australia. Republicans will recognize the long friendship with these countries and will cultivate and strengthen our diplomatic and trade relationships.

We deplore the brutal acts of Communist Vietnam against the people of Cambodia and Laos. We recognize that the suffering of refugees from these ravaged countries represents a major moral challenge to the world and one of the great human tragedies of modern times. A Republican Administration will work actively to bring relief to these suffering people, especially those who have sought refuge in Thailand. We value the special contribution the people of Thailand have made to the refugees by opening their borders and saving hundreds of thousands of them from death, and we pledge to provide full economic aid and military material to assist Thailand in repelling Vietnamese aggression.

We believe that no expanded relations with Communist Vietnam should be pursued while it continues its course of brutal expansionism and genocide. We pledge that a Republican Administration will press for full accounting of Americans still listed as missing in action.

Recognizing the growing importance of the People's Republic of China in world affairs, Republicans—who took the historic initiative in opening the lines of communication with that nation—will continue the process of building a working relation with the PRC. Growing contacts between the United States and the People's Republic of China reflect the interests of both nations, as well as some common perceptions of recent changes in the global military balance. We will not ignore the profound differences in our respective philosophies, governmental institutions, policies, and concepts of individual liberty.

We will strive for the creation of conditions that will foster the peaceful elaboration of our relationship with the People's Republic of China. We will exercise due caution and prudence with respect to our own vital interests, especially in the field of expanding trade, including the transfer of sophisticated technology with potential offensive military applications. The relationship between the two countries must be based on mutual respect and reciprocity, with due regard for the need to maintain peace and stability in Asia.

At the same time, we deplore the Carter Administration's treatment of Taiwan, our long-time ally and friend. We pledge that our concern for the safety and security of the 17 million people of Taiwan will be constant. We would regard any attempt to alter Taiwan's status by force as a threat to peace in the region. We declare that the Republican Administration, in strengthening relations with Taiwan, will create conditions leading to the expansion of trade, and will give priority consideration to Taiwan's defense requirements.

Africa

The Republican Party supports the principle and process of self-determination in Africa. We reaffirm our commitment to this principle and pledge our strong opposition to the effort of the Soviet Union and its militant allies to subvert this process. Soviet bases, tens of thousands of Cuban troops, and Soviet-bloc subversion are unacceptable.

We recognize that much is at stake in Africa and that the United States and the industrial West have vital interests there—economically, strategically, and politically. Working closely with our allies, a Republican Administration will seek to assist the countries of Africa with our presence, our markets, our know-how, and our investment. We will work to create a climate of economic and political development and confidence. We will encourage and assist business to play a major role in support of regional industrial development programs, mineral complexes, and agricultural self-sufficiency.

Republicans believe that African nations, if given a choice, will reject the Marxist, totalitarian model being forcibly imposed by the Soviet Union and its surrogates including Cuban and Nicaraguan troops as well as East German secret police. We believe that they know the Communist powers have relatively little to offer them and that, for the most part, the African peoples are convinced that the West is central to the world stability and economic growth on which their own fortunes ultimately depend.

A Republican Administration will adhere to policies that reflect the complex origins of African conflicts, demonstrate that we know what U.S. interests are, and back those interests in meaningful ways. We will recognize the important role of economic and military assistance programs and will devote major resources to assisting African development and stability when such aid is given on a bilateral basis and contributes directly to American interests on the continent.

In Southern Africa, American policies must be guided by common sense and by our own humanitarian principles. Republicans believe that our history has meaning for Africa in demonstrating that a multiracial society with guarantees of individual rights is possible and can work. We must remain open and helpful to all parties, whether in the new Zimbabwe, in Namibia, or in the Republic of South Africa. A Republican Administration will not endorse situations or constitutions, in whatever society, which are racist in purpose or in effect. It will not expect miracles, but will press for genuine progress in achieving goals consistent with American ideals.

Foreign Assistance and Regional Security

The United States has included foreign assistance and regional security as a major element of its foreign policy for four decades. Properly administered and focused, foreign assistance can be an effective means of promoting United States foreign policy objectives, and serve to enhance American security by assisting friendly nations to become stronger and more capable of defending themselves and their regions against foreign subversion and attack.

The threat posed to individual Third World nations is beyond the means of any one of them to counter alone. A Republican Administration will seek to strengthen and assist regional security arrangements among nations prepared to assume the burden of their defense.

No longer should American foreign assistance programs seek to force acceptance of American governmental forms. The principal consideration should be whether or not extending assistance to a nation or group of nations will advance America's interests and objectives. The single-minded attempt to force acceptance of U.S. values and standards of democracy has undermined several friendly nations, and has made

possible the advance of Soviet interests in Asia, the Middle East, Africa, and in the Western Hemisphere in the past four years.

American foreign economic assistance is not a charitable venture; charity is most effectively carried out by private entities. Only by private economic development by the people of the nations involved has poverty ever been overcome. U.S. foreign economic assistance should have a catalytic effect on indigenous economic development, and should only be extended when it is consistent with America's foreign policy interest. America's foreign assistance programs should be a vehicle for exporting the American idea.

A Republican Administration will emphasize bilateral assistance programs whenever possible. Bilateral programs provide the best assurance that aid programs will be fully accountable to the American taxpayer, and wholly consistent with our foreign policy interests.

The effort of the Carter Administration to diminish the role of American military assistance and foreign military sales in our foreign policy has had several negative effects:

- it has resulted in the export of many thousands of American jobs as the Soviet Union, Britain, and France have taken sales prohibited to American manufacturers;
- it has reduced the ability of friendly nations to defend their independence against Soviet-sponsored subversion, resulting in several cases, in abject takeovers by overtly pro-Soviet regimes; and
- it has weakened the fabric of the U.S. alliance structure by making the U.S. appear to be an unreliable ally, a trend which can only lead to the undesirable attempt by nations fearful of their security to seek to acquire their own nuclear weapons.

Decisions to provide military assistance should be made on the basis of U.S. foreign policy objectives. Such assistance to any nation need not imply complete approval of a regime's domestic policy. Republicans pledge to strengthen America's presence abroad by well-constructed programs of military assistance to promote national and regional security.

The manipulation of foreign arms sales has been one of the most seriously abused policy initiatives of the Carter Administration. The establishment of arbitrary ceilings on foreign sales, and the complex procedural and policy guidelines governing such sales have impeded the support of U.S. foreign policy objectives abroad. Friendly and allied nations alike have had to turn elsewhere for arms. This has stimulated the growth of a new arms industry in developing nations. Republicans pledge to reform and rebuild U.S. military assistance and foreign arms sales policies so that they will serve American interests in promoting regional security arrangements and the individual defense needs of friendly nations.

International Economic Policy

The American economy has an abundance of human and material resources, but nevertheless, it is part of a larger global economy. Our domestic prosperity and international competitiveness depend upon our participation in the international economy. Moreover, our security interests are in part determined by international economic factors. Yet the Carter Administration has largely ignored the role of international economics in relations between the United States and friendly nations throughout the world. The Administration has conducted its international economic policy at cross-purposes with other dimensions of its foreign policy, resulting in strains within the Western Alliance and a general decline in the domestic prosperity. Under a Republican Administration, our international economic policy will be harmonized with our foreign and defense policies to leave no doubt as to the strategy and purpose of American policy.

The economic policy of the Carter Administration has led to the most serious decline in the value of the dollar in history. The ability of Americans to purchase goods and services or to invest abroad has been diminished by Carter Administration policies devaluing the dollar. Republicans will conduct international economic policy in a manner that will stabilize the value of the dollar at home and abroad.

The Republican Party believes the United States must adopt an aggressive export policy. For too long, our trade policy has been geared toward helping our foreign trading partners. Now, we have to put the United States back on the world export map. We helped pull other countries out of the post–World War II economic chaos; it is time to remedy our own crisis. Trade, especially exporting, must be high on our list of national priorities. The Republicans will put it there and will promote trade to ensure the long-term health of the U.S. economy.

Exports can play a key role in strengthening the U.S. economy, creating jobs and improving our standard of living. A $15 billion increase in exports can increase employment by 1,000,000, the Gross National Product by $37 billion per year, and private investment by $4 billion per year. Nevertheless, the Carter Administration has placed exporting at the bottom of its priority list. The present Administration's trade policies lack coordination, cohesiveness, and true commit-

ment to improving our export performance. Rather than helping to create strong exporters in the United States and thereby create more jobs for Americans, the Carter Administration's trade policies have discouraged traders. At best, the Administration has adopted a passive approach to trade, merely reacting to changing world economies rather than actively seeking to promote a global structure that best addresses America's needs. As a result, we lag seriously behind our foreign competitors in trade performance and economic strength. Export promotion will be a central objective of international economic policy in a Republican Administration.

A Republican Administration will emphasize a policy of free trade, but will expect our trading partners to do so as well. The failure of the Carter Administration energetically to pursue negotiations designed to improve the access of American exports to foreign markets has contributed, in part, to protectionist sentiment.

Domestic problems—over-burdensome government regulations, excessive taxation, inflationary monetary policy, and an unstable economy—have contributed to the protectionist sentiments as well. We realize that protectionist legislation has engendered retaliation by America's trading partners in the past resulting in the "beggar thy neighbor" policies that had such disastrous consequences in the 1930s.

Republicans are committed to protect American jobs and American workers first and foremost. The Republican Party believes in free trade, and we will insist that our trade policy be based on the principles of reciprocity and equity. We oppose subsidies, tariff and non-tariff barriers that unfairly restrict access of American products to foreign markets. We will not stand idly by as the jobs of millions of Americans in domestic industries, such as automobiles, textiles, steel, and electronics are jeopardized and lost. We pledge to strengthen trade agreements and to change the Carter economic policies that have undermined the capability of American agriculture and industry to compete abroad.

Republicans believe that this nation's international trade balance can be improved through the elimination of disincentives for exporters. Statutory and regulatory requirements that inhibit exports should be reviewed and, where practical, eliminated. We further recognize that government can play a role in promoting international trade by establishing incentives for exports, especially those for small and medium-size business. We pledge also to work with our trading partners to eliminate subsidies to exports and dumping.

The ability of the United States to compete in foreign markets is hampered by the excessive taxation of

Americans working abroad who contribute to our domestic well-being by promoting international trade. Increased exports to our trading partners result in jobs and a rising standard of living at home. Carter Administration policy has the effect of discouraging the presence of American businessmen abroad due to the unfairly high level of taxation levied against them. A Republican Administration will support legislation designed to eliminate this inequity so that American citizens can fully participate in international commerce without fear of discriminatory taxation.

The Security of Energy and Raw Materials Access

The security of America's foreign sources of energy and raw material supply can no longer be ignored. The United States imports 50 percent of its domestic petroleum requirements, and depends upon foreign sources for 22 of the 74 non-fuel raw materials essential to a modern industrial economy. Nine of the most critical raw materials are almost entirely (i.e., more than 90 percent) located abroad. In contrast, the Soviet Union imports only 2 critical minerals at a level in excess of 50 percent of domestic consumption.

Reducing reliance on uncertain foreign sources and assuring access to foreign energy and raw materials requires the harmonization of economic policy with our defense and foreign policy. Domestic economic and regulatory policy must be adjusted to remove impediments to greater development of our own energy and raw materials resources. Democratic policies for federal land management, taxation, monetary policy, and economic regulation have served to increase America's dependence on foreign sources of energy and raw materials. Republicans pledge to work to eliminate domestic disincentives to the exploitation of these resources.

Multilateral negotiations have thus far insufficiently focused attention on U.S. long-term security requirements. A pertinent example of this phenomenon is the Law of the Sea Conference, where negotiations have served to inhibit U.S. exploitation of the seabed for its abundant mineral resources. Too much concern has been lavished on nations unable to carry out seabed mining with insufficient attention paid to gaining early American access to it. A Republican Administration will conduct multilateral negotiations in a manner that reflects America's abilities and long-term interest in access to raw material and energy resources.

Resource access will assume an important place in defense and economic planning under a Republican Administration. Since America's allies are, in most cases, more dependent than the U.S. on foreign sources of energy and raw materials, they too have a vital interest in the defense of their access to these critical resources. Republicans pledge to promote allied defense cooperation to assure protection from military threats to overseas resources.

— 1984 —

PREAMBLE

This year, the American people will choose between two diametrically opposed visions of what America should be.

The Republican Party looks at our people and sees a new dawn of the American spirit.

The Democratic Party looks at our nation and sees the twilight of the American soul.

Republicans affirm that now, as throughout history, the spiritual and intellectual genius of the American people will create a better nation and maintain a just peace. To Republicans, creativity and growth are imperatives for a new era of opportunity for all.

The Republican Party's vision of America's future, the heart of our 1984 Platform, begins with a basic premise:

> From freedom comes opportunity;
> from opportunity comes growth;
> from growth comes progress.

This is not some abstract formula. It is the vibrant, beating heart of the American experience. No matter how complex our problems, no matter how difficult our tasks, it is freedom that inspires and guides the American Dream.

If everything depends on freedom—and it does—then securing freedom, at home and around the world, is one of the most important endeavors a free people can undertake.

Thus, the title of our Platform, "America's Future: Free and Secure," is more than a summary of our Platform's message. It is the essence.

The Democratic Party understands none of this. It thinks our country has passed its peak. It offers Americans redistribution instead of expansion, contraction instead of growth, and despair instead of hope. In foreign policy it asserts the rhetoric of freedom, but in practice it follows a policy of withdrawal and isolation.

The Democratic Party, in its 1984 Platform, has tried to expropriate the optimism and vision that marked the 1980 Republican Platform.

Rhetorical pilfering of Republican ideals cannot disguise one of history's major ironies: the party whose 1932 standard-bearer told the American people, as president, that all we have to fear is fear itself has itself become the party of fear.

Today we declare ourselves the Party of Hope—not for some but for all.

It has been said that mercy must have a human heart and pity a human face. We agree. Democrats measure social programs in terms of government activity alone. But the divine command to help our neighbor is directed to each individual and not to a bureaucratic machine. Not every problem cries out for a federal solution.

We must help the poor *escape* poverty by building an economy which creates more jobs, the greatest poverty fighter of them all. Not to help the poor is to abandon them and demean our society; but to help the poor without offering them a chance to escape poverty is ultimately to degrade us all.

The great tasks of compassion must be accomplished both by people who care and by policies which foster economic growth to enhance all human development.

In all these areas, at home and abroad, Ronald Reagan has demonstrated the boldness of vision, the optimism for our future, and the confidence in the American people that can transform human lives and the life of a nation. That is what we expect from a President who, wounded by an assassin, walked his way into a hospital and cheerfully assured the world that he and his country would not be deterred from their destiny.

His example has shaped the 1984 Republican Platform, given it meaning and inspired its vision. We stand with President Reagan and with Vice President Bush to make it a reality.

ECONOMIC FREEDOM AND PROSPERITY

Free Enterprise, Democracy, and the Role of Government

Free enterprise is fundamental to the American way of life. It is inseparable from the social, religious, political, and judicial institutions which form the bedrock of a nation dedicated to individual freedom and human rights.

Economic growth enables all citizens to share in the nation's great physical and spiritual wealth, and it is maximized by giving them the fullest opportunity to engage in economic activities and to retain the rewards of their labor.

Our society provides both a ladder of opportunity on which all can climb to success and a safety net of assistance for those who need it. To safeguard both, government must protect property rights, provide a sound currency, and minimize its intrusions into individual decisions to work, save, invest, and take risks.

The role of the federal government should be limited. We reaffirm our conviction that State and local governments closest to the people are the best and most efficient. While President Reagan has done much to alleviate federal regulatory and bureaucratic burdens on individuals and businesses, Congress has failed to act. The size and scope of the federal government remains much too large and must be reduced.

During the Carter–Mondale Administration, no group of Americans was spared from the impact of a failing economy. Family budgets were stretched to the limit to keep pace with increases in taxes and costs of food, energy, and housing. For the first time, owning a home slipped out of reach for millions. Working people saw their wage increases outpaced by inflation. Older Americans saw their savings and retirement incomes consumed by basic living costs. Young people found job opportunities narrowing. Disadvantaged Americans faced an inefficient and wasteful bureaucracy which perpetuated programs of dependency. American business and industry faced recession, unemployment, and upheaval, as high interest rates, inflation, government regulation, and foreign competition combined to smother all enterprise and strike at our basic industries.

When President Reagan took office in 1981, our economy was in a disastrous state. Inflation raged at 12.4 percent. The cost of living had jumped 45 percent in the Carter–Mondale years. The prime rate was 21.5 percent. Federal spending increases of 17 percent per year, massive tax rate increases due to inflation, and a monetary policy debasing the dollar had destroyed our economic stability.

We brought about a new beginning. Americans are better off than they were four years ago, and they're still improving. Almost six and one-half million have found jobs since the recovery began, the largest increase in our history. One and one-half million have come in manufacturing—a part of our economy designated for stagnation and government control by Democrats. More than 107 million Americans, more than ever before, are working. Their industry proves that policies which increase incentives for work, saving, and investment do lead to economic growth, while the redistributionist policies of the past did cause unemployment, declining incomes, and idle industries.

We will therefore continue to return control over the

economy to the people. Our policies will maximize the role of the individual and build on the success of the past four years: (a) the most rapid decline in unemployment of any post–World War II recovery; (b) inflation dramatically reduced; (c) interest rates significantly cut; (d) a 25 percent cut in federal tax rates; (e) automatic tax increases eliminated by indexing tax rates; (f) the financial holdings of American families increased by over $1.8 trillion; (g) oil prices down 35 percent in real terms; and (h) 300 million hours once devoted to government paperwork returned to individuals and business.

Our most important economic goal is to expand and continue the economic recovery and move the nation to full employment without inflation. We therefore oppose any attempts to increase taxes, which would harm the recovery and reverse the trend to restoring control of the economy to individual Americans. We favor reducing deficits by continuing and expanding the strong economic recovery brought about by the policies of this Administration and by eliminating wasteful and unnecessary government spending. Mondale–Ferraro, by contrast, boast that they will raise taxes, with ruinous effects on the economy.

To assure workers and entrepreneurs the capital required to provide jobs and growth, we will further expand incentives for personal saving. We will expand coverage of the Individual Retirement Account, especially to homemakers, and increase and index the annual limits on IRA contributions. We will increase the incentives for savings by moving toward the reduction of taxation of interest income. We will work for indexation of capital assets and elimination of the double taxation of dividends to increase the attractiveness of equity investments for small investors.

We oppose withholding on dividend and interest income. It would discourage saving and investment, create needless paperwork, and rob savers of their due benefits. A higher personal saving rate is key to deficit control. We therefore oppose any disincentives to thrift.

History has proven again and again that wage and price controls will not stop inflation. Such controls only cause shortages, inequities, and ultimately high prices. We remain firmly opposed to the imposition of wage and price controls.

We are committed to bringing the benefits of economic growth to all Americans. Therefore, we support policies which will increase opportunities for the poorest in our society to climb the economic ladder. We will work to establish enterprise zones in urban and rural America; we will work to enable those living in government-owned or subsidized housing to purchase their homes. As part of our effort to reform the tax system, we will reduce disincentives to employment which too often result in a poverty trap for poor American families.

Fiscal and Monetary Policy

Taxation

A major goal of all Republicans in 1980 was to reduce the oppressive tax rates strangling Americans. The tax burden, which had increased steadily during the Carter–Mondale Administration, was at a record high and scheduled to go even higher. Taxes as a percentage of GNP rose from 18.2 percent in 1976 to 21 percent in 1981 and would have reached 24 percent by 1984. The tax bill for the median-income family of four had risen from $1,713 in 1976 to $2,778 in 1980 and would have reached $3,943 in 1984.

Double-digit inflation had pushed individuals into ever higher marginal tax brackets. High marginal tax rates reduced the incentive for work, saving, and investment, and retarded economic growth, productivity, and job creation.

With the Economic Recovery Tax Act of 1981, we carried out the first phase of tax reduction and reform by cutting marginal tax rates by 25 percent. Tax brackets were indexed to prevent tax hikes through bracket creep. In addition, families received further relief by reducing the marriage penalty and lowering estate and gift taxes.

Businesses and workers benefited when we replaced outdated depreciation systems with the accelerated cost recovery system, reduced capital gains tax rates, and lowered the pressures which high tax rates place on wage demands. Investment in plants and equipment has increased 16.5 percent since 1982, resulting in 6.3 million new jobs.

In 1980, we promised the American people a tax cut which would be progressive and fair, reducing tax rates across the board. Despite Democrat opposition we succeeded in reducing the tax rates of all taxpayers by about 25 percent with low-income taxpayers receiving a slightly larger percentage tax reduction than high-income taxpayers. These sound economic policies have succeeded. We will continue our efforts to further reduce tax rates and now foresee no economic circumstances which would call for increased taxation.

The bulk of the tax cut goes to those who pay most of the taxes: middle-income taxpayers. Nearly three-fourths of its benefits go to taxpayers earning less than $50,000. In fact, these taxpayers now pay a smaller percentage of total income taxes than they did in 1980; and those earning more than $50,000 pay a larger percentage of total income taxes than they did in 1980.

As a result, the income tax system is fairer now than it was under Carter–Mondale. To keep it fair, Republicans indexed the tax code: starting in 1985, individual tax brackets, the zero bracket amount, and the personal exemption will be adjusted annually for inflation. As a result, cost of living raises will no longer push taxpayers into higher brackets.

For years, congressional big spenders used inflation as a silent partner to raise taxes without taking the heat for passing tax increases. With indexing, taxpayers will be protected against that theft. Low- and moderate-income taxpayers benefit the most from indexing and would bear the brunt of the hidden tax increases if it were repealed.

Nearly 80 percent of the tax increase from the repeal of indexing would fall on taxpayers earning less than $50,000. For a family of four earning $10,000, repeal of indexing would result in a staggering 40 percent tax increase over the next five years. We pledge to preserve tax indexing. We will fight any attempt to repeal, modify, or defer it.

The Republican Party pledges to continue our efforts to lower tax rates, change and modernize the tax system, and eliminate the incentive-destroying effects of graduated tax rates. We therefore support tax reform that will lead to a fair and simple tax system and believe a modified flat tax—with specific exemptions for such items as mortgage interest—is a most promising approach.

For families, we will restore the value of personal exemptions, raising it to a minimum of $2,000 and indexing to prevent further erosion. We will preserve the deduction for mortgage interest payments. We will propose an employment income exclusion to assure that tax burdens are not shifted to the poor. Tax reform must not be a guise for tax increases. We believe such an approach will enhance the income and opportunities of families and low- and middle-income Americans.

We oppose taxation of churches, religious schools, or any other religious institutions. However, we do believe that any business income unrelated to the religious function of the institution should be subject to the same taxes paid by competing businesses.

We oppose the setting of artificially high interest rates which would drastically curtail the ability of sellers to finance sales of their own property. Rather, we encourage marketplace transfer of homes, farms, and smaller commercial properties.

Spending and Budget

The Republican Party believes the federal budget must be balanced. We are committed to eliminating deficits and the excessive spending that causes them. In 1980,

federal spending was out of control, increasing at a rate of over 17 percent. We have cut that growth rate by almost two-thirds.

But Congress ignored many of the President's budget reforms. It scaled back and delayed the tax cuts. As a result, we began to pay the price for the irresponsible spending and tax policies of the Carter–Mondale Administration. The resulting recession dramatically increased the deficit, and government spending continues at an unacceptable level.

Democrats claim deficits are caused by Americans' paying too little in taxes. Nonsense. We categorically reject proposals to increase taxes in a misguided effort to balance the budget. Tax and spending increases would reduce incentives for economic activity and threaten the recovery.

Even when we achieve full employment and even with robust economic growth, federal spending—including credit programs and other off-budget items—will remain too high. As a percentage of GNP, it must be reduced.

The congressional budget process is bankrupt. Its implementation has not brought spending under control, and it must be thoroughly reformed. We will work for the constitutional amendment requiring a balanced federal budget passed by the Republican Senate but blocked by the Democrat-controlled House and denounced by the Democrat Platform. If Congress fails to act on this issue, a constitutional convention should be convened to address only this issue in order to bring deficit spending under control.

The President is denied proper control over the federal budget. To remedy this, we support enhanced authority to prevent wasteful spending, including a line-item veto.

Monetary Policy

Our 1980 Platform promised to bring inflation under control. We did it. This cruelest tax—hitting hardest at the poor, the aged, and those on fixed incomes—ranged up to 13.3 percent under Carter–Mondale. We have brought it down to about 4 percent and we strive for lower levels. The effects of our program have been dramatic. Real, after-tax incomes are rising. Food prices are stable. Interest rates have fallen dramatically, leading to a resurgence in home building, auto purchases, and capital investment.

Just as our tax policy has only laid the groundwork for a new era of prosperity, reducing inflation is only the first step in restoring a stable currency. A dollar now should be worth a dollar in the future. This allows real economic growth without inflation and is the primary goal of our monetary policy.

The Federal Reserve Board's destabilizing actions must therefore stop. We need coordination between fiscal and monetary policy, timely information about Fed decisions, and an end to the uncertainties people face in obtaining money and credit. The Gold Standard may be a useful mechanism for realizing the Federal Reserve's determination to adopt monetary policies needed to sustain price stability.

Domestically, a stable dollar will mean lower interest rates, rising real wages, guaranteed value for retirement and education savings, growth of assets through productive investment, affordable housing, and greater job security.

Internationally, a stable dollar will mean stable exchange rates, protection for contract prices, commodity prices which change only when real production changes, greater resources devoted to job-creating investment, less protectionist pressure, and increased trade and income for all nations.

Regulatory Reform

Our 1980 Platform declared that "excessive regulation remains a major component of our nation's spiraling inflation and continues to stifle private initiatives, individual freedom, and State and local government autonomy." President Reagan's regulatory reform program contributed significantly to economic recovery by removing bureaucratic roadblocks and encouraging efficiency.

In many fields, government regulation either did not achieve its goals or made limited improvements at exorbitant costs. We have worked with industry and labor to get better results through cooperation rather than coercion.

The flood of regulation has stopped. The number of new regulations has been halved. Unrestrained growth in the size and spending of the regulatory workforce has stopped. Some $150 billion will thereby be saved over the next decade by consumers and businesses. In the past four years alone, 300 million hours of government-mandated paperwork were eliminated. We have reduced the regulatory burden on Americans by making government rules as cost-effective as possible. We must maintain this progress through comprehensive regulatory reform legislation and a constitutional procedure which will enable Congress to properly oversee executive branch rules by reviewing and, if necessary, overturning them.

So consumers can have the widest choice of services at the lowest possible prices, Republicans commit themselves to breaking down artificial barriers to entry created by antiquated regulations. With the explo-sion of computer technologies just beginning to enhance our way of life, we will encourage rather than hinder innovative competition in telecommunications and financial services.

There are still federal statutes that keep Americans out of the workforce. Arbitrary minimum wage rates, for example, have eliminated hundreds of thousands of jobs and, with them, the opportunity for young people to get productive skills, good work habits, and a weekly paycheck. We encourage the adoption of a youth opportunity wage to encourage employers to hire and train inexperienced workers.

We demand repeal of prohibitions against household manufacturing. Restrictions on work in the home are intolerable intrusions into our private lives and limit economic opportunity, especially for women and the homebound.

Support for Small Business

America's small business entrepreneurs have led the way in fueling economic recovery. Almost all the 11 million non-farm businesses in the United States are small, but they provide over 50 million jobs. We must keep them strong to ensure lasting prosperity. Republicans reaffirm our historic ties with independent business people and pledge continued efforts to help this energetic segment of our economy.

We have created a climate conducive to small business growth. Our tax rate reductions increased incentives for entrepreneurial activity and provided investment capital through incentives to save. Reduced capital gains taxes further stimulated capital formation and increased the return on small business investment. Greater depreciation allowances encouraged modernization. Estate tax changes will allow families to keep the rewards of their labors.

We have insisted on less federal interference with small business. As a result, burdensome regulations were reduced, and runaway agencies like OSHA were reined in. We have ensured that the federal government pays its bills on time or pays interest penalties.

Presidential action has focused needed attention on increased government procurement from small and minority businesses. In FY 1983 the Small Business Administration directed $2.3 billion in federal sole-source contracts to minority firms through its 8(a) program—a 45 percent increase over 1980. This record amount was achieved along with management improvements that eliminated past abuses in that program.

Three million women business owners are generating $40 billion in annual receipts and creating many new jobs. Yet, their enterprises face barriers in credit, access to capital, and technical assistance. They lag far behind in federal procurement contracts. We are dedicated to helping them become full partners in the economic mainstream of small business.

To them and to all who make America grow, we reaffirm our commitment to reduce marginal tax rates further. We oppose any scheme to roll back the estate tax cuts and will seek further reductions for family businesses. Moreover, we support lower capital gains tax rates and indexation of asset values to protect investors from inflation.

We will create enterprise zones to revitalize economically depressed areas by offering simplified regulations and lower taxes for small businesses that relocate there.

We will make it easier for small businesses to compete for government contracts, not only to assist the private sector but also to provide competition and greater cost control in federal purchases.

In a continuing effort to offset our balance of trade deficit, we reaffirm our strong support for this nation's tourism industry.

Science and Technology

We pledge to continue the Reagan Administration's science and technology policies, which have enhanced economic recovery and our nation's research capability.

We have refocused federal research and development spending on basic research, and it has increased more than 50 percent.

We propose to extend the incremental research and development tax credit to stimulate greater activity in the private sector.

To allow U.S. firms to compete on an equal footing with foreign companies, we will permit U.S. firms to cooperate in joint research and development projects.

Energy

In 1980, energy prices were at all-time highs and rising rapidly. The OPEC cartel had an iron grip on free world economies, Oil imports rose, and domestic production fell under Carter–Mondale price controls and allocations. Competition in energy markets declined.

We have all but eliminated those disastrous policies. President Reagan's immediate decontrol of oil prices precipitated a decline in real oil prices and increased competition in all energy markets. Oil price decontrol crippled the OPEC cartel.

The results have been dramatic. Imported oil prices are down 35 percent in real terms. The real price of gasoline is at a five-year low. Energy consumption has declined relative to economic growth. Energy efficiency increased by 12 percent since 1980, with lower costs to businesses and families. The Strategic Petroleum Reserve is now four times larger than in 1980, providing significant protection against any disruption in imports.

We will complete America's energy agenda. Natural gas should be responsibly decontrolled as rapidly as possible so that families and businesses can enjoy the full benefits of lower prices and greater production, as with decontrolled oil. We are committed to the repeal of the confiscatory windfall profits tax, which has forced the American consumer to pay more for less and left us vulnerable to the energy and economic stranglehold of foreign producers.

While protecting the environment, we should permit abundant American coal to be mined and consumed. Environmentally sound development of oil and natural gas on federal properties (which has brought the taxpayers $20 billion in revenue in the last four years) should continue. We believe that as controls have been lifted from the energy marketplace, conservation and alternative sources of energy, such as solar, wind, and geothermal, have become increasingly cost-effective. We further take pride in the fact that Reagan Administration economic policies have created an environment most favorable to the small businesses that pioneer these alternative technologies.

We now have a sound, long-term program for disposal of nuclear waste. We will work to eliminate unnecessary regulatory procedures so that nuclear plants can be brought on line quickly, efficiently, and safely. We call for an energy policy, the stability and continuity of which will restore and encourage public confidence in the fiscal stability of the nuclear industry.

We are committed to the termination of the Department of Energy. President Reagan has succeeded in abolishing that part which was telling Americans what to buy, where to buy it, and at what price—the regulatory part of DOE. Then he reduced the number of bureaucrats by 25 percent. Now is the time to complete the job.

Agriculture

Securing a Prosperous Rural America

The Republican Party is thankful for, and proud of, the ability of American farmers and ranchers to provide abundant, high quality, and nutritious food and fiber for all our citizens and millions more throughout the world. This unmatched ability to produce is basic to this country's high standard of living. We recognize that a prosperous agriculture is essential to the future of America and to the health and welfare of its people. We have set the stage for securing prosperity in rural America. In 1979, farm and ranch production costs increased 19 percent, in 1983 they actually declined by almost 3 percent. The prime interest rate has been brought down from 21.5 percent to 13 percent. Our reputation as a reliable world food and fiber supplier has been restored. Despite that remarkable beginning, much remains to be done.

We believe well-managed, efficient American farm and ranch operations are the most cost-effective and productive food and fiber suppliers in the world, and therefore have the inherent economic capability and right to make a profit from their labor, management, and investments. The primary responsibility of government with respect to agriculture is to create the opportunity for a free and competitive economic and policy environment supportive of the American farmers' and ranchers' industrious and independent spirit and innovative talent. We further believe that, to the extent some well-managed and efficient farms and ranches are temporarily unable to make a profit in the marketplace, it is in the public interest to provide reasonable and targeted assistance.

The Carter–Mondale Administration, and 28 years of a Congress rigidly controlled by the Democrats and out of touch with the people, brought farmers and ranchers to the hardest times since the Great Depression. Farm and ranch incomes fell to disastrous levels. Uncontrolled inflation and the highest interest rates in over a century prevented farmers from operating at a profit, and 300,000 of them went out of business under Carter–Mondale.

In the span of but four devastating years, the Carter–Mondale Administration managed to jeopardize this country's agricultural heritage by putting America's farmers $78 billion further in debt (a 75 percent increase) and inflating farmers' annual food and fiber production costs by $46 billion (a 55 percent increase). These irresponsible inflationary policies led to spiraling land values and to the illusion of enhanced debt-bearing wealth. This paper wealth was converted into very real and unavoidable debt. Debt payments, combined with record cost of production levels, have presented many farmers and ranchers with severe cash flow problems. On top of all that came the Carter–Mondale grain embargo of 1980. Thus, one begins to understand the origins of the financial stress farmers and ranchers are experiencing today. Adding insult to injury, farmers and ranchers found themselves blamed as Carter–Mondale inflation ballooned consumer food costs by $115 billion, a 50 percent increase in four years.

Republicans support a sound agricultural credit policy, including the Farm Credit System, to meet agriculture's expanded credit needs. We support an extensive examination of agricultural and rural credit and crop insurance programs to assure they are adequately serving our farmers and rural residents.

Interest Rates and Farm and Ranch Indebtedness

The magnitude of indebtedness and the level of interest rates significantly influence farm and ranch profitability. The interrelationship between high interest rates and the high value of the dollar has caused an erosion in our competitive position in export markets. Republicans recognize that lower interest rates are vital to a healthy farm and ranch economy and pledge that an economic priority of the first order will be the further lowering of interest rates by intensifying our efforts to cut federal spending to achieve a balanced budget and by reforming Federal Reserve policy.

Republicans are very much aware of the devastating impact which high interest rates have had, and continue to have, on the viability of America's farmers and ranchers. We also realize that, unless interest rates decline significantly in the near future, the character of American agriculture and rural life will be tragically changed. For these reasons, we pledge to pursue every possible course of action, including the consideration of temporary interest rate reductions, to ensure that the American farmer or rancher is not a patient that dies in the course of a successful economic operation.

Republicans are cognizant that there are many well-managed, efficient farm and ranch operations which face bankruptcy and foreclosure. The foreclosures and resulting land sales will jeopardize the equity positions of neighboring farms and ranches, compounding financial problems in agriculture. Republicans pledge to implement comprehensive Farmers Home Administration and commercial farm and ranch debt restructuring procedures, including the establishment of local community farm and ranch finance committees, which will advise borrowers, lenders, and government officials regarding debt restructuring alternatives and farmer and rancher eligibility.

Setting the Stage for Farm and Ranch Recovery

Sensitive to the needs of farmers and ranchers, we have made the best of the tools available to deal with the Carter–Mondale failure. Among the many specific accomplishments of the Reagan Administration in agriculture, Republicans are proud to have:

- Lifted the Carter–Mondale grain embargo and demonstrated by word and deed that farm and ranch product embargoes will not be used as a tool of foreign policy, negotiated a long-term agreement with the Soviet Union, and strengthened our credibility as a reliable supplier by enacting contract sanctity legislation.

- Increased food assistance and agricultural export financing programs to over $7 billion, a record level.
- Challenged unfair export subsidy practices and aggressively countered them with "blended credit" and other export expansion programs.
- Achieved major breakthroughs in Japan's beef and citrus quotas, allowing our exports to double over four years.
- Resisted protectionist efforts by other industries, such as domestic content legislation, that would cause a backlash against U.S. farm and ranch exports.
- Developed and implemented the PIK program to draw down burdensome reserve stocks of major commodities created by the Carter–Mondale embargo.
- Reformed bankruptcy law to provide for accelerated distribution of farm products in bankrupt elevators, acceptance of warehouse receipts and scale tickets as proof of ownership, and allowing a lien against elevator assets for unpaid farmers.
- Eliminated the marriage tax penalty for a surviving spouse and protected family farms and ranches by exempting, by 1987, up to $600,000 from estate taxes.
- Accelerated depreciation of farm and ranch equipment and buildings and increased the exemption for agricultural vehicles from the heavy vehicle use tax.
- Increased the gasoline tax exemption by 50 percent for alcohol fuels, stimulating demand for domestic grain production and reducing dependency on foreign oil.
- Worked with rural credit and farm and ranch lending institutions to assure adequate capital at the lowest possible interest rates.
- Responded to the emergency financial needs of farmers and ranchers stricken by drought and flood.

We want real profits for farmers and ranchers. We have begun the turnaround on farm and ranch incomes. Sound fiscal, monetary, and growth-oriented tax policies are essential if farmers and ranchers are to realize sufficient and enduring profits. We support legislation to permit farmers, ranchers, and other self-employed individuals to deduct from their gross income up to one-half of the cost of their personal hospitalization insurance premiums.

Government policies should strengthen the ability of farmers and ranchers to provide quality products at reasonable rates of return in an expanding economy.

We believe that federal farm programs should be tailored to meet the economic needs and requirements of today's structurally diverse and internationally oriented agriculture. These programs must be sensitive to potential impacts on all agriculture, especially nonprogram commodities, livestock, agribusiness, and rural communities.

Republicans believe that the future of American agriculture lies in the utilization of our rich farmland, advanced technology, and hard-working farm and ranch people, to supply food and fiber to the world. Traditional farm programs have threatened the confidence of America's farmers and ranchers and exhausted the patience of American taxpayers. We reject the policy of more of the same, and we further reject the Democrats' public utility vision of agriculture, which views it as a problem to be minimized by further political and bureaucratic management. Our new programs will bring the flexibility to adjust to rapidly changing export market conditions and opportunities, and, in a timely and effective manner, respond to the inherent, uncontrollable risks of farming and ranching.

Rural Americans impart a special strength to our national character, important to us all. Whether farmers or not, all rural citizens should have the same consideration as those who live in towns and cities in economic development, energy, credit, transportation availability, and employment. Opportunities for non-farm jobs have become increasingly important to farm and ranch families, enhancing life and work in rural America.

Toward Fair and Expanded Markets and Responding to Hunger

Agriculture is an international advantage for the United States. But a successful farm and ranch policy demands earnest attention to building on the strength of our domestic production capacity and to developing world markets, for American agriculture cannot be prosperous without exports.

Our farmers and ranchers must have full access to world markets and should not have to face unfair export subsidies and predatory dumping by other producing nations without redress. Republicans believe that unfair trade practices and non-tariff barriers are so serious that a comprehensive renegotiation of multilateral trade arrangements must be undertaken to revitalize the free, fair, and open trade critical to worldwide economic growth.

The Republican Party is unalterably opposed to the use of embargoes of grain or other agricultural products as a tool of foreign policy. The Carter–Mondale grain embargo is still—more than any other factor—the cause of the present difficulties in American agriculture and possibly the irretrievable loss of foreign markets. Republicans say, "Never again." The Democratic Platform says nothing.

America has a long history of helping those in need, and the responsibility for food assistance has been shared by federal and State governments and neighborhood volunteers. Federal expenditures in this area exceeded $19 billion in 1983, the highest amount ever. Numerous private and public efforts assure that adequate food is available. This expresses faith in our future and reflects our people's goodness.

We will provide adequate resources in programs ranging from food stamps to school lunches for the truly needy. We also recognize that fraud and abuse must be eliminated from those programs. We stress maximum local control consistent with national objectives.

Reducing Excessive Regulation in Agriculture

Excessive federal regulations, many imposed by the Carter–Mondale Administration, have been a crushing burden.

In 1980, we pledged to make sensible reductions in regulations that drained the profitability from farming, ranching, and commercial fishing. We did just that. We restored balance to the Interior Department's ineffective predator-control policies, and we moderated the EPA's and the FDA's excessive adherence to "zero risk" standards concerning the use of pesticides, antibiotics, food additives, and preservatives.

Republicans favor modernizing our food-safety laws, providing guidelines for risk–benefit assessment, peer review, and regulatory flexibility consistent with other health and safety policies.

Soil and Water Conservation

Agriculture must be both economically and environmentally sustainable. The soil and water stewardship of our farmers, ranchers, watermen, and rural people is commendable. Republicans believe that long-term soil, water, and other conservation policies, emphasizing environmentally sound agricultural productivity, rangeland protection, fish and wildlife habitat, and balanced forestry management, must be a top priority. Conservation practices must be intensified and integrated with farm programs to safeguard our most valuable resources. Volunteer participation, emphasizing State and local control and adequate incentives, is essential to effective conservation.

Water Policy

In 1980, we pledged a water policy which addressed our national diversity in climate, geography, reclamation needs, and patterns of land ownership. We promised a partnership between the States and federal government which would not destroy traditional State

supremacy in water law, and which would avert a water crisis in the coming decades. That partnership is now working to meet these challenges.

The Future of Farming

American agriculture is the world's most successful because of the hard work and creativity of family farmers and ranchers. They have benefited immensely from agricultural research, extension, and teaching, unequaled in the world. Cooperative extension, operating in every country, brings the results of USDA and Land Grant University research to rural America. We support these programs, with special attention to marketing efficiencies, reduced production costs, and new uses for farm and ranch commodities. We also encourage the establishment of regional international research and export trade centers.

Our agricultural people have developed the ideals of free enterprise and have based their enterprise on our culture's basic element, the family. The family farm and ranch is defined as a unit of agricultural production managed as an enterprise where labor and management have an equity interest in the business and a direct gain or loss from its operation. Family farms and ranches are the heart, soul, and backbone of American agriculture; it is the family farm that makes our system work better than any other.

Our rural and coastal people developed a great diversity of support organizations. They organized farm and ranch cooperatives, and rural electric and telephone cooperatives to provide essential services. They established farm and ranch organizations to work for better farm policies and to improve the quality of rural life. Republicans note with particular pride and enthusiasm the vital impact women have always had in American farming and ranching, and we support efforts to increase their role.

American agriculture has always relied upon the hardworking people who harvest seasonal and perishable crops. Republicans support comprehensive farm-labor legislation, fair to workers and employers, to protect consumers from work stoppages which disrupt the flow of food.

Republicans also recognize the tremendous efforts of commercial fishers to bring nutritious seafood products to market, thus strengthening America's food base.

Our agriculture is both a global resource and a tremendous opportunity. Only America possesses the natural, technological, management, and labor resources to commercially develop agriculture's next frontier.

We are encouraged by innovation in agriculture, and applaud its diversity, creativity, and enterprise.

Commercial applications of new technology and marketing and management innovations are creating additional opportunities for farming and ranching. Republicans have set the stage for building a new prosperity into our fundamentally strong agricultural system. We renew our national commitment to American farmers and ranchers.

International Economic Policy

The recent tremendous expansion of international trade has increased the standard of living worldwide. Our strong economy is attracting investment in the United States, which is providing capital needed for new jobs, technology, higher wages, and more competitive products.

We are committed to a free and open international trading system. All Americans benefit from the free flow of goods, services and capital, and the efficiencies of a vigorous international market. We will work with all of our international trading partners to eliminate barriers to trade, both tariff and non-tariff. As a first step, we call on our trading partners to join in a new round of trade negotiations to revise the General Agreement on Tariffs and Trade in order to strengthen it. And we further call on our trading partners to join us in reviewing trade with totalitarian regimes.

But free trade must be fair trade. It works only when all trading partners accept open markets for goods, services, and investments. We will review existing trade agreements and vigorously enforce trade laws including assurance of access to all markets for our service industries. We will pursue domestic and international policies that will allow our American manufacturing and agricultural industries to compete in international markets. We will not tolerate the loss of American jobs to nationalized, subsidized, protected foreign industries, particularly in steel, automobiles, mining, footwear, textiles, and other basic industries. This production is sometimes financed with our own tax dollars through international institutions. We will work to stop funding of those projects which are detrimental to our own economy.

The greatest danger today to our international trade is a growing protectionist sentiment. Tremendous fluctuations in exchange rates have rendered long-term international contracts virtually useless. We therefore urge our trading partners to join us in evaluating and correcting the structural problems of the international monetary system, to base it on more stable exchange rates and free capital markets.

Further, we support reorganization of trade responsibilities in order to reduce overlap, duplication, and waste in the conduct of international trade and industry.

Revisions in that system will stabilize trade relations so that debtor nations can repay their debts. These debts are the direct result of their domestic policies, often mandated by multilateral institutions, combined with the breakdown of the international monetary system. Slower economic growth, reduced imports, and higher taxes will not relieve debt burdens, but worsen them. The only way to repay the debts is to create productive capacity to generate new wealth through economic expansion, as America has done.

Austerity should be imposed not on people, but on governments. Debtor nations seeking our assistance must increase incentives for growth by encouraging private investment, reducing taxes, and eliminating subsidies, price controls, and politically motivated development projects.

SECURITY FOR THE INDIVIDUAL

America was built on the institutions of home, family, religion, and neighborhood. From these basic building blocks came self-reliant individuals, prepared to exercise both rights and responsibilities.

In the community of individuals and families, every generation has relearned the art of self-government. In our neighborhoods, Americans have traditionally taken care of their needs and aided the less fortunate. In the process we developed, independent of government, the remarkable network of "mediating institutions"—religious groups, unions, community and professional associations. Prominent among them have been innumerable volunteer groups, from fire departments and neighborhood watch patrols to meals-on-wheels and the little leagues.

Public policy long ignored these foundations of American life. Especially during the two decades preceding Ronald Reagan's election, the federal government eroded their authority, ignored their rights, and attempted to supplant their functions with programs at once intrusive and ineffectual. It thereby disrupted our traditional patterns of caring, sharing, and helping. It elbowed out the voluntary providers of services and aid instead of working through them.

By centralizing responsibility for social programs in Washington, liberal experimenters destroyed the sense of community that sustains local institutions. In many cases, they literally broke up neighborhoods and devastated rural communities.

Washington's governing elite thought they knew better than the people how to spend the people's money. They played fast and loose with our schools, with law enforcement, with welfare, with housing.

The results were declining literacy and learning, an epidemic of crime, a massive increase in dependency, and the slumming of our cities.

Worst of all, they tried to build their brave new world by assaulting our basic values. They mocked the work ethic. They scorned frugality. They attacked the integrity of the family and parental rights. They ignored traditional morality. And they still do.

Our 1980 Republican Platform offered a renewed vision. We based it upon home, family, and community as the surest guarantees of both individual rights and national greatness. We asserted, as we do now, the ethical dimension of public policy: the need to return to enduring principles of conduct and firm standards of judgment.

The American people responded with enthusiasm. They knew that our roots, in family, home, and neighborhood, do not tie us down. They give us strength. Once more we call upon our people to assert their supervision over government, to affirm their rights against government, to uphold their interests within government.

Housing and Homeownership

Homeownership is part of the American Dream. For the last two decades, that dream has been endangered by bad public policy. Government unleashed a dreadful inflation upon homebuyers, driving mortgage rates beyond the reach of average families, as the prime rate rose more than 300 percent (from 6.5 percent to 21.5 percent). The American worker's purchasing power fell every year from 1977 through 1980.

No wonder the housing industry was crippled. Its workers faced recurrent recessions. The boom-and-bust cycle made saving foolish, investment risky, and housing scarce.

Federal housing blighted stable low-income neighborhoods, disrupting communities which people had held together for generations. Only government could have wasted billions of dollars to create the instant slums which disgrace our cities.

In our 1980 Platform, we pledged to reverse this situation. We have begun to do so, despite obstructionism from those who believe that the taxpayer's home is government's castle.

We attacked the basic problem, not the symptoms. We cut tax rates and reduced inflation to a fraction of the Carter–Mondale years. The median price house that would cost $94,800 if Carter–Mondale inflation had continued now costs $74,200. The average monthly mortgage payment, which rose by $342 during the Carter–Mondale years, has increased just $24 since January 1981. The American Dream has made a comeback. To sustain it, we must finish the people's agenda.

We reaffirm our commitment to the federal-tax deductibility of mortgage interest payments. In the States, we stand with those working to lower property taxes that strike hardest at the poor, the elderly, and large families. We stand, as well, with Americans earning possession of their homes through "sweat-equity" programs.

We will, over time, replace subsidies and welfare projects with a voucher system, returning public housing to the free market.

Despite billions of dollars poured into public housing developments, conditions remain deplorable for many low-income Americans who live in them. These projects have become breeding grounds for the very problems they were meant to eliminate. Their dilapidated and crumbling structures testify to decades of corrupt or incompetent management by poverty bureaucrats.

Some residents of public housing developments have reversed these conditions by successfully managing their own housing units through creative self-help efforts. It is abundantly clear that their pride of ownership has been the most important factor contributing to the efficiency of operation, enhancing the quality of housing, improving community morale, and providing incentives for their self-improvement. The Republican Party therefore supports the development of programs which will lead to homeownership of public housing developments by current residents.

We strongly believe in open housing. We will vigorously enforce all fair housing laws and will not tolerate their distortion into quotas and controls.

Rent controls promise housing below its market cost but inevitably result in a shortage of decent homes. Our people should not have to underwrite any community which erodes its own housing supply by rent control.

Sound economic policy is good housing policy. In our expanding economy, where people are free to work and save, they will shelter their families without government intrusion.

Welfare

Helping the less fortunate is one of America's noblest endeavors, made possible by the abundance of our free and competitive economy. Aid should be swift and adequate to ensure the necessities of a decent life.

Over the past two decades, welfare became a nightmare for the taxpayer and the poor alike. Fraud and abuse were rampant. The costs of public assistance are astronomical, in large part because resources often benefit the welfare industry rather than the poor.

During the 1970s, the number of people receiving federal assistance increased by almost 300 percent, from 9 million to 35 million, while our population increased by only 11.4 percent. This was a fantastic and unsustainable universalization of welfare.

Welfare's indirect effects were equally as bad. It became a substitute for urgently needed economic reforms to create more entry-level jobs. Government created a hellish cycle of dependency. Family cohesion was shattered, both by providing economic incentives to set up maternal households and by usurping the breadwinner's economic role in intact families.

The cruelest result was the materialization of poverty, worsened by the breakdown of the family and accelerated by destructive patterns of conduct too long tolerated by permissive liberals. We endorse programs to assist female-headed households to build self-sufficiency, such as efforts by localities to enable participants to achieve permanent employment.

We have begun to clean up the welfare mess. We have dramatically reduced the poor's worst enemy—inflation—thereby protecting their purchasing power. Our resurgent economy has created over six million new jobs and reduced unemployment by 30 percent.

We have launched real welfare reforms. We have targeted benefits to the needy through tighter eligibility standards, enforced child-support laws, and encouraged "workfare" in the States. We gave States more leeway in managing welfare programs, more assistance with fraud control, and more incentives to hold down costs.

Only sustained economic growth, continuing our vigorous recovery, can give credible hope to those at the bottom of the opportunity ladder.

The working poor deserve special consideration, as do low-income families struggling to provide for their children. As part of a comprehensive simplification of the federal tax code, we will restore the real value of their personal tax exemptions so that families, particularly young families, can establish their economic independence.

Federal administration of welfare is the worst possible, detached from community needs and careless with the public's money. Our long tradition of State and local administration of aid programs must be restored. Programs and resources must be returned to State and local governments and not merely exchanged with them. We will support block grants to combine duplicative programs under State administration.

We must also recognize and stimulate the talents and energy of low-income neighborhoods. We must provide new incentives for self-help activities that flow naturally when people realize they can make a difference. This is especially critical in foster care and adoption.

Because there are different reasons for poverty, our programs address different needs and must never be replaced with a unitary income guarantee. That would betray the interests of the poor and the taxpayers alike.

We will employ the latest technology to combat welfare fraud in order to protect the needy from the greedy.

Whenever possible, public assistance must be a transition to the world of work, except in cases, particularly with the aged and disabled, where that is not appropriate. In other cases, it is long overdue.

Remedying poverty requires that we sustain and broaden economic recovery, hold families together, get government's hand out of their pocketbooks, and restore the work ethic.

Health

Our tremendous investment in health care has brought us almost miraculous advances. Although costs are still too high, we have dramatically enhanced the length and quality of life for all.

Faced with Medicare and Medicaid mismanagement, government tried to ration health care through arbitrary cuts in eligibility and benefits. Meanwhile, inflation drove up medical bills for us all. Economic incentives were backwards, with little awareness of costs by individual patients. Reimbursement mechanisms were based on expenses incurred, rather than set prospectively. Conspicuously absent were free-market incentives to respond to consumer wishes. Instead, government's heavy hand was everywhere.

We narrowly averted disaster. We moved creatively and carefully to restructure incentives, to free competition, to encourage flexible new approaches in the States, and to identify better means of health-care delivery. Applying these principles, we will preserve Medicare and Medicaid. We will eliminate the excesses and inefficiencies which drove costs unacceptably high in those programs. In order to assure their solvency and to avoid placing undue burdens on beneficiaries, reform must be a priority. The Republican Party reaffirms its commitment to assure a basic level of high quality health care for all Americans. We reaffirm as well our opposition to any proposals for compulsory national health insurance.

While Republicans held the line against government takeover of health care, the American people found private ways to meet new challenges. There has been a laudable surge in preventive health care and an emphasis on personal responsibility for maintaining one's health. Compassionate innovation has developed insurance against catastrophic illness, and capitated "at risk" plans are encouraging innovation and creativity.

We will maintain our commitment to health excellence by fostering research into yet-unconquered diseases. There is no better investment we as a nation can make than in programs which hold the promise of sounder health and longer life. For every dollar we spend on health research, we save many more in health care costs. Thus, what we invest in medical research today will yield billions of dollars in individual productivity as well as in savings in Medicare and Medicaid. The federal government has been the major source of support for biomedical research since 1945. That research effort holds great promise for combating cancer, heart disease, brain disorders, mental illness, diabetes, Alzheimer's disease, sickle cell anemia, and numerous other illnesses which threaten our nation's welfare. We commit to its continuance.

Many health problems arise within the family and should be dealt with there. We affirm the right and responsibility of parents to participate in decisions about the treatment of children. We will not tolerate the use of federal funds, taxed away from parents, to abrogate their role in family health care.

Republicans have secured for the hospice movement an important role in federal health programs. We must do more to enable persons to remain within the unbroken family circle. For those elderly confined to nursing homes or hospitals, we insist that they be treated with dignity and full medical assistance.

Discrimination in health care is unacceptable; we guarantee, especially for the handicapped, non-discrimination in the compassionate healing that marks American medicine.

Government must not impose cumbersome health planning that causes major delays, increases construction costs, and stifles competition. It should not unduly delay the approval of new medicines, nor adhere to outdated safety standards hindering rapidly advancing technology.

We must address ailments, not symptoms, in health-care policy. Drug and alcohol abuse costs thousands of lives and billions of dollars every year. We reaffirm our vigorous commitment to alcohol and drug abuse prevention and education efforts. We salute the citizens' campaign, launched from America's grassroots, against drunk driving. We applaud those States which raised the legal drinking age.

Much illness, especially among the elderly, is related to poor nutrition. The reasons are more often social than economic: isolation, separation from family, and often a mismatch between nutritional needs and available assistance. This reinforces our efforts to protect federal nutrition programs from fraud and abuse, so that their benefits can be concentrated upon the truly needy.

A supportive environment linking family, home, neighborhood, and workplace is essential to a sound health policy. The other essential step is to encourage the individual responsibility and group assistance that are uniquely American.

Environment

It is part of the Republican philosophy to preserve the best of our heritage, including our natural resources. The environment is not just a scientific or technological issue; it is a human one. Republicans put the needs of people at the center of environmental concerns. We assert the people's stewardship of our God-given natural resources. We pledge to meet the challenges of environmental protection, economic growth, regulatory reform, enhancement of our scenic and recreational areas, conservation of our non-renewable resources, and preservation of our irreplaceable natural heritage.

Americans were environmentalists long before it became fashionable. Our farmers cared for the earth and made it the world's most bountiful. Our families cared for their neighborhoods as an investment in our children's future. We pioneered the conservation that replenished our forests, preserved our wildlife, and created our national park system.

The American people have joined together in a great national effort to protect the promise of our future by conserving the rich beauty and bounty of our heritage. As a result, by almost any measure, the air is cleaner than it was 10 years ago, and fish are returning to rivers where they had not been seen for generations.

Within the last four years, dramatic progress has been made in protecting coastal barrier islands, and we began the Park Preservation and Restoration Program to restore the most celebrated symbols of our heritage. We support programs to restore and protect the nation's estuaries, wetland resources, and beaches.

The Republican Party endorses a strong effort to control and clean up toxic wastes. We have already tripled funding to clean up hazardous waste dumps, quadrupled funding for acid rain research, and launched the rebirth of the Chesapeake Bay.

The environmental policy of our nation originated with the Republican Party under the inspiration of Theodore Roosevelt. We hold it a privilege to build upon the foundation we have laid. The Republican Party supports the continued commitment to clean air and clean water.

This support includes the implementation of meaningful clean air and clean water acts. We will continue to offer leadership to reduce the threat to our environment and our economy from acid rain, while at the same time preventing economic dislocation.

Even as many environmental problems have been brought under control, new ones have been detected. And all the while, the growth and shifts of population and economic expansion, as well as the development of new industries, will further intensify the competing demands on our national resources.

Continued progress will be much more difficult. The environmental challenges of the 1980s are much more complex than the ones we tried to address in the 1970s, and they will not yield quickly to our efforts. As the science and administration of environmental protection have become more sophisticated, we have learned of many subtle and potentially more dangerous threats to public health and the environment.

In setting out to find solutions to the environmental issues of the 1980s and 1990s, we start with a healthy appreciation of the difficulties involved. Detecting contamination, assessing the threat, correcting the damage, and setting up preventive measures, all raise questions of science, technology, and public policy that are as difficult as they are important. However, the health and well-being of our citizens must be a high priority.

The number of people served by waste water treatment systems has nearly doubled just since 1970. The federal government should offer assistance to State and local governments in planning for the disposal of solid and liquid wastes. A top priority nationwide should be to eliminate the dumping of raw sewage.

We encourage recycling of materials and support programs which will allow our economic system to reward resource conservation.

We also commit ourselves to the development of renewable and efficient energy sources and to the protection of endangered or threatened species of plants and wildlife.

We will be responsible to future generations, but at the same time, we must remember that quality of life means more than protection and preservation. As Teddy Roosevelt put it, "Conservation means development as much as it does protection." Quality of life also means a good job, a decent place to live, accommodation for a growing population, and the continued economic and technological development essential to our standard of living, which is the envy of the whole world.

Transportation

America's overall transportation system is unequaled. Generating over 20 percent of our GNP and employ-ing one of every nine people in the work force, it promotes the unity amid diversity that uniquely characterizes our country. We travel widely, and we move the products of field and factory more efficiently and economically than any other people on earth.

And yet, four years ago, the future of American transportation was threatened. Over several decades, its vigor and creativity had been stunted by the intrusion of government regulation. The results were terribly expensive, and consumers paid the price. Our skies and highways were becoming dangerous and congested. With the same vision that marked President Eisenhower's beginning of the Interstate Highway System, the Reagan Administration launched a massive modernization of America's transport systems.

An expanded highway program is rebuilding the nation's roads and bridges and creating several hundred thousand jobs in construction and related fields. Driving mileage has increased by 8 percent, but greater attention to safety has led to a 17 percent reduction in fatalities, saving more than 8,000 lives yearly.

In public transit, we have redefined the federal role to emphasize support for capital investment, while restoring day-to-day responsibility to local authorities.

Our National Airspace Plan is revolutionizing air traffic control. It will improve flight safety and double the nation's flight capacity, providing better air service and stimulating economic growth.

Regulatory reform is revitalizing American transportation. Federal agencies had protected monopolies by erecting regulatory barriers that hindered the entry of new competitors. Small businesses and minority enterprises were virtually excluded. Prices were set, not by the public through free exchange, but by Washington clerks through green eyeshades.

Republicans led the successful fight to break government's stranglehold. The deregulation of airline economics (not their safety!) will be completed on December 30, 1984, when the Civil Aeronautics Board closes its doors forever. Through our regulatory reform efforts, the rail and trucking industries are now allowed to compete in both price and service. We also led the fight to deregulate interstate bus operations by enacting the Bus Regulatory Reform Act of 1982. While returning to a more free and competitive marketplace, we have ensured that small communities in rural America will retain necessary services through transitional assistance like the Essential Air Service Program, which will continue for four more years.

The Shipping Act of 1984 secured the first major reform of maritime law, as it applies to the U.S. liner trade, since 1916. This major step introduces genuine competition to the maritime industry, while enhancing our ability to compete against international cartels. Important in peacetime, critical in times of conflict, one of our proudest industries had long been neglected. We have expanded employment and brought hope of a future worthy of its past. The Reagan defense program now provides more work for our shipyards than at any time since World War II. We seek to halt the decline of our commercial fleet and restore it to economic strength and strategic capacity to fulfill its national obligations. We also seek to maximize the use of our nation's existing port facilities and shipbuilding and repair capability as a vital transportation resource that should be preserved in the best long-term interest of this country.

The American people benefit from regulatory reform. Air travelers now have a remarkable range of options, and flight is within reach of the average family budget. In the trucking business, increased competition has lowered prices and improved service.

The future of America's freight rail system is again bright. As a result of our reforms, the major private railroads have climbed back to profitability. Government red tape caused their red ink; by cutting the former, we are wiping out the latter. In addition, we transformed Conrail from a multi-billion dollar drain on the taxpayers into an efficient, competitive freight railroad. Returning Conrail as a financially sound single entity to private ownership, with service and jobs secure, will provide the nation with an improved rail freight system to promote economic growth. It will also return to the Treasury a significant portion of the taxpayers' investment, virtually unheard of for a federal project. We support improved passenger rail service where economically justified. We have made substantial progress in reducing the taxpayers' subsidy to Amtrak while maintaining services for which there is genuine demand. The Reagan Administration is selling the Alaska Railroad to the State of Alaska and transferring Conrail's commuter lines to the jurisdictions they serve.

The Republican Party believes that the nation's long-term economic growth will depend heavily on the adequacy of its public works infrastructure. We will continue to work to reverse the long-term decline that has occurred. We should foster development of better information on the magnitude and effectiveness of current federal, State, and local government capital expenditures and innovative financing mechanisms which would improve our capacity to leverage limited federal funds more effectively.

America's leadership in space depends upon the vi-

tality of free enterprise. That is why we encourage a commercial space-transportation industry. We share President Reagan's vision of a permanent manned space station within a decade, viewing it as the first stepping-stone toward creating a multi-billion dollar private economy in space. The permanent presence of man in space is crucial both to developing a visionary program of space commercialization and to creating an opportunity society on Earth of benefit to all mankind. We are, after all, the people who hewed roads out of the wilderness. Our families crossed ocean, prairie, and desert no less dangerous than today's space frontier to reach a new world of opportunity. And every route they took became a highway of liberty.

Like them, we know where we are going: forward, toward a future in our hands. Because of them, and because of us, our children's children will use space transportation to build both prosperity and peace on earth.

Education and Youth

Our children are our hope and our future. For their sake, President Reagan has led a national renewal to get back to the "basics" and excellence in education. Young people have turned away from the rebellion of the 1960s and the pessimism of the 1970s. Their hopeful enthusiasm speaks better for a bright future than any government program.

During the Reagan Administration, we restored education to prominence in public policy. This change will clearly benefit our youth and our country. By using the spotlight of the Oval Office, the Reagan Administration turned the nation's attention to the quality of education and gave its support to local and State improvement efforts. Parents and all segments of American society responded overwhelmingly to the findings of the National Commission on Excellence in Education, appointed by President Reagan. Its report, along with others from prominent experts and foundations, provided the impetus for educational reform.

Ronald Reagan's significant and innovative leadership has encouraged and sustained the reform movement. He catapulted education to the forefront of the national agenda and will be remembered as a president who improved education.

Unlike the Carter–Mondale Democrats, Republicans have leveled with parents and students about the problems we face together. We find remedies to these problems in the common sense of those most concerned: parents and local leaders. We support the decentralization necessary to put education back on the right track. We urge local school communities, including parents, teachers, students, administrators, and business and civic leaders, to evaluate school curricula—including extracurricular activities and the time spent in them—and their ultimate effect upon students and the learning process. We recognize the need to get "back to basics" and applaud the dramatic improvements that this approach has already made in some jurisdictions.

In schools, school districts, and States throughout our land, the past year and one-half has been marked by unprecedented response to identified education deficiencies. *The Nation Responds*, a recent report by the Reagan Administration, referred to a "tidalwave of school reform which promises to renew American education." According to that report:

- Forty-eight States are considering new high school graduation requirements and 35 have approved changes.
- Twenty-one States report initiatives to improve textbooks and instructional material.
- Eight States have approved lengthening the school day, seven are lengthening the school year, and 18 have mandates affecting the amount of time for instruction.
- Twenty-four States are examining master teacher or career ladder programs, and six have begun statewide or pilot programs.
- Thirteen States are considering changes in academic requirements for extracurricular and athletic programs, and five have already adopted more rigorous standards.

Education is a matter of choice, and choice in education is inevitably political. All of education is a passing on of ideas from one generation to another. Since the storehouse of knowledge is vast, a selection must be made of what to pass on. Those doing the selecting bring with them their own politics. Therefore, the more centralized the selection process, the greater the threat of tyranny. The more diversified the selection process, the greater the chance for a thriving free marketplace of ideas as the best insurance for excellence in education.

We believe that education is a local function, a State responsibility, and a federal concern. The federal role in education should be limited. It includes helping parents and local authorities ensure high standards, protecting civil rights, and ensuring family rights. Ignoring that principle, from 1965 to 1980, the United States indulged in a disastrous experiment with centralized direction of our schools. During the Carter–Mondale Administration, spending continued to increase, but test scores steadily declined.

This decline was not limited to academic matters. Many schools lost sight of their traditional task of developing good character and moral discernment. The result for many was a decline in personal responsibility.

The key to the success of educational reform lies in accountability: for students, parents, educators, school boards, and all governmental units. All must be held accountable in order to achieve excellence in education. Restoring local control of education will allow parents to resume the exercise of their responsibility for the basic education, discipline, and moral guidance of their children.

Parents have the primary right and responsibility for the education of their children; and States, localities, and private institutions have the primary responsibility for supporting that parental role. America has been a land of opportunity because America has been a land of learning. It has given us the most prosperous and dynamic society in the world.

The Republican Party recognizes the importance of good teachers, and we acknowledge the great effort many put forth to achieve excellence in the classroom. We applaud their numerous contributions and achievements in education. Unfortunately, many teachers are exhausted by their efforts to support excellence and elect to leave the classroom setting. Our best teachers have been frustrated by lowered standards, widespread indifference, and compensation below the true value of their contribution to society. In 1980–81 alone, 4 percent of the nation's math and science teachers quit the classroom. To keep the best possible teachers for our children, we support those education reforms which will result in increased student learning, including appropriate class sizes, appropriate and adequate learning and teaching materials, appropriate and consistent grading practices, and proper teacher compensation, including rewarding exceptional efforts and results in the classroom.

Classroom materials should be developed and produced by the private sector in the public marketplace, and then selections should be made at the State, local, and school levels.

We commend those States and local governments that have initiated challenging and rigorous high school programs, and we encourage all States to take initiatives that address the special educational needs of the gifted and talented.

We have enacted legislation to guarantee equal access to school facilities by student religious groups. Mindful of our religious diversity, we reaffirm our commitment to the freedoms of religion and speech guaranteed by the Constitution of the United States and firmly support the rights of students to openly practice the same, including the right to engage in voluntary prayer in schools.

While much has been accomplished, the agenda is only begun. We must complete the block-grant process begun in 1981. We will return revenue sources to State and local governments to make them independent of federal funds and of the control that inevitably follows.

The Republican Party believes that developing the individual dignity and potential of disabled Americans is an urgent responsibility. To this end, the Republican Party commits itself to prompt and vigorous enforcement of the rights of disabled citizens, particularly those rights established under the Education for All Handicapped Children Act, Section 504 of the Rehabilitation Act of 1973, and the Civil Rights of Institutionalized Persons Act. We insist on the highest standards of quality for services supported with federal funds.

In addition, government should seek out disabled persons and their parents to make them knowledgeable of their rights.

We will work toward providing federal funds to State and local governments sufficient to meet the degree of fiscal participation already promised in law.

We are committed to excellence in education for all our children within their own communities and neighborhoods. No child should be assigned to, or barred from, a school because of race.

In education, as in other activities, competition fosters excellence. We therefore support the President's proposal for tuition tax credits. We will convert the Chapter One grants to vouchers, thereby giving poor parents the ability to choose the best schooling available. Discrimination cannot be condoned, nor may public policies encourage its practice. Civil rights enforcement must not be twisted into excessive interference in the education process.

Teachers cannot teach and students cannot learn in an undisciplined environment. We applaud the President's promise to provide protection to teachers and administrators against suits from the unruly few who seek to disrupt the education of the overwhelming majority of students.

We urge the aggressive enforcement of the Protection of Pupil Rights amendment (also known as the Hatch Amendment, 20 U.S.C. 1232h) in order to protect pupils' and parents' rights. The amendment prohibits requiring any pupil to reveal personal or family information as part of any federally supported program, test, treatment, or psychological examination unless the school first obtains written consent of the pupil's parents.

The recent Grove City and Hillsdale College cases have raised questions about the extension of federal interference with private colleges, universities, and schools. Since federal aid, no matter how indirect, is now being linked to nearly every aspect of American life, great care must be taken in defining such terms as "federal financial assistance," "indirect" assistance, and "recipient" of assistance. We are deeply concerned that this kind of federal involvement in the affairs of some of the nation's fine private universities, colleges, and schools, many of which have remained stubbornly free of federal entanglements, can only bring with it unintended results. As the historical party of Lincoln and individual rights, we support enactment of legislation which would ensure protection of those covered under Title IX.

We urge States to establish partnerships with the scientific and business worlds to increase the number of teachers in these critical areas of learning. We also recognize a vast reservoir of talent and experience among retirees and other Americans competent to teach in these areas and ready to be tapped.

We endorse experiments with education such as enterprise zones and Cities-in-Schools. We reaffirm our commitment to wipe out illiteracy in our society. Further, we encourage the Congress and the States to reassess the process for aiding education, awarding funds on the basis of academic improvement rather than on daily attendance.

We are aware that good intentions do not always produce the desired results. We therefore urge our schools to evaluate their sex education programs to determine their impact on escalating teenage pregnancy rates. We urge that school officials take appropriate action to ensure parent involvement and responsibility in finding solutions to this national dilemma.

We support and encourage volunteerism in the schools. President Reagan's Adopt-a-School program is an example of how private initiative can revitalize our schools, particularly inner-city schools, and we commend him for his example.

Our emphasis on excellence includes the nation's colleges and universities. Although their achievements are unequaled in the world—in research, in proportion of citizens enrolled, in their contribution to our democratic society—we call upon them for accountability in good teaching and quality curricula that will ensure competent graduates in the world of work.

We pledge to keep our colleges and universities strong. They have been far too dependent on federal assistance and thus have been tied up in federal red tape. Their independence is an essential part of our liberty. Through regulatory reform, we are holding down the costs of higher education and reestablishing academic freedom from government. This is especially important for small schools, religious institutions, and the historically black colleges, for which President Reagan's Executive Order 12320 has meant new hope and vigor. We further reaffirm and support a regular Black College Day which honors a vital part of our educational community.

Republicans applaud the information explosion. This literacy-based knowledge revolution, made possible by computers, tapes, television, satellites, and other high technology innovations, buttressed by training programs through the business sector and foundations, is a tribute to American ingenuity. We urge our schools to educate for the ever-changing demands of our society and to resist using these innovations as substitutes for reasoning, logic, and mastery of basic skills.

We encourage excellence in the vocational and technical education that has contributed to the self-esteem and productivity of millions. We believe the best vocational and technical education programs are rooted in strong academic fundamentals. Business and industry stand ready to establish training partnerships with our schools. Their leadership is essential to keep America competitive in the future.

In an age when individuals may have four or five different jobs in their working career, vocational education and opportunities for adult learning will be more important than ever. The challenge of learning for citizenship and for work in an age of change will require new adaptations and innovations in the process of education. We urge the teaching profession and educational institutions at all levels to develop the maximum use of new learning opportunities available through learning-focused high technology. This technology in education and in the workplace is making possible, and necessary, the continuing education of our adult population.

The participation by adults in educational offerings within their communities will strengthen the linkages among the places where Americans live, work, and study.

Important as technology is, by itself it is inadequate for a free society. The arts and humanities flourish in the private sector, where a free market in ideas is the best guarantee of vigorous creativity. Private support for the arts and humanities has increased over the last four years, and we encourage its growth.

We support the National Endowments for the Arts and Humanities in their efforts to correct past abuses and focus on developing the cultural values that are the foundation of our free society. We must ensure that these programs bring the arts and humanities to people in rural areas, the inner-city poor, and other underserved populations.

Crime

One of the major responsibilities of government is to ensure the safety of its citizens. Their security is vital to their health and to the well-being of their neighborhoods and communities. The Reagan Administration is committed to making America safe for families and individuals. And Republican programs are paying dividends.

For the first time in the history of recorded federal crime statistics, rates of serious crime have dropped for two consecutive years. In 1983, the overall crime rate dropped 7 percent; and in 1982, the overall crime rate dropped 3 percent. In 1982 (the latest year for which figures are available), the murder rate dropped 5 percent, the robbery rate was down 6 percent, and forcible rape dropped 5 percent. Property crimes also declined: burglary decreased 9 percent, auto theft declined 2 percent, and theft dropped 1 percent.

Republicans believe that individuals are responsible for their actions. Those who commit crimes should be held strictly accountable by our system of justice. The primary objective of the criminal law is public safety; and those convicted of serious offenses must be jailed swiftly, surely, and long enough to assure public safety.

Republicans respect the authority of State and local law enforcement officials. The proper federal role is to provide strong support and coordination for their efforts and to vigorously enforce federal criminal laws. By concentrating on repeat offenders, we are determined to take career criminals off the street.

Additionally, the federal law enforcement budget has been increased by nearly 50 percent. We added 1,900 new investigators and prosecutors to the federal fight against crime. We arrested more offenders and sent more of them to prison. Convictions in organized crime cases have tripled under the Reagan Administration. We set up task forces to strike at organized crime and narcotics. In the year since, 3,000 major drug traffickers have been indicted, and nearly 1,000 have already been convicted. We are helping local authorities search for missing children. We have a tough new law against child pornography. Republicans initiated a system for pooling information from local, State and federal law enforcement agencies: the Violent Criminal Apprehension Program (VI-CAP). Under this program, State and local agencies have the primary law enforcement responsibility, but cross-jurisdictional information is shared rapidly so that serial murderers and other violent criminals can be identified quickly and then apprehended.

Under the outstanding leadership of President Reagan and Vice President Bush's Task Force on Organized Crime, the Administration established the National Narcotics Border Interdiction System. We set up an aggressive Marijuana Eradication and Suppression Program, gave the FBI authority to investigate drugs, and coordinated FBI and DEA efforts. We reaffirm that the eradication of illegal drug traffic is a top national priority.

We have leveled with the American people about the involvement of foreign governments, especially Communist dictators, in narcotics traffic: Cuba, the Soviet Union, Bulgaria—and now the Sandinistas in Nicaragua are international "pushers," selling slow death to young Americans in an effort to undermine our free society.

The Republican Party has deep concern about gratuitous sex and violence in the entertainment media, both of which contribute to the problem of crime against children and women. To the victims of such crimes who need protection, we gladly offer it.

We have begun to restore confidence in the criminal justice system. The Carter–Mondale legal policy had more concern for abstract criminal rights than for the victims of crime. It hurt those least able to defend themselves: the poor, the elderly, school children, and minorities. Republican leadership has redressed that imbalance. We have advanced such reforms as restitution by convicted criminals to their victims; providing victims with full explanations of what will occur before, during, and after trial; and assuring that they may testify at both trial and sentencing.

The Republican Senate has twice passed, with one dissenting vote, a comprehensive federal anti-crime package which would:

- Establish uniform, predictable and fair sentencing procedures, while abolishing the inconsistencies and anomalies of the current parole system;
- Strengthen the current bail procedures to allow the detention of dangerous criminals, who under current law are allowed to roam the streets pending trial;
- Increase dramatically the penalties for narcotic traffickers and enhance the ability of society to recoup ill-gotten gains from drug trafficking;
- Narrow the overly broad insanity defense; and
- Provide limited assistance to States and localities for the implementation of anti-crime programs of proven effectiveness.

In addition, the Republican Senate has overwhelmingly passed Administration-backed legislation which would:

- Restore a constitutionally valid federal death penalty;
- Modify the exclusionary rule in a way recently approved by the Supreme Court; and
- Curtail abuses by prisoners of federal *habeas corpus* procedures.

The Democrat bosses of the House of Representatives have refused to allow a vote on our initiatives by the House Judiciary Committee, perennial graveyard for effective anti-crime legislation, or by the full House despite our pressure and the public's demand.

The best way to deter crime is to increase the probability of detection and to make punishment certain and swift. As a matter of basic philosophy, we advocate preventive rather than merely corrective measures. Republicans advocate sentencing reform and secure, adequate prison construction. We concur with the American people's approval of capital punishment where appropriate and will ensure that it is carried out humanely.

Republicans will continue to defend the constitutional right to keep and bear arms. When this right is abused and armed felonies are committed, we believe in stiff, mandatory sentencing. Law-abiding citizens exercising their constitutional rights must not be blamed for crime. Republicans will continue to seek repeal of legislation that restrains innocent citizens more than violent criminals.

Older Americans

We reaffirm our commitment to the financial security, physical well-being, and quality of life of older Americans. Valuing them as a treasure of wisdom and experience, we pledge to utilize their unique talents to the fullest.

During the Carter–Mondale years, the silent thief of inflation ruthlessly preyed on the elderly's savings and benefits, robbing them of their retirement dollars and making many dependent on government handouts.

No more. Due to the success of Reaganomics, a retiree's private pension benefits are worth almost $1,000 more than if the 1980 inflation rate had continued. Average monthly Social Security benefits have increased by about $180 for a couple and by $100 a month for an individual. Because President Reagan forged a hard-won solution to the Social Security crisis, our elderly will not be repeatedly threatened with the program's impending bankruptcy as they were under the irresponsible policies of the Carter–Mondale Administration. We will work to repeal the Democrats' Social Security earnings-limitation, which penalizes the elderly by taking one dollar of their income for every two dollars earned.

Older Americans are vital contributors to society. We will continue to remove artificial barriers which discourage their participation in community life. We reaffirm our traditional opposition to mandatory retirement.

For those who are unable to care for themselves, we favor incentives to encourage home-based care.

We are combating insidious crime against the elderly, many of whom are virtual prisoners in their own homes for fear of violence. We demand passage of the President's Comprehensive Crime Control package, stalled by the Democrat-controlled House Judiciary Committee. We support local initiatives to fight crime against the elderly.

Older Americans want to contribute, to live with the dignity and respect they have earned, and to have their special needs recognized. The Republican Party must never turn its back on our elderly, and we ensure that we will adequately provide for them during their golden years so they can continue to enjoy our country's high standard of living, which their labors have helped provide.

Advancing Opportunity

Throughout this Platform are initiatives to provide an opportunity ladder for the poor, particularly among minorities, in both urban and rural areas. Unlike the Carter–Mondale Administration that locked them into the welfare trap, Republicans believe compassion dictates our offering real opportunities to minorities and the urban poor to achieve the American Dream.

We have begun that effort; and as a pledge of its continuance, this Platform commits us, not to a war of class against class, but to a crusade for prosperity for all.

For far too long, the poor have been trapped by the policies of the Democratic Party which treat those in the ghetto as if their interests were somehow different from our own. That is unfair to us all and an insult to the needy. Their goals are ours; their aspirations we share.

To emphasize our common bond, we have addressed their needs in virtually every section of this Platform, rather than segregating them in a token plank. To those who would see the Republican future for urban America, and for those who deserve a better break, we offer the commitments that make up the sinew of this Platform.

Congress must pass enterprise zones, to draw a green line of prosperity around the red-lined areas of our cities and to help create jobs and entrepreneurial opportunities.

We offer the boldest breakthrough in housing policy since VA mortgages: we offer opportunities for private ownership of housing projects by the poor themselves.

We pledge comprehensive tax reform that will give America back what was its post-war glory: a pro-family tax code with a dramatic work incentive for low-income and welfare families.

We offer hope, not despair; more opportunities for education through vouchers and tuition tax relief; and increased participation in the private enterprise system through the reform of counterproductive taxes and regulations.

Together with our emphatic commitment to civil rights, Republican programs will achieve, for those who feel left out of our society's progress, what President Reagan has already secured for our country: a new beginning to move America to full employment and honest money for all.

A FREE AND JUST SOCIETY

In 1980, the Republican Party offered a vision of America's future that applied our traditions to today's problems. It is the vision of a society more free and more just than any in history. It required a break with the worn-out past, to redefine the role of government and its relationship with individuals and their institutions. Under President Reagan's leadership, the American people are making that vision a reality.

The American people want an opportunity society, not a welfare state. They want government to foster an environment in which individuals can develop their potential without hindrance.

The Constitution is the ultimate safeguard of individual rights. As we approach the Constitutional Bicentennial in 1987, Republicans are restoring its vitality, which had been transgressed by Democrats in Congress, the executive, and in the courts.

We are renewing the federal system, strengthening the States, and returning power to the people. That is the surest course to our common goal: a free and just society.

Individual Rights

The Republican Party is the party of equal rights. From its founding in 1854, we have promoted equality of opportunity.

The Republican Party reaffirms its support of the pluralism and freedom that have been part and parcel of this great country. In so doing, it repudiates and completely disassociates itself from people, organizations, publications, and entities which promulgate the practice of any form of bigotry, racism, anti-Semitism, or religious intolerance.

Americans demand a civil rights policy premised on the letter of the Civil Rights Act of 1964. That law requires equal rights; and it is our policy to end discrimination on account of sex, race, color, creed, or national origin. We have vigorously enforced civil rights statutes. The Equal Employment Opportunity Commission has recovered record amounts of back pay and other compensation for victims of employment discrimination.

Just as we must guarantee opportunity, we oppose attempts to dictate results. We will resist efforts to replace equal rights with discriminatory quota systems and preferential treatment. Quotas are the most insidious form of discrimination: reverse discrimination against the innocent. We must always remember that, in a free society, different individual goals will yield different results.

The Republican Party has an historic commitment to equal rights for women. Republicans pioneered the right of women to vote, and our party was the first major party to advocate equal pay for equal work, regardless of sex.

President Reagan believes, as do we, that all members of our party are free to work individually for women's progress. As a party, we demand that there be no detriment to that progress or inhibition of women's rights to full opportunity and advancement within this society.

Participation by women in policy making is a strong commitment by the Republican Party and by President Reagan. He pledged to appoint a woman to the United States Supreme Court. His promise was not made lightly; and when a vacancy occurred, he quickly filled it with the eminently qualified Sandra Day O'Connor of Arizona.

His Administration has also sought the largest number of women in history to serve in appointive positions within the executive branch of government. Three women serve at Cabinet level, the most ever in history. Jeane Kirkpatrick, the U.S. Representative to the United Nations, Elizabeth Dole, Secretary of Transportation, and Margaret Heckler, Secretary of Health and Human Services, head a list of over 1,600 women who direct policy and operations of the federal government.

The Republican Party continues to search for interested and qualified women for all government positions. We will continue to increase the number of first-time appointments for women serving in government at all levels.

Our record of economic recovery and growth is an additional important accomplishment for women. It provides a stark contrast to the Carter–Mondale legacy to women: a shrinking economy, limited job opportunities, and a declining standard of living.

Whether working in or outside the home, women have benefited enormously from the economic progress of the past four years. The Republican economic expansion added over six million new jobs to the economy. It increased labor force participation by women to historic highs. Women's employment has risen by almost four and one-half million since the last Carter–Mondale year. They obtained almost one million more new jobs than men did. Economic growth due to Republican economic policies has produced a record number of jobs so that women who want to work outside the home now have unmatched opportunity. In fact, more than 50 percent of all women now have jobs outside the home.

The spectacular decline in inflation has immeasurably benefited women working both in and outside the home. Under President Reagan, the cost increase in everyday essentials—food, clothing, housing, utilities has been cut from the Carter–Mondale highs of over 10 percent a year to just over 4 percent today. We have ushered in an era of price stability that is stretching take-home pay hundreds of dollars farther. In 1982, for the first time in 10 years, women experienced a real increase in wages over inflation.

Lower interest rates have made it possible for more women, single and married, to own their homes and to buy their own automobiles and other consumer goods.

Our 25 percent reduction in marginal tax rates provided important benefits to women, as did the virtual elimination of the "widow's tax," which had jeopardized retirement savings of senior women. At the same time, we raised the maximum child care tax credit from $400 to $720 per family. We will continue to actively seek the elimination of discrimination against homemakers with regard to Individual Retirement Accounts so that single-income couples can invest the same amount in IRAs as two-income couples.

In addition, President Reagan has won enactment of the Retirement Equity Act of 1984. That legislation, strongly supported by congressional Republicans, makes a comprehensive reform of private pension plans to recognize the special needs of women.

Our record of accomplishment during the last four years is clear, but we intend to do even better over the next four.

We will further reduce the "marriage penalty," a burden upon two-income, working families. We will work to remove artificial impediments in business and industry, such as occupational licensing laws, that limit job opportunities for women, minorities, and youth or prevent them from entering the labor force in the first place.

For low-income women, the Reagan Administration has already given States and localities the authority, through the Job Training Partnership Act, to train more recipients of Aid to Families with Dependent Children for permanent, not make-work, jobs. We have increased child support collections from $1.5 billion to $2.4 billion and enacted a strong child support enforcement law. We will continue to stress welfare reforms which promote individual initiative, the real solution to breaking the cycle of welfare dependency.

With women comprising an increasing share of the work force, it is essential that the employment opportunities created by our free market system be open to individuals without regard to their sex, race, religion, or ethnic origin. We firmly support an equal opportunity approach which gives women and minorities equal access to all jobs—including the traditionally higher-paying technical, managerial, and professional positions, and which guarantees that workers in those jobs will be compensated in accord with the laws requiring equal pay for equal work under Title VII of the Civil Rights Act.

We are creating an environment in which individual talents and creativity can be tapped to the fullest, while assuring that women have equal opportunity, security, and real choices for the promising future. For all Americans, we demand equal pay for equal work. With equal emphasis, we oppose the concept of "comparable worth." We believe that the free market system can determine the value of jobs better than any government authority.

The Department of Justice has identified 140 federal statutes with gender-based distinctions. Proposed legislation will correct all but 18; six are still under study; the rest, which actually favor women, will remain as is. President Reagan's Fifty States Project, designed to identify State laws discriminating against women, has encouraged 42 States to start searches, and 26 have begun amending their laws. The Department has filed more cases dealing with sex discrimination in employment than were filed during a comparable period in the Carter–Mondale Administration.

Working with Republicans in Congress, President Reagan has declared 1983–1992 the Decade of Disabled Persons. All Americans stand to gain when disabled citizens are assured equal opportunity.

The Reagan Administration has an outstanding record in achieving accessibility for the handicapped. During the past two years, minimum guidelines have at last been adopted, and the Uniform Federal Accessibility Standard has become fact.

The Republican Party realizes the great potential of members of the disabled community in this country. We support all efforts being made at the federal level to remove artificial barriers from our society so that disabled individuals may reach their potential and participate at the maximum level of their abilities in education, employment, and recreation. This includes the removal, insofar as practicable, of architectural, transportation, communication and attitudinal barriers. We also support efforts to provide disabled Americans full access to voting facilities.

We deplore discrimination because of handicap. The Reagan Administration was the first to combat the insidious practice of denying medical care or even food and water to disabled infants. This issue has vast implications for medical ethics, family autonomy, and civil rights. But we find no basis, whether in law or medicine or ethics, for denying necessities to an infant because of the child's handicap.

We are committed to enforcing statutory prohibitions barring discrimination against any otherwise qualified handicapped individuals, in any program receiving federal financial assistance, solely by reason of their handicap.

We recognize the need for watchful care regarding the procedural due process rights of persons with handicaps both to prevent their placement into inappropriate programs or settings and to ensure that their rights are represented by guardians or other advocates, if necessary.

For handicapped persons who need care, we favor family-based care where possible, supported by appropriate and adequate incentives. We increased the tax credit for caring for dependents or spouses physically or mentally unable to care for themselves. We also provided a deduction of up to $1,500 per year for adopting a child with special needs that may otherwise make adoption difficult.

We are committed to seeking out gifted children and their parents to make them knowledgeable of their educational rights.

We reaffirm the right of all individuals freely to form, join, or assist labor organizations to bargain collectively, consistent with State laws and free from unnecessary government involvement. We support the fundamental principle of fairness in labor relations. We will continue the Reagan Administration's "open door" policy toward organized labor and its leaders. We reaffirm our longstanding support for the right of States to enact "Right-to-Work" laws under section 14(b) of the Taft–Hartley Act.

The political freedom of every worker must be protected. Therefore, we strongly oppose the practice of using compulsory dues and fees for partisan political purposes. Also, the protection of all workers must be secured. Therefore, no worker should be coerced by violence or intimidation by any party to a labor dispute.

The healthy mix of America's ethnic, cultural, and social heritage has always been the backbone of our nation and its progress throughout our history. Without the contributions of innumerable ethnic and cultural groups, our country would not be where it is today.

For millions of black Americans, Hispanic Americans, Asian Americans, and members of other minority groups, the past four years have seen a dramatic improvement in their ability to secure for themselves and for their children a better tomorrow.

That is the American Dream. The policies of the Reagan Administration have opened literally millions of doors of opportunity for these Americans, doors which either did not exist or were rapidly being slammed shut by the no-growth policies of the Carter–Mondale Administration.

We Republicans are proud of our efforts on behalf of all minority groups, and we pledge to do even more during the next four years.

We will continue to press for enactment of economic and social policies that promote growth and stress individual initiative of minority Americans. Our tax system will continue to be overhauled and reformed by making it fairer and simpler, enabling the families of minorities to work and save for their future. We will continue to push for passage of enterprise zone legislation, now bottled up in the Democrat-controlled House of Representatives. That bill, discussed elsewhere in this platform, will help minority Americans living in cities and urban areas to get jobs, to start their own businesses, and to reap the fruits of entrepreneurship by tapping their individual initiative, energy, and creativity.

We honor and respect the contributions of minority Americans and will do all we can to see that our diversity is enhanced during the next four years. Active contributions by minorities are the threads that weave the fabric that is America and make us stronger as a nation. We recognize these individuals and their contributions and will continue to promote the kinds of policies that will make their dreams for a better America a reality. The party of Lincoln will remain the party of equal rights for all.

We continue to favor whatever legislation may be necessary to permit American citizens residing in the Virgin Islands, Guam, and Puerto Rico to vote for president and vice president in national elections.

We support the right of Indian Tribes to manage their own affairs and resources. Recognizing the government-to-government trust responsibility, we are equally committed to working towards the elimination of the conditions of dependency produced by federal control. The social and economic advancement of Native Americans depends upon changes they will chart for themselves. Recognizing their diversity, we support the President's policy of responsibly removing impediments to their self-sufficiency. We urge the nations of the Americas to learn from our past mistakes and to protect native populations from exploitation and abuse.

Native Hawaiians are the only indigenous people of our country who are not officially designated as Native Americans. They should share that honored title. We endorse efforts to preserve their culture as a unique element in the human tapestry that is America.

Family Protection

Republicans affirm the family as the natural and indispensable institution for human development. A society is only as strong as its families, for they nurture those qualities necessary to maintain and advance civilization.

Healthy families inculcate values—integrity, responsibility, concern for others—in our youth and build social cohesion. We give high priority to their well-being. During the 1970s, America's families were ravaged by worsening economic conditions and a Washington elite unconcerned with them.

We support the concept of creating Family Education Accounts which would allow tax-deferred savings for investment in America's most crucial asset, our children, to assist low- and middle-income families in becoming self-reliant in meeting the costs of higher education.

In addition, to further assist the young families of America in securing the dream of homeownership, we would like to review the concept of Family Housing Accounts which would allow tax-exempt savings for a family's first home.

Preventing family dissolution, a leading cause of poverty, is vital. It has had a particularly tragic impact on the elderly, women, and minorities. Welfare programs have devastated low-income families and induced single parenthood among teens. We will review legislation and regulations to examine their impact on families and on parental rights and responsibilities. We seek to eliminate incentives for family break-up and to reverse the alarming rate of pregnancy outside marriage. Meanwhile, the Republican Party believes that society must do all that is possible to guarantee those young parents the opportunity to achieve their full educational and parental potential.

Because of Republican tax cuts, single people and

married people without dependents will have in 1984 basically the same average tax rates they had in 1960. The marriage penalty has been reduced. However, a couple with dependents still pays a greater portion of their income in taxes than in 1960. We reaffirm that the personal exemption for children be no less than for adults, and we will at least double its current level. The President's tax program also increased tax credits for child care expenses. We will encourage private sector initiatives to expand on-site child care facilities and options for working parents.

The problem of physical and sexual abuse of children and spouses requires careful consideration of its causes. In particular, gratuitous sex and violence in entertainment media contribute to this sad development.

We and the vast majority of Americans are repulsed by pornography. We will vigorously enforce constitutional laws to control obscene materials which degrade everyone, particularly women, and depict the exploitation of children. We commend the Reagan Administration for creating a commission on pornography and the President for signing the new law to eliminate child pornography. We stand with our President in his determination to solve the problem.

We call upon the Federal Communications Commission, and all other federal, State, and local agencies with proper authority, to strictly enforce the law regarding cable pornography and to implement rules and regulations to clean up cable pornography and the abuse of telephone service for obscene purposes.

Immigration

Our history is a story about immigrants. We are proud that America still symbolizes hope and promise to the world. We have shown unparalleled generosity to the persecuted and to those seeking a better life. In return, they have helped to make a great land greater still.

We affirm our country's absolute right to control its borders. Those desiring to enter must comply with our immigration laws. Failure to do so not only is an offense to the American people but is fundamentally unjust to those in foreign lands patiently waiting for legal entry. We will preserve the principle of family reunification.

With the estimates of the number of illegal aliens in the United States ranging as high as 12 million and better than one million more entering each year, we believe it is critical that responsible reforms of our immigration laws be made to enable us to regain control of our borders.

The flight of oppressed people in search of freedom has created pressures beyond the capacity of any one nation. The refugee problem is global and requires the cooperation of all democratic nations. We commend the President for encouraging other countries to assume greater refugee responsibilities.

Our Constitutional System

Our Constitution, now almost 200 years old, provides for a federal system, with a separation of powers among the three branches of the national government. In that system, judicial power must be exercised with deference towards State and local officials; it must not expand at the expense of our representative institutions. It is not a judicial function to reorder the economic, political, and social priorities of our nation. The intrusion of the courts into such areas undermines the stature of the judiciary and erodes respect for the rule of law. Where appropriate, we support congressional efforts to restrict the jurisdiction of federal courts.

We commend the President for appointing federal judges committed to the rights of law-abiding citizens and traditional family values. We share the public's dissatisfaction with an elitist and unresponsive federal judiciary. If our legal institutions are to regain respect, they must respect the people's legitimate interests in a stable, orderly society. In his second term, President Reagan will continue to appoint Supreme Court and other federal judges who share our commitment to judicial restraint.

The Republican Party firmly believes that the best governments are those most accountable to the people. We heed Thomas Jefferson's warning: "When all government, in little as in great things, shall be drawn to Washington as the center of all power, it will render powerless the checks provided of one government of another."

For more responsible government, non-essential federal functions should be returned to the States and localities wherever prudent. They have the capability, knowledge, and sensitivity to local needs required to better administer and deliver public services. Their diverse problems require local understanding. The transfer of rights, responsibilities, and revenues to the "home front" will recognize the abilities of local government and the limitations of a distant federal government.

We commend the President for the bold initiatives of his "New Federalism." The enacted block grants discussed elsewhere in this Platform are a positive step. But the job of making government more accountable to the people has just begun. We strongly favor the expansion of block-grant funding and other means to restore our nation's federal foundation.

More than 40 years ago, a grave injustice was done to many Americans of Japanese ancestry. Uprooted from their homes in a time of crisis, loyal citizens and residents were treated in a way which contravened the fundamental principles of our people. We join them and their descendants in assuring that the deprivation of rights they suffered shall never again be permitted in this land of liberty.

To benefit all Americans, we support the privatization of government services whenever possible. This maximizes consumer freedom and choice. It reduces the size and cost of government, thus lessening the burden on taxpayers. It stimulates the private sector, increases prosperity, and creates jobs. It demonstrates the primacy of individual action which, within a free market economy, can address human needs most effectively.

Within the executive branch, the Reagan Administration has made government work more efficiently. Under the direction of the Office of Personnel Management, non-defense government employment was reduced by over 100,000. The overwhelming majority of federal employees are dedicated and hardworking. Indeed, we have proposed to base their pay and retention upon performance so that outstanding federal employees may be properly rewarded.

The federal government owns almost a third of our nation's land. With due recognition of the needs of the federal government and mindful of environmental, recreational, and national defense needs, we believe the sale of some surplus land will increase productivity and increase State and local tax bases. It will also unleash the creative talents of free enterprise in defense of resource and environmental protection.

The expression of individual political views is guaranteed by the First Amendment; government should protect, not impinge upon First Amendment rights. Free individuals must have unrestricted access to the process of self-government. We deplore the growing labyrinth of bewildering regulations and obstacles which have increased the power of political professionals and discouraged the participation of average Americans. Even well-intentioned restrictions on campaign activity stifle free speech and have a chilling effect on spontaneous political involvement by our citizens.

The holding of public office in our country demands the highest degree of commitment to integrity, openness, and honesty by candidates running for all elective offices. Without such a commitment, public confidence rapidly erodes. Republicans therefore reaffirm our commitment to the fair and consistent application of financial disclosure laws. We will continue our support for full disclosure by all high officials of the government and candidates in positions of public trust. This extends to the financial holdings of spouses or dependents, of which the official has knowledge, financial interest, or benefit. We will continue to hold all public officials to the highest ethical standards and will oppose the inconsistent application of those standards on the basis of gender.

Republicans want to encourage, not restrict, free discourse and association. The interplay of concerned individuals, sometimes acting collectively to pursue their goals, has led to healthy and vigorous debate and better understanding of complex issues. We will remove obstacles to grassroots participation in federal elections and will reduce, not increase, the federal role.

Republicans believe that strong, competitive political parties contribute mightily to coherent national policies, effective representation, and responsive government. Forced taxpayer financing of campaign activities is political tyranny. We oppose it.

In light of the inhibiting role federal election laws and regulations have had, Congress should consider abolishing the Federal Election Commission.

We are the party of limited government. We are deeply suspicious of the amount of information which governments collect. Governments limited in size and scope best ensure our people's privacy. Particularly in the computer age, we must ensure that no unnecessary information is demanded and that no disclosure is made which is not approved. We oppose national identification cards.

We support reasonable methods to fight those who undermine national security, prevent crosschecks of government benefit records to conceal welfare fraud, or misuse financial secrecy laws to hide their narcotics profits under the guise of a right to privacy.

Private property is the cornerstone of our liberty and the free enterprise system. The right of property safeguards for citizens all things of value: their land, merchandise and money, their religious convictions, their safety and liberty, and their right of contract to produce and sell goods and services. Republicans reaffirm this God-given and inalienable right.

The unborn child has a fundamental individual right to life which cannot be infringed. We therefore reaffirm our support for a human life amendment to the Constitution, and we endorse legislation to make clear that the Fourteenth Amendment's protections apply to unborn children. We oppose the use of public revenues for abortion and will eliminate funding for organizations which advocate or support abortion. We commend the efforts of those individuals and religious and private organizations that are providing positive alternatives to abortion by meeting the physical, emotional, and financial needs of pregnant women and offering adoption services where needed.

We applaud President Reagan's fine record of judicial appointments, and we reaffirm our support for the appointment of judges at all levels of the judiciary who respect traditional family values and the sanctity of innocent human life.

AMERICA SECURE AND THE WORLD AT PEACE

The Future of Our Foreign Policy

President Reagan has restored the American people's faith in the principles of liberal democracy. Today, we have more confidence in the self-evident truths of democracy than at any time since World War II.

The first principle of that faith is that all human beings are created equal in the natural human right to govern themselves.

Just as we assert the right of self-government, it follows that all people throughout the world should enjoy that same human right. This moral principle must be the ideal by which our policy toward other nations is directed.

We Republicans emphasize that there is a profound moral difference between the actions and ideals of Marxist-Leninist regimes and those of democratic governments, and we reject the notions of guilt and apology which animate so much of the foreign policy of the Democratic Party. We believe American foreign policy can only succeed when it is based on unquestioned faith in a single idea: the idea that all human beings are created equal, the founding idea of democracy.

The supreme purpose of our foreign policy must be to maintain our freedom in a peaceful international environment in which the United States and our allies and friends are secure against military threats, and democratic governments are flourishing in a world of increasing prosperity.

This we pledge to our people and to future generations: we shall keep the peace by keeping our country stronger than any potential adversary.

The Americas

Our future is intimately tied to the future of the Americas. Family, language, culture, and trade link us closely with both Canada, our largest trading partner, and our southern neighbors.

The people of both Mexico and Canada are of fundamental importance to the people of the United States of America, not just because we share a common border, but because we are neighbors who share both history and a common interest for the present and future. Under President Reagan, our relations with both countries are being carried out in a serious, straightforward manner in a climate of mutual respect. As our countries seek solutions to common problems on the basis of our mutual interests, we recognize that each country has a unique contribution to make in working together to resolve mutual problems.

The security and freedom of Central America are indispensable to our own. In addition to our concern for the freedom and overall welfare of our neighbors to the south, two-thirds of our foreign trade passes through the Caribbean and the Panama Canal. The entire region, however, is gravely threatened by Communist expansion, inspired and supported by the Soviet Union and Cuba. We endorse the principles of the Monroe Doctrine as the strongest foundation for United States policy throughout the hemisphere.

We encourage even closer ties with the countries of South America and consider the strengthening of representative governments there as a contribution to the peace and security of us all. We applaud the Organization of American States for its efforts to bring peace and freedom to the entire hemisphere.

Republicans have no illusions about Castro's brutal dictatorship in Cuba. Only our firmness will thwart his attempts to export terrorism and subversion, to destroy democracy, and to smuggle narcotics into the United States. But we also extend a constructive, hopeful policy toward the Cuban people. Castro resents and resists their desire for freedom. He fears Radio Marti, President Reagan's initiative to bring truth to our Cuban neighbors. He is humiliated by the example of Cuban-born Americans, whose spiritual and material accomplishments contrast starkly with Communist failures in their birthplace. We believe in friendship between the Cuban and the American peoples, and we envision a genuine democracy in Cuba's future.

We support the President in following the unanimous findings of the Bipartisan Commission on Central America, first proposed by the late Senator Henry "Scoop" Jackson of Washington.

Today, democracy is under assault throughout the hemisphere. Marxist Nicaragua threatens not only Costa Rica and Honduras, but also El Salvador and Guatemala. The Sandinista regime is building the largest military force in Central America, importing Soviet equipment, Eastern bloc and PLO advisors, and thousands of Cuban mercenaries. The Sandinista government has been increasingly brazen in its embrace of Marxism–Leninism. The Sandinistas have systematically persecuted free institutions, including synagogue and church, schools, the private sector, the free press, minorities, and families and tribes throughout Nicaragua. We support continued assistance to the democratic freedom fighters in Nicaragua. Nicaragua cannot be allowed to remain a Communist sanctuary, exporting terror and arms throughout the region. We condemn the Sandinista government's smuggling of illegal drugs into the United States as a crime against American society and international law.

The heroic effort to build democracy in El Salvador has been brutally attacked by Communist guerrillas supported by Cuba and the Sandinistas. Their violence jeopardizes improvements in human rights, delays economic growth, and impedes the consolidation of democracy. El Salvador is nearer to Texas than Texas is to New England, and we cannot be indifferent to its fate. In the tradition of President Truman's postwar aid to Europe, President Reagan has helped the people of El Salvador defend themselves. Our opponents object to that assistance, citing concern for human rights. We share that concern, and more than that, we have taken steps to help curb abuses. We have firmly and actively encouraged human rights reform, and results have been achieved. In judicial reform, the murderers of the American nuns in 1980 have been convicted and sentenced; and in political reform, the right to vote has been exercised by 80 percent of the voters in the fair, open elections of 1982 and 1984. Most important, if the Communists seize power there, human rights will be extinguished, and tens of thousands will be driven from their homes. We therefore support the President in his determination that the Salvadoran people will shape their own future.

We affirm President Reagan's declaration at Normandy: there is a profound moral difference between the use of force for liberation and the use of force for conquest and territorial expansion. We applaud the liberation of man and mind from oppression everywhere.

We applaud the liberation of Grenada, and we honor those who took part in it. Grenada is small, and its people few; but we believe the principle established there, that freedom is worth defending, is of monumental importance. It challenges the Brezhnev doctrine. It is an example to the world.

The Caribbean Basin Initiative is a sound program for the strengthening of democratic institutions through economic development based on free people and free market principles. The Republican Party strongly supports this program of integrated, mutually reinforcing measures in the fields of trade, investment, and financial assistance.

We recognize our special-valued relationship with Puerto Rico and the Virgin Islands; and we will support special measures to ensure that they will benefit and prosper from the Caribbean Basin Initiative, thereby reinforcing a stronghold of democracy and free enterprise in the Caribbean. The Republican Party reaffirms its support of the right of Puerto Rico to be admitted into the Union after it freely so determines, through the passage of an admission bill which will provide for a smooth fiscal transition, recognize the concept of a multicultural society for its citizens, and secure the opportunity to retain their Spanish language and traditions.

The Soviet Union

Stable and peaceful relations with the Soviet Union are possible and desirable, but they depend upon the credibility of American strength and determination. As our power waned in the 1970s, our very weakness was provocative. The Soviets exploited it in Afghanistan, the Middle East, Africa, Southeast Asia, and the Western Hemisphere. Our policy of peace through strength encourages freedom-loving people everywhere and provides hope for those who look forward one day to enjoying the fruits of self-government.

We hold a sober view of the Soviet Union. Its globalist ideology and its leadership obsessed with military power make it a threat to freedom and peace on every continent. The Carter–Mondale Administration ignored that threat, and the Democratic candidates underestimate it today. The Carter–Mondale illusion that the Soviet leaders share our ideals and aspirations is not only false but a profound danger to world peace.

Republicans reaffirm our belief that Soviet behavior at the negotiating table cannot be divorced from Soviet behavior elsewhere. Overeagerness to sign agreements with the Soviets at any price, fashionable in the Carter–Mondale Administration, should never blind us to this reality. Any future agreement with the Soviets must require full compliance, be fully verifiable, and contain suitable sanctions for non-compliance. Carter–Mondale efforts to cover up Soviet violations of the 1972 Strategic Arms Limitations agreement and Anti-ballistic Missile Treaty emboldened the Soviets to strengthen their military posture. We condemn these violations, as well as recent violations of chemical and toxic weapons treaties in Afghanistan, Southeast Asia, and the Iran–Iraq war. We insist on full Soviet compliance with all treaties and executive agreements.

We seek to deflect Soviet policy away from aggression and toward peaceful international conduct. To that end, we will seek substantial reductions in nuclear weapons, rather than merely freezing nuclear weapons at their present dangerous level. We will continue multilateral efforts to deny advanced Western technology to the Soviet war machine.

We will press for Soviet compliance with all international agreements, including the 1975 Helsinki Final Act and the U.N. Declaration on Human Rights. We will continue to protest Soviet anti-Semitism and human rights violations. We admire the courage of such people as Andrei Sakharov, his wife Yelena Bonner, Anatole Shcharansky, Ida Nudel and Josef Begun, whose defiance of Soviet repression stands as a testament to the greatness of the human spirit. We will press the Soviet Union to permit free emigration of Jews, Christians, and oppressed national minorities. Finally, because the peoples of the Soviet empire share our hope for the future, we will strengthen our information channels to encourage them in their struggle for individual freedom, national self-determination, and peace.

Europe

Forty years after D-Day, our troops remain in Europe. It has been a long watch, but a successful one. For four decades, we have kept the peace where, twice before, our valiant fought and died. We learned from their sacrifice.

We would be in mortal danger were Western Europe to come under Soviet domination. Fragmenting NATO is the immediate objective of the Soviet military buildup and Soviet subversion. During the Carter–Mondale years, the Soviets gained a substantial military and diplomatic advantage in Europe. They now have three times as many tanks as we do and almost a monopoly on long-range theater nuclear forces. To keep the peace, the Reagan–Bush Administration is offsetting the Soviet military threat with the defensive power of the Alliance. We are deploying Pershing II and Cruise missiles. Remembering the Nazi Reich, informed voters on both sides of the Atlantic know they cannot accept Soviet military superiority in Europe. That is why the British, Italian, and West German parliaments have approved Euromissile deployments, and why new NATO base agreements were concluded successfully in Portugal, Spain, Turkey, and Greece. This is a victory for the Reagan–Bush Administration and our European friends.

The United States again leads the Alliance by offering hope of a safer future. As America's strength is restored, so is our allies' confidence in the future of freedom. We will encourage them to increase their contributions to our common defense.

To strengthen NATO's Southern Flank, we place the highest priority on resolving the Cyprus dispute and maintaining our support for both Greece and Turkey, with non-recognition of regimes imposed in occupied territory.

We share a deep concern for peace and justice in Northern Ireland and condemn all violence and terrorism in that strife-torn land.

We stand in solidarity with the peoples of Eastern Europe: the Poles, Hungarians, East Germans, Czechs, Rumanians, Yugoslavs, Bulgarians, Ukrainians, Baltic peoples, Armenians, and all captive nations who struggle daily against their Soviet masters. The heroic efforts of Lech Walesa and the Solidarity movement in Poland are an inspiration to all people yearning to be free. We are not neutral in their struggle, wherever the flame of liberty brightens the black night of Soviet oppression.

The tragic repression of the Polish people by the Soviet-inspired military dictatorship in Poland has touched the American people. We support policies to provide relief for Polish nationals seeking asylum and refuge in the United States.

The Middle East

President Reagan's Middle East policy has been flexible enough to adapt to rapidly changing circumstances, yet consistent and credible so that all nations recognize our determination to protect our vital interests. The President's skillful crisis management throughout the Iran–Iraq war has kept that conflict from damaging our vital interests. His peace efforts have won strong bipartisan support and international applause. And his willingness to stand up to Libya has made peace-loving states in the region feel more secure.

The 1979 Soviet invasion of Afghanistan, which surprised the Carter–Mondale Administration, brought Soviet forces less than 400 miles from the strategic Straits of Hormuz. The seizure of American hostages in Iran that year caught the United States unprepared and unable to respond. Lebanon is still in turmoil, despite our best efforts to foster stability in that unhappy country. With the Syrian leadership increasingly subject to Soviet influence, and the Palestine Liberation Organization and its homicidal subsidiaries taking up residence in Syria, U.S. policy toward the region must remain vigilant and strong. Republicans reaffirm that the United States should not recognize or negotiate with the PLO so long as that organization continues to promote terrorism, rejects Israel's right to exist, and refuses to accept U.N. Resolutions 242 and 338.

The bedrock of that protection remains, as it has for over three decades, our moral and strategic relationship with Israel. We are allies in the defense of freedom. Israel's strength, coupled with United States assistance, is the main obstacle to Soviet domination of the region. The sovereignty, security, and integrity of the state of Israel are moral imperatives. We pledge to help maintain Israel's qualitative military edge over its adversaries.

Today, relations between the United States and Israel are closer than ever before. Under President Reagan, we have moved beyond mere words to extensive political, military, and diplomatic cooperation. U.S.–Israeli strategic planning groups are coordinating our joint defense efforts, and we are directly supporting projects to augment Israel's defense industrial base. We support the legislation pending for an Israel–U.S. free trade area.

We recognize that attacks in the U.N. against Israel are but thinly disguised attacks against the United States, for it is our shared ideals and democratic way of life that are their true target. Thus, when a U.N. agency denied Israel's right to participate, we withheld our financial support until that action was corrected. And we have worked behind the scenes and in public in other international organizations to defeat discriminatory attacks against our ally.

Our determination to participate actively in the peace process begun at Camp David has won us support over the past four years from moderate Arab states. Israel's partner in the Camp David Accords, Egypt, with American support, has been a constructive force for stability. We pledge continued support to Egypt and other moderate regimes against Soviet and Libyan subversion, and we look to them to contribute to our efforts for a long-term settlement of the region's destructive disputes.

We believe that Jerusalem should remain an undivided city with free and unimpeded access to all holy places by people of all faiths.

Asia and the Pacific

Free Asia is a tremendous success. Emulating the United States economically and politically, our friends in East Asia have had the world's highest economic growth rates. Their economies represent the dynamism of free markets and free people, in stark contrast to the dreary rigidity and economic failures of centrally planned socialism. U.S. investments in Asia now exceed $30 billion, and our annual trade surpasses that with any other region.

Unable to match this progress, the Soviet Union, North Korea, and Vietnam threaten the region with military aggression and political intimidation. The Soviet rape of Afghanistan, the criminal destruction of

the KAL airliner, the genocide in Vietnam, Cambodia and Laos, the steady growth of Soviet SS-20 forces in East Asia, the rapid increase of the Soviet Pacific Fleet, the continuing build-up of North Korean forces and the brutal bombing of South Korean leaders in Rangoon, the recent deployment of Soviet forces at Cam Ranh Bay, the continued occupation of Cambodia by the Vietnamese, and chemical and biological weapons attacks against defenseless civilian populations in Afghanistan and Southeast Asia are some of the more obvious threats to the peace of Asia and to America's friends there.

Republicans salute the brave people of Afghanistan, struggling to regain their freedom and independence. We will continue to support the freedom fighters and pledge our continuing humanitarian aid to the thousands of Afghan refugees who have sought sanctuary in Pakistan and elsewhere.

To preserve free Asia's economic gains and enhance our security, we will continue economic and security assistance programs with the frontline states of Korea, Thailand, and Pakistan. We will maintain defense facilities in Korea, Japan, the Philippines, and the Indian Ocean to protect vital sea lanes.

We will promote economic growth while we strengthen human rights and the commitment to both democracy and free markets. We will help friendly nations deal with refugees and secure their help against drug cultivation and trafficking.

Our relations with Japan are central to America's role in the Far East, and they have never been better. The world's second-largest industrial power can make an increasingly important contribution to peace and economic development over much of Asia. We applaud Japan's commitment to defend its territory, air space, and sea lanes. We are heartened by its increases in defense spending and urge Japan to further expand its contribution to the region's defense. We have made progress in our trade relations and affirm that, with good will on both sides, broader agreement is likely.

In keeping with the pledge of the 1980 Platform, President Reagan has continued the process of developing our relationship with the People's Republic of China. We commend the President's initiatives to build a solid foundation for the long-term relations between the United States and the People's Republic, emphasizing peaceful trade and other policies to promote regional peace. Despite fundamental differences in many areas, both nations share an important common objective: opposition to Soviet expansionism.

At the same time, we specifically reaffirm our concern for, and our moral commitment to, the safety and security of the 18 million people on Taiwan. We pledge that this concern will be constant, and we will continue to regard any attempt to alter Taiwan's status by force as a threat to regional peace. We endorse, with enthusiasm, President Reagan's affirmation that it is the policy of the United States to support and fully implement the provisions of the Taiwan Relations Act. In addition, we fully support self-determination for the people of Hong Kong.

The Republic of Korea is a stalwart ally. To deter aggression, we will maintain our forces there which contribute to our common defense. Our growing economic relations are good for both countries and enhance our influence to foster a democratic evolution there.

We prize our special relationship with the Philippines. We will make every effort to promote economic development and democratic principles they seek. Because the Clark and Subic Bay bases are vital to American interests in the Western Pacific, we are committed to their continued security.

We recognize the close and special ties we have maintained with Thailand since the days of Abraham Lincoln. Thailand stands tall against the imperialist aggression of Vietnam and the Soviet Union in Southeast Asia.

We hail the economic achievements of the Association of Southeast Asian Nations. We will strengthen economic and political ties to them and support their opposition to the Vietnamese occupation of Cambodia.

Almost a decade after our withdrawal from Vietnam, thousands of Americans still do not know the fate of their fathers, brothers, and sons missing in action. Our united people call upon Vietnam and Laos with one voice: return our men, end the grief of the innocent, and give a full accounting of our POW–MIAs. We will press for access to investigate crash sites throughout Indochina. We support the efforts of our private citizens who have worked tirelessly for many years on this issue.

Africa

Africa faces a new colonialism. The tripartite axis of the Soviet Union, Cuba, and Libya has unleashed war and privation upon the continent. We are committed to democracy in Africa and to the economic development that will help it flourish. That is why we will foster free market, growth-oriented, and liberalized trading policies.

As part of reforming the policies of the International Development Association, we have assisted in directing a larger proportion of its resources to sub-Saharan Africa. To nurture the spirit of individual initiative in Africa, our newly created African Development Foundation will work with African entrepreneurs at the village level. In addition, through our rejection of the austerity programs of international organizations, we are bringing new hope to the people of Africa that they will join in the benefits of the growing, dynamic world economy.

We will continue to provide necessary security and economic assistance to African nations with which we maintain good relations to help them develop the infrastructure of democratic capitalism so essential to economic growth and individual accomplishment. We will encourage our allies in Europe and East Asia to coordinate their assistance efforts so that the industrialized countries will be able to contribute effectively to the economic development of the continent. We believe that, if given the choice, the nations of Africa will reject the model of Marxist state-controlled economies in favor of the prosperity and quality of life that free economies and free people can achieve.

We will continue to assist threatened African governments to protect themselves and will work with them to protect their continent from subversion and to safeguard their strategic minerals. The Reagan–Bush Administration will continue its vigorous efforts to achieve Namibian independence and the expulsion of Cubans from occupied Angola.

We reaffirm our commitment to the rights of all South Africans. Apartheid is repugnant. In South Africa, as elsewhere on the continent, we support well-conceived efforts to foster peace, prosperity, and stability.

Foreign Assistance and Regional Security

Developing nations look to the United States for counsel and guidance in achieving economic opportunity, prosperity, and political freedom. Democratic capitalism has demonstrated, in the United States and elsewhere, an unparalleled ability to achieve political and civil rights and long-term prosperity for ever-growing numbers of people. We are confident that democracy and free enterprise can succeed everywhere. A central element in our programs of economic assistance should be to share with others the beneficial ideas of democratic capitalism, which have led the United States to economic prosperity and political freedom.

Our bilateral economic assistance program should be directed at promoting economic growth and prosperity in developing nations. Therefore, we support recently enacted legislation untying our programs from the policies of austerity of international organizations such as the International Monetary Fund.

We have changed the Carter–Mondale policy of

channeling increasing proportions of U.S. assistance through multinational institutions beyond our control. We strongly support President Reagan's decision not to increase funding for the International Development Association because of its predilection for nations with state-dominated economic systems. Our contribution to the International Fund for Agricultural Development will be eliminated due to its consistent bias toward non-market economies. And the anti-American bureaucracy of the U.N.'s Educational, Scientific and Cultural Organization (UNESCO) will no longer be supported by U.S. taxpayers. We will not support international organizations inconsistent with our interests. In particular, we will work to eliminate their funding of Communist states.

Prominent among American ideals is the sanctity of the family. Decisions on family size should be made freely by each family. We support efforts to enhance the freedom of such family decisions. We will endeavor to assure that, those who are responsible for our programs are more sensitive to the cultural needs of the countries to which we give assistance.

As part of our commitment to the family and our opposition to abortion, we will eliminate all U.S. funding for organizations which in any way support abortion or research on abortion methods.

To strengthen bilateral foreign assistance, we will reduce or eliminate assistance to nations with foreign policies contrary to our interests and strengthen the Secretary of State's hand by ensuring his direct control over assistance programs.

Foreign military assistance strengthens our security by enabling friendly nations to provide for their own defense, including defense against terrorism.

Terrorism is a new form of warfare against the democracies. Supported by the Soviet Union and others, it ranges from PLO murder to the attempted assassination of the Pope. Combating it requires an integrated effort of our diplomacy, armed forces, intelligence services, and law enforcement organizations. Legislative obstacles to international cooperation against terrorism must be repealed, followed by a vigorous program to enhance friendly nations' counter-terrorist forces. In particular, we seek the cooperation of our hemispheric neighbors to deal comprehensively with the Soviet and Cuban terrorism now afflicting us.

International Organizations

Americans cannot count on the international organizations to guarantee our security or adequately protect our interests. The United States hosts the headquarters of the United Nations, pays a fourth of its budget, and is proportionally the largest contributor to most international organizations; but many members consistently vote against us. As Soviet influence in these organizations has grown, cynicism and the double standard have become their way of life.

This is why President Reagan announced that we will leave the worst of these organizations, UNESCO. He has put the U.N. on notice that the U.S. will strongly oppose the use of the U.N. to foster anti-Semitism, Soviet espionage, and hostility to the United States. The President decisively rejected the U.N. Convention on the Law of the Sea and embarked instead on a dynamic national oceans policy, animated by our traditional commitment to freedom of the seas. That pattern will be followed with regard to U.N. meddling in Antarctica and outer space. Enthusiastically endorsing those steps, we will apply the same standards to all international organizations. We will monitor their votes and activities, and particularly the votes of member states which receive U.S. aid. Americans will no longer silently suffer the hypocrisy of many of these organizations.

Human Rights

The American people believe that United States foreign policy should be animated by the cause of human rights for all the world's peoples.

A well-rounded human rights policy is concerned with specific individuals whose rights are denied by governments of the right or left, and with entire peoples whose Communist governments deny their claim to human rights as individuals and acknowledge only the "rights" derived from membership in an economic class. Republicans support a human rights policy which includes both these concerns.

Republican concern for human rights also extends to the institutions of free societies—political parties, the free press, business and labor organizations—which embody and protect the exercise of individual rights. The National Endowment for Democracy and other instruments of U.S. diplomacy foster the growth of these vital institutions.

By focusing solely on the shortcomings of non-Communist governments, Democrats have missed the forest for the trees, failing to recognize that the greatest threat to human rights is the Communist system itself.

Republicans understand that the East–West struggle has profound human rights implications. We know that Communist nations, which profess dedication to human rights, actually use their totalitarian systems to violate human rights in an organized, systematic fashion.

The Reagan–Bush Administration has worked for positive human rights changes worldwide. Our efforts have ranged from support for the Helsinki Accords to our support of judicial and political reform in El Salvador.

The Republican Party commends President Reagan for accepting the Honorary Chairmanship of the campaign to erect a U.S. Holocaust Memorial in Washington, D.C. and supports the efforts of the U.S. Holocaust Council in erecting such a museum and educational center. The museum will bear witness to the victims and survivors of the Holocaust.

For Republicans, the struggle for human freedom is more than an end in itself. It is part of a policy that builds a foundation for peace. When people are free to express themselves and choose democratic governments, their free private institutions and electoral power constitute a constraint against the excesses of autocratic rulers. We agree with President Truman, who said: "In the long run our security and the world's hopes for peace lie not in measures of defense or in the control of weapons, but in the growth and expansion of freedom and self-government."

To this end, we pledge our continued effort to secure for all people the inherent, God-given rights that Americans have been privileged to enjoy for two centuries.

Advocacy for Democracy

To promote and sustain the cause of democracy, America must be an active participant in the political competition between the principles of Communism and of democracy.

To do this, America needs a strong voice and active instruments of public diplomacy to counter the Communist bloc's massive effort to disinform and deceive world public opinion. Republicans believe that truth is America's most powerful weapon.

The Reagan–Bush Administration has elevated the stature of public diplomacy in the councils of government and increased the United States Information Agency budget by 44 percent in four years. New programs have been launched in television, citizen exchanges, and dissemination of written information. The National Endowment for Democracy has enlisted the talent of private American institutions, including the AFL-CIO and the U.S. Chamber of Commerce, to educate our friends overseas in the ways of democratic institutions. A sustained billion-dollar effort is modernizing and expanding the Voice of America, strengthening the Voice's signal, lengthening its broadcasts, improving its content, adding new language services and replacing antiquated equipment. Radio Marti, the new broadcast service to Cuba, will begin to broadcast the truth about Cuba to the Cuban people.

Initial steps have been taken to improve the capabilities of Radio Free Europe and Radio Liberty, which serve the captive nations of the Soviet bloc. We pledge to carry out a thorough improvement program for these radios, including new transmitters and other means of penetrating the jamming which denies the RFE/RL signal to millions of captive people, including the increasingly discontented Soviet minorities, behind the Iron Curtain.

Because of the importance we place on people-to-people exchange programs, Republicans support the dedicated work of Peace Corps volunteers. America must nurture good relations not only with foreign governments but with other peoples as well. By encouraging the free flow of ideas and information, America is helping to build the infrastructure of democracy and demonstrating the strength of our belief in the democratic example. The United States Peace Corps, reflecting traditional American values, will follow the White House initiative promoting free enterprise development overseas in third world countries.

The tradition of addressing the world's peoples, advocating the principles and goals of democracy and freedom, is as old as our Republic. Thomas Jefferson wrote the Declaration of Independence "with a decent respect to the opinions of mankind." This popular advocacy is even more important today in the global struggle between totalitarianism and freedom.

The Future of Our National Security

Republicans look to the future with confidence that we have the will, the weapons, and the technology to preserve America as the land of the free and the home of the brave. We stand united with President Reagan in his hope that American scientists and engineers can produce the technology and the hardware to make nuclear war obsolete.

The prospect for peace is excellent because America is strong again. America's defenses have only one purpose: to assure that our people and free institutions survive and flourish.

Our security requires both the capability to defend against aggression and the will to do so. Together, will and capability deter aggression. That is why the danger of war has grown more remote under President Reagan.

When he took office, defense policy was in disarray. The Carter–Mondale Administration had diminished our military capability and had confused the pursuit of peace with accommodating totalitarianism. It could not respond to the determined growth of Soviet military power and a more aggressive Soviet foreign policy.

We are proud of a strong America. Our military strength exists for the high moral purpose of deterring conflict, not initiating war. The deterrence of aggression is ethically imperative. That is why we have restored America's defense capability and renewed our country's will. Americans are again proud to serve in the Armed Forces and proud of those who serve.

We reaffirm the principle that the national security policy of the United States should be based upon a strategy of peace through strength, a goal of the 1980 Republican Platform.

Maintaining a technological superiority, the historical foundation of our policy of deterrence, remains essential. In other areas, such as our maritime forces, we should continue to strive for qualitative superiority.

President Reagan committed our nation to a modernized strategic and theater nuclear force sufficient to deter attack against the United States and our allies, while pursuing negotiations for balanced, verifiable reductions of nuclear weapons under arms control agreements.

In order to deter, we must be sufficiently strong to convince a potential adversary that under no circumstances would it be to its advantage to initiate conflict at any level.

We pledge to do everything necessary so that, in case of conflict, the United States would clearly prevail.

We will continue to modernize our deterrent capability, while negotiating for verifiable arms control. We will continue the policies that have given fresh confidence and new hope to freedom-loving people everywhere.

Arms Control for the Future

Americans, while caring deeply about arms control, realize that it is not an end in itself, but can be a major component of a foreign and defense policy which keeps America free, strong, and independent.

Sharing the American people's realistic view of the Soviet Union, the Reagan Administration has pursued arms control agreements that would reduce the level of nuclear weaponry possessed by the superpowers. President Reagan has negotiated with flexibility, and always from a position of strength.

In the European theater, President Reagan proposed the complete elimination of intermediate-range nuclear missiles. In the START talks with the Soviet Union, he proposed the "build-down" which would eliminate from the U.S. and Soviet arsenals two existing nuclear warheads for each new warhead.

The Soviet Union has rejected every invitation by President Reagan to resume talks, refusing to return

unless we remove the Pershing II and Cruise missiles which we have placed in Europe at the request of our NATO allies. Soviet intransigence is designed to force concessions from the United States even before negotiations begin. We will not succumb to this strategy. The Soviet Union will return to the bargaining table only when it recognizes that the United States will not make unilateral concessions or allow the Soviet Union to achieve nuclear superiority.

The Soviet Union, by engaging in a sustained pattern of violations of arms control agreements, has cast severe doubt on its own willingness to negotiate and comply with new agreements in a spirit of good faith. Agreements violated by the Soviet Union include SALT, the Anti-Ballistic Missile Treaty of 1972, the Helsinki Accords, and the Biological and Toxin Weapons Convention of 1972. This pattern of Soviet behavior is clearly designed to obtain a Soviet strategic advantage.

To deter Soviet violations of arms control agreements, the United States must maintain the capability to verify, display a willingness to respond to Soviet violations which have military significance, and adopt a policy whereby the defense of the United States is not constrained by arms control agreements violated by the Soviet Union.

We support the President's efforts to curb the spread of nuclear weapons and to improve international controls and safeguards over sensitive nuclear technologies. The President's non-proliferation policy has emphasized results, rather than rhetoric, as symbolized by the successful meeting of nuclear supplier states in Luxembourg in July of this year. We endorse the President's initiative on comprehensive safeguards and his efforts to encourage other supplier states to support such measures.

Defense Resources

The first duty of government is to provide for the common defense. That solemn responsibility was neglected during the Carter–Mondale years. At the end of the Eisenhower era, nearly 48 percent of the federal budget was devoted to defense programs, representing 9.1 percent of our gross national product. By 1980, under Carter–Mondale, defense spending had fallen to only 5 percent of gross national product and represented only 24 percent of the federal budget. The Reagan Administration has begun to correct the weaknesses caused by that situation by prudently increasing defense resources. We must continue to devote the resources essential to deter a Soviet threat—a threat which has grown and should be met by an improved and modernized U.S. defense capability. Even so, the percentage of the Reagan Administration budget spent on defense is only about half that of the Eisenhower–Kennedy era.

Readiness. In 1980, our military forces were not ready to perform their missions in the event of emergency. Many planes could not fly for lack of spare parts; ships could not sail for lack of skilled personnel; supplies were insufficient, for essential training or sustained combat. Today, readiness and sustainability have improved dramatically. We not only have more equipment, but it is in operating condition. Our military personnel have better training, pride, and confidence. We have improved their pay and benefits. Recruiting and retaining competent personnel is no longer a problem.

Under the Democrats, the All-Volunteer Force was headed for disastrous failure. Because of the Carter–Mondale intransigence on military pay and benefits, we saw the shameful spectacle of patriotic service families being forced below the poverty level, relying on food stamps and other welfare programs. The quality of life for our military has been substantially improved under the Reagan Administration. We wholeheartedly support the all-volunteer armed force and are proud of our historic initiative to bring it to pass.

From the worst levels of retention and recruiting in post-war history in 1979, we have moved to the highest ever recorded. We are meeting 100 percent of our recruiting needs, and 92 percent of our recruits are high school graduates capable of mastering the skills needed in the modern armed services. In 1980, 13 percent of our ships and 25 percent of our aircraft squadrons reported themselves not combat ready because of personnel shortages. Today, those figures have dropped to less than 1 percent and 4 percent respectively.

Today, the United States leads the world in integrating women into the military. They serve in a variety of noncombat assignments. We have made significant strides in numbers of women and their level of responsibility. Female officer strength has grown by 24 percent under the Reagan Administration and is projected to increase, with even greater increases for noncommissioned officers.

Conventional and Strategic Modernization. In 1980, we had a "hollow Army," a Navy half its numbers of a decade earlier, and an Air Force badly in need of upgrading. The Army is now receiving the most modern tanks, fighting vehicles, and artillery. The Navy has grown to 513 ships with 79 more under construction this year, well on its way toward the 600-ship, 15-carrier force necessary for our maritime strategy. The Air Force has procured advanced tactical aircraft. By decade's end, our intertheater lift capacity will have increased by 75 percent. We pledge to rescue a shipbuilding industry consigned to extinction by the Carter–Mondale team.

Since the end of World War II, America's nuclear arsenal has caused the Soviet Union to exercise caution to avoid direct military confrontation with us and our close allies.

Our nuclear arms are a vital element of the Free World's security system.

Throughout the 1970s and up to the present, the Soviet Union has engaged in a vast buildup of nuclear arms. In the naive hope that unilateral restraint by the United States would cause the Soviet Union to reverse course, the Carter–Mondale Administration delayed significant major features of the strategic modernization our country needed. There was no arms race because only the Soviet Union was racing, determined to achieve an intimidating advantage over the Free World. As a result, in 1980, America was moving toward a position of clear nuclear inferiority to the Soviets.

President Reagan moved swiftly to reverse this alarming situation and to reestablish an effective margin of safety before 1990. Despite obstruction from many congressional Democrats, we have restored the credibility of our deterrent.

Reserve and Guard Forces. We salute the men and women of the National Guard and the Reserves. The Carter–Mondale team completely neglected our vital Reserve and Guard forces, leaving them with obsolete equipment, frozen pay, and thousands of vacancies.

The Reagan Administration has transformed our Reserve and National Guard. The Naval Reserve will ultimately operate 40 of the fleet's 600 ships. Navy and Marine Air Reserve units now receive the most modern aircraft, as do the Air Force Reserve and Guard. Army Reserve and Guard units now receive the latest tanks, infantry fighting vehicles, and artillery. Reserve pay has increased 30 percent, and reserve components are having record success in filling their positions. Our country counts on the Reserves and the Guard, and they can count on us.

Management Reform. The Republican Party advocates a strong defense and fiscal responsibility at the same time. This Administration has already made major advances in eliminating the deep-rooted procurement problems we inherited. Republicans have changed the way the Pentagon does business, encouraging greater economy and efficiency, stretching the taxpayer's dollar.

Learning nothing from past mistakes, the Carter–Mondale Administration returned to centralized defense management. The predictable result: competition fell to only 15 percent of Pentagon procurement; programs were mired in disastrous cost overruns and disputes; outrageous and exorbitant prices were paid for spare parts; and the taxpayers' money was wasted on a grand scale.

We have tackled this problem head-on. We returned management to the Services and began far-reaching reforms. To hold down costs, we more than doubled competition in Pentagon procurement. We appointed Competition Advocate Generals in each Service and an overall Inspector General for the Pentagon. We increased incentives for excellent performance by contractors, and we have applied immediate penalty for poor performance. Our innovative approaches have already saved the taxpayers billions of dollars.

Spare parts acquisition has undergone thorough reform. Improving spare parts management, involving a Department of Defense inventory of almost four million items, is a complex and massive management challenge. The Pentagon's new 10-point program is already working. Old contracts are being revamped to allow competition, high prices are being challenged, and rigorous audits are continuing. As an example, a stool cap for a navigator's chair, once priced at $1,100, was challenged by an alert Air Force sergeant. It now costs us 31 cents. The Pentagon obtained a full refund and gave the sergeant a cash reward.

Our men and women in uniform deserve the best and most reliable weapons that this country can offer. We must improve the reliability and performance of our weapons systems, and warranties can be a very positive contribution to defense procurement practices, as can be the independent office of operational testing and evaluation, which was another positive Republican initiative.

The acquisition improvement program now includes program stability, multi-year procurement, economic production rates, realistic budgeting, and increased competition. The B-1B bomber, replacing our aging B-52 force, is ahead of schedule and under cost. We support our antisubmarine warfare effort and urge its funding at its current level. For the last two years, the Navy has received nearly 50 ships more than three years ahead of schedule and nearly $1 billion under budget. The *U.S.S. Theodore Roosevelt*, our newest aircraft carrier, is 17 months ahead of schedule and almost $74 million under cost.

We have reformed inefficient procurement practices established decades ago, and we will continue to ensure the most gain from each defense dollar.

The Tasks Ahead. The damage to our defenses through unilateral disarmament cannot be repaired quickly. The hollow Army of the Carter–Mondale Administration is hollow no more, and our Navy is moving toward a 600-ship force.

We share President Reagan's determination to restore credible security for our country. Our choice is not between a strong defense or a strong economy; we must succeed in both, or we will succeed in neither.

Our forces must be second to none, and we condemn the notion that one-sided military reduction will induce the Soviets to seek peace. Our military strength not only provides the deterrent necessary for a more peaceful world, but is also the best incentive for the Soviets to agree to arms reduction.

Veterans

America is free because of its veterans. We owe them more than thanks. After answering the call to arms, they brought leadership and patriotism back to their communities. They are a continuing resource for America. Through their membership in veterans' service activities, they have strongly supported President Reagan's defense policy. Knowing firsthand the sacrifices of war, they have spoken out frequently for a strong national defense.

Veterans have earned their benefits; these must not be taken away. The help we give them is an investment which pays our nation unlimited dividends.

We have accomplished a great deal. We are meeting the needs of women veterans and ensuring them equal treatment. We must prepare to meet the needs of aging veterans.

We are addressing the unique readjustment problems of Vietnam veterans by expanding the store-front readjustment counseling program, extending vocational training and job placement assistance, and targeting research toward understanding delayed stress reaction in combat veterans. We have moved to alleviate the uncertainty of veterans exposed to Agent Orange by providing nearly 129,000 medical exams and by launching an all-out, government-wide research effort.

We are making major strides in improving health care for veterans. VA hospital construction has expanded to meet community needs, and benefits for disabled veterans have been improved.

We will maintain the veterans' preference for federal hiring and will improve health, education, and other benefits. We support the Reagan Administration's actions to make home ownership attainable by more veterans, as well as our program to help veterans in small business compete for government contracts. We will extend to all veterans of recent conflicts, such as Lebanon and Grenada, the same assistance.

In recognition of the unique commitment and personal sacrifices of military spouses, President Reagan has called upon the nation to honor them and proclaimed a day of tribute. We will remember them and advance their interests.

National Intelligence

Knowing our adversaries' capabilities and intentions is our first line of defense. A strong intelligence community focuses our diplomacy and saves billions of defense dollars. This critical asset was gravely weakened during the Carter–Mondale years.

We will continue to strengthen our intelligence services. We will remove statutory obstacles to the effective management, performance, and security of intelligence sources and methods. We will further improve our ability to influence international events in support of our foreign policy objectives, and we will strengthen our counterintelligence facilities.

Strategic Trade

By encouraging commerce in militarily significant technology, the Carter–Mondale Administration actually improved Soviet military power. Because of that terrible error, we are now exposed to significant risk and must spend billions of defense dollars that would otherwise have been unnecessary.

The Reagan Administration halted the Carter–Mondale folly. We have strengthened cooperative efforts with our allies to restrict diversion of militarily critical technologies. We will increase law-enforcement and counterintelligence efforts to halt Soviet commercial espionage and illegal exploitation of our technology.

Terrorism

International terrorism is not a random phenomenon but a new form of warfare waged by the forces of totalitarianism against the democracies.

In recent years, certain states have sponsored terrorist actions in pursuit of their strategic goals. The international links among terrorist groups are now clearly understood; and the Soviet link, direct and indirect, is also clearly understood. The Soviets use terrorist groups to weaken democracy and undermine world stability.

Purely passive measures do not deter terrorists. It is time to think about appropriate preventive or preemptive actions against terrorist groups before they strike.

Terrorism is an international problem. No one country can successfully combat it. We must lead the free nations in a concerted effort to pressure members of the League of Terror to cease their sponsorship and support of terrorism.

A Secure Future

During the Carter–Mondale Administration, the Soviets built more weapons, and more modern ones, than the United States. President Reagan has begun to reverse this dangerous trend. More important, he has begun a process that, over time, will gradually but dramatically reduce the Soviet Union's ability to threaten our lives with nuclear arms.

His leadership came none too soon. The combined damage of a decade of neglect and of relentless Soviet buildup, despite treaties and our restraint, will not be undone easily.

Today, the Soviet Union possesses over 5,000 intercontinental nuclear warheads powerful and accurate enough to destroy hard military targets, and it is flight-testing a whole new generation of missiles. The Carter–Mondale Administration left this country at a decided disadvantage, without a credible deterrent. That is why President Reagan embarked on a modernization program covering all three legs of the strategic triad.

Republicans understand that our nuclear deterrent forces are the ultimate military guarantor of America's security and that of our allies. That is why we will continue to support the programs necessary to modernize our strategic forces and reduce the vulnerabilities. This includes the earliest possible deployment of a new small mobile ICBM.

While the Carter–Mondale team hid beneath an umbrella of wishful thinking, the Soviet Union made every effort to protect itself in case of conflict. It has an operational anti-satellite system; the United States does not. A network of huge ultra-modern radars, new anti-missile interceptors, new surface-to-air missiles, all evidence the Soviet commitment to self-protection.

President Reagan has launched a bold new Strategic Defense Initiative to defend against nuclear attack. We enthusiastically support President Reagan's Strategic Defense Initiative. We enthusiastically support the development of non-nuclear, space-based defensive systems to protect the United States by destroying incoming missiles. Recognizing the need for close consultation with our allies, we support a comprehensive and intensive effort to render obsolete the doctrine of Mutual Assured Destruction (MAD). The Democratic Party embraces Mutual Assured Destruction. The Republican Party rejects the strategy of despair and supports instead the strategy of hope and survival.

We will begin to eliminate the threat posed by strategic nuclear missiles as soon as possible. Our only purpose (one all people share) is to reduce the danger of nuclear war. To that end, we will use superior American technology to achieve space-based and ground-based defensive systems as soon as possible to protect the lives of the American people and our allies.

President Reagan has asked, "Would it not be better to save lives than to avenge them?" The Republican Party answers, "Yes!"

— 1988 —

PREAMBLE

An election is about the future, about change. But it is also about the values we will carry with us as we journey into tomorrow and about continuity with the best from our past.

On the threshold of a new century, we live in a time of unprecedented technological, social, and cultural development, and a rapidly emerging global economy. This election will bring change. The question is: Will it be change and progress with the Republicans or change and chaos with the Democrats?

Americans want leadership to direct the forces of change, on America's terms, guided by American values. The next stage of the American experiment will be a new dynamic partnership in which people direct government and government empowers people to solve their own problems and to have more choices in their lives.

In 1984, we said, "From freedom comes opportunity; from opportunity comes growth; from growth comes progress."

In 1988, we reaffirm that truth. *Freedom works.* This is not sloganeering, but a verifiable fact. It has been abundantly documented during the Reagan–Bush Administration in terms of real jobs and real progress for individuals, families, and communities urban and rural. Our platform reflects on every page our continuing faith in the creative power of human freedom.

Defending and expanding freedom is our first priority. During the last eight years, the American people joined with the Reagan–Bush Administration in advancing the cause of freedom at home and around the world. Our platform reflects George Bush's belief that military strength, diplomatic resoluteness, and firm leadership are necessary to keep our country and our allies free.

Republicans know the United States is a nation of communities—churches, neighborhoods, social and charitable organizations, professional groups, unions and private and voluntary organizations in city, sub-

urb, and countryside. It is We, the people, building the future in freedom. It is from these innumerable American communities, made up of people with good heads and good hearts, that innovation, creativity, and the works of social justice and mercy naturally flow and flourish. This is why George Bush and all Republicans believe in empowering people and not bureaucracies.

At the very heart of this platform is our belief that the strength of America is its people: free men and women, with faith in God, working for themselves and their families, believing in the inestimable value of every human being from the very young to the very old, building and sustaining communities, quietly performing those "little, nameless, unremembered acts of kindness and love" that make up the best portion of our lives, defending freedom, proud of their diverse heritages. They are still eager to grasp the future, to seize life's challenges and, through faith and love and work, to transform them into the valuable, the useful, and the beautiful.

This is what the American people do quietly, patiently, without headlines, as a nation of communities, every day. This is the continuing American revolution of continuity and change.

This is the American people's true miracle of freedom. It is to them that we dedicate this platform.

JOBS, GROWTH, AND OPPORTUNITY FOR ALL

America again leads the world, confident of our abilities, proud of our products, sure of our future, the pacesetter for all mankind. Moving toward the threshold of the 21st century, the American people are poised to fulfill their dreams to a degree unparalleled in human history.

Our nation of communities is prosperous and free. In the sixth year of unprecedented economic expansion, more people are working than ever before, real family income has risen; inflation is tamed. By almost any measure, Americans are better off than they were eight years ago. The Reagan Revolution has become a Republican renaissance. Our country's back—back in business and back on top again.

Government didn't work this economic wonder. The people did. Republicans got government out of the way, off the backs of households and entrepreneurs, so the people could take charge. Once again our people have the freedom to grow. From that freedom come prosperity and security.

From freedom comes opportunity; from opportunity comes growth; from growth comes progress.

Freedom is not an abstract concept. No, freedom is the inescapable essence of the American spirit, the driving force which makes Americans different from any other people on the face of the globe.

The restoration of our country's tradition of democratic capitalism has ushered in a new age of optimistic expansion. Based on free enterprise, free markets, and limited government, that tradition regards people as a resource, not a problem. And it works.

On every continent, governments are beginning to follow some degree of America's formula to cut tax rates, loosen regulation, free the private sector, and trust the people.

Remember the Carter–Mondale years:

- Taxes skyrocketed every year as the Democrats' inflation pushed everyone into higher tax brackets.
- Prices spiraled, financially strangling those people least able to keep up. This was heightened by the spending mania of a Democrat-controlled Congress. Savings plunged as prices rose. A dollar saved in 1977 was worth only half by 1981.
- 21.5 percent interest rates—levels not seen before or since—placed the basic needs of life beyond the means of many American families.
- The Democrats threatened workers, investors, and consumers with "industrial policies" that centralized economic planning.
- Joblessness eroded the earnings and dignity of millions under the Democrat Administration.
- The number of poor households grew dramatically during the Democrats' years in power.
- Economic stagnation caused by the Democrats' policies made it harder to find a job, get a promotion, buy a home, raise a family, or plan for old age.

In addition to all of these problems, the Democrats were telling us that there was something wrong with America and something wrong with its people.

Something *was* terribly wrong, but not with the people. A half-century of destructive policies, pitting Americans against one another for the benefit of the Democrats' political machine, had come to a dead end. The Democrats couldn't find a way out, so the voters showed them the door.

Now the ideological heirs of Carter and Mondale are trying again to sell the public a false bill of goods. These liberals call America's prosperity an illusion. They fantasize our economy is declining. They claim our future is in the hands of other nations. They aren't operating in the real world.

They can't build the future on fear. Americans know that and are constructing their futures on the solid foundation Republicans have already set in place:

- We are in the midst of the longest peacetime expansion in our country's history. Where once we mea-

sured new businesses in the thousands, we now count millions. These small businesses have helped create more than 17 million well-paying, high-quality new jobs, more than twice the number of jobs that were created during that time in Japan, Canada, and Western Europe combined! Small business has accounted for 80 percent of the jobs created during the recovery. Who says America has lost its competitive edge?

- More Americans are working than ever before. Because of Republican growth policies, the unemployment rate has plunged to its lowest level in 14 years.
- Since 1983, 3 million people have risen above the government poverty level. The poverty rate is down for the third consecutive year. The Republican economic program has been the most successful war on poverty.
- Under a Republican Administration, family incomes are growing at the fastest pace recorded in 15 years.
- Under Republican leadership, tax reform removed 6 million low-income people from the income tax rolls and brought financial relief to tens of millions more.
- The typical family is now paying almost $2,000 less per year in income taxes than it would if the Democrats' antiquated income tax system of the 1970s were still in place.
- The Carter "misery index"—the sum of the inflation and unemployment rates—is half of what it was in 1980. Republican economic policies have turned it into a "prosperity index."
- Republicans reduced inflation to one-third of its 1980 level, helping not only average Americans but also low-income Americans and elderly Americans on fixed incomes, who spend most of their income on necessities.
- Interest rates are lower by nearly two-thirds than under the Democrats in 1980.
- Exports are booming. World sales create local jobs!
- Productivity is rising three times as fast under Republican policies as it did during the late 1970s.
- Industrial output increased by one-third during the current expansion.
- Business investment is increasing 20 percent faster, in real terms, than before the Republican economic resurgence.
- The manufacturing sector is now accounting for 23 percent of GNP. U.S. manufacturing jobs have increased overall since 1982. The Democrats are wrong about America losing its industrial base, except in Massachusetts, where the Democrat governor of that State has presided over a net decline of 94,000 manufacturing jobs.

This is not a portrait of a people in decline. It is the profile of a can-do country, hopeful and compassionate, on the move. It is America resurgent, renewed, revitalized by an idea: the belief that free men and women, caring for families and supporting voluntary institutions in a nation of communities, constitute the most powerful force for human progress.

In 1980, Ronald Reagan and George Bush called upon us all to recover from a failed political system the power rightly belonging to the people. Now we call upon our fellow citizens, at the bicentennial of our Constitution, in the words of its preamble, to "secure the blessings of liberty to ourselves and our posterity" by opening new vistas of opportunity.

These "blessings of liberty"—the chance to make a decent living, provide for the family, buy a home, give children a superior education, build a secure retirement, help a generation reach farther and build higher than we were able to—these are the goals that George Bush and the Republican Party seek for every American.

But this prosperity is not an end in itself. It is a beginning. It frees us to grow and be better than we are, to develop things of the spirit and heart. This is the direction in which George Bush will lead our country. It is prosperity with a purpose.

Jobs

The Republican Party puts the creation of jobs and opportunity first. In our 1980 and 1984 platforms, we promised to put Americans back to work by restoring economic growth without inflation. We delivered on our promise:

- Small business entrepreneurs have led the way in creating new job opportunities, particularly for women, minorities, and youths.
- Over 17 million new jobs have been created.
- More than 60 percent of these new jobs since 1982 are held by women.
- More Americans are working now than at any time in our history.
- The unemployment rate is at its lowest level in 14 years.
- Statistics show that the great majority of the jobs we have created are full-time, quality jobs, paying more than $20,000 per year.

Job growth for minority and ethnic Americans has been even more impressive:

- Minority workers have been finding jobs twice as fast as others.
- Black unemployment has been cut almost in half

since 1982. Black Americans gained 2.3 million new jobs in the last few years.
- Black teen unemployment is at its lowest level in 15 years.
- Sales from the top 100 black firms rose 15 percent between 1982 and 1986. The 7.9 percent growth rate for all black businesses compares to an overall rate of 5 percent for all business.
- Family incomes of Asian-Americans rank among the highest of all ethnic groups in the United States.
- Hispanic employment increased nearly three times as fast as for all civilian workers. More Hispanics are at work now than at any time since recordkeeping began.

We will use new technologies, such as computer data bases and telecommunications, to strengthen and streamline job banks matching people who want to work with available jobs.

We advocate incentives for educating, training, and retraining workers for new and better jobs—through programs like the Job Training Partnership Act, which provides for a public/private partnership—as our country surges ahead.

The best jobs program—the one that created more than 17 million jobs since 1982—is lower taxes on people. We believe that every person who wants a job should have the opportunity to get a job. We reject the notion that putting more Americans to work causes inflation. The failure of government make-work programs proves that jobs are created by people in a free market.

Opportunity for All

With its message of economic growth and opportunity, the GOP is the natural champion of blacks, minorities, women and ethnic Americans. We urge Republican candidates and officials at all levels to extend to minority Americans everywhere the historic invitation for full participation in our party.

A free economy helps defeat discrimination by fostering opportunity for all. That's why real income for black families has risen 14 percent since 1982. It's why members of minority groups have been gaining jobs in the Republican recovery twice as fast as everyone else. Upward mobility for all Americans has come back strong.

We are the party of real social progress. Republicans welcome the millions of forward-looking Americans who want an "opportunity society," not a welfare state. We believe our country's greatest resource is its people—all its people. Their ingenuity and imagination are needed to make the most of our common future. So we will remove disincentives that keep the less fortunate out of the productive economy:

- Families struggling near the poverty line are always hurt most by tax increases. Six million poor have been removed from the tax rolls in the 1986 Tax Reform Act—the largest income transfer to lower-income Americans since the early 1970s. We will continue to reduce their burden.
- We advocate a youth training wage to expand opportunities and enable unskilled young people to enter the work force.
- As an alternative to inflationary—and job-destroying—increases in the minimum wage, we will work to boost the incomes of the working poor through the Earned Income Tax Credit, especially for earners who support children. This will mean higher take-home pay for millions of working families.
- We will reform welfare to encourage work as the ticket that guarantees full participation in American life.
- We will undertake a long overdue reform of the unemployment insurance program to reward workers who find new jobs quickly.
- We insist upon the right of Americans to work at home. The Home Work Rule, banning sale of certain items made at home, must go. It idles willing workers, prevents mothers from working and caring for their children in their own homes, limits the country's output, and penalizes innocent persons to please special interests.
- We will fight to end the Social Security earnings limitation for the elderly. It discourages older persons from reentering or remaining in the work force, where their experience and wisdom are increasingly needed. As a first step, we will remove the earnings limitation for those whose income is from child care.
- We will continue our efforts, already marked with success, to revitalize our cities. We support, on the federal, State and local levels, enterprise zones to promote investment and job creation in beleaguered neighborhoods.

Entrepreneurship

Our country's 18 million small business entrepreneurs are the superstars of job creation. In the past decade, they created two out of three new jobs. When they are free to invest and innovate, everyone is better off. They are today's pathfinders, the explorers of America's economic future.

Republicans encourage the women and men in small businesses to think big. To help them create jobs, we will cut to 15 percent the current counterproduc-

tive capital gains tax. This will foster investment in new and untried ventures, which often are the cutting edge of constructive change. It will also build the retirement value of workers' pension funds and raise revenues for the federal government.

We will increase, strengthen, and reinvigorate minority business development efforts to afford socially and economically disadvantaged individuals the opportunity for full participation in our free enterprise system.

Work-place benefits should be freely negotiated by employee–employer bargaining. We oppose government requirements that shrink workers' paychecks by diverting money away from wages to pay for federal requirements. These hidden taxes add to labor costs without paying those who labor. That is the liberals' way of replacing collective bargaining with congressional edicts about what's good for employees. It reduces the number of jobs and dishonestly imposes on others the costs of programs that Congress can't afford.

We call for a reasonable State and federal product liability standard that will be fair to small business, including professional and amateur sports, and to all who are in liability contests. We propose to return the fault-based standard to the civil justice system. Jobs are being lost, useful and sometimes lifesaving products are being discontinued, and America's ability to compete is being adversely affected. Reform will lower costs for all and will return fairness to the system for the benefit of everyone. Republicans recognize the basic right of all Americans to seek redress in the courts; however, we strongly oppose frivolous litigation. In addition, we support enactment of fair and balanced reforms of the tort system at the State level.

The remarkable resurgence of small business under the Republican renaissance of the 1980s highlights the key to the future: plant openings, thousands of them in every part of this land, as small businesses lead the way toward yet another decade of compassionate prosperity.

Reducing the Burden of Taxes

The Republican Party restates the unequivocal promise we made in 1984: *We oppose any attempts to increase taxes.* Tax increases harm the economic expansion and reverse the trend to restoring control of the economy to individual Americans.

We reject calls for higher taxes from all quarters—including "bipartisan commissions." The decisions of our government should not be left to a body of unelected officials.

The American people deserve to know, *before the election,* where all candidates stand on the question of tax increases. Republicans unequivocally reiterate the no-tax pledge we have proudly taken. While we wouldn't believe the Democrats even if they took the pledge, they haven't taken it.

The crowning economic achievement of the Republican Party under Ronald Reagan and George Bush has been the dramatic reduction in personal income taxes. The Reagan–Bush Administration has cut the top marginal tax rate from 70 percent to 28 percent. We got government's heavy hand out of the wallets and purses of all our people. That single step has sparked the longest peacetime expansion in our history.

We not only lowered tax rates for all. We tied them to the cost of living so congressional Democrats couldn't secretly boost taxes by pushing people into higher brackets through inflation. We took millions of low-income families off the tax rolls, and we doubled the personal exemption for all.

As a result, by 1986 the income tax bill of a typical middle-income family had declined by one-quarter. If the Democrats had defeated our economic recovery program, that family would have paid nearly $6,000 more in taxes between 1982 and 1987. Meanwhile, average Americans and the working poor carry substantially less of the burden. Upper-income Americans now pay a larger share of federal taxes than they did in 1980.

Our policies have become the model for much of the world. Through the power of capitalism, governments are rushing to reduce tax rates to save their stagnating economies. This is good for America, for their recovery will make them better trading partners for our own exuberant economy.

Many economists advising the Democrat Party have publicly called for a national sales tax or European-style Value-Added Tax (VAT), which would take billions of dollars out of the hands of American consumers. Such a tax has been imposed on many nations in Europe and has resulted in higher prices, fewer jobs, and higher levels of government spending. We reject the idea of putting a VAT on the backs of the American people.

Republicans know that sustaining the American economic miracle requires a growing pool of private savings. From bank accounts, small stock purchases, and piggy banks, the streams of thrift must flow together and form a mighty tide of capital. That rushing force pushes our society ahead, lifting everyone as it goes. To keep it going:

- We support incentives for private savings, such as our deductibility for IRA contributions.
- We oppose tax withholding on savings.

- To protect savings by ensuring the soundness of our financial system, the federal government must continue to play an active role through its regulatory responsibilities and supervisory duties. We demand stern punishment for those persons, whether in financial institutions or in Congress, whose wheeling and dealing have betrayed the public trust.

Income Taxes Slashed for Typical Family

- We will reduce to 15 percent the rates for long-term capital to promote investments in jobs and to raise revenue for the federal government by touching off another surge of economic expansion. In 1978, we cut the capital gains tax from 49.1 percent to 28 percent; in 1981, it was slashed again to 20 percent. The cuts injected a new vitality into the economy, with the result that revenues from this tax rose 184 percent from 1978 to 1985.
- We call for a taxpayers' bill of rights to give everyone simple and inexpensive means to resolve disputes with government. Democrats, using the Massachusetts Revenue Department as a model, intend to squeeze more out of the public by making the IRS more intrusive. Republicans will not tolerate tax cheating by anyone, but we know most Americans responsibly pay their fair share. By restoring their confidence in frugal, limited government, we will enhance compliance with tax laws that are simple and fair.

Beating Inflation

Today, the dollar is sound again. The Republican economic program brought inflation under control and lowered interest rates. Ten million more American families have bought homes for the first time. Inflation has been forced down from over 13 percent to 4 percent. Interest rates are only half of what they were at the end of the Carter years.

If the Democrats' inflation rates had continued all these years, a family of four would now be paying an average of $200 a month more for food and over $300 a month more for housing. That's the real cost of the Democrats' bad policies.

The Democrats would drag us back to those dreadful years when inflation was robbing workers of their earnings, consumers of their spending power, and families of their savings. Skyrocketing interest rates were stalling the economy and pushing decent housing out of reach for millions.

We can't let them do it again. To sustain the country's economic expansion, confidence in American monetary policy is vital. The possibility of imprudent action by government breeds fear, and that fear can shake the stock and commodity markets worldwide. To keep markets on an even keel, we urge objective Federal Reserve policies to achieve long-run price stability.

Regulatory Reform

This is a success story for the entire nation. Eight years ago, the country was strangling in red tape. Decades of rules and regulations from official Washington smothered enterprise, hindered job creation, and crippled small businesses. Even worse, the federal bureaucracy was spreading its intrusion into schools, religious institutions, and neighborhoods.

At the outset of his Administration, President Reagan asked Vice President Bush to take charge of an unprecedented exercise in liberty: relieving Americans from oppressive and unnecessary regulations and controls. With George Bush's leadership, Republicans turned the tables on the regulators.

We saved consumers tens of billions of dollars in needless regulatory costs that had been added to the price of virtually every product and service.

- In banking, we ensured that savers would get a fair return on their savings through market interest rates in place of artificially low rates capped by government.
- In energy, transportation, telecommunications, and financial services, we made fundamental changes in the way Americans could do business. We trusted them. We hacked away at artificial rules that stifled innovation, thwarted competition, and drove up consumer prices. Indeed, telecommunications and computer technology innovations have improved economic performance in nearly every American industry and business.
- In education, housing, and health care, we reduced the chilling effect of regulation upon the private sector and communities. Despite opposition from liberals in the Congress, we have at least slowed the expansion of federal control.
- We turned dozens of narrow programs, full of strings attached, into a few block grants with leeway for State and local administration.

The job isn't over yet. We will resist the calls of Democrats to turn back or eliminate the benefits that reducing regulations has brought to Americans from every walk of life—in transportation, finance, energy and many other areas. We want to reduce further the intrusion of government into the lives of citizens. Consistent with the maintenance of a competitive mar-

ketplace, we are committed to breaking down unnecessary barriers to entry created by regulations, statutes, and judicial decisions, to free up capital for productive investment. Let Democrats trust the federal bureaucracy. Republicans trust the creative energy of workers and investors in a free market.

We are committed to further return power from the federal government to State and local governments, which are more responsive to the public and better able to administer critical public services.

Competition in Public Services

Republicans recognize that the American people, in their families, communities, places of work, and voluntary associations, solve problems better and faster than government. That's why the Republican Party trusts people to deal with the needs of individuals and communities, as they have done for centuries.

In recent decades, however, big government elbowed aside the private sector. In the process, it made public services both expensive and inefficient. The federal government should follow the lead of those cities and States which are contracting out for a wide range of activities.

We resolve to defederalize, denationalize, and decentralize government monopolies that poorly serve the public and waste the taxpayers' dollars. To that end, we will foster competition wherever possible.

We advocate privatizing those government assets that would be more productive and better maintained in private ownership. This is especially true of those public properties that have deteriorated under government control, and of public housing, where residents should have the option of managing their own projects. In other areas as well, citizens and employees should be able to become stockholders and managers of government enterprises that would be more efficiently operated by private enterprise. We will not initiate production of goods and delivery of services by the federal government if they can be procured from the private sector.

Housing

The best housing policy is sound economic policy. Low interest rates, low inflation rates, and the availability of a job with a good paycheck that makes a mortgage affordable are the best housing programs of all.

That has been the key to the rebirth of housing during the Reagan–Bush Administration. If things had continued the way they were in 1980, the average family today would have to pay over $300 more for housing every month. Instead, we curbed inflation, pulled down interest rates, and made housing affordable to more Americans than ever before. We promoted homeownership by stoking the engines of economic growth. The results have been spectacular.

- Mortgage rates have fallen from 17.5 percent to single digits today.
- Homeownership has become affordable for more than 10 million additional families.
- Our regulatory reform campaign, in cooperation with local government and the housing industry, has pointed the way to lower housing costs through removal of needless rules that inflate prices.

That's only the beginning. We want to foster greater choice in housing for all:

- First and foremost, Republicans stand united in defense of the homeowner's deduction for mortgage interest. That separates us from the Democrats who are already planning to raise taxes by limiting its deductibility.
- We will continue our successful drive for lower interest rates.
- We support the efforts of those in the States who fight to lower property taxes, which strike hardest at the poor, the elderly, families with children, and family farmers.
- We support programs to allow low-income families to earn possession of their homes through urban and rural homesteading, cooperative ventures in construction and rehabilitation, and other pioneering projects that demonstrate the vitality of the private sector and individual initiative.
- We support the FHA mortgage insurance program, the Government National Mortgage Association, the VA guarantee program, and other programs that enhance housing choices for all Americans.
- We pledge to continue to expand opportunities for homeownership and to maintain the strength of savings institutions, including thrifts.
- We call on the Departments of Treasury, Housing and Urban Development, Agriculture, and the Federal Home Loan Bank Board to develop incentives for the private sector to bring housing stock foreclosed on by federal agencies back into service for low- and moderate-income citizens.
- We call for repeal of rent control laws, which always cause a shortage of decent housing by favoring the affluent with low rents, denying persons with modest incomes access to the housing market.

In public housing, we have turned away from the disasters of the past, when whole neighborhoods be-

came instant slums through federal meddling. We have promoted a long-range program of tenant management with encouraging results already. We pledge to continue that drive and to move toward resident ownership of public housing units, which was initiated under Ronald Reagan and George Bush.

We are determined to replace hand-out housing with vouchers that will make low-income families neighbors in communities, not strangers in projects.

To ensure that federal housing funds assist communities, rather than disrupt them, we advocate merging programs into a block grant at the disposal of States and localities for a wide range of needs.

We reaffirm our commitment to open housing as an essential part of the opportunity we seek for all. The Reagan–Bush Administration sponsored a major strengthening of the federal fair housing law. We will enforce it vigorously and will not allow its distortion into quotas or controls.

Controlling Federal Spending

The Reagan–Bush policies of economic growth have finally turned around the deficit problem. Through Republican-initiated constraints on spending, the federal budget deficit dropped by over 25 percent last year. With the help of the Gramm–Rudman law and a flexible budget freeze, a balanced budget can be expected by 1993.

But the relentless spending of congressional Democrats can undo our best efforts. No president can cause deficits; Congress votes to spend money. The American people must prevent big-spending congressional Democrats from bringing back big budget deficits; we must return both the Senate and the House of Representatives to Republican control for the first time in 36 years.

In 1981, we inherited a federal spending machine that was out of control. During the Carter–Mondale years, spending grew by 13.6 percent annually. We cut that growth rate in half, but the cancer still expands, as it has in some States such as Massachusetts, where the budget has increased more than twice as fast as the federal budget. We will not be content until government establishes a balanced budget and reduces its demands upon the productivity and earnings of the American people.

We categorically reject the notion that Congress knows how to spend money better than the American people do. Tax hikes are like addictive drugs. Every shot makes Congress want to spend more. Even with the Republican tax cuts of 1981, revenues have increased by about $50 billion every year. But congressional spending has increased even more! For every $1 Congress takes in new taxes, it spends $1.25.

That's why congressional Democrats have sabotaged the Republican program to control the federal budget. They refuse to put any reasonable restrains on appropriations. They smuggle through pork barrel deals in huge "continuing resolutions" larded for the special interests. They oppose the balanced budget amendment and all reforms in the bankrupt process. They mock the restraints legally mandated by our Gramm–Rudman budget plan.

Enough is enough. It's time to push through the Republican agenda for budget reform to teach the Congress the kind of financial responsibility that characterizes the American family:

- We call for structural changes to control government waste, including a two-year budget cycle, a super-majority requirement for raising taxes, a legislatively enacted line-item veto, individual transmission of spending bills, greater rescission authority for the chief executive and other reforms.
- We call for a flexible freeze on current government spending. We insist on the discipline to provide stable funding for important government programs, increasing spending only for true national priorities. We oppose any increase in taxes, so that the economy will continue to expand and so revenues from a growing tax base will reduce the deficit.
- We believe the Grace Commission report to eliminate waste, inefficiency, and mismanagement in the federal government must be re-examined: its recommendations should be given a high profile by public policy officials.
- We call for a balanced budget amendment to the Constitution. If congressional Democrats continue to block it, we urge the States to renew their calls for a constitutional convention limited to consideration of such an amendment.
- We will use all constitutional authority to control congressional spending. This will include consideration of the inherent line-item veto power of the president.

Opening Markets Abroad

America's best years lie ahead. Because Republicans have faith in individuals, we welcome the challenge of world competition with confidence in our country's ability to out-produce, out-manage, out-think, and out-sell anyone.

This is the voter's choice in 1988: compete or retreat. The American people and the Republican Party are not about to retreat.

To make the 1990s America's decade in international trade, Republicans will advance trade through strength. We will not accept the loss of American jobs to nationalized, subsidized, protected foreign industries and will continue to negotiate assertively the destruction of trade barriers:

- We negotiated a sweeping free trade agreement with Canada, our largest trading partner. Under this agreement, Americans will be able to trade, invest, and prosper, with no barriers to competition and economic growth.
- We have sought enforcement of U.S. international trade rights more vigorously than any previous Administration. The Reagan–Bush Administration was the first to self-initiate formal trade actions against unfair foreign market barriers.
- We launched the "Uruguay Round" of trade talks to promote a more open trading system and to address new trade problems that stifle world economic progress.
- We negotiated long and hard to beat back the most protectionist provisions in trade legislation and produced a bill that focuses on opening markets around the world.
- We support multilateral actions to open up foreign markets to U.S. products through the General Agreement on Tariffs and Trade. We will use GATT as well to deal with problems involving agricultural subsidies, trade in services, intellectual property rights, and economic relations with countries that mis-manage their economies by suppressing market forces.

We will not tolerate unfair trade and will use free trade as a weapon against it. To ensure that rapid progress is forthcoming from our work in GATT, we stand ready to pursue bilateral arrangements with nations which share our commitment to free trade. We have begun with the U.S.–Israel and U.S.–Canada free trade agreements. These agreements should be used as a model by the entire Western Hemisphere as it moves toward becoming a free trade zone, a powerhouse of productivity that can spur economic growth throughout the continents. We are prepared to negotiate free trade agreements with partners like the Republic of China on Taiwan and the Association of South East Asian Nations (ASEAN) countries if they are willing to open their markets to U.S. products.

The emerging global economy has required American workers and consumers to adapt to far-reaching transformations on every continent. These changes will accelerate in the years ahead as nations with free economic systems rush toward a future of incredible promise. International trade among market economies is the driving force behind an unprecedented expansion of opportunity and income.

Unfortunately, international markets are still restricted by antiquated policies: protective tariffs, quotas, and subsidies. These hinder world trade and hurt everyone, producers and consumers alike. It is the politicians and special interests who use protectionism to cover up their failures and enrich themselves at the expense of the country as a whole.

We propose that the General Accounting Office be required to issue regular statistics on the costs of U.S. trade restrictions to American workers, consumers, and businesses.

The bosses of the Democrat Party have thrown in the towel and abandoned the American worker and producer. They have begun a full-scale retreat into protectionism, an economic narcotic that saps the life out of commerce, closes foreign markets to U.S. producers and growers, and costs American consumers billions of dollars. The Democrats' plans would endanger 200,000 jobs and $8 billion in economic activity in agriculture alone! Over the past year, U.S. exports have expanded by 30 percent. The Democrats would reverse that growth by cowering behind barriers.

The bottom line in international trade must be American excellence. Every part of our economy is challenged to renew its commitment to quality. We must redouble our efforts to cut regulation, keep taxes low, and promote capital formation to sustain the advance of science and technology. Changes in both the managing of business and our approach to work, together with a new emphasis on quality and pleasing the customer, are creating a new work place ethic in our country. We will meet the challenges of international competition by know-how and cooperation, enterprise and daring, and trust in a well-trained work force to achieve more than government can even attempt.

International Economic Policy

Eight years ago, Ronald Reagan and George Bush offered visionary leadership to make a clean break with the failed past of international economics.

Our economic success is now acknowledged worldwide. Countries all over the world, even the Soviet Union, are abandoning worn-out industrial policy planning by government in favor of the market-oriented policies underlying what foreign leaders call the "American Miracle."

We encouraged the major economic powers to draw greater guidance for their monetary policies from commodity prices. This was an important step toward ensuring price stability, eliminating volatility of exchange rates, and removing excessive trade imbalances.

We support the Administration's efforts to improve coordination among the industrialized nations regarding their basic economic policies as a means of sustaining non-inflationary growth. It is important that we continue and refine efforts to dampen the volatility of exchange rate fluctuations, which have at times impeded improvements in investment and trade. Further, it is important to guard against the possibility of inflation in all currencies by comparing them with a basket of commodities, including gold.

International price stability will set the stage for developing countries to participate in the transforming process of economic growth. We will not turn our backs on the Third World, where Soviet imperialism preys upon stagnation and poverty. The massive debt of some emerging nations not only cripples their progress but also disrupts world trade and finance.

We will use U.S. economic aid, whether bilateral or through international organizations, to promote free market reforms: lower marginal tax rates, less regulation, reduced trade barriers. We will work with developing nations to make their economies attractive to private investment—both domestic and foreign—as the only lasting way to ensure that these nations can secure capital for growth. We support innovations to facilitate repayment of loans, including "debt for equity" swaps. We urge our representatives in all multilateral organizations such as the World Bank to support conditionality with all loans to encourage democracy, private sector development, and individual enterprise. As part of our commitment to the family as the building block of economic progress, we believe decisions on family size should be made freely by each family, and we remain opposed to U.S. funding for organizations involved in abortion.

To dig their way out of debt, those nations must do more than take out additional loans. They need America's greatest export: capitalism. While sharing the pie of prosperity with others, we will teach its recipe. It is this simple: Where democracy and free markets take root, people live better. Where people live better, they produce and trade more. As capitalism spreads throughout the world, more nations are prospering, international commerce is booming, and U.S. trade is breaking records.

But even more important than economic progress is the advance of freedom. Republicans want not only a better life for the people of developing lands; we want a freer and more peaceful future for them, too. Those goals are inextricably linked. It is a case of all or nothing, and we believe that free people can have it all.

From all over the world, capital flows into the United States because of confidence in our future. Direct investment in America creates important econ-omywide benefits: jobs, growth, and lower interest rates. We oppose shortsighted attempts to restrict or overly regulate this investment in America that helps our people work, earn, and live better.

Most important, we will lead by example. We will keep the United States a shining model of individual freedom and economic liberty to encourage other peoples of the world to assert their own economic rights and secure opportunity for all.

STRONG FAMILIES AND STRONG COMMUNITIES

Strong families build strong communities. They make us a confident, caring society by fostering the values and character—integrity, responsibility, sharing and altruism—essential for the survival of democracy. America's place in the 21st century will be determined by the family's place in public policy today.

Republicans believe, as did the framers of the Constitution, that the God-given rights of the family come before those of government. That separates us from liberal Democrats. We seek to strengthen the family. Democrats try to supplant it. In the 1960s and 1970s, the family bore the brunt of liberal attacks on everything the American people cherished. Our whole society paid dearly.

It's time to put things together again. Republicans have started this critical task:

- We brought fairness to the tax code, removed millions of low-income families from the rolls, and cut tax rates dramatically.
- We reestablished a pro-family tax system. We doubled the exemption for dependents and protected families from backdoor tax hikes by indexing the exemption to inflation.
- We tamed inflation to lower interest rates, protected the savings of the elderly, and made housing more affordable for millions of households.
- We fought to reverse crime rates and launched the nation's first all-out war on drug abuse, though there is still much more to do.
- We appointed judges who respect family rights, family values, and the rights of victims of crime.
- We brought education back to basics, back to parents, and strengthened the principle of local control.
- Through President Reagan's historic executive order on the family, we set standards in law for deter-

mining whether policies help or hurt the American family.

Republicans have brought hope to families on the front lines of America's social reconstruction. We pledge to fulfill that hope and to keep the family at its proper place at the center of public policy.

Caring for Children

The family's most important function is to raise the next generation of Americans, handing on to them the Judeo-Christian values of Western civilization and our ideals of liberty. More than anything else, the ability of America's families to accomplish those goals will determine the course our country takes in the century ahead.

Our society is in an era of sweeping change. In this era of unprecedented opportunity, more women than ever before have entered the work force. As a result, many households depend upon some form of non-parental care for their youngsters. Relatives, neighbors, churches and synagogues, employers and others in the private sector, are helping to meet the demand for quality care. In the process, we are learning more about the needs of children and about the impact of various forms of care. That knowledge should guide public policy and private options on many issues affecting the way we work and raise our families.

Republicans affirm these common sense principles of child care:

- The more options families have in child care, the better. Government must not constrain their decisions. Individual choice should determine child care arrangements for the family.
- The best care for most children, especially in the early years, is parental. Government must never hinder it.
- Public policy must acknowledge the full range of family situations. Mothers or fathers who stay at home, who work part-time, or who work full-time, should all receive the same respect and consideration in public policy.
- Child care by close relatives, religious organizations, and other community groups should never be inhibited by government programs or policies.

In sum, this is a perfect example of the difference between the two parties. Republicans want to empower individuals, not bureaucrats. We seek to minimize the financial burdens imposed by government upon families, ensure their options, and preserve the role of our traditional voluntary institutions. Democrats propose a new federal program that negates parental choice and disdains religious participation. Republicans would never bar aid to any family for choosing child care that includes a simple prayer.

In returning to our traditional commitment to children, the Republican Party proposes a radically different approach:

- Establish a toddler tax credit for preschool children as proposed by Vice President Bush, available to all families of modest means, to help them support and care for their children in a manner best suited to their families' values and traditions.
- Establishment of a plan that does not discriminate against single-earner families with one parent in the home.
- Continue to reverse the Democrats' 30-year erosion of the dependent tax exemption. That exemption has been doubled under Republican leadership. This will empower parents to care for their families in a way public services can never do.
- Make the dependent care tax credit available to low-income families with young children.
- Eliminate disincentives for grandparents and other seniors to care for children by repealing the earnings limitation for Social Security recipients.
- Encourage States to promote child care programs which allow teen-age mothers to remain in school.
- Promote in-home care—preferred by almost all parents—by allowing annual, instead of quarterly, payments of income taxes by employees and withholding taxes by employers.
- Encourage employers, including government agencies, to voluntarily address their employees' child care needs and use more flexible work schedules and job sharing to recognize the household demands upon their work force.
- Reform the tort liability system to prevent excessive litigation that discourages child care by groups who stand ready to meet the needs of working parents.
- Reform Federal Home Mortgage Association rules to retain mortgage eligibility for homeowners who offer family child care.

Adoption

Adoption is a special form of caring for children. We recognize the tremendous contributions of adoptive parents and foster parents. The Reagan–Bush Administration has given unprecedented attention to adoption through a presidential task force, whose recommendations point the way toward vastly expanding opportunities for children in need.

Republicans are determined to cut through red tape to facilitate the adoption for those who can offer strong family life based on traditional values. Trapping minority and special needs children in the foster care system, when there are families ready to adopt these youngsters, is a national disgrace. We urge States to remove obstacles to the permanent placement of foster children and to reform antiquated regulations that make adoption needlessly difficult.

Pornography

America's children deserve to be free from pornography. We applaud Republicans in the 100th Congress who took the lead to ban interstate dial-a-porn. We endorse legislative and regulatory efforts to anchor more securely a standard of decency in telecommunications and to prohibit the sale of sexually explicit materials in outlets operated on federal property. We commend those who refuse to sell pornographic material. We support the rigorous enforcement of "community standards" against pornography.

Health

Americans are accustomed to miracles in health care. The relentless advance of science, boosted by space age technology, has transformed the quality of health care and broadened the exercise of our compassion. By the year 2000, more than 100,000 Americans will be more than 100 years old. Yesterday's science fiction regularly becomes today's medical routine.

The American people almost lost all that in the 1960s and 1970s, when political demagogues offered quack cures for the ills of our health care system. They tried to impose here the nationalized medicine that was disastrous in other countries.

Republicans believe in reduced government control of health care while maintaining an unequivocal commitment to quality health care:

- We fostered competition and consumer choice as the only way to hold down the medical price spiral generated by government's open-ended spending on health programs.
- We gave the hospice movement its important role in federal programs.
- We launched a national campaign to ensure quality treatment and to prevent abuse in nursing homes.
- We led the way to enacting landmark legislation for catastrophic health insurance under Medicare.
- We speeded up the regulatory process for experimental drugs for life-threatening illness and loosened import controls to allow greater choice by patients.
- We promoted health care through pilot projects in the States. We took steps to ensure home health care

so that chronically ill children under Medicaid would not have to stay in the hospital.

Republicans will continue the recovery of America's health care system from the Democrats' mistakes of the past:

- We will promote continuing innovation to ensure that tomorrow's miracles are affordable and accessible to all. We are encouraged by advances in communications which enable small or isolated facilities to tap the resources of the world's greatest centers of healing. Many breakthroughs in recent years have dramatically reduced the incidence of surgery and replaced lengthy hospital stays with out-patient treatment.
- We will work for continuing progress in providing the most cost-effective, high-quality care.
- We will lead the fight for reform of medical malpractice laws to stop the intolerable escalation of malpractice insurance. It has artificially boosted costs for patients, driven many good doctors out of fields such as obstetrics and other high-risk specialties, and made care unavailable for many patients.
- We are opposed to the establishment of government mandated professional practice fees and services requirements as a condition of professional licensure or license renewal.
- We are committed to avoiding the medical crisis facing Massachusetts—a State for which the American Medical Association observed a "moment of silence" at its annual meeting—a State where the decline in the availability of medical care has reached a dangerous level.
- We will continue to seek opportunities for private and public cooperation in support of hospices.
- We are committed to improving the quality and financing of long-term care. We will remove regulatory and tax burdens to encourage private health insurance policies for acute or long-term care. We will work for convertibility of savings, IRAs, life insurance, and pensions to pay for long-term care.
- We will encourage the trend in the private sector to expand opportunities for home health care to protect the integrity of the family and to provide a less expensive alternative to hospital stays. We want to ensure flexibility for both Medicare and Medicaid in the provision of services to those who need them at home or elsewhere.
- We will foster employee choice in selecting health plans to promote responsibility for wellness.
- Recognizing that medical catastrophes can strike regardless of age, we empathize with the plight of the thousands of American families with catastrophi-

cally ill children and will work toward making catastrophic health care coverage available to our youngest citizens.
- Recognizing that inequities may exist in the current treatment of health insurance costs for those who are self-employed, including farmers, we will study ways to more appropriately balance such costs.
- We will continue to promote alternative forms of group health care that foster competition and lower costs.
- We will make special provision for relief of rural hospitals and health care providers who have been unduly burdened by federal cost containment efforts. The availability of health services, especially during a crisis like the current drought, is essential for rural America.
- We will continue generous funding for the National Institutes of Health.
- We will hold down Medicaid costs by promoting State pilot programs to give low-income persons the opportunity to secure health insurance. We demand tough penalties against providers who defraud this and other health programs.
- We will work to assure access to health care for all Americans through public and private initiatives.
- We will promote wellness, especially for the nation's youth. Personal responsibility in behavior and diet will dramatically reduce the incidence of avoidable disease and curb health care costs in decades ahead.
- We will call on the Food and Drug Administration to accelerate its certification of technically sound alternatives to animal testing of drugs and cosmetics when considering data regarding product safety and efficacy.

AIDS

Those who suffer from AIDS, their families, and the men and women of medicine who care for the afflicted deserve our compassion and help. The Reagan–Bush Administration launched the nation's fight against AIDS, committing more than $5 billion in the last years. For 1989, the President's budget recommends a 42 percent increase in current funding.

We will vigorously fight against AIDS, recognizing that the enemy is one of the deadliest diseases to challenge medical research. Continued research on the virus is vital. We will continue as well to provide experimental drugs that may prolong life. We will establish within the Food and Drug Administration a process for expedited review of drugs which may benefit AIDS patients. We will allow supervised usage of experimental treatments.

We must not only marshal our scientific resources against AIDS, but must also protect those who do not have the disease. In this regard, education plays a critical role. AIDS education should emphasize that abstinence from drug abuse and sexual activity outside of marriage is the safest way to avoid infection with the AIDS virus. It is extremely important that testing and contact tracing measures be carried out and be appropriately confidential, as is the case with the longstanding public health measures to control other communicable diseases that are less dangerous than AIDS.

We will remove barriers to making use of one's own (autologous) blood or blood from a designated donor, and we call for penalties for knowingly donating tainted blood or otherwise deliberately endangering others.

The latency period between infection with the virus and onset of AIDS can be lengthy. People should be encouraged to seek early diagnosis and to remain on the job or in school as long as they are functionally capable.

Healthy Children, Healthy Families

As we strengthen the American family, we improve the health of the nation. From prenatal care to old age, strong family life is the lynchpin of wellness and compassion.

This is especially important with regard to babies. We have reduced infant mortality, but it remains a serious problem in areas where alcohol, drugs, and neglect take a fearful toll on newborns. We will target federal health programs to help mothers and infants get a good start in life. We will assist neighborhood institutions, including religious groups, in reaching out to those on the margins of society to save their children, especially from fetal alcohol syndrome, the major cause of birth defects in this country.

Inadequate prenatal care for expectant mothers is the cause of untold numbers of premature and low-birth-weight babies. These newborns start life at a severe disadvantage and often require massive health care investments to have a chance for normal childhood. We continue to endorse the provision of adequate prenatal care for all expectant mothers, especially the poor and young.

We hail the way fetal medicine is revolutionizing care of children and dramatically expanding our knowledge of human development. Accordingly, we call for fetal protection, both in the work place and in scientific research.

Many of the health problems of young people today stem from poverty, moral confusion, and family dis-

ruption. Republicans are ready to address the root causes of today's youth crisis:

- We will assert absolutes of right and wrong concerning drug abuse and other forms of self-destructive behavior.
- We will require parental consent for unemancipated minors to receive contraceptives from federally funded family planning clinics.
- We support efforts like the Adolescent Family Life program to teach teens the traditional values of restraint and the sanctity of marriage.
- We urge all branches of the entertainment and communications industry to exercise greater responsibility in addressing the youth market.

To prepare for tomorrow's expanding opportunities, today's young Americans must be challenged by high values with the support that comes from strong families. That is the surest way to guide them to their own affirmation of life.

Older Americans

Older Americans are both our bridge to all that is precious in our history and the enduring foundation on which we build the future. Young Americans see most clearly when they stand on the shoulders of the past.

After eight years of President Reagan's youthful leadership, older Americans are safer and more secure. In 1980, we promised to put Social Security back on a sound financial footing. We delivered. We established the national commission that developed the plan to restore the system and led the way in enacting its recommendations into law.

Now that Social Security is in healthy shape, congressional Democrats are plotting ways to use its short-term revenue surplus for their own purposes. We make this promise: They shall not do so. We pledge to preserve the integrity of the Social Security trust funds. We encourage public officials at all levels to safeguard the integrity of public and private pension funds against raiding by anyone, in labor, business, or government. such as in Massachusetts where the current Democrat governor has raided $29 million from the State pension reserves to fund his enormous deficit in the State budget.

We will not allow liberal Democrats to imperil the other gains the elderly have made during the Reagan–Bush Administration:

- Inflation, the despoiler of household budgets for the aged, has been reduced to less than one-third its peak rate under the last Democrat Administration.
- Passage of our anti-crime legislation has helped tar-

get resources to fight crime against the elderly, many of whom have been prisoners in their own homes.

- As a result of the Republican economic program, the poverty rate for older Americans has declined by 20 percent during the Republican Administration. When the value of non-cash benefits is counted, the poverty rate is the lowest in history: 3 percent.
- We dramatically cut estate taxes so surviving spouses will not have to sell off the property they worked a lifetime to enjoy just to pay the IRS.
- President Reagan led the Congress in expanding Medicare coverage to include catastrophic health costs.
- Effective spending on Medicare has more than doubled. We have, however, saved money for both taxpayers and beneficiaries through reforms in Medicare procedures.
- Congressional Republicans have supported reauthorization of the broad range of programs under the Older Americans Act.
- The Republican Party reaffirms its long-standing opposition to the earnings test for Social Security recipients. Industrious older persons should not be penalized for continuing to contribute their skills and experience to society.

The 1990s should be the best decade ever for America's older worker. Older Americans will be our natural teachers. In a civilization headed for the stars, they will help us keep our feet on the ground.

The Homeless

Republicans are determined to help the homeless as a matter of ethical commitment, as well as sound public policy. The Reagan–Bush Administration has been at the forefront of the effort:

- In 1987, President Reagan signed a $1 billion aid package to help local governments aid the homeless.
- In 1988, the federal government will spend $400 million on emergency shelters and medical care alone. Today, a total of 45 federally assisted programs are potentially available to the homeless.
- In 1983, we launched an Emergency Food and Shelter Program under the Federal Emergency Management Administration.
- The General Services Administration has donated both buildings and equipment for shelters.
- In 1985, the Department of Housing and Urban Development (HUD) began to lease single-family homes at a nominal rent for use as shelters.

- The Department of Agriculture has provided hundreds of millions of dollars worth of surplus food—more than 1.1 billion pounds to soup kitchens and shelters.
- The Alcohol, Drug Abuse and Mental Health Administration gives the States about a half-billion dollars a year to offset the lack of outpatient services.

Homelessness demonstrates the failure of liberalism. It is the result of Democrat policies in the 1960s and 1970s that disrupted mental health care, family stability, low-cost housing, and the authority of towns and cities to deal with people in need. Republicans are ready to deal with the root causes of the problem:

- Our top priority must be homeless families. As part of an overall emphasis on family responsibility, we will strongly enforce child support laws. We call for development of a model divorce reform law that will adequately safeguard the economic and social interests of mothers and children while securing fairness to fathers in decisions concerning child custody and support.
- We will improve safety in federally assisted shelters for the good of all, particularly families.
- We will work with State and local governments to ensure that education is available to homeless children. All appropriate federal education and health programs must make provision for the special needs of these youngsters.
- We will create, as a national emergency effort, a regulatory reform task force drawn from all levels of government to break through the restrictions that keep 1.7 million housing units unrehabilitated and out of use. We will explore incentives for the private sector to put these housing units back into service.
- As detailed elsewhere in this platform, we will advance tenant management and resident ownership of public housing as a proven means of upgrading the living environment of low-income families.
- We favor expanding Community Development Block Grants for acquiring or rehabilitating buildings for shelters. We urge work requirements, no matter how modest, for shelter residents so they can retain skills and a sense of responsibility for their future.
- Rent controls promise housing below its market cost, but inevitably result in a shortage of decent homes. Our people should not have to underwrite any community which erodes its own housing supply by rent control.

We call upon the courts to cooperate with local officials and police departments in arranging for treatment for persons whose actions disrupt the community or endanger their own or others' safety.

CONSTITUTIONAL GOVERNMENT AND INDIVIDUAL RIGHTS

Equal Rights

Since its inception, the Republican Party has stood for the worth of every person. On that ground, we support the pluralism and diversity that have been part of our country's greatness. "Deep in our hearts, we do believe":

- That bigotry has no place in American life. We denounce those persons, organizations, publications, and movements which practice or promote racism, anti-Semitism or religious intolerance.
- That the Pledge of Allegiance should be recited daily in schools in all States. Students who learn we are "one nation, under God, indivisible, with liberty and justice for all" will shun the politics of fear.
- In equal rights for all. The Reagan–Bush Administration has taken to court a record number of civil rights and employment discrimination. We will continue our vigorous enforcement of statutes to prevent illegal discrimination on account of sex, race, creed, or national origin.
- In guaranteeing opportunity, not dictating the results of fair competition. We will resist efforts to replace equal rights with discriminatory quota systems and preferential treatment. Quotas are the most insidious form of reverse discrimination against the innocent.
- In defending religious freedom. Mindful of our religious diversity, we firmly support the right of students to engage in voluntary prayer in schools. We call for full enforcement of the Republican legislation that now guarantees equal access to school facilities by student religious groups.
- That the unborn child has a fundamental individual right to life which cannot be infringed. We therefore reaffirm our support for a human life amendment to the Constitution, and we endorse legislation to make clear that the Fourteenth Amendment's protections apply to unborn children. We oppose the use of public revenues for abortion and will eliminate funding for organizations which advocate or support abortion. We commend the efforts of those individuals and religious and private organizations that are providing positive alternatives to abortion by meeting the physical, emotional, and financial

needs of pregnant women and offering adoption services where needed.
- We applaud President Reagan's fine record of judicial appointments, and we reaffirm our support for the appointment of judges at all levels of the judiciary who respect traditional family values and the sanctity of innocent human life.
- That churches, religious schools and any other religious institution should not be taxed. We reject as wrong, bigoted, and a massive violation of the First Amendment the current attempt by the American Civil Liberties Union to tax the Roman Catholic Church or any other religious institutions it targets in the future.

Private Property

We believe the right of private property is the cornerstone of liberty. It safeguards for citizens everything of value, including their right of contract to produce and sell goods and services. We want to expand ownership to all Americans, for that is the key for individuals to control their own future.

To advance private stewardship of natural resources, we call for a reduction in the amount of land controlled by government, especially in our western States. Private ownership is best for our economy, best for our environment, and best for our communities. We likewise consider water rights a State issue, not a federal one.

Women's Rights

We renew our historic commitment to equal rights for women. The Republican Party pioneered the right of women to vote and initiated the rights now in the Equal Pay Act, requiring equal pay for equal work. But legal rights mean nothing without opportunity, and that has been the of hallmark of Republican policy. In government, the Reagan–Bush team has broken all records for the advancement of women to the most important positions: 28 percent of the top policy-level appointments went to women. But far more important than what we've done in government is what women have accomplished with the economic freedom and incentives our policies have provided them.

We must remove remaining obstacles to women's achieving their full potential and full reward. That does not include the notion of federally mandated comparable worth, which would substitute the decisions of bureaucrats for the judgment of individuals. It does include equal rights for women who work for the

Congress. We call upon the Democrat leadership of the House and Senate to join Republican members in applying to Congress the civil rights laws that apply to the rest of the nation. Women should not be second-class citizens anywhere in our country, but least of all beneath the dome of the Capitol.

- Recognizing that women represent less than 5 percent of the U.S. Congress, only 12 percent of the nation's statewide offices, plus 15 percent of State legislative positions, the Republican Party strongly supports the achievements of women in seeking an equal role in the governing of our country and is committed to the vigorous recruitment, training, and campaign support of women candidates at all levels.

Americans With Disabilities

One measure of our country's greatness is the way it treats its disabled citizens.

Our citizens are the nation's most precious resource. As Republicans, we are committed to ensuring increased opportunities for every individual to reach his or her maximum potential. This commitment includes providing opportunities for individuals with disabilities. The 1980s have been a revolution, a declaration of independence for persons with disabilities, and Republicans have initiated policies which remove barriers so that such persons are more independent.

The most effective way to increase opportunities for such persons is to remove intentional and unintentional barriers to education, employment, housing, transportation, health care, and other basic services. Republicans have played an important role in removing such barriers:

- Republicans supported the creation of a new program to provide early intervention services to infants and toddlers with disabilities.
- Republicans initiated a supported employment program that allows individuals with severe disabilities to earn competitive wages in integrated work settings, thus, in many instances, creating first-time taxpayers.
- Republicans initiated changes in the Social Security Act that now permit individuals with disabilities to work without losing health insurance coverage.
- Republicans developed legislation to increase the availability of technology-related assistance for individuals with disabilities, thereby increasing their ability to do things for themselves, others, and their communities.
- Republicans have made a sustained commitment to policies that create opportunities for individuals

with disabilities to lead productive and creative lives.

Republicans will continue to support such policies:

- We recognize the great potential of disabled persons and support efforts to remove artificial barriers that inhibit them from reaching their potential, and making their contributions, in education, employment and recreation. This includes the removal, insofar as practicable, of architectural, transportation, communication and attitudinal barriers.
- We support efforts to provide disabled voters full access to the polls and opportunity to participate in all aspects of the political process.
- By promoting vigorous economic growth, we will provide incentives for the scientific and technological research that may reverse or compensate for many disabilities.
- We pledge to fight discrimination in health care. Following the example of President Reagan, we insist upon full treatment for disabled infants. We find no basis, whether in law or medicine or ethics, for denying care or treatment to any medically dependent or disabled person because of handicap, age, or infirmity.
- We will strongly enforce statutory prohibitions barring discrimination because of handicap in any program receiving federal financial assistance.
- We will protect the rights established under the Education for All Handicapped Children Act, Section 504 of the Rehabilitation Act of 1973, and the Civil Rights of Institutionalized Persons Act. We will balance those rights against the public's right to be protected against diseases and conditions which directly threaten the health and safety of others.
- We recognize the need to procedural due process rights of persons with disabilities both to prevent their placement into inappropriate programs or settings and to ensure that their rights are represented by guardians or other advocates when necessary.

We endorse policies that give individuals with disabilities the right to participate in decisions related to their education, the right to affect how and where they live and the right to choose or change a job or career.

To further promote the independence and productivity of people with disabilities and their integration into the mainstream of life, the Republican Party supports legislation to remove the bias in the Medicaid program toward serving disabled individuals in isolated institutional settings and ensure that appropriate, community-based services are reimbursable through Medicaid.

Native Americans

We support self-determination for Indian Tribes in managing their own affairs and resources. Recognizing the government-to-government trust responsibility, we will work to end dependency fostered by federal controls. Reservations should be free to become enterprise zones so their people can fully share in America's prosperity. We will work with tribal governments to improve environmental conditions and will ensure equitable participation by Native Americans in federal programs in health, housing, job training and education.

We endorse efforts to preserve the culture of native Hawaiians and to ensure their equitable participation in federal programs that can recognize and preserve their unique place in the life of our nation.

The Right of Gun Ownership

Republicans defend the constitutional right to keep and bear arms. When this right is abused by an individual who uses a gun in the commission of a crime, we call for stiff, mandatory penalties.

The Rights of Workers

We affirm the right of all freely to form, join or assist labor organizations to bargain collectively, consistent with State laws. Labor relations must be based on fairness and mutual respect. We renew our long-standing support for the right of States to enact "Right-to-Work" laws. To protect the political rights of every worker, we oppose the use of compulsory dues or fees for partisan purposes. Workers should not have to pay for political activity they oppose, and no worker should be coerced by violence or intimidation by any party to a labor dispute.

The Republican Party supports legislation to amend the Hobbs Act, so that union officials, like all other Americans, are once again subject to the law's prohibition against extortion and violence in labor disputes.

We also support amendments to the National Labor Relations Act to provide greater protection from labor violence for workers who choose to work during strikes.

The Right to Political Participation

Republicans want to broaden involvement in the political process. We oppose government controls that make it harder for average citizens to be politically active. We especially condemn the congressional Democrats' scheme to force taxpayer funding of campaigns.

Because we support citizen participation in politics,

we continue to favor whatever legislation may be necessary to permit American citizens residing in Guam, the Virgin Islands, American Samoa, the Northern Marianas Islands, and Puerto Rico to vote for president and vice president in national elections and permit their elected federal delegate to have the rights and privileges—except for voting on the floor—of other members of Congress.

Puerto Rico has been a territory of the United States since 1898. The Republican Party vigorously supports the right of the United States citizens of Puerto Rico to be admitted into the Union as a fully sovereign State after they freely so determine. Therefore, we support the establishment of a presidential task force to prepare the necessary legislation to ensure that the people of Puerto Rico have the opportunity to exercise at the earliest possible date their right to apply for admission into the Union.

We also pledge that a decision of the people of Puerto Rico in favor of statehood will be implemented through an admission bill that would provide for a smooth fiscal transition, recognize the concept of a multi-cultural society for its citizens, and ensure the right to retain their Spanish language and traditions.

We recognize that the people of Guam have voted for a closer relationship with the United States of America, and we reaffirm our support of their right to improve their political relationship through a commonwealth status.

The Republican Party welcomes, as the newest member of the American family, the people of the Commonwealth of the Northern Marianas Islands, who became U.S. citizens with President Reagan's 1986 presidential proclamation.

Immigration

We welcome those from other lands who bring to America their ideals and industry. At the same time, we insist upon our country's absolute right to control its borders. We call upon our allies to join us in the responsibility shared by all democratic nations for resettlement of refugees, especially those fleeing communism in Southeast Asia.

Restoring the Constitution

We reassert adherence to the Tenth Amendment, reserving to the States and to the people all powers not expressly delegated to the national government.

Our Constitution provides for a separation of powers among the three branches of government. In that system, judicial power must be exercised with deference toward State and local authority; it must not expand at the expense of our representative institutions. When the courts try to reorder the priorities of the American people, they undermine the stature of the judiciary and erode respect for the rule of law. That is why we commend the Reagan–Bush team for naming to the federal courts distinguished women and men committed to judicial restraint, the rights of law-abiding citizens, and traditional family values. We pledge to continue their record. Where appropriate, we support congressional use of Article III, Section 2 of the Constitution to restrict the jurisdiction of federal courts.

Government Ethics and Congressional Reform

As the United States celebrates the bicentennial of the U.S. Congress, many Americans are becoming painfully aware that they are being disenfranchised and inadequately represented by their elected officials.

Indeed, the process of government has broken down on Capitol Hill. The founding fathers of the United States Constitution would be shocked by congressional behavior:

- The Democrat congressional leaders exempt themselves from the laws they impose on the people in areas like health, safety and civil rights.
- Salaries and staff keep growing. Lavish free mailing privileges and other power perks help most incumbents hold onto their offices, election after election.
- Out of 91 appropriations bills in the past seven years, only seven made it to the president's desk on time.
- A catch-all bill to fund the government for 1988 was 2,100 pages long, lumping together 13 money bills that should have been separately subject to presidential review.
- $44 billion is currently being spent for programs not authorized by legislation.
- Special interest spending and pork-barrel deals are larded throughout massive bills in chaotic late-night sessions.
- Vetoed bills are not dealt with directly by the Congress but are buried in other pending legislation.
- Phony numbers are used to estimate budgets and to cover up the true costs of legislation.

Even worse, outright offenses against ethical standards and public laws are treated lightly. National security leaks go unpunished. In the House of Representatives, the Ethics Committee has become a shield for Democrats who get caught but don't get punished.

After 36 years of one-party rule, the House of Representatives is no longer the people's branch of government. It is the broken branch. It is an arrogant oligarchy that has subverted the Constitution. The Democrat congressional leaders:

- Stole a congressional seat from the people of Indiana by barring a duly elected, and officially certified, Republican member.
- Flagrantly abuse every standard of accepted procedure by adjourning and, contrary to 200 years of House tradition, immediately reconvening in order to create a "new day" and pass legislation previously defeated.
- Deny the century-old right of the minority party to offer its final alternatives to bills.
- Change House rules to prevent debate and thwart the offering of amendments.
- Rig adoption of substantive legislation on mere procedural votes, so their followers won't be accountable on controversial votes to the people back home.
- Protect their cronies charged with personal misconduct or criminal activities.
- Refuse to allow the House to vote on issues of tremendous concern to the American people and viciously penalize independent Democrats who vote their conscience.
- Rig the subcommittee system to give themselves artificial majorities and additional staff members.

Republicans want to hold accountable to the people, the Congress and every other element of government. We will:

- Extend the independent counsel law to Congress.
- Apply health and safety laws and civil rights statutes to the Congress.
- Give to whistleblowers on Capitol Hill the same legal protection they have in the executive branch, to encourage employees to report illegalities, corruption and sexual harassment.
- Implement the budget reform agenda outlined elsewhere in this platform—a balanced budget amendment, line-item veto, and other steps—to restore accountability, order, and truth in government to the way Congress spends the people's money.
- Support citizen efforts in the Senate to defeat the gerrymanders that steal seats for Democrat congressmen by denying fair representation to the voters.
- Force democracy into the committee system of the House so that committees and staffs reflect the overall composition of the House.
- We favor a constitutional amendment which would place some restriction on the number of consecutive

terms a man or woman may serve in the U.S. House of Representatives or the U.S. Senate.

EDUCATING FOR THE FUTURE

Republican leadership has launched a new era in American education. Our vision of excellence has brought education back to parents, back to basics, and back on a track of excellence leading to a brighter and stronger future for America.

Because education is the key to opportunity, we must make America a nation of learners, ready to compete in the rapidly changing world of the future. Our goal is to combine traditional values and enduring truths with the most modern techniques and technology for teaching and learning.

This challenge will be immense. For two decades before 1981, poor public policies had led to an alarming decline in performance in our schools. Unfocused federal spending seemed to worsen the situation, hamstringing education with regulations and wasting resources in faddish programs top-heavy with administrative overhead.

Then President Reagan and Vice President Bush rallied our "nation at risk." The response was in the best tradition of the American people. In every State, indeed, in every community, individuals and organizations have launched a neighborhood movement for education reform. It has brought together Americans of every race and creed in a crusade for our children's future. Since 1980, average salaries for elementary and secondary teachers have increased to over $28,000, an increase of 20 percent after inflation. We can enhance this record of accomplishment by committing ourselves to these principles:

- Parents have the primary right and responsibility for education. Private institutions, communities, States, and the federal government must support and stimulate that parental role. We support the right of parents to educate their children at home.
- Choice and competition in education foster quality and protect consumers' rights.
- Accountability and evaluation of performance at all levels of education is the key to continuing reform in education. We must reward excellence in learning, in teaching, and in administration.
- Values are the core of good education. A free society needs a moral foundation for its learning. We oppose any programs in public schools which provide birth control or abortion services or referrals. Our "first line of defense" to protect our youth from con-

tracting AIDS and other sexually communicable diseases, from teen pregnancy, and from illegal drug use must be abstinence education.
- Quality in education should be available to all our children within their communities and neighborhoods. Federal policy should empower low-income families to choose quality and demand accountability in their children's schooling.
- Throughout all levels of education we must initiate action to reduce the deplorable dropout rate which deprives young people of their full potential.
- Federal programs must focus on students at special risk, especially those with physical disabilities or language deficits, to increase their chance at a productive future in the mainstream of American life.
- Because America's future will require increasingly competent leadership in all walks of life, national policy should emphasize the need to provide our most talented students with special programs to challenge their abilities.

Based on those principles, the Republican agenda for better education looks first to home and family, then to communities and States. In States and localities, we support practical, down-to-earth reforms that have made a proven difference in actual operation:

- Choice in education, especially for poor families, fosters the involvement that is essential for student success, and States should consider enacting voucher systems or other means of encouraging competition among public schools.
- Performance testing, both for students and teachers, measures progress, assures accountability to parents and the public, and keeps standards high.
- Merit pay, career ladders, or other rewards for superior teachers acknowledge our esteem for them and encourage others to follow their example of dedication to a profession that is critical to our nation's future.
- Making use of volunteerism from the private sector and providing opportunity for accelerated accreditation for those with needed expertise broadens the classroom experience and encourages excellence.
- Expansions of curriculum to include the teaching of the history, culture, geography and, particularly, the languages of key nations of the world is a necessity. To compete successfully throughout the world, we must acquire the ability to speak the languages of our customers.
- Excellence in the teaching of geography is essential to equipping our people with the ability to capture new markets in all parts of the world.
- Discipline is a prerequisite for learning. Our schools

must be models of order and decorum, not jungles of drugs and violence.

On the federal level, Republicans have worked to facilitate State and local reform movements:

- We kept the spotlight on the reform movement through White House leadership, and we refocused the Department of Education to recognize and foster excellence.
- We enacted legislation to ensure equal access to schools for student religious groups and led congressional efforts to restore voluntary school prayer.
- We led a national crusade against illiteracy, following the example of Barbara Bush.
- We put into law protection for pupils in federally funded programs, to shield students and their families from intrusive research and offensive psychological testing.
- We strengthened education programs by proposing to replace federal aid to schools with direct assistance that would give choice to low-income parents.
- We broke new ground in early childhood development programs, such as Even Start, that emphasize the involvement of parents in the learning process and address adult illiteracy and school readiness education holistically.
- We intervened in court cases to defend the right of students to learn in a safe, drug-free environment.

We will continue to advance that agenda and to expand horizons for learning, teaching, and mastering the future:

- We will protect the Pledge of Allegiance in all schools as a reminder of the values which must be at the core of learning for a free society.
- We will use federal programs to foster excellence, rewarding "Merit Schools" which significantly improve education for their students.
- We will urge our local school districts to recognize the value of kindergarten and pre-kindergarten programs.
- We will direct federal matching funds to promote magnet schools that turn students toward the challenges of the future rather than the failures of the past.
- We will support laboratories of educational excellence in every State by refocusing federal funds for educational research.
- We will increase funding for the Head Start program to help children get a fair chance at learning, right from the beginning.
- We will work with local schools and the private sec-

tor to develop models for evaluating teachers and other school officials.
- We will continue to support tuition tax credits for parents who choose to educate their children in private educational institutions.
- We would establish a public–private partnership using the Department of Labor's Job Training Partnership Act funds to encourage youth to stay in school and graduate. The Labor Department funds would be made available to local employers and business groups to hire high school students after school and during the summer with the requirement that they keep their grades at a "C" average or above until graduation.

In higher education, Republicans want to promote both opportunity and responsibility:

- We will keep resources focused on low-income students and address the barriers that discourage minority students from entering and succeeding in institutions of higher education.
- We are determined to reverse the intolerable rates of default in the guaranteed student loan program to make more money available to those who really need to borrow it.
- We will keep the spotlight of public attention on the college cost spiral—running far ahead of inflation overall—and challenge administration to exercise more fiscal responsibility.
- We will create a College Savings Bond program, with tax-exempt interest, to help families save for their children's higher education.
- We will condition federal aid to post-secondary institutions upon their good faith effort to maintain safe and drug-free campuses.
- We will insist that freedom of speech is not only a fundamental right, it is one of the first lines of education. This freedom should be afforded to all speakers with a minimum of harassment.
- We will continue education benefits for veterans of military service and advance the principle that those who serve their country in the armed forces have first call on federal education assistance.
- We will continue the Reagan–Bush policy of emphasizing vocational-technical education. A large number of jobs in our society require secondary and post-secondary vocational-technical education. Federal programs and policies must recognize and enhance vocational-technical students.
- We will support educational programs in federal prisons that will allow prisoners the opportunity to become literate and to learn an employable skill. We encourage similar programs at the State level.

To compete globally, our society must prepare our children for the world of work. We cannot allow one of every eight 17-year-olds to remain functionally illiterate. We cannot allow 1 million students to drop out of high school every year, most of them without basic skills; therefore, we must teach them reading, writing, and mathematics. We must reestablish their obligation to learn.

Education for the future means more than formal schooling in classrooms. About 75 percent of our current work force will need some degree of retraining by the year 2000. More than half of all jobs we will create in the 1990s will require some education beyond high school, and much of that will be obtained outside of regular educational institutions. Unprecedented flexibility in working arrangements, changes, and a stampede of technological advance are ushering us into a era of lifelong learning. Therefore, we support employment training programs at all levels of government such as the Job Training Partnership Act and the recently restructured Worker Adjustment Program for dislocated workers. The placement success of these programs can be directly traced to their public/private sector partnerships and local involvement in their program development and implementation.

In the 1960s and 1970s, we learned what doesn't solve the problems of education: federal financing and regimentation of our schools. In the 1980s, we asserted what works: parental responsibility, community support and local control, good teachers and determined administrators, and a return to the basic values and content of Western civilization. That combination gave generations of Americans the world's greatest opportunities for learning. It can guarantee the same for future generations.

Arts and Humanities

Republicans consider the resurgence of the arts and humanities a vital part of getting back to basics in education. Our young people must acquire more than information and skills. They must learn to reason and to appreciate the intellectual achievements that express the enduring values of our civilization. To that end, we will:

• Continue the Republican economic renaissance which has made possible a tremendous outpouring of support for the arts and humanities.
• Support full deductibility for donations to tax-exempt cultural institutions in order to encourage the private support of arts and humanities.
• Support the National Endowments for the Arts and Humanities and the Institute of Museum Services in their effort to support America's cultural institutions, artists, and scholars.
• Guard against the misuse of governmental grants by those who attack or derogate any race or creed and oppose the politicization of the National Endowments for the Arts and Humanities.

While recognizing the diversity of our people, we encourage educational institutions to emphasize in the arts and humanities those ideas and cultural accomplishments that address the ethical foundations of our culture.

Science and Technology

Our nation's continuing progress depends on scientific and technological innovation. It is America's economic fountain of youth. Republicans advocate a creative partnership between government and the private sector to ensure the dynamism, and creativity of scientific research and technology:

• We recognize that excellence in education, and especially scientific literacy, is a precondition for progress, and that economic growth makes possible the nation's continuing advancement in scientific research.
• We consider a key priority in any increased funding for the National Science Foundation the retooling of science and engineering labs at colleges and universities.
• We endorse major national projects like the superconducting Super Collider.
• We will ensure that tax policy gives optimum incentives for the private sector to fund a high level of advanced research. Toward that end, we will make permanent the current tax credit for research and development and extend it to cooperative research ventures.
• We will strengthen the role of science and engineering in national policy by reinforcing the Office of the President's Science Adviser with the addition of a Science Advisory Council.
• We will encourage exchange of scientific information, especially between business and academic institutions, to speed up the application of research to benefit the public.
• We will improve the acquisition of scientific and technical information from other countries through expedited translation services and more aggressive outreach by federal agencies.
• We will include international technology flows as part of U.S. trade negotiations to ensure that the benefits of foreign advances are available to Americans.

- We will encourage innovation by strengthening protection for intellectual property at home and abroad. We will promote the public benefits that come from commercialization of research conducted under federal sponsorship by allowing private ownership of intellectual property developed in that manner.
- We will oppose regulation which stifles competition and hinders breakthroughs that can transform life for the better in areas like biotechnology.

This is an agenda for more than science and technology: It will broaden economic opportunity, sustain our ability to compete globally, and enhance the quality of life for all.

Space

The Republican Party will reestablish U.S. preeminence in space. It is our nation's frontier, our manifest destiny. President Reagan has set ambitious goals for a space comeback. We are determined to meet them and move on to even greater challenges.

We support further development of the space station, the National Aerospace Plane, Project Pathfinder, a replacement shuttle, and the development of alternate launch vehicles. We endorse Mission to Planet Earth for space science to advance our understanding of environmental and climatic forces.

A resurgent America, renewed economically and in spirit, must get on with its business of greatness. We must commit to a manned flight to Mars around the year 2000 and to continue exploration of the moon.

These goals will be achievable only with full participation by private initiative. We welcome the Reagan–Bush initiative to increase the role of the private sector in transport, particularly in the launch of commercial satellites. The Reagan–Bush Administration's proposed space station will allow the private sector additional opportunities in the area of research and manufacturing.

Our program for freedom in space will allow millions of American investors to put their money on the future. That's one of the ways to lift the conquest of space out of the congressional budget logjam. Republicans believe that America must have a clear vision for the future of the space program, well-defined goals, and streamlined implementation, as we reach for the stars.

Strong Communities and Neighborhood Crime

Republicans want a free and open society for every American. That means more than economic advance-

ment alone. It requires the safety and security of persons and their property. It demands an end to crime.

Republicans stand with the men and women who put their lives on the line every day, in State and local police forces and in federal law enforcement agencies. We are determined to reestablish safety in the streets of those communities where the poor, the hard-working, and the elderly now live in fear. Despite opposition from liberal Democrats, we've made a start:

- The rate of violent crime has fallen 20 percent since 1981. Personal thefts fell 21 percent, robberies fell 31 percent, assaults fell 17 percent, and household burglaries fell 30 percent.
- In 1986, crimes against individuals reached their lowest level in 14 years.
- The Reagan–Bush Administration has crusaded for victims' rights in trials and sentencing procedures and has advocated restitution by felons to their victims.
- We have been tough on white-collar crime, too. We have filed more criminal anti-trust cases than the previous Administration.
- We pushed a historic reform of toughened sentencing procedures for federal courts to make the punishment fit the crime.
- We appointed to the courts judges who have been sensitive to the rights of victims and law-abiding citizens.
- We will forge ahead with the Republican anti-crime agenda.
- We must never allow the presidency and the Department of Justice to fall into the hands of those who coddle hardened criminals. Republicans oppose furloughs for those criminals convicted of first degree murder and others who are serving a life sentence without possibility of parole. We believe that victims' rights should not be accorded less importance than those of convicted felons.
- We will reestablish the federal death penalty.
- We will reform the exclusionary rule, to prevent the release of guilty felons on technicalities.
- We will reform cumbersome *habeas corpus* procedures, used to delay cases and prevent punishment of the guilty.
- We support State laws implementing preventive detention to allow courts to deny bail to those considered dangerous and likely to commit additional crimes.

The election of 1988 will determine which way our country deals with crime. A Republican President and a Republican Congress can lay the foundation for a safer future.

Drug-Free America

The Republican Party is committed to a drug-free America. Our policy is strict accountability, for users of illegal drugs as well as for those who profit by that usage.

The drug epidemic didn't just happen. It was fueled by the liberal attitudes of the 1960s and 1970s that tolerated drug usage. Drug abuse directly threatens the fabric of our society. It is part of a worldwide narcotics empire whose $300 billion business makes one of the largest industries on earth.

The Reagan–Bush Administration has set out to destroy it. In the past six years, federal drug arrests have increased by two-thirds. Compared to 1980, two-and-a-half times as many drug offenders were sent to prison in 1987. Federal spending for drug enforcement programs more than tripled in the last seven years. And we have broken new ground by enlisting U.S. intelligence agencies in the fight against drug trafficking.

Drug usage in our armed forces has plummeted as a direct result of an aggressive education and random testing program. In 1983, we instituted random drug testing in the Coast Guard. At that time, 10.3 percent of the tests showed positive drug usage. As a result of this testing program, the positive usage rate fell dramatically to 2.9 percent in 1987. The Reagan–Bush Administration has also undertaken efforts to insure that all those in safety-related positions in our transportation system are covered by similar drug testing requirements. We commend this effort.

We are determined to finish the job:

- The Republican Party unequivocally opposes legalizing or decriminalizing any illicit drug.
- We support strong penalties, including the death penalty for major drug traffickers.
- User accountability for drug usage is long overdue. Conviction for any drug crime should make the offender ineligible for discretionary federal assistance, grants, loans, and contracts for a period of time.
- To impress young Americans with the seriousness of our fight against drugs, we urge States to suspend eligibility for a driver's license to anyone convicted of a drug offense.
- We urge school districts to get tough on illegal drug use by notifying parents and police whenever it is discovered.
- We will encourage tougher penalties for those who use children in illegal narcotics operations.
- We will require federal contractors and grantees to establish a drug-free work place with the goal that no American will have to work around drug abuse.
- We will suspend passports from those convicted of major drug offenses.
- To protect residents of public housing, we will evict persons dealing in drugs. We will foster resident review committees to screen out drug abusers and dealers. We will promote tenant management as the surest cure for the drug plague in public projects.
- We will strengthen interdiction of foreign drugs and expand the military's role in stopping traffickers.
- We will work with foreign governments to eradicate drug crops in their countries.
- In a summit of Western Hemisphere nations, we will seek total cooperation from other governments in wiping out the international drug empire.
- In addition to our enforcement activities, we encourage drug education in our schools. These programs should begin as early as the elementary school years, before children are subjected to peer pressure to experiment with drugs, and should continue through high school. Cutting down on the demand for drugs will be of great assistance as we increase our enforcement efforts to reduce drug supply.
- We will encourage seizure and forfeiture programs by the Department of the Treasury and each State to take the profits out of illicit drug sales.

We commend our fellow citizens who are actively joining the war against drugs. Drug dealers are domestic terrorists, and we salute the heroic residents of poor neighborhoods who have boldly shut down crack houses and run traffickers out of their communities.

We recognize the need to improve the availability of drug rehabilitation and treatment.

There's a bright side to the picture. We know the most powerful deterrent to drug abuse: strong, stable family life, along with the absolute approach summed up in "Just Say No." Nancy Reagan has made that phrase the battle-cry of the war against drugs, and it is echoed by more than 10,000 Just Say No clubs. We salute her for pointing the way to our nation's drug-free future.

OPPORTUNITY AND ASSISTANCE

Our country's economic miracle of the last eight years has been the most successful assault on poverty in our era. Millions of families have worked their way into the mainstream of national life. The poverty rate continues to decline. However, many remain in poverty, and we pledge to help them in their struggle for self-sufficiency and independence.

For most of our country's history, helping those less fortunate was a community responsibility. Strong families pulled together, and strong communities cared for those in need. That is more than a description of the past. It is a prescription for the future, pointing the way toward real reform of today's welfare mess through these Republican principles:

- We support the maintenance of income assistance programs for those who cannot work. In particular, we recognize our responsibility to ensure a decent standard of living for the aged, the disabled, and children dependent upon the community.
- Poverty can be addressed by income assistance or in-kind services. Dependency, on the other hand, requires a comprehensive strategy to change patterns of attitude and behavior. We will work to address both poverty and dependency.
- Work is an essential component of welfare reform, and education is an essential component of employability. Welfare reform must require participation in education and work, and provide day care assistance and continued access to Medicaid during the transition to full independence.
- Fathers of welfare dependent children must be held accountable by mandating paternity determinations and requiring the participation of unemployed fathers in education and work programs.
- State and local administration of education, work, and welfare programs is best for both the taxpayers and those in need.
- State and local pilot programs in welfare are the cutting edge of welfare reform. States should be granted the authority by the federal government to pursue innovative programs which return teen mothers to school and welfare recipients to work. Congressional Democrats are blocking the expansion of this vital process. A Republican Congress will give the States authority to meet local needs.
- Welfare fraud is an offense against both the taxpayers and the poor. Whether perpetrated by participants or providers of services, its eradication is an essential component of a compassionate welfare policy.

We are committed to assisting those in need. We are equally committed to addressing the root causes of poverty. Divorce, desertion, and illegitimacy have been responsible for almost all the increase in child poverty in the last 15 years. Because strong family life is the most remarkable anti-poverty force in history, Republicans will make the reinforcement of family rights and responsibilities an essential component of public policy. Stronger enforcement of child support laws must be an important part of that effort, along with the revision of State laws which have left many women and children vulnerable to economic distress.

Children in poverty deserve our strongest support. We are committed to safer neighborhoods and full prosecution for child abuse and exploitation. We will reach out to these children through Head Start and targeted education, basic health and nutrition assistance, local community efforts and individual concern. But something more is required to fulfill the hope for self-sufficiency: a job in an expanding economy. The compassionate policy for children in need is the chance for families to stand on their own feet in a society filled with opportunity.

Fighting poverty means much more than distributing cash. It includes education and work programs. It means reducing illiteracy, the single greatest indicator of lifelong poverty. It involves combating crime so that the homes and earnings of the poor are secure. It includes Republican reforms in public housing, like resident management and ownership. It requires regulatory reforms to open up opportunities for those on the margins of the work force. It means streamlining adoption rules and ensuring poor parents a real say in their children's education. Above all, it means maintaining a strong, healthy economy that creates jobs.

Urban Revitalization

Urban America is center stage of our country's future. That is why we address its problems and potential throughout this platform, rather than limiting our concern to a particular section. In doing so, Republicans follow three broad principles:

- Economic growth is the most important urban program. Because we cut taxes, a new prosperity has transformed many towns and cities. Because we forced down inflation, cities pay much lower bond rates. Because we created 17.5 million new jobs through a thriving economy, millions of urban residents have seized the opportunity to escape welfare and unemployment. Because we slashed regulatory burdens, enterprise is transforming areas untouched by government programs of past years.
- Local control is the best form of administration. That's why we merged federal programs into block grants for community development and housing.
- Citizen choice is the key to successful government. Options in education empower parents and attract new residents. Options in public housing transform slums into real communities, bustling with enterprise and hope.

Building on those principles, Republicans will advance our urban opportunity agenda which includes:

- Enterprise zones, where tax incentives and regulatory reforms open the way for creating jobs and rebuilding neighborhoods from the ground up which have been blocked by the Democrats in Congress.
- Resident control—both management and ownership—of public housing, with a goal transferring one-third of the country's public housing space to tenants by 1995.
- Urban homesteading and other programs to ensure affordable housing opportunities in our cities.
- Emergency waiver of Davis–Bacon wage requirements for cities with severe deterioration of the public infrastructure.
- Contracting out public services to workers in the private sector.
- Education assistance directed to low-income households instead of aid to institutions that fail to meet their needs.
- Continued reduction in crime rates, especially street crime and the violence that destroys community life.
- Unrelenting war on drugs.
- Greater control by local government in federally assisted programs, especially transportation and housing.
- Steady environmental progress to ensure clean air and clean water to our cities and assist local governments in solving their solid waste problems in order to make our cities safe and healthy places to live.
- Special attention to urban residents in the national census, to ensure that cities are not shortchanged in federal representation or in federal programs based upon population.

RURAL COMMUNITY DEVELOPMENT AND THE FAMILY FARM

Republicans see a robust future for American agriculture. Rural America is our country's heartland and pillar of economic and moral strength. From its small towns and communities comes more than the world's greatest bounty of food. From them also comes a commitment to the land by a proud and independent people.

For much of this century, the first line of defense against world hunger has been the American farmer and rancher. In the future as in the past, the enterprise of rural Americans will be crucial to the progress of our country and of mankind. The entire nation—and indeed the world—benefits from their unsurpassed productivity.

When farmers and ranchers face adversity, the communities that depend on them do, too. When farmers' income falls, the earnings of others follow. When agriculture suffers, the tax base and public services of whole regions decline.

That is why the current drought is an emergency for our entire country. It will affect every American: the way we live, the food we eat, the land we cherish. We cannot promise to bring rain, but we can bend every arm of government to provide for the expeditious relief of farmers and ranchers in trouble. We pledge to do so. We will focus assistance on those most seriously hurt by the drought. With strong Republican support in the House and Senate, a major relief bill has been signed by President Reagan.

The Record

Some disasters are manmade. In the late 1970s, American agriculture bore the brunt of bad public policy. Long thereafter, farmers suffered the consequences of those four years of devastating Democrat mismanagement. Inflation drove production costs and farm debt to their highest levels in history. To top it off, the Democrats' embargo of grain and other agricultural products dealt a blow to the nation's heartland from which many farmers never recovered.

NEVER AGAIN!

For eight years, Ronald Reagan and George Bush have provided the leadership to turn that situation around. Despite strong Democrat opposition, Republicans have made a good beginning. Because of Republican policies, America's farm and rural sector is coming alive again:

- Inflation, unemployment, and interest rates are at their lowest levels in years. Our dollar exchange rate is more competitive.
- Land values, the best indicator of farm prospects, have stabilized and are rising in many areas.
- Farm credit institutions, both public and private, are back on their feet.
- Farm debt has been reduced from $193 billion in 1983 to a projected $137 billion in 1988.
- Net farm income increased to its highest level ever in 1987, reaching $46 billion, while net cash income was also a record at $57 billion.
- We have reduced price-depressing surpluses to their lowest levels in many years. Total grain surpluses have been cut in half from their high in 1986.

In summary, increased agricultural exports, higher commodity and livestock prices, increased profits and land values, declining farm debt and surpluses, all these point to a healthier outlook for the rural economy.

The recovery is no accident. Republicans have acted decisively in the interest of rural America. Look at the record:

- In 1981, we immediately halted the Democrats' embargo on grain and other agricultural products and kept our pledge always to be a reliable supplier. We now reaffirm our promise never to use food as a weapon as was done by the last Democrat Administration.
- We have successfully opened more markets for our agricultural commodities and value-added products around the world through competitive pricing, aggressive use of the Export Enhancement Program, the Targeted Export Assistance Program, marketing loans, and generic commodity certificates.
- Through tough trade negotiations, we have opened markets abroad, including the Japanese beef and citrus markets. Numerous markets for specialty products have also been opened.
- We ended the notorious "widow's tax" so surviving spouses don't have to sell family farms and ranches to meet inheritance taxes. We also reduced other burdensome inheritance taxes for farm and ranch families.
- In 1985, President Reagan signed one of the most successful farm bills in modern history. The dual goals of protecting farm income while gaining back our lost markets are being achieved.
- We have given farmers the opportunity to profitably retire millions of acres of erodible and generally less productive land through the Conservation Reserve Program, and we enacted legislation to ensure that dollars will not be used to subsidize soil erosion or otherwise damage the environment that makes rural America a place where people want to live.

The Democrats offer nothing for the future of farming. Their plan for mandatory production controls would make productive and efficient American farmers beat a full-scale retreat from the world market:

- It would be a boon to family farms—in Argentina, Brazil, Canada, the European Community, Australia, and other competitor nations.
- It would pull the plug on rural Americans. It would sound a death-knell for rural towns and cities as land is taken from production. According to a United States Department of Agriculture study, it would reduce Gross National Product by $64 billion and wipe out 2.1 million jobs in the private sector.

In short, Democrats want to put farmers on welfare while Republicans want to look after the welfare of all rural Americans.

Our Global Economy

Better than most people, agriculturists know we live in a global economy. America's farmers, ranchers, foresters, and fishermen can compete against anyone in the world if trade rules are fair.

We recognize the historical contribution of agricultural exports to a positive national trade balance and will work on all fronts to improve agricultural trade.

Republicans will aggressively pursue fair and free trade for all U.S. products:

- We will insist that production-, consumption-, and trade-distorting agricultural subsidies of the European Economic Community and others be phased out simultaneously with the phasing out of our farm and export assistance programs.
- We will continue to put free and fair trade for farmers and ranchers on the agenda of every international conference on trade.
- We will use free agreements with good trading partners as leverage to open markets elsewhere.
- We will be a reliable supplier of agricultural products to world markets and will not use food as a weapon of foreign policy.

In short, instead of retreat, Republicans promise a full-scale assault on foreign markets.

The Future

Republicans will work to improve agricultural income through market returns at home and abroad, not government controls and subsidies:

- We pledge early action to renew and improve the successful farm programs set to expire in 1990.
- We pledge to continue international food assistance, including programs through the Eisenhower Food for Peace program, to feed the world's hungry and develop markets abroad.
- We will continue to provide leadership in the effort to improve standards of quality for grain and other agricultural products in order to meet international competition.
- We call for greater planting flexibility in federal programs to allow more diversity in farming and more freedom for farmers to grow what they want to grow and to sell their products to whoever will buy them.
- We recognize the need for appropriate multiple-use

policy on federal range lands and retention of a fair and equitable grazing fee policy as has been established by the Reagan Administration.

- We support a States' review of the adequacy of crop irrigation capacity under severe water shortage conditions, such as the 1988 drought, to identify areas of potential need and development.
- Water use policy formulation belongs to the States without federal interference; we recognize traditional State supremacy in water law, which is the best bulwark against future water crises.
- We resolve to lower tax for long-term capital gains and to work for fairer preproductive expense capitalization laws, including the so-called "heifer tax" as just one example, to promote investment in the production of food and fiber.
- We stand with the nation's foresters and the communities that depend on the forest products industry in supporting an annual timber harvest and multiple-use policy that meets national needs both for a sustained yield of wood products and for sound environmental management.
- We will continue our strong support for agricultural research, including increased emphasis on developing new uses for farm products, such as alternative fuels, food, non-food and industrial products. The agricultural industry is, and always has been, on the leading edge of the technological revolution, and it must continue this tradition in order to be internationally competitive.
- We will encourage public and private research and technical assistance to ensure that the resource base of American agriculture is preserved. Sound stewardship of our land and water resources is important for this and future generations. The soil and water resources of our nation must provide profit for farmers and ranchers and a safe and wholesome food supply. Our Land Grant institutions, working with the private sector, can provide more environmentally safe and biodegradable agrichemicals and improved farming techniques that will help preserve the quality of our underground and surface water supplies.
- We pledge that State farm home exemption and redemption rights shall remain inviolate from federal interference.

Rural Economic Development

Republicans realize that rural communities face challenges that go beyond agricultural concerns. Rural economic development is about more than jobs; it is also about the quality of life. We are ready to address the needs of rural America with creativity and compassion:

- The best jobs program for rural Americans is a good farm program.
- The key to rural development is effective local leadership working in partnership with private business and federal, State, and local governments. We will advance, in Congress and at the State level, rural enterprise zones to attract investment and create jobs geared to the opportunities of the century ahead.
- Education is the crucial element in ensuring that rural Americans will be tn the mainstream of our national future. We must assure rural youngsters quality education and good schools.
- The roads, bridges, schools, sewer and water systems, and other public works of many rural communities have deteriorated. We will ensure that those communities receive their fair share of aid under federal assistance programs.
- Discrimination against rural hospitals and medical practices in federal reimbursement of health care costs has contributed to reduced medical services in rural America. We pledge to help rural Americans meet their health care needs and will ensure fair treatment for their health care institutions under federal health programs.
- To have full participation in our country's unbounded future, rural people will need access to modern telecommunications and satellite communications systems including commercial decryption devices. Adequate supplies of reasonably priced electric power are also a necessity. We continue to support a strong rural electrification and telephone program. We believe the network of local rural electric and telephone cooperatives that provide these services represents a vital public/private partnership necessary to assure growth and development of the rural economy.
- We will energetically use the Job Training Partnership Act and a newly enacted worker retraining program to ensure that rural workers are fully integrated into the work force of the future.
- We will continue to support programs that enhance housing, business, and industry opportunities for rural Americans; and we will adapt urban homesteading programs to rural communities.
- Sound agricultural policy for rural America demands sound economic policy for all America. We will continue to stabilize fiscal and monetary policies in order to keep inflation in check and interest rates stable. This foundation of economic stability must underlie all rural initiatives by levels of government.

This is our pledge for the continuing renewal of a prosperous rural America.

ENERGY FOR THE FUTURE

To make real their vision for the future, the American people need adequate, safe, and reliable supplies of energy. Both the security of our nation and the prosperity of our households will depend upon clean and affordable power to light the way ahead and speed a daring society toward its goals. We recognize that energy is a security issue as well as an economic issue. We cannot have a strong nation if we are not energy independent.

We are partway there. In 1981, Republican leadership replaced the Democrats' energy crisis with energy consensus. We rejected scarcity, fostered growth, and set course for an expansive future. We left behind the days of gasoline lines, building-temperature controls, the multi-billion dollar boondoggle of the Synfuels Corporation, and the cancellation of night baseball games.

The Carter–Mondale years of crippling regulation and exorbitant costs are a thing of the past. We returned the country to policies that encourage rather than discourage domestic production of energy. With a free, more competitive system of producing and marketing energy, American consumers gained a wider range of energy choices at lower prices.

During the Reagan–Bush years, we loosened OPEC's hold on the world's petroleum markets. The United States built up its Strategic Petroleum Reserve and persuaded its allies to increase their emergency petroleum stocks as both a deterrent and a cushion against supply disruptions. When President Reagan and Vice President Bush took office, the Strategic Petroleum Reserve held only 79 million barrels. Now it contains almost 550 million, a three-month cushion in the event of a crisis.

Conservation and energy efficiency, stimulated by the oil shocks of the 1970s, made impressive gains. The nation now consumes less oil, and no more energy in total, than it did in 1977, even with the remarkable growth in our economy under the Reagan–Bush Administration.

Despite the gains, much hard work remains. A strong energy policy is required to assure that the needs of our society are met. Because of low prices, domestic oil and gas production has declined significantly. New initiatives will be required to halt the erosion of the domestic oil reserve base, to restore the vitality of the domestic oil and gas industry, to slow the rise in oil imports, and to prevent a return to the vulnerabilities of the 1970s. We must maintain the progress made in conservation and

rely more heavily on secure American fuels: domestic oil, natural gas, coal, nuclear energy, alternative sources and renewables.

Oil

The United States is heavily dependent on oil, which represents 40 percent of our total energy consumption. We must have a healthy domestic industry to assure the availability of this fuel to meet our needs. The decline in oil prices has brought exploratory drilling in the country to a virtual standstill, and continuing low prices threaten the hundreds of thousands of small wells that make up the most of U.S. production.

We will set an energy policy for the United States to maintain a viable core industry and to ensure greater energy self-sufficiency through private initiatives. We will adopt forceful initiatives to reverse the decline of our domestic oil production. Republicans support:

- Repeal of the counterproductive Windfall Profits Tax.
- Maintenance of our schedule for filling the Strategic Petroleum Reserve to reach 750 million barrels by 1993 and encouragement of our allies to maintain similar reserves.
- Tax incentives to save marginal wells, to encourage exploration for new oil, and to improve the recovery of oil still in place.
- Repeal of the Transfer Rule prohibiting independent producers from using certain tax provisions on acquired properties.
- Elimination of 80 percent of intangible drilling costs as an alternative minimum tax preference item.
- Exploration and development in promising areas, including federal lands and waters, particularly in the Arctic, in a manner that is protective of our environment and is in the best national interest.

Such continued exploration and development of new domestic oil and gas reserves are essential to keep our nation from becoming more dependent on foreign energy sources. Indeed, tax incentives can make our investment in U.S. oil and gas exploration competitive with other countries. They can stimulate drilling, put people back to work, and help maintain our leadership in oilfield technology and services. Incentives and opportunities for increased domestic exploration can also help limit the rise in imports, discourage oil price shocks, and enhance energy security.

Natural Gas

Natural gas is a clean, abundant, and reasonably priced fuel secure within the borders of the nation.

Increased reliance on gas can have significant national security and environmental benefits. While U.S. gas resources are plentiful and recoverable at competitive prices, regulatory burdens and price controls still impede development.

More progress must be made in deregulation of natural gas:

- We support fully decontrolling prices and providing more open access to transportation.
- We also support the flexible use of natural gas to fuel automobiles and boilers.

Over the longer term, natural gas as an alternative fuel could significantly reduce overdependence on imported oil, while also improving air quality. We should support cost-effective development and greater use of this fuel.

Coal

The United States enjoys a rich national endowment of enormous supplies of coal, which can provide a secure source of energy for hundreds of years.

- We should aggressively pursue the clean-coal technology initiative successfully launched by the Reagan–Bush Administration as part of the solution to coal's environmental problems.
- A major effort should be made to encourage coal exports, which could improve the trade balance, put Americans to work, and provide reliable supplies to our allies.

Nuclear Power

We must preserve nuclear power as a safe and economic option to meet future electricity needs. It generates 20 percent of our electricity, and we anticipate the continued expansion of renewable energy and environmentally safe nuclear power. We will promote the adoption of standardized, cost-effective, and environmentally safe nuclear plant designs. We should enhance our efforts to manage nuclear waste and will insist on the highest standards of safety.

Technology, Alternatives, Conservation, and Regulation

Technology is America's competitive edge, and it should be encouraged in finding new solutions to our energy problems. Energy efficiency improvements such as more efficient cars, better insulated homes, and more efficient industrial processes, have resulted in substantial savings, making the U.S. economy more competitive.

- We support funding for research and development, particularly where current market economics preclude private initiative.
- We will set priorities and, where cost-effective, support research and development for alternative fuels such as ethanol, methanol, and compressed natural gas, particularly for use in transportation.
- We will also support research and development for energy efficiency, conservation, renewables, fusion and superconductivity.
- We encourage the improvements of our national electricity transportation network, to achieve the economic and environmental efficiencies and reliability of linking electricity-exporting regions with importers.

Substantial progress has been made in eliminating the intrusive and costly regulative functions of the Department of Energy and should be continued. Efforts should be made to streamline the department's functions and evaluate its long institutional role in setting national energy policy, in discouraging a return to regulation, and in promoting long-term scientific research.

We believe continued economic progress requires an adequate and secure supply of electricity from every possible source in addition to energy conservation. Conservation alone cannot meet the energy needs of a growing economy. Witness the case of Massachusetts, where the State government's energy policy of stopping construction of any significant electric generating plants of all kinds has caused a dangerous shortage.

PRESERVING AND PROTECTING THE ENVIRONMENT

The Republican Party has a long and honored tradition of preserving our nation's natural resources and environment. We recognize that the preservation, conservation, and protection of our environment contribute to our health and well-being and that, as citizens, we all share in the responsibility to safeguard our God-given resources. A great Republican President, Teddy Roosevelt, once characterized our environmental challenge as "the great central task of leaving this land even a better land for our descendants than it is for us." Satisfying this imperative requires dedication and a commitment both to the protection of our environment and to the development of economic opportunities for all through a growing economy.

Republicans have led the efforts to protect the environment.

- We have dramatically reduced airborne lead contamination. This reduction has been perhaps the most important contribution to the health of Americans living in urban areas.

- By almost any measure, the air is vastly improved from the 1970s. Carbon monoxide, sulphur dioxide, ozone, nitrogen dioxide, and other emissions have declined substantially.
- We brought record numbers of enforcement cases against toxic polluters based on the principle that polluters should pay for the damages they cause.
- We pioneered an international accord for the protection of the stratospheric ozone layer, the first such international agreement.
- Dramatic progress has been made in protecting coastal barrier islands, in reducing coastal erosion, and in protecting estuaries.
- We have led the fight to clean up our Great Lakes and the Chesapeake and Narragansett Bays, some of the most unique and productive ecosystems on earth.
- We encouraged agricultural conservation, enhanced our wetlands, and preserved and restored our National Parks, which had suffered tragic neglect in the years preceding the Reagan–Bush Administration.
- Under Republican leadership, the most important soil conservation measure of the last half-century became law as the Conservation Title of the 1985 Farm Bill.
- We established 34 national wildlife refugees in 21 States and territories.
- We reformed U.S. and international aid programs to assist developing nations to assure environmental protection.

Republicans look to the environmental future with confidence in the American people and with a renewed commitment to world leadership in environmental protection. We recognize the necessary role of the federal government only in matters that cannot be managed by regional cooperation or by levels of government closer to the people. Cooperative action by all is needed to advance the nation's agenda for a cleaner, safer environment.

The toughest challenges lie ahead of us. Republicans propose the following program for the environment in the 1990s:

- We will work for further reductions in air and water pollution and effective actions against the threats posed by acid rain. These goals can and must be achieved without harmful economic dislocation.
- We are committed to minimizing the release of toxins into the environment.
- We will continue to lead the effort to develop new clean-coal technologies and to remove the barriers

that prevent cleaner, alternative fuels from being used.

- We support a comprehensive plan of action to fight coastal erosion and to protect and restore the nation's beaches, coral reefs, bodies of water, wetlands, and estuaries such as the Louisiana coast, Chesapeake Bay, the Great Lakes, San Francisco Bay, Puget Sound, Narragansett Bay, and other environmentally sensitive areas. The restoration of these areas will continue to be a priority.
- A top priority of our country must be the continued improvement of our National Parks and wildlife areas. We must upgrade our recreation, fisheries, and wildlife programs in parks, wildlife refuges, forests, and other public lands. We support efforts, including innovative public–private partnerships, to restore declining waterfowl populations and enhance recreational fisheries.
- We will fight to protect endangered species and to sustain biological diversity worldwide.
- We support federal, State, and local policies, including tax code provisions, which lead to the renewal and revitalization of our environment through restoration, and which encourage scenic easements designed to preserve farmland and open spaces.
- We believe public lands should not be transferred to any special group in a manner inconsistent with current Reagan–Bush Administration policy. To the extent possible, consistent with current policy, we should keep public lands open and accessible.
- We will protect the productive capacity of our lands by minimizing erosion.
- We are committed to the historic preservation of our American heritage, including our architectural, archeological, and maritime resources.
- We support strong enforcement of our environmental laws and will accelerate the pace of our national effort to clean up hazardous waste sites and to protect our groundwater. We will promote proper use of fertilizers and pesticides to minimize pollution of groundwater.
- Republicans recognize that toxic and hazardous waste production is increasing. Therefore, we will utilize the nation's scientific community to develop solutions to this waste disposal dilemma as an alternative to the continued burying, exporting, and ocean dumping of these dangerous substances, as they are no more than stop-gap measures with extremely tragic potential.
- We are committed to solving our country's increasing problem of waste disposal. By 1995, half of our existing landfills will be closed, and municipalities will have increased difficulty finding new sites. This

is an issue which will require the dedication and re-solve of our local communities, the private sector, and all of us as citizens. Resource recovery, recycling, and waste minimization are critical elements of our solution, and we will work to ensure that innovative approaches to the problem are encouraged.

- We are determined to prevent dumping off our coasts and in international waters. Ocean dumping poses a hazard not only to marine life, but also to those who live along our coasts and to those who use them for recreation. Where federal laws have been violated, we will prosecute polluters to the full extent of the law, including adherence to the 1991 federal ban on ocean dumping of sewage sludge. Where laws need to be strengthened, we will work in the federal, State, and local levels to do so.
- We will support all serious efforts to cope with the special problems of illegal dumping of hospital and medical waste. We pledge close cooperation by the Environmental Protection Agency with States and industry groups to develop new approaches to the most cost-effective means for the safe disposal by responsible medical facilities. Those who continue to dump illegally threaten the very life and health of our communities, and we call for enactment of the States of tough new felony laws that will permit swift prosecution of these criminals.
- We will require that federal departments and agencies meet or exceed the environmental standards set for citizens in the private sector.

Many of the most serious environmental problems that will confront us in the years ahead are global in scope. For example, degradation of the stratospheric ozone layer poses a health hazard not only to Americans, but to all peoples around the globe. The Reagan–Bush Administration successfully pioneered an agreement to attack this problem through world-wide action. In addition, we will continue to lead this effort by promoting private sector initiatives to de-velop new technologies and adopt processes which protect the ozone layer. A similar ability to develop in-ternational agreements to solve complex global prob-lems such as tropical forest destruction, ocean dump-ing, climate change, and earthquakes will be increasingly vital in the years ahead. All of these ef-forts will require strong and experienced leadership to lead the other nations of the world in a common effort to combat ecological dangers that threaten all peoples. The Republican Party believes that, toward this end, the National Oceanic and Atmospheric Adminis-tration should be joined with the Environmental Protection Agency.

We all have a stake in maintaining the environmen-tal balance and ecological health of our planet and our country. As Republicans, we hold that it is of critical importance to preserve our national heritage. We must assure that programs for economic growth and oppor-tunity sustain the natural abundance of our land and waters and protect the health and well-being of our citizens. As a nation, we should take pride in our ac-complishments and look forward to fulfilling our obligation of leaving this land an even better place for our children and future generations.

TRANSPORTATION FOR AMERICA

Republican leadership has revitalized America's trans-portation system. Through regulatory reform, we in-creased efficiency in all major modes of transportation. By making our national transportation system safer, more convenient, and less expensive, we have both strengthened our economy and served the interests of all the American people:

- Aviation deregulation now saves consumers $11 bil-lion annually through improved productivity and lower air fares. Millions more Americans can now afford to fly. Even though more people are flying, the overall safety record for commercial aviation during the past four years has been the best in his-tory.
- The National Airspace System (NAS) Plan is up-grading virtually all the equipment in the air traffic control system to meet safety and capacity needs into the next century.
- Rail freight service has been rescued from the brink of insolvency and revitalized. Railroads have low-ered rates for many shippers, helping to keep the transportation cost of coal-generated electric power down and making America's farmers more compet-itive abroad.
- The creation of regional and short-line railroads has been encouraged by the Reagan–Bush Adminis-tration. The development of these small businesses has been a welcome alternative to railroad aban-donments, and we will continue to encourage their growth.
- The Reagan–Bush Administration achieved new rail safety legislation, which expands federal jurisdic-tion over drug, alcohol, and safety violations.
- America's trucking industry has also been im-proved. The number of motor carriers has more than doubled since regulatory barriers to competi-tion were removed. Many of these new carriers are

small or minority-owned businesses. Private enterprise has thus been able to restructure routes, reduce empty backhauls, and simplify rates. Reduced regulation saves the American consumer $37 billion annually in lower freight bills, making businesses in every part of America more competitive.

- The successful sale of Conrail through a public offering recouped nearly $2 billion dollars of the taxpayers' investment in bankrupt railroads from the 1970s.
- The Reagan–Bush Administration has undertaken a comprehensive program to upgrade federal interstate highways and bridges.
- Through highway improvements, education, and federal encouragement of tougher State laws against drunk driving, highway safety has vastly improved.

As we look to the future, the Republican Party will continue to press for improved transportation safety, reduced costs, and greater availability and convenience of transportation through more open markets and other mechanisms. The Republican Party believes that:

- Americans demand that those entrusted with their safety while operating commercial motor vehicles, railroads, or aircraft not use drugs or alcohol. While we will protect individual rights, the Republican Party supports comprehensive efforts to curb drug and alcohol abuse in transportation, including drug and alcohol testing of all those in safety-related positions.
- Our transportation system is based upon a vast public and private investment in infrastructure, which must continue to grow and to be maintained to meet America's needs. We advocate greater local autonomy in decision making concerning the Highway Trust Fund and the Airport and Airway Trust Fund, and we oppose diversion of their resources to other purposes.
- Research should be developed for new technologies to deal with urban gridlock and congested highways.
- The travel and tourism industry is a positive force in enhancing cultural understanding and sustaining economic prosperity. We recognize its important contributions and should work to encourage its continued growth.
- The federal government and local communities must work together to develop additional airport capacity of all types. At the same time, we support timely completion of the National Airspace System Plan and continuing augmentation of air traffic control and aircraft inspection personnel.

- We will further increase American jobs and trade opportunity by assuring that American air carriers are afforded full and fair access to international route authorities.
- We will not abandon the economic flexibility that has so enormously strengthened the health of our railroads and so powerfully benefited the American economy.
- Development of high speed rail systems to meet the needs of intercity travel should be encouraged.
- Year by year since 1981, Amtrak operations have shown improvement. Amtrak's ratio of revenues to costs stood at 48 percent in 1981. Last year, 65 percent of the costs were covered by revenues. Fiscal year 1988 will see the ratio pushing 70 percent. We recognize that intercity rail passenger service plays an important role in our transportation system. At the same time, we support continued reductions in public subsidies.
- A new spirit of competitive enterprise in transportation throughout all levels of government should be encouraged. We will encourage both States and cities to utilize private companies, where effective, to operate commuter bus and transit services at substantial savings over what publicly funded systems cost.
- The engines of innovation powered by regulatory reform have brought forth exciting advances in the technology of trucking, rail, and shipping, particularly as they work together as an integrated system for the movement of goods domestically and abroad. Alternative fuels that are clean and efficient will both improve air quality and reduce our dependence on imported oil in meeting transportation needs. These technological approaches are far preferable to outmoded regulation, such as the current design of Corporate Average Fuel Economy (CAFE) standards, which create substantial advantages for foreign auto manufacturers and actually promote the export of U.S. jobs.
- We consider a privately owned merchant fleet and domestic shipbuilding capacity necessary to carry our nation's commerce in peace and to support our defense responsibilities. We will support programs to give the American maritime industry greater flexibility and freedom in meeting foreign competition.
- We are committed to continuing the Reagan–Bush Administration efforts to stop foreign protectionism that inhibits U.S. flag vessels from fairly competing abroad.
- Maritime safety, search and rescue, military preparedness, environmental and fisheries enforcement, and drug interdiction have long been the respons-

ibility of the U.S. Coast Guard. The Republican Party supports all of these vital roles, and will support funding and manpower adequate to enable the Coast Guard to carry out its responsibilities.

AMERICA LEADING THE WORLD

Under the leadership of President Ronald Reagan and Vice President George Bush, America has led the world through eight years of peace and prosperity.

In the years since 1980, our nation has become in fact what it has always been in principle, "the last best hope of mankind on earth."

Republicans know that free nations are peace loving and do not threaten other democracies. To the extent, therefore, that democracies are established in the world, America will be safer. Consequently, our nation has a compelling interest to encourage and help actively to build the conditions of democracy wherever people strive for freedom.

In 1961, President John Kennedy said, "We shall pay any price, bear any burden, meet any hardship, support any friend, oppose any foe to assure the survival and success of liberty." Seeds sown by the Reagan–Bush Administration to make good on that promise are now bearing fruit.

Today's Republican Party has the only legitimate claim to this legacy, for our opposition to totalitarianism is resolute. For those Democrats who came of age politically under the party of Truman and Kennedy, the message is clear: The old Democrat world view of realistic anticommunism, with real freedom as its goal, has been abandoned by today's national Democrat Party.

In the tradition of the Republican Party, we have long-term foreign policy goals and objectives which provide vision and leadership. We also have a *realistic*, long-term strategy to match those goals. The primary objectives of foreign policy must be defending the United States of America and its people; protecting America's vital national interests abroad; and fostering peace, stability and security throughout the world through democratic self-determination and economic prosperity.

To accomplish these goals, we believe our policies must be built upon three basic pillars: strength, realism, and dialogue.

Republican foreign policy, based on a peace preserved by steadfastly providing for our own security, brought us the INF treaty, which eliminated an entire class of nuclear weapons. America's determination and will, coupled with our European allies' staunch cooperation, brought the Soviets to the bargaining table and won meaningful reductions in nuclear weapons. The INF treaty was not won by unilateral concessions or the unilateral canceling of weapons programs.

Today's Republican foreign policy has been tested and validated. Our formula for success is based on a realistic assessment of the world as it is, not as some would like it to be. The Soviet retreat from Afghanistan is not the result of luck or the need of the Kremlin to save a few rubles. It is a direct result of a Republican policy known as the Reagan Doctrine: our determination to provide meaningful aid to people who would rather die on their feet than live on their knees under the yoke of Soviet-supported oppression. Support for freedom-fighters, coupled with an openness to negotiate, will be the model for our resistance to Marxist expansionism elsewhere.

The world expects the United States to lead. Republicans believe it is in our country's best interest to continue to do so. For this reason, we will engage both our adversaries and friends. We share a common interest in survival and peaceful competition. However, the Reagan–Bush administration has shown that dialogue and engagement can be successful only if undertaken from a position of strength. We know something the national Democrats seem to have forgotten: If a foreign policy is based upon weakness or unrealistic assumptions about the world, it is doomed to failure. If it is based upon naivete, it will be doomed to disaster.

Under our constitutional system, the execution of foreign policy is the prime responsibility of the executive branch. We therefore denounce the excessive interference in this function by the current Democrat majority in the Congress, as it creates the appearance of weakness and confusion and endangers the successful conduct of American foreign policy.

The world in 1988 shows the success of peace through strength and the Reagan Doctrine advancing America's national interests. Our relations with the Soviets are now based on these determined and realistic policies. Results such as the INF treaty are a concrete example of the soundness of this approach:

- The Afghan people are on the verge of ridding their country of Soviet occupation, and with our continued support they can secure true liberty.
- In Southeast Asia, our policies of isolation toward Vietnam and our support for the Cambodian resistance have contributed to Vietnam's decision to get out of Cambodia.
- In southern Africa, Cuban troops may soon be leaving Angola; Namibia may soon enjoy independence.

- The Iran–Iraq war is closer to a settlement due to the strong leadership of the Reagan–Bush Administration in the United Nations and the American presence in the Persian Gulf.

The party Abraham Lincoln helped to establish—the party of Teddy Roosevelt, Dwight Eisenhower, Ronald Reagan, and George Bush—today offers the United States of America continued leadership, strong and effective. The President of the United States must be a good Commander-in-Chief; the Oval Office is no place for on-the-job training. The Republican Party, tempered by real-world experience, accustomed to making tough choices, is prepared to lead America forward into the 1990s.

The Americas

Our future is intimately tied to the future of the Americas. Family, language, culture, environment, and trade link us closely with both Canada and Mexico. Our relations with both of these friends will be based upon continuing cooperation and our mutually shared interests. Our attention to trade and environmental issues will contribute to strong economic growth and prosperity throughout the Americas.

Today, more Latin Americans than ever before live free because of their partnership with the United States to promote self-determination, democracy, and an end to subversion. The Republican Party reaffirms its strong support for the Monroe Doctrine as the foundation for our policy throughout the hemisphere, and pledges to conduct foreign policy in accord with its principles. We thereby seek not only to provide for our own security, but also to create a climate for democracy and self-determination throughout the Americas.

Central America has always been a region of strategic importance to the United States. There, Nicaragua has become a Soviet client state like Cuba. Democratic progress in the region is threatened directly by the Sandinista military machine and armed subversion exported from Nicaragua, Cuba, and the Soviet Union. The Sandinistas are now equipped with Soviet arms which, in quality and quantity, are far in excess of their own defense requirements.

The people of Nicaragua are denied basic human, religious, and political rights by the Sandinista junta. Today, thousands of Nicaraguans are united in a struggle to free their homeland from a totalitarian regime. The Republican Party stands shoulder to shoulder with them in this struggle and is committed to assist them with both humanitarian and military aid. Peace without freedom for the Nicaraguan people is not good enough.

If democracy does not prevail, if Nicaragua remains a communist dictatorship dedicated to exporting revolution, the fragile democracies in Central America will be jeopardized. The Republican Party stands with them in their struggle for peace, freedom, and economic growth. We express our emphatic support for the people and government of El Salvador, a target of foreign-directed insurgency. Under Republican leadership, the United States should respond to requests from our Central American neighbors for security assistance to protect their emerging democracies against insurgencies sponsored by the Soviets, Cuba, or others.

Democracy continues to prosper in El Salvador, Guatemala, Honduras, and in Costa Rica, the region's oldest democracy. However, economic growth in these countries has not matched their political progress. The United States must take the lead in strengthening democratic institutions through economic development based on free-market principles. We pledge our continued support to the peoples of the Americas who embrace and sustain democratic principles in their self-government.

A Republican Administration will continue to promote policy reforms to free the private sector in Central America, such as deregulation of enterprise and privatization of government operations. We will assist friendly democracies in reviving the institutions of regional economic cooperation and integration, and will allow Nicaragua to participate when it enjoys a free, pluralist society and respects free-market principles.

The growth of democracy and freedom throughout Latin America is one of the most positive foreign policy developments of the 1980s. Republican leadership has created the environment necessary for this growth. Over the past decade, Latin Americans have moved boldly toward democracy, with 26 of 33 nations now democratic or in transition toward democracy. Mexico has a special strategic and economic importance to the United States, and we encourage close cooperation across a wide variety of fronts in order to strengthen further this critical relationship.

We believe the governments of Latin America must band together to defeat the drug trade which now flourishes in the region. We must pledge our full cooperation and support for efforts to induce producers of illicit drug crops to substitute other methods of generating income.

Republicans will continue to oppose any normalization of relations with the government of Cuba as long as Fidel Castro continues to oppress the Cuban people at home and to support international terrorism and drug trafficking abroad. We will vigorously continue our support for establishment of a genuinely representative government directly elected by the Cuban people. We reiterate our support of Radio Marti and urge the creation of TV Marti to better reach the oppressed people of Cuba.

Panama now poses a different challenge to the regional progress made over the past eight years. Our policy must be as firm with respect to military authoritarianism and narco-terrorism as it is with communist tyranny and guerrilla subversion. That policy must include a determined effort to bring to justice any identified narco-terrorist or drug dealer within his or her country of residence or in the courts of the United States of America. Republicans view the Panama Canal as a critical, strategic artery connecting the Atlantic and Pacific. We believe that U.S. access to the Panama Canal must remain free and unencumbered, consistent with the foremost principle of the Canal Treaty. We acknowledge, however, the historical partnership and friendship between the American and Panamanian people.

Republicans believe that an active, engaged America, clear of purpose and steady in action, is essential to continued progress in Latin America. Passivity and neglect are a sure prescription for the reversal of freedom and peace in Latin America.

The Soviet Union: New Challenges and Enduring Realities

Steady American leadership is needed now more than ever to deal with the challenges posed by a rapidly changing Soviet Union. Americans cannot afford a future administration which eagerly attempts to embrace perceived, but as yet unproven, changes in Soviet policy. Nor can we indulge naive inexperience or an overly enthusiastic endorsement of current Soviet rhetoric.

The current leaders in the Soviet Union came to power while the United States was undergoing an unsurpassed political, economic, and military resurgence. The Reagan–Bush success story—new jobs and unprecedented economic growth combined with reasserted leadership of the free world—was not lost on the new Soviet regime. It had inherited a bankrupt economy, a society with a Third-World standard of living, and military power based upon the sweat of the Soviet worker. Confronted by the failure of their system, the new Soviet leaders have been forced to search for new solutions.

Republicans are proud that it was a Republican President who extended freedom's hand and message to the Soviet Union. It will be a new Republican President who can best build on that progress, ever

cautious of communism's long history of expansionism and false promises. We are prepared to embrace real reform, but we will not leave America unprepared should reform prove illusory.

Soviet calls for global peace and harmony ring hollow when compared with ongoing Soviet support for communist guerrillas and governments throughout the Third World. Even in Afghanistan, the Soviet Union is in retreat not as a result of a more benevolent Soviet worldview, but because of the courage of determined Mujahidin freedom-fighters fully supported by the United States.

The Soviet military continues to grow. Tanks and aircraft continue to roll off Soviet production lines at a rate two to three times that of the United States. Soviet military doctrine remains offensive in nature, as illustrated by the intimidating presence of massed Soviet tank divisions in Eastern Europe. This is the reality of Soviet military posture.

With a realistic view of the Soviet Union and the appropriate role of arms reductions in the U.S.-Soviet relationship, the Reagan–Bush administration concluded the historic INF agreement with the Soviet Union. Ongoing negotiations with the Soviet Union to reduce strategic nuclear weapons by 50 percent are possible because the American people trust Republican leadership. The American people know that, for Republicans, no agreement is better than an agreement detrimental to the security of the free world. To pursue arms control for its own sake or at any cost is naive and dangerous.

Republicans will continue to work with the new Soviet leadership. But the terms of the relationship will be based upon persistent and steady attention to certain fundamental principles:

- Human and religious rights in the Soviet Union.
- Economic reform in the Soviet Union.
- Cessation of Soviet support for communist regimes, radical groups, and terrorists.
- Verified full compliance with all arms control agreements.
- The right of free emigration for all Soviet citizens.
- Reduction in the Soviets' massive offensive strategic and conventional capability. In other words, Soviet military doctrine must match its rhetoric.
- An end to untied credits, particularly general purpose loans which provide the Soviet Union with desperately needed hard currency to bolster its weak economy and facilitate illicit Soviet purchase of U.S. technology.

Republicans proudly reaffirm the Reagan Doctrine: America's commitment to aid freedom-fighters against the communist oppression which destroys freedom and the human spirit. We salute the liberation of Grenada. We affirm our support for the heroic fighters in the Afghan resistance and pledge to see them through to the end of their struggle. We pledge political and material support to democratic liberation movements around the world.

Republicans believe human rights are advanced most where freedom is advanced first. We call on the Soviet government to release political prisoners, allow free emigration for "refuseniks" and others, and introduce full religious tolerance. Soviet Jews, Christians, Armenians, and other ethnic and religious groups are systematically persecuted, denied the right to emigrate, and prevented from freely practicing their religious beliefs. This situation is intolerable, and Republicans demand an end to all of these discriminatory practices.

We support the desire for freedom and self-determination of all those living in captive nations. The Republican Party denounces the oppression of the national free will of Poles, Hungarians, Czechoslovakians, East Germans, Bulgarians, Romanians, and Albanians. We support the desire for freedom of Estonians, Latvians, Lithuanians, Ukrainians, the people of the Caucasus, and other peoples held captive in the Soviet Union. We support the Solidarity free trade union movement in Poland.

We find the violation of human rights on the basis of religion or culture to be morally repugnant to the values we hold. Historical tragedies—like the Holocaust or the terrible persecution suffered by the Armenian people—vividly remind us of the need for vigilance in protecting and promoting human rights. We and others must ensure that such tragedies occur never again.

The Republican Party commends the Reagan–Bush Administration for its far-sighted efforts to modernize our electronic tools of public diplomacy to reach the captive nations. The Voice of America, Worldnet, Radio Free Europe and Radio Liberty are on the leading edge of our public diplomacy efforts. These electronic means of communication are force-multipliers of truth. They attack one of the darkest pillars of totalitarianism: the oppression of people through the control of information. We urge the further use of advanced technologies such as direct broadcast satellites and videotape, as well as continuing use of television and radio broadcasting, to articulate the values of individual liberty throughout the world.

Combating Narcotics: Defending Our Children

By eradication at the source, interdiction in transit, education and deterrence against use, prompt extradition of drug kingpins, or rehabilitation, America must be drug free. No nation can remain free when its children are enslaved by drugs.

We consider drugs a major national security threat to the United States.

We urge all nations to unite against this evil. Although we salute our hemispheric neighbors who are fighting the war on drugs, we expect all nations to help stop this deadly commerce. We pledge aggressive interdiction and eradication, with strong penalties against countries which shield or condone the narcotics traffic.

Republicans are proud of the fact that we have dramatically increased the interdiction of dangerous drugs. For example, over the past six years, our annual seizure of cocaine has increased by over 1,500 percent. While much has been accomplished in eradicating drugs at the source and in transit, much more remains to be done.

We will use our armed forces in the war on drugs to the maximum extent possible. We must emphasize their special capabilities in surveillance and command and control for interdiction and in special operations for eradication of drugs at the source.

To fight international drug trade, we will stress the swift extradition of traffickers. We support a comprehensive use of America's resources to apprehend and convict drug dealers. To enforce anti-drug policy, we pledge to enhance eradication efforts with increased herbicide use; regulate exports of "precursor chemicals" used in the manufacture of illicit drugs; train and equip cooperating government law-enforcement agencies; emphasize a strategy to "choke off" drug supply routes; and impose the death penalty for drug kingpins and those who kill federal law enforcement agents.

Europe and the Defense of the West

The United States and Europe share a wide array of political, economic, and military relationships, all vitally important to the United States. Together they represent a growing, multifaceted bond between America and the European democracies.

Culturally, as well as militarily, we share common goals with Western Europe. The preservation of liberty is first among these. We will not allow the cultural, economic, or political domination of Western Europe by the Soviet Union. Our own national security requires it, for our democracy cannot flourish in isolation. The United States, led by the Reagan–Bush Administration, and our European allies have successfully reasserted democracy's ideological appeal. This formula is without equal for political and economic progress.

Republicans believe that the continued growth of trade between Europe and the United States is in the best interest of both the American people and their European friends. However, this economic relationship must be based upon the principle of free and fair trade. Protectionism and other barriers to American products will not be tolerated. The American people demand economic fair play in U.S.-European trade.

The recently signed INF treaty has proven that NATO's dual track policy of improving NATO nuclear forces in Europe, while negotiating arms reductions with the Soviet Union, was the only way to make the Soviet leadership accept meaningful nuclear arms reductions. NATO's cohesion as an alliance, when assaulted by Soviet propaganda attacks during the 1980s, proved its resilience. Bolstered by the strong leadership of the United States, Europe stood firm in opposing Soviet demands for a nuclear freeze and unilateral disarmament.

American aid and European industriousness have restored Western Europe to a position of global strength. In accord with this, the Republican Party believes that all members of NATO should bear their fair share of the defense burden.

Republicans consider consultation and cooperation with our allies and friends to stop the proliferation of ballistic missile technology a crucial allied goal. We believe that continued support for the Strategic Defense Initiative will yield the type of defensive insurance policy the American people want for themselves and their allies.

We share a deep concern for peace and justice in Northern Ireland and condemn all violence and terrorism in that strife-torn land. We support the process of peace and reconciliation established by the Anglo-Irish Agreement, and we encourage new investment and economic reconstruction in Northern Ireland on the basis of strict equality of opportunity and nondiscrimination in employment.

The Republican Party strongly encourages the peaceful settlement of the long-standing dispute on Cyprus.

The future of U.S. relations with Europe is one of endless opportunity and potential. Increased cooperation and consultation will necessarily lead to greater economic, political and military integration, thus strengthening the natural bonds between the democratic peoples on both sides of the Atlantic. This will require a seasoned American leadership, able to build on the achievements of the Reagan–Bush Administration and prepared to lead the alliance into the 1990s and beyond.

Asia and the Pacific

Democratic capitalism is transforming Asia. Nations of the Pacific Rim have become colleagues in the enterprise of freedom. They have shown a strong capacity for economic growth and capital development.

The Asia-Pacific arena continues to be a vital strategic interest for the U.S. and is an area of increased military, economic, and diplomatic activity for the Soviet Union.

Japan has assumed the role earned by her people as a world economic power. The GOP believes that our relations can only be strengthened by attacking trade barriers, both tariff and non-tariff, which not only hurt the U.S. now but also will eventually distort Japan's own economy. We believe that it is time for Japan to assume a greater role in this region and elsewhere. This should include a greater commitment to its own defense, commitment to leading the way in alleviating Third World debt, and fostering economic growth in fragile democracies.

Today, democracy is renewed on Taiwan, the Philippines, and South Korea, and is emerging elsewhere in the area. We pledge full cooperation in mutual defense of the Philippines and South Korea, and the maintenance of our troops and bases vital for deterring aggression. The United States, with its friends and allies, will strengthen democratic institutions in the Philippines by assisting in its economic development and growth. We reaffirm our commitment to the security of Taiwan and other key friends and allies in the region. We regard any attempt to alter Taiwan's status by force as a threat to the entire region. We adhere to the Taiwan Relations Act, the basis for our continuing cooperation with those who have loyally stood with us, and fought at our side, for half a century.

Today, the communist regime of the People's Republic of China looks to free-market practices to salvage its future from stagnant Marxism. We welcome this development. As we draw closer in our relationship, the Republican Party believes that we must continue to encourage the abandonment of political repression in the People's Republic of China and movement toward a free market. We also look toward continued improvement in mutually beneficial trade between our two nations.

We recognize the significant progress made by the Reagan–Bush Administration to assure the end of the Soviet occupation of Afghanistan. We will continue to press for self-determination and the establishment of a genuinely representative government directly elected by the Afghan people. We pledge to continue full military and humanitarian support and supplies for the resistance until complete Soviet withdrawal is realized.

We commend the government of Pakistan for its opposition to the Soviet occupation of Afghanistan and its support of the Afghan people, particularly its refugees. We reaffirm our friendship and will continue the strong security assistance relationship between the United States and Pakistan.

We will press for the withdrawal of Vietnamese occupation of Laos and Cambodia and will continue support for the efforts of the non-communist resistance.

Republicans insist that Vietnam, Laos, and Cambodia must provide adequate information on American POWs and MIAs. The grief of the POW and MIA families is a constant reminder to all Americans of the patriotic sacrifice made by their missing loved ones. Republicans will not rest until we know the fate of those missing in Indochina. We will continue to press relentlessly for a full accounting of America's POWs and MIAs. We put the government of Vietnam on notice that there will be no improvement in U.S.–Vietnam relations until such a satisfactory full accounting has been provided by the government of Vietnam.

Republicans are committed to providing assistance for refugees fleeing Vietnam, Laos, and Cambodia. Republicans strongly believe that the promise of asylum for these refugees must be met by adequate resources and vigorous administration of refugee programs. We will increase efforts to resettle Vietnamese refugees under the orderly departure program. We are particularly committed to assisting the resettlement of Amerasian children against whom brutal discrimination is practiced.

We recognize the close and special ties we have maintained with Thailand since the days of Abraham Lincoln. Thailand stands tall against the imperialist aggression of Vietnam and the Soviet Union in Southeast Asia.

Republicans strongly support our traditional, close bilateral relations with our ally Australia. We also look forward to a rejuvenation of the ANZUS alliance with its benefits and responsibilities to all partners.

The Middle East

The foundation of our policy in the Middle East has been and must remain the promotion of a stable and lasting peace, recognizing our moral and strategic relationship with Israel. More than any of its predecessors, the Reagan–Bush Administration solidified this partnership. As a result, the relations between the United States and Israel are closer than ever before.

We will continue to maintain Israel's qualitative advantage over any adversary or coalition of adversaries.

We will continue to solidify our strategic relationship with Israel by taking additional concrete steps to further institutionalize the partnership. This will include maintaining adequate levels of security and eco-

nomic assistance; continuing our meetings on military, political and economic cooperation and coordination; prepositioning military equipment; developing joint contingency plans; and increasing joint naval and air exercises. The growth of the Soviet military presence in the Eastern Mediterranean and along NATO's southern flank has demonstrated the importance of developing and expanding the U.S.–Israel strategic relationship.

We oppose the creation of an independent Palestinian state; its establishment is inimical to the security interests of Israel, Jordan and the U.S. We will not support the creation of any Palestinian entity that could place Israel's security in jeopardy.

Republicans will build upon the efforts of the Reagan–Bush Administration and work for peace between Israel and her Arab neighbors based upon the following principles:

- A just and lasting peace is essential, urgent, and can be reached only through direct negotiations between Israel and the Arab nations.
- Peace treaties must be reached through direct negotiations and must never be imposed upon unwilling partners.
- The PLO should have no role in the peace process unless it recognizes Israel's right to exist, accepts United Nations Security Council resolutions 242 and 338, renounces terrorism, and removes language from its charter demanding Israel's destruction.

Under Republican leadership, the United States will explore every opportunity to move forward the peace process toward direct negotiations as long as the security of Israel is not compromised. Much work remains to establish a climate in the Middle East where the legitimate rights of all parties, including the Palestinians, can be equitably addressed.

We recognize that Israel votes with the United States at the United Nations more frequently than any other nation. The Reagan–Bush Administration supported legislation mandating that if the U.N. and its agencies were to deny Israel's right to participate, the United States would withhold financial support and withdraw from those bodies until their action was rectified. The Republican Party reaffirms its support for the rescission of U.N. Resolution 3379, which equates Zionism with racism. Failure to repeal that resolution will justify attenuation of our support for the U.N.

We believe that Jerusalem should remain an undivided city, with free and unimpeded access to all holy places by people of all faiths.

Republicans see Egypt as a catalyst in the Arab world for advancing the cause of regional peace and security. For this reason, we believe that the United States has a significant stake in Egypt's continuing economic development and growth. As the only Arab nation to have formally made peace with Israel, it is reaping the benefits. Egypt's support of the Camp David Accords demonstrates that an Arab nation can make peace with Israel, be an ally of the United States, and remain in good standing in the Arab world. Republicans support the Reagan–Bush Administration's formal designation of Egypt as a major non-NATO ally.

Our continued support of Egypt and other pro-Western Arab states is an essential component of Republican policy. In support of that policy, we deployed a naval task force to join with allies to keep the sea lanes open during the Iran–Iraq war. We also recognize the important role the moderate Arab states play in supporting U.S. security interests.

Republicans will continue to build on the Reagan–Bush achievement of increased security cooperation with the pro-Western Arab states. We recognize that these Arab nations maintain friendly relations with the United States in the face of potential retaliation attempts by radical elements in the Middle East.

Continuing strife in Lebanon is not in the interest of the U.S. Until order is established, Lebanon will be a source of international terrorism and regional instability. To reestablish normalcy in Lebanon, the U.S. must strengthen the hand of the overwhelming majority of Lebanese, who are committed to an independent, peaceful, and democratic Lebanon.

In order to achieve this goal, we will base the policy of the United States on the principles of the unity of Lebanon; the withdrawal of all foreign forces; the territorial integrity of Lebanon; the reestablishment of its government's authority; and the reassertion of Lebanese sovereignty throughout the nation, with recognition that its safekeeping must be the responsibility of the Lebanese government. We will strive to help Lebanon restore its society so that, in the future as in the past, religious groups will live in harmony, international commerce will flourish and international terrorism will not exist.

For nearly four decades, U.S. policy in the Persian Gulf has reflected American strategic, economic, and political interests in the area. Republican policy has three fundamental objectives:

- Maintaining the free flow of oil.
- Preventing the expansion of Soviet influence.
- Supporting the independence and stability of the states in the region.

By pursuing these goals, we have created the political leverage to begin the process of ending the Iran–Iraq war. Our re-flagging of Kuwaiti ships limited the expansion of both Iranian and Soviet influence in the region.

Africa

Republicans have three priorities in our country's relations with Africa. The first is to oppose the forces of Marxist imperialism, which sustain the march of tyranny in Africa. This priority includes giving strong assistance to groups which oppose Soviet and Cuban-sponsored oppression in Africa.

Our second priority is the need to develop and sustain democracies in Africa. Democrats have often taken the view that democracy is unattainable because of Africa's economic condition, yet at the same time they refuse to promote the conditions in which democracies can flourish. Economic freedom and market-based economies are the key to the development of democracy throughout Africa.

Our third area of concern is humanitarian assistance, especially food aid, to African nations. The Reagan–Bush Administration has always provided this assistance.

Republicans salute the Reagan–Bush Administration for responding with characteristic American compassion to famine conditions in Africa by providing record amounts of food, medical supplies, and other lifesaving assistance. In spite of our efforts, the people of Africa continue to suffer. Republicans condemn the cynical Marxist governments, especially in Ethiopia, which used planned starvation as a weapon of war and a tool for forced migration.

The recent African drought and resulting famine were not just natural disasters. They were made worse by poorly conceived development projects which stripped lands of their productive capacity. Republicans recognize that protecting the natural resource base of developing nations is essential to protecting future economic opportunities and assuring stable societies. We are leading the fight worldwide to require sound environmental planning as part of foreign development programs.

We believe that peace in southern Africa can best be achieved by the withdrawal of all foreign forces from Angola, complete independence and self-determination for the people of Namibia, a rapid process of internal reconciliation, and free and fair elections in both places. The Reagan–Bush Administration has worked tirelessly to achieve this outcome; and while obstacles remain, we are closer than ever to a comprehensive settlement of these interrelated conflicts. America's strong support for Angolan freedom-fighters has helped make this progress possible. We also oppose the maintenance of communist forces and influence in Mozambique.

Republicans deplore the apartheid system of South Africa and consider it morally repugnant. All who value human liberty understand the evil of apartheid, and we will not rest until apartheid is eliminated from South Africa. That will remain our goal. Republicans call for an effective and coordinated policy that will promote equal rights and a peaceful transition to a truly representative constitutional form of government for all South Africans and the citizens of all nations throughout Africa. We deplore violence employed against innocent blacks and whites from whatever source.

We believe firmly that one element in the evolution of black political progress must be black economic progress; actions designed to pressure the government of South Africa must not have the effect of adversely affecting the rising aspirations and achievements of black South African entrepreneurs and workers and their families. We should also encourage the development of strong democratic black political institutions to aid in the peaceful transition to majority rule. Republicans believe that it is wrong to punish innocent black South Africans for the policies of the apartheid government of South Africa.

Child Survival Program

The health of children in the developing countries of Asia, Africa, the Near East, Latin America and the Caribbean has been a priority of the Reagan–Bush Administration. Republicans have designated the Child Survival Program as one of our highest foreign assistance priorities. With the creation of the Child Survival Fund in early 1985, we have helped to ensure that children in developing countries worldwide get a decent start in life.

Our commitment to the Child Survival Program is more than a compassionate response to this challenge. It is in part an indication of the success of the program. Child Survival funding has been put to good use, and it is making a difference. Experience has shown that a few dollars go a long way in saving a child's life.

Republican efforts have seen results. The pilot studies begun by the Reagan–Bush Administration a few years ago have resulted in child survival programs that today are reaching hundreds of thousands of women and children in the developing world. Policies are in place, health workers are trained, and host gov-

ernments throughout the world are committed to child survival programs.

Republicans are committed to continuing our contribution to this vital program. As we look forward to the 1990s, many countries will have achieved what only a few years ago seemed like unattainable goals. Those countries need to find ways to sustain those achievements. It will not be easy. For other countries, the road to these goals will be longer as they strive to give every child what should be his or her birthright, a chance to thrive.

We can help them. We can provide leadership and support. We are committed to sustaining this effort to save and improve the lives of the world's children.

We commend the Reagan–Bush Administration for its courageous defense of human life in population programs around the world. We support its refusal to fund international organizations involved in abortion.

Stopping International Terrorism and Dealing with Low-Intensity Conflict

The nature of warfare itself has changed. Terrorism is a unique form of warfare that attacks and threatens security and stability around the world. Ranging from the attempted assassination of the Pope and car-bomb attacks on American USO clubs, to narco-subversion in the nations of the West, terrorism seeks to silence freedom as an inalienable right of Man.

The world of totalitarianism and anti-Western fanatics have joined forces in this campaign of terror. The goals of their undeclared war against the democracies are the withdrawal of our presence internationally and the retraction of our freedoms domestically.

The Republican Party believes that, in order to prevent terrorist attacks, the United States must maintain an unsurpassed intelligence capability. In cases of terrorism where prevention and deterrence are not enough, we believe that the United States must be prepared to use an appropriate mix of diplomatic, political, and military pressure and action to defeat the terrorist attack. The United States must continue to push for a Western commitment to a "no-concessions" policy on terrorism.

The Republican Party understands that many problems facing our country are centered on "Low-Intensity Conflicts." These include insurgencies, organized terrorism, paramilitary actions, sabotage, and other forms of violence in the gray area between peace and declared conventional warfare. Unlike the Democrat Party, Republicans understand that the threat against the vital interests of the United States covers a broad spectrum of conflict. We are committed to defending the people of the United States at all levels. To implement that commitment, we will rely on the planning and strategy of the U.S. Special Operations Command, the recently established Office of Assistant Secretary of Defense for Special Operations and Low-Intensity Conflict and other Department of Defense offices.

We commend the Reagan–Bush Administration for its willingness to provide a measured response to terrorists such as Libya's Colonel Qadhafi. We affirm our determination to continue isolating his outlaw regime. We applaud the Reagan–Bush Administration's dispatch in implementing the Omnibus Diplomatic Security and Anti-Terrorism Act of 1986. We are strongly committed to obtaining the freedom of all Americans held captive by terrorist elements in the Middle East. Where possible, we will hold accountable those responsible for such heinous acts. We also support foreign military assistance that enables friendly nations to provide for their own defense, including defense against terrorism.

We recognize the increasing threat of terrorism to our overall security. We will pursue a forward-leaning posture toward terrorism, and are prepared to act in concert with other nations or unilaterally, as necessary, to prevent or respond to terrorist attacks. Our policy will emphasize pre-emptive anti-terrorist measures; allied and international cooperation; negotiation toward an international agreement to facilitate pre-emptive and proactive measures against terrorists and narco-terrorists; and creation of a multi-national strike force, on the authority granted in a multi-national agreement, specializing in counterterrorism, intelligence and narcotics control.

Republicans believe that, when necessary, our own armed forces must have the capability to meet terrorist crises. Our support for defense forces specifically equipped and trained to conduct unconventional warfare has resulted in important improvements in this critical area. Under the Reagan–Bush Administration, major improvements have been made in the special operations force's readiness, manning, and modernization.

The Republican Party is strongly committed to increased support of unconventional forces by streamlining the bureaucracy which supports them, building the weapons and platforms which are a minimal requirement for their success, and funding the research and development needed for their future vigor. We wholeheartedly support greater international cooperation to counter terrorism and to ensure the safety of innocent citizens traveling abroad.

State Department Organization

The United States depends upon effective diplomacy to protect and advance its interests abroad. Modern diplomacy requires an institution capable of integrating the international dimension of our national values and concerns into a coherent foreign policy. That institution must be made fully responsive to the guidance and direction provided by our country's political leadership.

This requires a truly hierarchical decision-making structure in the Department of State to assure that issues not directly decided by the Secretary of State are not out of reach of politically accountable authority.

Republicans commend the efforts initiated by the Reagan Administration, and in particular the Secretary of State, to restructure and streamline management of the department in order to provide for greater flexibility, efficiency and accountability.

We will continue these efforts in the areas of organization, personnel, and responsiveness as part of a long-term program to make the Department of State more immediately responsive to a complex and changing world.

PEACE THROUGH STRENGTH— A PROVEN POLICY

Peace through strength is now a proven policy. We have modernized our forces, revitalized our military infrastructure, recruited and trained the most capable fighting force in American history. And we have used these tools with care, responsibility, and restraint.

The Reagan–Bush national security program has restored America's credibility in the world. Our security and that of our allies have been dramatically enhanced; the opportunities for the United States to be a positive force for freedom and democracy throughout the world have expanded, and the chances for new breakthroughs for peace have risen dramatically.

Republicans will build upon this record and advance the cause of world freedom and world peace by using our military credibility as a vehicle for security at home and peace abroad.

These new opportunities for peace and world freedom pose new challenges to America.

The INF Treaty, the first treaty to actually reduce the number of nuclear weapons, was made possible by our commitment to peace through strength. It will impose new demands on our armed forces. We will redouble our commitment to correct a dangerous imbalance of conventional forces both through negotiation and through force improvements.

The Carter administration left our armed forces in a dangerously weakened position. Ten of the Army's 16 divisions were rated as "not combat ready" due to shortages of skilled manpower, spare parts, fuel, ammunition, and training. For the same reasons, more than 40 percent of the U.S. Air Force and Navy combat aircraft were not fully mission-capable.

The vacillating, ineffectual defense policies of the Democrat presidential nominee would similarly weaken our national security. His ideas about strategic weapons are not only out of step with the thinking of the vast majority of Americans, but also in direct conflict with those of his vice presidential running mate and most of the leading Democrats on the Senate and House Armed Services Committees.

Republicans will support U.S. defense capabilities by keeping our economy strong and inflation rates low. Continued economic growth will allow more dollars to be available for defense without consuming a larger portion of the GNP or the federal budget; continued efficiency and economy will assure those dollars are well spent.

Even as we engage in dialogue with our adversaries to reduce the risks of war, we must continue to rely on nuclear weapons as our chief form of deterrence. This reliance will, however, move toward non-nuclear defensive weapon systems as we deploy the Strategic Defense System. We will greatly enhance security by making the transition from an all-offensive balance of nuclear terror to a deterrent that emphasizes non-nuclear defense against attack.

We must improve conventional deterrence that would prevent our adversaries from being able to advance successfully into allied territory. We stand in unity with our European allies in the conviction that neither a nuclear war nor a conventional war should be fought. Nonetheless, we must stay on the cutting edge of weapon system development and deployment to deter Soviet aggression in Europe and throughout the free world.

Only by maintaining our strength and resolve can we secure peace in the years ahead. Republicans will provide the steady leadership needed to move our nation effectively into the 21st century.

America Defended

We have begun a historic transition from an America threatened by nuclear weapons to an America defended against the possibility of a devastating nuclear attack.

We understand the ominous implications of the proliferation of ballistic missile technology in the Third World. The Reagan–Bush Administration has succeeded in negotiating an agreement among the seven leading industrial countries to stop the spread of this technology. This underscores the need for deployment of the Strategic Defense System commonly known as SDI. SDI represents America's single most important defense program and is the most significant investment we can make in our nation's future security.

SDI is already working for America. It brought the Soviets back to the bargaining table, and it has energized and challenged our research and technology community as never before. It has started to reverse the trend of unmatched heavy Soviet investment in strategic defense. Republicans insist it is unacceptable that today the citizens of Moscow are protected against ballistic missile attack while Americans have no such protection.

The SDI program has been structured to facilitate a smooth transition to a safer world. It emphasizes deployments based upon the following objectives:

- Providing protection against an accidental or unauthorized launch of a nuclear missile or an attack by a rogue nation.
- Changing the emphasis of our deterrent from nuclear offense to non-nuclear defensive weapons and providing the only real safeguard against cheating on offensive arms control agreements.
- Ultimately, providing a comprehensive defense against all ballistic missile attacks.

We are committed to rapid and certain deployment of SDI as technologies permit, and we will determine the exact architecture of the system as technologies are tested and proven.

In response to the dangerous proliferation of ballistic missiles, a joint U.S.–Israel effort is now underway to produce the free world's first anti-tactical ballistic missile system, "Project Arrow." We will support this use of SDI research funds.

The Democrat nominee for president opposes deployment of any SDI system. He opposes deployment of even a limited ballistic missile defense system to protect Americans against missile attacks that might be launched accidentally or by an outlaw ruler with access to a few nuclear weapons. His position contradicts the sponsorship by certain Democrats in Congress of a system to protect Americans from such missile attacks.

In recognition of our responsibility to provide optimum protection for the American people from terrorists, accidents and—should deterrence fail—from war, we also believe that a high priority should be given to civil defense.

Republicans want to begin with protection and add to deterrence. We applaud the leaders of the scientific community for their confidence in the ability of U.S. technology to enhance deterrence and to provide effective defenses. We urge the universities of our country to continue to cooperate with the government and the private sector in establishing the SDI system.

A Strategy for Deterrence

Republicans will implement a strategic modernization program, emphasizing offensive and defensive strategic forces that are affordable and credible and that provide for a more stable balance. In contrast with the Democrat nominee and his party, we will not jeopardize America's security and undermine the advances we have made for peace and freedom by permitting erosion of our nuclear deterrent.

Over the past 30 years, every administration—Democrat and Republican alike—has understood the importance of maintaining a strategic triad: a mix of ground, air and sea retaliatory forces. Republicans know our country needs a survivable land-based leg of the triad. The current Democrat leadership rejects this integral element of our strategic force posture. This will destroy the triad by neglecting necessary modernization and foregoing the strategic forces essential for preserving deterrence.

The most critical element in enabling the President to preserve peace is to assure his ability to communicate with foreign leaders and our armed forces under the most adverse circumstances. The Democrat nominee has acted to prevent a future President from having this ability by denying the federal government the needed approval to deploy key elements of the Ground Wave Emergency Network (GWEN) in Massachusetts. By doing so, he has demonstrated a shocking disregard for the security of all Americans. This nation cannot afford such irresponsible leadership from one who aspires to be our Commander-in-Chief.

To end our historic reliance on massive nuclear retaliation, we need to develop a comprehensive strategic defense system. This system will deter and protect us against deliberate or accidental ballistic missile attack, from whatever source.

In the conventional area, we need to ensure that our ground, naval, and air forces are outfitted with the finest equipment and weapons that modern technology can provide; we must also assure that they are fully capable of meeting any threats they may face. We put special emphasis on integrating the guard and reserves into effective combat forces. We must sustain and accelerate the progress we have already made to ensure that all of our forces are prepared for special operations warfare. In addition, advances in conventional weapons technology, specifically, "smart," highly accurate weaponry, must be accelerated. These new weapons will deter our adversaries by threatening significant targets with very precise conventional weapons. We must provide sealift and airlift capability needed to project and support U.S. forces anywhere in the world.

We must also deal with the reality of chemical and biological weapons. We must have a deterrent capability; that requires modernization of our own chemical weapons. But we must also strengthen our efforts to achieve a verifiable agreement to eliminate all chemical and biological weapons. Getting a completely verifiable agreement will be difficult, requiring tough, on-site, on-demand verification. It is, however, essential that we press ahead, particularly given the growing proclivity in some quarters to use chemical and biological weapons.

In each aspect of our deterrent force, Republicans propose to foster and take advantage of our technology and our democratic alliance systems to develop competing strategies for most effectively defending freedom around the world.

An Arms Reduction Strategy

Arms reduction can be an important aspect of our national policy only when agreements enhance the security of the United States and its allies. This is the Reagan–Bush legacy; true arms reductions as a means to improve U.S. security, not just the perception of East–West détente. Clear objectives, steady purpose, and tough negotiating, backed up by the Republican defense program, produced the INF Treaty. This is the first real nuclear arms reduction treaty in history. Until 1981, we had accepted arms "control" as simply a "managed" arms build-up, always waiting for the next agreement to reverse the trend. Republicans insist on mutual arms reduction. We have proven that there are no barriers to mutual reductions except a lack of will and strength to safely achieve them.

We cannot afford to return to failed Democrat approaches to arms control. Democrats treat arms control as an end in itself, overemphasizing the atmospherics of East–West relations, making unilateral concessions, and reneging on the traditional U.S. commitment to those forces essential to U.S. and allied security. Notwithstanding their stated intentions, the Democrats' approach—particularly a nuclear freeze—would make nuclear war more, not less, likely.

Republicans are committed to completing the work the Reagan–Bush Administration has begun on an unprecedented 50 percent cut in strategic nuclear weapons. We will achieve verifiable and stable reductions by implementing the Republican agenda for a secure America:

- We will consistently undertake necessary improvements in our forces to maintain the effectiveness of our deterrent.
- We will not negotiate in areas which jeopardize our security. In particular, we will not compromise plans for the research, testing, or the rapid and certain deployment of SDI.
- We will insist on effective verification of compliance with any and all treaties and will take proportional, compensatory actions in cases of noncompliance. Specifically, the Soviet ABM radar at Krasnoyarsk poses a clear violation of the ABM Treaty and, if not corrected, would constitute a "material breach" of the treaty.
- We will place special emphasis on negotiating asymmetrical Soviet cutbacks in those areas where a dangerous imbalance exists. For example, during the three-year regime of Mikhail Gorbachev, the Soviet military has added more new conventional weapons than currently exist in the entire armed forces of France and West Germany.
- We will reject naive and dangerous proposals such as those offered by the Democrat nominee to ban the testing of weapons and delivery systems. Those simplistic and destabilizing proposals are designed only for domestic political appeal and would actually jeopardize achievement of stable arms reductions. The accuracies and efficiencies achieved by testing have in fact resulted in 25 percent fewer warheads and 75 percent less megatonnage than 20 years ago. Our more accurate weapons of today enhance stability.

We must always remember—and ever remind our fellow citizens—that when the future of our country is at stake, no treaty at all is preferable to a bad treaty.

The Space Challenge

The Republican Party is determined to lead our country and the world into the 21st century with a revitalized space program. The American people have never turned back from a frontier.

Our exploration of space has kept this country on the leading edge of science, research, and technology.

Our access to space is essential to our national security. In the coming decade, nations around the world will compete for the economic and military advantages afforded by space.

The free and unchallenged use of space offers to the free world, and the Soviet bloc as well, unprecedented strategic, scientific, and economic advantages. The Soviets openly seek these advantages, which must not be denied to the United States and other free nations. Our goal is for the United States to acquire the means to assure that we can enforce a stable and secure space environment for all peoples.

We must establish a permanent manned space station in orbit during the 1990s for a commercial and governmental space presence.

U.S. satellites currently act as the "eyes and ears" for our strategic forces. The survivability of U.S. space assets is vital to American interests.

We believe the U.S. needs an antisatellite (ASAT) capability to protect our space assets from an operational Soviet threat, and we intend to deploy it rapidly. Furthermore, we encourage the responsible Democrat members of Congress to join us in this effort. Our country's advance in space is essential to achieve the economic transformations which await us in the new century ahead.

Two powerful engines that can reenergize the space program will be competitive free enterprise and SDI. The United States must regain assured access to space through a balanced mix of space shuttles and unmanned vehicles. We must also expand the role—in investment, operation, and control—of the private sector. Republicans believe that this nation can and must develop a private sector capability to compete effectively in the world marketplace as a provider of launches and other services.

We applaud those who have pioneered America's rendezvous with the future. We salute those who have lifted the nation's spirit by raising its sights. We remember in special honor those who gave their lives to give our country a leading role in space.

America: A Strong Leader and Reliable Partner

NATO remains the United States' most important political and military alliance. Republican commitment to NATO is unwavering, reflecting shared political and democratic values which link Europe, Canada, and the United States. NATO pools our collective military resources and capabilities, stretching in Europe from Norway in the north to Turkey, our strategic friend and pillar in the south.

Our challenge is to assure that today's positive signals from the Soviets translate into a tangible reduction of their military threat tomorrow. Soviet conventional superiority remains a serious problem for NATO. Soviet–Warsaw Pact military doctrine continues to be predicated upon the Soviet Union's ability to mount a massive conventional offensive against the NATO allies. The NATO allies must strengthen their conventional forces, modernize their remaining nuclear systems, and promote rationalization, standardization and interoperability.

On the critical issues of defense burden sharing, Republicans reflect the belief of the American people that, although we must maintain a strong presence, the alliance has now evolved to a point where our European and Japanese allies, blessed with advanced economies and high standards of living, are capable of shouldering their fair share of our common defense burden.

We are committed to supporting the network of liberty through balanced regional or bilateral alliances with nations sharing our values in all parts of the world, especially our neighbors in Central America. The Republican Party reiterates its support of the people of Central America in their quest for freedom and democracy in their countries.

We are proud of the great economic and democratic progress throughout the world during the Reagan–Bush Administration, and we are committed to strengthening the defensive ties that have thwarted Soviet expansion in the past seven years.

Keeping the Sea Lanes Free

The United States has always been a maritime nation. We have rebuilt our Navy to permit continued freedom of the seas. Our focus has correctly been on the fighting ships our Navy would use in the event of a conflict. Our successful peace mission in the Persian Gulf is eloquent testimony to the benefits of a blue water Navy.

To protect American interests in remote areas of the world, we require a 600-ship Navy with 15 aircraft carrier battle groups. This number enables us to operate in areas where we lack the infrastructure of bases we enjoy in Western Europe and the western Pacific. A force of this size will enable us to meet both our security interests and commitments into the 21st century. Republicans are also committed to the strategic homeporting of our forces throughout the United States. Notwithstanding the Democrat nominee's claim to support conventional arms improvements. U.S. security interests are jeopardized by his proposal to cancel two aircraft carriers previously authorized and funded by Congress.

Providing new policies for the maritime industry is crucial to this nation's defense capability and its economic strength. These policies must include leadership to help make the industries competitive through reform of government programs, aggressive efforts to remove barriers to the U.S. flag merchant fleet, and a commitment to cooperate with the industries themselves to improve their efficiency, productivity, and competitive positions.

A national commitment to revitalize the commercial shipbuilding industry is needed in this country. Shipyards and the supplier base for marine equipment necessary to build and maintain a merchant marine must survive and prosper. Our merchant marine must be significantly enlarged and become more competitive in order to vastly increase the amount and proportion of our foreign trade it carries.

Sealift is needed to supply our troops and transport commercial cargo during a prolonged national emergency. As a nation, we must be willing to pay for the strategic sealift capability we require. We can do this by ensuring that the needed ships are built and by helping to sustain the ships and their crews in commercial operation. We must return this nation to its foremost place among the world maritime powers through a comprehensive maritime policy.

Last year Congress slashed the Administration's budget request for the Coast Guard. We urge Congress to adjust the budget process to protect the Coast Guard appropriation, thereby removing the temptation to siphon its funds and personnel into other programs and ensuring improved coordination of government agencies in our nation's war against drugs.

Our Nation's Technology Base

Science and technology are the keys to a better future for all. Many of the miracles we take for granted in everyday life originated in defense and space research. They have not only helped preserve the peace, but also have made America's standard of living the envy of the world.

Because of advances in science and technology, our defense budget today is actually one-third lower, as a fraction of the gross national product, than it was a generation ago.

Today, national security and technological superiority are increasingly linked by the relationship between technology and key strategies of credible and flexible deterrence, defenses against ballistic missiles, and space pre-eminence.

Investment in defense research and development must be maintained at a level commensurate with the

Reagan–Bush years. This investment should be focused on efficient and effective areas such as ballistic missile defense, space, command and control, and "smart" munitions.

We support a defense budget with the necessary funds and incentives for industry to invest in new technologies and new plants and equipment. This is needed to preserve and expand our competitive edge, thereby assuring future opportunities for America's next generation in science, engineering, and manufacturing.

Our nation will benefit greatly from patent royalties and technological progress that will be developed through spinoffs, especially in the fields of micro-miniaturization and superconductivity, which are vital in order for U.S. industry to compete in the world.

We regard the education of American students in the fields of science and technology as vital to our national security.

Our investment in militarily critical knowledge and technology must be safeguarded against transfer to the Soviet Union and other unfriendly countries.

Defense Acquisition

Americans are prepared to support defense spending adequate to meet the needs of our security. Americans have a right—and the government has a duty—to ensure that their hard-earned tax dollars are well spent. We Republicans recognize that waste and fraud in the defense acquisition process cheat the American people and weaken our national security. Neither can be tolerated.

Those who loot national security funds must be prosecuted and punished. Mismanagement must also be rooted out. The planning and budgeting process must be improved, and the acquisition process reformed, recognizing that congressionally mandated waste contributes mightily to inefficiencies in the system.

We will sustain necessary appropriations in the defense budget to avoid the destructive impact of wildly fluctuating and unpredictable annual funding.

The Packard Commission recommended a series of important reforms for improved defense management. We are committed to ensuring that these reforms are fully implemented—by Congress, the Defense Department and the defense industry. Most particularly we call for submission of a two-year budget for defense to help us meet these goals. Persons involved in the federal government procurement process must be subject to "revolving door" legislation.

Procurement today is constrained by an adversarial relationship between the Congress and the Defense Department. The result is micromanagement by Congress, which has resulted in thousands of regulations that add expensive and time consuming red tape without adding value. Republicans support a firm policy of cooperation, treating members of Congress as full partners in the acquisition process. This will result in more efficiency and better weapons. An example of what can be accomplished with this partnership is the new base closing legislation.

To make real these reforms, we will once again depend on the professionalism, the diligence, and the patriotism of the men and women who comprise the vast majority of our defense establishment.

Armed Forces Personnel for the Nineties

A free society defends itself freely. That is why Republicans created an all-volunteer force of men and women in the 1970s, and why it has proven to be a tremendous success in the 1980s.

From Grenada to the Persian Gulf, the readiness of those in uniform has made America proud again. Despite a demographic decline in the number of those eligible for service, military recruitment and retention rates are at all time highes. Quality is outstanding, and all sectors of society are participating.

We will continue to make the military family a special priority, recognizing strong home life as an essential component in the morale and performance of the armed forces.

Republicans deplore and reject the efforts of those who would support either a numerical cap or a reduction of the number of military dependents able to accompany U.S. servicemen and women overseas. We recognize that a stable and happy family life is the most important prerequisite for retaining these dedicated men and women in the service of our country.

Republicans recognize that a secure national defense depends upon healthy military personnel. We commend the United States Armed Forces for their leadership in proving the utility of testing active duty personnel and applicants for disease and substance abuse.

Republicans will never take the military for granted. We support an all-volunteer force and we will continue to insist on fairness in pay and benefits for military personnel and their families, always striving to keep compensation in line with the civilian economy.

The National Guard and Reserve are essential to the integrated force concept of our armed services. Prior to 1981, the Guard and Reserve were deprived of both modern equipment and integration into the active forces. This policy has been changed to enable the Guard and Reserve to make their full contribution to our security. We recognize the major role played by the men and women of the Guard and Reserves in the total defense policy. These improvements will be sustained.

Veterans

Veterans have paid the price for the freedoms we enjoy. They have earned the benefits they receive, and we will be vigilant in protecting these programs of health care, education and housing.

We believe men and women veterans have earned the right to be heard at the highest levels of government. With the personal support of President Reagan, American's veterans will now have a seat in the president's Cabinet.

The health needs of our aging veterans are of special importance, and Republicans will not retreat from this national commitment. We encourage the new Secretary of the Veterans Department to work with the Federal Council on the Aging, and other agencies and organizations, to assure that the development of new facilities and treatment programs meet the special needs of our elderly veterans.

Republicans support the policy that, in all areas where there are no VA hospitals or long-term care facilities, veterans needing medical attention for service-connected disabilities should have the option of receiving medical care within their communities with adequate funding.

We must continue to address the unique readjustment problems of Vietnam veterans by continuing the storefront counseling, vocational training and job placement programs. We support veterans' preference in federal employment and are vigilant about the serious problems associated with delayed stress reaction in combat veterans, particularly disabled and Vietnam veterans. An intense scientific effort must continue with respect to disabilities that may be related to exposure to ionizing radiation or herbicides.

The Republican Party supports sufficient funding to maintain the integrity of the VA hospital and medical care system and the entitlement and beneficiary system. We also support the efforts of the Department of Labor to properly meet the needs of unemployed veterans, particularly disabled and Vietnam veterans.

Our commitment to America's veterans extends to the men and women of all generations.

Intelligence: An Indispensable Resource at a Critical Time

A crucial part of the Reagan–Bush Administration's rebuilding of a strong America has been the restoration of the nation's intelligence capabilities after years of neglect and downgrading by the Carter–Mondale administration. This renewed emphasis has been essential in conducting diplomacy, supporting our armed forces, confronting terrorism, stopping narcotics traffic, battling Soviet subversion, and influencing events in support of other national policies. Our vital intelligence capability will continue to prevent tragedies and save lives.

In the years ahead, the United States will face a widening range of national security challenges and opportunities. Scores of foreign intelligence services will seek to uncover our secrets and steal our technology. But there will also be opportunities to advance U.S. interests, for freedom and democracy are on the march. Both the threats and the opportunities will place demands on our intelligence capabilities as never before.

The Republican Party endorses covert action as one method of implementing U.S. national security policy. We reject legislative measures that impinge on the president's constitutional prerogatives. Our country must be able to collect from both technical and human sources the vital information which is denied to us by closed societies in troubled regions of the world. Our senior national security officials must be informed about trends in foreign societies, opportunities to advance U.S. interests, and the vulnerabilities of those who seek to harm our interests. This information can then be used, through the proper chain of command, to support our national policies.

To strengthen the decision-making process and further limit access to classified information, we support the concept of a single joint committee for intelligence, made up of appropriate congressional leaders and analogous to the former Joint Atomic Energy Committee.

We will continue to enhance the nation's capability for counterintelligence. Congressional intrusion into the administration of counterintelligence must be kept to a minimum.

Leaks of highly sensitive and classified national security information and materials have increased at an alarming rate in recent years. Such leaks often compromise matters critical to our defense and national security; they can result in the tragic loss of life. We advocate a law making it a felony for any present or former officer or employee of the federal government, including members of Congress, to knowingly disclose classified information or material to a person not authorized to have access to it.

The U.S. must continue to provide political, military, and economic assistance to friends abroad and to those seeking to help us against our adversaries. These activities must always be in support of our national policy, and the U.S. has the right to expect reciprocity wherever possible.

To the extent the Congress requires the president to inform its members of activities sensitive to national security, the president is entitled to require that Congress will respect that sensitivity.

National Security Strategy for the Future

We have set forth the foreign and defense policies of the Republican Party in the two preceding sections of this Platform. To implement those policies, we propose this integrated national security strategy for the future.

The long-term security of our nation is the most important responsibility of the U.S. government. The domestic well-being of the American people cannot be ensured unless our country is secure from external attack. To guard our borders, preserve our freedom, protect America from ballistic missile attack, foster a climate of international stability and tranquility—so that nations and individuals may develop, interact, and prosper free from the threat of war or intimidation— these are the most important goals of America's foreign and defense policy.

We dare not abandon to others our leadership in pursuit of these goals. International peace and stability require our country's engagement at many levels. While we cannot resolve all issues unilaterally, neither can we abdicate our responsibilities by retrenchment or by relying on the United Nations to secure our interests abroad. Those who advocate America's disengagement from the world forget the dangers that would be unleashed by America's retreat—dangers which inevitably increase the costs and risks of the necessary reassertion of U.S. power.

Republicans learned this lesson well as we implemented the most successful national security policy since World War II. In 1981, we had to deal with the consequences of the Democrats' retreat. We inherited an American in decline, with a crisis of confidence at home and a loss of respect abroad. Reestablishing America's strength, its belief in itself, and its leadership role was the first and most important task facing the Reagan–Bush Administration. We met that task. We repaired our defenses, modernized our stategic nuclear forces, improved our strategy for deterrence with our development of the Strategic Defense Initiative, deployed INF missiles in Europe, and restored pride in our nation's military service.

We also met that task by a policy of engagement. We worked with allies, not against them. We supported friends instead of accommodating foes. We fostered the achievement of genuine self-determination and democracy rather than merely preaching about human rights in the Third World.

The Reagan–Bush approach produced dramatic results. Our policy is proven: to foster peace while resolutely providing for the security of our country and its allies. We have significantly enhanced that security. We have expanded the opportunities for the United States to be a positive force for freedom and democracy throughout the world, and the chances for new breakthroughs for peace have risen dramatically.

We secured the first arms reduction agreement, eliminating an entire class of Soviet and U.S. nuclear weapons. We laid the basis in START for unprecedented, radical reductions in strategic nuclear arms.

In regional conflicts, a humiliating Soviet retreat from Afghanistan, made possible by our unyielding support for the Mujahidin, helped to sober the Soviet rulers about the costs of their adventurism. Our protection of vital U.S. interests in the Persian Gulf against Iranian aggression led to the agreement to start resolving the Persian Gulf War. Our support for freedom fighters in Angola has resulted in the chance of a settlement there and elsewhere in southern Africa. Our isolation of Vietnam has led to the prospect of its withdrawal from Cambodia.

In human rights and the building of democracy, Republican leadership has turned the tide against terror in Central America, aided the restoration of democracy in the Philippines and South Korea, and liberated the island of Grenada from a Cuban-controlled dictatorship.

This is a remarkable record of achievement. It shows that our policies of achieving peace through strength have worked. By rebuilding American strength and restoring American self-confidence. Republicans achieved a remarkable series of foreign policy objectives critical to our country's security. The resurgence of American leadership has changed the world and is shaping the future, creating new opportunities not dreamt of eight years ago. This is a true measure of competence.

Although we have established a framework for the future, we cannot afford to rest on our laurels. The young democracies we have helped to flourish may yet be overcome by authoritarian pressures. The Soviet Union can easily revert to past practices. Its current effort of internal restructuring could create a more powerful adversary with unchanged objectives. Arms reductions could again become an excuse for reducing our commitment to defense, thus creating dangerous instabilities. Economic competition could easily slip into protectionism and mercantilism. Both to meet those challenges and to build upon the opportunities created by our success, the U.S. must continue in the strong leadership role it has assumed over the past eight years.

As we face the opportunities and challenges of the future, our policies must be guided by realism, strength, dialogue, and engagement. We must be realistic about the Soviet Union and the world we face. Hostile forces remain in that world. Soviet military capabilities are still dangerous to us. It must be clear to all, except the leadership of the Democrat Party, that we are not beyond the era of threats to the security of the United States.

Our country must have all the military strength that is necessary to deter war and protect our vital interests abroad. Republicans will continue to improve our defense capabilities. We will carefully set priorities within a framework of fiscal conservatism, and improved management of defense resources.

We will continue modernizing our strategic forces, emphasizing a mix of offensive and defensive forces, effective and survivable, employing unique U.S. technological advantages. We will redouble our commitment through force improvements to correct the dangerous imbalance that exists in conventional forces.

At the same time, we will pursue negotiations designed to eliminate destabilizing asymmetries in strategic and conventional forces. Arms reductions can contribute to our national security only if they are designed to reduce the risk of war and result in greater stability. They must be part of a process of broader dialogue with the Soviet Union, as well as other nations, a process in which we explore possible opportunities to reduce tensions and create more stable, predictable, and enduring relationships.

As we shape our foreign and defense policies, we must never lose sight of the unique leadership role the United States plays in the world community. No other nation can assume that role. Whether we are dealing with security challenges in the Persian Gulf or terrorism or the scourge of drugs, the willingness of other nations to act resolutely will depend on the readiness of America to lead, to remain vigorously engaged, and to shoulder its unique responsibilities in the world.

The American people and the Republican Party, in the tradition of Ronald Reagan and with the leadership of George Bush, are indeed ready to do so.

— 1992 —

PREAMBLE

Abraham Lincoln, our first Republican President, expressed the philosophy that inspires Republicans to this day: "The legitimate object of Government is to do for a community of people whatever they need to have done, but cannot do at all, or cannot so well do, for themselves in their separate and individual capacities. But in all that people can individually do as well for themselves, Government ought not to interfere."

We believe that most problems of human making are within the capacity of human ingenuity to solve.

For good reason, millions of new Americans have flocked to our shores: America has always been an opportunity society. Republicans have always believed that economic prosperity comes from individual enterprise, not government programs. We have defended our core principles for 138 years; but never has this country, and the world, been so receptive to our message.

The fall of the Berlin Wall symbolizes an epochal change in the way people live. More important, it liberates the way people think. We see with new clarity that centralized government bureaucracies created in this century are not the wave of the future. Never again will people trust planners and paper shufflers more than they trust themselves. We all watched as the statue of Soviet hangman Feliks Dzherzhinsky was toppled in front of Moscow's KGB headquarters by the very people his evil empire sought to enslave. Its sightless eyes symbolized the moral blindness of totalitarians around the world. They could never see the indomitable spirit of people determined to be free from government control—free to build a better future with their own heads, hands, and hearts.

We Republicans saw clearly the dangers of collectivism; not only the military threat, but the deeper threat to the souls of people bound in dependence. Here at home, we warned against Big Government, because we knew concentrated decision making, no matter how well intentioned, was a danger to liberty and prosperity. Republicans stood at the rampart of freedom, defending the individual against the domineering state. While we did not always prevail, we always stood our ground, faithful to our principles and confident of history's ultimate verdict.

Our opponents declared that the dogmas of the Left were the final and victorious faith. From kremlins and ivory towers, their planners proclaimed the bureaucratic millennium. But in a tragic century of illusion, Five Year Plans and Great Leaps Forward failed to summon a Brave New World. One hundred and fifty years of slogans and manifestos came crashing down in an ironic cascade of unintended consequences. All that is left are the ruins of a failed scoundrel ideology.

As May Day lapses back into just another spring festival, the Fourth of July emerges as the common holiday of free men and women. Yet, in 1992, when the self-governing individual has overcome the paternalistic state, liberals here at home simply do not get it. Indeed, their party seeks to turn the clock back. But their ideas are old and tired. Like planets still orbiting a dying star, the believers in state power turn their faces to a distant and diminishing light.

The Democrats would revise history to rationalize a return to bigger government, higher taxes, and moral relativism. The Democrat Party has forgotten its origins as a party of work, thrift, and self-reliance. But they have not forgotten their art for dissembling and distortion. The Democrats are trapped in their compact with the ideology of trickle-down government, but they are clever enough to know that the voters would shun them if their true markings were revealed.

America had its rendezvous with destiny in 1980. Faced with crisis at home and abroad, Americans turned to Republican leadership in the White House. Presidents Reagan and Bush turned our nation away from the path of overtaxation, hyperregulation, and megagovernment. Instead, we moved in a new direction. We cut taxes, reduced red tape, put people above bureaucracy. And so we vanquished the idea of the almighty state as the supervisor of our daily lives. In choosing hope over fear, Americans raised a beacon, reminding the world that we are a shining city on a hill, the last best hope for man on earth.

Contrary to statist Democrat propaganda, the American people know that the 1980s were a rising tide, a magnificent decade for freedom and entrepreneurial creativity. We are confident that, knowing this, they will never consciously retreat to the bad old days of tax and spend. Our Platform will clarify the choice before our fellow citizens.

We have learned that ideas do indeed have consequences. Thus, our words are important not for their prose but for what they reveal about the thinking of our President and our Party.

Two years ago, President Bush described the key elements of what he called "our new paradigm," a fresh approach that aims to put new ideas to work in the service of enduring principles—principles that were upheld throughout the long twilight struggle, principles George Bush has acted decisively to advance. Thus we honor the Founders and their vision.

Unlike our opponents, we are inspired by a commitment to profound change. Our mission combines timeless beliefs with a positive vision of a vigorous America: prosperous and tolerant, just and compassionate. We believe that individual freedom, hard work, and personal responsibility—basic to free society—are also basic to effective government. We believe in the fundamental goodness of the American people. We believe in traditional family values and in the Judeo-Christian heritage that informs our culture. We believe in the Constitution and its guarantee of color-blind equal opportunity. We believe in free markets. We believe in constructive change, in both true conservatism and true reform. We believe government has a legitimate role to play in our national life, but government must never dominate that life.

While our goals are constant, we are willing to innovate, experiment, and learn. We have learned that bigger is not better, that quantity and quality are different things, that more money does not guarantee better outcomes. We have learned the importance of individual choice—in education, health care, child care—and that bureaucracy is the enemy of initiative and self-reliance. We believe in empowerment, including home ownership for as many as possible. We believe in decentralized authority, and a bottom-line, principled commitment to what works for people.

We believe in the American people: free men and women with faith in God, working for themselves and their families, believing in the value of every human being from the very young to the very old.

We believe the founders intended Congress to be responsive, flexible and foresighted. After decades of Democrat misrule, the Congress is none of these things. Dominated by reactionaries, obsessed with the failed policies and structures of the past, the Democrat majority displays a "do-nothing" doggedness: they intend to learn nothing and forget nothing. Seeking to build a better America, we seek to elect a better Congress.

Finally, we believe in a President who represents the national interest, not just the aggregation of well-connected special interests; a President who brings unity to the American purpose.

America faces many challenges. Republicans, under the strong leadership of President Bush, are responding with this bold Platform of new ideas that infuses our commitment to individual freedom and market forces with an equal commitment to a decent, just way of life for every American.

With a firm faith that the American people will always choose hope over fear, we Republicans dedicate ourselves to this forward-looking agenda for America in the 1990s, transcending old, static ideas with a shared vision of hope, optimism, and opportunity.

UNITING OUR FAMILY

As the family goes, so goes the Nation. Strong families and strong communities make a strong America. An old adage says, "America is great because she is good;

If America ceases to be good, she will cease to be great."

Our greatness starts at home—literally. So Republicans believe government should strengthen families, not replace them. Today, more than ever, the traditional family is under assault. We believe our laws should reflect what makes our Nation prosperous and wholesome: faith in God, hard work, service to others, and limited government.

Parents bring reality to these principles when they pass them on to their children. As the Book of Proverbs proclaims, "Train up a child in the way he should go: and when he is old, he will not depart from it."

Imagine the America we could create if all parents taught their children the importance of honesty, work, responsibility, and respect for others. We would have less violence in our homes and streets; less illegal drug use; fewer teen pregnancies forcing girls and boys to be adults before they have graduated from high school. Instead, we would have an America of families, friends, and communities that care about one another.

That kind of future is not a matter of chance; it is a question of personal responsibility. Barbara Bush captured the importance of that stewardship when she said, "At the end of your life you will never regret not having passed one more test, not winning one more verdict, or not closing one more deal. You will regret time not spent with a husband, a child, a friend, or a parent."

The Republican Party has espoused these principles since its founding. Families built on solid, spiritual foundations are central to our Party's inspiration. At this time of great national and global transition, we renew our commitment to these fundamental principles, which will guide our family, our country, our world into the next century.

Family: The Home of Freedom

The Rights of the Family

Our national renewal starts with the family. It is where each new generation gains its moral anchor. It is the school of citizenship, the engine of economic progress, a permanent haven when everything is changing.

Change can be good, when it liberates the energy and commitment of family members to build better futures. We welcome change that corrects the mistakes of the past, particularly those at war against the family. For more than three decades, the liberal philosophy has assaulted the family on every side.

Today, its more vocal advocates believe children should be able to sue their parents over decisions about schooling, cosmetic surgery, employment, and other family matters. They deny parental authority and responsibility, fracturing the family into isolated individuals, each of them dependent upon—and helpless before—government. This is the ultimate agenda of contemporary socialism under all its masks to liberate youth from traditional family values by replacing family functions with bureaucratic social services. That is why today's liberal Democrats are hostile toward any institution government cannot control, like private child care or religious schools.

The Republican Party responds, as it has since 1980, with an unabashed commitment to the family's economic liberty and moral rights. Republicans trust parents and believe they, not courts and lawyers, know what is best for their children. That is why we will work to ensure that the Congress and the States shall enact no law abridging the rights of the family formed by blood, marriage, adoption, or legal custody—rights which are anterior and superior to those of government. Republicans oppose and resist the efforts of the Democrat Party to redefine the traditional American family.

The Right to a Family

Every child deserves a family in a home filled with love and free from abuse. Today, many children do not enjoy that right. We are determined to change that. While government cannot legislate love and compassion, we can provide the leadership to encourage the development of healthy, nurturing families. We applaud the fine example of family values and family virtue as lived by the President and the First Lady.

We will promote whole, caring families by eliminating biases that have crept into our legal and tax codes. We will advance adoption through significant tax credits, insurance reforms, and legal reforms. We encourage adoption for those unprepared or unwilling to bear the emotional, financial, or physical demands of raising a child and will work to revive maternity homes to ensure care for both mothers and babies.

We applaud the commitment of foster care parents who provide family environments for foster care children. We abhor the disgraceful bureaucratic mismanagement for foster care. Big city mayors have spent billions on social service bureaucrats who have lost track of many children. Many have no health records, no real residence, not even the simplest personal possessions. Shuttled from house to house, they lack discipline and identity and are ripe for lives of crime. We are determined to reform this system to help these children.

Broken homes can have a devastating emotional and economic impact upon children and are the breeding ground for gang members. We urge State legislatures to explore ways to promote marital stability. Because the intergenerational family is a vital element of social cohesion, we urge greater respect for the rights and the roles of grandparents.

Republicans recognize the importance of having fathers and mothers in the home. The two-parent family still provides the best environment of stability, discipline, responsibility, and character. Documentation shows that where the father has deserted his family, children are more likely to commit a crime, to drop out of school, to become violent, to become teen parents, to take illegal drugs, to become enmired in poverty, or to have emotional or behavioral problems. We support the courageous efforts of single-parent families to have a stable home.

Caring for Children

George Bush secured the American family's most important victory of the last four years: his child care bill. He won landmark legislation—a voucher system for low-income households, allowing parents to choose what's best for their children, including care given by neighbors or churches. The Democrat Party opposed that legislation and instead sought government control of child care and fewer choices for parents.

The President also advanced equity for families that forego a second income to care for their children at home through his Young Child Tax Credit. Congressional Democrats are already trying to repeal it.

The demands of employment and commuting often make it hard for parents to spend time with their children. Republicans advocate maximum flexibility in working and child care arrangements so that families can make the most of their schedules. We support pro-family policies: job sharing, telecommuting, compressed work weeks, parental leave negotiated between employer and employees, and flextime. We reject the Democrats' one-size-fits-all approach that puts mandates on employers and takes choices away from employees.

Most parents prefer in-home care of their children but often encounter government obstacles. Republicans will promote in-home care by allowing payment annually, instead of quarterly, of income taxes by employees and withholding taxes by employers. Our proposals for tort reform, now blocked by the Democrat Congress, will prevent excessive litigation that hampers the growth of child care opportunities. By taking care of our children, we are taking care of our future.

Family Security

Over the last several decades, liberal Democrats have increasingly shifted economic burdens onto the American family. Indeed, the liberal Democrat tax-and-spend policies have forced millions of women into the workplace just to make ends meet. Because of their policies in Congress, fathers and mothers have a tougher time bringing home what they work so hard for.

Between 1948 and 1990, under the Democrat controlled Congress for most of those years, federal taxes on the average family of four rose from 2 percent to 24 percent of income. When State and local levies are included, the tax burden exceeds one-third of family income. The increase in the effective federal tax rate since 1950 has now swallowed up an ever increasing share of a family's earnings. Instead of working to improve their family's standard of living, they must work to feed government's gluttonous appetite.

This is a scandal. In the 1980s, two Republican Presidents kept Democrats from making matters worse. Presidents Reagan and Bush led the way to increase the personal exemption for dependents. We pledge to go farther to restore the value, as a percentage of average household income, it had 50 years ago. The value of the dependent deduction has eroded to a fraction of its original worth to families. Republicans call for a complete restoration, in real dollars, to its original value. Rather than fatten government bureaucracies with new programs to "help" families, we want to expand the Young Child Tax Credit to $500 per child and make it available to all families with children under the age of ten.

When the Democrats establish tax policy that makes marriage more expensive than living together, they discourage traditional commitment and stable home life. We will remove the marriage penalty in the tax code, so a married couple will receive as large a standard deduction as their unmarried counterparts. Together, these changes will empower parents to care for their families in a way public services never can.

Achieving Educational Excellence

In the earliest American communities, pioneers would establish a church, then a school. Parents wanted their children to have the best possible education, to learn what they needed to know to make a better life. Virtually every newly arrived immigrant family thought of education as the American way from the back to the front of the line. Americans have come to believe that only a country that successfully educates its sons and daughters can count on a strong, competitive economy, a vibrant culture, and a solid civic life.

As a result of this popular demand for education, Americans have created the most extensive and widely accessible educational system in the world. The people have insisted that primary responsibility for education properly remain with families, communities, and States, although, from early times, the national government has played a role in encouraging innovation and access. In the 18th century, the Northwest Ordinance assured that school bells would ring amid frontier forests. In the 19th century, President Lincoln signed the Morrill Act establishing 50 land-grant colleges. In the 20th century, President Eisenhower signed the National Defense Education Act, providing millions with a chance at higher education; and President Nixon signed legislation that today provides federal grants and loans to half our full-time college students. In the 21st century, the promotion of educational excellence will be more crucial than ever before in our Nation's history.

Recognizing what every parent knows, that our current educational system is not educating our children, President Bush is leading an education revolution. We applaud the President's bold vision to change radically our education system. Our parents want it, our communities want it, our States want it, and our children want it—but the Democrat leadership in the House and the Senate continues to thwart the will of the American people for radical change in the way we educate our children.

The Republican strategy is based on sound principle. Parents have the right to choose the best school for their children. Schools should teach right from wrong. Schools should reinforce parental authority, not replace it. We should increase flexibility from federal regulation. We should explore a new generation of break-the-mold New American Schools. Standards and assessments should be raised, not reduced to a lowest common denominator. Communities should be empowered to find what works. The pursuit of excellence in education is a fundamental goal. Good teachers should be rewarded for teaching well. Alternative certification can bring desperately needed new people into the teaching profession. America needs public, private, and parochial schools.

Education is a joint responsibility of the individual, the family, and the community. Parents are the first and most important teachers of their children. They should have the right not only to participate in their child's education, but to choose for their children among the broadest array of educational choices, without regard to their income. We also support the right of parents to provide quality education through home-based schools.

The Bush Administration has sent to Congress several legislative proposals embodying these principles. The proposals, in spite of the fact that 1,500 communities across the Nation have developed local committees to support them through the AMERICA 2000 strategy, languish in the Democrat Congress. And they are opposed by special interest unions which have a power-grip on the failed policies of the past.

Improving America by Improving Our Schools

For America to maintain her preeminence into the next century, our educational system must be revolutionized. Too many schools still teach in an outdated manner. Too many government and union rules have burdened our schools. And too much influence by lobbyists has blocked true reform. Even the most inspiring teachers are working within a system that stymies their creativity and fails to challenge their students.

Creating the Best Schools in the World

We applaud President Bush's consistent and determined leadership in setting a new direction for American education. Our overriding purpose is clear: to create the best schools in the world for our children by the turn of the century.

To do so, the President has established a bold strategy, AMERICA 2000, which challenges communities in every State to take charge to achieve our ambitious national education goals. The success of AMERICA 2000 will depend upon the local community, where implementation and ultimate responsibility rest.

We have seen real progress. Perhaps most important, though, is that President Bush has fostered a national debate on education that has challenged every American to get involved. He has called forth American traits of ingenuity and ambition to create better lives for our children. As a result, a new generation of break-the-mold New American Schools is taking shape. New and tougher standards and assessments are being established for what our children should know. The number of strings attached to federal school aid is being reduced.

The President has shown unprecedented leadership for the most important education goal of all: helping middle and low income families enjoy the same choice of schools—public, private, or religious—that families with more resources already have. The President's proposed "GI Bill for Children" will provide $1,000 scholarships to middle- and low-income families, enabling their children to attend the school of their choice. This innovative plan will not only drive schools to excel as they compete, but will also give every parent consumer power to obtain an excellent education for his or her child.

Republican leadership has nearly doubled funds for Head Start, making it possible, for the first time, for all eligible four-year-olds to participate, should their parents choose to enroll them. The Bush Administration has put a college education within reach of millions more students, young and old. The President has proposed allowing families to deduct the interest they pay on student loans, and penalty-free withdrawal of IRA funds for educational expenses.

Ensuring High Standards in Knowledge and Skills

For America to compete in a world where 85 percent of all jobs will require high skills, we believe that students not planning to attend college need better opportunities. America's college graduates set the world pace for knowledge and skills. But we also have a strong commitment to the "forgotten half" of the students in our schools, students who will graduate from high school ill-prepared for work. We must build a well-educated, high-skills workforce to ensure a new century of prosperity for America.

The President has developed a sweeping youth apprenticeship strategy to meet this goal. His plan will ensure that students meet the high standards demanded of all high school students, while training them with a skill as well. We strongly support youth apprenticeships that include a year of college, to encourage a lifetime of learning and opportunity for students.

Our Educational Beliefs

We are confident that the United States can, by the end of this decade, reach the six national education goals that President Bush and the nation's governors have established: that all children should arrive at school ready to learn; that high school graduation rates should be at least 90 percent; that all children should learn challenging subject matter and become responsible citizens; that American children should be first in the world in math and science; that there must be a literate and skilled workforce; and that schools must be disciplined and free of drugs and violence.

We have an uncompromising commitment to improve public education—which means assuring that our schools produce well-educated, responsible citizens—not the maintenance of a government monopoly over the means of educating. American families must be given choice in education. We value the important role played by our private, independent, and parochial schools, colleges, and universities. We believe that their quality is best encouraged by minimizing government regulation.

We believe distance learning is a valuable tool in the fight to bring equal educational opportunity to every student regardless of wealth or geographic location. Distance learning provides students access to the vast educational resources of our Nation.

We encourage the use of modern technology to meet the goal of educational excellence. We support policies that provide access for all instructional and educational programmers to permit them to provide the greatest choice of programming and material to schools and teachers. We also support policies which will encourage the use of all advanced technologies for the delivery of educational and instructional programming in order to give schools and teachers the greatest flexibility in providing creative and innovative instruction. We encourage local school boards to ensure review of these materials by parents and educators.

We support efforts to open the teaching profession by reforming the certification system now barring many talented men and women from the classroom.

Schools should be—as they have been traditionally—academic institutions. Families and communities err when by neglect or design they transfer to the school responsibilities that belong in the home and in the community. Schools were created to help and strengthen families, not to undermine or substitute for them.

Accordingly, we oppose programs in public schools that provide birth control or abortion services or referrals. Instead, we encourage abstinence education programs with proven track records in protecting youth from disease, pregnancy, and drug use.

The critical public mission in education is to set tough, clear standards of achievement and ensure that those who educate our children are accountable for meeting them. This is not just a matter of plans or dollars. Competency testing and merit pay for teachers are essential elements of such accountability.

We are proud of our many dedicated, professional teachers and educators who have committed their lives to educating America's children. We also believe that powerful unions and liberal special interest groups should not be the driving force in education reform.

Just as spiritual principles—our moral compass—help guide public policy, learning must have a moral basis. America must remain neutral toward particular religions, but we must not remain neutral toward religion itself or the values religion supports. Mindful of our country's Judeo-Christian heritage and rich religious pluralism, we support the right of students to engage in voluntary prayer in schools and the right of the community to do so at commencements or other occasions. We will strongly enforce the law guaranteeing equal access to school facilities. We also advocate recitation of the Pledge of Allegiance in schools as a reminder of the principles that sustain us as one Nation under God.

Our ambitious vision for America works, however, only in a society of well-educated citizens. The Democrat Party, beholden to the special interests who resist change, can never accomplish the improvements in education which our schools and our children so desperately need. Indeed, they have no plan. The Republican Party has started an education revolution. We have presented a detailed plan which is even now becoming reality. The future of our Nation demands no less. The President is leading the country on an education crusade, a crusade the American people have joined.

For Healthier Families: Promote Health, Prevent Disease, Reform Health Care

Americans receive the finest medical care in the world. We have the best health care providers, the best hospitals, and the best medical technology. People come here from Canada, from Europe, from every part of the globe to seek procedures and treatments that are either unavailable or strictly rationed in their home countries.

But we must do better. Costs are soaring. Many Americans, responsible for children and aging parents, worry about the quality and price of care. The 1992 election presents all of us with a clear choice. Democrats want a costly, coercive system, imported from abroad, with a budget set by Congress and policies set by bureaucrats. That is a prescription for misery. It would imperil jobs, require billions in new taxes, lower the quality of health care overall, drive health care providers out of the profession, and result in rationing.

The congressional Democrats' health care reform proposal would exclude themselves from coverage under their own program. They refuse to live with the scheme they are trying to force on the rest of the country.

Republicans believe government control of health care is irresponsible and ineffective. We believe health care choices should remain in the hands of the people, not government bureaucrats. This issue truly represents a fundamental difference between the two parties.

We endorse President Bush's comprehensive health care plan, which solves the two major problems of the current system—access and affordability—while preserving the high quality care Americans now enjoy. The President's plan will make health care *more affordable* through tax credits and deductions that will offset insurance costs for 95 million Americans; and make health care *more accessible*, especially for small businesses, by reducing insurance costs and eliminating workers' worries of losing insurance if they change jobs. This plan will expand access to health care by:

- Creating new tax credits and deductions to help low- and middle-income Americans. These tax credits would be available in the form of vouchers for low-income people who work.
- Providing insurance security for working

Americans by requiring insurers to cover preexisting conditions.
- Making health insurance premiums fully deductible for the self-employed.
- Making it easier for small firms to purchase coverage for their employees. The proposal would allow small businesses to form health insurance purchasing pools that would make insurance more affordable. It also would guarantee the availability and renewability of insurance for small firms, set premium standards, preempt State mandated-benefit laws, establish minimum coverage plans, and require States to establish risk pools to spread risks broadly across health insurers.
- Addressing the medical malpractice problem by a cap on noneconomic damage recoveries in malpractice claims and an alternative dispute resolution before going to court.

In short, the President aims to make coverage available to all guaranteed, renewable, with no preconditions. Under this plan, no one will have to go broke to get well.

The Democrats' plan stands in stark philosophical contrast. Instead of preserving individual options, it would rely on government bureaucrats. Instead of preserving quality care, it would lead to rationing and waiting lines. And instead of enhancing the health care security of American workers, it would require a massive increase in payroll taxes that would destroy hundreds of thousands of jobs.

The Democrats' so-called "play or pay" proposal would require employers either to provide health insurance for their workers or pay a new tax that would fund in part a new government-run health program. According to a study prepared by the Urban Institute, this mandate would require new federal taxes—or new federal borrowing—of $36 billion in the first year alone. Nearly 52 million Americans who now have private health insurance would be dumped by their employers onto the government-run plan. Additional costs to employers—particularly small employers—would total an estimated $30 billion in the first year. The Republican staff of Congress' Joint Economic Committee estimates that 712,000 people would lose their jobs because of the "play or pay" mandate.

Republicans are also determined to resolve the crisis in medical liability, allowing physicians and certified midwives to deliver babies and practice in underserved areas. Meaningful medical tort reform would assure that doctors would not have to practice medicine under a cloud of potential litigation. We will reduce administrative expenses and paperwork by adopting a uniform claim and data system. We pledge our support for rehabilitation and long-term care coverage. We will curb costs through better prenatal and other preventive care. We encourage the application of the Good Samaritan law to protect health care providers who wish to volunteer their time to provide patient care to the community. We encourage coordinated care in public programs and private insurance. We further support regulatory reforms to speed the development of new drugs and medical technology.

The health care safety net must be secure for those who need preventive, acute, and long-term care. Special consideration should be given to abolishing or reforming programs which prohibit or discourage individuals from seeking to work their way out of poverty and dependency. We will reduce paperwork burdens and redirect those resources to actual services. We will enhance access to medical care through community health centers, which provide primary care in medically underserved areas. We will modify outdated antitrust rules that prohibit hospitals from merging their resources to provide improved, cost-effective health care.

We encourage the use of telecommunications technology to link hospitals in larger communities with health care facilities in smaller communities. Advanced communications networks will facilitate the sharing of resources, will improve access to affordable health care through the transmission of medical imaging and diagnostics, and will ensure that Americans living in rural areas have the same access to doctors and the latest medical procedures as Americans living in urban areas.

Republicans focus on health, not just health care. We want not only to treat disease and disability, but to reduce and prevent them. Through funding for NIH, we invest in research to cure a range of diseases, from cancer to heart disease, from multiple sclerosis to lupus. We support efforts which foster early cancer detection. Even more important, we rely on individuals to lower the incidence of preventable illness and injury. A large part of our health care costs, public and private, is caused by behavior. Good judgment can save billions of dollars—and perhaps millions of lives.

AIDS

The HIV/AIDS epidemic has exploded over the past decade into a crisis of tragic proportions. In our country, AIDS has already claimed more than 150,000 lives, and as many as one million more Americans may have been infected with the virus.

Epidemics have, throughout history, challenged governments, which have too often been powerless to combat them. Science—and human wisdom—have advanced, however, and we have met this crisis not only with a massive commitment of resources but also with a personal determination on the part of the President. That commitment and leadership will continue.

AIDS should be treated like any other communicable or sexually transmitted disease, while at the same time preserving patient confidentiality. We are committed to ensure that our Nation's response to AIDS is shaped by compassion, not fear or ignorance, and will oppose, as a matter of decency and honor, any discrimination against Americans who are its victims.

We encourage State legislatures to enact legislation which makes it a criminal act for anyone knowingly to transmit the AIDS virus.

We will seek to ensure that medical personnel, and the people who trust in their care, will be protected against infection.

This disease also challenges America scientifically. We must succeed in slowing the epidemic's spread. The Administration has thus placed great emphasis on a variety of prevention efforts to do so. We must recognize, also, that prevention is linked ultimately to personal responsibility and moral behavior. We reject the notion that the distribution of clean needles and condoms are the solution to stopping the spread of AIDS. Education designed to curb the spread of this disease should stress marital fidelity, abstinence, and a drug free lifestyle. There must be a means for successfully treating the virus, and this has led to a threefold increase in research and steps to speed the approval process for new drugs that could make a crucial difference to those infected. Above all, a cure must be found. We have committed enormous resources—$4.2 billion over the past four years for research alone, more than for any disease except cancer. In keeping with the American spirit, our fellow citizens with HIV/AIDS deserve our compassion and our care, and they deserve our united commitment to a cure.

Healthy Families

Responsible families are the key to wellness. They are the best guard against infant mortality and child abuse. We support programs to help mothers and their babies get a good start in life, and we call for strong action, at all levels of government, to enforce parental responsibility with regard to alcohol, drugs, and neglect.

We applaud the President's initiatives to require the involvement of more women in clinical trials and to create within NIH a center to combat breast and cervical cancer. We also call for expanded research on various diseases, common to both men and women, but whose effects on women have yet to be determined.

We call for fetal protection in the workplace and in scientific research.

The Homeless

The Bush Administration has worked vigorously to address this tragedy, believing that involuntary homelessness in America is unacceptable. Accordingly, the Administration has proposed $4 billion in homeless assistance, an amount cut back by the Democrat-controlled Congress. We have also implemented a SHELTER PLUS CARE program designed to assist homeless persons who are mentally ill, chemically dependent, or stricken with AIDS. Republicans remain determined to help the homeless as a matter of ethical commitment as well as sound public policy.

Older Americans

The interests of older Americans are addressed throughout this Platform, for the elderly play an honored role in all walks of American life. From reducing inflation to fighting crime, from quality health care to a cleaner environment, the Republican agenda for all has particular relevance to those who have worked the longest and grown the wisest.

We reaffirm our commitment to a strong Social Security system. To stop penalizing grandparents and other seniors who care for children, we pledge to continue the Republican crusade to end the earnings limitation for Social Security recipients. More than ever, our Nation needs older Americans in its schools and workplaces. There should be no barriers to their full participation in our country's future. We pledge support for greater availability of long-term care and for research to combat Alzheimer's disease. Republicans also took the lead in expanding home health care in government programs, and we want to build on that accomplishment.

Promoting Cultural Values

The culture of our Nation has traditionally supported those pillars on which civilized society is built: personal responsibility, morality, and the family. Today, however, these pillars are under assault. Elements within the media, the entertainment industry, academia, and the Democrat Party are waging a guerrilla war against American values. They deny personal responsibility, disparage traditional morality, denigrate religion, and promote hostility toward the family's way of life. Children, the members of our society most vulnerable to cultural influences, are barraged with violence and promiscuity, encouraging reckless and irresponsible behavior. This undermines the authority of parents, the ones most responsible for passing on to their offspring a sense of right and wrong. The lesson our Party draws is important—that all of us, individuals and corporations alike, have a responsibility to reflect the values we expect our fellow citizens to exhibit. And if children grow to adulthood reflecting not the values of their parents but the amorality with which they are bombarded, those who send such messages cannot duck culpability.

One example is the advocacy of violence against law enforcement officers, promoted by a corporation more interested in profits than the possible consequences of such a message. We believe, in the spirit of Theodore Roosevelt, that corporations, like individuals, have responsibilities to society, and that conscience alone should prevent such outrages.

We also stand united with those private organizations, such as the Boy Scouts of America, who are defending decency in fulfillment of their own moral responsibilities. We reject the irresponsible position of those corporations that have cut off contributions to such organizations because of their courageous stand for family values. Moreover, we oppose efforts by the Democrat Party to include sexual preference as a protected minority receiving preferential status under civil rights statutes at the federal, State, and local level.

We oppose any legislation or law which legally recognizes same-sex marriages and allows such couples to adopt children or provide foster care.

We must recognize that the time has come for a national crusade against pornography. Some would have us believe that obscenity and pornography have no social impact. But if hard-core pornography does not cheapen the human spirit, then neither does Shakespeare elevate it. We call on federal agencies to halt the sale, under government auspices, of pornographic materials. We endorse Republican legislation, the Pornography Victims Compensation Act, allowing victims of pornography to seek damages from those who make or sell it, especially since the Commission on Pornography, in 1986, found a direct link between pornography and violent crimes committed against women and children. Further, we propose a computerized federal registry to track persons convicted of molesting children. We also believe that the various State legislatures should create a civil cause of action against makers and distributors of pornography when their material incites a violent crime.

Government has a responsibility, as well, to ensure that it promotes the common moral values that bind us together as a Nation. We therefore condemn the use of public funds to subsidize obscenity and blasphemy masquerading as art. The fine arts, including those with public support, can certainly enrich our society.

However, no artist has an inherent right to claim taxpayer support for his or her private vision of art if that vision mocks the moral and spiritual basis on which our society is founded. We believe a free market in art—with neither suppression no favoritism by government—is the best way to foster the cultural revival our country needs.

Individual Rights, Good Homes and Safer Streets

At a time when the rest of the world has rejected socialism, there are communities here at home where free markets have not been permitted to flourish. Decades of liberalism have left us with two economies. The pro-growth economy rewards effort, promotes thrift, and supports strong families. The other economy stifles initiative and is anti-work and anti-family. In one economy, people are free to be owners and entrepreneurs. In the other economy, people are at the mercy of government. We are determined to elevate the poor into the pro-growth economy.

Republicans will lead a new national consensus around economic opportunity, greater access to property, home ownership and housing, jobs and entrepreneurship. We must bring the great promise of America to every city, every small town, and to all our people.

Our agenda for equality of opportunity runs throughout this Platform and applies to all Americans. There is no such thing as segregated success. We reject the Democrats' politics of division, envy and conflict. They believe that America is split into classes and can be healed only through the redistribution of wealth. We believe in the economics of multiplication: free markets expand opportunity and wealth for all.

That is true liberation. It frees poor people not only from want but also from government control. That is why liberal Democrats have fought us every step of the way, refusing congressional action on enterprise zones until Los Angeles burned—and then mocking the expectations of the poor by gutting that critical proposal. They can kill bills, but they cannot kill hope. We are determined to pass that legislation for the sake of all who are awaiting their chance for the American Dream.

We will eliminate laws that keep Americans out of jobs, like the outdated ban on home work. The antiquated Davis–Bacon Act inflates taxpayer costs and keeps willing workers from getting jobs in federally assisted projects. It must go. Unlike the Democrats, we believe the private sector, not the federal government, should set prevailing wage rates.

As explained elsewhere in this Platform, low-income families must gain control of their future through choice in their children's education.

Rebuilding the Dream

Our Party has always championed the American dream of home ownership. Abraham Lincoln wanted all families to have access to property, because it would give them a tangible stake in their family's future. As families built homes and improved the land, they built a brighter future for themselves and a legacy for their children. Lincoln's Homestead Act of 1862 did all this without enlarging government. It empowered families.

In the tradition of Lincoln, President Bush has replicated the American dream of home ownership. For first-time home buyers, he has proposed a $5,000 tax credit. For lower-income families, he has worked to restore opportunity through HOPE, his initiative to help tenants now dependent on federal aid to buy their own homes; Mortgage Revenue Bonds, to assist more than 1.9 million families to buy a first home; Low Income Housing Tax Credits, already producing more than 420,000 decent apartments at affordable prices; and HOME, a partnership among all levels of government to help low-income families secure better housing.

For everyone, but especially for the poor, the best housing policy is non-inflationary economic growth with low interest rates, the heart of our opportunity agenda.

Ending Dependency

Welfare is the enemy of opportunity and stable family life. Two decades ago, decisions about public assistance were taken away from States and communities and given to Washington officials. Since then, almost everything has gone wrong. Since 1965, we have spent $3.5 trillion on welfare. It bought a horrendous expansion of dependence, especially among mothers and children.

Today's welfare system is anti-work and anti-marriage. It taxes families to subsidize illegitimacy. It rewards unethical behavior and penalizes initiative. It cannot be merely tinkered with by Congress, it must be recreated by States and localities. Republican governors and legislators in several States have already launched dramatic reforms, especially with workfare and learnfare. Welfare can no longer be a check in the mail with no responsibility.

We believe fathers and mothers must be held responsible for their children. We support strongest enforcement of child support laws. We call for strong enforcement and tough penalties against welfare fraud and insist that work must be a mandatory part of public assistance for all who are able to work. Because divorce, desertion, and illegitimacy account for almost all the increase in child poverty over the last 20 years, we put the highest priority upon enforcement of family rights and responsibilities.

Among these responsibilities is the obligation to get an education—a key to avoiding dependency. Families on welfare with school-age children must be required to send them to school or provide adequate home education in keeping with various State laws in order to continue receiving public assistance. Young adult heads of welfare households should be required to complete appropriate education or training programs.

Safe Homes and Streets

One of the first duties of government is to protect the public security—to maintain law and order so that citizens are free to pursue the fruits of life and liberty. The Democrats have forsaken this solemn pledge. Instead of protecting society from hardened criminals, they blame society and refuse to hold accountable for their actions individuals who have chosen to engage in violent and criminal conduct. This has led to the state of affairs in which we find ourselves today.

Violent crime is the gravest domestic threat to our way of life. It has turned our communities into battlegrounds, playgrounds into graveyards. It threatens everyone, but especially the very young, the elderly, the weak. It destroys business and suffocates economic opportunity in struggling communities. It is a travesty that some American children have to sleep in bathtubs for protection from stray bullets. The poverty of values that justifies drive-by shootings and random violence holds us hostage and insecure, even in our own homes. We must work to develop community-help projects designed to instill a sense of responsibility and pride.

This is the legacy of a liberalism that elevates criminals' rights above victims' rights, that justifies soft-on-crime judges' approving early-release prison programs, and that leaves law enforcement officers powerless to deter crime with the threat of certain punishment.

For twelve years, two Republican Presidents have fought to reverse this trend, along with Republican officials in the States. They have named tough law-and-order judges, pushed for minimum mandatory sentences, expanded federal assistance to States and localities, sought to help States redress court orders on prison overcrowding, and devoted record resources that are turning the tide against drugs. They have repeatedly proposed legislation, consistently rejected by congressional Democrats, to restore the severest penalties for the most heinous crimes, to ensure swift and certain punishment, and to end the legal loopholes that let criminals go free.

Congressional Democrats reject Republican reform of the exclusionary rule that prohibits use of relevant evidence obtained in good faith and allows criminals, even murderers, to go free on a technicality. They reject our reform of *habeas corpus* law to prevent the appellate process from becoming a lawyers' game to thwart justice through endless appeals and procedural delays. They refuse to enact effective procedures to reinstate the death penalty for the most heinous crimes. They reject tougher, mandatory sentences for career criminals. Instead, congressional Democrats actually voted to create more loopholes for vicious thugs and fewer protections for victims of crime and have opposed mandatory restitution for victims. Their crime legislation, which we emphatically reject, cripples law enforcement by overturning over twenty United States Supreme Court cases that have helped to reduce crime and keep violent criminal offenders off the streets.

For too long our criminal justice system has carefully protected the rights of criminals and neglected the suffering of the innocent victims of crime and their families. We support the rights of crime victims to be present, heard, and informed throughout the criminal justice process and to be provided with restitution and services to aid their recovery.

We believe in giving police the resources to do their job. Law enforcement must remain primarily a State and local responsibility. With 95 percent of all violent crimes within the jurisdiction of the States, we have led efforts to increase the number of police protecting our citizens. We also support incentives to encourage personnel leaving the armed forces to continue to defend their country—against the enemy within—by entering the law enforcement profession.

Narcotics traffic drives street crime. President Bush has, for the first time, used the resources of our armed forces against the international drug trade. By our insistence, multilateral control of precursor chemicals and money laundering is now an international priority. We decry efforts by congressional Democrats to slash international anti-narcotics funding and inhibit the most vital control efforts in Peru. We support efforts to work with South and Central American leaders to eradicate crops used to produce illegal narcotics.

The Republican Party is committed to a drug free America. During the last twelve years, we have radically reversed the Democrats' attitude of tolerance toward narcotics, vastly increased federal operations against drugs, cleaned up the military, and launched mandatory testing for employees in various fields, including White House personnel. As a result, overall drug abuse is falling. We urge that States and communities emphasize anti-drug education by police officers and others in schools to educate young children to the dangers of the drug culture. Dope is no longer trendy.

We oppose legalizing or decriminalizing drugs. That is a morally abhorrent idea, the last vestige of an ill-conceived philosophy that counseled the legitimacy of permissiveness. Today, a similarly dysfunctional morality explains away drug dealing as an escape, and drive-by shootings as an act of political violence. There is no excuse for the wanton destruction of human life. We therefore support the stiffest penalities, including the death penalty, for major drug traffickers.

Drug users must face punishment, including fines and imprisonment, for contributing to the demand that makes the drug trade profitable. Among possible sanctions should be the loss of government assistance and suspension of drivers' licenses. Residents of public housing should be able to protect their families against drugs by screening out abusers and dealers. We support grassroots action to drive dealers and crack-houses out of operation.

Safe streets also mean highways that are free of drunken drivers and drivers under the influence of illegal drugs. Republicans support the toughest possible State laws to deal with drunken drivers and users of illegal drugs, who deserve no sympathy from our courts or State legislatures. We also oppose the illicit abuse of legal drugs.

White-collar crime threatens homes and families in a different way. It steals secretly, forcing up prices, rigging contracts, swindling consumers, and harming the overwhelming majority of business people, who play fair and obey the law. We support imprisonment for those who steal from the American people. We pledge an all-out fight against it, especially within the political machines that control many of our major cities. We will continue to bring to justice corrupt politicians and those who collude with them to plunder savings and loans.

New Members of the American Family
Our Nation of immigrants continues to welcome those seeking a better life. This reflects our past, when some newcomers fled intolerance; some sought prosperity; some came as slaves. All suffered and sacrificed but hoped their children would have a better life. All searched for a shared vision—and found one in America. Today we are stronger for our diversity.

Illegal entry into the United States, on the other hand, threatens the social compact on which immigration is based. That is, the nation accepts immigrants and is enriched by their determination and values. Illegal immigration, on the other hand, undermines

the integrity of border communities and already crowded urban neighborhoods. We will build on the already announced strengthening of the Border Patrol to better coordinate interdiction of illegal entrants through greater cross-border cooperation. Specifically, we will increase the size of the Border Patrol in order to meet the increasing need to stop illegal immigration and we will equip the Border Patrol with the tools, technologies, and structures necessary to secure the border.

We will seek stiff penalities for those who smuggle illegal aliens into the country, and for those who produce or sell fraudulent documents. We also will reduce incentives to enter the United States by promoting initiatives like the North American Free Trade Agreement. In creating new economic opportunity in Mexico, a NAFTA removes the incentive to cross the border illegally in search of work.

Individual Rights
The protection of individual rights is the foundation for opportunity and security.

The Republican Party is unique in this regard. Since its inception, it has respected every person, even when that proposition was not universally popular. Today, as the day of Lincoln, we insist that no American's rights are negotiable.

That is why we declare that bigotry and prejudice have no place in American life. We denounce all who practice or promote racism, anti-Semitism, or religious intolerance. We believe churches and religious schools should not be taxed; we defend the right of religious leaders to speak out on public issues; and we condemn the cowardly desecration of places of worship that has shocked our country in recent years.

Asserting equal rights for all, we support the Bush Administration's vigorous enforcement of statutes to prevent illegal discrimination on account of sex, race, creed, or national origin. Promoting opportunity, we reject efforts to replace equal rights with quotas or other preferential treatment. That is why President Bush fought so long against the Democrat Congress to win a civil rights bill worthy of that name.

We renew the historic Republican commitment to the rights of women, from the early days of the suffragist movement to the present. Because legal rights mean little without opportunity, we assert economic growth as the key to the continued progress of women in all fields of American life.

We believe the unborn child has a fundamental individual right to life which cannot be infringed. We therefore reaffirm our support for a human life amendment to the Constitution, and we endorse legislation to make clear that the Fourteenth Amendment's protections apply to unborn children. We oppose using public revenues for abortion and will not fund organizations which advocate it. We commend those who provide alternatives for abortion by meeting the needs of mothers and offering adoption services. We reaffirm our support for appointment of judges who respect traditional family values and the sanctity of innocent human life.

President Bush signed into law the greatest advance ever for disabled persons: the Americans with Disabilities Act, a milestone in removing barriers to full participation in our country's life. We will fully implement it, with sensitivity to the needs of small businesses, just as we have earlier legal protections for the disabled in federal programs. We oppose the nonconsensual withholding of health care or treatment from any person because of handicap, age, or infirmity, just as we oppose euthanasia and assisted suicide.

We support full access to the polls, and the entire political process, by disabled voters. We will ensure that students with disabilities benefit from AMERICA 2000's new emphasis on testing for excellence and accountability for results.

Promoting the rights of the disabled requires, before all else, an expanding economy, both to advance assistive technology and to create opportunities for personal advancement. That is another reason why Republicans are committed to growth.

We reaffirm our commitment to the Fifth Amendment to the Constitution: "No person shall be . . . deprived of life, or property, without due process of law; nor shall private property be taken for public use, without just compensation." We support strong enforcement of this Takings clause to keep citizens secure in the use and development of their property. We also seek to reduce the amount of land owned or controlled by the government, especially in the western States. We insist upon prompt payment for private lands certified as critical for preserving essential parks and preserves.

Republicans defend the constitutional right to keep and bear arms. We call for stiff mandatory sentences for those who use firearms in a crime. We note that those who seek to disarm citizens in their homes are the same liberals who tried to disarm our Nation during the Cold War and are today seeking to cut our national defense below safe levels. We applaud congressional Republicans for overturning the District of Columbia's law blaming firearm manufacturers for street crime.

We affirm the right of individuals to form, join, or assist labor organizations to bargain collectively, consistent with State laws. We support the right of States to enact Right-to-Work laws.

A Republican Congress will amend the Hobbs Act, so that union officials will not be exempt from the law's prohibition against extortion and violence. We call for greater legal protection from violence for workers who stay on the job during strikes.

We support self-determination for Indian Tribes in managing their own affairs and resources. Recognizing the government-to-government trust responsibility, we aim to end dependency fostered by federal controls. Reservations and tribal lands held in trust should be free to become enterprise zones so their people can fully share in the Nation's prosperity. We will work with tribal governments to improve education, health, economic opportunity, and environmental conditions. We endorse efforts to preserve the culture and languages of Native Americans and Hawaiians and to ensure their equitable participation in federal programs.

UNITING OUR COUNTRY

Over the last four years, the United States has achieved our overriding objective since the end of World War II. Communism and other forms of planned economies lie in the ash heap of history, defeated not only by our military strength but by the force of our ideas—democracy and free enterprise.

Now a huge international market is evolving. Combined with America's low inflation and low interest rate environment, it presents us with unprecedented economic opportunity. We commit to the proposition that the American economy will remain first in the world. This is our goal. Achieving it will ensure that our people will enjoy the jobs, benefits, and economic growth to sustain the American dream for themselves and their posterity.

Republicans believe that the greatest engine for social change and economic progress is the entrepreneurial economy. We believe that America has broken down the lines of class to a greater degree than any society on earth, not because of government but because of an economic system that allows men and women to create wealth for themselves and their communities. We believe that positive change can occur and benefit all Americans if we continue to remove governmental barriers to entrepreneurship and, thus, economic growth.

Our cause embraces traditional ideals and modern realities. It both reforms and innovates. We aim to shape history through faith in one another. Because we look forward, we emphasize saving, investment, and job creation. We encourage innovation and the entre-preneurial spirit that are, together, part of our national character. We both conserve and develop our natural resources. Because we have learned from the past, we are determined to change what desperately needs changing in government.

Government does not have all the answers, but we know where to find them: in the spirit of our people. We know the weapons for this battle: economic and political liberty in the pursuit of happiness. We understand that material gain improves life only if it lifts us all to pursue higher ends: self-respect, work and study, a decent life and future for our children, and a useful old age.

So we rededicate ourselves to the truths the Nation keeps coming back to—the simple, spiritual truths about our family, our country, our world—for upon them we will build our more perfect union.

Security and Opportunity in a Changing Economy

Our economy is people, not statistics. The American people, not government, rescued the United States from an economic collapse triggered by Democrats in the 1970s. Crippled by taxes, robbed by inflation, threatened by controls, stunned by interest rates, the people ended America's decline and restored hope across our country and around our world.

We launched an era of growth and prosperity such as the world had never seen: 20 million new jobs in the longest peacetime economic expansion in the history of the Republic. We curbed the size and power of the federal establishment. We lowered tax rates. We restored a sound dollar. We unleashed the might of free people to produce, compete, and triumph in free markets. We gave them the tools, they completed the job.

During the 1980s and into the present decade, the U.S. economy once again became the engine of global growth. Inflation has fallen to its lowest level in 30 years. Interest rates dropped 15 percentage points. Productivity has sharply risen. Exports are booming. Despite a global downturn in late 1990, real economic growth resumed last year and has continued for five consecutive quarters. With low interest rates and low inflation, the American economy is poised for stronger growth through the rest of the 1990s. Keeping inflation and interest rates low and stable through a sound monetary policy is essential for economic growth.

These gains were made in spite of the leaders of the Democrat Party. They continue to delay and defeat the President's agenda for growth, jobs, and prosperity. Spending faster than ever, they blocked Republican re-forms that would have saved billions of wasted tax-payer dollars. They refused to give the President a line-item veto to curb their self-serving pork-barrel projects.

The congressional Democrat leadership killed the Taxpayer Protection Amendment for a balanced budget in the Democrat-controlled House of Representatives. It was supported by 98 percent of the Republican members; 57 percent of the Democrat members voted no. Then they rigged parliamentary procedures to forbid a vote on that Amendment in the Democrat-controlled Senate. Every Republican Senator voted twice to end the filibuster, while more than 70 percent of the Democrats voted, twice, to keep the filibuster going. Their nominee this year for the Vice Presidency supported the filibuster and spurned the Balanced Budget Amendment.

They played citizens against one another, wallowing in the politics of hate and envy to smear the wonder of social mobility. They lied about America's achievement in the 1980s, rewriting history to erase the true accomplishments of the American people.

Keeping What You Earn

The test of economic policy is whether it promotes economic growth and expands job opportunities. Lower taxes and an expanding economy depend on long-term, consistent restraint in the growth of federal spending.

In 1990, as the deficit was threatening to balloon and further harm the economy, the President pushed for cuts in government spending overall and for caps on mandatory spending. The Democrat Congress insisted, however, on a tax hike as their price for controlling spending. In short, the Democrats held the U.S. economy—and U.S. jobs—hostage in order to raise taxes, much as they had done to President Reagan.

Just as they did with President Reagan, the Democrat-controlled Congress promised President Bush they would abide by binding controls on federal spending; and just as with President Reagan, they broke their word. Republicans will not again agree to such a program.

This year, to create jobs and promote growth, President Bush submitted a program of tax cuts and incentives designed to get the economy moving again—a program very similar to one he had sent to Congress in early 1990. The Democrats' response was predictable—instead of cutting taxes, they passed a $100 billion tax increase that would have smothered growth and jobs. The President, true to our Republican philosophy, vetoed this tax hike, and sustained his veto with the support of Republicans in Congress.

Now a new Democrat nominee comes forward with his plan for the economy. With a clean piece of paper, and every opportunity to end his party's romance with taxes, he has instead proposed the largest tax increase in American history. His tax increases, his proposed mandated benefits on small firms, and his further reductions in defense would cost the jobs of 2.6 million Americans. With his present spending increases, his plan would greatly increase the federal budget and the deficit.

The simple truth for the American people is this: The only safeguard between themselves and Democrat tax increases is the use of the veto by George Bush and enough Republican votes in Congress to sustain it.

The truth is that the Democrat philosophy of bigger government and rigorous redistribution of income requires them to push for ever increasing spending and ever higher taxes.

The choice is clear—between George Bush, who vetoes tax increases, and his opponent, who proposes a $150 billion tax increase.

Our Republican position is equally clear: we will oppose any attempt to increase taxes. Furthermore, Republicans believe that the taxes insisted on by the Democrats in the 1990 budget agreement were recessionary. The Democrat Congress held President Bush and indeed all American hostage, refusing to take even modest steps to control spending, unless taxes were increased. The American economy suffered as a result. We believe the tax increases of 1990 should ultimately be repealed.

Just as history shows that tax increases destroy jobs and economic growth, it also shows that the proper path to create jobs and growth is tax rate reduction.

We commend those congressional and senatorial candidates who pledge to oppose tax rate increases.

As the deficit comes under control, we aspire to further tax rate cuts, strengthening incentives to work, save, invest, and innovate. We also support President Bush's efforts to reduce federal spending and to cap the growth of non–Social Security entitlements.

Republicans want individuals and families to control their own economic destiny. Only long-term expansion of our economy and jobs can make the American dream a reality for generations to come. That is why we demand that the Congress do what President Bush called for last January, open a new era of growth and opportunity by enacting his comprehensive plan for economic recovery, including a reduction in the capital gains tax; and investment tax allowance; a $5,000 tax credit for first-time home buyers; a needed modification of the "passive loss rule"; a $500 increase in the personal income tax exemption; making permanent the research and development tax credit; and the passage of federal enterprise zone legislation.

We support restoring the deductibility of IRAs for all Americans, including full-time homemakers, and encourage savings for education and home ownership through Family Savings Accounts. The President's Family Savings Accounts will be an impetus to the economy. Let families use their IRAs for first-time home purchases, for college education, and for medical emergencies.

We will cut the capital gains tax rate to 15 percent—zero in enterprise zones—and index it so government cannot profit from inflation by taxing phantom capital gains, literally stealing from savings and pensions.

We reject the notion advanced by Democrats that this enhances the wealthy. To the contrary, it would encourage investment, create new jobs, make capital available for business expansion, and contribute to economic expansion.

Reducing the tax on investment will be the biggest possible boost for the new technologies, businesses, and jobs we need for the next century. If government taxes capital gains at such a high rate that there is no incentive to take risks, to build businesses, to invest, to create jobs, or to better oneself, then jobs and small businesses vanish and everyone's opportunities are diminished.

Cutting the rate, on the other hand, will help supply seed capital where it is needed most—in our poorest communities. Refusing to cut it will handcuff America in international competition and will shackle aspiring entrepreneurs in inner cities and poor rural areas. To encourage investment in new technologies, we will make permanent the research and development tax credit. For the same reason, we want to expand deductibility for investments in new plants and equipment.

We support further tax simplification. The tax code should create jobs for Americans, not profits for tax lawyers, lobbyists, and tax-shelters. Small businesses should spend more time hiring and producing, not filling out IRS forms.

We oppose taxing religious and ethnic fraternal benefit societies because of their vital role in fostering charity and patriotism.

We also oppose tax withholding on savings and dividends.

We applaud the efforts by President Bush to help workers who change jobs by enhancing the portability of pensions.

Leading Democrat members of Congress have called for a national sales tax, or European-style Value Added Tax (VAT), which would take billions of dollars out of the hands of American consumers. Such a tax has been imposed on many nations in Europe and has resulted in higher prices, fewer jobs, and higher levels of government spending. Republicans oppose the idea of putting a VAT on the backs of the American people.

Republicans believe in expanding the economy. Jobs and growth are our answer to the future.

The Future Is the Family

The most dramatic change in the tax code in our lifetime is one that has never been explicitly enacted by Congress or reported as a specific news event. It is the gradual, year-by-year erosion of the personal exemption, until it was indexed by a Republican Administration in 1986.

Republicans also led the way in the 1980s by increasing the personal exemption from $1,500 to $2,000. This platform calls for another immediate increase of $500, but in the long run we are committed to fully restoring the inflation-adjusted value of the personal exemption. This will require reductions in federal spending, which is why the best hope for tax fairness for America's families lies in a Republican Congress.

Liberation Through Deregulation

Government regulation is a hidden tax on American families, costing each household more than $5,000 every year. It stifles job creation and hobbles our national competitiveness. The "Iron Triangle" of special interests, federal bureaucrats and Democrat congressional staff is robbing consumers and producers alike.

We support President Bush's freeze on new regulations. We applaud his Competitiveness Council, under Vice President Quayle, for fighting the regulatory mania, saving the public $20 billion with its initial 90 day moratorium on new regulations and billions more under the current 120 day freeze. We call for a permanent moratorium until our regulatory reforms are fully in place. They include market-based regulation, cost benefit analysis of all new rule making, and a Regulatory Budget that will make Congress admit—and correct—the harm it does by legislation that destroys jobs and competitiveness.

We recognize that property rights are being endangered by government overregulation. We reaffirm the constitutional right to private ownership of property; this right is paramount in our free society. Every rule that reduces the value of private property is what our Constitution calls a "taking." This under-the-table taxation is unfair, immoral, and economically destructive. We support legislation to require full compensation of property owners who are victims of regulatory takings.

Home Ownership

The best housing policy is a non-inflationary, growing economy that has produced low mortgage rates and has made housing more affordable.

We demand Congress enact President Bush's housing program introduced as part of his pro-growth package in January.

Provide a $5,000 tax credit for first-time home buyers and allow them penalty-free IRA withdrawals.

Set a modified "passive loss rule" for active real estate investors.

Extend tax preferences for mortgage revenue bonds and low-income housing.

And allow deductions for losses on personal residences.

The average American's home is his or her primary asset. That asset should be completely shielded from federal taxation, allowing the homeowner to maintain it or access it as he or she sees fit. We call for the complete elimination of the capital gains tax on the sale of a principal residence.

Owning a home is not just an investment. It is a commitment to the community, a guard against crime, a statement about family life. It is a crucial component of upward mobility. To advance these goals, Republicans are determined to preserve deductibility of mortgage interest.

Bureaucratic government imposes too many regulatory barriers to affordable housing. These barriers must come down.

We applaud efforts in the States to lower property taxes, which strike hardest at the poor, elderly, families with children, and family farmers. We advocate repeal of rent control laws, which help the affluent and hurt low-income families by causing housing shortages.

We support the FHA mortgage insurance program, the Government National Mortgage Association, the VA guarantee program, and other programs that enhance housing choices for all. We urge federal departments and agencies to work with the private sector to bring foreclosed housing stock back into service as soon as possible.

We reaffirm our commitment to open housing, without quotas or controls, as part of the opportunity we seek for all.

For low-income families, the Republican Party stands for a revolution in housing by converting public housing into homes owned by low-income Americans. President Bush is eager to work closely with the States to fight and win a new conservative war on poverty. The truest measure of our success will not be how many families we add to housing assistance rolls but, rather, how many families move into the ranks of homeownership. But every part of that opportunity agenda has been thwarted by landlord Democrats in Congress. We ask the electorate: End the strangulation of divided government. Give Republicans the chance to move housing policy off the Democrat Party plantation into the mainstream of American life. Resident management and ownership of public housing reflect this American mission, not only to assure political freedom but to allow all our fellow citizens to build a better life for themselves and their children.

Congressional Democrats have consistently blocked efforts to repeal the earnings test which prevents people over age 65 from keeping their jobs and remaining productive members of the workforce. The Social Security earnings test discriminates against senior citizens. These senior citizens have to pay the highest marginal tax rate of any Americans. We support repeal of the Social Security earnings test.

Controlling Government Spending

For 12 years, Republicans in the White House and Congress have battled a Democrat system corrupt and contemptuous of the American taxpayer. Our Republican Presidents have vetoed one reckless bill after another. But liberal Democrats still control a rigged machine that keeps on spending the public's money.

The only solution is for the voters to end divided government so that a Republican Congress can enact the Balanced Budget Amendment, requiring a supermajority for any future tax increases. And since the Democrat-controlled Congress has consistently voted down a line item veto amendment for the President to control specific wasteful pork-barrel spending, a Republican Congress will adopt a line-item veto for the presidency, restore presidential power to rescind spending and to lower specific appropriations.

Deficits have grown as Democrat Congresses have converted government assistance programs into entitlements and allowed spending to become uncontrolled. A Republican Congress, working with a Republican President, will consider non–Social Security mandatory spending portions of the federal budget when looking for savings.

When legislators and bureaucrats waste tax money, they deserve to lose their jobs. When they save money, they deserve praise. When federal programs have outlived their usefulness, they deserve a decent burial. When federal judges dare to seize the power of the purse, by ordering the imposition of taxes, they should be removed from office by the procedures provided by the Constitution.

The latest Democrat scam is to raise taxes for "investment"—a code word for more government spending. A Republican Congress will foster investment where it does the most good, by individuals within the private sector.

Job Creation and Small Business Opportunities

The engines of growth in a free economy are small businesses and jobs. Almost 99 percent of all businesses in America are considered small. Small business is the backbone of the American economy. For the past 12 years it has led the way in economic growth.

Small business generates 67 percent of all new jobs. Employment in industries dominated by small business increased more than twice as fast as in industries dominated by large businesses. Small business plays a critical role in America's economic health. What happens on Main Street drives what happens on Wall Street.

To create jobs and keep small business growing, the Republican Party supports increased access to capital for business expansion, exporting, long-term investment, opportunity capital for the disadvantaged, and capital to bring new products and new technology to the market.

The Republican Party enthusiastically encourages the passage of federal enterprise zones. Enterprise zones have been effective programs for promoting growth in urban and rural America. Republicans believe that the concept of enterprise zones is based on unyielding faith in the entrepreneurial spirit of all Americans. Enterprise zones foster individual initiative and government deregulation. The States have come a long way in developing successful enterprise zone programs. State programs could only benefit from federal efforts. Congress should follow the lead of President Bush and HUD Secretary Jack Kemp in passing the federal enterprise zone program that will empower communities by reducing government regulation and taxation.

The implementation of enterprise zones as an incentive for job creation and business development is also essential to further job and business opportunities. These efforts are bolstered by continued support of job training and minority business development programs, which have been created and implemented by the President's Administration within the last three years. This is of special import to women, who own 32 percent of the Nation's businesses, most of them small ones.

Because the regulation of securities markets bars most small businesses from easy access to capital, we also support the Small Business Administration's Section 7(a) loan guarantee program and similar efforts that essentially compensate for the burdens government itself imposes upon entrepreneurs.

Leading the Information Age

The Nation's telecommunications infrastructure will be essential to growth and competitiveness in the information age. The most far-reaching transformation of daily life since the harnessing of electricity will mean unprecedented opportunity for rural areas, reduced commuting, health care in the home, and empowerment for the disabled.

Today, however, government policy at both the federal and State levels is standing in the way of this telecommunications progress. Existing judicial, legislative, and regulatory market allocation schemes constitute a counterproductive industrial policy by prohibiting the full participation by all providers in all segments of the telecommunications marketplace. We need to liberate this future-oriented technology and, in turn, empower the American people by giving consumers a truly competitive choice and lower prices.

As a result, we Republicans believe that full and open competition in the telecommunications marketplace is the most effective means for the U.S. to achieve our goal of having the most technologically advanced telecommunications infrastructure in the world.

Jobs Through Science and Technology

We believe technology holds the key to America's future—and the future is bright. America is not in decline. America is still the land of opportunity. The new horizon is science and technology. New discoveries, new challenges, and new opportunities await us. Science and technology offer us change—exciting, dramatic, and positive change in the well-being of every American.

Scientific research and development in genetics, biotechnology, and electronics will provide better, more affordable health care for all Americans. Distance learning, through technology, will help bring exciting, quality, affordable education to all students, even in rural areas and inner cities. Technology will help us conquer disease, protect the environment, and provide a more abundant, healthier food supply. And technology will lead to better jobs and a better quality of life for all of us—and for our children and our children's children.

Scientific and technological developments in telecommunications, high performance computers, high speed data networks, digitization, advanced software, biotechnology, high energy physics, advanced materials, superconductors, manufacturing processes, energy, transportation, agriculture, oceanography, atmospheric studies, geological research, space, and the environment are some of the keys to increases in productivity. And increases in productivity will create economic growth and a higher standard of living for all of us. Technology is also critical to our national defense.

We believe America must make technological development one of its highest priorities. We therefore support efforts to promote science and technology—providing funding for basic research, supporting investment in emerging technologies, improving education in science and engineering, enhancing tax credits for research and development, eliminating unnecessary regulation to create competitive markets, and protecting intellectual property. We further support efforts to increase the pace of technology transfer from the government to the private sector, where the fruits of this research can be used in the free market to create new processes, products, and most important, jobs.

We believe these policies will make us internationally competitive and will lead to a bright and prosperous future for our Nation.

President Bush has provided leadership in this arena by developing budgets allocating major new resources to scientific endeavors. The National Science Foundation, the National Institutes of Health, the National Aeronautics and Space Administration (NASA), and the research and development program in the Departments of Energy and Commerce have all become budget priorities under the President's leadership. The sad fact is, however, that the Democrat Congress has cut steadily and sharply in science areas in order to expand spending on social programs. This is short-sighted; the truth is that American innovation in science and engineering will expand our economy and jobs to greater social advantage to all Americans. A Republican Congress working with President Bush would reflect our interest in advancing scientific inquiry and assuring the resulting economic benefits for all Americans.

Space

We are a pioneer people. Today's telecommunications revolution began with the first satellites of the Eisenhower years. So too, what we now do—or fail to do—in space will determine the future for generations to come.

That is why President Bush established the National Space Council under Vice President Quayle. Together, they rescued a floundering program, revamped NASA, opened up competition, and engaged the best minds of academia and research in a twofold mission for mankind. Mission to Planet Earth will define and perhaps mitigate effects on our fragile environment. Mission from Planet Earth will open space for science and industry. Especially in this Columbia year, we hail the President's decision "to return to the moon, this time to stay, and then a journey to tomorrow, a mission to Mars."

Investments in space, though aimed at the future, pay dividends right now—in research and medicine, in international competitiveness and domestic opportunity. This must not be diverted to political pork barrels. The journey to the stars used to be a bipartisan adventure, but many Democrat officeholders have jumped ship.

Republicans, by contrast, are determined to complete Space Station Freedom within this decade. Our agenda is to lower the cost of access to space, and to broaden that access to the private sector, with a family of new launchers; to build and fly sensors for the global environment; and to advance cutting-edge capabilities like the National Aerospace Plane and single-stage-to-orbit rockets, so technological breakthroughs can be quickly exploited. We will promote space-based industry and ensure that space remains a frontier for private enterprise, not a restricted preserve for government. We will continue international cooperation in space ventures and welcome Russia's cosmonauts and citizens of other nations to fly for freedom.

Banking and Job Creation

Job creation and economic growth are dependent on a healthy and competitive financial services system that can respond to the needs of the market. The Democrat Congress stalled Republican legislation to prevent the savings and loan crisis. Then, last year, the Congress refused to pass the Republican Administration's comprehensive financial sector reform bill to strengthen our banking industry and let it compete, both domestically and internationally, consistent with the principles of safety and soundness.

We applaud the President's efforts to alleviate the continuing problems caused by a lack of funds available to creditworthy borrowers in small businesses and the housing industry. We endorse his efforts to restrain overzealous regulators, reduce regulatory compliance costs, strengthen financial institutions through diversification, and reduce unnecessary barriers to lending.

Trade: A New World of Growth

Four years ago, the American people faced an historic decision: compete or retreat. They chose, with President Bush, to compete in the international arena. Rather than retreat with the Democrats to the limits of yesteryear, they decided to attack the international marketplace with characteristic American vigor. Just as George Bush is a proven world leader on the military front, equally he is an economic world leader.

The results are spectacular. We have cut the trade deficit in half in just four years. The United States is again the world's top exporter. Exports drive our economy. Every $1 billion in exports creates 20,000 new jobs for Americans. Exports have created nearly two million new jobs at home since 1988.

We are tough free traders, battling to sweep away barriers to our exports. We are waging the Uruguay Round of the General Agreement on Tariffs and Trade (GATT) negotiations to win worldwide reductions in tariffs, elimination of subsidies, and protection of American intellectual property rights. We are fighting to reduce farm subsidies in the European Community and to break up their government-industry collusion in production of civil aircraft. We firmly endorse President Bush's policy to support the Republic of China on Taiwan in international trade and her accession to GATT. Major market access gains have been made with Japan, with American manufacturing exports tripling since 1985. Throughout the world, we enforced greater compliance with U.S. trade rights. And we are making every effort to bring home a Uruguay Round agreement that is not only good for America, but great for tomorrow's entrepreneurs everywhere.

The free trade agenda for the next four years starts with the signing of a North American Free Trade Agreement (NAFTA) with Mexico, completing the establishment of a free trade area which already includes Canada. NAFTA will create the largest market in the world, greater than the European Community, with 360 million consumers and a total output of six trillion dollars. It means a net gain of hundreds of thousands of American jobs.

We acknowledge the possible effects on regional markets, specifically agriculture. We encourage our negotiators to be sensitive to those market concerns.

We will continue to fill the Pacific Rim with American exports, negotiating trade agreements with other Asian economies, and will complete our efforts—such as the Structural Impediments Initiative with Japan—to reduce barriers to American goods and services. And we will continue to negotiate the Enterprise for the Americas Initiative with Latin America as a first step in creating a hemispheric free trade zone.

Congress should report to the American people the cost to workers, consumers, and businesses of every Democrat trade restriction, trade tax, or trade quota bill it considers. We will not tolerate their obstructing the greatest expansion of international trade in history. Republicans welcome this opportunity; for we know America's workers, thinkers, and builders will make the most of it.

International Economic Policy

Twelve years ago, we unleashed a tidal wave of freedom around the world—not just political, but economic liberty as well. What works in America—personal responsibility, limited government, competition—works throughout the world.

Because the world economy is interdependent, the United States has been affected by downturns elsewhere, particularly since 1990 with the crash of the Japanese stock market and Germany's economic difficulties. Now, as progress resumes, the Republican plan for global growth is vital for all nations, developed or otherwise. The continuing prosperity of our neighborhoods will depend in part upon the masterful diplomacy we have come to expect from President Bush.

Economic freedom is an essential link to our foreign policy. It means expanded trade, but it also means dynamic growth based on shared values—a coming together of nations in the commonwealth of peaceful progress. To that end, U.S. aid, whether bilateral or through international organizations, should promote market reforms, limit regulation, and encourage free trade.

Chief among these market reforms should be the privatization of state-owned industries such as telecommunications, power, mining, and refining. Privatization should afford American companies the opportunity to purchase some of these assets, bring competition to these countries, and substantially reduce our trade deficit. The United States government should take all possible steps to assist American companies wishing to invest in privatized industries by adopting policies, rules, and regulations that will equitably facilitate these ventures, especially for small businesses.

We will work with developing nations to make their economies attractive to private investment and will support innovations to guarantee repayment of their loans, including debt for equity swaps. Our experience can help them develop environmentally rational strategies for growth.

Because we uphold the family as the building block of economic progress, we protect its rights in international programs and will continue to withhold funds from organizations involved in abortion.

Most important, we encourage developing nations to adopt both democracy and free markets. The two are inextricably tied and afford all people the greatest opportunities.

Reforming Government and the Legal System

Two centuries ago, the American people created a miracle—a system of government, founded on limited authority and the rule of law, a system that made government the servant of the people. Today it is in shambles. Citizens feel overwhelmed by vast bureaucracies. Congress insulates incumbents from public judgment. Huge problems get worse while committee chairmen play partisan games. The current legal system tends to breed delay, cost, confusion, and jargon—everything but justice. Many of our once great cities are controlled by one-party machines that promote and encourage corruption and incompetence.

The Republic has not failed, the Democrat Party bosses failed the Republic.

The Republican Party, now as at its founding, challenges a debased status quo. In Congress, the States, our cities, our courtrooms, we fight for the basics of self-government.

We rely on what works, judging programs by how well they do instead of how much they spend. The Democrats believe in more government. Republicans believe in leaner, more effective government.

We decentralize authority, returning decisions to States, localities, and private institutions. The Democrat bosses want to concentrate power on Capitol Hill. Republicans place it in town halls and the American home.

Republicans favor the free-enterprise system. We choose market forces—consumer rights—over red tape. The Democrats argue that government must constantly override the market. Republicans regard the worst market failure as the failure to have a market.

We replace dependency with empowerment. The Democrats see an America filled with wards of the State. Republicans see an America peopled by citizens and consumers eager for the chance to chart their own course.

We make electoral systems understandable and accountable to the voter. The Democrats fear proposals that would limit the tenure and hidden power of incumbent politicians. Republicans want the ballot box to prevail over the cloakroom.

Cleaning Up the Imperial Congress

The Democrats have controlled the House of Representatives for 38 years—five years longer than Castro has held Cuba. They have held the Senate for 32 of those 38. Their entrenched power has produced a Congress arrogant, out of touch, hopelessly entangled in a web of PACs, perks, privileges, partisanship, paralysis, and pork. No wonder they hid their congressional leaders during the Democrat convention of 1992. They didn't want Americans to remember who has been running the Congress.

The Democrats have transformed what the Framers of the Constitution intended as the people's House into a pathological institution. They have grossly increased their staffing, their payrolls, their allied bureaucracies in little-known congressional agencies. Congress has ballooned to 284 congressional committees and subcommittees, almost 40,000 legislative branch employees and staff, and $2.5 billion in taxpayer financing, amounting to approximately $5 million per lawmaker per year. Incumbents have abused free mailing privileges for personal political gain. Twenty-two Democrats, with a total of 585 years in power, rule over a committee system that blocks every attempt at reform.

The Democrats have trampled the traditions of the House, rigging rules, forbidding votes on crucial amendments, denying fair apportionment of committee seats and resources. They have stacked campaign laws to benefit themselves. The Democrat leadership of the House has been tainted with scandal and has resisted efforts to investigate scandals once disclosed. Some in their leadership have resigned in well-earned disgrace.

The Democrat leadership of the Congress has turned the healthy competition of constitutional separation of powers into mean-spirited politics of innuendo and inquisition. Committee hearings are no longer for fact-finding; they are political sideshows. "Advise and consent" has been replaced by "slash and burn."

Republicans want to change all that. We reaffirm our support for a constitutional amendment to limit the number of terms House members and Senators may serve. We want a citizens' Congress, free of bloated pensions and perpetual perks.

Congress must stop exempting itself from laws such as the minimum wage and the civil rights statutes, as well as laws which apply to the executive branch. The Independent Counsel Act is a case in point. It has permitted rogue prosecutors to spend tremendous amounts to hound some of the Nation's finest public servants. If that act is reauthorized, it must be extended to Congress as well. Safety and health regulations, civil rights and minimum wage laws are further examples of areas where Congress has set itself apart from the people. This practice must end.

Congress must slash its own bureaucracy. Its employees operate in a maze of overlapping jurisdictions. A Republican Congress will cut expenses by 25 percent, reduce the number of committees and subcommittees, and assign staff in accurate proportion to party strength.

We will restore integrity to the House of Representatives, reforming its rules, allowing open debate and amendment. The committee system, both in Congress and in Democrat-controlled State legisla-

tures, has been abused by chairpersons who have arbitrarily killed legislation which would have passed. Committees are a place for open and free discussion, not a closet for Democrats to stash Republican legislation. Democracy itself is endangered by these abuses, and Republicans condemn these practices. Both houses of Congress must guarantee protection to whistleblowers to encourage employees to report illegality, corruption, sexual harassment, and discrimination.

The Democrat rulers of Congress have blocked or stalled presidential initiatives in many areas, including education, housing, crime control, economic recovery, job creation, and budget reform. They care more about scoring petty partisan points for themselves and their party than about achieving real progress for the Nation. To accomplish change, we need a change in Congress.

Reforming the Congressional Budget Process

At the heart of the Democrats' corruption of Congress is a fraudulent budget process. They do not want the public to understand how they spend the public's money. At a time when the Nation's future depends on reduction deficits, the lords of the Capitol still play the old shell game.

Republicans vigorously support a balanced budget, a Balanced Budget Constitutional Amendment, and a line-item veto for the President.

Republicans believe this balancing of the budget should be achieved, not by increasing taxes to match spending, but by cutting spending to current levels of revenue. We prefer a Balanced Budget Amendment which contains a supermajority requirement to raise taxes.

We also propose procedural reforms. We support legislation that would require Congress to pass a legally binding budget before it can consider spending bills. The budget's spending ceilings shall not be exceeded without a supermajority vote of both chambers. If Congress fails to pass any appropriation bill, funding for its programs will automatically be frozen at the previous year's level. The key to prosperity for the rest of this century and for the next generation of Americans is a budget strategy that restores sanity to the budget process and checks the growth of government.

Congress should be forced to confront basic arithmetic through Truth in Counting. The Democrats measure all changes in funding against a "current services baseline," with built-in increases for inflation and other factors. If they want a $1 million program to grow to $2 million, they then count an increase to $1.5 million as a half-million dollar cut. This is the accounting system of Wonderland, where words mean exactly what the Democrat Speaker says they mean. The double-talk must end with zero-based budgeting. We also support "sunset laws" that require government agencies to be reviewed periodically and reauthorized only if they can be rejustified.

Cleaning Up Politics: The Gerrymander

After more than a half-century of distortion by power-hungry Democrats, the political system is increasingly rigged.

Throughout the 1980s, voters were cheated out of dozens of seats in the House of Representatives and in State legislatures because districts were oddly shaped to guarantee election of Democrats. It was swindle by law. We support State-level appointment of nonpartisan redistricting commissions to apply clear standards for compactness of districts, competitiveness between the parties, and protection of community interests.

Cleaning Up Politics: Campaign Reform

We crusade for clean elections. We support State efforts to increase voter participation but condemn Democrat attempts to perpetrate vote fraud through schemes that override the States' safeguards of orderly voter registration. And it is critical that the States retain the authority to tailor voter registration procedures to unique local circumstances.

Most of all, we condemn the Democrats' shameless plots to make taxpayers foot the bills for their campaigns. Their campaign finance bill would have given $1 billion, over six years, in subsidies to candidates. President Bush vetoed that bill. Campaign financing does need reform. It does not need a hand in the public's pocketbook.

We will require congressional candidates to raise most of their funds from individuals within their home constituencies. This will limit outside special-interest money and result in less expensive campaigns, with less padding for incumbents. To the same end, we will strengthen the role of political parties to remove pressure on candidates to spend so much time soliciting funds. We will eliminate political action committees supported by corporations, unions, or trade associations, and restrict the practice of bundling.

To restore competition in elections by attacking the unfair advantages of incumbency, we will stop incumbents from warding off challengers merely by amassing huge war chests. Congressional candidates will be forbidden from carrying campaign funds from one election to the next. We will oppose arbitrary spending limits—cynical devices which hobble challengers to keep politicians in office.

We will fully implement the Supreme Court's decision in the *Beck* case, ensuring that workers have the right to stop the use of their union dues for political or other noncollective bargaining purposes.

Managing Government in the Public Interest

The focus of government must shift from quantity to quality, from spending to service. Americans should expect measurable, published standards for services provided by government at all levels. Performance standards and rules, commonplace in the private sector, must be applied to government activities as well. Because federal government employees should not be a privileged caste, we will remove the bar to garnishing their wages to ensure payment of their debts.

The Quality Revolution in American business has quietly but profoundly transformed American culture over the past decade. Millions of American workers have benefited from the more cooperative spirit the Quality Revolution has brought to tens of thousands of workplaces; and every American has benefited from the lower costs, higher-quality service, and greater level of competitiveness it has produced. Republicans are proud to have played a leading role in this transformation, especially through the annual Malcolm Baldrige National Quality Award, which recognizes companies that best represent the principles of Quality.

The Quality Revolution in the private sector, with its concepts of Continuous Improvement, Profound Knowledge, and "Doing the Right Thing Right the First Time," stands in stark contrast to the outmoded practices, insensitivity and outright waste, abuse, and corruption endemic in the bureaucratic welfare state. The Republican Party is firmly committed to bringing the Quality Revolution into government at every level by creating a "Quality Workers for a Quality America" coalition whose aim will be to transform the bureaucratic welfare state into a government that is customer-friendly, cost-effective, and improving constantly.

Privatization is an important alternative to higher taxes and reduced services. If private enterprise can perform better and more cheaply than government, let it do so. This is especially true of properties now decaying under government control, such as public housing, where residents should have the option to manage their own projects. These citizens should have the chance to become stockholders and managers of government enterprises and to run them more efficiently as private enterprises. We applaud President Bush's initiative to allow States and localities to privatize facilities built with federal aid.

Where it advances both efficiency and safety, we will advocate privatization of airport operation and management.

We deplore the blatant political bias of the government-sponsored radio and television networks. It is especially outrageous that taxpayers are now forced to underwrite this biased broadcasting through the Corporation for Public Broadcasting (CPB). We call for sweeping reform of CPB, including greater accountability through application of the Freedom of Information Act, a one-year funding cycle, and enforcement of rigorous fairness standards for all CPB-supported programming. We look forward to the day when public broadcasting is self-sufficient.

Always trusting the initiative of the American people over the ways of government, we will not initiate production of goods or delivery of services by the federal government if they can be procured from the private sector.

We will not initiate any federal activity that can be conducted better on the State or local level. In doing so, we reassert the crucial importance of the Tenth Amendment. We oppose costly federal mandates that stifle innovation and force tax hikes upon States and localities. We require that Congress calculate the cost of mandated initiatives upon communities affected and provide adequate financial support for mandates invoked. We will continue the process of returning power to local voters by replacing federal programs with block grants.

Reforming the Legal System

The United States, with 5 percent of the world's population, has two-thirds of the world's lawyers. Litigation has become an industry, an end in itself. The number of civil cases in federal district courts has more than tripled in the past thirty years. It now takes more than a year to resolve the average lawsuit. Delays of three to five years are commonplace.

The current legal system forces consumers to pay higher prices for everything from basic goods to medical treatment. Direct litigation and inflated insurance premiums sock American consumers for an estimated $80 billion a year. All told, our legal system costs, directly and indirectly, $300 billion a year. What it costs us in the world marketplace, by hindering our competitiveness, is beyond calculation.

We therefore endorse the President's proposals for legal reform as developed by Vice President Quayle, and we salute his principled challenge to the American Bar Association to clean up its own house. We support the Fairness Rule, to allow the winning party to a lawsuit to recover the costs of litigation from the losing party. This will discourage needless suits, freeing legal resources for people with genuine cases.

We believe complainants should have a choice of ways to settle problems through alternative dispute programs that will permit parties to pursue less costly and less complicated ways to resolve conflicts. We also call for greater use of judicial sanctions to stop frivolous lawsuits. We call for changes to the federal Racketeer Influenced and Corrupt Organizations (RICO) law to limit its use in civil litigation by requiring proof of all elements by clear and convincing proof.

We seek to restore fairness and predictability to punitive damages by placing appropriate limits on them, dividing trials into two phases to determine liability separately from damages, and requiring clear proof of wrongdoing. This will go a long way to reduce insurance premiums for professional and product liability and for all malpractice, including medical, thereby lowering costs for consumers throughout the economy, while preserving the ability of injured persons to obtain damages. It will also foster the creation of new products for the American marketplace, perhaps cures for the diseases we most fear.

The Republican Party commends President Bush and Vice President Qualye for their continued leadership in helping volunteers overcome their concern that their good acts and voluntary donations of time on behalf of civic groups, community organizations, and churches will result in civil liability and lawsuits. We encourage the State legislatures to pass the Administration's model bill, "The Volunteerism Act."

We will throw out "junk science" by requiring courts to verify the legitimacy of persons called as expert witnesses. To restore integrity to courtroom testimony, we will ban the practice of paying fees to experts only if a successful verdict is obtained. We will maintain diversity jurisdiction for citizens of different States to ensure access to the federal courts when appropriate.

Because four-fifths of the time and cost of a lawsuit involves discovery—pretrial investigation of the facts—we will require automatic disclosure, by both sides, of basic information. We will ban abuses of the discovery process used to intimidate opponents and drive up their costs.

We will fight rising health care costs—and equally important, help dedicated doctors to keep practicing in critical areas like obstetrics—by providing incentives for States to reform their liability laws. This will reduce the practice of "defensive medicine," requiring patients to be tested for every conceivable ailment at their own enormous expense to guard against the mere possibility of a lawsuit.

Recognizing that legal reform can solve only parts of the larger problem, we support a federal product liability law. The cost of product liability protection is a great expense to the American consumer and seriously impedes our international competitiveness. For example, a consumer pays an additional 17 percent to cover the liability insurance of an ordinary stepladder. If thirteen European nations can enact uniform product liability laws to give them a competitive edge against the United States, we can do it here too—once we break the Democrat hold on the Congress so Republicans can put the interests of workers and consumers ahead of trial lawyers.

Some of the problems in our legal system are rooted in a declining sense of, and respect for, individual responsibility. We reaffirm that all Americans are first and finally responsible for their own behavior.

The Nation's Capital

We call for closer and responsible congressional scrutiny of the city, federal oversight of its law enforcement and courts, and tighter fiscal restraints over its expenditures. We oppose statehood as inconsistent with the original intent of the Framers of the Constitution and with the need for a federal city belonging to all the people as our Nation's Capital.

A New Era for the Territories

We welcome greater participation in all aspects of the political process by Americans residing in Guam, the Virgin Islands, American Samoa, the Northern Marianas, and Puerto Rico. Because territorial America is far-flung and divergent, we know that any single approach to the future will not necessarily meet the needs of all. Republicans therefore emphasize respect for the wishes of those who reside in the territories regarding their relationship to the rest of the Union.

We affirm the right of American citizens in the United States territories to seek the full extension of the Constitution with the accompanying rights and responsibilities, and we support all necessary legislation to permit them to do so.

The Republican Party supports the right of the United States citizens of Puerto Rico to be admitted to the Union as a fully sovereign State after they freely so determine.

We recognize that the people of Guam have voted for a closer relationship with the United States of America, and we reaffirm our support of their right to mutually improve their political relationship through commonwealth.

We support American Samoa's efforts to advance toward economic self-reliance through a multi-year plan, while ensuring the protection afforded to the people of American Samoa by the original treaty of cession.

We support the full extension of rights and responsibilities under the U.S. Constitution to American citizens of the Virgin Islands.

We commend President Bush for the successful development of self-government in Micronesia and the Marshall Islands and for efforts to conclude the United Nations' last trusteeship in Palau consistent with the people's right of self-determination.

Our Land, Food, and Resources

We hold the resources of our country in stewardship. Our heritage from the past must be our legacy to generations to come. Our people have always known that, as they cherished their land and turned earth and rock into food, fiber, and power. In the process, they built the world's most formidable economy, sustained by its raw materials, driven by its energy resources. They brought comfort to the home, transformed the Nation, and fed the world.

Agriculture and energy remain building blocks of modern life. Their vitality is crucial to the Nation's growth. Indeed, to its survival. While supporting conservation, we reject the notion that there are limits to growth. Human ingenuity is the ultimate resource, and it knows no limits. The true measure of America's economic success is not whether austerity can be shared by many, but whether prosperity can be achieved for all.

We advocate privatizing those government agencies and assets that would be more productive and better maintained in private ownership. We support efforts to decentralize government monopolies that poorly serve the public and waste taxpayers' dollars.

Agriculture

The Republican Party is the home of the farmer, rancher, and forester. We have long championed their right to pursue growth, efficiency, and competitiveness through market incentives, diversification, and personal ingenuity. And for good reason. Their industry provides consumers with the highest-quality food and fiber for the smallest percentage of disposable income of any nation in the history of the world.

They have been pioneer environmentalists. They have turned over to their children and grandchildren land that has been nurtured to expand its productivity while conserving this vital resource. Even more important, they have cultivated in their homes strong family life and moral virtues. We endorse American Samoa's time-honored land tenure system, which fosters self-reliance and strong extended family values. When we lose farmers, we lose much more than agriculture. We are committed to bringing our farm families the full benefit of a growing and diversified rural economy.

Our rural families also deserve to be brought into the mainstream of health care, with tax policies that provide all who are self-employed full deductibility of their health insurance premiums.

We stand with farmers against attempts by liberal Democrats to repeal the laws of economics by dictating price levels and restricting production. We stand with them against agricultural embargoes. We reject the notion that elected officials and bureaucrats make better farm managers than farmers themselves.

We remain strong in our support of livestock agriculture. We believe in the humane treatment of animals, but we oppose attempts by animal rights extremists to impose excessive restrictions on animal husbandry practices.

Our Omnibus Farm Bills of 1985 and 1990 gave farmers greater flexibility in decisions concerning management of their farms and marketing of their commodities. We have reduced government control and ownership of commodity inventories. Export sales and profitability have improved significantly. Agricultural debt has fallen by 30 percent. Under this President and sound Republican policies, net farm income has reached record levels.

At the same time, we cut by two-thirds the cost of government commodity programs. Only one-half of one percent of the federal budget is now spent on those programs. By reducing dependency on government, we have created a healthier agricultural sector. We will build upon our 1985 and 1990 legislation and repeal obsolete or unworkable statutes while continuing to provide a viable base of support for U.S. farmers.

Agricultural prosperity is essential to the Nation's global competitiveness. We will continue to expand the growth of American agriculture through exports, development of new products, and new markets. Commodity exports this year will hit $40 billion, a 50 percent increase over the levels of five years ago. There has never been an annual deficit in our balance of agricultural trade, and the positive balance this year will be $18 billion.

We pledge to fight unfair competition and to bring down the walls of protectionism around the world that unfairly inhibit competitiveness of U.S. farm exports. We pledge continued pressure to open world markets through the Uruguay Round, the North American Free Trade Agreement, and bilateral negotiations. We affirm that there will be no GATT agreement unless it improves opportunities for U.S. farmers to compete in world markets. We repeat our demand for cutbacks in export subsidies by the European Community and elsewhere, and we will fight the use of arbitrary health and sanitation standards to sabotage U.S. exports.

New markets for agricultural products will also be created as producers translate technological breakthroughs into new uses, such as soy oil diesel and biodegradable plastics. We support the widest possible use of ethanol in the U.S. motor fuel market, including in oxygenated fuels programs and as ethanol blends in reformulated gasolines. In addition, the Republican Party supports increased research and development to reduce ethanol production costs and expand its use in motor fuel markets. Such use will greatly help American farmers, improve the rural economy, and reduce our dependence on imported oil.

Building our farm economy requires meeting our farmers' financing needs. Critical to these needs are competitive, reasonable interest rates for U.S. producers. Under George Bush, interest rates have been dramatically reduced, thereby contributing substantially to improving the net income of American farm and ranch families. We will continue working to ensure that farmers have access to credit, with particular consideration to the needs of young and beginning farmers.

We recognize the importance of efficient, equitable transportation systems to the economic viability of agricultural exports, and we will work to achieve greater efficiencies within the U.S. maritime industry and to decrease the cost to agriculture of shipping services.

We support farm conservation efforts, both those pioneered in our 1985 Farm Bill and entirely voluntary undertakings, which result in three times as much erosion control as those mandated by law. We support the Conservation Reserve, with more than 35 million acres now enrolled. It shows what farmers can do through incentives rather than government controls.

We value our Nation's real wetlands habitat and the diversity of our native animal and plant life. We oppose, however, bureaucratic harassment of farm, ranch, and timber families under statutes regarding endangered species; we recognize that jobs can be lost, communities displaced, and economic progress for all denied. Accordingly, prior to the implementation of a recovery plan for a species declared to be endangered, we will require the Congress to affirm the priority of the species on the endangered list and the specific measures to be taken in any recovery plan. These acts should not rest with the rubber stamp of a bureaucrat.

With regard to wetlands, following our principle that environmental protection be reasonable, land that is not truly wet should not be classified as a wetland. Protection of environmentally sensitive wetlands must not come at the price of disparaging landowners' property rights. Thus, we endorse, as President Bush has done, legislation to discourage government activities that ignore property rights. We also find intolerable the use of taxpayer funds, through the Legal Services Corporation, to attack the agricultural community.

Power for Progress

Energy sustains life as we know it: our standard of living, the prospect for economic growth, the way our children will live in the century ahead. Republican energy policy, now as in the past, reflects the common sense aspirations of the American people.

Our goals address our fundamental needs: an energy supply, available to all, that remains reasonably priced, secure, and clean, produced by strong energy industries on which the country can rely, operating in an environmentally responsible manner and producing from domestically available energy resources to the maximum extent practicable.

Anyone older than a teenager can remember the energy upheavals of the bad old days, when political games threw the Nation into a tailspin. Stranded in gasoline lines, shocked by home heating bills, shutting down factory operations, America's motorists, homeowners, and workers rightly blamed official Washington for wrecking something which had always worked so efficiently that it was taken for granted.

Today, after 12 years of Republican reform, we can again have confidence in our energy policies. The average household spends 11 percent less on energy, as adjusted for inflation, than it did in 1980, because of both conservation and lower costs.

We broke the shackles of bureaucratic regulation by ending petroleum price and allocation controls, deregulating natural gas wellhead prices, and repealing restrictions on the use of clean-burning natural gas by industry and utilities. We repealed the Windfall Profit Tax on crude oil that penalized investment in domestic oil production. We promoted free competition in an open marketplace and ended the public subsidy to the "synthetic fuels" program. And we broke the back of OPEC, the international energy cartel.

And, equally important, we undertook a reevaluation of estimates of our domestic energy resource base, which the Carter Administration had determined to be inadequate. The Republican Administration correctly found that we can indeed continue to supply a significant amount of our domestically available energy resources, including natural gas and coal, for all energy consumption needs well into the next century.

When Iraq's dictator moved to seize the world's energy lifeline by controlling the Persian Gulf, George Bush did more than liberate Kuwait. He prevented energy crisis and economic shutdown in America. Now his National Energy Strategy leads toward continued growth in the century ahead. It provides the Nation with a comprehensive and balanced strategy for America's energy future. Specifically, it promotes adequate energy supplies and reduces consumer costs by relying on market forces, diversifying domestic energy sources, and improving the efficiency and flexibility of energy consumption. We seek to foster greater competition and increased output, in the interest of producers and consumers alike.

The domestic oil and gas industry saves us from total dependence on unreliable foreign imports. But over the past decade, it has lost more than 300,000 jobs. Drilling rigs are still. Crippled by environmental rules and taxes, independent producers have been devastated and major companies are moving operations overseas. We will reverse that situation by allowing access, under environmental safeguards, to the coastal plain of the Arctic National Wildlife Refuge, possibly one of the largest petroleum reserves in our country, and to selected areas of the Outer Continental Shelf (OCS). We support incentives to encourage domestic investment for onshore and OCS oil and gas exploration and development, including relief from the alternative minimum tax, credits for enhanced oil recovery and geological exploration under known geological oil fields and producing geological structures, and modified percentage depletion rules to benefit marginal production. We will ensure that royalty payments on federal lands remain consistent with changing economic conditions.

Most important, unlike Democrat no-growth fanatics, we know what is most at stake in the energy debate: the family's standard of living, including job opportunities, household income, and the environment in which we live.

That is why we have been supporting complete decontrol of wellhead prices for clean natural gas, which have already declined 10 percent in the last four years while consumption increased by the same amount. We support replacing government controls with the power of the market to determine transactions between buyers and sellers of natural gas. We encourage the use of natural gas for both vehicles and electricity generation, and the expansion of research, development, and demonstration for end-use natural gas technologies. We will foster more public–private partnerships to advance use of natural gas.

The Republican Party has a deep and abiding commitment to America's mining industry. We support the original intent of the Mining Law of 1872: to provide the security necessary for miners to risk capital investment on federal lands, thus preserving jobs and bolstering the domestic economy.

We support clean-coal technologies to allow greater use of America's most abundant fossil fuel within standards required by the Clean Air Act. We encourage the export of U.S. coal. We support acceleration of the international transfer of coal-related technologies to boost exports for U.S. coal, in order to capitalize on America's leadership in these technologies.

We oppose any attempt to impose a carbon tax as proposed by liberal Democrats.

We endorse major national projects, like the Super Conducting Super Collider, which offer the promise of developing more efficient ways to store, transport, and use energy.

We will hasten development of the next generation of nuclear power plants—one of the cleanest, safest energy sources of all. Republicans back reform of the nuclear licensing process. We will site and license a permanent waste depository and a monitored retrievable storage facility. We reject the scare tactics used against nuclear power by those who want to shut down this essential contributor to the American future.

We endorse development of renewable energy sources and research on fuel cells, conservation, hydro, solar, hydrogen, and wind power as components of our overall plan for energy security and environmental quality.

Public Lands

The millions of acres that constitute this Nation's public lands must continue to provide for a number of uses. We are committed to the multiple use of our public lands. We believe that recreation, forestry, ranching, mining, oil and gas exploration, and production on our public lands can be conducted in a way compatible with their conservation. The United States has some of the richest mineral resources in the world. Our public lands should not be arbitrarily locked up and put off limits to responsible uses.

Approximately 50 percent of the lands in the West are owned by the federal government. These lands are a deeply intermingled pathwork quilt of public and private ownership. In order to provide an economic base for the people of the West, a public–private cooperative partnership on these lands for multiple use in an environmentally sound manner is imperative.

Transportation

From its founding, the Republican Party has considered the Nation's transportation system crucial to economic opportunity for all. That is why our 1860 Platform endorsed the Transcontinental Railroad. It is why President Eisenhower signed the Interstate and Defense Highway Act, bringing America closer together and launching a lengthy economic expansion.

Today, America's transportation system is safer, more efficient, more reliable than that of any other country. It employs one of every ten workers and accounts for $800 billion in spending. It enables us to compete in the world market and gives us more choices in our daily lives.

Under President Bush, that system has been strengthened by revolutionary legislation to pave the way into the century ahead. Providing $151 billion for highways and transit systems, it is the most extensive transportation improvement project in our Nation's history—and a tremendous jobs program as well.

Highway death rates have dropped to an all time low, largely due to better road design and stronger safety programs. This progress would be wiped out by the Democrats' draconian plan for higher Corporate Average Fuel Economy (CAFE) standards. Their national nominees want to require a 45 miles-per-gallon standard. That means unsafe vehicles, reduced consumer choice, higher car costs, and a loss of 300,000 jobs in the auto industry here at home.

To reduce the congestion that still chokes urban areas, we established a National Highway System of 155,000 miles, giving States and localities greater voice in decisions about projects. It will improve connections between ports and highways, airports and railways, spur development of new airports and reduce their environmental impact, promote private investment in transportation, and foster high-tech solutions to congestion.

To keep America on the move, we assert the same principle that guides us in all other sectors of the economy: consumers benefit through competition within the private sector. That is why we will complete the job of trucking deregulation. We will also abolish the Interstate Commerce Commission, finally freeing shippers and consumers from horse-and-buggy regulation. We applaud the President's executive order that will assist communities to privatize government-controlled ventures, such as airports and toll roads.

Our tough trade campaign, along with regulatory reforms, will assure U.S. air carriers fair access to international routes and allow the U.S. merchant marine to sail over foreign protectionism. The President has proposed and will aggressively pursue a comprehensive revision of existing maritime policy.

Regulatory reform of airlines now allows more people to fly more safely, at better prices. Tough laws for drug and alcohol testing are making all modes of transportation safer than ever. Disabled persons will have greater access to the entire transportation network under the Americans with Disabilities Act.

Wherever possible, the market should allocate investment in transportation, steering the development of passenger rail, mass transit, and highways to best suit consumers. States and localities should have discretion in using Highway Trust Fund revenues to construct new roads, expand existing ones, or invest in mass transit facilities, as they see fit. We advocate development of high-speed rail systems, through private investment, to serve intercity travel. We also advocate development of short-haul aircraft with verticle take-off and landing capability, to bring commerce and jobs to communities large and small.

We will continue aggressively to support development of intelligent highway systems, an efficient battery for electric cars, perfected natural gas vehicles, greater private investment in space travel, and removal of regulatory impediments to intermodal transport.

Because Republicans advocate personal responsibility, we salute groups, organizations, and individuals that take direct action to improve safe driving and street safety.

Environment

Cleaning up America is a labor of love for family, neighborhood, and Nation. In the Republican tradition of conserving the past to enrich the future, we have made the United States the world's leader in environmental progress.

We spend more than any other country on environmental protection. Over the last 20 years, our country has spent $1 trillion to clean its air, water, and land. We increased GNP by 70 percent while cutting lead in the air by 97 percent. Our rivers run cleaner than ever in memory. We've preserved parks, wilderness, and wildlife. The price of progress is now about $115 billion a year, almost 2 percent of GNP, and that will grow to 3 percent by 2000.

Clearly we have led the world in investment in environmental protection. We have taught the world three vital lessons. First, environmental progress is integrally related to economic advancement. Second, economic growth generates the capital to pay for environmental gains. Third, private ownership and economic freedom are the best security against environmental degradation. The ghastly truth about state socialism is now exposed in what used to be the Soviet Union: dead rivers and seas, poisoned land, dying people.

Liberal Democrats think people are the problem. We know people are the solution. Respecting the people's rights and views, we applied market-based solutions to environmental problems. President Bush's landmark Clean Air Act Amendments of 1990, the toughest environmental law ever enacted, uses an innovative system of emission credits to achieve its dramatic reductions. This will save $1 billion over the Democrats' command-and-control approach. Other provisions of that law will cut acid rain emissions in half, reduce toxic pollutants by 90 percent, reduce smog, and speed the use of cleaner fuels.

The President's leadership has doubled spending for real wetlands and targeted one million acres for a wetlands reserve through his Farm Bill of 1990. We have collected more civil penalties from polluters in two years than in the previous twenty, begun the phase-out of substances that harm the ozone layer, and launched a long-term campaign to expand and improve national parks, forests, and recreation areas, adding 1.5 million acres. President Bush has dramatically increased spending for cleaning up past environmental damage caused by federal facilities.

Our reforestation drive will plant one billion trees a year across America. Our moratorium on offshore drilling in sensitive offshore areas has brought time for technology to master environmental challenges. Our farm policies have begun a new era in sound agricultural environmentalism.

Because the environment knows no boundaries, President Bush has accelerated U.S. research on global climate change, spending $2.7 billion in the last three years and requesting $1.4 billion for 1993, more than the rest of the world put together. Under his leadership, we have assisted nations from the Third World to Eastern Europe in correcting the environmental damage inflicted by socialism. We proposed a worldwide forestry convention and gave almost half a billion dollars to forest conservation. We won debt-for-nature swaps and environmental trust funds in Latin America and the Caribbean. We secured prohibitions against unilateral export or dumping of hazardous waste. We led the international ban on trade in ivory, persuaded Japan to end driftnet fishing, streamlined response to oil spills, and increased environmental protection for Antarctica.

Adverse changes in climate must be the common concern of mankind. At the same time, we applaud our President for personally confronting the international bureaucrats at the Rio Conference. He refused to accept their anti-American demands for income redistribution and won instead a global climate treaty that relies on real action plans rather than arbitrary targets hostile to U.S. growth and workers.

Following his example, a Republican Senate will not ratify any treaty that moves environmental decisions beyond our democratic process or transfers beyond our shores authority over U.S. property. The

Democrats' national candidates, on the other hand, insist the U.S. must do what our foreign competitors refuse to do: abolish 300,000 to 1,000,000 jobs to get a modest reduction in "greenhouse gasses."

Environmental progress must continue in tandem with economic growth. Crippling an industry is no solution at all. Bankrupt facilities only worsen environmental situations. Unemployment is a form of pollution too, poisoning families and contaminating whole communities.

Some in our own country still refuse to face those facts. They try to hijack environmentalism, making it anti-growth and anti-jobs. Although the average family of four now pays $1,000 a year for environmental controls, liberal Democrats want to tighten the squeeze. They use junk science to foster hysteria instead of reason, demanding rigid controls, more taxes, and less resource production.

However, with billions of dollars at stake in national production and jobs, not to mention our quality of life, our decisions to spend on environmental protection must not be determined by the politics of the moment. We will use scientifically respectable risk–benefit assessments to settle environmental controversies. It is time to replace knee-jerk reactions with the kind of scientific analysis that helps businesses, individuals and communities contribute to economic and environmental progress through flexible application of laws. We must base our environmental policies on real risks to human health, determined by sound, peer-reviewed science, including procedures for what is an acceptable risk.

We will require federal agencies to promptly compensate, from their own budgets, for any taking of private property, including the denial of use.

We will legislatively overhaul the Superfund program to speed the cleanup of hazardous waste and more efficiently use Superfund dollars. We will develop greenways of parks and open space in urban areas to further improve the quality of life in our cities. We will work with U.S. industry and labor to identify promising markets abroad where America's environmental know-how can carry our success story to the rest of planet earth.

Private Property Rights

We reaffirm our commitment to the Fifth Amendment to the Constitution: "No person shall be . . . deprived of life, liberty, or property, without due process of law; nor shall private property be taken for public use, without just compensation." We support strong enforcement of his Takings clause to keep citizens secure in the use and development of their property.

The right to own, use, and dispose of property inheres in mankind by nature and is a fundamental political tenet of all free nations. We applaud the wisdom of the First Congress for incorporating this guarantee of individual liberty in the Bill of Rights. We remind all government officials that property rights are not granted by government; rather, government is directed by the governed to protect the rights of private property owners.

The vigilant protection of private property rights safeguards for citizens everything of value, including their right of contract to produce and sell the fruits of their labor. The historic collapse of Communism and other command-and-control economies is absolute evidence of the failure of economic systems that lack a recognition of the natural rights of property owners.

We also seek to reduce the amount of land owned or controlled by the government, especially in the western states. We insist upon prompt payment for private lands certified as critical for preserving essential parks and preserves.

UNITING OUR WORLD

The world is now our neighborhood. Its triumphs and tragedies affect our communities, our jobs, and the security of our families. That is why Republicans want America to shape the international future: Because we put America first.

Not everyone does. Just twelve years ago, the forces of freedom were in tattered retreat. A failed foreign policy by a Democrat White House and Democrat-controlled Congress had left our allies uncertain, our friends betrayed, our foes emboldened. It was a frightening era, in some ways the worst of times. We all remember the flickering television images of blindfolded Americans being degraded by thugs. When voters make their choice in this year's elections, they should ask themselves: Are we safer and stronger today, in 1992, than we were in 1980, when Jimmy Carter was the Democrat President?

Republicans are proud to answer those questions. The Nation's international position has not just improved since the Democrats left office. It has been transformed. Never in this century has the United States enjoyed such security from foreign enemies. With President Bush leading the free world, the Soviet empire has collapsed, as Ronald Reagan predicted, into the dustbin of history. Eastern Europe is liberated. Germany is peacefully united. The former Soviet armies are returning home. Nuclear arsenals are being cut to fractions of their former size.

A democratically elected Russian president sits in the Kremlin. Ukraine, Armenia, and the Baltic states take their rightful place among the family of nations. Israel and all of its Arab neighbors talk face to face for the first time. Nicaragua and Panama celebrate democracy.

It might very well not have turned out this way. Only the naive believe that history is an inevitable tide or a series of accidents. Our crusade of a half-century, to champion freedom and civilization against the dark night of totalitarianism, is now victorious. An American President led the free world to this great triumph. George Bush was that man.

Freedom's victory begins a new chapter in the epic of America, full of both promise and peril. This different and unpredictable world demands visionary, experienced leadership, tested and strengthened, careful and cool. At stake is nothing less than our security, our prosperity, and our children's future. Americans can trust President Bush with that awesome responsibility.

The Triumph of Freedom

No other President in the long history of our country has achieved so many of the enduring objectives of American foreign policy in so short a time as has George Bush. He made it look easy, even destined. It was neither.

Building on the legacy of Ronald Reagan, George Bush saw the chance to sweep away decadent Communism. He was the first Western leader to declare his determination to fashion "a Europe whole and free." He took the free world beyond containment, led the way in aiding democracy in Eastern Europe, and punched holes through the rusting Iron Curtain. We all remember the joy we felt when we saw the people of Berlin dancing on top of the crumbling Wall that had symbolized four decades of Communist oppression.

He championed Germany's right to become again one nation and orchestrated the diplomacy to make it happen, on Western terms, in one astounding year. Foreseeing revolutionary change in the Soviet Union itself, he carefully pushed its rulers to open the way to the democratic future. When crisis came, in August 1991, George Bush, in the words of Boris Yeltsin, "was the first to understand the true meaning of the victory of the Russian people" and gave his decisive backing to the cause of democracy.

The world had never before faced the disintegration of a nuclear superpower. Today, thanks in large part to President Bush's initiatives, nuclear weapons are found in only four countries of the former Soviet Union—not fourteen. Because of his efforts all but Russia are giving up any claim to these weapons, and

Russia has agreed to destroy the most dangerous missiles ever built. The balance of terror is fading away. The ideals of liberty, both political and economic, are the dominant moral and intellectual force around the globe.

George Bush made it happen.

Yet now that we have won the Cold War, we must also win the peace. We must not repeat the mistake of the past by throwing away victory through complacency. A new world beckons, unlike any we have ever known, filled with uncertainties. Old passions have reemerged. New democracies struggle to decide their destiny. Nations are torn asunder. Migrants and refugees strain the social fabric of continents. Tyrants work to build nuclear, chemical, and even biological weapons to threaten us and our neighbors. Drug trafficking and terrorism, often linked, menace Americans at home and abroad.

Great transitions in world affairs are rarely tidy. They challenge statesmanship, require steadiness and wisdom. History teaches that when the United States shrinks from the world, we hasten the emergence of new dangers. Republicans remember the lesson taught by our founders: that eternal vigilance is the price of liberty.

Meeting the Challenge

The Gulf War showed the world how much is at stake when voters choose their President. George Bush had known war first hand. So he tried the way of peace— months of negotiations and economic sanctions—then did what a President must do. He led from powerful convictions based on American values. The United States, in a preeminent position of world leadership, forged a new strategy of collective engagement which invigorated the United Nations.

This was not the same United States held hostage in 1980, when the Democrats controlled both the White House and the Congress. No helpless giant here. The President charted a path that wrecked Saddam Hussein's dreams of conquest and nuclear aggression while keeping America from the quagmire of indefinite military occupation of Iraq.

President Bush, trusting the military commanders he had chosen, was Commander-in-Chief of one of the finest achievements in the distinguished history of our armed forces. Americans will never forget that, of the 323 congressional Democrats, only 96 voted to support Operation Desert Storm and 227 voted to oppose it. If the Democrats had prevailed, Saddam Hussein would still be in Kuwait, armed with nuclear weapons. Everyone discovered what difference a vote for President can make.

Leadership through Partnership

A new era demands a new agenda. Our post–Cold War strategy both reflects our country's ideals and guards its interests.

Building a commonwealth of freedom differs greatly from the old concept of containment. It rests on a stable balance of power but goes beyond it to emphasize, above all, the supremacy of an idea: a common conception of how to make freedom work for all the nations moving with us into a radically changing future.

Republicans understand that objective cannot be pursued by the United States alone. We therefore have harnessed the free world's strength to American leadership. But such a strategy requires a President whose lead others will trust and follow. By forging consensus whenever possible, we multiply the impact of our Nation's power and principles. But if necessary we will act alone to protect American interests. Consistent with our policy and traditions, we oppose any actions that would undermine America's sovereignty, either in political or economic matters. Leadership through partnership allows us to project American ideals and protect American interests abroad, at less cost to our taxpayers.

That is how we will secure the victory of democracy as the best guarantee of a world without war. It is how we will open the world for American business to ensure prosperity in an open international economy. And it is how we will banish the nuclear nightmare, limit the danger from weapons of mass destruction, and safely manage a critical transition in our Nation's defenses.

Securing the Victory of Democracy

The spread of democracy and economic liberty is the best guarantee of peace. It can mean speaking out of applying economic pressure to encourage peaceful change, aiding democratic forces, or being ready, as a last resort, to take military action where vital American interests are at stake, as when President Bush restored the rule of law to Panama. Republican Presidents have used all these tools in a comprehensive, consistent campaign to promote democracy worldwide.

New tests lie ahead. On past occasions, the tide of liberty has ebbed as dictators recaptured much of what they had lost. We want freedom's wave to roll on to reach countries like China, Cuba, North Korea, Vietnam, and others. We want to keep drawing attention to serious human rights violations around the world, spurring other governments to make and fulfill the promise of liberty to their people. We want to prevent any new technology of authoritarianism from drawing any of the world's people to a grim and vengeful vision of our future.

This is the challenge we face in the next four years. It is why President Bush led the way in promoting assistance to the fledgling democracies of Eastern Europe. It is why he has persuaded the Congress to invest in the democratic future of nations reborn from Communism. To the peoples of those nations, and to the Russian people in particular, we declare: If you stay on the path to freedom, we stand ready to help.

We rejoice especially with the people of Latvia, Lithuania, and Estonia, whose nationhood we have always upheld in law and in our hearts.

In Western Europe, we reaffirm the NATO alliance. While we reduce our troop commitments on the continent—a thousand soldiers are coming home every week—we must keep a powerful force deployed there. The United States must remain a European power in the broadest sense, able to influence the policies and events that affect the livelihood and security of future generations of Americans.

The violence in what used to be Yugoslavia is an affront to humanity. We condemn those responsible for the carnage there and call for an immediate international investigation of atrocities. We support the United Nations peacekeeping effort and urge an immediate cease-fire by all parties. The United States should continue to demand respect for international law and fundamental human rights in this agonizing conflict.

We encourage a peaceful settlement for Cyprus and respect by all parties for the wishes of the Cypriot people.

We urge peace and justice for Northern Ireland. We welcome the newly begun process of constitutional dialogue that holds so much promise. We encourage investment and reconstruction to create opportunity for all.

In the Middle East, prospects for peace have been transformed by the determined statesmanship of George Bush. Without the leadership of President Bush, Iraq would today threaten world peace, the peace and security of the Middle East, and the very survival of Israel with a huge conventional army and nuclear weapons. Direct peace talks, on terms Israel rightly had sought for more than four decades, would not be a reality. Soviet Jewish emigration likely would have been interrupted. The rescue of Ethiopian Jewry might not have happened. And the equation of Zionism to racism still would be a grotesque stain on the United Nations.

Although much has changed for the better, the Middle East remains an area of high tensions—many unrelated to the Arab-Israeli conflict—where regional conflicts can escalate to threaten the vital interests of the United States. As Saddam Hussein's aggression against Kuwait demonstrated, heavily armed radical regimes are capable of independent aggressive action. In this environment, Israel's demonstrated strategic importance to the United States, as our most reliable and capable ally in this part of the world, is more important than ever. This strategic relationship, with its unique moral dimension, explains the understandable support Israel receives from millions of Americans who participate in our political process. The strong ties between the U.S. and Israel were demonstrated during the Gulf War when Israel chose not to retaliate against repeated missile attacks, even though they caused severe damage and loss of life. We will continue to broaden and deepen the strategic relationship with our ally Israel—the only true democracy in the Middle East—by taking additional concrete steps to further institutionalize the partnership. This will include maintaining adequate levels of security and economic assistance; continuing our meetings on military, political and economic assistance; continuing our meetings on military, political and economic cooperation and coordination; prepositioning military equipment; developing joint contingency plans; and increasing joint naval and air exercises.

Consistent with our strategic relationship, the United States should continue to provide large-scale security assistance to Israel, maintaining Israel's qualitative military advantage over any adversary or coalition of adversaries. We also will continue to negotiate with the major arms supplying nations to reach an agreement on limiting arms sales to the Middle East and preventing the proliferation of non-conventional weapons.

We applaud the President's leadership in fostering unprecedented direct talks between Israel and its Arab neighbors. The United States is prepared to use its good offices to mediate disputes at their request. We do not believe the U.S. should attempt to impose a solution on the parties.

The basis for negotiations must be U.N. Security Council Resolutions 242 and 338. Peace must come from direct negotiations. It will be up to the negotiators to determine exactly what is required to satisfy these resolutions, but we firmly believe Israel has a right to exist in secure and recognized borders. As President Bush stated in Madrid, our objective is not simply to end the state of war; rather, it is to establish real peace, one with treaties, security, diplomatic relations, trade, investment, cultural exchange, even tourism. We want the Middle East to become a place where people lead normal lives.

A meaningful peace must assure Israel's security while recognizing the legitimate rights of the Palestinian people. We oppose the creation of an independent Palestinian state. Nor will we support the creation of any political entity that would jeopardize Israel's security. As Israelis and Palestinians negotiate interim self-government, no party will be required to commit itself to any specific final outcome of direct negotiations. Israel should not be forced to negotiate with any party. In this regard, the United States will have no dialogue with the PLO until it satisfies in full the conditions laid out by President Bush in 1990. We believe Jerusalem should remain an undivided city, with free and unimpeded access to all holy places by people of all faiths. No genuine peace would deny Jews the right to live anywhere in the special city of Jerusalem.

Peace in the Middle East entails cooperation between all the parties in the region. To this end, we have worked to bring all of the states of the area together with Israel to hold multilateral negotiations on issues of common concern such as regional development, water, refugees, arms control and the environment. We support these forums as a means of encouraging Arab acceptance of Israel and solving common regional problems.

We continue to back legislation mandating that if the U.N. and its agencies were to deny Israel's right to participate, the United States would withhold financial support and withdraw from those bodies until their action was rectified.

Republicans believe freedom of emigration is a fundamental human right and that Jews from any nation should be free to travel to Israel. Republicans are proud we have maintained our historic and moral commitment to the resettlement in Israel of persecuted Jews. We congratulate President Bush and Secretary Baker on the agreement with Israel for a generous package of loan guarantees that will provide new immigrants with needed humanitarian assistance.

We also should maintain our close ties with and generous aid for Egypt, which properly reaps the benefits of its courageous peace with Israel. We continue to support Egypt and other pro-Western states in the region against subversion and aggression and call for an end to the Arab boycott of Israel. We also support establishment of a strong central government in Lebanon, democratically elected and representative of its citizens.

We salute all the countries in the Middle East who contributed to the success of Desert Storm and share our goal of stability in the region. With them, we hope to build upon that triumph a new future for the

Middle East, founded on mutual respect and a common longing for peace. To promote this goal, we should settle for nothing less than full, unconditional, immediate, and verified Iraqi compliance with all aspects of the cease-fire laid out in U.N. resolutions.

In the Western Hemisphere, as elsewhere, we must promote democratic values. We will continue to seek cooperation in the common battle against the drug lords. We will also lower barriers to trade and investment, knowing that our exports to Latin America are helping to lead our economic recovery at home. The President's Enterprise for the American initiative and the North American Free Trade Agreement mean, for the United States, billions in new trade, hundreds of thousands of new jobs, and a long-term solution to the economic pressures behind illegal immigration.

We welcome positive changes, economic and political, in Mexico, and salute the people of Panama on their recovery of free institutions after Operation Just Cause. We commend President Bush for the decisive military action that led to the end of the corrupt Noriega regime and freedom for democratically minded Panamanians. We will uphold free and unencumbered U.S. access to the Canal. We hail the patriots of El Salvador and Nicaragua, whose bravery and blood thwarted Communism and Castro despite the inconstancy of congressional Democrats. Together with other members of the Organization of American States, we will work to restore democracy to Haiti.

The Monroe Doctrine remains a cardinal principle of our foreign policy, and we continue to strive toward the day when the alien ideology of Communism and Fidel Castro's regime will be purged from Cuba, and Americans can welcome the Cuban people back into the family of free nations. Toward that end, we support Radio and TV Marti and the spirit of Cuba Libre.

In Asia, we remain committed to the spread of political and economic liberty. We will work with Japan for common progress and maintain our military presence in Japan and in Asia. We also will promote greater Japanese responsibility for self-defense and worldwide prosperity.

We reaffirm our commitment to the security of Taiwan and regard any attempt to alter its status by force as a threat to the center region. We adhere to the Taiwan Relations Act, the basis for continuing cooperation with those who have stood loyally with us for half a century.

Our policy toward China is based on support for democratic reform. We need to maintain the relationship with China so that we can effectively encourage such reform. We will continue to work toward the day when the Chinese people will finally complete their journey to an open society, free of the deplorable restrictions on personal liberties that still exist.

We will maintain our close relationship with the Republic of Korea, helping to deter aggression from the north. North Korea remains an outlaw state and must not be permitted to acquire nuclear weapons.

With the people of the Philippines, we will maintain our special ties of history and affection.

We support the movement in Cambodia toward peace and democracy.

We demand the fullest possible accounting for America's POWs and MIAs in Southeast Asia. The grief of their families touches all of us. We will seek complete information in all forums and from all sources. Our President has put the government of Vietnam on notice: improved relations depend upon this goal.

In Africa, despite opposition from Congressional Democrats, we armed freedom fighters and helped force the withdrawal of Cuban troops. Now we enter the long season of building, trying to revive faith in democracy on a continent ravaged by Marxist wars, looted by local dictators, and misled by socialist ideology. Political and economic liberty are the keys.

We will support responsible efforts by the international community to help end the anarchy in Somalia and to address the plight of the people of that country suffering from drought and starvation. We condemn those who are using armed force to impede food distribution.

In South Africa, the Republican policy of constructive engagement—opposing apartheid while fostering peaceful change—has been successful. That nation's prospects have been transformed for the better, though many difficulties lie ahead. We condemn all violence against the innocent and applaud those who seek reconciliation to create a new, democratic South Africa. We encourage economic reform as crucial to both security and prosperity in the new South Africa.

We recognize that foreign aid must have a reasonable relationship to our national interests. We therefore support an ongoing review of such programs so that they can be both effectual and justified. We promote financial contribution from other democracies of the world to share the cost of the American burden for peacekeeping and foreign aid.

We support efforts by private voluntary agencies to help meet the needs of countries newly liberated from Communism, and of the developing world, in such areas as medical, agricultural, educational, and entrepreneurial assistance.

Opening the World to American Business

The triumph of democracy is also a victory for economic freedom. All the world over, people in search of a better life are rejecting politicians' control of their future. This will mean a broader horizon for American opportunity. The whole world has become our marketplace.

The election of 1992 will determine whether our country seizes this tremendous opportunity or retreats from it. Republicans trust individuals and families to make their own economic decisions; Democrat politicans do not. We reject their program of strangled trade, industrial policy, high taxes, and regulation. We reject punitive taxes on foreign businesses in this country that only invite retaliatory taxes against U.S. businesses abroad. Trade war is the road to international depression—and for keeping American workers dependent on government handouts. We do not want to replace the arms race with a subsidies race.

Putting Americans first means keeping the national interest ahead of the special interests. It means opening the world to American goods within a system of free and expanding trade. Just as Ronald Reagan declared in Berlin, "Tear down this wall," so George Bush is dismantling the walls of protectionism in order to continue expanding our exports.

Our strong commitment to free trade also encompasses vigorous enforcement of U.S. trade laws. We expect a fair and level playing field in our trade with other nations and will work to ensure that foreign markets are just as open to our goods as U.S. markets are to theirs. In all negotiations concerning trade, we will put the interests of America first.

Throughout the world, as here at home, the Republican Party stands for growth. America's families have nothing to fear—and everything to gain—from the new era of free enterprise and prosperity that will emerge as free people compete, excel, and progress.

Banishing the Nuclear Nightmare

The world has moved from the brink of disaster to the threshold of historic opportunity. For almost half a century, we lived under the shadow of nuclear destruction. Today, that specter is fading. We will not stop here. We will banish the threat of nuclear annihilation from the face of the earth—not by salvaging our military, as some Democrats might insist, but by building on the historic diplomatic achievements of Presidents Bush and Reagan.

This means assuring stable command and control of the former Soviet arsenal, complete acceptance and verified implementation of all treaty obligations by the successor states to the USSR, and achieving the additional 50 percent reduction in strategic forces now

agreed upon. We must assist in dismantling weapons, transforming the massive Soviet war machine into an engine of peace and civilian revival. We will cooperate with our former adversaries both to curtail proliferation and to move beyond the ABM treaty toward effective ballistic missile defenses.

We will not permit the Soviet nuclear nightmare to be replaced by another one. Outlaw nations—North Korea, Iran, Iraq, Libya and others—lust for weapons of mass destruction. This is the nightmare of proliferation: nuclear, chemical, and biological weapons that, together with ballistic missiles, can deliver death across whole continents, including our own.

We will renew and strengthen the Nuclear Nonproliferation Treaty. We will design security policies to counter proliferation dangers. We will reinforce multilateral accords like the Missile Technology Control Regime. And most important, we will develop and deploy global defenses against ballistic missiles. Despite the opposition of the Democrat Party and congressional Democrats, we will deploy an effective strategic defense system for the American people.

America's Security

Because America won the Cold War, our homes and neighborhoods are more secure than they have been for half a century. Our children are safer. The greatest peace dividend is peace itself. For it, we thank God.

Victory was never inevitable. It was won in blood and treasure, over five decades, by the American people—from the military on the front lines to the taxpayers sustaining the forces of freedom. It was also secured, and the course of mankind profoundly changed for the better, because two successive Republican Presidents, Ronald Reagan and George Bush, were dedicated to peace through strength.

"Peace through strength" was more than a slogan. It was the calculated Republican plan for, first, the survival and, then, the triumph, of America. But freedom did not come cheaply, and the new world we celebrate today required great sacrifice.

In 1981 we inherited from Jimmy Carter and anti-defense Democrats a crippled military: demoralized, underfunded, ill-equipped. Republicans told the truth to the American people; they heeded our call to arms. We restored our armed forces to their proper place in both the budget and the pride of the Nation. Our men and women in uniform today are the equals of the finest soldiers, sailors, and airmen who ever wore the uniform of our country.

Like earlier generations in 1918 and 1945, they won a great victory. Now, as in the aftermath of those earlier conflicts, comes the difficult task of reducing both the size and cost of defense without letting down America's guard. In the past, terrible mistakes were made, and we paid dearly for them when war came to Korea. We will not allow that to happen again.

America Challenged

The greatest danger to America's security is here at home, among those who would leave the Nation unprepared for the new realities of the post–Cold War world. The ruthless demagogues in rogue regimes are real; and so are the nuclear, chemical, and biological weapons they seek. The danger of nuclear proliferation is real, especially with the dispersal of nuclear know-how after the collapse of the USSR. That is why the Republican Party, whose leaders like Dan Quayle insisted upon fielding a new Patriot missile in the 1980s, now calls for a new generation of defense against the Scuds of tomorrow.

Rather than admit their mistakes of the past, the same liberal Democrats who sought to disarm America against the Soviet threat now compound their errors with a new campaign—half audacity, half mendacity—to leave the Nation unprotected in a still dangerous world.

Republicans call for a controlled defense drawdown, not a freefall. That is why President Bush proposes to carefully reduce defense spending over the next four years by an additional $34 billion, including $18 billion in outlays, with a 25 percent reduction in personnel. He has already eliminated over 100 weapon systems. Around the world, American forces are coming home from the frontiers of the Cold War. More than 550 overseas bases are being closed or realigned. Yet U.S. forces retain the ability to meet the challenge of another Desert Storm with equal success.

U.S. defense spending already has been reduced significantly. Five years ago, it was more than a quarter of the federal budget. By 1997 it will be less than a sixth. Spending on defense and intelligence, as a proportion of Gross Domestic Product, will be the lowest it has been since before World War II.

Yet any defense budget, however lean, is still too much for the Democrats. They want to start by cutting defense outlays over the next four years by nearly $60 billion beyond the President's cuts, throwing as many as one million additional Americans out of work. And this may be just the beginning, as the Democrats use the defense budget as a bottomless piggybank to try to beat swords into pork barrels. This is folly. It would take us back to the "hollow military" of the Carter era. Once American defenses are allowed to decay, they cannot be rebuilt overnight. Effective arsenals, like effective leaders, require years of patient development. And our greatest asset of all, the people on whom our security depends, deserve a constant long-term investment in their quality, morale, and safety. Republicans pledge to provide it.

America Secure

Because the U.S. will rely on a smaller force of offensive nuclear weapons to deter aggression in the post–Cold War era, we will maintain the triad of land-, sea-, and air-based strategic forces. We will continue to test the safety, reliability, and effectiveness of our nuclear weapons.

With a smaller military, modernization of conventional forces is more important than ever. Desert Storm showed the importance of "force multipliers" like smart munitions, stealth technology, and night fighting capabilities. We will upgrade existing weapons and selectively procure those that hold the promise of dramatic forward leaps in capability. Under no circumstances will we yield our technological superiority.

We must remain ready to defend American citizens and interests wherever they may be threatened. Essential to that readiness is maintenance of a strong, global navy and modernization of vital airlift and sealift capacity. We remain committed to combating terrorism in all its forms wherever it threatens U.S. citizens or interests.

Republicans will preserve the Nation's access to space for defense, as well as for other purposes, and ensure that space technology does not fall into dangerous hands.

Transformed by the collapse of Communism, our Strategic Defense Initiative is now designed to provide the U.S. and our allies with global defenses against limited ballistic missile attacks. SDI is the greatest investment in peace we could ever make. This system will be our shield against technoterrorism. Russia has agreed to be our partner in it, sharing early warning information and jointly moving forward to stop those who would rain death upon the innocent.

We will use missile defenses to assure threatened nations that they do not need to acquire ballistic missiles of their own. We will move beyond the ABM Treaty to deploy effective defenses with the goal of someday eliminating, not merely reducing, the threat of nuclear holocaust.

We support efforts to reduce armaments, both conventional and otherwise, but the most effective arms control of all over the long run is democracy. Free nations do not attack one another. That is why the promotion of democracy on every continent is an essential part of the Republican defense agenda.

Managing the Peace

A new era in defense requires new approaches to management, to get more out of every dollar in a shrinking budget. That calls for dramatically different ways of doing business. For example, President Bush's reforms in defense management and acquisition already mean massive savings—$70 billion through 1997—without sacrificing combat capability.

Our armed forces will still depend on our superb industrial base for everything from belt buckles to submarines. We cannot lose that engineering and manufacturing capability. This is especially true of the high technology, demonstrated in Desert Storm, that made our enemies realize they had been left behind in the race for the future. We therefore pledge to maintain America's technological lead, preserve its defense industrial base, and maintain robust levels of investment in research and development.

We will attack the problem of waste in the military, especially at its root in the pork-barrel politics of Capitol Hill. A Republican Congress will end the costly micromanagement of defense programs and reduce the number and scope of oversight committees. We will urge the Department of Defense to encourage a broader constituency for saving and to continue genuine procurement reforms based on performance rather than unreasonable regulations imposed by the Democrat Congress. We will continue the successful effort to eliminate redundancy and streamline all facets of defense management.

We applaud the President's efforts to assist all individuals and communities adversely affected by the ongoing defense builddown, with more than 30 defense adjustment programs already in place and over $7 billion committed to the effort in just the next two years.

The Men and Women of Defense

Republicans created the all-volunteer Army and we hail its success. We pledge to keep faith with the men and women volunteers and with their families, for they are the backbone of the nation's defense. We oppose Democrat efforts to bring back the draft, whether directly or through the subterfuge of compulsory domestic service.

The armed forces are a color-blind meritocracy, a model for the rest of our society. Its enlistees should receive preference in federal education and retraining programs. We applaud the advancement of women in the military and single out for special recognition the outstanding contribution of women in Operations Desert Shield/Desert Storm. However, we oppose liberal Democrat attempts to place women in combat positions just to make an ideological point. Unlike the Democrat Party and its candidate, we support the continued exclusion of homosexuals from the military as a matter of good order and discipline.

The Department of Defense will not be an exception to our assertion of family values. Republicans will not tolerate sexual harassment or misconduct toward any individual in the ranks. We demand both its prevention and its punishment. To drive home that point, we urge a halt to the sale, in military facilities, of sexually explicit materials. We call for greater consideration of the needs of families when parents are called to duty.

We must ensure that all of the various benefits, including medical, that were promised to the men and women who chose to make the military and the defense of their Nation a career are fulfilled even upon retirement.

In the Republican tradition of support for America's veterans, we proposed and created a Department of Veterans' Affairs so their concerns would be represented at the Cabinet table. We affirm our support for veterans' preference in federal employment and for sufficient funding to maintain the integrity of the veterans hospital and medical care system. We strongly endorse programs to meet the needs of unemployed veterans.

Intelligence

Desert Storm reminded us that our intelligence community is a national asset of critical importance to our security.

Assuring the availability of timely and reliable information on regional threats and unrest, drug trafficking, terrorism, technology transfer, proliferation, and a host of other issues—this is one of our highest national priorities in the post–Cold War world. U.S. policymakers also must have the best possible understanding of international trade, investment, industrial, financial, and other developments that affect our economic security.

We must and will maintain the full range of our traditional intelligence capabilities, including covert action, to ensure our security in a dangerous and unpredictable world. We reject the Democrat candidate's proposal to cripple U.S. intelligence and decry the deep spending cuts to the intelligence budget sponsored by Democrats in Congress.

Proven Leadership

George Bush has been the most important architect of Western aspirations and designs for the challenging world we are now entering. His record is clear. President Bush has shown he understands how to lead in this new era, where the preeminent position of the

United States offers new opportunities to build an international consensus on key issues. President Bush, with experienced Republican leadership, has proven he knows how to place our Nation at the center of effective coalitions where our power is multiplied.

The test of international leadership is on the field, not in a playbook. The Oval Office is no place for on-the-job training—not in carrying out the presidential duty to protect and defend our Nation, not in managing the arsenal of the supreme nuclear power. There are those who talk and those who perform. George Bush has clearly performed for America, making the right calls in a series of tough decisions that helped transform the world.

Now that we have won the Cold War, we must secure the peace that follows. History has shown that the years following conflict are often critical—where the choices made can either lay the foundation for lasting peace or sow the seeds of future war. In this period of high hopes and great challenges ahead, the Nation needs the tested and experienced leadership of President Bush and the Republican Party.

William McKinley Campaigning in 1896. *Source:* Smithsonian Institution.

ELECTIONS

— 1856 —

Out of the remnants of the Whig and Free Soil parties, a new political party, the Republicans, nominated their first presidential candidate, John C. Frémont, in 1856. The Democrats nominated a southern-sympathizing northerner, James Buchanan of Pennsylvania. In a close contest, Frémont lost by 500,000 votes, securing 1.3 million votes, or 33.1%, to Buchanan's plurality of 1.8 million, or 45.3%. Millard Fillmore ran as the candidate of the Whig-American Party, securing 870,000 votes, or 21.5% of the popular vote. The electoral college was equally tight, with Buchanan winning 174 votes to Frémont's 114. Fillmore was only able to win Maryland and its 8 electoral votes. Frémont ran well in the North, where his antislavery views were well received.

In addition to a campaign seeking to limit the expansion of slavery into the territories, Frémont portrayed the election as a choice between democracy and southern aristocracy. True to his career, Frémont's 1856 campaign was a pathfinding one that laid the groundwork for a Republican victory in 1860, when the issue of slavery came to a head.

— 1860 —

The election of 1860 was the most critical election in American history. The outcome of this contest led to the secession of the southern states and a long and

Republican Candidates for President and Vice President, 1860: Lincoln and Hamlin. *Source:* Library of Congress.

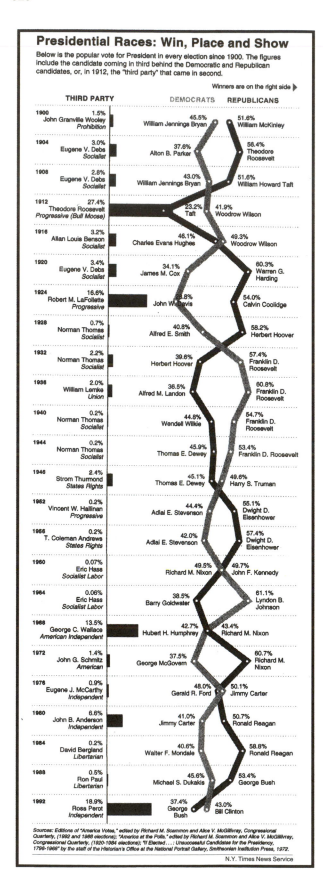

Presidential Races: Win, Place and Show

Below is the popular vote for President in every election since 1900. The figures include the candidate coming in third behind the Democratic and Republican candidates, or, in 1912, the "third party" that came in second.

Winners are on the right side ▶

THIRD PARTY	DEMOCRATS	REPUBLICANS
1900 1.5% John Granville Wooley *Prohibition*	45.5% William Jennings Bryan	51.6% William McKinley
1904 3.0% Eugene V. Debs *Socialist*	37.6% Alton B. Parker	56.4% Theodore Roosevelt
1908 2.8% Eugene V. Debs *Socialist*	43.0% William Jennings Bryan	51.6% William Howard Taft
1912 27.4% Theodore Roosevelt *Progressive (Bull Moose)*	23.2% Taft 41.9% Woodrow Wilson	
1916 3.2% Allan Louis Benson *Socialist*	46.1% Charles Evans Hughes	49.3% Woodrow Wilson
1920 3.4% Eugene V. Debs *Socialist*	34.1% James M. Cox	60.3% Warren G. Harding
1924 16.6% Robert M. LaFollette *Progressive*	38.8% John W. Davis	54.0% Calvin Coolidge
1928 0.7% Norman Thomas *Socialist*	40.8% Alfred E. Smith	58.2% Herbert Hoover
1932 2.2% Norman Thomas *Socialist*	39.6% Herbert Hoover	57.4% Franklin D. Roosevelt
1936 2.0% William Lemke *Union*	36.5% Alfred M. Landon	60.8% Franklin D. Roosevelt
1940 0.2% Norman Thomas *Socialist*	44.8% Wendell Willkie	54.7% Franklin D. Roosevelt
1944 0.2% Norman Thomas *Socialist*	45.9% Thomas E. Dewey	53.4% Franklin D. Roosevelt
1948 2.4% Strom Thurmond *States Rights*	45.1% Thomas E. Dewey	49.6% Harry S. Truman
1952 0.2% Vincent W. Hallinan *Progressive*	44.4% Adlai E. Stevenson	55.1% Dwight D. Eisenhower
1956 0.2% T. Coleman Andrews *States Rights*	42.0% Adlai E. Stevenson	57.4% Dwight D. Eisenhower
1960 0.07% Eric Hass *Socialist Labor*	49.5% Richard M. Nixon	49.7% John F. Kennedy
1964 0.06% Eric Hass *Socialist Labor*	38.5% Barry Goldwater	61.1% Lyndon B. Johnson
1968 13.5% George C. Wallace *American Independent*	42.7% Hubert H. Humphrey	43.4% Richard M. Nixon
1972 1.4% John G. Schmitz *American*	37.5% George McGovern	60.7% Richard M. Nixon
1976 0.9% Eugene J. McCarthy *Independent*	48.0% Gerald R. Ford	50.1% Jimmy Carter
1980 6.6% John B. Anderson *Independent*	41.0% Jimmy Carter	50.7% Ronald Reagan
1984 0.2% David Bergland *Libertarian*	40.6% Walter F. Mondale	58.8% Ronald Reagan
1988 0.5% Ron Paul *Libertarian*	45.6% Michael S. Dukakis	53.4% George Bush
1992 18.9% Ross Perot *Independent*	37.4% George Bush	43.0% Bill Clinton

Sources: Editions of "America Votes," edited by Richard M. Scammon and Alice V. McGillivray, Congressional Quarterly, (1992 and 1988 elections); "America at the Polls," edited by Richard M. Scammon and Alice V. McGillivray, Congressional Quarterly, (1920-1984 elections); "If Elected...: Unsuccessful Candidates for the Presidency, 1796-1968" by the staff of the Historian's Office at the National Portrait Gallery, Smithsonian Institution Press, 1972.

N.Y. Times News Service

bloody Civil War. The embryotic Republican Party that had nominated John C. Frémont in 1856 turned to Representative Abraham Lincoln, a rising star in the party, made famous by his debates in a Senate race against Stephen A. Douglas of Illinois. The 1860 presidential race pitted Lincoln against Douglas in an election that would dramatically affect the United States. Senator Douglas had been nominated by the Democratic Party regulars, and southern Democrats who had bolted the convention after Douglas was nominated offered Buchanan's vice president, John Breckinridge of Kentucky, as a third candidate. Lincoln was the electoral benefactor of the split in the Democratic vote. He garnered more than 1.8 million votes, or 39.8% of the popular vote, to Douglas's nearly 1.4 million, or 29.5%, and Breckinridge's 800,000, or 18.1%. In the electoral college Lincoln won the election with 180 electoral votes, capturing the electoral-rich northern states. He failed to win a single state outside of the North and Midwest. Douglas was able to capture only

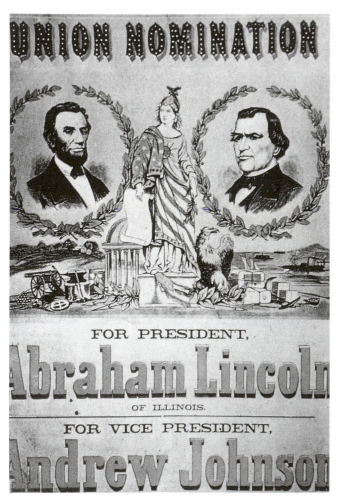

Poster, 1864. *Source:* Smithsonian Institution.

Republican Candidates for President and Vice President, 1868: Grant and Colfax. *Source:* Library of Congress.

12 electoral votes, while Breckinridge secured 72 and the Constitutional Union Party candidate, John Bell, garnered 39 votes.

The campaign focused exclusively on the issue of slavery and continuance of the Union if Lincoln were elected. Lincoln called on voters not to resort to disunion. He stated that he had no intention to abolish slavery if elected president. He did, however, believe that its extension into the territories had to be curtailed. In the end, southern voters saw the two ideas linked and could not remain in the Union with Lincoln as president.

— 1864 —

With the 11 Confederate states not voting, the election of 1864 pitted incumbent Republican President Abraham Lincon against a former Union general and copperhead, George B. McClellan, for the Democrats. McClellan was able to win 1.8 million votes (45%), but it was not enough to beat Lincoln's 2.2 million (55%). In the electoral college, McClellan was able to win the votes of only three states, Kentucky, New Jersey, and

Delaware, and their 21 votes, while Lincoln was successful in securing 212 electoral votes.

Although American voters were displeased with Lincoln's handling of the war, they saw no real alternative in McClellan. Lincoln's campaign was helped by successes on the battlefields just before the November election.

— 1868 —

The Republican Party nominated for president the strongest candidate any party could have selected. Civil War hero General Ulysses S. Grant faced little opposition from the Democratic presidential nominee, former New York Governor Horatio Seymour. With three states—Virginia, Texas, and Mississippi—still not voting because of Reconstruction, the election of 1868 marked the first occasion where blacks were enfranchised. Nearly 500,000 southern blacks voted in the election, which Grant won by only 306,000 votes. There were wide claims of fraud, and the southern states' ballots were counted by Congress. The electoral count was a rout, with Grant taking 214 votes to

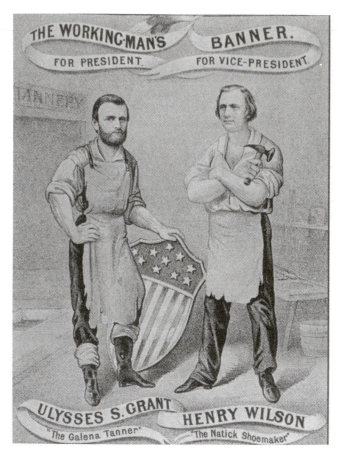

Grant and Wilson Campaign Poster, 1872. *Source:* Library of Congress.

Seymour's 80. The electoral college vote probably would have been even more lopsided if voter fraud had not carried New York and Georgia for the Democratic nominee.

The campaign focused mostly on rhetoric, with Republicans waving the "bloody shirt" to remind voters that it was their party that had saved the Union and brought peace to the land. In addition, the activities of the Ku Klux Klan were used by Republicans to show the true nature of southerners. With the memories of the Civil War still fresh in the minds of many voters, Grant, the savior of the Republic, had little to do but stand for election.

— 1872 —

The election of 1872 was never in doubt. Despite allegations of widespread corruption in his administration, incumbent Republican President Ulysses S. Grant trounced the nominee of the Liberal Republican Party and the Democratic Party, publisher Horace Greeley. Grant won the popular vote by nearly 700,000

votes (56% to 44%). Before the electoral votes could be cast, however, Greeley died. His 63 votes were splintered among four candidates. Grant handily won the electoral college, taking 286 ballots. In the election, Congress chose not to count the votes of Arkansas and Louisiana because of voter fraud.

Grant's campaign was a replay of the 1868 election wherein Republicans waved the "bloody shirt" to remind voters that it was Grant who had brought peace to the nation. Despite Democratic attempts to focus on a set of new political issues facing the nation, such as tariffs, monetary policy, civil service reform, foreign policy, and territorial expansion, the campaign focused on personalities. Greeley learned, as had Seymour in 1868, that he was no match for Grant, the savior of the Union.

— 1876 —

The election of 1876 was the most controversial election in the history of the Republic. The Democratic nominee, Governor Samuel J. Tilden of New York, won a majority of the popular vote. He outpaced his

Republican Candidates for President and Vice President, 1876: Hayes and Wheeler. *Source:* Library of Congress.

Garfield–Arthur Poster from the 1880 Election. *Source:* Library of Congress.

Republican opponent, Rutherford B. Hayes, by a count of 4,288,546 (51%) to 4,034,311 (48%). But in a much-disputed count of the electoral votes, Hayes was declared the winner by 185 electoral votes to 184. The electoral votes of Oregon, Florida, Louisiana, and South Carolina were determined by a special commission established in 1877 to resolve the conflict over who had won the votes. By consistent votes of 8 to 7, the commission of five senators, five representatives, and five Supreme Court justices decided the votes belonged to Hayes. Hayes and Tilden, practical politicians, made a deal that in return for Tilden's quietly accepting the results, Hayes would remove U.S. troops from the South, ending Reconstruction.

During the campaign, Republicans used the rhetoric of the "bloody shirt" to stir an emotion-based support for their candidate. This emotional appeal had great effect because Hayes, unlike Tilden, had served as a Union officer and was wounded at the battle of South Mountain and cited for gallantry at the battles of Fisher's Hill and Cedar Creek. Hayes also brought with him a reputation of being an honest man, an important attribute after the scandals of the Grant administration.

— 1880 —

After a protracted convention in which delegates rejected a third term for President Ulysses S. Grant and

James G. Blaine of Maine, Republicans nominated Representative James A. Garfield of Ohio as their candidate for president in 1880. In the election, Garfield faced the Democratic nominee, Civil War General Winfield Scott. In a popular vote of more than 9.2 million votes cast, Garfield won by fewer than 2,000 votes. The results in the electoral college were not as close, however, as Scott won only 155 electoral votes to Garfield's 214. Garfield won the more populated and electoral-rich states of the East and Midwest.

Garfield's campaign portrayed him as a moderate reformer of the civil service and as a continuation of Republican leadership. The success of his campaign was his ability to unite the two major factions of the Republican Party, the Half Breeds and the Stalwarts, behind his candidacy.

— 1884 —

The election of 1884 pitted two men of extraordinary political accomplishments against each other. The Republicans gave the nod to Speaker of the House James G. Blaine of Maine, while the Democrats nominated Governor Grover Cleveland of New York. In a close race where Cleveland's home state of New York would decide the election, Blaine's campaign lost New York and the election because of two events. First, in a meeting with the Reverend Samuel D.

Republican Candidates for President and Vice President, 1884: Blaine and Logan. *Source:* Library of Congress.

Bouchard, a Presbyterian minister from Brooklyn, who visited Blaine to endorse him, Bouchard offended thousands of voters by claiming that the Republican Party was not a place for the people of rum (consumers of alcohol), Romanism (Catholics) and rebellion (southerners). Bouchard's endorsement hurt Blaine's electoral chances. Additionally, Blaine attended a lavish dinner affair the night after Bouchard's comments. With the country in a period of hard times, voters did not react well to the luxurious banquet. Blaine lost the election by less than 30,000 votes. In the electoral college the margin of victory was also narrow, 219 to 182.

Blaine's personal life was a major campaign issue. Critics reported that Blaine had benefited financially from the corrupt deals he had made on behalf of robber barons. Democrats emphasized this link by chanting, "Blaine, Blaine, James G. Blaine, the continental liar from the state of Maine." In addition, reform-minded Republicans known as Mugwumps deserted the Blaine campaign. In the end, the election turned on

the economic hard times that gripped the nation. Voters sought a change from the Republican leadership in the White House, which had been steady for more than two decades.

— 1888 —

Republicans resorted to a time-honored tradition in politics by nominating a Civil War veteran and a man with an honorable political name, Benjamin Harrison, the grandson of President William Henry Harrison. In the election of 1888 the Democrats renominated President Grover Cleveland. In a close election, the contest turned on the outcomes of two states, Indiana, which was Harrison's home state, and New York, which was Cleveland's home state. Harrison won his home state as favorite son and won New York because of political disputes between Cleveland and the Tammany machine in New York City. Despite the fact that Cleveland won a plurality of the popular vote 5,234,488 (48.6%) to Harrison's 5,443,892 (47.8%), the result in the electoral college was for Harrison, 233 to 168.

The Harrison campaign was well organized and well financed through the efforts of Matther Quay of Pennsylvania. Harrison conducted a front-porch campaign in Indianapolis, while millions of pieces of campaign literature were distributed to counter Cleveland's antitariff efforts. Torchlight parades and brass bands in uniforms were common events in the election campaign.

— 1892 —

The election of 1892 was a rematch of the 1888 election. Incumbent Republican President Benjamin Harrison was pitted against former Democratic President Grover Cleveland. Harrison had fallen out of favor with many political leaders of his party. With the Cleveland campaign well financed and organized, Harrison lost the election by nearly 380,000 votes and the electoral college by 277 to 145.

Little separated the two candidates in terms of issues. The Cleveland reconciliation with Tammany and the political ties with western populists gave the Democratic nominee a second term. Additionally, the death of Harrison's wife in 1892 limited Harrison's participation in the reelection bid.

— 1896 —

With the behind-the-scenes deal making of Cleveland businessman Mark Hanna, the Republican Party nominated William McKinley for president. The Democratic Party nominated William Jennings Bryan, a

Republican Candidates for President and Vice President, 1888: Harrison and Morton. *Source:* Library of Congress.

member of the populist, free-silver wing of the party. McKinley won a close election with 51% of the popular vote to Bryan's 47%. If 21,000 votes in six states had been cast differently, Bryan would have won the electoral college. Instead, it went to McKinley, 271 to 176.

Hanna ran a masterful campaign for McKinley. While Bryan was actively traveling throughout the country making more than 600 speeches, McKinley stayed at home in Canton, Ohio. From his front porch, McKinley would meet with the media, which printed his words throughout the country. McKinley offered a conservative, stable alternative to the perceived radicalness of Bryan. Additionally, Hanna brought professionalism to the campaign by hiring thousands of workers to canvass the electorate and distribute millions of pamphlets.

— 1900 —

The election of 1900 was a rematch of the 1896 election, which pitted populist Democrat William Jennings Bryan of Nebraska against incumbent Republican President William McKinley. McKinley decisively de-

feated Bryan by winning 7.2 million votes, or 51.7% of the popular vote, to Bryan's 6.4 million, or 45.5%. In the electoral college, McKinley easily won by a margin of 292 to 155.

McKinley's 1900 reelection hailed the era of prosperity and imperialism. His election slogan of the "full dinner pail" that all Americans were enjoying under his administration was a powerful symbol. Millions of McKinley–Roosevelt dinner pails, which doubled as lanterns, were distributed. In addition, McKinley defended U.S. entry into the Spanish-American War and annexation of Puerto Rico, Guam, and the Philippines. Americans seemed to care little about American expansion as long as there was prosperity at home.

— 1904 —

In the election of 1904, incumbent Republican President Theodore Roosevelt, who had assumed the presidency after McKinley's assassination in 1901, faced the Democratic Party nominee, New York court of appeals chief justice Alton C. Parker. Roosevelt thoroughly beat fellow New Yorker Parker, winning 7.6

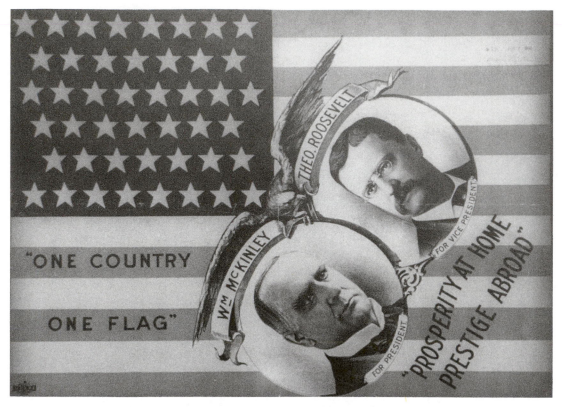

Republican Candidates for President and Vice President, 1900: McKinley and Roosevelt. *Source:* Library of Congress.

Republican Candidates for President and Vice President, 1904: Roosevelt and Fairbanks. *Source:* Library of Congress.

million votes, or 56.4% of the popular vote, to Parker's 5.1 million, or 37.6%. In the electoral college, Parker was only able to garner the votes of the southern states and their 140 electoral votes, while Roosevelt won big with 336 votes.

Roosevelt ran on the successes of the McKinley and Roosevelt administrations. He emphasized his progressive ideas of reform, while being able to appeal to traditional, conservative Republican voters. In Roosevelt, voters saw a strong leader who asserted America's newfound role in the world with vigor. With the country enjoying prosperity, there was little reason for voters to turn away from the popular Teddy Roosevelt.

— 1908 —

Republicans nominated the hand-picked successor of Theodore Roosevelt, William Howard Taft of Ohio, while the Democratic Party nominated, for a third time, populist William Jennings Bryan. The results of the election were not even close, as Taft outpolled Bryan by more than 1 million votes and orchestrated an electoral college landslide of 321 to 162.

The campaign saw both major candidates on the stump. Taft's campaign held to the themes of the Roosevelt administration. Critics argued that Taft stood for "Take advice from Theodore." Roosevelt entered the campaign by attacking corruption in the Democratic National Committee; its treasurer, C.N. Haskell, had been implicated in a bribery scandal involving Standard Oil. With Roosevelt and Bryan clashing in the press, Taft gave speeches outlining the differences between him and his "radical" opponent.

— 1912 —

The Republican Party committed the fatal error of not unifying behind a single candidate in the election of 1912. The progressive wing of the Republicans sought the nomination of Theodore Roosevelt, while the conservative wing wanted the renomination of incumbent President William Howard Taft. The Taft forces were victorious in his nomination, but the Roosevelt supporters bolted the convention and nominated Roosevelt on a third-party ticket. This party split led to the victory of the Democratic nominee, Governor Woodrow Wilson of New Jersey. Taft ran third in most states, winning only Utah and Vermont. In the end, the vote in the electoral college was not even close, as Wilson won 435 votes to Roosevelt's 88 and Taft's 8.

Republican Candidates for President and Vice President, 1908: Taft and Sherman. *Source:* Library of Congress.

The campaign was dominated by a strong progressive force that was taking control of the country. While little separated Wilson from Roosevelt, the differences between Wilson and Taft were more marked. Despite the remarkable trust-busting record of Taft, he was unable to shake his image as the lackey of big business.

— 1916 —

In the election of 1916, Republicans nominated Supreme Court Justice Charles Evans Hughes to face incumbent Democratic President Woodrow Wilson. In a close election, Hughes lost the popular vote to Wilson, who garnered 9.1 million votes, or 49.2%, to Hughes's 8.5 million votes, or 45.1%. In the all-important electoral college, the vote was even closer. Wilson was able to eke out a victory of 277 votes to 254. Wilson won 30 states including the South and West, but Hughes made the race close by winning the more populous eastern and midwestern states.

The Hughes campaign was highly critical of the Wilson administration's policies. Additionally, the candidate promised neutrality in the hostilities in Europe, while seeking to strengthen the military readiness of America. Since the primary issue of the election was the war in Europe, and with both parties seeking to stay out of it, voters saw little reason to switch to the Republicans.

— 1920 —

The election of 1920 pitted two Ohioans for the presidency. The Republicans had nominated on the tenth ballot Senator Warren G. Harding, while the Democratic Party, after a protracted convention, nominated Governor James M. Cox. Harding soundly defeated his fellow Ohioan by nearly 7 million popular votes and a 404-to-127 electoral college trouncing.

The campaign focused largely on the Democratic Party's commitment to the Treaty of Versailles and the League of Nations. Harding and the party were critical of the Wilson administration and argued that his election would be a return to normalcy.

— 1924 —

In the election of 1924, Republicans nominated incumbent President Calvin "Silent Cal" Coolidge, who had assumed the office after Harding's death in 1923. Coolidge faced John W. Davis of New York, who secured the Democratic nomination on the 103rd ballot. Coolidge won a resounding electoral victory in a

three-man race that included Progressive candidate Robert La Follette of Wisconsin. Davis could muster only 8.4 million popular votes, or 28.9%, to Coolidge's 15.7 million votes, or 54.1%. La Follette garnered 4.8 million votes, or 16.6% of the popular returns. In the electoral college, the defeat was equally humiliating for the Democratic nominee. Coolidge won 382 electoral votes to Davis's 136 votes—all from the South. La Follette won the 13 electoral votes of his home state of Wisconsin.

Coolidge's campaign was characteristically silent. Since his general political philosophy was that government ought to do as little as possible, he offered no new agenda for administration. With his Democratic opponent also a conservative, there was little that separated the two. American voters, as is their propensity, chose to stay with the man already in charge.

— 1928 —

The Republican Party nominated wartime food administrator and secretary of commerce under President Calvin Coolidge, Herbert Hoover. The Democrats nominated the first Roman Catholic candidate, New York Governor Alfred E. Smith. Hoover crushed Smith in the election, winning by more than 6 million votes (58.2% to 40.8%). Hoover won 40 states and 444 electoral votes to Smith's 8 states and 87 electoral votes.

Hoover Campaigning, 1932. *Source:* Library of Congress.

Hoover promised the continued prosperity that the Republicans had brought to the country since the 1920 election of Warren G. Harding. Additionally, Smith's religion and position against Prohibition were used against him. Hoover was the electoral benefactor of the economic prosperity that would soon come to a dramatic end with the stock market crash of 1929.

— 1932 —

The election of 1932 saw an end to the Republican Party stranglehold on the White House that had existed since the Civil War. Growing dissatisfaction with the Republican Party and its candidate, President Herbert Hoover, gave the Democratic nominee, Franklin Delano Roosevelt, a landslide victory. Hoover suffered a humiliating defeat, losing by more than 7 million votes. In the electoral college, Roosevelt whipped Hoover 472 to 59. Hoover carried only the three northern New England states of Vermont, New Hampshire, and Maine, plus Pennsylvania and a split of Connecticut.

Landon–Knox Campaign Poster from the 1936 Election. *Source:* Smithsonian Institution.

Hoover could do little during the campaign to improve his electoral chances. He was fatally linked to the economic depression that was gripping the country and the world. His lack of responsiveness to the onset of the depression cost the Republicans the White House for two decades.

— 1936 —

In 1936, Republicans nominated the only candidate they could find, Governor Alfred M. Landon, nicknamed the "Silent Cal" of Kansas. Landon, the only Republican governor reelected in 1934, never stood a chance of defeating incumbent Democratic President Franklin D. Roosevelt. Landon was beaten by more than 10 million votes, able to carry only two stalwart Republican states, Vermont and Maine. Mocking the stubbornness of the two states, New Hampshire citizens placed road signs on the border between the states announcing to travelers that they were about to enter the United States. In the electoral college, Roosevelt's victory was 523 to 8.

While accepting some of the New Deal programs as beneficial, Landon ran a campaign that highlighted the dangers of a continued reliance on the federal government as the solution to the nation's problems. Citing that the nation was in peril of becoming a socialist country was an argument that fell on deaf ears in 1936.

— 1940 —

Faced with the renomination of Democratic President Franklin D. Roosevelt for an unprecedented third term, Republicans nominated a lifelong Democrat turned Republican, Wendell L. Willkie. Willkie had come to national attention through his opposition to the New Deal policies of government-run utilities. While the election results in 1940 were not as overwhelming as those of 1936, Willkie still lost to Roosevelt by 5 million votes and the electoral college 449 to 82.

Willkie's campaign focused on two things. First, he stressed that many of the goals of the New Deal could be achieved but that they had to be carried out by the private sector. Second, the campaign stressed the danger of breaking the tradition of limiting presidents to two terms. To reinforce this notion, Republicans pointed to the political excesses of the New Deal, especially the Court-packing plan.

Willkie Campaigning, 1940. *Source:* Museum of Modern Art.

— 1944 —

The election of 1944, which saw the Democrats nominate Franklin D. Roosevelt for a fourth term, pitted the popular incumbent against the Republican nominee, New York Governor Thomas Dewey. While the margin of victory was not as large as those of 1936 or 1940, Roosevelt handily and decisively defeated Dewey by more than 3.5 million votes, or 53.4% of the popular vote for Roosevelt and 45.9% for Dewey. The electoral college was 432 for Roosevelt and 99 for Dewey.

While Dewey supported much of the New Deal program as being beneficial, during his campaign he criticized its scope, believing that it destroyed individual self-reliance. In the end, Dewey lost because the country was unwilling to change presidents in the middle of a war.

— 1948 —

In 1948 the Republicans believed they had the best chance of regaining the White House after 16 years of Democratic domination. They nominated moderate New York Governor Thomas Dewey, whose polling numbers showed he had a large lead over incumbent Democratic President Harry S. Truman. Despite pre-

dictions of a Republican victory, Truman defeated Dewey in a plurality vote. Truman won the popular totals with slightly more than 24 million votes to Dewey's nearly 22 million votes. In the electoral college, Truman garnered 303 votes to Dewey's 189. States' rights Democratic candidate Strom Thurmond won 39 electoral votes.

Dewey and the Republicans were unable to defeat Truman, despite the president's high negatives with the American voter. Perhaps the candidate and the party were misled by the dated polling numbers showing an electoral victory. In the end, with voter turnout low, Dewey was unable to distinguish himself as a strong alternative to the status quo.

— 1952 —

The Republican Party returned to a tried-and-true formula for electoral success in 1952 by nominating a World War II hero, General Dwight D. Eisenhower. Eisenhower, who had been approached by the Democratic Party four years earlier, was a moderate, inexperienced politician. In the 1952 election, he was pitted against a reluctant Democratic candidate, Governor Adlai E. Stevenson of Illinois. The resulting election was a landslide victory for "Ike," who garnered 442 electoral votes to Stevenson's 89. Stevenson was able to win only 9 states, all from the South. In terms of the popular vote, Eisenhower captured 6 million more votes than Stevenson.

Ike promised action on three main issues, "communism, corrupton, and Korea." These played well with voters. While Stevenson showed himself to be an eloquent speaker, he learned the tough political rule of never running against a war hero.

— 1956 —

In a rematch of the 1952 election, Democratic nominee Adlai E. Stevenson was once again trounced by Republican Dwight D. Eisenhower. Ike added to his electoral victories of 1952 by ceding to Stevenson only seven states (North Carolina, South Carolina, Georgia, Alabama, Mississippi, Arkansas, and Missouri) and their 73 electoral votes to Ike's 41 states and 457 electoral votes. In terms of popular votes, Stevenson garnered 26 million votes, or 42% of the vote, to the president's 35.6 million, or 57.4%.

Little had changed in campaign strategies from 1952 to 1956. America was prospering and was at peace. Ike's campaign needed to do little in order to secure victory. One issue that faced the popular president was concern for his health, as he had suffered a heart attack in September 1955. But his quick recovery allayed any fears that the public might have entertained.

— 1960 —

The election contest of 1960 between Republican Vice President Richard M. Nixon and the Democratic nominee, Senator John F. Kennedy of Massachusetts, was one of the closest in American history. Kennedy narrowly defeated Nixon in the popular vote polling by a mere 115,000 votes (49.7% to 49.6%). The votes in the electoral college did not reflect this closeness, as Kennedy was able to win elector-rich Illinois and Texas. Some historians argue that Illinois had widespread voter fraud that favored Kennedy. Nixon, however, quietly accepted the results of the electoral college, where he lost to Kennedy by 303 to 219.

Nixon's campaign emphasized his experience as vice president and his close association with the popular President Eisenhower. In a series of four televised debates—the first in American political history—however, Kennedy was able to discount the experience of Nixon while appealing to voters. Nixon did not make Kennedy's religion, Roman Catholicism, a campaign issue, despite the advice of some of his managers.

— 1964 —

The Republican Party determined the outcome of the 1964 presidential election when it nominated Senator Barry Goldwater of Arizona. Goldwater, a staunch conservative, had only limited appeal within his own party. The Democrats knew that there was no contest. They offered a sitting president, Lyndon B. Johnson,

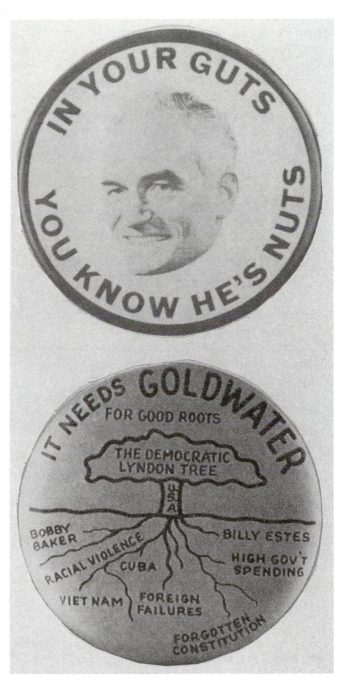

Campaign Buttons Against and For Goldwater, 1964.
Source: National Archives.

who had assumed the office in 1963, after Kennedy was assassinated. The final outcome of the election was a landslide victory for Johnson, who won 61% of the popular vote and 486 of the 538 electoral votes. Goldwater was able to carry only six states, five from the Deep South that were angered by Johnson's desegration stances (South Carolina, Georgia, Alabama, Mississippi, and Louisiana) and his home state of Arizona.

Goldwater did not try to moderate his image during the campaign. In fact, he exacerbated it when, in his acceptance speech, he declared, "Extremism in the defense of liberty is no vice! . . . Moderation in the pursuit of justice is no virtue." Goldwater appeared on television in a half-hour broadcast to explain his positions to the American public. While contributions from the convinced continued to come in, he failed to convert many followers.

— 1968 —

After the Goldwater disaster of 1964, Republicans turned to former Vice President Richard M. Nixon to face the Democratic nominee, Vice President Hubert Humphrey, who had just emerged from the violence-scarred Chicago National Convention. Nixon won in a close race where a mere 500,000 popular votes separated him and Humphrey. But the electoral college totals overwhelmingly supported Nixon's victory, 301 to 191. Governor George Wallace, who had run as an independent, pulled 46 electoral votes and nearly 10 million votes in the South.

With a large lead over his opponent, Nixon ran a conservative campaign that focused on staged events that his managers could control. In addition, he conceded the South to independent George Wallace and focused his attention on the border states. For the first time in American political history, the candidates of both parties hired Madison Avenue ad agencies to handle the making and the broadcasting of television commercials. In the end, the division in the Democratic Party caused by the 1968 convention was too great a chasm for Humphrey to bridge.

— 1972 —

The Republican candidate, President Richard M. Nixon, faced little challenge for reelection from the Democratic nominee, Senator George McGovern of South Dakota. McGovern was simply too liberal to be elected, just as Republican Barry Goldwater had been too conservative to be elected in 1964. Nixon crushed

Nixon–Agnew Campaign Buttons, 1968. *Source:* National Archives.

his opponent, garnering nearly 61% of the poplar vote and 520 electoral votes. McGovern was able to win only Massachusetts and the District of Columbia for 17 electoral votes.

The Nixon campaign successfully painted McGovern as too radical for the post of president. Most

President and Mrs. Ford on Primary Campaign Trip in Michigan, 1976. *Source:* Witten (National Archives).

Americans agreed with the Nixon spin. Despite the fact that the Nixon campaign had little to fear from McGovern, it committed a fatal error by breaking into the Democratic National Campaign Headquarters at the Watergate building. This mistake led to a congressional investigation and, for the first time in American history, the resignation of a president.

— 1976 —

The Republican standard-bearer for the 1976 election was President Gerald R. Ford, who had assumed the office after Nixon resigned. Ford thus became the first person to hold the office of president who had not been elected. (Ford had been appointed after Nixon Vice President Spiro Agnew resigned on charges of tax fraud.) The Democratic Party believed that the election offered a chance to redeem itself after the humiliating McGovern run of 1972. They nominated a political outsider, former Governor James E. "Jimmy" Carter, for president. Ford began the contest a 33-point underdog and managed to close the gap, making the election a toss-up. In the end, however, the political

unknown captured a majority (50.1%) of the popular vote and dominated the electoral college 297 to 240.

Ford's campaign focused on Carter's inexperience as a key factor in the election. But many voters were reminded of Ford's pardon of former President Nixon and the Republican scarlet letter of Watergate. Ford was unable to overcome "the Nixon issue" that continually haunted his campaign.

— 1980 —

With the economy in a recession and American pride at a low, the Republican Party believed that its candidate, former Governor Ronald Reagan of California, would be the first challenger to oust a sitting president since 1932. The Democratic incumbent, President James E. "Jimmy" Carter, lost a lopsided election to Reagan, who garnered 8 million more votes than Carter as well as 489 electoral votes to Carter's 49. In the end, Carter was able to win only six states (Minnesota, Maryland, West Virginia, Georgia, Hawaii, and part of Rhode Island) plus the District of Columbia.

Ronald and Nancy Reagan at Liberty State Park, NJ, 1980. *Source: New York Times.*

The Reagan campaign accomplished two things very well. First, it showed the domestic and foreign policy failures of the Carter administration in a stark light. Reagan asked voters to ask themselves whether or not they were better off in 1980 than they had been in 1976. Second, Reagan offered the American voter a vision of the future that recaptured America's status as a place of hope and opportunity. He used his extensive rhetoric skill to inspire a vision of America as "the shining city on the hill." His message appealed to traditional Democrats as well as Republicans.

— 1984 —

The Republicans had little doubt that their candidate, President Ronald Reagan, would win a stunning re-election over the Democratic nominee, former Carter Vice President Walter Mondale. Despite the historic step of choosing a female running mate, Representative Geraldine Ferraro of New York, the Democratic ticket generated little enthusiasm with the American voter. In the end, incumbent Republican President Ronald Reagan won in the biggest landslide in

American history. Reagan won the popular election by nearly 17 million votes and the electoral college 525 to 13. Mondale was able to win only his home state of Minnesota and the Democratic bastion of the District of Columbia.

The Reagan campaign benefited from a strong economic recovery and a resurgence in American pride. Mondale's campaign to scare voters with concerns over Reagan's age and the growing national debt were criticisms that slid off the president, earning him the nickname "the Teflon president." In the end, voters asked themselves if they were better off in 1984 than in 1980. Most of them responded positively and voted that way.

— 1988 —

Even though Republican President Ronald Reagan was ineligible to run again, the 1988 election was still a referendum on him. The Democrats nominated a political outsider, Governor Michael Dukakis of Massachusetts, to run against Reagan Vice President George Bush. Bush won the election handily by more than 7 million popular votes and a 426-to-112 vote in the electoral college. Dukakis won only nine states plus the District of Columbia. Nevertheless, his defeat had not been as severe as those of Carter and Mondale against the more popular Reagan.

The most interesting part of the 1988 campaign was Bush's selection of little-known Senator Dan Quayle of Indiana as his vice presidential running mate. While there was no contest between Bush and Dukakis, Dukakis's running mate, Senator Lloyd Benson of Texas, stood head and shoulders above Senator Quayle. Bush focused on the theme of continuity, family values, and international leadership. With the economy humming along nicely and the "world" at peace, he had little difficulty convincing voters that he was the better choice.

— 1992 —

In the beginning of 1992, the prospects for a Democratic takeover of the White House in November looked bleak. An incumbent Republican president, George Bush, was at his height of popularity, having successfully won the Gulf War. The Democrats nominated the little-known governor of Arkansas, William J. "Bill" Clinton. By election time, Clinton had cut into Bush's popularity and scored an electoral victory few would have predicted months earlier. In a three-way race that included an independent candidate, H. Ross Perot, Clinton garnered a plurality of nearly 45 million (43%)

of the popular vote, outdistancing Bush's 39 million (37.5%) and Perot's nearly 20 million (18.9%). In the electoral college, Clinton won 370 votes to Bush's 168.

Bush was no match for the gifted Democratic campaigner. In the debates, Bush had a difficult time articulating his vision of the future. Additionally, his campaign lacked the edge that had marked his 1988 electoral victory. Some believe that without the aid of Lee Atwater, Bush's friend and campaign guru, who had died of a brain tumor, Bush lacked the direction and stomach for a tough campaign. While emphasizing his successes in foreign relations, his broken "no new taxes" pledge and failure to recognize the growing concern over the economy cost him reelection.

APPENDIXES

APPENDIX 1

The Rules of the Republican Party
Adopted by the 1992 Republican National Convention, Held at Houston, Texas, August 17–20, 1992

PREAMBLE

BE IT RESOLVED, That the Republican Party is the party of the open door. Ours is the party of equality of opportunity for all and favoritism for none.

It is the intent and purpose of these rules to encourage the broadest possible participation of all voters in Republican Party activities at all levels and to assure that the Republican Party is open, accessible to all, and answerable ultimately to the people in the true American tradition.

It is the further purpose of these rules to ensure that the Republican Party stands for the principle that, as we are the party open to all, we are also the party of opportunity for all: opportunity for everyone of every race, religion, color, national origin, age, and sex.

These rules provide for full participation with equal opportunity for men and women, for minorities and heritage groups, and for all Americans regardless of age or social or economic status.

These rules mandate that the Republican Party shall be a nationwide party, purposeful and strong in all sections of the country, North, South, East, and West.

These rules maintain the Republican Party as an instrument for the political realization of that concept of individual liberty on which our constitutional government is founded.

BE IT FURTHER RESOLVED, That the following be and they hereby are adopted as The Rules of the Republican Party, comprised of the rules of business of this national convention, the rules for the election and government of the Republican National Committee until the next national convention, the rules under which delegates and alternate delegates shall be allotted to the respective states in the next national convention, and the rules under which such delegates and alternate delegates shall be elected and under which contests shall be considered.

PROCEEDINGS OF THE CONVENTION

Rule No. 1

Order of Business

The convention shall proceed in the order of business prepared and printed by the Republican National Committee.

Rule No. 2

Committee Reports

The report of the Committee on Credentials shall be disposed of before the report of the Committee on Rules and Order of Business is acted upon, the report of the Committee on Rules and Order of Business shall be disposed of before the report of the Committee on Resolutions is acted upon, and the report of the Committee on Resolutions shall be disposed of before the convention proceeds to the nomination of candidates for President of the United States and Vice President of the United States.

Rule No. 3

Definition of "States"

Whenever used in these rules, "state" or "states" shall be taken to include American Samoa, the District of Columbia, Guam, Puerto Rico, and the Virgin Islands, except in Rule No. 31 and unless the context in which the word "state" or "states" is used clearly makes such inclusion inappropriate.

Rule No. 4

Admission to Convention Hall

(a) No person except members of the several delegations, officers of the convention, members of the

Republican National Committee and, beginning at the 1992 Republican National Convention, incumbent Republican governors, incumbent Republican United States Senators, and incumbent Republican members of the United States House of Representatives, shall be admitted to the section of the convention hall restricted to delegates.

(b) Press and staff shall be admitted to the section(s) of the hall authorized for them.

(c) The chairman of the Republican National Committee shall insure that guest passes to the convention are distributed in an equitable fashion. Each delegate and alternate delegate to the convention shall receive at least one guest pass to each session of the convention.

Rule No. 5

Voting

(a) Each delegate to the convention shall be entitled to one (1) vote, which may be cast by an alternate delegate in the absence of the delegate.

(b) In the absence of any delegate at large or any delegate from any Congressional district, the roll of alternate delegates for the state or district shall be called in the order in which the names are placed upon the roll of the convention, unless the law governing the state or district electing the absent delegate, the state or district convention, or the Republican state committee or governing committee shall otherwise provide, or the delegation shall otherwise direct at the time of certification, in which event the alternative delegates from the state or district shall vote in the order established pursuant to the foregoing, as set forth in the delegation's certification. The form of certificate provided by the Republican National Committee shall provide a means by which an order for voting by alternate delegates may therein be specified.

Rule No. 6

Rules of Order

The Rules of the House of Representatives of the United States shall be the rules of the convention, except that the current edition of *Robert's Rules of Order, Newly Revised*, ("*Robert's Rules of Order*") shall be the rules for committees and subcommittees of the convention, insofar as they are applicable and not inconsistent with the rules herein set forth; provided, however, that the convention may adopt its own rules concerning the reading of committee reports and resolutions.

Rule No. 7

Length of Debate

No delegate shall speak more than once or longer than five (5) minutes upon the same question, unless by leave of the convention, except in the presentation of the name of a candidate for nomination for President of the United States or Vice President of the United States.

Rule No. 8

Suspension of Rules

A motion to suspend the rules shall always be in order but only when made by authority of a majority of the delegates from any state and seconded by a majority of the delegates from each of five (5) or more other states, severally.

Rule No. 9

Platform Resolutions

All proposed resolutions relating to the platform shall be submitted in writing to the Committee on Resolutions without reading and without debate.

Rule No. 10

Minority Reports; Amendments

No resolution or amendment pertaining to the report of the Committee on Resolutions or the Committee on Rules and Order of Business shall be reported out or made a part of any report of such committee or otherwise read or debated before the convention, unless the same shall have been submitted to the chairman, vice chairman, or secretary of such committee or to the secretary of the convention in writing not later than one hour after the time at which such committee votes on its report to the convention and shall have been accompanied by a petition evidencing the affirmative written support of a minimum of twenty-five percent (25%) of the membership of such committee.

Rule No. 11

Motion to Table

It shall be in order to lay on the table a proposed amendment to a pending measure and such motion, if adopted, shall not carry with it or prejudice such original measure.

Rule No. 12

Previous Question

When the previous question shall be demanded by a majority of the delegates from any state, and the demand is likewise seconded by a majority of delegates from each of two (2) or more other states, severally, and the call is sustained by a majority of the delegates to the convention, the question shall then be proceeded with and disposed of according to the Rules of the House of Representatives of the United States in similar cases.

Rule No. 13

Roll Call

(a) Upon all subjects before the convention requiring a roll call, the states shall be called in alphabetical order.

(b) In the balloting, the vote of each state shall be announced by the chairman of such state's delegation; and in case the vote of any state shall be divided, the chairman shall announce the number of votes for each candidate, or for or against any proposition; but if exception is taken by any delegate from that state to the correctness of such announcement by the chairman of that delegation, the chairman of the convention shall direct the roll of members of such delegation to be called, and the result shall be recorded in accordance with the vote of the several delegates in such delegation.

(c) In balloting, if any delegation shall pass when its name is called, then at the conclusion of the roll call all delegations which passed shall be called in the order herein before established and no delegation shall be allowed to change its vote until all delegations which passed shall have been given a second opportunity to vote.

(d) Except in a roll call for nomination for President of the United States and Vice President of the United States, or where the majority of delegates of fifteen (15) or more states severally have requested that a roll call be conducted by voice call of the roll, the chairman of the convention may order that the balloting on any subject placed before the convention requiring a roll call be conducted by electronic, telephonic or computer device which will display votes to the convention simultaneously. Each delegation chairman shall record and tally any such votes of the delegation on official roll call tally sheets provided by the secretary of the convention, showing the individual vote of the delegates, and file such tally sheets with the secretary of the convention not more than thirty (30) minutes after the completion of the roll call vote.

Rule No. 14

Unit Rule

No delegate or alternate delegate shall be bound by any attempt of any state or Congressional district to impose the unit rule.

Rule No. 15

Record Vote

If a majority of the delegates of any six (6) states severally shall demand a roll call vote, the same shall be taken of the states in the order hereinbefore established.

Rule No. 16

Nominations

(a) In making the nominations for President of the United States and Vice President of the United States and voting thereon, the roll of the states shall be called, separately in each case; provided, however, that if there is only one candidate for nomination for Vice President of the United States who has demonstrated the support required by paragraph (b) of this rule, a motion to nominate for such office by acclamation shall be in order and no calling of the roll with respect to such office shall be required.

(b) Each candidate for nomination for President of the United States and Vice President of the United States shall demonstrate the support of a majority of the delegates from each of five (5) or more states, severally, prior to the presentation of the name of that candidate for nomination.

(c) The total time of the nominating speech and seconding speeches for any candidate for nomination for President of the United States or Vice President of the United States shall not exceed fifteen (15) minutes.

(d) When it appears at the close of a roll call that any candidate for nomination for President of the United States or Vice President of the United States has received a majority of the votes entitled to be cast in the convention, the chairman of the convention shall declare that the candidate has been nominated.

(e) If no candidate shall have received such majority, the chairman of the convention shall direct the roll of the states be called again and shall repeat the calling of the roll until a candidate shall have received a majority of the votes entitled to be cast in the convention.

Rule No. 17

Convention Committees

(a) The delegates elected to the convention from each state, immediately after they are elected, shall elect from the delegation their members of the Committees on Resolutions, Credentials, Rules and Order of Business, and Permanent Organization of the convention, consisting of one (1) man and one (1) woman for each committee, and shall file notice of such selection with the secretary of the Republican National Committee; provided, however, that no delegate may serve on more than one (1) committee of the convention; except that the delegates from each of American Samoa, Guam, and the Virgin Islands shall select as hereinabove provided one (1) member of each such committee. Alternate delegates may not serve as members of the convention committees.

(b) Committees and subcommittees may set time limits for speaking on any question by a simple majority vote; provided, however, that not less than twenty (20) minutes, equally divided between proponents and opponents on any question, shall be allowed in any case on any debatable motion, order, or appeal.

(c) Upon request of one-fifth ($\frac{1}{5}$) of the members of a committee or subcommittee of the convention, a vote shall be recorded in the manner provided by these rules, and no votes in the committees or subcommittees of the convention shall be taken by secret ballot.

Rule No. 18

Temporary Rules

Rules No. 1 through No. 17 shall be the temporary rules of the next national convention and its committees and subcommittees.

THE REPUBLICAN NATIONAL COMMITTEE

Rule No. 19

Organization of the Republican National Committee

The Republican National Committee shall have the general management of the Republican Party, subject to direction from the national convention. The members of the Republican National Committee shall consist of one (1) national committeeman and one (1) national committeewoman from, and the chairman of the state Republican Party of, each state.

Rule No. 20

Method of Election

(a) Where the rules adopted by a state Republican Party provide a method of election of the national committeeman and the national committeewoman, they shall be elected pursuant to such method.

(b) Where the rules adopted by a state Republican Party do not provide a method of election of the national committeeman and the national committeewoman, and where state laws do provide such a method of election, they shall be elected pursuant to such method provided by state laws.

(c) Where neither the rules adopted by a state Republican Party nor state laws provide a method of election of the national committeeman and the national committeewoman, the national convention delegation from such state shall elect them.

(d) At each convention, the roll shall be called and the delegation from each state shall report through its chairman the names of the elected national committee members whose election shall be ratified by the convention if otherwise in accordance with these rules.

Rule No. 21

Term of Office

(a) National committeemen and national committeewomen shall serve from the adjournment of the national convention until the adjournment of the following national convention, and until their successors shall have been elected and qualified.

(b) The duly elected and acting chairman of each state Republican Party shall be a member of the Republican National Committee during his or her tenure in office.

Rule No. 22

Vacancies

(a) Election of members to fill vacancies in the Republican National Committee shall be ratified by the Republican National Committee upon their election by the state Republican Party in and for the state in which the vacancy occurs.

(b) The Republican National Committee shall have the power to declare vacant the seat of any member who refuses to support the Republican nominee for President of the United States or Vice President of the United States.

(c) In the event of the death, resignation, disqualification, or disability of any officer or committee member of the Republican National Committee, as enumerated in Rule No. 23 and Rule No. 29, such vacancy shall be filled by the same body and in the same manner as provided therein for the election of such officer or officers or committee members in the first instance.

Rule No. 23

Officers of the Republican National Committee

(a) The officers of the Republican National Committee shall consist of:

(1) A chairman and a co-chairman of the opposite sex who shall be elected by the members of the Republican National Committee. Except as otherwise ordered by a majority of the members of the Republican National Committee present and voting on the matter, the chairman and the co-chairman shall be full-time, paid employees of the Republican National Committee. The chairman shall be the chief executive officer of the Republican National Committee. The chairman or co-chairman may be removed from office only by a two-thirds ($\frac{2}{3}$) vote of the entire Republican National Committee.

(2) Eight (8) vice chairmen, comprising one (1) man and one (1) woman from each of the following four (4) regions:

The Western States Association: Alaska, American Samoa, Arizona, California, Colorado, Guam, Hawaii, Idaho, Montana, Nevada, New Mexico, Oregon, Utah, Washington, and Wyoming;

The Midwestern States Association: Illinois, Indiana, Iowa, Kansas, Michigan, Minnesota, Missouri, Nebraska, North Dakota, Ohio, South Dakota, West Virginia, and Wisconsin;

The Northeastern States Association: Connecticut, Delaware, the District of Columbia, Maine, Maryland, Massachusetts, New Hampshire, New Jersey, New York, Pennsylvania, Puerto Rico, Rhode Island, Vermont, and the Virgin Islands; and

The Southern States Association: Alabama, Arkansas, Florida, Georgia, Kentucky, Louisiana, Mississippi, North Carolina, Oklahoma, South Carolina, Tennessee, Texas, and Virginia.

(3) A secretary, a treasurer, and such other officers as the Republican National Committee shall deem necessary, all to be elected by the Republican National Committee.

(b) The chairman, co-chairman, and all other officers shall be elected in January of each odd-numbered year. All officers except the vice chairman shall be nominated from the floor, and candidates must have at least two (2) votes in three (3) states in order to have their names put in nomination. There shall be no nominating committee.

(c) The eight (8) vice chairmen shall be elected at regional caucuses by the Republican National Committee members of the four (4) regions and shall be residents of and Republican National Committee members from their respective regions. The election shall take place in January of each odd-numbered year commencing in January 1997. The election of vice chairmen shall not require confirmation by the Republican National Committee.

(d) The chairman shall appoint a general counsel for the Republican National Committee and a chairman of the Republican Finance Committee, both of whom shall be confirmed by the Republican National Committee.

Rule No. 24

Chairman's Executive Council; Executive Committee

(a) There shall be a Chairman's Executive Council of the Republican National Committee to consist of eleven (11) members of the Republican National Committee, three (3) to be appointed by the chairman and eight (8) additional members to consist of one (1) man and one (1) woman elected by and from each of the four (4) regional caucuses. In addition, the following shall serve as ex-officio members of the Chairman's Executive Council: the chairman, the co-chairman, the general counsel, the chairman of the Republican Finance Committee, the chairman of the Republican State Chairmen's Advisory Committee, the chairman of the Budget Committee, and the president of the National Federation of Republican Women.

(b) The Chairman's Executive Council may exercise all the executive and administrative functions required of the Republican National Committee between meetings of the Republican National Committee, with the exception of the following:

(1) election of officers of the Republican National Committee;

(2) ratification of the election of members of the Republican National Committee;

(3) issuance of the call and designation of the time and place for holding the national convention; and

(4) filling a vacancy in the office of Republican candidate for President of the United States, or Republican candidate for Vice President of the United States.

(c) The Chairman's Executive Council shall meet on the call of the chairman and such meetings shall be held at least twice in each year. In addition, upon written petition of at least twenty-five percent (25%) of the members of the Chairman's Executive Council, the chairman, within ten (10) days of his receipt of said petition, shall call a meeting of the Chairman's Executive Council to be held in a city to be designated by the chairman. The date of such meeting shall fall between ten (10) and twenty (20) days from the date of the call. The minutes of all Chairman's Executive Council meetings shall be distributed as promptly as practicable to all members of the Republican National Committee.

(d) There shall be an Executive Committee, which shall be composed of the members of the Chairman's Executive Council, the president of the National Federation of Republican Women, the chairman of the Young Republican National Federation, the chairman of the College Republican National Committee, the chairman of the National Republican Heritage Groups Council, the chairman of the National Black Republican Council, the chairman of the Republican National Hispanic Assembly, the president of the National Federation of the Grand Order of Pachyderm Clubs, the president of the National Conference of Republican Mayors, the Republican leader of the United States Senate, the Republican leader of the United States House of Representatives, the chairman of the Republican Governors Association, the president of the National Conference of Republican County Officials, the president of the National Republican Legislators Association, the president of the National Association of Urban Republican County Chairmen, the chairman of the Republican Labor Council, the chairman of Republicans Abroad, and a representative of Jewish-Americans appointed by the Chairman of the Republican National Committee. Additional groups and organizations may be granted representation on or removed from the Executive Committee by the Republican National Committee, subject to ratification by the next Republican national convention. Groups and organizations represented on the Executive Committee may be referred to as "Auxiliaries of the Republican National Committee." The Executive Committee shall consult with and offer advice to the chairman of the Republican National Committee with respect to the executive and administrative functions of the Republican National Committee.

(e) The Executive Committee shall meet on the call of the chairman of the Republican National Committee. In addition, upon written petition of at least twenty-five percent (25%) of the members of the Executive Committee, the chairman, within ten (10) days of receipt of said petition, shall call a meeting of the Executive Committee to be held in a city to be designated by the chairman. The date of such meeting shall fall between ten (10) and twenty (20) days from the date of the call.

(f) There shall be a Republican Labor Council which shall be composed of working men and women, all supportive of the Republican Presidential nominee, balanced between union and non-union members, appointed by the chairman of the Republican National Committee with the approval of the Republican National Committee. This Council shall elect its chairman from among its members.

Rule No. 25

Rules of Order

(a) *Robert's Rules of Order* shall govern in all meetings of the Republican National Committee and its committees insofar as they are applicable and not inconsistent with these rules.

(b) All meetings of the Republican National Committee and all of its committees shall be open meetings, except as provided for by *Robert's Rules of Order*.

(c) A member of the Republican National Committee may give a written and witnessed proxy to a legal and qualified voter of the same state, which shall be effective for one meeting and which shall be filed with the secretary of the Republican National Committee.

(d) No votes (except elections to office when properly ordered pursuant to the provisions of *Robert's Rules of Order*) shall be taken by secret ballot in any open meeting of the Republican National Committee or of any committee thereof.

Rule No. 26

Meetings of the Republican National Committee

(a) The Republican National Committee shall meet at least twice in each year. A tentative agenda for each meeting shall be mailed to the membership at least ten (10) days prior to such meeting. The minutes, including all resolutions and motions, shall be mailed to all members of the Republican National Committee within thirty (30) days after the close of the meeting.

(b) The first meeting of the Republican National Committee shall take place within five (5) days after the adjournment of the national convention. Such meeting and all other meetings of the Republican National Committee shall take place upon call of the chairman or, in case of a vacancy in the chairmanship, upon call of the co-chairman or, in case of a vacancy in the chairmanship and the co-chairmanship, upon call of the vice chairman senior in time of service as a member of the Republican National Committee; provided, however, that such call shall be issued at least ten (10) days in advance of the date of the proposed meeting, except that if one of the purposes of a meeting of the Republican National Committee is to fill a vacancy in the office of Republican candidate for President of the United States or Republican candidate for Vice President of the United States, then only five (5) days' notice of the purpose, date, and place of said meeting shall be required. Upon written petition of sixteen (16) or more members of the Republican National Committee, representing no fewer than sixteen (16) states, filed jointly or severally with the chairman, requesting a meeting of the Republican National Committee, it shall be the duty of the chairman, within ten (10) days from receipt of said petition, to issue a call for a meeting of the Republican National Committee, to be held in a city to be designated by the chairman, the date of such called meeting to be not later than twenty (20) days or earlier than ten (10) days from the date of the call.

Rule No. 27

Filling Vacancies in Nominations

(a) The Republican National Committee is hereby authorized and empowered to fill any and all vacancies which may occur by reason of death, declination, or otherwise in the office of Republican candidate for President of the United States or Republican candidate for Vice President of the United States, as nominated by the national convention, or the Republican National Committee may reconvene the national convention for the purpose of filling any such vacancies.

(b) In voting under this rule, the Republican National Committee members representing any state shall be entitled to cast the same number of votes as said state was entitled to cast in the national convention.

(c) In the event that the members of the Republican National Committee from any state shall not be in agreement in the casting of votes hereunder, the votes of such state shall be divided equally, including fractional votes, among the members of the Republican National Committee present or voting by proxy.

(d) No candidate shall be chosen to fill any such vacancy except upon receiving a majority of the votes entitled to be cast in the election.

Rule No. 28

Committees of the Republican National Committee

(a) There shall be the following committees:

(1) There shall be a Standing Committee on Rules of the Republican National Committee, composed of one (1) member of the Republican National Committee from each state, to review and propose recommendations with respect to The Rules of the Republican Party. The members of the Republican National Committee from each state shall caucus and by majority vote choose from their number within eight (8) months following the national convention appointees to serve on this committee. If the members of the Republican National Committee from any state do not within this period submit to the chairman of the Republican National Committee their choice to serve on the Standing Committee on Rules, the chairman of the Republican National Committee shall select, from among the members of the Republican National Committee from each such state, one (1) member to serve on the Standing Committee on Rules. The chairman of the Standing Committee on Rules shall be elected by the committee from among its members.

(2) There shall be a Committee on Arrangements to plan for and manage the next national convention. The chairman and the co-chairman of the Republican National Committee shall be members of the Committee on Arrangements and the chairman of the Republican National Committee shall appoint to the Committee on Arrangements at least one (1) member of the Republican National Committee from each state. The chairmen of the Committee on Arrangements and of its subcommittees shall be appointed by and serve at the pleasure of the chairman of the Republican National Committee from among the members of the Committee on Arrangements and, together with such other officers as shall be elected by the Committee on Arrangements, shall be members of the executive committee of the Committee on Arrangements. The chairman of the Standing Committee on Rules and the chairman of the Committee on Contests shall also be members of the Committee on Arrangements.

(3) There shall be a Committee on the Call, composed of a chairman and at least seven (7) members of the Republican National Committee who shall be appointed by the chairman of the Republican National Committee. This committee shall assist the Republican National Committee in connection with issuance of the call for the next national convention pursuant to Rule No. 30. This committee shall be appointed after the selection of the Committees on Rules and Arrangements.

(4) There shall be a Committee on Contests, which shall be composed of two (2) members of the Republican National Committee from each of the

four (4) regions described in Rule No. 23, elected by members of the Republican National Committee from each such region, and a chairman appointed by the chairman of the Republican National Committee from among the members or officers of the Republican National Committee. This committee shall perform the duties relating to the resolution of contests prescribed in Rule No. 39. This committee shall be elected after the selection of the Committees on Rules and Arrangements.

(5) There shall be a Committee on the Site of the Republican National Convention, which shall be composed of two (2) members of the Republican National Committee from each of the four (4) regions described in Rule No. 23, elected by the members of the Republican National Committee from each such region, and a chairman appointed by the chairman of the Republican National Committee from among the members or officers of the Republican National Committee. This committee shall be responsible for investigating potential sites for the next national convention, and for recommending a site to the Republican National Committee for selection. This committee shall be selected no later than two (2) years following the Presidential election.

(6) Each member of the Republican National Committee shall be a member of at least one (1) of the above-mentioned committees. The general counsel of the Republican National Committee shall be counsel to each of such committees. The minutes of these committees shall be distributed as promptly as practicable to all members of the Republican National Committee. Any of these committees may meet and act by telephone conference upon twenty-four (24) hours' notice.

(b) The chairman of the Republican National Committee, with the approval of the Republican National Committee, may appoint such other committees and assistants as he or she may deem necessary, and whenever such committees are appointed, they shall consist of a chairman and an equal number of men and women.

Rule No. 29

Finance and Budget

(a) The Republican National Committee shall create a Republican Finance Committee and any subcommittees thereof which it deems desirable, to which it may delegate the responsibility of developing and implementing a broad-based fundraising plan. The chair-

man of the Republican Finance Committee shall be appointed pursuant to the provisions of Rule No. 23(d).

(b) The Republican National Committee shall create a Budget Committee and any subcommittees thereof which it deems desirable, to which it may delegate the responsibility of developing a budget and reviewing income and expenditures of the Republican National Committee. The Budget Committee shall be composed of seven (7) members of the Republican National Committee, three (3) of whom shall be appointed by the chairman of the Republican National Committee and one (1) of whom shall be elected by each of the four (4) regional caucuses in January of each odd-numbered year. In addition, the following shall serve as ex-officio members of the Budget Committee: the chairman, co-chairman, and treasurer of the Republican National Committee, and the chairman of the Republican Finance Committee. The chairman of the Republican National Committee shall make every effort in his appointments to ensure that an equal number of men and women serve on the Budget Committee. The chairman of the Republican National Committee shall appoint the chairman of the Budget Committee from among the members thereof.

(c) The annual budget shall be approved at the first meeting of the Republican National Committee held in each year. The proposed budget, in reasonable detail, shall be mailed to all members of the Republican National Committee at least ten (10) days prior to such meeting.

(d) The Republican National Committee shall not, without prior written and filed approval of all members of the Republican National Committee from the state involved, contribute money or in-kind aid to any candidate for public or party office except the nominee of the Republican Party or a candidate who is unopposed in the Republican primary after the filing deadline for that office.

CONVENING OF THE NEXT NATIONAL CONVENTION

Rule No. 30

Call of Next Convention

The Republican National Committee shall issue the call for the next national convention to nominate candidates for President of the United States and Vice President of the United States prior to January 1 of the year in which the national convention is to be held. The Republican National Committee shall issue and promulgate the call in a manner consistent with these rules, which call shall include the text of the rules relating to the convening and the proceedings of the national convention.

Rule No. 31

Membership in Convention

The membership of the next national convention shall consist of:

(a) Delegates.

(1) Six (6) delegates at large from each of the fifty (50) states.

(2) Three (3) district delegates for each Representative in the United States House of Representatives from each state.

(3) Four (4) delegates at large from American Samoa, fourteen (14) delegates at large from the District of Columbia, four (4) delegates at large from Guam, fourteen (14) delegates at large from Puerto Rico, and four (4) delegates at large from the Virgin Islands; provided, however, that if Puerto Rico shall become a state prior to the next national convention, the number of delegates from Puerto Rico shall be calculated in accordance with the same formula used for the other states.

(4) From each state having cast its electoral votes, or a majority thereof, for the Republican nominee for President of the United States in the last preceding election: four and one-half ($4\frac{1}{2}$) delegates at large plus a number of the delegates at large equal to sixty percent (60%) of the number of electoral votes of that state; provided, however, that if Puerto Rico shall become a state prior to the next national convention, it shall be presumed that it would have cast its electoral votes, or a majority thereof, for the Republican nominee in the last preceding election. (In the computation of the number of delegates at large, any sum of the four and one-half ($4\frac{1}{2}$) plus the sixty percent (60%) representing a fraction shall be increased to the next whole number.) In addition, one (1) delegate at large shall be awarded to a state for any and each of the following public officials elected by such state in the year of the last preceding Presidential election or at any subsequent election held prior to January 1 of the year in which the next national convention is held:

  (i) Each Republican United States Senator; provided that no such additional delegate at large award to any state shall exceed two (2);

  (ii) A Republican governor; provided that no such additional delegate at large award to any state shall exceed one (1);

  (iii) Membership in the Republican Party of at least one-half ($\frac{1}{2}$) of the Representatives representing a state in the United States House of Representatives; provided that no such additional delegate at large award to any state shall exceed one (1); and

  (iv) Membership in the Republican Party of a majority of the members of any chamber of a state legislature, if such chamber has been organized, and is presided over (if the presiding officer is elected by the chamber), by Republicans; or, if the membership in the Republican Party of the members of any chamber of a state legislature increases by twenty-five percent (25%) or more, so long as twenty-five percent (25%) equals at least two (2) legislators; provided that no such additional delegate at large award to any state shall exceed one (1).

(5) In addition from the District of Columbia, if the District of Columbia shall have cast its electoral votes, or a majority thereof, for the Republican nominee for President of the United States in the last preceding Presidential election: four and one-half ($4\frac{1}{2}$) delegates at large plus the number of delegates at large equal to thirty percent (30%) of the fourteen (14) delegates at large allotted to the District of Columbia. (In the computation of the number of delegates at large, any sum of the four and one-half ($4\frac{1}{2}$) plus the thirty percent (30%) representing a fraction shall be increased to the next whole number.)

(6) Any state which would receive fewer delegates under all provisions of this rule than it received to the 1972 Republican National Convention shall have its number of delegates increased to the same number of delegates it received to the 1972 Republican National Convention.

(b) Alternate Delegates.

One (1) alternate delegate for each delegate to the national convention.

Rule No. 32

Election of Delegates and Alternate Delegates

(a) Order of Precedence.

Delegates at large and their alternate delegates and delegates from Congressional districts and their alternate delegates to the national convention shall be elected in the following manner:

(1) In accordance with any applicable laws of a state, insofar as the same are not inconsistent with these rules; or

(2) To the extent not provided for in the applicable laws of a state, in accordance with any applicable Republican Party rules of a state, insofar as the same are not inconsistent with these rules; or

(3) By a combination of the methods set forth in paragraphs (a)(1) or (a)(2) of this rule; or

(4) To the extent not provided by state law or party rules, as set forth in paragraph (c) of this rule.

(b) General.

In all elections of delegates or alternate delegates to the national convention, the following rules shall apply:

(1) In any jurisdiction in which Republican representation upon the board of judges or inspectors of elections for primary elections is denied by law, delegates and alternate delegates shall be elected as provided in paragraph (a)(2) or (a)(4) of this rule.

(2) In selecting delegates and alternate delegates to the national convention, no state law shall be observed which hinders, abridges, or denies to any citizen of the United States, eligible under the Constitution of the United States to hold the office of President of the United States or Vice President of the United States, the right or privilege of being a candidate under such state law for the nomination for President of the United States or Vice President of the United States or which authorizes the election of a number of delegates or alternate delegates from any state to the national convention different from that fixed in these rules.

(3) Alternate delegates shall be elected to the national convention for each unit of representation equal in number to the number of delegates elected therein and shall be chosen in the same manner and at the same time as the delegates, and under the same rules; provided, however, that if the law of any state shall prescribe another method of choosing alternate delegates they may be chosen in accordance with the provisions of the law of the state in which the election occurs.

(4) Delegates and alternate delegates at large to the national convention when serving as delegates and alternate delegates shall be residents of and duly qualified voters in their respective states. All delegates and alternate delegates allocated as delegates and alternate delegates at large shall be elected at large in the several states; provided, however, that such allocation and method of election may be varied in any state to the extent, and only to the extent, necessary to avoid conflict with state law applicable to the selection of national convention delegates if such varying allocation

and method of election were those pursuant to which delegates at large and alternate delegates at large were elected to the 1988 Republican National Convention from that state.

(5) Delegates and alternate delegates to the national convention representing Congressional districts shall be residents of and qualified voters in said districts respectively when elected and when serving as delegates and alternate delegates. There shall be three (3) delegates and three (3) alternate delegates allocated to represent each Congressional district of the several states, who shall be elected by each such Congressional district; provided, however, that such number of delegates and alternate delegates allocated to represent, and elected by, any Congressional district of a state may be reduced or increased to the extent, and only to the extent, necessary to avoid conflict with state law applicable to the selection of national convention delegates if such varying allocation was that pursuant to which district delegates and alternate district delegates were elected to the 1988 Republican National Convention from the state.

(6) No delegate or alternate delegate to the national convention shall be required to pay an assessment or fee in excess of that provided by the law of the state in which his or her election occurs as a condition of serving as a delegate or alternate delegate to the national convention.

(7) There shall be no automatic delegates to the national convention who serve by virtue of party position or elective office.

(8) Delegates and alternate delegates to the national convention may be elected only in one of the following manners:
   (i) by primary election;
   (ii) by the Republican state committee, where specifically provided by state law;
   (iii) by state and Congressional district conventions;
   (iv) by any method consistent with these rules by which delegates and alternate delegates were selected to the 1984 Republican National Convention in that state.

(9) No state law shall be observed which permits any person to participate in a primary delegate and alternate delegate selection process that also permits that person at the same primary to participate in the choosing of nominees of any other party for other elective office. Delegates and alternate delegates shall in that event be elected by Congressional district or state conventions pursuant to paragraph (c) of this rule.

(10) No delegates or alternate delegates shall be se-

lected pursuant to any Republican Party rule of a state or state law which materially changes the method of selecting delegates or alternate delegates and was adopted or made effective more than seven days after the issue of the call for the next national convention in the year before the year in which the national convention is to be held. Where it is not possible to select delegates or alternate delegates in the manner in effect in that state before the date seven days after the issue of the call for the next national convention, delegates or alternate delegates shall be selected in the same manner as was used for the immediately next preceding national convention or, if it is not possible to select delegates or alternate delegates in the same manner as was used for the immediately next preceding national convention, then delegates or alternate delegates shall be selected by Congressional district or state conventions pursuant to paragraph (c) of this rule.

(11) Except with respect to delegates and alternate delegates elected under paragraph (b)(8)(ii) of this rule and if consistent with paragraph (c)(5) of this rule, the selection process for choosing those who will select delegates or alternate delegates shall not begin before September 1 of the year before the year in which the national convention is to be held.

(12) Notwithstanding the provisions of Rule 32(a), a state party may select its delegates and alternate delegates by rules inconsistent with Rule 32(a)(1), provided that those state party rules are not otherwise inconsistent with the Rules of the Republican Party, and provided that the Republican National Committee, after determining that the state law being waived hereunder is adverse to the best interests of the Republican Party in that state, has granted that state party a waiver of Rule 32(a)(1) of these rules.

(c) Conventions.

Wherever state law permits or the Republican Party rules of a state require the election of delegates and alternate delegates by convention or there is no applicable state law or Republican Party rule, delegates and alternate delegates to the national convention shall be elected by Congressional district or state conventions pursuant to the following rules:

(1) Congressional district or state conventions shall be called by the Republican state committee.

(2) Delegates to Congressional district conventions may be elected in precinct caucuses, mass meetings, mass conventions, or county conventions in which only eligible voters in such precinct, county, or district as the case may be shall vote.

(3) Notices of the call for any such caucus, meeting, or convention shall be published in a newspaper or newspapers of general circulation in the county, district, or state as the case may be, not less than fifteen (15) days prior to the date of such caucus, meeting, or convention.

(4) Only legal and qualified voters who are deemed to be Republicans pursuant to state law or by party rules of a state shall participate in any Republican caucus, mass meeting, or mass convention held for the purpose of selecting delegates to county, district, or state conventions and only such legal and qualified voters shall be elected as delegates to county, district, and state conventions; provided, however, that in addition to the qualifications provided herein, the governing Republican committee of each state shall have the authority to prescribe additional qualifications not inconsistent with law. Such additional qualifications shall be adopted and published in at least one (1) daily newspaper having a general circulation throughout the state, such publication to be at least ninety (90) days before such qualifications become effective.

(5) No delegates shall be deemed eligible to participate in any Congressional district or state convention the purpose of which is to elect delegates to the national convention who are elected prior to the date of the issuance of the call of such national convention.

(6) Congressional district conventions shall be composed of delegates who are legal and qualified voters therein, and delegates to state conventions shall be qualified voters in the respective districts which they represent in said state conventions. Such delegates shall be apportioned by the state Republican Party among counties, parishes, and cities of the state or district having regard to the Republican vote or the population therein.

(7) There shall be no proxies at any district or state convention (which shall not include meetings of a Republican state committee) held for the purpose of selecting delegates to the national convention. If alternate delegates to such selection convention are selected, the alternate delegate and no other shall vote in the absence of the delegate.

(d) On or before September 1 of the year before the year in which the national convention is to be held, each Republican state committee shall adopt rules, procedures, policies, and instructive materials (prepared pursuant to Rule No. 34(a) governing the selection of delegates and alternate delegates to the national convention to convene during the following year, and shall certify and file with the secretary of the Republican National Committee true copies of the same and of all statutes governing the selection of such delegates and alternate delegates. Any subsequent amendments to or changes in such statutes, rules, procedures, policies, and materials shall be filed with the secretary of the Republican National Committee within twenty-one (21) days after the date of the amendment or change.

Rule No. 33

Election of Excess Delegates and Alternate Delegates

(a) No state shall elect a greater number of persons to act as delegates and alternate delegates than the actual number of delegates and alternate delegates respectively to which it is entitled under the call for the national convention, and no unit of representation may elect any delegate or delegates, or their alternate delegates, with permission to cast a fractional vote.

(b) Where more than the authorized number of delegates from any state is certified and forwarded to the secretary of the Republican National Committee in the manner provided in Rule No. 35, a contest shall be deemed to exist and the secretary shall notify the several claimants so reported and shall submit all such credentials and claims to the whole Republican National Committee for decision as to which claimants reported shall be placed upon the temporary roll of the national convention.

Rule No. 34

Participation

(a) The Republican National Committee shall assist the states in their efforts to inform all citizens as to how they may participate in delegate-selection procedures. The states, in cooperation with the Republican National Committee, shall prepare instructive material on delegate-selection methods and make it available for distribution.

(b) Participation in a Republican primary, caucus, or any meeting or convention held for the purpose of selecting delegates and alternate delegates to a county, district, state, or national convention shall in no way be abridged for reasons of sex, race, religion, color, age, or national origin. The Republican National Committee and the Republican state committee or governing committee of each state shall take positive action to achieve the broadest possible participation by men and women, young people, minority and heritage groups, senior citizens, and all other citizens in the delegate-selection process.

(c) Unless otherwise provided by the laws of the state in which the election occurs, in those states where delegates and alternate delegates are elected through the convention system or a combination of convention and primary systems, the precinct, ward, township, or county meetings shall be open meetings, and all citizens who are qualified shall be urged to participate.

(d) Each state shall endeavor to have equal representation of men and women in its delegation to the Republican National Convention.

(e) The provisions of these rules are not intended to be the basis of any kind of quota system.

Rule No. 35

Certification of Election

(a) All delegates and alternate delegates shall be elected not later than thirty-five (35) days before the date of the meeting of the national convention, unless otherwise provided by the laws of the state in which the election occurs.

(b) Election of delegates and alternate delegates shall be certified:

(1) in every case where they are elected by convention, by the chairman and secretary of such convention or by the chairman and secretary of the Republican state committee, and forwarded to the secretary of the Republican National Committee;

(2) in every case where they are elected by primary, by the canvassing board or officer created or designated by the law of the state in which the election occurs, to canvass the returns and issue certificates of election to delegates or alternate delegates to national conventions of political parties, and all certificates shall be forwarded by said duly elected delegates and alternate delegates in the manner herein provided; and

(3) in every case where they are elected by the Republican state committee, by the chairman and secretary of the Republican state committee, and forwarded to the secretary of the Republican National Committee.

(c) No later than thirty (30) days before the time set for the meeting of the national convention, the credentials of each delegate and alternate delegate shall be filed with the secretary of the Republican National Committee for use by the secretary in making up the temporary roll of the national convention, except in the case of delegates or alternate delegates elected at a time or times in accordance with the laws of the state in which the election occurs rendering impossible the filing of credentials within the time above specified.

Rule No. 36

Contests: Resolution by States

All contests arising in any state electing district delegates by district conventions shall be decided by its state convention, or if the state convention shall not meet prior to the national convention, then by its state committee; and only contests affecting delegates elected at large shall be presented to the Republican National Committee; provided, however, if the contest regarding a district delegate arises out of the irregular or unlawful action of the state committee or state convention, the Republican National Committee may take jurisdiction thereof and hear and determine the same under the procedures provided in Rules No. 38 and No. 39.

Rule No. 37

Temporary Roll

(a) The names of the delegates and alternate delegates presenting certificates of election from the officials designated in Rule No. 35 shall be placed upon the temporary roll of the national convention by the Republican National Committee.

(b) No person on the temporary roll of the national convention and whose right to be seated as a delegate or alternate delegate is being contested shall be entitled to vote in the national convention or in any committee thereof until by vote of the national convention the contest as to such person has been finally decided and such person has been permanently seated, except that any such person may be accorded the right to so vote, except in matters involving the credentials of that person, by an affirmative vote of a majority of the members of the Republican National Committee or the Committee on Credentials.

Rule No. 38

Contest Filing

(a) Notices of contests shall state the grounds of the contest and shall be filed, no later than thirty (30) days before the time set for the meeting of the national convention, with the secretary of the Republican National Committee, except in the case of delegates or alternate delegates elected at a time or times in accordance with applicable state law rendering impossible the filing of the notice of contest within the time above specified.

(b) Notices of contests may be filed only by a resident of the state whose delegation is challenged who was eligible to participate at any level in the delegate selection process of that state.

(c) Only contests that are timely filed under these rules shall be considered.

(d) For purposes of the rules relating to contests and credentials, the term "party" shall mean a person or persons who shall have filed a notice of contest pursuant to this Rule No. 38, and the person or persons whose right to be seated as a delegate or alternate delegate is the subject of such notice of contest.

Rule No. 39

Contest Procedure

(a) The Committee on Contests shall have the power to adopt procedural rules, not inconsistent with these rules, which shall govern the expeditious prosecution of contests before the Committee on Contests. When any deadline set out in this rule falls on a Sunday or legal holiday, such deadline shall be extended to the following day.

(b) No later than twenty-two (22) days before the convening of the national convention (or, in the case of delegates or alternate delegates elected at a time or times in accordance with applicable state law rendering impossible compliance with this requirement, within five (5) days after such election), each of the parties shall file with the secretary of the Republican National Committee at least three (3) printed or typewritten copies of the statement of position in support of the party's claim to sit as delegates or alternate delegates to the national convention together with such affidavits or other evidence as desired. The secretary of the Republican National Committee, upon receiving the statement of position of a party, shall furnish the opposing party a copy of said statement of position.

Each statement of position shall begin with a summary of not more than one thousand (1,000) words setting forth succinctly a synopsis of the statement of position and a specific statement of the points relied upon.

(c) The Committee on Contests shall promptly hear the matter, decide what issues are involved, either of law or fact, or both, decide upon its recommendation for resolution of such issues, and submit such issues and its recommendations for resolution to the Republican National Committee. The issues so submitted by the Committee on Contests shall be the sole issues passed upon and determined by the Republican National Committee unless the Republican National Committee shall, by a majority vote, extend or change the same.

If the Committee on Contests for any reason shall fail to state the issues either of law or fact, the Republican National Committee shall decide upon what issues the contest shall be tried, and the hearing shall be limited to such issues unless the Republican National Committee, by a majority vote, shall decide otherwise.

(d) The Committee on Contests shall make up a report of each contest filed, showing the grounds of contest; the statute and rule, if any, under which the contest is waged; and the contentions of each party thereto. The report shall conclude with a statement of the points of issue in the contest, both of fact and law, and a statement of the recommendation of the Committee on Contests as to resolution of such points of issue, and shall be signed by the chairman or his designee. When the Committee on Contests has prepared such report stating the issues of law and fact, a copy of the statement of such issues shall be submitted forthwith to a person in the convention city, whom the parties must appoint at the time of filing the contest to receive such statement, and a copy shall be served forthwith by the chairman of the Committee on Contests upon the parties by the most expeditious method available, providing for written evidence of receipt including, but not limited to, overnight delivery service.

(e) The parties shall have eight (8) days to file written objections to the Committee on Contests' statement of the issues of fact or law, or both, unless the Republican National Committee is called to act upon the contest sooner, in which case such objections shall be made before the meeting of the whole committee. If the parties reside in American Samoa, Guam, Alaska, Hawaii, Puerto Rico, or the Virgin Islands, they shall be entitled to ten (10) days to file written objections.

The objections shall contain any additional statement of issues of either law or fact, or both, claimed by the party submitting the same to be involved in and necessary to be decided in the contest.

(f) When the Republican National Committee is called to pass upon any contest that may arise, the members of the Committee on Credentials shall also be notified of the time and place of such meeting and shall have the right to attend all hearings of all contests but without the right to participate in the discussion or the vote.

Rule No. 40

Convention Committee on Credentials

(a) When the national convention shall have assembled, the secretary of the Republican National Committee shall deliver to the Committee on Credentials all credentials and other papers forwarded under Rule No. 35(c).

(b) An appeal may be taken to the Committee on Credentials from any ruling of the Republican National Committee on any contest, by and only by a party to such contest in the proceedings conducted pursuant to Rules No. 38 and No. 39, provided, however, that notice of such appeal must be filed with the secretary of the Republican National Committee within twenty-four (24) hours after the decision, that such notice shall specify the grounds upon which the appeal is taken, and that only the grounds so specified shall be heard by the Committee on Credentials upon such appeal. No evidence other than that taken before the Republican National Committee shall be taken up by the Committee on Credentials unless it shall, by a majority vote of all of its members, so direct.

(c) No issue involving the status of one or more delegates or alternate delegates or any contest relating thereto may originate before the Committee on Credentials of the national convention. All contests must first be presented to the Committee on Contests of the Republican National Committee or to the whole Republican National Committee.

APPENDIX 2

Republican Leaders and Whips of the House of Representatives

Congress	Majority/Minority	Leader	Whip
56th	Majority	Sereno E. Payne	James A. Tawney
57th	Majority	Sereno E. Payne	James A. Tawney

Congress	Majority/Minority	Leader	Whip
58th	Majority	Sereno E. Payne	James A. Tawney
59th	Majority	Sereno E. Payne	James E. Watson
60th	Majority	Sereno E. Payne	James E. Watson
61st	Majority	Sereno E. Payne	John W. Dwight
62nd	Minority	James R. Mann	John W. Dwight
63rd	Minority	James R. Mann	Charles H. Burke
64th	Minority	James R. Mann	Charles M. Hamilton
65th	Minority	James R. Mann	Charles M. Hamilton
66th	Majority	Franklin W. Mondell	Harold Knutson
67th	Majority	Franklin W. Mondell	Harold Knutson
68th	Majority	Nicholas Longworth	Albert H. Vestal
69th	Majority	John Q. Tilson	Albert H. Vestal
70th	Majority	John Q. Tilson	Albert H. Vestal
71st	Majority	John Q. Tilson	Albert H. Vestal
72nd	Minority	Bertrand H. Snell	Carl B. Bachmann
73rd	Minority	Bertrand H. Snell	Harry L. Englebright
74th	Minority	Bertrand H. Snell	Harry L. Englebright
75th	Minority	Bertrand H. Snell	Harry L. Englebright
76th	Minority	Joseph W. Martin	Harry L. Englebright
77th	Minority	Joseph W. Martin	Harry L. Englebright
78th	Minority	Joseph W. Martin	Leslie C. Arends
79th	Minority	Joseph W. Martin	Leslie C. Arends
80th	Majority	Charles A. Halleck	Leslie C. Arends
81st	Minority	Joseph W. Martin	Leslie C. Arends
82nd	Minority	Joseph W. Martin	Leslie C. Arends
83rd	Majority	Charles A. Halleck	Leslie C. Arends
84th	Minority	Joseph W. Martin	Leslie C. Arends
85th	Minority	Joseph W. Martin	Leslie C. Arends
86th	Minority	Charles A. Halleck	Leslie C. Arends
87th	Minority	Charles A. Halleck	Leslie C. Arends
88th	Minority	Charles A. Halleck	Leslie C. Arends
89th	Minority	Gerald A. Ford	Leslie C. Arends
90th	Minority	Gerald A. Ford	Leslie C. Arends
91st	Minority	Gerald A. Ford	Leslie C. Arends
92nd	Minority	Gerald A. Ford	Leslie C. Arends
93rd	Minority	Ford/John J. Rhodes	Leslie C. Arends
94th	Minority	John J. Rhodes	Robert H. Michel
95th	Minority	John J. Rhodes	Robert H. Michel
96th	Minority	John J. Rhodes	Robert H. Michel
97th	Minority	Robert H. Michel	Trent Lott
98th	Minority	Robert H. Michel	Trent Lott
99th	Minority	Robert H. Michel	Trent Lott
100th	Minority	Robert H. Michel	Trent Lott
101st	Minority	Robert H. Michel	Newt Gingrich
102nd	Minority	Robert H. Michel	Newt Gingrich
103rd	Minority	Robert H. Michel	Newt Gingrich
104th	Majority	Dick Armey	Tom DeLay

APPENDIX 3

Republican Leaders of the Senate

Congress	Majority/Minority	Leader	Whip
62nd	Majority	Shelby M. Cullom	None
63rd	Minority	Jacob H. Gallinger	None
64th	Minority	Jacob H. Gallinger	James W. Wadsworth
65th	Minority	Jacob H. Gallinger	Charles Curtis
66th	Majority	Henry Cabot Lodge	Charles Curtis
67th	Majority	Henry Cabot Lodge	Charles Curtis
68th	Majority	Lodge/Charles Curtis	Curtis/Wesley L. Jones
69th	Majority	Charles Curtis	Wesley L. Jones
70th	Majority	Charles Curtis	Wesley L. Jones
71st	Majority	James E. Watson	Simeon D. Fess
72nd	Majority	James E. Watson	Simeon D. Fess
73rd	Minority	Charles L. McNary	Felix Hebert
74th	Minority	Charles L. McNary	None
75th	Minority	Charles L. McNary	None
76th	Minority	Charles L. McNary	None
77th	Minority	Charles L. McNary	None
78th	Minority	Charles L. McNary	Kenneth Wherry
79th	Minority	Wallace H. White Jr.	Kenneth Wherry
80th	Majority	Wallace H. White Jr.	Kenneth Wherry
81st	Minority	Kenneth Wherry	Leverett Saltonstall
82nd	Minority	Wherry/Styles Bridges	Leverett Saltonstall
83rd	Majority	Robert A. Taft/William F. Knowland	Leverett Saltonstall
84th	Minority	William F. Knowland	Leverett Saltonstall
85th	Minority	William F. Knowland	Everett McKinley Dirksen
86th	Minority	Everett McKinley Dirksen	Thomas H. Kuchel
87th	Minority	Everett McKinley Dirksen	Thomas H. Kuchel
88th	Minority	Everett McKinley Dirksen	Thomas H. Kuchel
89th	Minority	Everett McKinley Dirksen	Thomas H. Kuchel
90th	Minority	Everett McKinley Dirksen	Thomas H. Kuchel
91st	Minority	Dirksen/Hugh Scott	Hugh Scott/Robert P. Griffin
92nd	Minority	Hugh Scott	Robert P. Griffin
93rd	Minority	Hugh Scott	Robert P. Griffin
94th	Minority	Hugh Scott	Robert P. Griffin
95th	Minority	Howard H. Baker Jr.	Ted Stevens
96th	Minority	Howard H. Baker Jr.	Ted Stevens
97th	Majority	Howard H. Baker Jr.	Ted Stevens
98th	Majority	Howard H. Baker Jr.	Ted Stevens
99th	Majority	Robert Dole	Alan K. Simpson
100th	Minority	Robert Dole	Alan K. Simpson
101st	Minority	Robert Dole	Alan K. Simpson
102nd	Minority	Robert Dole	Alan K. Simpson
103rd	Minority	Robert Dole	Alan K. Simspon
104th	Majority	Dole/Trent Lott	Trent Lott/Don Nickles

APPENDIX 4

Party Defections in Congress

Name	State	Year	House/Senate	Direction
Wayne Morse	OR	1952	Senate	$R \rightarrow I \rightarrow D$
Strom Thurmond	SC	1964	Senate	$D \rightarrow R$
Albert W. Watson	SC	1965	House	$D \rightarrow R$
Harry F. Byrd Jr.	VA	1970	Senate	$D \rightarrow I$
Ogden R. Reid	NY	1972	House	$R \rightarrow D$
Donald W. Reigle	MI	1973	House	$R \rightarrow D$
John Jarman	OK	1975	House	$D \rightarrow R$
Peter A. Peyser	NY	1976	House	$R \rightarrow D$
Eugene A. Atkinson	PA	1981	House	$D \rightarrow R$
Bob Stump	AZ	1981	House	$D \rightarrow R$
Phil Gramm	TX	1983	House	$D \rightarrow R$
Andy Ireland	FL	1984	House	$D \rightarrow R$
Bill Grant	FL	1989	House	$D \rightarrow R$
Tommy Robinson	OK	1989	House	$D \rightarrow R$
Richard Shelby	AL	1994	Senate	$D \rightarrow R$
Ben Nighthorse Campbell	CO	1995	Senate	$D \rightarrow R$
Greg Laughlin	TX	1995	House	$D \rightarrow R$
Berry Tauzin	LA	1995	House	$D \rightarrow R$
Mike Parker	MS	1995	House	$D \rightarrow R$
Jimmy Hayes	LA	1995	House	$D \rightarrow R$

APPENDIX 5

Republican Party Convention Sites and Dates

1856
Music Fund Hall
Philadelphia, PA
June 17–19

1860
The Wigwam
Chicago, IL
May 16–18

1864
Front Street Theater
Baltimore, MD
June 7–8

1868
Crosby's Opera House
Chicago, IL
May 20–21

1872
Academy of Music
Philadelphia, PA
June 5–6

1876
Exposition Hall
Cincinnati, OH
June 14–16

1880
Exposition Hall
Chicago, IL
June 2–5, 7–8

1884
Exposition Hall
Chicago, IL
June 3–6

1888
Civic Auditorium
Chicago, IL
June 19–25

1892
Industrial Exposition Hall
Minneapolis, MN
June 7–10

1896
Specially Built Auditorium
St. Louis, MO
June 16–18

1900
Exposition Auditorium
Philadelphia, PA
June 19–21

1904
The Coliseum
Chicago, IL
June 21–23

1908
The Coliseum
Chicago, IL
June 16–19

1912
The Coliseum
Chicago, IL
June 18–22

1916
The Coliseum
Chicago, IL
June 7–10

1920
The Coliseum
Chicago, IL
June 8–12

1924
Municipal Auditorium
Cleveland, OH
June 10–12

1928
Civic Auditorium
Kansas City, MO
June 12–15

1932
Chicago Stadium
Chicago, IL
June 14–16

1936
Municipal Auditorium
Cleveland, OH
June 9–12

1940
Convention Hall
Philadelphia, PA
June 24–28

1944
Chicago Stadium
Chicago, IL
June 26–28

1948
Convention Hall
Philadelphia, PA
June 21–25

1952
International Amphitheater
Chicago, IL
July 7–11

1956
Cow Palace
San Francisco, CA
August 20–23

1960
International Amphitheater
Chicago, IL
July 25–28

1964
Cow Palace
San Francisco, CA
July 13–16

1968
Convention Hall
Miami Beach, FL
August 5–8

1972
Convention Hall
Miami Beach, FL
August 21–23

1976
Kemper Arena
Kansas City, MO
August 16–19

1980
Joe Louis Arena
Detroit, MI
July 14–17

1984
Dallas Convention Center
Dallas, TX
August 20–23

1988
Louisiana Superdome
New Orleans, LA
August 15–18

1992
Houston Astrodome
Houston, TX
August 17–20

1996
Convention Center
San Diego, CA
August 13–15

APPENDIX 6

Chairs of the Republican National Committees

1856–64	Edwin D. Morgan	1932–34	Everett Sanders
1864–66	Henry J. Raymond	1934–36	Henry P. Fletcher
1866–68	Marcus L. Ward	1936–40	John Hamilton
1868–72	William Claflin	1940–42	Joseph W. Martin Jr.
1872–76	Edwin D. Morgan	1942–44	Harrison E. Spangler
1876–79	Zachariah Chandler	1944–46	Herbert Brownell Jr.
1879–80	J. Donald Cameron	1946–48	B. Carroll Reece
1880–83	Marshall Jewell	1948–49	Hugh D. Scott Jr.
1883–84	D. M. Sabin	1949–52	Guy George Gabrielson
1884–88	Benjamin Franklin Jones	1952–53	Arthur E. Summerfield
1888–91	Matthew S. Quay	1953	C. Wesley Roberts
1891–92	James S. Clarkson	1953–57	Leonard W. Hall
1892–96	Thomas H. Carter	1957–59	H. Meade Alcorn
1896–1904	Marcus A. Hanna	1959–61	Thruston B. Morton
1904	Henry C. Payne	1961–64	William E. Miller
1904–7	George B. Cortelyou	1964–65	Dean Burch
1907–8	Harry S. New	1965–69	Ray C. Bliss
1908–9	Frank H. Hitchcock	1969–71	Rogers C. B. Morton
1909–12	John F. Hill	1971–73	Robert Dole
1912	Victor Rosewater	1973–74	George Bush
1912–16	Charles D. Hilles	1974–77	Mary Louise Smith
1916–18	William R. Wilcox	1977–81	Bill Brock
1918–21	Will Hays	1981–83	Richard Richards
1921–24	John T. Adams	1983–89	Frank J. Fahrenkopf Jr.
1924–28	William M. Butler	1989–91	H. Lee Atwater
1928–29	Herbert Work	1991–92	Clayton Yeutter
1929–30	Claudius H. Huston	1992–93	Rich Bond
1930–32	Simeon D. Fess	1993–	Haley Barbour

APPENDIX 7

Republican State Committee Headquarters

Alabama
P.O. Box 320800
Birmingham, AL 35232-0800
(202) 324-1984

Alaska
750 East Firewood Lane, Suite 102
Anchorage, AK 99503
(907) 276-4467

American Samoa
P.O. Box 3820
Pago Pago, AS 96799
(684) 633-4116

Arizona
3501 North 24th Street
Phoenix, AZ 85016-6607
(602) 957-7770

Arkansas
One Riverfront Place, Suite 550
North Little Rock, AR 72114
(501) 372-7301

California
1903 West Magnolia
Burbank, CA 91506
(818) 841-5210

Colorado
1275 Tremont Place
Denver, CO 80204
(303) 893-1776

Connecticut
508 Tolland Street
East Hartford, CT 06108
(201) 289-6552

Delaware
2 Mill Road
Wilmington, DE 19806
(302) 651-0260

District of Columbia
440 First Street NW, 4th Floor
Washington, DC 20001
(202) 662-1382

Florida
P.O. Box 311
Tallahassee, FL 32302
(904) 222-7920

Georgia
3091 Maple Drive N.E., Suite 315
Atlanta, GA 30305
(404) 365-7700

Guam
P.O. Box 2846
Agana, GU 96910
(671) 472-3450

Hawaii
100 North Beretania Street, Suite 203
Honolulu, HI 96817
(805) 526-1755

Idaho
P.O. Box 2267
Boise, ID 83702
(208) 343-6405

Illinois
233 South Third Street
Springfield, IL 62701
(217) 525-0011

Indiana
One North Capitol, Suite 1260
Indianapolis, IN 46204
(317) 635-7561

Iowa
521 East Locust Street
Des Moines, IA 50309
(515) 282-8105

Kansas
214 West Sixth Street
Topeka, KS 66603
(913) 234-3416

Kentucky
P. O. Box 1068, 105 West Third
Frankfort, KY 40602
(502) 875-5130

Louisiana
650 North Sixth Street
Baton Rouge, LA 70802
(504) 383-7234

Maine
24 Stone Street
Augusta, ME 04330
(207) 622-6247

Maryland
60 West Street, Suite 201
Annapolis, MD 21401
(301) 269-0113

Massachusetts
9 Galen Street, Suite 320
Watertown, MA 02172
(617) 924-8683

Michigan
2121 East Grand River
Lansing, MI 48912
(517) 487-5413

Minnesota
8030 Cedar Avenue, Suite 202
Bloomington, MN 55425
(612) 854-1446

Mississippi
P. O. Box 60
Jackson, MS 39205
(601) 948-5191

Missouri
P. O. Box 73
Jefferson City, MO 65102
(314) 636-3146

Montana
1425 Helena Avenue
Helena, MT 59601
(406) 442-6469

Nebraska
421 South 9th Street, Suite 102
Lincoln, NE 68508
(402) 475-2122

Nevada
953 East Sahara Avenue, Suite 13B
Las Vegas, NV 89104
(702) 737-7031

New Hampshire
134 North Main Street
Concord, NH 03301
(603) 225-9341

New Jersey
310 West State Street
Trenton, NJ 08618
(609) 989-7300

New Mexico
P.O. Box 36900
Albuquerque, NM 87176
(505) 883-7345

New York
315 State Street
Albany, NY 12210
(518) 449-2601

North Carolina
P. O. Box 12905, 1410 Hillsborough Street
Raleigh, NC 27605
(919) 828-6423

North Dakota
P. O. Box 1917
Bismarck, ND 58502
(701) 255-0030

Ohio
172 East State Street, 4th Fl.
Columbus, OH 43215
(614) 228-2481

Oklahoma
4031 North Lincoln Blvd.
Oklahoma City, OK 73105
(405) 528-3501

Oregon
10550 SW Allen Blvd., Room 224
Beaverton, OR 97005
(503) 627-0745

Pennsylvania
P. O. Box 1624
Harrisburg, PA 17105
(717) 234-4901

Rhode Island
400 Smith Street
Providence, RI 02908
(401) 421-2570

South Carolina
P. O. Box 21765
Columbus, SC 29250
(803) 789-8999

South Dakota
P. O. Box 1099
Pierre, SD 57501
(605) 224-7347

Tennessee
2817 West End Avenue
Nashville, TN 37203
(651) 321-4521

Texas
211 East 7th Street, Suite 620
Austin, TX 78701
(512) 477-9821

Utah
640 East 400, South Suite A
Salt Lake City, UT 84102
(801) 533-9777

Vermont
P. O. Box 70
Montpelier, VT 05602
(802) 223-3411

Virginia
115 East Grace Street
Richmond, VA 23219
(804) 780-0111

Washington
9 Lake Bellevue Drive, Suite 203
Bellevue, WA 98005
(206) 451-1988

West Virginia
101 Dee Drive
Charleston, WV 25311
(304) 344-3446

Wisconsin
P. O. Box 31
Madison, WI 53701
(608) 257-4765

Wyoming
P. O. Box 241
Casper, WY 82602
(307) 234-9166

APPENDIX 8

House Election Victories by Party, 1860–1996

Between 1860 and 1996, 27,025 House elections were held in the United States. Of these, 13,976 were won by the Democrats and 12,400 by the Republicans. The remaining 649 elections were won by independents and third parties (ITPs). Interestingly, the growing duopoly of the electoral system is proved by the fact that over the years, the number of electoral victories by ITPs has dwindled to a trickle. Between 1860 and 1895 the ITPs won 509 seats. The relative number was 100 between 1895 and 1931, 38 between 1932 and 1965, and only 2 since 1966.

While the two major parties have maintained some measure of parity in most states, there are a number of exceptions, particularly in the South and in the Midwest and Northeast. Thus, Vermont has returned only one Democrat to the House since 1860, while on the other end of the spectrum Texas has sent 1,067 Democrats but only 104 Republicans. Right in the middle is New York, which has elected exactly 1,290 Republicans and 1,290 Democrats in the 136-year period.

State	Democrat	Republican	State	Democrat	Republican
Alabama	476	64	Nebraska	65	181
Alaska	6	14	Nevada	36	30
Arizona	59	70	New Hampshire	24	120
Arkansas	327	24	New Jersey	333	440
California	676	672	New Mexico	50	28
Colorado	105	108	New York	1290	1290
Connecticut	157	192	North Carolina	537	106
Delaware	34	35	North Dakota	11	98
Florida	341	117	Ohio	566	885
Georgia	614	39	Oklahoma	247	366
Hawaii	34	2	Oregon	77	119
Idaho	31	84	Pennsylvania	693	1281
Illinois	658	907	Rhode Island	74	76
Indiana	366	421	South Carolina	325	64
Iowa	97	484	South Dakota	28	91
Kansas	55	320	Tennessee	420	180
Kentucky	469	140	Texas	1067	104
Louisiana	432	52	Utah	44	57
Maine	27	206	Vermont	1	106
Maryland	304	132	Virginia	470	127
Massachusetts	332	546	Washington	142	157
Michigan	313	638	West Virginia	202	109
Minnesota	132	339	Wisconsin	177	442
Mississippi	381	35	Wyoming	9	44
Missouri	608	217			
Montana	54	41	Total	13,976	12,400

APPENDIX 9

Party Affiliations in Congress, 1860–1996

In the 136 years from 1860 to 1996, the Democrats controlled the House of Representatives for 80 years and the Republicans for 56 years. In contrast, the Republicans controlled the Senate for 72 years and the Democrats for 62 years; Republicans and Democrats were equally divided in the Senate of the 47th Congress (1881 to 1883), with 37 members each. To provide a framework for comparison, the Republicans have held the White House for 84 years and the Democrats for 52 years.

Both parties have had their sojourns in the political wilderness for extended periods of time. The Democrats, crippled by the Civil War, never really tasted power until the New Deal. (The Wilson era was in fact a gift from Theodore Roosevelt to the Democratic Party.) But having gained power in 1932, the Democrats have held on to it with rare tenacity. For a period of 62 years between 1932 and 1994 (with the exception of the 80th and 83rd Congresses), the Democrats have reigned on the Hill and dominated the legislative agendas. This is a record of longevity unmatched in the annals of political parties.

		House		Senate	
Year	Congress	Democrat	Republican	Democrat	Republican
1861–63	37th	43	105	10	31
1863–65	38th	75	102	9	36
1865–67	39th	42	149	10	42
1867–69	40th	49	143	11	42
1869–71	41st	63	149	11	56
1871–73	42nd	104	134	17	52
1873–75	43rd	92	194	19	49
1875–77	44th	169	109	29	45
1877–79	45th	153	140	36	39
1879–81	46th	149	130	42	33
1881–83	47th	135	147	37	37
1883–85	48th	197	118	36	38
1885–87	49th	183	140	34	43
1887–89	50th	169	152	37	39
1889–91	51st	159	166	37	39
1891–93	52nd	235	88	39	47
1893–95	53rd	218	127	44	38
1895–97	54th	105	244	39	43
1897–99	55th	113	204	34	47
1899–1901	56th	163	185	26	53
1901–03	57th	151	197	31	55
1903–05	58th	178	208	33	57
1905–07	59th	136	250	33	57
1907–09	60th	164	222	31	61
1909–11	61st	172	219	32	61
1911–13	62nd	228	161	41	51
1913–15	63rd	291	127	51	44
1915–17	64th	230	196	56	40
1917–19	65th	216	210	53	42
1919–21	66th	190	240	47	49
1921–23	67th	301	131	37	59

Year	Congress	House		Senate	
		Democrat	Republican	Democrat	Republican
1923–25	68th	205	225	43	51
1925–27	69th	183	247	39	56
1927–29	70th	195	237	46	49
1929–31	71st	167	267	39	56
1931–33	72nd	220	214	47	48
1933–35	73rd	310	117	60	35
1935–37	74th	319	103	69	25
1937–39	75th	331	89	76	16
1939–41	76th	261	164	69	23
1941–43	77th	268	162	66	28
1943–45	78th	218	208	58	37
1945–47	79th	242	190	56	38
1947–49	80th	188	245	45	51
1949–51	81st	263	171	54	42
1951–53	82nd	234	199	49	47
1953–55	83rd	211	221	47	48
1955–57	84th	232	203	48	47
1957–59	85th	233	200	49	47
1959–61	86th	283	153	64	34
1961–63	87th	263	174	65	35
1963–65	88th	258	177	67	33
1965–67	89th	295	140	68	32
1967–69	90th	247	187	64	36
1969–71	91st	243	192	57	43
1971–73	92nd	254	180	54	44
1973–75	93rd	239	192	56	42
1975–77	94th	291	144	60	37
1977–79	95th	292	143	61	38
1979–81	96th	276	157	58	41
1981–83	97th	243	192	53	46
1983–85	98th	269	165	54	46
1985–87	99th	252	182	53	47
1987–89	100th	258	177	55	45
1989–91	101st	259	174	55	45
1991–93	102nd	267	167	56	44
1993–95	103rd	258	176	57	43
1995–97	104th	199	233	46	53

GENERAL INDEX

Numbers in bold indicate volume; page numbers in italic indicate illustration.

Numbers in bold indicate volume; page numbers in italic indicate illustration.

Numbers in bold indicate volume; page numbers in italic indicate illustration.

F

Fascism, **1**:42

"Fair Deal" policies, Truman's, **1**:44

Fair Labor Standards Act of 1938, **1**:141

Fair-play amendment, **1**:48, **2**:433

Fairbanks, Charles W., **1**:260–61, **2**:428, 430, *834*

Fairfield, Vermont, President Arthur's birthplace, **1**:203

Fairness Doctrine, **1**:126, 140

Fall, Albert B., **1**:32, 226

Fallinger, Richard, **1**:253

Family Cap, **1**:197

Family Support Act of 1988, **1**:197

Family values, **1**:173; Bush and, **1**:209; 1976 platform on the family, **2**:641; 1980 platform on strong families, **2**:668, 671; 1984 platform on family protection, **2**:727–28; 1988 platform on families, **2**:750, 753; 1992 platform on families, **2**:790–96; Quayle and, **1**:264; traditional, **1**:198, 201

Farm relief: Coolidge and, **1**:32–33, 211–12; 1908 platform on, **2**:468; 1920 platform on agriculture, **2**:481–82; 1924 platform on agriculture, **2**:491–92; 1928 platform on agriculture, **2**:499–500; 1932 platform on agriculture, **2**:507–8; 1936 platform on agriculture, **2**:518; 1940 platform on agriculture, **2**:522–23; 1944 platform on agriculture, **2**:528; 1952 platform on agriculture, **2**:540; 1956 platform on agriculture, **2**:549–51; 1960 platform on agriculture, **2**:565–66; 1968 platform on agriculture, **2**:595–96; 1972 platform on agriculture, **2**:619–20; 1976 platform on agriculture and rural development, **2**:636–37; 1980 platform on agriculture, **2**:679–81; 1984 platform on agriculture, **2**:710–14; 1988 platform on rural community and family farm, **2**:765–68; 1992 platform on agriculture, **2**:812–14

Farmer–Labor alliance, **1**:19

Farmer–Labor Party, **1**:187

Farrakhan, Louis, **1**:71–72

Faubus, Orval, **1**:214

FECA Amendments, **1**:85, 86, 100

Federal Building, Oklahoma City, bombing of, **1**:113

Federal candidates, campaign finance and, **1**:84

Federal Communications Commission (FCC), **1**:71, 126, 140, 300

Federal Corrupt Practices Act of 1925, **1**:82, 83, 85, 293

Federal deficit, **1**:54. *See also* Budget deficit

Federal Election Campaign Act of 1971, **1**:83–85, 186–87

Federal Election Commission, **1**:85

Federal Highway System, **1**:49, 80

Federal involvement in education, **1**:117–21

Federal Reserve Act of 1913, **1**:28

Federal Reserve Board, **1**:144, 169, **2**:439

Federal Trade Commission (FTC), **2**:472; food and drug advertising, **1**:140

The Federalist Papers (Madison), **1**:153, 154

Federalist Party, **1**:1; electioneering practices, **1**:97, 98; Federalist trade policy, **1**:190; Federalist and Whig foreign policy, **1**:122; minorities and the, **1**:149; states' rights, **1**:182–83

Felton, Rebecca Latimer, **1**:287

Fenno, John, **1**:98

Fenton, Reuben E., **1**:256, 293, 294

Ferraro, Geraldine A., **1**:97, 248, **2**:439

Ferris, Woodbridge N., **1**:299

Fess, Simeon D., **1**:287

Fessenden, William Pitt, **1**:5, 287

Fifteenth Amendment, **1**:7, 11, 73, 199, 229

Filibuster, **1**:261; record for longest, **1**:299

Filipino Americans, **1**:151

Fillmore, Millard, **1**:145, 190, 274, 278, 284, 285, **2**:827

Financial Crises and Periods of Industrial and Commercial Depression (T.E. Burton), **1**:283

Firefighters Local Union v. Stoots, **1**:71

First Amendment: freedom of speech, **1**:126–27; religion and politics under the, **1**:172; school prayer and the, **1**:174

First International American Conference (1889), **1**:122

First Monday, **1**:58

First National Bank of the United States, **1**:183

Fish, Hamilton, **1**:41, 126, 222, 257, 263

Fisher, Mary, **1**:209, **2**:440

Fisk, James, **1**:221

Flag Day, **1**:21

Flanigan, Peter, **1**:53

Flemming v. Nestor, **1**:180

Floaters, **1**:18

Floor votes, **1**:158

Florida: governors of, **1**:402; House election victories in, **2**:866; primary, **1**:162, 164; Republican state committee headquarters, **2**:864

Flynt, Jack, **1**:276

Foley, Thomas, **1**:185

Follett, Mary Parker, **1**:106

Food and Drug Administration (FDA), **1**:251

Foraker, Joseph B., **1**:22, 26, 224

Forand, Aime J., **1**:130

Forbes, Steve, **1**:86

Ford, Betty, **1**:68, 97, 217, **2**:*841*

Ford, Gerald R., **1**:*56–57*, 62, 75, 174, *215*–17, 291, 299; abortion and, **1**:68; campaign slogans, **1**:97; crime policy, **1**:112; Dole and, **1**:286; endorsement of ERA, **1**:200; foreign policy, **1**:125; health care and, **1**:131; as House minority leader, **1**:53, 156; 1976 convention and, **2**:437–38; 1976 election and, **2**:*841*; 1980 convention and, **2**:438;1984 convention and, **2**:439; 1988 convention and, **2**:439; Nixon and, **1**:56,

Ford, Gerald R. (*continued*) 162, 215, 216, 217, 246; nomination of, **1**:162; Reagan and, **1**:247; Rockefeller and, **1**:264–65; Social Security and, **1**:179, 181; Supreme Court appointee, **1**:68

Ford, Henry, **1**:37, 293

Fordney–McCumber Act of 1922, **1**:191, 225

Foreign debts: 1924 platform on, **2**:489; 1928 platform on, **2**:497

Foreign policy, **1**:121–22; Arthur's, **1**:205; bipartisan, **1**:41, 44, 49; Bush's, **1**:206–8; Coolidge's, **1**:212; 1892 platform on foreign relations, **2**:456; Eisenhower's, **1**:49, 214–15; Federalist and Whig, **1**:122; Grant's, **1**:222; Harding's, **1**:225; B. Harrison's, **1**:228; Hayes's, **1**:231; isolationists vs. internationalists, **1**:123–24; McKinley's, **1**:241–42; moderate and militant anticommunist Republicans, **1**:124–25; 1916 platform on foreign relations, **2**:475–76; 1920 platform on foreign relations, **2**:479–81; 1924 platform on foreign relations, **2**:490–91; 1928 platform on foreign policies, **2**:497–99; 1932 platform on foreign affairs, **2**:509; 1936 platform on foreign affairs, **2**:519–20; 1952 platform on, **2**:536–38; 1956 platform on, **2**:553–56; 1960 platform on, **2**:560–62; 1968 platform on, **2**:597–99; 1972 platform on, **2**:602–6; 1976 platform on, **2**:652–60; 1980 platform on, **2**:697–705; 1984 platform on, **2**:730–41; 1988 platform on, **2**:773–89; Nixon's, **1**:244–45; Reagan's, **1**:125, 248–49; Republican expansionism, **1**:122–23; R.A. Taft's, **1**:124; W.H. Taft's, **1**:253; Truman's, **1**:44; W. Wilson's, **1**:30

A Foreign Policy for Americans (R.A. Taft), **1**:298

Fort Donelson, Tennessee, **1**:221

Fort Sumter, **1**:239

Fortas, Abe, **1**:139

Fortune, **1**:42

Foster, James P., **1**:17

Four-power treaty, **1**:124

Fourteenth Amendment, **1**:7, 70, 71, 73, 199, 229, 235, 294

Fourth Circuit Court of Appeals, U.S., **1**:70

Framington, New Hampshire, **1**:266

France, **1**:263; Suez Canal and Anglo-French intervention, **1**:214

Free Labor ideology, Republican Party and, **1**:3, 4, 7, 12, 14, 38

Free Soil Party, **1**:1, 2, 22, 186, 267, 269, 290, 297

Free trade ideology, Democratic Party and, **1**:14, 17

Freedmen's Bureau, **1**:235, 267, 297

Freedom of speech, **1**:126–27; 1920 platform on alien agitation and, **2**:485; 1932 platform on, **2**:512; 1940 platform on, **2**:525

Frelinghuysen, Theodore, **1**:278
Frémont, Jesse Benton, **1**:3, 88, 269
Frémont, John C., **1**:269–70, 287, 290; campaign slogan and song, **1**:88; 1856 convention and, **2**:421–22; 1856 election and, **1**:2–3, **2**:827; nomination of, **1**:145
Fremont, Ohio, **1**:231
French Declaration of the Rights of Man of 1789, **1**:180
French Panama Canal Company, **1**:251
French Revolution, **1**:190
Fried, Charles, **1**:69
"Front porch" campaigns, **1**:99, 222, 227, **2**:833
Frye, William P., **1**:287, 300
Fullilove v. Klutznick, **1**:71
The Furtile System (Rhodes), **1**:295

G

Galena, Illinois, **1**:221
Gallant Man (recording), **1**:285
Gallup, George, **1**:192
Gallup polls, **1**:38, 45, 58, 80, 161
Gann, Paul, **1**:75
Garfield, James A., **1**:*14*, 89, *217*, *218*–20, 268, 284, 288, 294; Arthur and, **1**:204; assassination of, **1**:14, 220, 267; Crédit Mobilier scandal and, **1**:8; on disfranchisement of African Americans, **1**:73–74; education and, **1**:118; 1880 convention and, **2**:425; 1880 election and, **2**:*831*; front-porch speeches, **1**:99; Half-Breeds faction and, **1**:13, 204; nomination of, **1**:147, 220
Gaudet, Hazel, **1**:192–93
Gazette of the United States, **1**:98
Geauga Academy, Ohio, **1**:217
Gender gap, **1**:58, 97, 208
General Agreement on Tariffs and Trade (GATT), **1**:191, 192, 208
Geneva Conference of 1955, **1**:214
Georgetown University, **1**:282
Georgia: governors of, **1**:402; House election victories in, **2**:866; Republican state committee headquarters, **2**:864
German Americans, **1**:149
German immigration, nativists opposition against, **1**:1, 2
Germany: German reparations, **1**:259; U.S. declaration of war on, **1**:30
Gerrymander, **2**:810
Gettysburg Address, **1**:5
Gettysburg, Pennsylvania, **1**:215
GI Bill, **1**:118, 286
Gilded Age, **1**:79, 99, 149, 223
Gillett, Frederick H., **1**:275
Gilman, Charlotte Perkins, **1**:198
Gingrich, Newt, **1**:274, 275–76, 286; acceptance by American conservative Jewry, **1**:136; affirmative action and, **1**:76; anti-

Gingrich, Newt (*continued*)
big-government position, **1**:78; campaign finance reform and, **1**:87; Contract with America and, **1**:81, 104, 109–10, 114, 115, 121, 157, 276; crime policy, **1**:113–14; Dole and, **1**:158; drug policy, **1**:116–17; gun control and, **1**:128; health care and, **1**:132; as House Speaker, **1**:107–8, 156–57; media and, **1**:140; Michel and, **1**:156; new Republican congressional majority and, **1**:63–64; party discipline and, **1**:155; school prayer and, **1**:177; Social Security and, **1**:181; use of C-SPAN, **1**:108; welfare reform, **1**:197
Gingrich, Robert, **1**:275
Giuliani, Rudolph, **1**:132
Glen Falls, New York, **1**:271
Godkin, E.L., **1**:3, 15
Gold: "Black Friday" scandal, **1**:221; standard, **1**:20, 21, 144, 241, 242
Gold Standard Act of 1900, **1**:241, 242
Goldman, Emma, **1**:198
Goldwater, Barry, **1**:52–53, 58, 174, 175, *270*–71, 292; African American–GOP relations and, **1**:75; antiwelfare position, **1**:80; campaign materials, **1**:97; Cold War and, **1**:101; crime and, **1**:112; education and, **1**:120; Ford and Goldwater campaign, **1**:217; foreign policy and, **1**:124–25; health care and, **1**:130; 1960 convention and, **2**:435; 1964 convention and, **2**:435–36; 1964 election and, **2**:*839*–40; nomination of, **1**:161–62; Reagan and Goldwater campaign, **1**:247; Rhodes and, **1**:294, 296; Rockefeller and, **1**:50, 51, 52; states' rights and, **1**:184
Gompers, Samuel, **1**:210
Goodell, Charles, **1**:216, 217
GOPAC, **1**:63
Gorbachev, Mikhail, **1**:102, 207, 248
Gordon, Irving Wexler "Waxy," **1**:268
Gordon, Slade, **1**:189
Gorman, Arthur Pue, **1**:15
Gould, Jay, **1**:221
Government: 1924 platform on, **2**:492, 494; 1928 platform on honesty in, **2**:502–3; 1932 platform on reorganization of government bureaus, **2**:514; 1940 platform on, **2**:524, 525; 1952 platform on reorganization of, **2**:543; 1956 platform on federal, **2**:551; 1960 platform on, **2**:567–69; 1968 platform on the individual and, **2**:593–94; 1972 platform on, **2**:611–12, 625–26; 1976 platform on taxes and government spending, **2**:636; 1980 platform on the, **2**:679, 682–84, 688–89; 1988 platform on federal spending, **2**:747–48; 1992 platform on government spending, **2**:805; 1992 platform on reforming government and the legal system, **2**:808–12. *See also* Big government
Governors, chronological list by state, **1**:400–420

Gramm, William Philip "Phil," **1**:58, 71, 121, 132, 283, **2**:439
Gramm–Rudman–Hollings Act of 1985, **1**:58
Grand Army of the Republic, **1**:7
Grand Rapids Herald, **1**:299
Grant, Ulysses S., **1**:*8*, *220*–23, 229, 263, 265, 283; Arthur's support for, **1**:203; campaign materials, **1**:89; campaign strategy, **1**:99; S. Colfax and, **1**:255, 256; education and, **1**:117–18; 1864 convention and, **2**:422; 1868 convention and, **2**:422, 423; 1868 election and, **2**:829–30; 1872 convention and, **2**:423; 1872 election and, **2**:*830*; 1880 convention and, **2**:424–25; freedom of speech and, **1**:126; Grantism (corruption), **1**:8, 9, 222; A. Johnson and, **1**:234, 235; nomination battle, **1**:147; pardon of suffragettes, **1**:199; presidency, **1**:7, 73, 219; Stalwarts and Half-Breeds factions and, **1**:12–13, 22, 204, 220, 222, 268
Grants-in-aid, **1**:78
Great Britain: British political parties, **1**:153–54, 155; Civil War damages from, **1**:263; Eisenhower and British relations, **1**:214; Grant and British relations, **1**:*222*; unemployment insurance to British workers, **1**:178
Great Depression, **1**:36–38; African Americans and, **1**:74; decline in Republican Party support and, **1**:167; education aid and, **1**:118; Hoover and, **1**:36–38, 93, 197; party identification and, **1**:170; F.D. Roosevelt and, **1**:79; social programs and, **1**:178; stock market crash of 1929 and, **1**:36, 184, 233
"Great Society" program, L.B. Johnson's, **1**:53, 80, 104, 112, 113, 178
Great Strike of 1877, **1**:230
Greeley, Horace, **1**:274; S. Colfax and, **1**:257; on Frémont in 1856 campaign, **1**:2–3; presidential nomination, **1**:9, 187, 219, 222, **2**:423, 830
Greenback–Labor Party, **1**:178
Greenbacks, **1**:230
Greenman v. Yuba Power Products Co., **1**:188
Greenville, North Carolina, **1**:234
Grenada, invasion of, **1**:60, 138, 248
Gresham, Walter Q., **1**:287–88, **2**:426
Griffin, Robert P., **1**:216, 288
Grow, Galusha A., **1**:256, 276–77
Guam: annexation of, **1**:123, 241, **2**:833; national committee membership, **1**:176; Republican state committee headquarters, **2**:864
Guatemala, CIA coup, **1**:214
Guiteau, Charles, **1**:14, 220
Gulf War, Persian, **1**:62, 163, 206, 207, **2**:440
Gun control, **1**:127–28; gun ownership, **2**:757
Gun Control Act of 1968, **1**:127

H

Hadley, Herbert S., **1:**288

Hague, Frank, **1:**82

Hague treaties, **2:**469

Haig, Alexander, **1:**245

Haiti, **1:**125, 207

Haldeman, H.R., **1:**245

Half-Breeds, **1:**12–13, 14, 204, 268, **2:**424, 831

Hall, Leonard Wood, **1:**49

Halleck, Charles, **1:**42, 53, 156, 217, 288

Hamilton, Alexander, **1:**98, 182, 183, 190

Hamilton College, **1:**279

Hamilton, John D.M., **1:**39, 40, 41, 174

Hamiltonian approach to government, **1:**27, 32, 283

Hamlin, Ellen, **1:**261

Hamlin, Hannibal, **1:**238, 256, 261, **2:**422, *827*

Hampton, Wade, **1:**230

Hancock, Winfield Scott, **1:**14, 73, 204, 220

Handicapped citizens. *See* Disabilities, Americans with

Hanna, Marcus A. "Mark," **1:**23, 33, 258, 288; McKinley campaign and, **1:**21, 22, 82, 99, 241, 288, **2:**427, 428, 832, 833

Harbord, James G., **2:**431

Harding, Warren G., **1:***31,* 34, 126, 167, *223–26,* 259, 271, 283, 287, 289; African American–GOP relations and, **1:**74; cabinet, **1:**32; campaign slogans, **1:**92, 224; Coolidge and, **1:**211; death of, **1:**32; education and, **1:**118; election of, **1:**30–32, 254; foreign policy, **1:**124; Hoover and, **1:**232; 1912 convention and, **2:**429; 1916 convention and, **2:**429; 1920 convention and, **2:**430; 1920 election and, **2:**836; trade policy, **1:**191

Hardwick, Thomas W., **1:**287

Harlan, James, **1:**280

Harmon, Judson, **1:**224

Harper's Weekly, **1:**15, 27, 87

Harriman, Averill, **1:**264

Harriman, E.H., **1:**24

Harris v. McRae, **1:**67

Harrisburg, Pennsylvania, **1:**283; Gingrich's birthplace, **1:**275

Harrison, Benjamin, **1:**10, *16,* 226–28, 262, 288, 294; Blaine and, **1:**268; campaign slogan, **1:**89–90, 98; campaign strategy, **1:**99; education and, **1:**118; 1888 convention and, **2:**426; 1888 election and, **2:**832, *833;* 1892 convention and, **2:**426–27; 1892 election and, **2:**832; L.P. Morton and, **1:**263; patronage demands and, **1:**18; renomination of, **1:**19; T. Roosevelt and, **1:**250; support for African American voting rights, **1:**74; W.H. Taft and, **1:**252; tariff battle and, **1:**16, 17, 18

Harrison, Caroline Scott, **1:**226, 228

Harrison, Mary Lord Dimmick, **1:**228

Harrison Narcotics Act, **1:**111, 116

Harrison, William Henry, **1:**89, 98, 122, 145, 226, **2:**832

Hartley, Fred, **1:**119

Harvard University, **1:**250, 277, 291; Law School, **1:**229, 275

Hascell, Asa, **1:**265

Hatch Act, **1:**41

Hatch, Orrin G., **1:**114, 132, 141, 177

Hatfield, Mark O., **1:**138, 177, 288–89

Hawaii: annexation of, **1:**122–23, 228, 241, 268, 279, 296; governors of, **1:**402; House election victories in, **2:**866; 1920 platform on, **2:**487–88; 1928 platform on, **2:**504; 1932 platform on, **2:**514; 1940 platform on, **2:**524; 1944 platform on, **2:**531; 1956 platform on, **2:**552; 1972 platform on Hawaiians, **2:**631–32; Republican state committee headquarters, **2:**864

"Hawks," **1:**60, 217, 245

Hay, John, **1:**20, 22, 137, 191, 241, 242

Hayes, Helen, **2:**439

Hayes, Lucy Ware Webb, **1:**228, 229

Hayes, Rutherford B., **1:**73, 222, *228–31,* 266, 268, 270, 274, 284; Arthur and, **1:**203; the Camerons and, **1:**283; campaign slogan, **1:**89; education and, **1:**118; electoral dispute of 1876 and presidency, **1:**9–10, 219, 229, **2:**424, *830–31;* B. Harrison and, **1:**226; New York Customhouse appointments, **1:**13, 203, 230; nomination of, **1:**145, 147; Reconstruction policy, **1:**89, 228, 230, 266; John Sherman and, **1:**297

Hayes, Rutherford, Jr., **1:**229

Hayes, Sophia Birchard, **1:**229

Hays, Will, **1:**30, 31, 33, 57, 174, **2:**430

Health care, **1:**128–33, **2:**469; 1920 platform on education and health, **2:**487; 1952 platform on health, **2:**542; 1956 platform on health, education and welfare, **2:**548–49; 1960 platform on health, **2:**571, 572; 1968 platform on health, **2:**592; 1972 platform on, **2:**613–14; 1976 platform on, **2:**642–43; 1980 platform on health, **2:**669–70; 1984 platform on health, **2:**716–17; 1988 platform on health, **2:**751–52; 1992 platform on, **2:**795–97

Health Maintenance Organization Act of 1973, **1:**131

Health maintenance organizations (HMOs), **1:**131

Hearst, William Randolph, **1:**54, 138, 271

Heckler, Margaret, **1:**201

Helms, Jesse A., **1:**127, 139, 177, 289, **2:**438

Helvering v. Davis, **1:**179

Henderson, David B., **1:**277

Henderson, Leon, **1:**42

Hennessy, Bernard C., **1:**174

Henningsen v. Bloomfield Motors, **1:**188

Heritage Foundation, **1:**136

Heritage Group, **1:**152

Herndon, William H., **1:**237

Herter, Christian A., **1:**296, **2:**434

Highway Act of 1956, **1:**49

Highway Trust Fund, **1:**49

Hill, Anita, **1:**201, 208

Hill, David B., **1:**20

Hill, Lester, **1:**129

Hill–Burton Act, **1:**131

Hinckley, John, Jr., **1:**247–48

Hiram College, Ohio, **1:**218

Hispanic Americans, **1:**148; 1976 platform on, **2:**644; 1980 platform on, **2:**666; Republican Party and, **1:**150–51

Hiss, Alger, **1:**46, 101, 127, 136, 213, 244, 282

History of the Anti-Slave Measures of the Thirty-seventh and Thirty-eighth United States Congress (H. Wilson), **1:**267

History of the Rise and Fall of Slave Power in the United States (H. Wilson), **1:**267

Hoar, George F., **1:**117–18, 138, 275, 289

Hobart, Addison W., **1:**261

Hobart, Garret A., **1:**241, 242, 261–62, **2:**427, 428

Hobart, Jennie Tuttle, **1:**261–62

Hobart, Sophia Vanderveer, **1:**261

Hodgenville, Kentucky, **1:**236

Hoekstra, Peter, **1:**78

Hoeven, Charles, **1:**217

Hofstadter, Richard, **1:**20

Hollywood, California: communism in, **1:**137; Dole campaign on sex and violence in, **1:**139

Holman, William S., **1:**300

Holmes, Oliver Wendell, **1:**230

Home rule, **2:**504–5

Homeless, the, **2:**754–55, 797

Homestead Act of 1862, **1:**7, 183, 239, 276

Homosexuality, **1:**209

Hoover, Herbert, **1:***35,* 167, *231–34,* 259, 260, 285, 289, 299; African American–GOP relations and, **1:**74; big government and, **1:**79; campaign materials, **1:**93; Coolidge and, **1:**212; crime policy, **1:**111; education and, **1:**118–19; foreign policy, **1:**124; Great Depression and, **1:**36–38, 184; in Harding and Coolidge cabinets, **1:**32, 34; health care and, **1:**129; Hoover Commissions, **1:**79, 231, 234; "Hoovervilles," **1:**37; 1928 campaign, **1:**34–35; 1928 convention and, **2:**431; 1928 election and, **2:**836–37; 1932 election and, **2:**837; 1940 convention and, **2:***432;* party identification and, **1:**170; Progressivism, **1:**34, 38, 39; Radio Act of 1927 and, **1:**126; as secretary of commerce, **1:**232; Supreme Court appointee, **1:**272; R.A. Taft and, **1:**298; welfare system and, **1:**195, 196

Hoover Institution, **1:**233

Horton, Willie, **1:**61, 76, 206

Hotel Blackstone, **1:**224

House of Representatives, U.S.: campaigns for Republican candidates, **1:**100; congressional elections, **1:**103–5; first woman elected to the, **1:**294; House election victories by party, **2:**866; House Judiciary Committee, **1:**112; House leaders,

Numbers in bold indicate volume; page numbers in italic indicate illustration.

Numbers in bold indicate volume; page numbers in italic indicate illustration.

N

Numbers in bold indicate volume; page numbers in italic indicate illustration.

Spanish-speaking Americans, 1972 platform on, **2**:631

Speakers of the House, biographies of the, **1**:274–80

Special Health Revenue Sharing Act of 1975, **1**:131

Spellman, Francis Cardinal, **1**:139

Spence, Floyd, **1**:115

Spencer, Herbert, **1**:12

Spencer, Stuart, **1**:57, 58

Split-ticket voting, **1**:50, 55, 170, 171

Spooner, John C., **1**:24, 129, 280

Sputnik, **1**:51, 118, 119, 214

"Square Deal" policies, T. Roosevelt's, **1**:23, 92, 251

Stafford v. Wallace, **1**:254

Stalin, Joseph, **1**:214

Stalwarts, **1**:12–13, 14, 204, 205, 220, 222, 229, 268, **2**:831

Standard Oil, **2**:835

Standpatters, **1**:24, 26, 29, 152

Stanford University, **1**:228, 232, 233

Stans, Maurice, **1**:83

Stanton, Edwin, **1**:221, 235, 239, 297

Stanton, Elizabeth Cady, **1**:198, 199

"Star Wars" (Strategic Defense Initiative), **1**:77, 207

Stassen, Harold E., **1**:45, 48, **2**:433, 434

States' rights, **1**:182–84

Stearns, Frank, **1**:33

Steiger, William A., **2**:437

Stevens, John Paul, **1**:68

Stevens, Thaddeus, **1**:5, 73, 256, 297

Stevenson, Adlai E.: Eisenhower and, **1**:49, 50, 51, 95, 213, 214, **2**:838–39; Nixon and, **1**:244; on Republican elephant, **1**:88

Stewart Machine Company v. Davis, **1**:179

Stimpson, Alan, **1**:135

Stimson accords, **1**:212

Stimson, Henry, **1**:41

Stimson, James A., **1**:170, 193

Stock market: Great Depression and crash of 1929, **1**:36, 184, 233; October 1987 crash, **1**:192

Stockman, David, **1**:60–61, 169

Stockton, Robert F., **1**:269

Stokes, Donald E., **1**:141–42, 170, 193, 194

Stone, Lucy, **1**:199

STOP ERA, **1**:200

Strategic Arms Limitation Talks I (SALT I), **1**:125, 245, 248

Strategic Arms Limitation Talks II (SALT II), **1**:125

Strategic Arms Reduction Treaty I (START I), **1**:77, 102, 115

Strategic Arms Reduction Treaty II (START II), **1**:77, 115

Strategic Defense Initiative (SDI), **1**:77, 78, 102, 115, 125, 207, 248, **2**:782–83

Straus, Oscar, **1**:26

Strikes, **1**:230

Structural Impediments Initiative, **1**:192

Stuart, John Todd, **1**:237

Study of Television and Social Behavior, **1**:139

Subsidies, direct or indirect, **1**:195

Suez Canal, **1**:214

Sugar trusts, **1**:260

Summerfield, Arthur E., **1**:48, 49

Sumner, Charles, **1**:5, 7, 73, 256–57, 297

Sumner, William Graham, **1**:12

Sunday, Billy, **1**:35

"Super 301," **1**:192

Super Tuesday contests, **1**:160–61, 163

Superfund program, **1**:59

Supplemental Security Income (SSI), **1**:195

Supply-side economics, **1**:61, 168, 248

Supreme Court, U.S.: affirmative action and, **1**:70, 71, 72; *Brown v. Board of Education*, **1**:184, 213–14, 299; Bush's Court appointee, **1**:201, 208; campaign finance and, **1**:85–86; *Dred Scott* decision, **1**:238; Ford's Court appointee, **1**:68; Grant's Court appointments, **1**:221; gun control and, **1**:128; Hoover's Court appointee, **1**:272; media and, **1**:138, 139; Nixon's Court appointees, **1**:174, 184; open primaries and, **1**:160; Reagan's Court appointees, **1**:59, 68, 174, 249; *Roe v. Wade* decision, **1**:67–70, 200–201; F.D. Roosevelt's Court-packing plan, **1**:39–40, 272, 290, **2**:837; school prayer and, **1**:174, 177; segregation and, **1**:184, 213–14; Social Security decision, **1**:179–80, 195; W.H. Taft on the, **1**:254; term limits and, **1**:186; Watergate and, **1**:246

Swainson, John B., **1**:295

Swing voters, **1**:18

T

Taft, Alfonso, **1**:252

Taft, Charles, **1**:28

Taft, Robert A., **1**:45, 49, 152, 161, 285, 298, 299; on anticommunist crusade, **1**:46; on Dewey and Truman, **1**:44; education and, **1**:119; Eisenhower and, **1**:47, 48, 213; foreign policy and, **1**:124, 253; health care and, **1**:129; isolationist position, **1**:40, 42, 100, 101; 1940 convention and, **2**:432; 1948 convention and, **2**:433; 1952 convention and, **2**:433; Republicanism of, **1**:142; as Supreme Court justice, **1**:254

Taft, Robert A., Jr., **1**:298

Taft, William Howard, **1**:25, 27, 252–54, 261, 265, 271, 277, 283, 288, 298, 300; campaign materials, **1**:92; expansionism under, **1**:123; 1908 convention and, **2**:428–29; 1908 election and, **2**:835; 1912 convention and, **2**:429; 1912 election and, **2**:835–36; nomination of, **1**:146, 147; presidency, **1**:25–26, 79; T. Roosevelt vs., **1**:26–28

Taft–Hartley Act, **1**:44, 213, **2**:433, 434

Taiwan, **1**:214

Tammany Hall, **1**:8, 82, 89, 145, **2**:832

Tanner, James R., **1**:227

Tariff reform: Dingley Tariff, **1**:191, 241; 1888 convention and issue of, **2**:426; Fordney–McCumber Act of 1922, **1**:191, 225; Greeley's opposition to tariff reduction, **1**:9; McKinley Tariff of 1890, **1**:18–19, 228, 240; 1908 platform on, **2**:466; 1912 platform on, **2**:472; 1916 platform on, **2**:477; 1920 platform on trade and, **2**:484–85; 1924 platform on, **2**:489–90; 1928 platform on, **2**:496–97; 1932 platform on, **2**:508–9; 1936 platform on, **2**:518–19; 1940 platform on trade and, **2**:523; Payne–Aldrich Tariff of 1909, **1**:26, 191, 253, 280; protectionism and tariff policy, **1**:14, 16; Smoot–Hawley Tariff of 1930, **1**:191, 233; states' rights and protective tariffs, **1**:183; Tariff of 1842, **1**:190; tariff fight of 1887–1888, **1**:16–18; tariffs of 1862 and 1865, **1**:14; trade policy and, **1**:189–92

Tashjian v. Republican Party of Connecticut, **1**:160

Tax Equity and Fiscal Responsibility Act of 1982, **1**:132

Tax Reform Act of 1986, **1**:248

Taxes: earned-income tax credit, **1**:141–42; federal excise taxes and national, **1**:7, 8; 1920 platform on taxation, **2**:483; 1924 platform on finance and taxation, **2**:488–89; 1928 platform on finance and taxation, **2**:496; 1940 platform on taxation, **2**:523; 1944 platform on finance and taxation, **2**:529; 1952 platform on monetary policy and taxation, **2**:539–40; 1956 platform on fiscal policy and taxation, **2**:546; 1972 platform on government spending and, **2**:611–12; 1976 platform on fiscal responsibility, **2**:652; 1976 platform on government spending and, **2**:636; 1980 platform on, **2**:662–63, 681, 688–89; 1984 platform on taxation, **2**:707–8; 1988 platform on, **2**:744; payroll, **1**:181; Revenue Act of 1926, **1**:34; tax reform of 1986, **1**:169; tax subsidies, **1**:195; tuition tax credit, **1**:120, 121

Taylor, Zachary, **1**:99, 122, 190, 238, 284, 296

Teapot Dome Scandal, **1**:32, 82, 226

Teapot Dome, Wyoming, **1**:32

Teeter, Robert, **1**:60

Television, **1**:140–41; commercialization of campaigns and, **1**:99–100; conventions and, **1**:148; Eisenhower's appeal on, **1**:213; Ford's campaign commercials, **1**:57; Kennedy–Nixon debates, **1**:51–52, 161, 244; public perception and, **1**:168; Study of Television and Social Behavior, **1**:139

Teller Amendment, **1**:123

Teller, Henry M., **2**:427

Tennessee: governors of, **1**:416; House election victories in, **2**:866; Republican state committee headquarters, **2**:865

U

V

Numbers in bold indicate volume; page numbers in italic indicate illustration.

Vice presidents, biographies of the, 1:254–67

Vietnam: 1968 platform on, 2:436, 599–600; 1972 platform on, 2:437

Vietnam War: Cold War and, 1:101–2; Eisenhower and, 1:124; Ford and amnesty for Vietnam War resisters, 1:217; Nixon and, 1:245; perceptions of Republican Party and, 1:167; Vietnam syndrome, 1:62, 248; Vietnamization policy, 1:54, 125; voting behavior and, 1:193

Vietnamese citizens, 1:151

Villard, Oswald, 1:24

Violence, on television, 1:139

Virgin Islands, national committee membership, 1:176

Virginia: governors of, 1:418; House election victories in, 2:866; Republican state committee headquarters, 2:865

Virginia House of Burgesses, 1:82

Vocal minority, 1:53

Volcker, Paul, 1:144

Volstead Act, 1:225, 275, 287

Volunteerism, 2:626

Voodoo economics, 1:69, 168

Voorhis, Jerry, 1:51, 243–44

Voting age, lowering of, 2:436

Voting behavior, 1:192–95

Voting Rights Act, 1:75, 150, 151

Voting rights, for African Americans, 1:7, 11, 73, 74, 199

Vouchers, school, 1:121

W

Wade, Benjamin F., 1:5, 7, 236, 256, 299–300, 2:423

Wade–Davis Bill/Wade–Davis Manifesto, 1:285, 297, 299

Wagner–Peyser Act, 1:178

Walkinson, Rev. M.R., 1:173

Wall, E.C., 1:20–21

Wall Street Journal, 1:32

Wallace, George, 1:53, 112, 184, 187, 2:840

Wallace, Henry, 1:95

Walsh, David I., 1:295

War of 1812, 1:122, 189–90

War on Drugs, 1:113, 116, 208

War on Poverty, L.B. Johnson's, 1:112, 130

War Powers Resolution, 1:102

Wards, precinct, 1:8–9

Warren, Charles B., 1:260

Warren, Earl, 1:45, 214, 290, 2:433

Washburn University, 1:286

Washington: blanket primary in, 1:164; governors of, 1:418–19; House election victories in, 2:866; Republican state committee headquarters, 2:865

Washington, Booker T., 1:29, 74

Washington Conference of 1921–22, 1:225

Washington, DC. *See* District of Columbia

Washington, George, 1:82, 122, 182, 190, 222, 237, 255

Washington Post, 1:28, 54, 55

Washington press corps, 1:54

Watergate: FECA and Watergate scandal, 1:85; Nixon and, 1:55–56, 68, 75, 104, 113, 154, 162, 167, 217, 243, 246, 2:841

Waterways: 1908 platform on natural resources and, 2:468; 1920 platform on, 2:484; 1924 platform on, 2:493; 1928 platform on, 2:501; 1932 platform on, 2:512

Watson, James E., 1:259, 300

Watson, Tom, 1:22

Wattenberg, Martin P., 1:167

Weaver, James, 1:19

Webb–Kenyon Act, 1:111

Webster, Daniel, 1:287

Webster v. Reproductive Health Services, 1:68, 69, 70, 201

Weed, Thurlow, 1:2, 4, 5, 98

Weicker, Lowell P., 1:177, 188

Weinberger, Caspar, 1:77, 209

Weld, William F., 1:69, 2:440

Welfare: 1968 platform on the poor and, 2:591–92; 1972 platform on welfare reform, 2:616–17; 1976 platform on welfare reform, 2:645–46; 1980 platform on the welfare system, 2:663–64, 671; 1984 platform on, 2:715–16; 1992 platform on ending dependency on, 2:798–99; Republican Party approach to, 1:196–98; what is, 1:195–96

Welles, Gideon, 1:5

Welliver, Judson, 1:32

West Branch, Iowa, Hoover's birthplace, 1:231

West Georgia College, 1:276

West Middlesex, Pennsylvania, 1:272

West Point, U.S. Military Academy at, 1:212, 220

West Virginia: governors of, 1:419; House election victories in, 2:866; Republican state committee headquarters, 2:866

Western Reserve Eclectic Institute, Hiram, Ohio, 1:217

Westfield, Massachusetts, 1:275

Wheeler, Burton K., 1:259

Wheeler Compromise, 1:266

Wheeler, William A., 1:265–66, 2:424, 830

Whig Party, 1:186, 267, 290; anti-immigration platform, 1:134; congressional leadership, 1:105; conventions, 1:145, 146, 159; demise of, 1:1–2, 296; electioneering practices, 1:97, 98–99; Federalist and Whig foreign policy, 1:122; A. Johnson and, 1:234; Lincoln and, 1:237, 238; minority group defection to the, 1:148, 149; Second National Bank controversy, 1:183; Seward's Whig candidacy, 1:296; states' rights, 1:182

Whiskey Ring, 1:8, 222

White, Byron R, 1:68, 201

White, Edward Douglas, 1:254

White, F. Clifton, 1:52

White, George, 1:73, 74

White House Conference on Education (1954), 1:119

White, Rick, 1:140

White Slave-Trade Act, 1:111

White supremacy, 1:53

White, Theodore H., 1:51, 152

White, Wallace H., Jr., 1:300

White, William Allen, 1:33

Whitman, Charles S., 1:29

Whittier College, California, 1:243

"Wide Awakes" marching clubs, 1:99

Wide-open primary, 1:164

Wilbur, Ray Lyman, 1:118

Wilcox, Clyde, 1:171–72

Wiley, Alexander, 1:111

Williams College, Massachusetts, 1:217

Williams, Richard, 1:256

Willkie Clubs, 1:40

Willkie, Wendell L., 1:40–41, 42, 161, 273, 298, 299; campaign materials, 1:93–94, 95; Ford and Willkie campaign, 1:216; isolationist position, 1:124; modern Republicanism and, 1:142; 1940 convention and, 2:432, 433; 1940 election and, 2:837; 1944 election and, 2:838; 1948 election and, 2:838

Wilmot Proviso, 1:238

Wilson, Charles E., 1:49

Wilson, Henry, 1:222, 256, 257, 266–67, 2:423, 830

Wilson, Peter B. "Pete," 1:71, 135

Wilson, Woodrow, 1:251, 259, 271, 275, 281, 287, 293; Democrats and, 1:211, 224; endorses Sedition Act of 1918, 1:126; 14 Points speech, 1:123; Harding's victory and, 1:32; Hoover and, 1:232; "New Freedom" policies, 1:28, 29, 30; 1912 election and, 2:835–36; 1916 election and, 2:836; nomination of, 1:146; presidency, 1:28–29, 30; W.H. Taft and, 1:253, 254; trade policy, 1:191

Wisconsin: governors of, 1:419–20; House election victories in, 2:866; La Follette's "Wisconsin idea," 1:28; Progressive Party, 1:187, 2:429, 431; Republican state committee headquarters, 2:866; Wisconsin primary, 1:164

Wolcott, Edward O., 2:427

Wolfe, Thomas, 1:11

Women: abortion, 1:59, 61, 67–70, 200–201, 208, 2:668; affirmative action, 1:70–72; Aid to Families with Dependent Children (AFDC), 1:196, 197; Coolidge campaign thimble, 1:211; creation of Prohibition Party, 1:186; election of women to the 1924 national committee, 2:431; Equal Rights Amendment (ERA), 1:163, 200, 290, 2:433, 437, 438, 439, 627–28; first American first lady college graduate, 1:229; first woman elected to the House of Representatives, 1:294; first

X

Y

Z

BIOGRAPHICAL INDEX

Numbers in bold indicate volume; page numbers in italic indicate illustration.

Buckingham, William, **1**:256

Buckley, James L., **1**:187

Burchard, Rev. Samuel D., Blaine and,
   1:15–16, 268, **2**:831–32

Burger, Warren, **1**:139

Burnham, Walter Dean, **1**:9

Burnside, Ambrose E., **1**:280

Burton, Harold H., **1**:129

Burton, Theodore E., **1**:283

Bush, Barbara, **1**:61, 69, 209, **2**:440

Bush, Columba, **2**:439

Bush, George, **1**:61–63, 160, 205, *206–9*, 275,
   281, 286; abortion and, **1**:61, 69; P.J.
   Buchanan and, **1**:282; campaign contributions to, **1**:86; campaign materials, **1**:97;
   campaign strategy, **1**:100; Cold War and,
   1:102; crime policy, **1**:113; drug policy,
   1:116; education and, **1**:120, 121; foreign
   policy, **1**:125; gun control and, **1**:128;
   health care and, **1**:132; Hispanic support
   for, **1**:151; Horton–Bush affair, **1**:61, 76,
   206; media and, **1**:138, 139, 140; minimum wage and, **1**:141; New Federalist
   programs, **1**:184; 1980 convention and,
   2:438; 1984 convention and, **2**:439; 1988
   congressional elections and, **1**:104; 1988
   convention and, **2**:439–40; 1988 election
   and, **1**:163, **2**:842; 1992 election and,
   2:842–43; "no new taxes" pledge, **1**:81,
   276, **2**:440, 843; perception of, **1**:168;
   Quayle and, **1**:263; Reagan and, **1**:247,
   249; as Reagan Republican, **1**:81;
   Reaganomics and, **1**:168; realignment
   and, **1**:170, 171; as Republican national
   chair, **1**:175; Supreme Court appointee,
   1:201; term-limit advocate, **1**:185; "thousand points of light," **1**:208; trade policy,
   1:191, 192; "voodoo economics," **1**:69,
   168; voting behavior and, **1**:193, 194; welfare reform, **1**:196

Bush, George, Jr., **1**:209

Bush, Jeb, **1**:209

Butler, Andrew, **1**:297

Butler, Nicholas Murray, **1**:283

Butler, William M., **1**:33

Byrnes, John W., **1**:131

C

Cahill, William, **1**:112

Calhoun, John C., **1**:183, 255, 283

Cameron, James Donald, **1**:283

Cameron, Simon, **1**:8, 12, 238, 283

Campbell, Angus, **1**:141–42, 170, 193, 194

Cannon, Joseph G. "Uncle Joe," **1**:265,
   274–75, 277, 293, 300; Cannonism, **1**:26,
   274; as House Speaker, **1**:23–24, 107;
   leadership style, **1**:106

Capone, Alphonse "Al," **1**:298

Capper, Arthur, **1**:283–84

Cardozo, Benjamin N., **1**:179

Carmines, Edward G., **1**:170, 193

Carson, Kit, **1**:269

Carter, Jimmy, **2**:440; anti-Carter campaign
   slogans, **1**:97; Asian American support
   of, **1**:152; Cold War and, **1**:102; education
   and, **1**:120; election of, **1**:162–63; Ford
   and, **1**:57, 75, **2**:438, 841; Gingrich and,
   1:276; health care and, **1**:131; media and,
   1:139; popularity decline, **1**:104; Reagan
   and, **1**:58, 75, 247, **2**:841; regulatory activity under, **1**:80; social services and, **1**:180;
   voting behavior and, **1**:193

Carville, James, **1**:208

Case, Clifford, **1**:52

Castro, Fidel, **1**:214–15

Cedras, Raul, **1**:207

Chairman, John, **1**:288

Chamberlain, Daniel, **1**:230

Chamberlain, Neville, **1**:76

Chamberlain, Sir Austen, **1**:259

Chamorro, Violeta Barrios de, **1**:207

Chandler, William E., **1**:7, 11, 13, 14

Chandler, Zachariah, **1**:10, 12, 21

Chase, Salmon P., **1**:238, 280, 299; 1856 convention and, **2**:421; in Lincoln cabinet,
   1:4, 173, 239

Chaves, Dennis, **1**:285

Cheney, Richard "Dick," **1**:57, 276

Clapper, Raymond, **1**:40–41

Clark, Daniel, **1**:284

Clarkson, James S., **1**:227

Clay, Cassius M., **2**:422

Clay, Henry, **1**:145, 146, 183, 190, 237, 278,
   284

Cleveland, Grover, **1**:10, 268, 280, 294; campaign materials, **1**:90; 1884 election and,
   1:15, **2**:831; 1888 election and, **2**:832; 1892
   election and, **1**:19–20, 228, **2**:832; gold
   standard and, **1**:20; Harding and, **1**:224;
   B. Harrison and, **1**:227, 228; tariff battle
   and, **1**:16, 18, 191

Clinton, Hillary Rodham, **1**:132, 209

Clinton, William Jefferson "Bill," **1**:276,
   2:440; affirmative action and, **1**:71, 72;
   Bush and, **1**:62, 63, 76, 163, 208, **2**:842–43;
   campaign contributions to, **1**:86; campaign finance reform and, **1**:87; Cold War
   and, **1**:102–3; congressional leadership
   under, **1**:105; crime policy, **1**:113, 114;
   drug policy, **1**:116; foreign policy, **1**:125;
   health care and, **1**:132; media and, **1**:140;
   minimum wage and, **1**:141; 1992 congressional elections and, **1**:104; perception of,
   1:167; Reaganomics and, **1**:169; "rein-
   venting government" policies, **1**:81; tort
   reform and, **1**:189; voting behavior and,
   1:193; welfare reform, **1**:196, 197

Coats, Daniel R., **1**:127

Cohen, Eliot V., **1**:46

Cohen, William S., **1**:177

Colfax, Schuyler, **1**:221, 222, 255–57, **2**:423,
   829

Colfax, William, **1**:255

Collie, Melissa P., **1**:106

Comstock, Anthony, **1**:139, 257

Conkling, Roscoe, **1**:*13*, 284, 293, 294;
   Arthur and, **1**:203; 1876 convention and,
   2:423–24; 1880 convention and, **2**:424;
   Garfield and, **1**:13; L.P. Morton and,
   1:263; on the party machine, **1**:8; Senate
   resignation, **1**:14, *15*; Stalwarts faction
   and, **1**:12, 204, 229

Connally, John, **1**:299

Converse, Philip E., **1**:141–42, 170, 193, 194

Coolidge, Calvin M., **1**:30, 167, 209, *210–12*,
   275, 277; book on, **1**:295; campaign materials, **1**:93; campaign slogan, **1**:32, 154,
   211; education and, **1**:118; foreign policy,
   1:124; health care and, **1**:129; Hoover
   and, **1**:232; 1920 convention and,
   2:430–31; 1924 convention and, **2**:431;
   1924 election and, **2**:836; 1928 convention
   and, **2**:431; presidency, **1**:32–33

Cooper, Joseph, **1**:106

Corcoran, Thomas, **1**:42

Cortelyou, George B., **1**:24

Cotter, Cornelius P., **1**:174

Coughlin, Charles, **1**:39

Cowles, Edwin, **1**:14

Cox, George B., **1**:277

Cox, James M., **1**:32, 92, 224, **2**:836

Cox, Sunset, **1**:256

Crittenden, John Jordan, **1**:284

Cronkite, Walter, **1**:58

Cullom, Shelby M., **1**:284

Cumming, Hugh, **1**:129

Cummins, Albert B., **1**:285

Curley, James, **1**:82

Curtin, Andrew G., **1**:294

Curtis, Charles, **1**:93, 257–58, 259, **2**:431

Curtis, George, **1**:15

Custer, George A., **1**:230

Cutting, Bronson M., **1**:285

Czolgosz, Leon, **1**:242

D

Daley, Richard, **1**:138, 244

D'Amato, Alphonse, **1**:57, 136

Danforth, John C., **1**:177, 180, 189

Dannemeyer, William E., **1**:132

Darman, Richard, **1**:60

Darwin, Charles, **1**:12

Daugherty, Harry M., **1**:32, 226

Davenport, Russell, **1**:41

David, Paul T., **1**:145

Davis, David, **1**:4, 238

Davis, Henry W., **1**:285, 299

Davis, James W., **1**:146

Davis, John W., **1**:33, 211, 259, **2**:836

Davis, Patti Reagan, **1**:247

Dawes, Carol Blymer, **1**:258

Dawes, Charles G., **1**:258–60, **2**:431

Dayton, William L., **2**:422

Numbers in bold indicate volume; page numbers in italic indicate illustration.

Numbers in bold indicate volume; page numbers in italic indicate illustration.

GEOGRAPHICAL INDEX

Numbers in bold indicate volume; page numbers in italic indicate illustration.

E

Eastern Europe, Bush's foreign policy, **1**:207
Eastford, Connecticut, **1**:276
Elkins, West Virginia, **1**:287
Elwood, Indiana, **1**:273
Estonia, **1**:207
Europe: 1956 platform on, **2**:554; 1984 platform on, **2**:732; 1988 platform on, **2**:776–77
Evanston, Illinois, **1**:258

F

Fairfield, Vermont, President Arthur's birthplace, **1**:203
Florida: governors of, **1**:402; House election victories in, **2**:866; primary, **1**:162, 164; Republican state committee headquarters, **2**:864
Framington, New Hampshire, **1**:266
France, **1**:263; Suez Canal and Anglo-French intervention, **1**:214
Fremont, Ohio, **1**:231

G

Galena, Illinois, **1**:221
Georgia: governors of, **1**:402; House election victories in, **2**:866; Republican state committee headquarters, **2**:864
Germany: German reparations, **1**:259; U.S. declaration of war on, **1**:30
Gettysburg, Pennsylvania, **1**:215
Glen Falls, New York, **1**:271
Greenville, North Carolina, **1**:234
Grenada, invasion of, **1**:60, 138, 248
Guam: annexation of, **1**:123, 241, **2**:833; national committee membership, **1**:176; Republican state committee headquarters, **2**:864
Guatemala, CIA coup, **1**:214

H

Haiti, **1**:125, 207
Harrisburg, Pennsylvania, **1**:283; Gingrich's birthplace, **1**:275
Hawaii: annexation of, **1**:122–23, 228, 241, 268, 279, 296; governors of, **1**:402; House election victories in, **2**:866; 1920 platform on, **2**:487–88; 1928 platform on, **2**:504; 1932 platform on, **2**:514; 1940 platform on, **2**:524; 1944 platform on, **2**:531; 1956 platform on, **2**:552; 1972 platform on Hawaiians, **2**:631–32; Republican state committee headquarters, **2**:864

Hodgenville, Kentucky, **1**:236
Hollywood, California: communism in, **1**:137; Dole campaign on sex and violence in, **1**:139
Houston, Texas, 1992 convention in, **2**:440, 863

I

Idaho: governors of, **1**:402–3; House election victories in, **2**:866; Republican state committee headquarters, **2**:864
Illinois: governors of, **1**:403; House election victories in, **2**:866; Republican state committee headquarters, **2**:864
Indiana: governors of, **1**:403–4; House election victories in, **2**:866; Republican state committee headquarters, **2**:864
Iowa: caucus, **1**:160, 163; governors of, **1**:404–5; House election victories in, **2**:866; Republican state committee headquarters, **2**:864
Iran: CIA coup, **1**:214; hostage crisis, **1**:97, 249
Iraq: invasion of Kuwait, **1**:125, 206; loan guarantees to, **1**:136; Operation Restore Hope, **1**:206–7
Israel, recognition of, **2**:433

J

Japan: Bush's foreign policy, **1**:208; McKinley's foreign policy, **1**:242; 1972 platform on, **2**:606

K

Kansas: bleeding, **1**:2; 1856 convention and slavery issues, **2**:421, 422; governors of, **1**:405; House election victories in, **2**:866; Republican state committee headquarters, **2**:864
Kansas City, Missouri: 1928 convention in, **2**:431, 862; 1976 convention in, **2**:437, 862
Kentucky: governors of, **1**:405; House election victories in, **2**:866; Republican state committee headquarters, **2**:864
Kettle Hill, charge on, **1**:250
Kuwait, **1**:163, 248–49; Iraqi invasion of, **1**:125, 206

L

Latin America, **1**:253; 1916 platform on, **2**:476; 1932 platform on, **2**:510; 1972 platform on, **2**:606

Latvia, **1**:207
Lebanon, **1**:249
Liberia, **1**:207
Libya, **1**:248
Lithuania, **1**:207
Little Rock, Arkansas, **1**:51, 184, 214
Long Branch, New Jersey, **1**:261
Louisiana: blanket primary in, **1**:164; governors of, **1**:406; House election victories in, **2**:866; Reconstruction and bayonet rule in, **1**:230; Republican state committee headquarters, **2**:864

M

Mackinac Island, Michigan, **1**:42
Maine: election of third-party governor, **1**:188; governors of, **1**:406–7; House election victories in, **2**:866; Republican state committee headquarters, **2**:864
Malone, New York, **1**:265
Marietta, Ohio, **1**:258
Maryland: governors of, **1**:407; House election victories in, **2**:866; Republican state committee headquarters, **2**:864
Massachusetts: governors of, **1**:407; House election victories in, **2**:866; Republican state committee headquarters, **2**:864
Mexico: 1912 platform on, **2**:476; 1920 platform on, **2**:480
Miami Beach, Florida: 1968 convention in, **2**:436, 862; 1972 convention in, **2**:437, 862
Michigan: first female representative from, **1**:288; governors of, **1**:408; House election victories in, **2**:866; Republican state committee headquarters, **2**:864
Middle East: 1956 platform on the, **2**:554; 1972 platform on the, **2**:605; 1976 platform on the, **2**:656–57; 1980 platform on the, **2**:699–700; 1984 platform on the, **2**:732–33; 1988 platform on the, **2**:778–79
Milton, Massachusetts, Bush's birthplace, **1**:205
Minneapolis, Minnesota, 1892 convention in, **2**:426, 427, 862
Minnesota: governors of, **1**:408–9; House election victories in, **2**:866; Republican state committee headquarters, **2**:864
Mississippi: flood relief and control, **2**:474, 501; governors of, **1**:409; House election victories in, **2**:866; Republican state committee headquarters, **2**:865
Missouri: governors of, **1**:409; House election victories in, **2**:866; Republican state committee headquarters, **2**:865
Montana: governors of, **1**:409; House election victories in, **2**:866; primary, **1**:160; Republican state committee headquarters, **2**:865
Mount McGregor, New York, Grant's death in, **1**:220

Numbers in bold indicate volume; page numbers in italic indicate illustration.

Numbers in bold indicate volume; page numbers in italic indicate illustration.

Numbers in bold indicate volume; page numbers in italic indicate illustration.

INDEX OF MINORITIES AND WOMEN

Numbers in bold indicate volume; page numbers in italic indicate illustration.

Numbers in bold indicate volume; page numbers in italic indicate illustration.